Visual Knowledge Modeling for Semantic Web Technologies:
Models and Ontologies

Gilbert Paquette
LICEF Research Center, Canada

INFORMATION SCIENCE REFERENCE

Hershey · New York

Director of Editorial Content:	Kristin Klinger
Director of Book Publications:	Julia Mosemann
Acquisitions Editor:	Lindsay Johnston
Development Editor:	Julia Mosemann
Publishing Assistant:	Tom Foley
Typesetter:	Deanna Jo Zombro
Production Editor:	Jamie Snavely
Cover Design:	Lisa Tosheff
Printed at:	Yurchak Printing Inc.

Published in the United States of America by
Information Science Reference (an imprint of IGI Global)
701 E. Chocolate Avenue
Hershey PA 17033
Tel: 717-533-8845
Fax: 717-533-8661
E-mail: cust@igi-global.com
Web site: http://www.igi-global.com

Library of Congress Cataloging-in-Publication Data

Paquette, Gilbert, 1942-
  Visual knowledge modeling for semantic web technologies : models and ontologies / by Gilbert Paquette.
     p. cm.
  Includes bibliographical references and index.
  Summary: "This book addresses how we can make the Web more useful, more intelligent, more knowledge intensive to fulfill our more and more demanding learning and working needs? It is based on the premise that representing knowledge visually is key for individuals and organizations to enable useful access to the knowledge era"--Provided by publisher. ISBN 978-1-61520-839-5 (hardcover) -- ISBN 978-1-61520-840-1 (ebook) 1. Semantic Web. 2. Ontologies (Information retrieval) I. Title.
  TK5105.88815.P367 2010
  025.042'7--dc22
                                    2009044837
British Cataloguing in Publication Data
A Cataloguing in Publication record for this book is available from the British Library.

All work contributed to this book is new, previously-unpublished material. The views expressed in this book are those of the authors, but not necessarily of the publisher.

Table of Contents

Preface ix

Acknowledgment xi

Introduction xiii

Section 1
Modelling Knowledge Visually

Chapter 1

Representing Knowledge 1
   Gilbert Paquette, LICEF Research Center, Canada
Language and the Representation of Knowledge 2
Examples of Graphic Representations 6
Knowledge Representation and Learning 14
Knowledge Representation and Instructional Engineering 17
Conclusion 20
References 20

Chapter 2

Modeling Using a Semi-Formal Visual Language 23
   Gilbert Paquette, LICEF Research Center, Canada
Theoretical Basis of the MOT Modeling System 24
Basic Object Types 26
Primitive Relations Between Knowledge Objects 27
Syntax Rules of the MOT Language 37
Representing Other Types of Models in MOT 42
Conclusion 47
References 48

Chapter 3

Types and Examples of Knowledge Models 49
   Gilbert Paquette, LICEF Research Center, Canada

Basis for a Classification of Models 50
Factual Systems 51
Conceptual Systems 53
Procedural Systems 55
Prescriptive Systems 58
Processes and Methods 61
Conclusion 63

Chapter 4
Modeling Tools and Techniques 66
    Gilbert Paquette, LICEF Research Center, Canada
The MOT+ Visual Model Editor 66
Overview of the Modeling Process 72
Identifying Knowledge Objects 73
Priorizing Knowledge Objects to be Developed Further 78
Expanding the Model 82
Defining and Co-Referencing Knowledge Objects in Other Domains 86
Validating and Documenting Models 89
Conclusion 91
References 91

Section 2
Modeling Competencies

Chapter 5
Knowledge, Skills, and Competency 93
    Gilbert Paquette, LICEF Research Center, Canada
Competencies in Business and the Workplace 94
Competencies in the Definition of Professions 96
Educational Competencies 98
Analysis of Competency Approaches 101
The Concept of Competency 104
Conclusion 105
References 106

Chapter 6
Taxonomies of Problems and Generic Skills 107
    Gilbert Paquette, LICEF Research Center, Canada
Generic Skills as Problem-Solving Processes 108
Generic Skills as Active Meta-Knowledge 111
Generic Skills as Action Verbs Related To Learning Objectives 114
An Integrated Cycle of Skills 116

Comparison of the Taxonomies Related to Generic Skills 117
The Concept of Generic Skill 119
Conclusion 121
References 122

Chapter 7
A Taxonomy of Generic Skills 124
    Gilbert Paquette, LICEF Research Center, Canada
Presentation of the Taxonomy of Generic Skills 126
Generic Skills and Meta-Domains 129
Towards a Library of Processes for Generic Skills 132
Relations Between Skills: Specialization and Composition 137
Giving an Operational Meaning to Competency Profiles 142
Conclusion 145
References 146

Chapter 8
Modeling Multi-Actor Activity Scenarios 147
    Gilbert Paquette and Olga Marino, LICEF Research Center, Canada
Instructional Engineering and Learning Scenarios 148
Multi-Actor Processes and Workflows 154
The MOT+LD and the TELOS Scenario Editors 159
A Scenario Modeling Process 170
Conclusion 172
References 172

Chapter 9
Competency-Driven Scenario and Actor Modeling 175
    Gilbert Paquette and Olga Marino, LICEF Research Center, Canada
Competency Gaps and Domain Modeling 176
Competency-Driven Scenario Modeling 180
Competency-Based Actor's Roles and Resources 183
Knowledge and Competency Actors Models 187
Conclusion 194
References 195

Section 3
Ontology Modeling and the Semantic Web

Chapter 10
Visual Ontology Modeling and the Semantic Web 198
    Gilbert Paquette, LICEF Research Center, Canada
The Semantic Web: Ontologies and Inferences 199

The MOT+OWL and MOWL Visual Ontology Editors 204
Ontology Examples 204
A Detailed Ontology for Competencies 215
Ontology Engineering 219
Conclusion 221
References 222

Chapter 11
Referencing Resources through Ontology Evolution 224
    Délia Rogozan and Gilbert Paquette, LICEF Research Center, Canada
A Model of Ontology Evolution 225
Compatibility Analysis and Change Propagation 229
An Ontology of Ontology Changes 232
A Framework for Managing the Ontology Changes and the Semantic Referencing of Resources 237
Conclusion 243
References 243

Chapter 12
Competency Equilibrium And Instructional Scenarios' Quality 245
    Julien Contamines and Gilbert Paquette, LICEF Research Center, Canada
Research on Instructional Scenarios's Quality 246
Competency-Driven Scenario Validation 249
Process for Scenario Validation 256
Conclusion 259
References 260

Chapter 13
Ontology-Based Software Component Aggregation 263
    Gilbert Paquette and Anis Masmoudi, LICEF Research Center, Canada
Software Component Aggregation Process 264
Metadata for Software Component Referencing 267
The Software Components Ontology 269
A Framework for Ontology-Driven Aggregation of Components 274
Conclusion 276
References 277

Chapter 14
From Semi-Formal Models to Formal Models 278
    Michel Héon and Gilbert Paquette, LICEF Research Center, Canada
Levels of KNOWLEDGE Formalization 279
Meta-modeling: A Transformation Tool Between Models 281
Method for Transforming Semi-Formal Models into Ontologies 286
Illustration of Machine-Assisted Ontology Formalization 297
Conclusion 299
References 300

Chapter 15

An Ontology-Driven System for E-Learning and Knowledge Management 302
    Gilbert Paquette, LICEF Research Center, Canada
Principles for an Operations System 303
Building the Architecture of TELOS 304
The TELOS Technical Ontology 307
TELOS Main Tools 311
Ontology-Driven Scenario Execution in the Task Manager 317
Conclusion 321
References 322

Section 4
Visual Modelling in Practice

Chapter 16

Modeling for Learning 325
    Josianne Basque and Béatrice Pudelko, LICEF Research Center, Canada
External Representations and Cognitive Tools 326
Knowledge Modeling as an Individual Learning Strategy for Distance Learners 329
Collaborative Knowledge Modeling as a Learning Strategy in Distance Education 331
Collaborative Knowledge Modeling in Face-to-Face Learning Situations 335
Conclusion 337
Acknowledgment 338
References 338

Chapter 17

Modeling for Instructional Engineering 344
    Richard Hotte, Karin Lundgren-Cayrol, Diane Rulland and Gilbert Paquette,
        LICEF Research Center, Canada
Building a Competency Profile fora Professional Training Program 345
Delivery Model for Virtual Campuses 353
A tutoring Scenario For -Web-Based Courses 358
Developing a Process Model to Design Competency-Based Learning 366
Conclusion 371
References 372

Chapter 18

Modeling for Learning Design Repositories 374
    Gilbert Paquette, LICEF Research Center, Canada
The IDLD Portal 375
Learning Design as Learning Objects 378
A Case Study: Producing and Reusing Patterns and Learning Designs 380

An Ontology for Learning Design Objects 383

Conclusion 390

References 391

Chapter 19

Modeling for Knowledge Management in Organizations 393

  Gilbert Paquette, Michel Léonard, Josianne Basque and Béatrice Pudelko,
   LICEF Research Center, Canada

Building a Knowledge Management Environment in a Large Company 394

Transfer of Expertise in Organizations Through Co-Modeling of Knowledge 399

Modelling a Computerized School 405

Conclusion 411

References 412

Chapter 20

Modeling for Tools and Environments Specification 414

  Karin Lundgren-Cayrol, Diane Ruelland, Geneviève Habel and François Magnan,
   LICEF Research Center, Canada

Modeling Learning Resource Management Tools 415

Modeling a Resource Repository Management Process 419

Modeling a Competency Self-Management Tool 426

Creating an Ontology-Based Learning Environment 431

Conclusion 435

References 436

Chapter 21

Modeling for Research and Communication 439

  Gilbert Paquette, LICEF Research Center, Canada

Modeling the MISA Instructional Engineering Method 440

Modeling Assistance for a Host System 447

Visual Modeling in Doctoral Research 459

Conclusion 462

References 463

About the Author 465

Index 466

Preface

This book is the result of a research program that I have led at the LICEF research Center of Télé-université since 1992. Télé-université is the oldest distance university in Canada, founded in 1972.

Learning and Teaching at a distance implies a very different context than in a Campus university, even though knowledge modeling is central in both cases, as in any educational or knowledge management situation. In distance learning, teachers and learners are not in a classroom at the same time. They interact in a Virtual Campus supported by information and communication technology. This implies that the courses must be carefully planned for autonomous study by the learner, and for networked interactions between learners and trainers or professors. On the professors' side, while keeping the general responsibility on the quality of learning, the teaching activities are shared with education professionals, media and technology specialists, and the tutors that interact directly with the learners. There are multiple interactions between these actors in three main processes: *design*, where courses and programs are conceived and planned; *production* where the learning material and environments are produced, and the *delivery* of these environments where learning take place.

The research program at LICEF has been influenced by this challenging context. Modeling is the central idea that provided the backbone of our research and application activities. Modeling multi-actor processes was necessary both to describe the flow of the activities between actors involved in design and production of on-line courses before learning occurs, as well as to define the learning processes themselves. These are seen also as multi-actor processes where learners achieve learning task supported by the learning material and the interaction with tutors, facilitators and peer learners. An instructional engineering method was build by modeling these processes, supported by a first visual modeling tool built by us at the beginning of the nineties. Modeling also proved critical to organize knowledge acquisition goals in the form of competencies, both to plan the activities and the design of the learning environments. Finally knowledge construction and competency acquisition was seen also as a learner's activity to be supported also by friendly visual modeling tools.

We soon found out that these tools and methods were useful outside the context of universities. Early in the nineties, we started interacting with large companies and professional organizations that were seeking similar approaches, most of the time in blended learning contexts involving some classroom activities, but mostly training outside the classroom. Our first projects were achieved in partnership with the DMR group, a large software consulting company, where we built a courseware support system integrating a visual modeling tool, and the Bank of Montreal, where our method and modeling tools served to design a training program for the personnel involved in a new set of banking services.

Later on, we interacted with 6 technology-based companies in the Multimedia Telecommunication project, with 7 laboratories in French Campus Universities within the HyperGuide-Recto project, and also with a large set of Canadian universities and companies grouped in the TeleLearning National Centers of Excellence (TL-NCE). We have also been leading the eduSource integration project on learning object repositories and worked on two projects with professional organizations to help them build knowledge-based competency profile and use it to orient a training program. The visual modeling tools have been translated in foreign languages and used in some European and Latin American countries.

More recently, in the last six years, we extended the generality of the Visual Modeling tools and methods to knowledge management and the Semantic Web, mainly through the LORNET research network that was led by the author and heavily founded by the Canadian Government.

Internationally, since the beginning of the century, an increasing number of organizations had recognized the importance of learning technologies and knowledge management in organization. This new awareness resulted in attempts to identify, structure, organize, and sustain knowledge by reengineering professional processes for work and training, supported by the increasingly ubiquitous online technologies. At the same time, an important international movement started to elaborate eLearning standards that would enable users from all over the world to interoperate and reuse computerized resources, "learning objects" or "knowledge objects" available in "learning object repositories" distributed on World Wide Web. Both these major movements converged and integrated another pervading trend, the construction of the next Web generation, the "Semantic Web", where knowledge models in the form of ontologies are the central element. These important international trends formed the core of the LORNET Research Program. They provided guidance to specify, structure and organize the scope, the goals, the objectives and the themes of the research program.

At the moment I write this book, we are involved in a three year project with Hydro-Quebec, a large public utility company, where we participate in building a knowledge management system based on the tools and methods developed in the LORNET network. We are also using visual knowledge modeling in other contexts such as a the Canada School of Public Services, or representing knowledge for a group of small manufacturing companies, as well as planning and support environment stages for young students. We also continue to apply Visual Modeling in our own teaching and research activities where we use knowledge and ontology modeling intensively.

I presented in short the history behind the book in order to emphasized that, although the tools and methods presented here have sound theoretical foundations, they have also practical value. They have been tested in a variety of contexts. They have been used outside university setting by professional in large or small, private and public organizations and in various cultural and linguistic contexts.

The reader interested in concrete examples will find throughout this book many references to Web sites that we maintain. In particular, the following link will lead the reader to tools, models and documents that will help him to follow up on the reading.

These are available free of charge at the following address: www.licef.ca/cice/

Gilbert Paquette
Montreal, October 2, 2009

Acknowledgment

For some of the chapters of this book, I have asked for the collaboration of other researchers at my research Center or from some of my doctoral students. Although I have revised all the texts and added some elements to facilitate their integration in the main thread of the book, I must pay credit for the quality of their involvement.

Here is a list of these chapters or chapter sections and their prime authors.

Section 8.2 and 9.4	Olga Marino
Chapter 11	Délia Rogozan
Chapter 12	Julien Contamines
Chapter 13	Anis Masmoudi
Chapter 14	Michel Héon
Chapter 16 and Section 19.2	Josianne Basque and Béatrice Pudelko
Section 17.3	Richard Hotte
Section 17.4	Karin Lundgren-Cayrol and Diane Ruelland
Section 19.1	Michel Léonard
Section 20.1 and 20.2	Karin Lundgren-Cayrol
Section 20.3	Diane Ruelland
Section 20.4	Geneviève Habel and François Magnan

In conclusion, I would like to thank all the researchers and students at the LICEF research Center and the CICE Research Chair who have used the concepts, tools and methods presented here. Besides the above contributors, I would like to underline the early contribution of Claire Aubin, Françoise Crevier and Ileana De la Teja who made important contributions to the MISA method and still use the MOT editors in their professional practice. I must also mention the steady and insightful contribution of Michel Léonard who supports the use of the MOT modeling tools by giving training to partner organizations in different parts of the world who are using it. All these persons, and also colleague researchers at TELUQ France Henri, Jacqueline Bourdeau and Hamadou Saliah-Hassane have contributed useful feedback from time to time.

Also many thanks to the computer architects, analysts and technicians who have produced versions of the visual modeling tools used in this book, in particular Eric Bleicher, Ioan Rosca, Alexis Miara, Frédéric Bergeron and François Magnan. Without their intelligent contribution, all these projects might have remained a theory instead of operational tools.

Finally, I must recognize the financial support of the organizations who financed various versions of the tools: the DMR Group and the Centre de recherche informatique de Montréal (CRIM), the Social

Sciences and Humanities Research Council (SSHRC), the Telelearning Network of Centers of Excellence (TL-NCE), the Canadian Defense Industrial Research Program (DIRP), Hydro-Quebec, Bell Canada and the Natural Science and Engineering Research Council (NSERC) of Canada.

Introduction

The beginning of this twenty-first century is characterized by the advent of what we have come to label "the knowledge society". Unlike other "golden ages" of human history, where creation was the affair of a small minority, the fascinating era we live in is a mass movement where we see governments building knowledge policies, companies putting tremendous efforts for the management of their knowledge considered as their main asset, and where individuals, using more and more mobile realistic media, acquire and use different information processing tools considered as indispensable means for the acquisition of knowledge and competency.

The Knowledge Society and the Ubiquitous Web

This mass movement is of course propelled by the arrival of the ubiquitous Web in almost everybody's life. The Internet provides us with a large part of the knowledge that humanity has built through the ages and is building right now. Within a few clicks, one can reach, all around the world, libraries, museums, journals, radio or television stations, universities and schools that provide a huge mass of information and knowledge.

The Internet is a universal tool for information access, but it does not supply by itself means to help us choose and handle information according to our rapidly changing needs, in particular our learning and working needs. One can regret that many people use the term "knowledge" for certain sites that only present information that is useless or misleading. Information is not the same as knowledge. Knowledge is more demanding. It involves changing our mental models, structuring information, developing generic skills and competencies to process information and knowledge.

This is the subject of this book. *How can we make the Web more useful, more intelligent, more knowledge intensive to fulfill our more and more demanding learning and working needs?* This book is based on the premise that representing knowledge visually is key for individuals and organizations to enable useful access to the knowledge era.

Representing Knowledge Visually

It is often said that a picture is worth a thousand words. That is true of sketches, diagrams, and graphs used in various fields of knowledge. Conceptual maps are widely used to represent and clarify relationships between concepts and to facilitate knowledge construction by the learners or the design of learning environments by educators. Flowcharts are graphical representations of procedural knowledge or algorithms, composed of actions and decisions that trigger series of actions in a dynamic rather than a static way. Decision trees constitute another form of representation used in various fields for decision-making systems, establishing influence or cause/effect relationships between variables.

All these representation methods are useful at an informal level, as thinking aids and as tools for the communication of ideas, but they have limitations. One is the imprecise meaning of the links between the entities that compose the model. Another one is the ambiguity in graphs where objects, actions on objects and statement of properties about them are all mixed-up and are not represented in a way that helps differentiate them and uncover their relationships.

Another difficulty is the impossibility to combine more than one representation in the same model. For example, concepts used in procedural flowcharts as entry, intermediate or terminal objects could be given a more precise meaning by developing them in conceptual sub-models of the procedure. The same is true of procedures present in conceptual models that could be developed as procedural sub-models described by flowcharts, combined or not with decision trees.

In software engineering, many visual representation formalisms have been proposed such as Entity-Relationship models, Modern structured analysis, Conceptual Graphs, Object modelling technique, KADS, or Unified Modeling Language UML. These representation systems have been built for the analysis and architectural design of complex software systems. The most recent ones require the use of up to eight different kinds of model and the links between them are hard to follow without considerable expertise.

Our goal is different. We need a visual representation system that is both simple enough to be used by educational specialists and learners who are not computer scientists, let general and powerful enough to represent the structure of knowledge and learning/working scenarios. The distinction and the integration of basic types of knowledge and links in the same language are here essential.

The visual representation language that constitutes the thread of this book has evolved and has been tested for many years in a vast array of modeling applications in various contexts. Visual tools have been built to build knowledge model of different types, translated in three languages and used in many countries. They are used by trainers for corporate training. Designers or professors have used them to prepare university courses or to propose modeling exercises to their students. They have served to model processes for the introduction of IT in a computer-supported high school, or to model instructional methods or research processes.

In this book I use the Modeling using Object Types (MOT) visual language and tools to present three major steps starting with informal visual modeling for the educated laymen, to help represent interesting knowledge. I then move to semi-formal modeling to help define target competencies and activity scenarios for knowledge and competency acquisition by learners and workers. Finally, I present the more formal visual models (ontologies) that can be used by software agents to insure the execution of knowledge-based processes on the Semantic Web. A host of real-life applications will be presented to show how modeling in practice can improve learning, instructional design, knowledge management in organisation, Web-based environments definition and research processes.

Facilitating Access to the Knowledge Web

The overall objective of the book is to make visual knowledge modeling available to a large public as an intellectual method and as a set of tools at different levels of formalization. It aims to provide to its readers a simple, yet powerful visual language to structure their thoughts, analyze information, transform it to personal knowledge, and communicate information to support knowledge acquisition in collaborative activities. A secondary objective is to understand the goals, methods and tools of the Semantic Web and to be able to participate in its evolution by modelling ontologies and exploiting their use for semantic referencing of the resources used and produced in learning or workflow scenarios.

A first unique characteristic of this book is to depart from literary and theoretical considerations about knowledge and competency to focus on the pragmatics and operational issues. The book is built around visual models with many examples and applications that have been developed in real projects by the author and his team of collaborators at the LICEF Research Center and the CICE Research Chair for the last fifteen years. To my knowledge, this team has had the longest and more profound involvement in knowledge modeling using visual tools for education and knowledge management.

Some readers might find too brief the general discussion of knowledge modeling provided at the beginning of the book. This is a vast subject that has been covered from different viewpoints by a number of authors. In this book, I synthesize the main ideas as long as they are useful to provide a solid foundation for a knowledge representation language. My firm belief is that insight into knowledge modeling can be best served by practical modeling activities in various domains. For this, the MOT modeling language and technique is introduced early in the first part of the book with a host of examples.

Just the same, this book will provide an overall and integrated view of emerging concepts that are at the forefront of the evolution of Internet technologies in the context of learning and knowledge management environments. Usually, these concepts are dispersed outside any structured framework that could help their understanding, use, evaluation and evolution. Providing such a framework will reinforce the effort to build a Semantic Web that is more knowledge intensive and to uncover new research orientations that need to be explored.

The themes proposed here have a great potential impact. This book will be the first one to present an integrated approach that brings the reader from informal modeling to formal modeling for Semantic Web applications. The use of a visual language, simple yet powerful, will encourage readers to get involve in modeling activities thus increasing there intellectual capacity to capture, structure and communicate knowledge. I hope that popularizing such activities will have an impact on the quality of knowledge resources on the Web and on the quality of learning and workplace scenario design. I have witness evidence of this impact in all the organizations that have used knowledge modeling visual tools.

The projected audience is composed of knowledge workers in a variety of area. In many countries, a majority of workers are involved in knowledge acquisition, organization, processing and communication activities. Any writer can structure a book, a study or a journal article using visual modeling. Process managers in all kinds of organization can plan or adapt workflows or scenario using visual modeling. And of course, professor, teachers, designers and learning managers need visual modeling to prepare effectively courses or training programs, and to plan Web-based educational environments. Finally, Web designers will need to move progressively to the Semantic Web where the content and the semantic of resources will be represented using knowledge models.

The potential benefits are for the reader to gain a clear view of different types and different levels of knowledge and their relationship, in whatever field he is involved at the moment. He will also gain a methodology and a set of tools for knowledge and competency modeling available on a companion Web site at www.licef.ca/cice/KM. These tools and examples can be used in his professional activities, as well as for his own knowledge and competency acquisition planning.

Organisation and Content of the Book

I now present the structure of the book and the interrelations between its chapters. The book is subdivided into four parts and 21 chapters. The following figure presents the main interrelations between these parts and chapters.

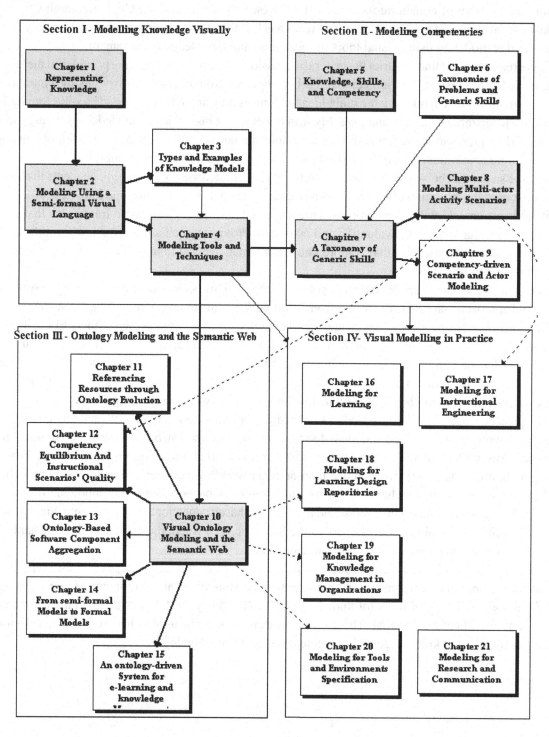

In the first section, *Modelling Knowledge Visually*, I present the basis of Visual Knowledge Modeling. Synthesising work in education and cognitive science modeling, I present various informal modeling languages that will help define the MOT visual language and discuss its properties, advantages and limits. Then I use the MOT language to build models equivalent to commonly used graphic representation and I present a taxonomy of model categories that can be built with the MOT language. The last chapter presents tools and techniques to facilitate knowledge modeling.

In Section II, *Modelling Competencies*, I start with an inventory of competency profiles examples in order to propose a structured concept of competency and to discuss the notion of generic skill applied to domain knowledge as a basis for building competency profiles. After a study of a number of previous proposals, I propose an integrated taxonomy of generic skills. Then I combine knowledge modeling and generic skills modeling to help build competency profiles. The last two chapters are applications of competency modeling, to guide the modeling of multi-actor activity scenarios, the modeling of a knowledge domain and the definition of actors' models.

In Section III, *Ontology Modeling and the Semantic Web*, I present a specialization of the visual language (MOT+OWL) that supports the representation of knowledge and competencies as ontologies, thus bringing the visual language at a formal and computational level. The other chapters are independent from one another. They address actual research issues about the use of ontologies for the semantic Web, stemming from the work of doctoral students supervised by the author. The first one concerns the maintenance of the referencing of resources using an ontology while it is evolving. The second addresses the quality of activity scenarios by referencing their components with ontologies and competency attachments. The third one uses ontology to guide the aggregation of software components. The fourth one presents a process to transform informal and semi-formal models, like the ones in parts I and II into ontologies. In the last chapter, the TELOS ontology-driven system is presented with its technical ontology that drives the system to produce Web-bases environments for learning and knowledge management.

Section IV, *Visual Modelling in Practice*, is composed of six chapters, independent from each others, that present applications and studies that have been conducted with colleagues and students at the LICEF research centers. They exploit the concepts, tools and methods presented in part I and II. Three of the chapters (18, 19 and 20) also contain ontology modeling applications, relying on part. Each chapter covers a different type of use of visual knowledge modeling: for learning, for instructional engineering, for learning design repositories, for knowledge management in organizations, for tools and environments specification and for research processes.

Use of the Book for Various Readers

The preceding figure provides a concept map of the parts and chapters of the book. Strong links are essential prerequisites, light links are useful prerequisite and dotted links mean that only a part of the chapter is necessary to understand part of a following chapter.

Using these links, the reader will be able to decide on a learning path that corresponds to his/her needs. Here are some examples

- The reader who wants a good overview at a first reading can start with the "colored" rectangles that correspond to chapters 1, 2, 4, 5, 7, 8, 10, and one of the chapters in Section IV.
- The reader interested mainly in ontologies and the Semantic Web, or the reader more technically inclined should read all the chapters of part I, chapter 8, and all the chapters in Section III.

- The reader interested mainly in educational applications of visual modeling should read all nine chapters of Section I and II, plus chapters 16, 17, 18 and 21.
- The reader interested mainly in knowledge management applications of visual modeling should read all nine chapters of Section I and II, plus chapters 19, 20.

Section 1
Modelling Knowledge Visually

Chapter 1
Representing Knowledge

Gilbert Paquette
LICEF Research Center, Canada

ABSTRACT

- Language and the Representation of Knowledge
  - Knowledge Representation
  - Grammar and Semantics
  - Formal Language: Propositions
- Examples of Graphic Representations
  - Semantic Trees and Conceptual Maps
  - Semantic Networks and Entity-relationship Diagrams
  - Algorithms and Flow Charts
  - Causal Diagrams and Decision Trees
  - Object-oriented Models
- Knowledge Representation and Learning
  - Schema Representation
  - Diagnosing and assessing knowledge
  - Structuring information transfer
  - Learning through knowledge representation
- Knowledge Representation and Instructional Engineering
  - Types of knowledge in education
  - Modeling Information Systems

The invention of writing more than 6,000 years in Mesopotamia is a recent phenomenon in human history. In the few million years that preceded this event, knowledge was passed on from generation to generation by oral tradition.

Writing was a huge factor in accelerating civilization and transferring knowledge by enabling us to externalize our thoughts first on stone, parchment,

DOI: 10.4018/978-1-61520-839-5.ch001

then paper, and finally by digitizing and recording them on optical disks and computer servers.

These media act as a kind of external memory that extends the storage capacity of our brain. This external memory can be accessed on demand, made permanent, changed in a multitude of ways, sent to others, used as a basis for mass communication orally or electronically, and distributed through print, analog, or digital media.

The purpose of this chapter is to broaden our understanding of knowledge representation through organized systems of symbols, to present these systems, and to describe how they are used to understand, communicate, and solve problems.

1.1 LANGUAGE AND THE REPRESENTATION OF KNOWLEDGE

In order to exchange, communicate, and process knowledge, we must represent it through a medium that is external to our brain and in a form that understandable. Before defining more precisely what language and representation systems are, let us first look at an example.

Mental Models and Representations

A user manual accompanying a television set has the following instructions: *If there is no image but only sound, check the brightness setting of the screen; if there is image but no sound, check the volume or mute controls. If there is no image or sound, make sure the unit is plugged in and the power switch is on.*

This text transmits a certain amount of *knowledge* required to solve a minor problem, in as much as the reader understands the meaning of the text. Figure 1 presents an alternative representation of the same knowledge. This second representation contains no English words and relies solely on an interpretation of the pictures.

This example (Paquette and Bergeron, 1989)

illustrates that there are two levels involved in the process of representation: *knowledge* and the various *representations* of that knowledge. In general, a body of knowledge can be represented by many forms, such as the accompanying text or the pictograms in Figure 1, and used for many purposes.

Representation in the form of sentences or symbols is useful for transmitting knowledge from one human being to another, but since we sometimes need to process this knowledge in more structured ways, we resort to other representations. Simply reading the text or icons in Figure 1 is not sufficient for applying the knowledge they describe—such knowledge must be *understood*. Human beings understand texts or pictograms through mental representations, i.e. sets of ideas they have about a situation.

Many hypotheses have been suggested as to the actual form of these mental representations; however, we can confirm their existence through a simple exercise. Without referring to the text in the manual or to Figure 1, try to transmit the same information to another person. You will probably not use the same words or pictures, but the information will be conveyed.

Through your mental representation of the situation, you are able to consider questions such as *My TV has no sound or picture, even though it is plugged in. Where is the problem?* By using

Figure 1. Pictorial representation of knowledge

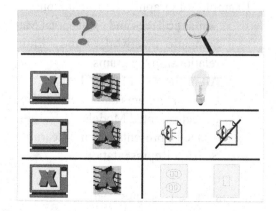

basic rules of inference, you are able to address the problem and deal with it in an appropriate manner.

Knowledge Representation

The mental representation of knowledge is a subject that has received much attention in cognitive science. Knowledge in neurology, cognitive psychology, linguistics, and artificial intelligence has converged around the associative nature of mental representations.

Two theories about mental representations—the symbolic hypothesis and the connectionist hypothesis—are often viewed as opposed. A discussion of these theories, which are moreover reconcilable (Anderson 1990), is beyond the scope of this chapter since we are interested here in the external representations of knowledge as it becomes information that can be manipulated and exchanges between people.

By symbolically representing a body of knowledge, we are defining a set of *expressions* in which each piece of knowledge corresponds to one or more expressions, and each expression corresponds to one or more pieces of knowledge. In the previous example, expressions consisted of either English sentences or pictures. The knowledge that a television set has no sound (a statement of fact) can be expressed by various combinations of words in natural language.

Unfortunately, words in English and other natural languages are often inadequate for describing certain kinds of knowledge, which is why, in many fields, other types of symbolism are used. For example, if a musical composition were described by words alone, it would quickly become a lengthy run-on novel: *Play a half-note C at the third octave, followed by E flat, etc.*

Virtually every sphere of human activity has its own formalized representation system—family trees in genealogy, definitions in dictionaries, blueprints in architecture, circuit diagrams in electronics, maps in geography, and so on.

Grammar and Semantics

In order to develop a representation system for learning and instructional engineering, we have to define its conventions and rules. This involves the following elements.

1. Defining a *lexicon:* a set of basic symbols that are used in the representation system. In English, this would include the letters of the alphabet, punctuation marks, and words accepted by an official dictionary; in music, the musical staff and the symbols representing key, pitch, rests, etc.

2. Defining a *grammar:* expressions considered acceptable when the basic symbols of the lexicon are combined. In English, this would mean using grammatically correct sentences; in chemistry, describing the molecular structure of chemical compounds using acceptable expressions consisting of a series of chemical symbols and numerical suffixes such as H_2O ou NaCl; in music, grammatical rules stipulating that a staff must contain a key signature, a time signature, and notes and rests that respect the musical subdivisions of time.

3. Defining *semantics:* a way to give meaning to grammatical expressions by associating them with intelligible mental representations and, conversely, to associate one or more grammatical expressions with knowledge that is part of the mental model of the individuals using the language.

It is through expressions of formal language that we are able to translate a fact or a piece of knowledge into useful information; it is what we call *representation* or *modeling*. The difficulty of representation lies in the complex nature of expressions and their ability or inability to convey nuances. Translation also involves a series of choices: What level of detail do we want? Which factors are important? Interestingly, if there were only one way to observe and describe a situation in natural language, literature would probably not exist.

The inverse operation is *interpretation*, the ability to mentally represent facts or knowledge implied by an expression of language. Here too, interpretation is rarely unambiguous, since expressions of language can have several possible meanings. However, certain languages require singular interpretations. An expression in a computer programming language, for example, can only have one meaning if we want the program to work. This is not necessarily true for the field of education, however, where precisely a *diversity* of interpretation can give rise to debate that is beneficial for learning.

In light of the inverse operations of representation and interpretation, a formal language must have the following properties to be useful:

- It must be able to convey all the relevant knowledge of a given field through expres-

sions of its representation system. In other words, the system must be *complete* with regard to the given field; lack of completeness can force us to use increasingly complex representation systems or use more than one system. In this regard, natural language is much more demanding than, for example, basic algebraic notation, which only seeks to express polynomial equality or inequality.

- Expressions of language must be easily generated and understood; in other words, an expression must be easily associated with a fact or a piece of knowledge, and vice versa. In some cases, expressions of language must be processed by computer, which usually implies strict definitions of acceptable expressions and their corresponding interpretations.

- Expressions of language should make explicit the important aspects of a field of knowledge, while masking the unnecessary aspects or details. For example, on a musical staff, the shape of the musical instrument or even the type of musical instrument is not essential to the representa-

Figure 2. Inverse operations of representation and interpretation

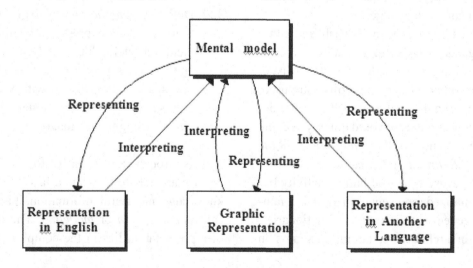

tion—but key and tempo are.

A Formal Language, Propositional Logic

Let us now illustrate the above example using a formal language known as *propositional logic*. This system allows us to represent various aspects of the situation through basic expressions.

Table 1 reformulates the sentences in Figure 1 relating to our television problem. The expressions in the second column translate the essential elements of the problem. "Details" such as articles, adjectives, and verbs (see, hear, check, etc.) are left out. The structure of the English text has been simplified to such an extent that the resulting expressions are no longer grammatically correct, yet they convey the essential information. Their simple yet highly structured format can be applied to other arguments, based on the following rules:

• If we know that the expressions "A" and "if A then B" are true, then regardless of what A and B symbolize, we can infer that B is true.

> This line of inference can perhaps be made clearer if we substitute A with "IT_IS_SNOWING" and B with "IT_IS_COLD." From "IT_IS_SNOWING" and "if IT_IS_SNOWING then IT_IS_COLD," we can easily infer that "IT_IS_COLD."

Note that the purpose of linking the words by underscores or giving them symbols such as "B" is that we are not concerned with the meaning of the individual words in, for example, "it is cold," but rather the overall meaning of the statement and its capacity to be true or false depending on the circumstances.

Likewise, if we know that the expressions "NOT A" and "A or B" are true, then regardless of what A and B symbolize, we can infer that B is true. If A represents "It is nice" and B "It is cloudy" and "it is not nice" (not A), we can infer "it is cloudy" (B).

The *lexicon* of propositional logic consists of two types of symbols:

• *Elementary propositions*—strings of one or more capital letters such as S, I, MI, MV, MA, MS, MI, or IT_IS_SNOWING.
• The *logical connectors* "not," "and," "or," and "if…then." The role of these connectiors is to link propositions together to form more complex propositions.

The *grammar* of propositional logic consists of rules for combining the terms of the lexicon and defining the correct expressions of the language.

Table 1. Representation of two simple statements

Natural language	Schematic language
If there is no image but only sound, check the brightness setting of the screen.	if not IMAGE and SOUND then ADJUST_BRIGHTNESS
If there is image but no sound, check the volume or "mute" controls.	if IMAGE and not SOUND then VOLUME or MUTE
If there is no image or sound, make sure the unit is plugged in and the power switch is on.	if not IMAGE and not SOUND then PLUG or ON
My TV has no sound or image, even though it is plugged in. Where is the problem?	not sound and not IMAGE and not PLUG

- The connector *no* can be placed before any simple or compound proposition surrounded by parentheses (like the minus sign before a number). The connectors *and*, *or*, and *if...then* can be placed between two simple or compound propositions surrounded by parentheses.

The *semantics* of propositional logic consists of interpreting each elementary proposition as either *true* of *false* in a given context. Excluded, therefore, are arguments based on multiple levels of certainty, on more than two truth values, or on variables representing classes of objects[1]. Such restrictions are unique to propositional logic. In addition, connectors have very precise meanings that are close, but not identical, to their meanings in English. The connector *if...then* expresses the idea of consequence, the first proposition being called the *antecedent* or *premise*, the second being called the *consequence* or *conclusion*. Propositions containing the connector *or* are true if either proposition is true. Propositions containing the connector *and* are true if both propositions are true. Propositions containing the connector *no* are true if the proposition following the "no" is not true.

Such a formal language helps to clarify the different types of arguments. Returning to our television example (Table 1), we can represent each simple proposition by its first letter. We obtain the following compound propositions:

(1) If (*not* I *and* S) then A
(2) If (I *and not* S) then (V or M)
(3) If (not I *and not* S) then (P or O)
(4) not P and not S
(5) not P

We then apply the above rules of inference:

- R1: From (A) and from (If A then B), we can infer B
- R2: From (not A) and from (A or B), we

can infer B

By applying rule R1 to propositions (3) and (4), we can infer:

- P or 0 (the unit is not plugged in or the power switch is not on)

By applying rule R2 to propositions (6) and (5), we can infer that between these two propositions, the power switch is not on.

Despite its simplicity, propositional logic allows us to sort out complex situations; its strength comes from focusing on simple propositional structures and establishing precise rules of grammar and interpretation. This approach is the basis for expert systems, in which propositions such as (1), (2), and (3) form the knowledge base (rules of the type IF...THEN) and statements such as (4) form the fact base. In an expert system, rules of deduction such as R1 and R2 constitute what is called the "inference engine." The same inference engine can process knowledge bases from very different fields, provided they are adequately represented in a formal language similar to the one presented here.

1.2 EXAMPLES OF GRAPHIC REPRESENTATIONS

It is often said that a picture is worth a thousand words. This is also true of the diagrams, charts, and graphs used in various fields of knowledge. In this section, we will present examples of graphic representations that are relevant to learning and instructional engineering. Our goal is to provide the basis for a system of graphic representation that is the subject of our next chapter.

Semantic Trees and Conceptual Maps

Semantic trees are widely used in education to categorize concepts and provide examples. They are graphic illustrations of the hierarchical links between concepts. The following is an example of a semantic tree:

The graph in Figure 3 depicts a hierarchy of categories, from the more general "Painters" to the individual artists representing various groups or schools of painting. Note that, as a language, this type of diagram can have several possible interpretations, for it does not specify the nature of the links. For readers less familiar or not at all familiar with the field, the distinction between the two types of links in the chart would probably go unnoticed. The upper links represent relationships between a class and its sub-classes (links of specialization, as we will later see), while the lower ones represent links of class membership (links of instanciation).

Semantic trees can be used in instructional engineering to provide a structure for a course, a book, or a website. They can also provide the basis for a learning strategy in which the learners discuss an area of knowledge then create a semantic tree to represent their concept of its structure.

Though more general than semantic trees, *conceptual maps* are also widely used in education to represent relationships between concepts. Conceptual maps are based on the theory of associative memory in cognitive psychology. According to this theory, new concepts have meaning only through their association with known concepts. By explicitly representing networks of association, conceptual maps facilitate the assimilation of new knowledge, whether presented or explained by an instructor or formulated and organized by the learner.

Conceptual maps are also graphs but not necessarily hierarchical in nature. In conceptual maps, nodes represent concepts, and links represent relationships between concepts. The nature of each link is indicated by a word placed on or near the line that graphically represents the link.

Figure 4 is a conceptual map describing the causal and influential relationships between different factors that affect climate change. These relationships reveal much about the structure of

Figure 3. Semantic tree in art history

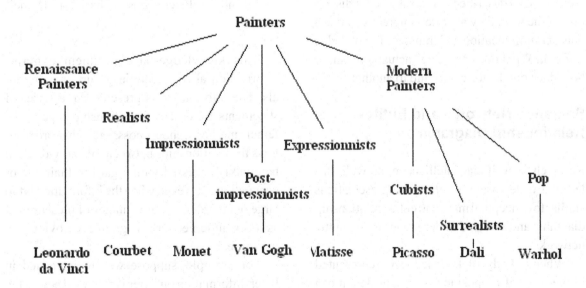

Figure 4. Conceptual map of climate change

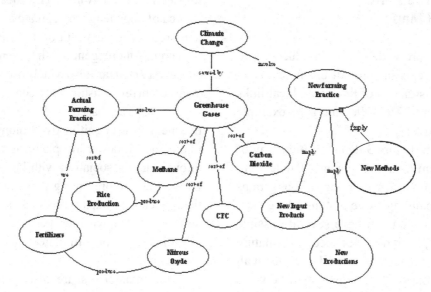

the field and serve as a preliminary outline or starting point for further analysis involving other factors or relationships.

Note that, since they also use non-directional links, conceptual maps are sometimes difficult to interpret. They must therefore include other contextual knowledge indicating, for example, that fertilizers produce nitrous oxide and not the opposite, or that the graph should be read from top to bottom or left to right. As well, since the terms used to describe the links are at the discretion of the user, they are often imprecise and can make communication and transfer of knowledge difficult. What does "involve" actually mean, or how does one factor contribute to another?

Semantic Networks and Entity-Relationship Diagrams

Research in artificial intelligence, as well, has led to a wide variety of graphic representations similar to conceptual maps and entity-relationship diagrams and grouped under the term "semantic networks."

When a body of knowledge is represented in the form of propositions or predicates, it can result in a rather long list of statements, as in the following fragment:

- Charles is 67. Mary is 63. Linda is 42. Diane is 37. Peter is 35. Julia is 12.
- Charles is Peter's father. Peter is Julia's father. Mary is Peter's mother, Diane is Julia's mother.
- Charles is male. Peter is male. Mary is female. Julia is female. Linda is female.
- Linda is Peter's boss. Charles is Diane's boss.

This knowledge-base fragment contains information about a certain group of individuals. The information is presented in a series of statements by order of relationship type—age, father, mother, gender, boss, etc. This order allows the relationships between the individuals to be quickly accessed with regard to their age or occupation. However, when the information is too large or complex, the advantages of presenting it as a semantic network diagram are obvious, as in Figure 5.

For example, suppose we are interested in Peter. Information on Peter is scattered across the

Figure 5. Example of a semantic network

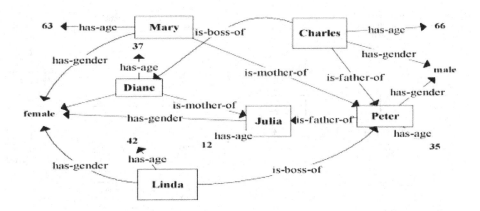

list of statements, and it is difficult to quickly see who and what is associated with Peter, and how. The following paragraph contains information about Peter:

Peter is a 35-year-old man; he is the son of Mary and Charles and has a daughter Julia. He works for Linda. Julia's mother is Diane, who works for Charles (thus her father-in-law).

The paragraph is a "reading" of all the information from the box above in the form of a network of associations. Using Peter as our starting point, we are able to see the relationships that involve him at an immediate level; we can then take note of the other objects that come into play, and so on. Objects that are accessed immediately are considered "near" the original object, while those that are accessed through successive associations are considered "distant." Julia is "near" to Peter, while Linda is rather "distant" from Julia. Such interpretations are possible because the network in Figure 5 highlights the *associations* implied in the information.

Similar representation systems are used in computer science to describe the basic structure of relational databases designed with programs such as ACCESS, ORACLE, and SYBASE. These are called *entity-relationship graphs* (Chen

1976*)*. Such graphs have stricter rules than other semantic networks because the structures they describe are often used in computers and form the basis of programs designed for responding to user requests. In particular, they specify the cardinality of links, which considerably increases programming efficiency.

Algorithms and Flow Charts

So far, we have examined graphic representations in the form of *conceptual* trees or networks. We will now present a well-known diagram used to describe *procedural* knowledge. A set of procedures is also called an algorithm. A convenient way to represent an algorithm is by a flow chart. Flow charts are used in introductory courses in programming, but also in other fields of knowledge, especially in education.

Below are two examples of simple flow charts. The first is a programmable algorithm used for calculating the sum of the first N positive integers, whatever the value of N. The second is a simplified version of a method used in instructional engineering called LVR (Learner Verification and Revision) for validating pedagogical material through a number of learner verification cycles and revisions.

These examples are quite different. The first

Figure 6. Two examples of simple flow charts

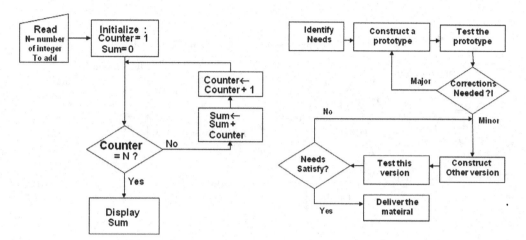

example has only one possible machine interpretation. It is intended for a computer that will perform the calculation loop several times within a more complex program. On the other hand, the second example is heuristic and imprecise. It is intended for humans requiring a good deal of judgment to make decisions at each cycle.

Yet both representations share features that distinguish them from the other examples we have presented thus far. They consist of actions and decisions that guide further action. They are dynamic rather than static. They take place in time and involve a number of cycles or loops that end when certain conditions are met, for example, when the list of numbers to add is exhausted or the requirements resulting from the tests are reasonably satisfied.

Such representations are necessary for learning procedures and methods. They also describe the processes used in instructional engineering and can guide programmers in developing highly complex telelearning systems.

Causal Diagrams and Decision Trees

This is another form of procedural representation used in many fields, especially for decision-support and expert systems, where describing the cause and effect and influence links between various factors is important. Decisions may be administrative, instructional, or otherwise. They can be used by a knowledge-based computer system or by a person who must take into account several factors. Figure 7a is an example of a causal diagram (partial) illustrating the causes of a car not starting.

The links are read from left to right and are interpreted as follows: A car not starting can be caused by carburetor, engine, or electrical failure. Engine failure can be caused by poor performance, complete failure, voltage or spark plug problems, oil problems, or fuel consumption. Oil problems can be caused by engine temperature, oil level, or oil pressure.

Values for each attribute can be indicated on the links as required. For example, the engine temperature may be normal or high, or oil may be normal or related to problems due to temperature, low level, or low pressure. In other cases, links could indicate the likelihood of a problem being caused by such or such an attribute.

In a causal diagram, each attribute and its dependent values form a constraint (Paquette & Roy, 1990), for example, "Oil" and its dependent attributes "Oil level," "Oil pressure," and "Engine temperature."

To construct an expert system, one can produce a decision tree for each constraint in a causal

Figure 7. A causal diagram and decision tree for identifying causes of failure

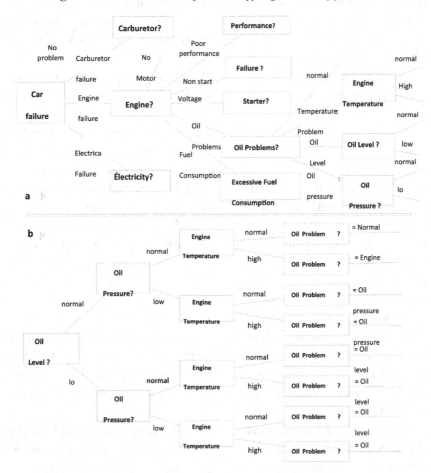

diagram. Figure 7b shows such a decision tree associated with the constraint "Oil Problem". To create such a decision tree, we begin with one of the attributes that influences the constraint (for example, oil level), and then draw an arch for each possible value to a second attribute (for example, oil pressure). We do the same for the second attribute. When all attributes are completed, we link each complete path of the tree to the main constraint attribute (in our example, "Oil Problem ?") and determine this value of the attribute in each case represent by a path from root to leave, i.e. the type of oil-related problem.

In fact, a decision tree can be used to directly construct a set of rules forming the knowledge base of an expert system. In our example, the following rules would be obtained from the decision tree:

- If *Oil-level* = normal and *Oil-pressure* = normal and *Engine-temp* = normal
  ○ Therefore, *Oil Problem = normal*
- If *Oil-level* = *normal* and *Oil-pressure* = *normal* and *Engine-temp* = *high*
  ○ Therefore, *Oil Problem = Engine Temperature*
- If *Oil-level* = *normal* and *Oil-pressure* = *low*
  ○ Therefore, *Oil Problem = Oil pressure*
- If *Oil-level* = low
  Therefore, *Oil Problem = Oil level.*

Causal diagrams can be used to divide the

11

task of decision-making into smaller sets of local decisions based on a constraint formed by single attribute and the attributes directly influencing it To complete the rule base, simply associate a decision tree with each of the constraints, for example, for the possible causes of engine or carburetor failure.

Inference Trees

Inference and problem solving are closely linked. Both may be graphically represented by diagrams similar to decision trees. Also called deduction trees, inference trees consist of statement nodes that are linked by arches on which the rules allowing the inference are indicated.

As we saw earlier, the inference rules for propositions are simple and generate quick results. Yet, who has not been surprised by the ending of a well-crafted detective novel? In the mind of the detective, facts identifying the culprit are linked with exquisite logic, while the reader is still struggling through plot twists and an avalanche of evidence. The strength of the detective is his ability to distinguish relevant information from irrelevant information, to make and test hypotheses, to reason by analogy, and to give importance to details that might otherwise appear insignificant.

Here is an example of facts gathered by our trusty sleuth. Can you find out "whodunit"?

If Andrew is innocent, then Bernard cannot be guilty because both said they were elsewhere together the night of the murder. For the same reason, Guy is innocent if Francis is. If Guy and Henry are innocent, then John is not guilty. On the other hand, if Bernard and Charles are innocent, so is Francis. Guy and Karen can prove the innocence of Larry if they themselves are innocent. If Andrew is innocent, so is Zoltan. It is certain that either William or John is guilty. On the other hand, it is proved beyond any doubt that Henry, Charles, and Andrew could not have committed the crime.

Let us represent the statement "X is innocent" by the initial of each suspect X. Then, let us represent each statement in propositional logic. The following ten statements are obtained:

• If A then B; If F then B; If G and H then J; If B and C then F; If G and K then L; If A then Z; W or J; H; C; A.

Figure 8. An inference tree

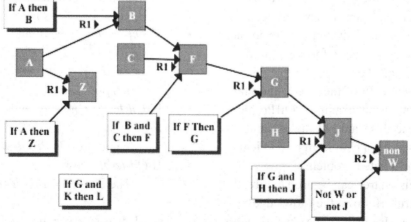

Figure 8 is an inference tree that connects these statements through links representing inference steps based on one or more of the following rules:

- **R1**: From (X) and (*if* X *then* Y), we can infer (Y)
- **R2**: From (*not* X) and (X *or* Y), we can infer (Y)

The above graph can be interpreted as follows: From "If A is innocent then B is innocent" and "A is innocent" we can infer from rule R1 that "B is innocent." The last step may be interpreted as follows: From "W is guilty (not innocent) or J is guilty" and "J is not guilty" we can infer from rule R2 that "W is guilty." A node is not attached to the rest because it is not used in the inference chain.

Object-Oriented Models

The rise of object-oriented programming has led to the development of highly precise graphic representational languages that are used in the design of complex computer systems. Examples of these include "Modern structured analysis" (Yourdon, 1989), "Object modeling technique (WTO)" (Rumbaugh, Blaha, Premerlani, Eddy, & Lorensen, 1991), KADS (Scheiber, Wielinga & Breuker, 1993), conceptual graphs (Sowa, 1984) to name a few. Recently, three of these methods were combined to create the UML (Unified Modeling Language), which has become the standard for object-oriented systems (Booch, Jacobson & Rumbaugh, 1999).

Figure 9 shows an example of this type of modeling. These methods propose representing computer systems through several models. The example here is one such model; it represents

Figure 9. An example of an object-oriented model

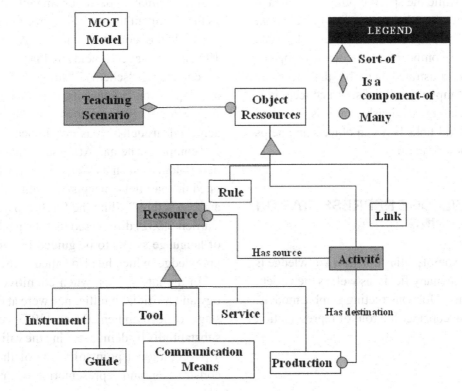

a *static* view of object classes; different models are required to represent the *dynamic* aspect of systems and to implement the corresponding code.

A teaching scenario is a kind of MOT model and shares the same basic properties. Because of the inheritance mechanism in object programming, these properties do not have to be recoded. A teaching scenario consists of objects that can be resources, activities, links, or rules. Activities are derived from resources that can be instruments, guide, tools, means of communication, services, or productions. Activities implement production-type resources.

Such graphs are useful for designing software based on structured objects because they provide an overview of the composition and relationships among the objects to be programmed. The example here shows three types of links common to most representation systems based on object modeling:

Inheritance, represented here by the "Sort-of" link, defines a relationship between a class and its subclasses in which the common properties of all resource types of the resource object share the same code, while the specific properties of each resource type are coded separately. *Aggregation*, represented here by the "Component-of" link, describes the composition of complex objects. *Association*, illustrated here by the "Derived from" and "Implements" links, is a concept borrowed from entity-relationship models; it is used to create lateral links between objects and helps to clarify their properties.

1.3 KNOWLEDGE REPRESENTATION AND LEARNING

The above examples illustrate how knowledge is represented in many fields, as well as the variety of methods used for constructing graphic models. We will now consider the role of representation in learning.

Schema Representation

Structured representation of knowledge and learning are inextricably linked. Understanding is impossible without identifying and classifying objects and ideas and linking them by association in some organized way—through structures. Without structures, it would be impossible to construct mental representations that make the world intelligible for us. Objects would have an identity, but we would not be able to link them together.

These mental structures or schemas vary in complexity. They can describe concrete or abstract concepts such as *computer*, *kindness*, or *economy*. They can combine a series of events into a scenario such as visiting an exhibition. They can represent complex procedures such as manufacturing newsprint or solving differential equations. They can also describe a set of laws or principles that make up a theory.

The concept of schema as the building block of mental structures is now well established in cognitive psychology. Indeed, the concept has marked the replacement of behaviorism with cognitivism as the dominant theoretical approach in psychology and other cognitive sciences. As early as the 1920s, Jean Piaget (Inhelder & Piaget, 1958) used the concepts of "schema," "structure," "strategy," and "operation" to describe cognitive processes. According to Piaget, growth of the intellect is achieved through increasingly logical, numerous, and complex schemas. At the same time, "gestalt" psychologists such as Wertheimer (1945) developed the parallel concepts of "entity," "pattern," and "structure," while the English psychologist, Bartlett (1932) discovered that the interpretation of language seems to be guided by pre-existing knowledge, which he also called "schemas."

In the late sixties, when cognitive psychology and artificial intelligence were at their early stages of development, Bruner (1973) contributed substantially by demonstrating the validity, from a psychological point of view, of the internal construction and representation of knowledge.

Along the same lines, Newell & Simon (1972) developed a representation of problem-solving tasks, while Minsky (1975) defined the concept of "frame" as essential to understanding perception and as a way to reconcile the notions of declarative knowledge and procedural knowledge (Winograd, 1985).

Schemas play a central role in the construction of knowledge (Rumelhart & Ortony, 1977), which in turn is essential to the learning process.

- Schemas guide perception, which is defined as an active, constructive, and selective process. Consider, for example, a group of pedestrians who are waiting for a bus and then see it appear above the cars in front of it. Only a few elements are required for the pedestrians to recognize it as a bus because they possess schemas that allow them to reconstruct the remaining elements.
- Schemas are the building blocks of memory and recall. Mental representations are organized in such a way as to allow easy access to them. The more schemas are interconnected with one another, the easier it is to remember.
- Schemas make understanding possible by allowing existing schemas to confront new experiences. If no schemas are associated with the experiences, they remain incomprehensible.
- Schemas provide support for problem-solving and performing complex tasks. They help to identify problems, set objectives, acknowledge constraints, and plan and implement solutions.

From the perspective of cognitive psychology, learning is the result of a process of construction and reconstruction of schemas; it involves an interaction with the physical and social world rather than simply a search and transfer of information.

How do we change or create our system of schemas, in other words, how do we learn? First, we use external experiences to give attribute values to existing schemas. We then try to complement these values in order to extract meaning from the experiences. This can be done by using the attribute values of other schemas in order to follow a procedure, make an inference, or create a slightly modified version of an existing schema. When this process of adaptation fails, when new experiences cannot be described using existing schemas, the latter can be restructured to create new schemas.

The link between knowledge representation and learning can be described in the following way: Learning is a process by which a representation of a certain knowledge representation is transformed into a another representation of that knowledge. Learning is a process, whereas the representation of knowledge is both the starting point and result.

Diagnosing and Assessing Knowledge

Knowledge representation plays a central role in learning. It can be used to diagnose or assess learner knowledge, convey structured information to the learner, or serve as a basis for learning strategies.

Diagnosing and assessing learner knowledge is a three-step process involving 1) extracting knowledge from the subject through various techniques; 2) representing it structurally; and 3) comparing this representation with an ideal model, for example, that provided by an expert in the field (Jonassen, Beissner, & Yacci, 1993). As an example, let us refer back to our conceptual map of climate change (Figure 4). This map could be used to diagnose learners' knowledge. A list of concepts from the field would be presented to the learner, who would then be asked to link the concepts. The type of link could be left open to the learner or selected from a fixed list such as "caused-by," "imply," "produce," "sort-of."

A learner who produced Table 2 would demonstrate knowledge about some of the effects

Table 2. Links between concepts

Concept A	Concept B	Link A to B?	Link B to A?
Climate change	Greenhouse gases	Caused by	N/A
Climate change	New farming practices	?	?
Greenhouse gases	New farming practices	?	?
Current farming practices	Fertilizers	Utilize	N/A
Fertilizers	Nitrous oxide	?	N/A
Greenhouse gases	Nitrous oxide	N/A	Sort-of
....	....	....	.....

of current farming practices but not about the solutions offered by new agricultural practices. A conceptual map demonstrating this knowledge would be different from the one in Figure 4. By comparing the two conceptual maps, we would obtain a "structural" diagnosis of the learner's weaknesses.

Structuring Information Transfer

The goal here is to structure learning content in order to present it to the learner or develop teaching material based on this structure. We can use various methods of representation in the form of lists, tables, or graphic representations such as semantic networks and cause-effect maps in order to provide an overview of the subject matter.

For example, the semantic tree shown in Figure 3, can be used to organize information related to art movements and representative painters for a course in art history. Using the term "advance organizer," Ausubel (1968) proposed the use of pre-existing structural representations at the beginning of a learning process to provide learners with an advanced reference schema for guiding further learning.

Learning through Knowledge Representation

A learning strategy is a set of mental operations used by a learner to acquire knowledge. Learning strategies are generalized skills that can be applied in different fields. They aim to increase the number of associations between new information and knowledge previously acquired. Among these strategies are various forms of graphical or tabular representations. In this case, however, it is the learner and not the instructor who creates such representations. Constructing semantic networks helps learners to develop these learning strategies.

For this purpose, Dansereau (1978) proposed a technique for knowledge representation. Students structure a particular field of learning by building a network in the form of a set of nodes connected by predefined links. The nodes represent a particular object, event, or idea. The links are non-oriented and are read from top to bottom using the following semantic rules:

- A P link connects a node that is part of or a component of the node above it;
- A T link connects a node that is a type of or an example of the node above it;
- An L link connects a node that leads to, precedes, or results in the node below it;
- An A link connects two nodes that are analogous or similar;
- A C link connects a node that is a characteristic or attribute of the node above it;
- An E link connects a node that is evidence or proof of the node above it.

By using this system of representation, learners are able to create semantic networks such as the following:

Dansereau and his colleagues also created a more complex system consisting of 13 types of links. An initial assessment revealed that learners found that the 6-link system inadequate but that the 13-link system was difficult to implement.

Further studies showed that the 6-link system was, in fact, effective and represented a good compromise, being neither too general nor too specific (Dansereau & Holley, 1982). Students using this representational technique remember concepts better than those who do not use it. As well, students consider that it is a useful technique for problem solving.

A less structured method was also tested, which allowed students to generate their own links instead of using the 6 predefined links. Results showed that students with poor verbal skills seem to benefit from the more structured approach, while those with better verbal skills benefit from the less structured one.

1.4 KNOWLEDGE REPRESENTATION AND INSTRUCTIONAL ENGINEERING

The MISA learning systems engineering method that will be presented in Chapter 8 can generate four learning models. Each of these models can used to construct a graphic model representing knowledge, pedagogical strategies, materials,

and knowledge delivery. To do this, we require a general method of knowledge representation of which we will now present the fundamentals.

Types of Knowledge in Education

Increasingly, knowledge in educational sciences uses the concept of schema while distinguishing different types of knowledge. The reason for classifying knowledge is to match teaching strategy with knowledge type.

The Component Display Theory (CDT), an instructional theory developed by Merrill (1994), is based on the idea that the products of learning can be classified into a finite number of categories and associated with different teaching strategies. It uses a two-dimensional matrix involving performance and content. Performance consists of three skill levels: remembering, using, and finding (or building/constructing). Skills apply to four types of content:

• *Facts*, for example the association between a date and an event, a number of objects, or the attribute value of an object;

Figure 10. Example of a learner-created semantic network (Jonassen, Beissner, & Yacci, 1993, p. 232)

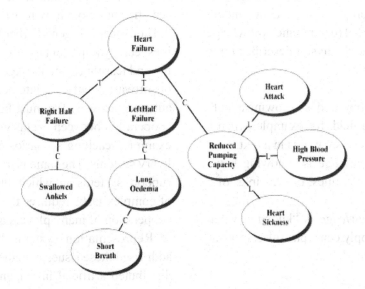

• *Concepts*, which are classes of objects, events, or symbols that share common characteristics;
• *Procedures*, which are steps that lead to action;
• *Principles*, which are cause and effect relationships in a process.

In a reference book widely used in instructional design, Romiszowski (1981) also presents a taxonomy of knowledge. Using expected post-learning performance as a basis, he describes two categories of skills—memory and understanding—associated respectively with factual knowledge and conceptual knowledge.

He then distinguishes between factual knowledge about objects, events, people, and procedures. Then, at a conceptual level, he describes the specific concepts that allow us to recognize instances of a phenomenon and the rules and principles that allow to us to link concepts and facts in order to predict or explain phenomena.

Finally, Romiszowski describes four types of knowledge—facts, procedures, concepts, and principles. These, he notes, represent the four categories of information used by Williams (1977) to extend the taxonomies of Bloom (1975) and Gagné (1970) and are similar to the categories of information previously used by Horn (1969) as the basis for his "information mappings."

Another leading researcher in education, Tennyson (1990), proposed a teaching model emphasizing contextual (or strategic) knowledge in learning activities. Tennyson describes three types of knowledge:

• *Declarative knowledge* is "knowing about" something in a field, for example, when a reader underlines key words in a text;
• *Procedural knowledge* is "knowing how" to apply concepts, rules, or principles of a field;
• *Contextual knowledge* is "knowing when and why" to apply concepts, rules, or principles of a field;

Other authors such as West, Farmer, & Wolff (1991) reaffirm these three categories:

• *Declarative knowledge* can be represented in memory by an associative network of propositions in which facts and concepts are organized (Anderson, 1985); networks can be semantic or episodic;
• *Procedural knowledge* is "knowing how" in the form of instructions carried out in a particular order and according to certain conditions;
  • *Conditional knowledge* is knowing when or why to use a procedure; it takes the form "if these conditions are met, then do such and such a thing."

Similar to Merrill (1994) and Romiszowski (1981), Tennyson (1990) and West *et al.* (1991) group facts and concepts under the term "declarative knowledge", and principles under the term "conditional knowledge."

Representing Interaction and Cooperation

Cooperation between agents is a dimension long overlooked in knowledge-based systems. More recently, it has been addressed in workflow representation notations as will be presented in chapter 9. The concept of agent (Ferber 1994; Sycara 1998) is especially important for instructional engineering and learning systems. Agents are the persons or software agents that interact in a process in an autonomous way. We must be able to represent cooperation between agents when designing, for example, teaching scenarios or telelearning delivery systems. The same is true for performance support systems in which the implementation of complex tasks requires the collaboration and cooperation of many players and agents.

Representation systems have increasingly addressed these issues, whether in the context of distributed artificial intelligence (Bond & Gasser, 1988; Gasser, 1991), cognitive or reactive multi-agent systems (Ferber, 1994), or software engineering.

Within the latter, the KADS method (Schreiber *et al.*, 1993) proposes a cooperation model as one of its seven model types. Central to this method are the *expertise model* and *cooperation model*, which define a system's principal components and future behavior. Combining these two sub-models into a coherent whole is the *conceptual model*. The cooperation model specifies the tasks that require cooperation and assigns them to the various agents of the system. It defines three elements:

- Task distribution among agents
- Communication between agents to ensure task dependencies; outputs of tasks can become inputs for other tasks;
- Control, achieved through local recognition agents performing each task.

The UML method also proposes collaboration diagrams made up of nodes and links. These diagrams contain both static and dynamic elements, including class societies, interface objects, and other elements that work together to produce a behavior greater than the sum of its parts. The diagrams are particularly useful for implementing use cases and describing agent roles in a system. In the same way, the knowledge representation system discussed throughout this book must also take into account the representation of actors, their roles and their interactions.

Modeling Information Systems

In a popular book on object-oriented programming (Booch *et al.*, 1999), the central role of modeling is explained in the following way: "Modeling is a central part of all the activities that lead up to the deployment of good software. We build models to communicate the desired structure and behavior of our systems. We build models to visualize and control the system's architecture. We build models to better understand the system we are building, often exposing opportunities for simplification and reuse. We build models to manage risk" (p. 4). The authors make the following analogy:

If you want to build a doghouse, you can pretty much start with a pile of lumber, some nails, and a few basic tools, such as a hammer, saw and tape measure. In a few hours, with little prior planning, you'll likely end up with a dog house that's reasonably functional, and you can probably do it with no one else's help. (…) If you want to build a house for your family, you can start with a pile of lumber, some nails and a few basic tools, but it's going to take you a lot longer and your family will certainly be more demanding that the dog. In this case, unless you've already done it a few dozen times before, you'll be better served by doing some detailed planning before you pound the first nail or lay the foundation. At the very least, you'll want to make some sketches of how you want the house to look.(…) If you want to build a high-rise office building, it would be infinitely stupid for you to start with a pile of lumber, some nails, and a few basic tools. You will want to do extensive planning, because the cost of failure is high. You will be just a part of a much large group responsible for developing and deploying the building, so the team will need all sorts of blueprints an models to comunicate with one another. Curiously, a lot of software development organizations start out wanting to build high rises but approach the problem as if they were knocking out a dog house. (pp. 8-9)

In most cases, models are necessary in order to have an overall understanding of a system. They help achieve four goals:

1. View the system as it is or as we would like it to be;

2. Specify the structure and behavior of the system;
3. Obtain outlines and models that will guide the development of the system;
4. Document decisions and actions.

For these reasons, modeling is at the core of the instructional engineering method presented in Chapter 4. Because of the complexity of telelearning systems, a representational method is required that takes into account the following principles.

- *The choice of model greatly influences how problems are dealt with and how solutions are found.* In the next Chapter, we will present a taxonomy of knowledge models. One of the key issues for instructional engineering is precisely to choose a model that corresponds to training objectives, i.e. that helps reduce the gap between current and targeted learner skills. As we will see in Part II, there is a direct relationship between a competency and a problem type.

- *Each model can have different levels of detail.* The challenge for instructional engineering is to find the right level of detail that both optimizes targeted knowledge and skills and takes into account the size of the proposed learning system (scope of the program, duration of the course or activity, etc.)

- *The best models are connected to reality.* When implemented, a model must reflect as closely as possible the learning system it was intended to represent. Ideally, one should be able to browse through the knowledge base as if it were a reference book, or simulate a teaching scenario.

- *No single model is sufficient. Each non-trivial system must be designed using a small number of quasi-independent models.* This is one of the principles highlighted in Chapter 4. The four models generated by the instructional engineering method are independent but associated. Though not constructed the same way, they all use the same representational technique, which we will discuss in the following chapters.

CONCLUSION

We have highlighted the central role of knowledge representation and the languages used to construct models of reality. We have also introduced the various graphical forms of knowledge representation applied in information sciences and education.

Knowledge representation is at the heart of learning. Schemas, which are mental representations, are the inputs and outputs of the learning process. They can be used to diagnose and assess current knowledge, to structure information according to targeted knowledge or skills, and ultimately, to support learning strategies that engage learners directly in knowledge representation activities.

Knowledge representation is also at the heart of instructional engineering. It must be able to produce learning system models that take into account the types of knowledge and relationships in a particular field and the interactions between the various agents involved in the learning process.

Particular attention must be given to the choice of models, their level of detail, their ability to reflect reality, and both their independence and inter-connectedness—all of which go into representing a learning system.

These guiding principles provide the basis for the "Modeling using Object Types" (MOT) system that will be presented in the next chapter.

REFERENCES

Anderson, J.A. (1985). *Cognitive psychology and its implications*. New York: Freeman.

Anderson, J. A. (1990). Hybrid computation in cognitive science: Neural networks and symbols. *Applied Cognitive Psychology, 4*, 337–347. doi:10.1002/acp.2350040408

Ausubel, D. (1968). *Educational psychology: a cognitive view*. New York: Holt, Rinehart and Winston.

Bartlett, F. C. (1932). *Remembering*. Cambridge, UK: Cambridge University Press.

Bloom, B. S. (1975). Taxonomy of Educational Objectives: The Classification of Educational Goals. New York: D.M

Bond, A. H., & Gasser, L. (Eds.). (1988). *Readings in Distributed Artificial Intelligence*. San Mateo, CA: Morgan Kaufman.

Booch, G., Jacobson, J., & Rumbaugh, I. (1999). *The Unified Modeling Language User Guide*. Reading, MA: Addison-Wesley.

Bruner, J. (1973). *Beyond the Information Given*. New York: Norton.

Chen, P. P. S. (1976). The entity-relationship model-toward a unified view of data. *ACM Transactions on Database Systems, 1*(1), 9–36. doi:10.1145/320434.320440

Dansereau, D. F. (1978). The development of a learning strategies curriculum . In O'Neil, H. F. Jr., (Ed.), *Learning Strategies* (pp. 1–29). New York: Academic Press.

Dansereau, D. F., & Holley, C. D. (1982). Development and evaluation of a text mapping strategy . In Flammer, A., & Kintsch, W. (Eds.), *Discourse Processing* (pp. 536–554). doi:10.1016/S0166-4115(08)62718-1

Ferber, J. (1994). Coopération réactive et émergence. *Intellectica, 2*, 19–52.

Gagné, R. M. (1970). *The Conditions of Learning* (2nd ed.). New York: Holt, Rhinehart & Winston.

Gasser, L. (1991). Social conceptions of knowledge and action: DAI foundations and open systems semantics. *Artificial Intelligence, 47*, 107–138. doi:10.1016/0004-3702(91)90052-L

Horn, R. E. (1969). *Information Mapping for Learning and Reference*. Lexington, MA: Information Resources Inc.

Inhelder, B., & Piaget, J. (1958). *The Growth of Logical Thinking from Childhood to Adolescence*. New York: Basic Books. doi:10.1037/10034-000

Jonassen, D. H., Beissner, K., & Yacci, M. (1993). *Structural Knowledge: techniques for representing, conveying, and acquiring structural knowledge*. Hillsdale, NJ: Lawrence Erlbaum Associates.

Merrill, M. D. (1994). *Principles of Instructional Design*. Englewood Cliffs, NJ: Educational Technology Publications.

Minsky, M. (1975). A Framework for Representing Knowledge . In Winston, P. H. (Ed.), *The Psychology of Computer Vision* (pp. 211–277). New York, NJ: McGraw-Hill.

Newell, A., & Simon, H. A. (1972). *Human problem solving*. Englewood Cliffs, NJ: Prentice-Hall.

Paquette, G., & Bergeron, G. (1989). *L'intelligence articielle- comprendre et prolonger l'intelligence humaine* (2nd ed.). Montréal, Canada: Beauchemin.

Paquette, G., & Roy, L. (1990). *Systèmes à base de connaissances*. Montréal, Canada: Beauchemin.

Pitrat, J. (1991). *Métaconnaissance, avenir de l'intelligence artificielle*. Paris: Hermès.

Romiszowski, A. J. (1981). *Designing Instructional Systems*. New York: Kogan Page and Nichols Publishing.

Rumbaugh, I., Blaha, M., Premerlani, W., Eddy, F., & Lorensen, W. (1991). *Object-oriented Modelling and Design*. Englewood Clliffs, NJ: Prentice-Hall.

Rumelhart, D. E., & Ortony, A. (1977). The representation of knowledge in memory. In R. C. Anderson, R. J. Spiro & W. E. Montague (Eds.), Schoolling and the acquisition of knowledge (pp.93-135). Hillsdale, NJ: Lawrence.

Schreiber, G., Wielinga, B., & Breuker, J. (1993). *KADS - A Principled Approach to Knowledge-based System Development*. San Diego, CA: Academic Press.

Sowa, J. F. (1984). *Conceptual Structures, Information Processing in Mind and Machine*. Reading, MA: Addison-Wesley.

Sycara, K. P. (1998). The many faces of Agents. *AI Magazine*, (Summer): 1998.

Tennyson, R. (1990). Cognitive learning theory linked to instructional theory. *Journal of Structural Learning*, *10*(3), 249–25.

Wertheimer, M. (1945). *Productive Thinking*. New York: Harper & Row.

West, C. K., Farmer, J. A., & Wolff, P. M. (1991). *Instructional design: implications from cognitive science*. Englewood Cliffs, NJ: Prentice Hall.

Williams, R. G. (1977). A behavioural typology of educational objectives for the cognitive domain. *Educational Technology*, *17*(6), 39–46.

Winograd, T. (1985). Beyond the declarative/procedural controversy . In Brachman, R. J., & Lévesque, H. J. (Eds.), *Readings in Knowledge Representation* (pp. 357–370). Los Altos, CA: Morgan Kaufman Publishers.

Yourdon, E. (1989). *Modern Structured Analysis*. Englewood Cliffs, NJ: Prentice Hall.

ENDNOTE

[1] For a discussion or other types of formal logic systems, the reader can consult online course material by P. Suber (http://www.earlham.edu/~peters/courses/log/loghome.htm) or books in Probabilistic Logic or Fuzzy Logic.

Chapter 2
Modeling Using a Semi-Formal Visual Language

Gilbert Paquette
LICEF Research Center, Canada

ABSTRACT

- Basis of the MOT Modeling System
  - Schema representation in MOT
  - Objectives of the representation system
  - Construction Principles
- Basic Knowledge Types and Relations
- Syntax Rules of the MOT Language
  - The MOT meta-model
  - Rules regarding the origin and destination of links
  - Rules regarding cycles and multiplicity of links
- Representing other types of models in MOT
  - Semantic trees and a conceptual maps
  - Semantic networks
  - Flow charts
  - Causal Diagrams and Decision Trees
  - Inference trees

In this chapter, we present a visual knowledge representation method that can be used by software designers to construct a learning system or task support system. The *Modeling using Object Types* (MOT) method can also be used in other contexts, especially as a support tool for learners or by experts wishing to represent a particular area of knowledge. In the context of constructivist pedagogy, such activities overlap. Because it places users in a problem-solving environment, a task support system allows them to construct *new* knowledge. Conversely, a constructivist

DOI: 10.4018/978-1-61520-839-5.ch002

learning system can use a task support system as a basis for learning activities that focus on solving *existing* problems, either real or imagined. Such an environment can also engage learners in instructional engineering activities per se by applying the principle that one understands what one can explain clearly to others.

The representational method presented here was developed in 1992 as part of a university course on integrating knowledge modeling into the field of instructional design. The method was further refined and became the basis for a modeling tool used in an instructional engineering workshop (Paquette, Crevier & Aubin, 1994). The tool is now integrated into the ADISA system (Distributed Workshop in Learning System Engineering), but also exists in two versions, MOT and MOT+, which will be presented in Chapter 8. More recently, this representation language has evolved into a scenario editor and ontology editor, first incorporated in MOT then adapted as a central tool in the TELOS system, which we will introduce in Part III.

In Chapter 1, we outlined various forms of knowledge representation used in education and computer engineering. The different models used by a project require modeling techniques that are distinct yet complementary. Instructional designers need an integrated formalism that is easily accessible and able to provide them with a coherent overview of key processes, concepts, and strategies that describe a learning system. Rather than distinguish between conceptual models, procedural models, and theoretical models, thus creating a proliferation of models, the system presented here stresses an integrated approach to different types of knowledge, notably concepts, procedures, and principles, and to their instantiation as facts. Such an approach is necessary in order to facilitate acquisition of the technique by learning system designers and users.

This effort at simplification is offset by the general nature of modeling using object types. Our representation system can serve the same function as many of the techniques presented in the previous chapter; indeed, these can be re-expressed as MOT models, and will be described more fully in this chapter.

In the MOT system, creating a typology of knowledge objects and links is essential because pedagogical treatment differs for each type. For example, if the knowledge object is a concept, we can construct it through a process of induction, alternating between the specific and the general through examples and counter examples. If the knowledge object is a process, we can simulate and construct it by solving increasingly complex problems. If the knowledge object is a principle, we can test it in various applications and then formulate it more precisely through discussion forums.

We will first present the basic principles of the representation system, then its main components and modeling rules. We will then conclude the chapter with an analysis of the possibilities and limits of the representation system with regard to certain criteria.

2.1 THEORETICAL BASIS OF THE MOT MODELING SYSTEM

In this section, we will present the basic principles of the MOT representation system. We will apply the concept of schema and identify the different types of knowledge and links used in other representation systems. We will then define the objectives and principles of the MOT system.

Schema Representation in MOT

The MOT representation system is based on the theory of schemas presented in the preceding chapter. The distinction between two broad categories of schemas—declarative or conceptual schemas, and procedural schemas—is now well accepted. The first category involves data, while the second includes the procedures and methods used in data processing to organize information.

More recently, a third category of "conditional" or "strategic" schemas has been proposed (Paris, Lipson & Wixson, 1983). These consist of principles having one or more conditions that describe the application context, and a sequence of procedures to apply or statements of properties that are a consequence of the condition(s). Two categories of principles can be distinguished:

- *operational principles*, describing when to apply certain procedures, e.g. "If the value 100 is reached, then stop adding whole numbers;
- *relational principles*, combining two or more concepts, in particular, the cause and effect relation, e.g. "If the light is red, then we should not cross the street."

Schemas are well suited to visual representation of knowledge—procedural or strategic—in which the main components, called *attributes*, as well as their *attribute values* are described. An attribute value is *concrete* if it is associated with an object from the real world, but more often, it is *abstract* (a number, a color, a form, etc.) and can be described by other schemas.

In the MOT representation system, there are four types of knowledge objects— facts, concepts, procedures, and principles—described through schemas. With regard to facts, we distinguish three types of facts corresponding to the attribute values of concepts, procedures, and principles. We speak of concept examples, procedural traces, and statements of principles. Similar categories of knowledge are described by Merrill (1994), Romiszowski (1981), and Tennyson (1994), whose work was discussed in the previous chapter. In the MOT representation system, actors and interactions are represented through principle-type knowledge objects in which the actors are seen as applying principles to control procedures or other principles. By linking these objects with the procedures they regulate (through *regulation* links), we are able represent

task distribution among agents. By decomposing a principle, we are able to describe in as much detail as necessary the communication and control strategies forming the basis of cooperation.

These schemas can be combined through six basic links—instantiation, specialization, composition, precedence, the input/output relation, and regulation. A seventh link—application—is used to link models to represent, for example, competencies, a subject that will be covered in Part II. Note that these links are also schemas having their own names, visual representations, origins, and destinations, and unlike those of other representation systems, they are directional.

Objectives of the Representation System

We have identified six major objectives of the representation system—simplicity, generality, completeness, ease of interpretation, standardization and communicability, and computability.

- *Simplicity.* The system must be easy to use by designers, learners, and instructors with a minimum of training. It must therefore contain a number of basic components that is neither too large, which would make the system difficult to use, nor too small, which would complicate the models artificially.
- *Ease of interpretation.* The components of the system must be easy to interpret by users. In particular, the links must be sufficiently distinct from one another in terms of their meaning. These meanings should be natural enough to explain them readily without ambiguity.
- *Genericity.* The system should perform the same functions with as much facility as the various representations used in education, including conceptual maps, semantic networks, inference trees, flow charts, decisions trees, and cause and effect diagrams,

as well as the dynamic component systems used in software engineering.

- *Completeness.* The system must be able to represent all relevant situations in a particular field of knowledge. Using only a few knowledge object types and links, one should be able to represent complex models of conceptual systems, processes (including cooperation between agents), methods, and theories.
- *Standardization and communicability.* The system should promote the communication of knowledge among users. Such communication is facilitated by the standardization of components and modeling rules. A well-constructed model by one person should be easily interpreted by another person with little documentation or instructions.
- *Computability.* Finally, the system must be able to produce symbolic representations that can be used by modern computer systems, either by translating the models into the XML format of MOT language, or into the more standardized XML format of the Ontology Web Language (OWL), a format which is used internationally for the majority of new knowledge processing tools.

Construction Principles

To achieve the above objectives, we have established a number of guiding principles for the representation system:

1. Knowledge objects are represented by schemas whose form is determined by the type of knowledge, whether a fact, concept, procedure, or principle.
2. Schema attributes are represented by links between knowledge objects; these include links of instantiation, specialization, composition, precedence, the input/output relation, regulation, and application. Abstract knowledge (concepts, procedures, and principles)

is instantiated to produce different sets of facts, respectively called examples, traces, and statements.

3. Abstract knowledge (concepts, procedures, and principles) are organized into hierarchies.
4. The notion of process is represented by procedural-type knowledge objects with their own inputs/outputs and operating principles. We prefer the term process to that of task. There is a distinction between the two—a task is a declarative description of a process to be performed, i.e. the *output* of a process, while the process has a more dynamic connotation representing all actions or group of actions, with their relationships required to perform a task or set of tasks
5. Inputs (or data) and outputs (or products) are represented by instantiated concepts as required by facts and according to the genericity of the procedure.
6. The control structure of a procedure is represented by principles regulating the procedure from the outside or incorporated into the procedure in the form of decision rules. Agents or actors in a distributed or cooperative system are represented by principle-type schemas when our concern is limited to the control aspects.

2.2 BASIC OBJECT TYPES

In the previous chapter, we discussed the components of natural and formal languages such as English, Morse code or computer programming. The same components will be used to describe the visual language of the MOT representation system. We will first present its *lexicon* or *vocabulary*, that is to say the different types of knowledge objects and links that it uses. We will then describe how these knowledge objects and links are interpreted in various situations, thus defining its semantics. In section 2.4, we will provide the grammar rules

Figure 1. Definition of abstract knowledge object-types and their graphic symbols

Abstract knowledge	Symbol
Concepts describe a domain's classes of objects (the "what" dimension) by their common properties, the "values" of an object's properties making it distinct from others.	
Procedures describe sets of operations that affect objects (the "how" dimension); they represent combinations of actions that may apply to several cases, each case distinguishing itself from others by the objects to which actions may apply and their resulting transformation.	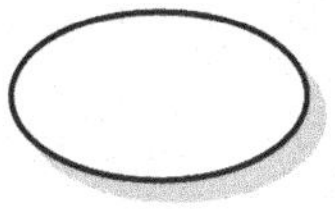
Principles are general *statements* intended to describe objects properties, establish cause-and-effect links between objects (the "why" dimension), or determine a procedure's application conditions (the "when" dimension); principles are most often formulated as "If *this* condition ...then *that* condition or *that* action."	

Figure 2. Definition of fact types and their graphic symbols

Facts	Symbol
Examples result from specifying values for each concept's attribute, i.e. from a set of facts that describe a concrete and precise object.	
Traces are obtained the same way, by specifying the input and output variables of all actions that compose a procedure, which results in a particular set of actions, inputs, and products, i.e. an execution trace.	
Statements are obtained the same way, by specifying a principle's variables, thus resulting in a cause-and-effect link between properties and values of particular objects, or between properties of a particular object and a precise executable action.	

for MOT. A language usually contains a procedural or *pragmatic* aspect that specifies the processes involved in constructing, modifying, or using a representation. We will present the pragmatic aspect of MOT in Chapter 4.

A MOT model consists of six knowledge object types[1] connected by seven relational or link types.

Knowledge objects are represented by various geometric figures. These may relate to abstract knowledge, to facts, or as we shall see later, to skills.

- **Abstract knowledge** represents classes of objects with particular attributes that describe their properties. There are three types of abstract knowledge—concepts, principles, and procedures (see Figure 1).

- **Facts** are data, comments, examples, prototypes, actions, or statements that describe a particular object. There are three types of facts, each corresponding to a type of abstract knowledge (see Figure 2).

Table 1. Interpretation of knowledge objects

Type	Interpretation and Examples
Concept	• classes of objects: countries, clothing, motor vehicles, etc. • types of documents: forms, brochures, images, etc. • categories of tools: text editors, TVs, etc. • categories of people: doctors, Europeans, etc. • classes of events: floods, conferences, etc.
Procedure	• generic operations: addition, motor assembly, etc. • general tasks: complete a report, supervise production, etc. • general activities: take an exam, teach a course, etc. • instructions: follow a recipe, assemble a piece of equipment, etc. • scenarios: a film, a meeting, etc.
Principle	• properties: taxpayer X has dependents, cars have four wheels, etc. • constraints: the task must be completed in 20 days, etc. • cause/effect relationships: if it rains for less than 5 days, then the crops will fail, etc. • laws: metals expand when heated, etc. • theories: laws of market economics, etc. • decisional rules: rules guiding an investment choice, etc. • prescriptions: principles of pedagogical design, etc. • regulating bodies or actors: author of a text.

Interpretation of Knowledge Objects

We will now present various interpretations of the graphic symbols defined above. Such interpretations allow different combinations of these symbols to be associated with objects in the real world. They also justify to a certain extent the rules of grammar and the exceptions that will be presented later.

The genericity of a representation system depends on the flexibility with which its symbols can be interpreted in different contexts. As such, knowledge objects in the MOT system can be used to represent different categories of objects in the real world, as shown in the table below.

Note that abstract knowledge is always interpreted by classes of objects, actions, or statements. Concepts, procedures, and principles must take into account the variability of individuals, actions, and procedures. If an instance is possible, it involves a set of facts (examples, traces, or statements).

2.3 PRIMITIVE RELATIONS BETWEEN KNOWLEDGE OBJECTS

Relations between knowledge objects are represented by directed links identified by the first letter of the relationship name. There are six basic types of relation between knowledge objects. A seventh link, which will be explored further in the chapter, connects knowledge objects between two domains; it is also used to connect skills that are generic to knowledge according to principles that will be discussed in Part II.

- The instanciation link (I) relates abstract knowledge to a group of facts obtained by giving values to attributes (variables) that define abstract knowledge. Abstract knowledge—concepts, procedures, or principles—is "instantiated" by sets of facts that are, respectively, examples, traces, or statements.
  ◦ Example: "John's car" is an instance of "Mustang cars."
- The composition link (C) connects knowledge to one of its components or parts. An object's attributes may be specified as

knowledge components by connecting the knowledge object to each of its attributes with the link "is composed of."

- Examples: A "car" is composed of a "body."
- "John's car" is composed of "the body of John's car."

- The specialization link (S) connects two abstract knowledge objects of the same type, where one is a particular case of the other. In other words, the second object is more general or abstract than the first.
  - Example: "Mustang" is a sort of "Car."

- The precedence link (P) connects two procedures or principles, where the first must be completed or satisfy before the second can begin.
  - Example: "Make an outline" precedes "Draft the text."

- The input/product link (I /P) connects a concept to a procedure. If the link's direction is from concept to procedure, the concept is an input to the procedure. If the direction is from procedure to concept, then the concept is the product of the procedure.
  - Example: "Outline" is an input to "Draft the text."
  - "Draft the text" produces "Text."

- The regulation link (R) is directed from a principle to a knowledge object (concept, procedure, or another principle), or vice versa. In the first case, the principle defines a concept by specifying constraints (sometimes called "integrity constraints"), or establishes a law or relation between two or several concepts. A regulation link from a principle to a procedure or another principle means that the principle exerts external control (regulates) on the execution of a procedure or the selection of other principles.
  - Examples: "Outline format rules" regulate "Outline."
  - "Traffic control rules" regulate "Permission for plane take off."
  - "Project management rules" regulate "Applicable design principles."

Interpretation of I Links

Abstract knowledge such as concept, procedure or principle is a schema, a mold for forming different instances. To produce an instance, all variable attributes of a concept, a procedure or a principle must receive a specific value, producing a single individual that is a member of a class that correspond to the concept, procedure or principle.

The instance effect is different depending on whether it is applied to a concept, procedure, or principle.

- In the case of a concept, the result is an individual member of the object class that represents the concept (an example). Each instance consists of a set of facts of the type "attribute = value."
- In the case of a procedure, the result is a set of actions for a particular case (a trace). Each instance consists of a series of actions that have been implemented for that particular case.
- In the case of a principle, the result is an affirmation that is either true or false (a statement). Each instance consists of statements obtained through instantiation of the "IF" condition and statements obtained through instantiation of the "THEN" condition or traces of procedures appearing in the "THEN" part of the principle.

The above three cases are illustrated in Table 2, showing the attributes of concepts, procedures, and principles with regard to the sets of facts resulting from instantiation.

Table 2 demonstrates that there are as many examples of the concept "metal object" as there are attribute values for it (length, thickness, type

Table 2. Interpretation of instance links (I)

Type	Knowledge objects and attributes	Instances (set of facts)
Concept	A metal object – Type of metal: X – Length: Y – Thickness: Z	• Type of metal = iron: Length = 1.6 m; Thickness = 1 mm • Type of metal = lead: Length = 2 mm; Thickness = 1 mm • …
Procedure	Measure the expansion of a heated metal – Select metal object – Heat to temperature B – Measure the expansion C	• Select an iron bar 1 mm x 1.6 m; Heat to 200° C; Measure the expansion = 0.5 mm • Select a lead bar 2 mm x 1 mm; Heat to 250° C; Measure the expansion = 0,8 mm • …
Principle	Law of expansion of metals – IF a metal object – IF heated to more than 150° C – THEN the object lengthens	• If Object is an iron bar 1.6 m x 1 mm; IF heated to more than 200° C; THEN Object lengthens; • IF Object is a lead bar 2 mm x 1mm; IF heated to 250° C, THEN Object lengthens • …

of metal, etc.). Similarly, there are as many traces of the procedure "heat a metal object" as there are sets of concrete actions obtained by varying the object and the temperature. Finally, there are as many statements of the principle "All metals expand when heated sufficiently" as there are specific statements indicating that a particular object will expand to such or such a length when heated to such or such a temperature.

We emphasize that the notions of concept and example are relative. For instance, in knowledge modeling, a "television set" or "to add" are examples of the concepts "Concept" and "Procedure," while in their respective domains they are simply "concepts" or "procedures." The same distinction exists between procedures and traces, and between principles and statements.

Interpretation of S Links

Specialization links have different interpretations depending on whether they connect a concept, procedure, or principle.

Table 3. Interpretation of specialization links (S)

Type	Specialized knowledge	Sort-of
Concept	automobile, motorcycle, etc. legislation, poem, etc. MS WORD word-processor, French word-processor, etc. taxpayer with spouse, wealthy taxpayer, etc. alkali metals, heavy metals, etc.	motor vehicle document word-processor taxpayer metal
Procedure	add whole numbers, add fractions, etc. write a history book, etc. manage a computer programming project, etc. follow a recipe for jam, etc.	add numbers write a book manage a project follow a recipe
Principle	definition of a primate, etc. projective geometry, etc. bond investment rules, etc. a metal object will expand if heated to more than 300° C, etc. IF goal is security, or investment is less than $5,000 THEN offer term deposit IF goal is security THEN offer a term deposit of less than 1 year	definition of a mammal mathematical theory investment rules a metal object will expand if heated to more than 200° C IF goal is security THEN offer a term deposit IF security THEN offer a term deposit

Table 4. Interpretation of composition links (C)

Type	Examples	Components
Concept	• motor vehicle • document} • word-processor • taxpayer • appointment	• motor, electrical system, steering, etc. • chapter, sections, paragraphs, page numbers, etc. • save, copy, price, etc. • age, income, dependents, etc. • time, place, subject, etc.
Procedure	• add • write a book • teach a course • follow a recipe • follow an agenda	• add units, tens, etc. • do research, make an outline, etc. • introduce the subject, give an exercise, etc. • gather the ingredients, prepare the sauce, etc. • adopt the agenda, discuss the first item, etc.
Principle	• definition of a mammal • geometry • investment rules • a metal object will expand if heated to more than 200° C • IF security THEN offer a term deposit	• the animal is hairy, the animal is viviparous, etc. • various definitions and theorems • various rules affecting investment choice • the object is metal, the temperature is > 200° C, the object expands • the client's goal is security, offer a term deposit

A specialization link between two concepts indicates that the class corresponding to the origin concept of the link is a subset of the destination link. For example, an automobile is a sort of motor vehicle, so all automobiles are also motor vehicles.

In the case of procedures, the interpretation is slightly different. Specialized procedures generally regulate only a portion (subset) of the cases regulated by the more general procedure. As such, the they contain more components, i.e. sub-procedures. For example, managing a computer-programming project involves specialized tasks that are not found in a general project management process.

In the case of principles, different situations may apply:

- For a *set* of principles, the interpretation of specialization is the opposite of set inclusion. For example, the definition of a primate or a rodent requires a longer list of properties (principles) than that of a mammal.
- For a *single* principle of the form "IF... THEN," the above table shows various ways that a more specialized principle, i.e. one that applies to fewer cases, can be derived from another principle: One can add additional conditions to a principle or replace an outcome with a more restrictive condition or a more specialized procedure.

Interpretation of C Links

Composition links have different interpretations depending on whether they connect a concept, procedure, or principle. Note that instances (set of facts resulting from instantiation) can be decomposed in a manner that is analogous to the abstract knowledge they are derived from.

A composition link is generally interpreted as connecting constituent parts of a knowledge object, i.e. one of its attributes, in the case of a concept; a sub-procedure, action, operation, or sub-task in the case of a procedure; a condition (principle) or action (procedure) defining a principle or set of principles. Some examples can be found in Table 4.

In the case of concepts and procedures, C links are interpreted directly. In the case of principles consisting of a set of principles (the first three cases in the above table), interpretation is also direct.

However, in the case of the last two principles in the above table, their interpretation needs to be clarified. This brings us to distinguish between

Figure 3. Example of a relational principle

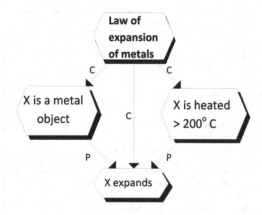

Figure 4. Example of a decision principle

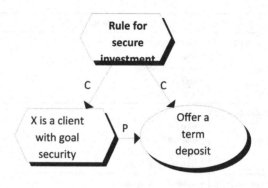

two kinds of principles—*relational principles* and *principles of operation*.

- A *relational principle* (*property* or *law*) is of the type "IF... THEN" and relates one or several attribute values to one or several objects. The properties following the "IF" are called conditions; the properties following the "THEN" are called outcomes.

For example, a "Law of expansion of metals" is composed of three properties shown in Figure 3:

- "X is a metal object"
- "X is heated > 200° C"
- "X expands"

The first two are the conditions, and the third is the outcome.

Precedence links (P) are added between the conditions and the outcome to replace the words "IF" and "THEN," which are not part of the graph. It express the idea that condition validation must precede outcome assertion.

P links are thus interpreted as follows: Outcome happens only when all the preceding conditions have been validated. In this way, one is able to visually (and operationally) represent causal or influence links between conditions and outcomes.

- An *operational principle* refers to principles of the form "IF... THEN" composed of conditions following the "IF" part and procedures following the "THEN", also called actions or operations.

For example, a "rule for secure investment" illustrated in Figure 4 consists of the condition "X is a client whose investment goal is security" and the action "Offer a term deposit."

As in the case of relational principles, the words "IF" and "THEN," which are not part of the visual representation, are replaced by a P link between the condition and the action. P links are interpreted as follows: the action(s) will be executed only when the conditions preceding the action(s) have been validated as true.

Interpretation of P Links

There are four possible situations involving precedence (P) links—a principle precedes a principle (illustrated in Figure 3), a principle precedes a procedure (illustrated in Figure 4).

The third situation, in which a precedence link connects two procedures, presents no difficulty of interpretation. The first procedure must be completed before executing the second one, as in the example in Figure 5

Let us now complete this example by representing to show a fourth case where a procedure

Figure 5. Example of P links between two procedures

precedes a principle. Figure 6 show a decomposition of a process "Heat the object" into three cases depending on whether the object is lead, iron, or another metal. We can replace the procedure "Heat object" by the three operational principles (also called decision rules) shown in Figure 6.

The model for the procedure "Measure the expansion of a heated metal" is interpreted as follows: Execute the procedure "Select object," then execute any of the three action principles in the center of the figure. Validate the condition at each step and then execute the corresponding action, followed by the final procedure "Measure the length." The procedure is therefore represented by the eight knowledge items in the model, five of which are procedures and three of which are principles.

Interpretation of I/P Links

Input/product links (I/P) are used in either of two situations—when a concept is an input to a procedure, or when a concept is a product of a procedure.

When a concept is an input to a procedure, it may be that the procedure transforms the objects represented by the concept, or uses them to transform other objects. The product is the result (the end product, the deliverable) of a transformation by a procedure.

In the example in Figure 7, a metal object is transformed by the procedure into another metal object since it no longer has the same length, though the two objects are both instances of the concept "metal object." On the other hand,

"temperature" is not modified, since it is used to effect the transformation, i.e. expand the object.

Note that the value of the component "Length" is both input and product of "Heat and measure the expansion of a heated metal." The term *procedural attachment* is used for a procedure that takes as input certain components of a concept and returns as product a new value for the component or another component of the same concept.

Figure 7 shows another example of a procedural attachment in which the input is the value of the three sides of a triangle and the product is its perimeter.

Interpretation of R Links

There are three possible situations involving regulation links (R) depending on whether a principle regulates one or more concepts, one or more procedures, or other principles.

When a principle regulates a concept, it can be interpreted as being at least partially a *definition* of the concept, such as the definition of a table on the left part of Figure 9. It can also be interpreted as a *standard* or *constraint* that all instances of the concept must adhere to, as shown in the right part of Figure 9. This model is read as "A slide is regulated by three principles: "Standard colors," Fonts are at least 20 points," and "One idea per slide."

As shown on Figure 10, when principles regulate a procedure they are interpreted as being a *control structure* of the procedure. Unlike the example in Figure 6, in which the principles are an internal part of the procedure, here the principles regulate a procedure from the outside and specify how the procedure and its components are to be executed.

Figure 10 illustrates two control structures for the same procedure "Heat and measure the expansion of a heated metal object." For the model on the left, the execution is sequential—we could just as easily have drawn precedence links between the sub-procedures (#1 select, #2 heat, #3 measure,

Figure 6. Example of P links between a procedure and a principle

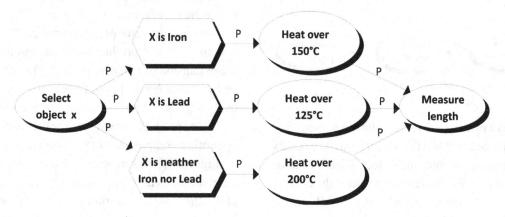

Figure 7. Interpretation of input/product links

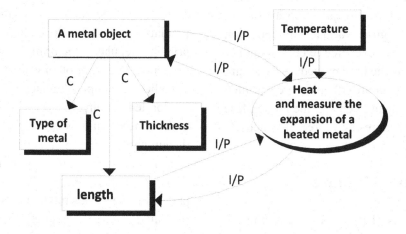

Figure 8. Input/product link and procedural attachment

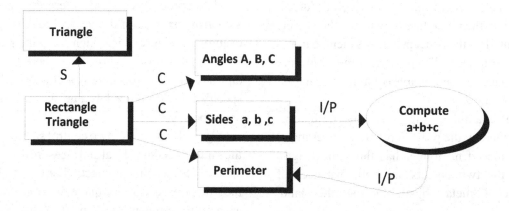

Figure 9. Principles regulating a concept

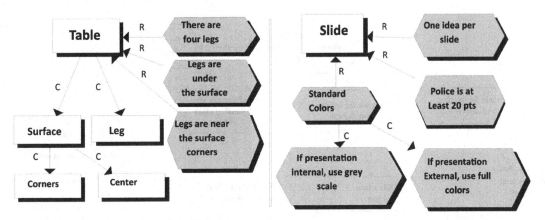

Figure 10. Principles regulating a procedure

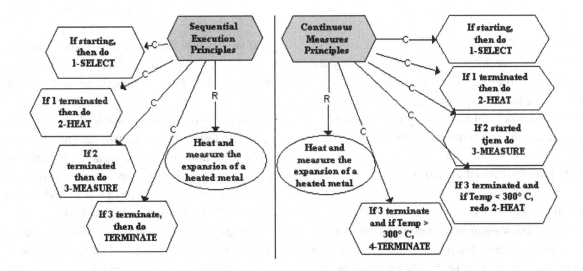

#4 terminate). For the model on the right, the sub-procedures are executed partially in sequence, partially parallel to one another, thus allowing for a continuous measurement, i.e. without stopping the metal from being heated until the threshold of 300° C is reached. Note that the principles of a control structure are connected by C links to the object representing that control structure, in this case, "Principles of sequential execution" and "Principles of continuous measurement."

Note that when a procedure is regulated externally by operational principles, we can avoid the restrictiveness of precedence links. Thus, in the same way as in rule-based expert systems, we can define control structures that specify any combination of execution, be it sequential, parallel, spiral, or otherwise.

We will now look at the remaining situation in which a principle regulates another principle. R links are thus interpreted as follows: A principle specifies the conditions for selecting the principles it regulates. If a condition is satisfied, it results in the selection of a principle followed by the execution of its conditions and outcomes.

Figure 11. Principles regulating other principles that control a procedure

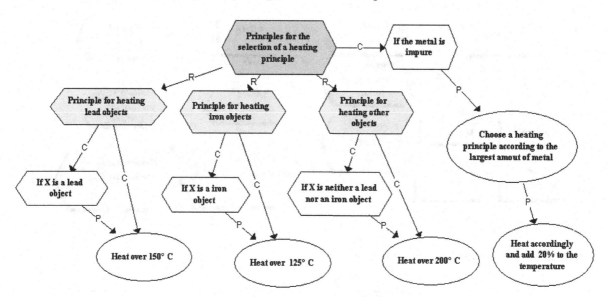

The originating principle of the R link can also modify the principles it regulates before they are applied, as in Figure 11. If the metal is impure, we choose the principle for heating the metal with the greatest portion and modify this principle by increasing the temperature by 20%.

Interpretation of A links

Unlike other links that establish relationships between knowledge in the same domain, A links are used to establish a relationship between two domains—a "meta-domain," whose objects are the origin of the link, and an "application domain," whose objects are associated by A links to the objects of the meta-domain (i.e. the "meta-objects").

All application domains such as physics, sociology, or law are constituted of knowledge and facts. The domain that studies knowledge per se is particularly important in learning. Knowledge about knowledge is called *meta-knowledge*. In particular, the domain of meta-knowledge studies the properties of knowledge such as genericity and validity, as well as the processes involved in transforming knowledge (the ability to generalize, to make analogies, etc.)

If we say that "simulate a procedure" applies (A link) to "perform an Internet search," we imply that the variable "procedure" in the meta-domain has a specific value—"perform an Internet search"—that will be used in the application field. The link between the two statements in the application domain simply means "simulate the procedure of performing an Internet search." In Part II, we will use this type of link to address the notions of competency and generic skill.

Since meta-knowledge is also knowledge (about knowledge), we can distinguish between three main categories of abstract meta-knowledge and their corresponding facts, as we do for knowledge. These are *meta-concepts*, *meta-procedures*, and *meta-principles*, used in connecting the meta-knowledge domain with the application domain

Meta-concepts, also named *knowledgeattributes* or *properties*, are concepts that define value systems which apply to knowledge from various fields. For instance, one may claim that some knowledge in physics or economics is a priority, is useful, is proven, or is known to all. A concept such as "priority" belongs neither to physics nor to economics but to the domain that studies knowledge. In effect, it is a knowledge *attribute*

Figure 12. Meta-concept of "knowledge priority" applied in two domains

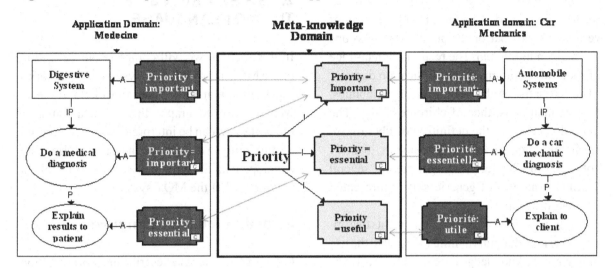

(variable), taking a value that can be defined, for example, using a three-level importance scale—useful, important, or essential. Figure 12 illustrates the application of such a meta-concept in two different application domains. The meta-concept "Priority" is identified in the meta-knowledge domain, where it instantiates to three values or meta-examples: Priority=important, Priority=essential, or Priority=useful.[2] These meta-concept/value pairs are reused in the application domains, as show by the bidirectional "reification" link.

Applied to the domain of auto mechanics, the meta-examples tell us that the ability to perform an automobile diagnosis is considered essential, that knowledge of the components of an automobile is considered important, and that the ability to explain the diagnosis to a customer is considered useful only in that it is usually done by a customer service representative. Applied to the domain of medicine, the meta-examples tell us that the ability to perform a medical diagnosis is considered important, that knowledge of the digestive system is considered important, and that the ability to explain the diagnosis to a patient is considered essential because it can influence treatment outcome.

Note that the values of the meta-concept "Priority" can be associated not only with concepts, but also with procedures, principles, or facts from the application domain. The type of meta-knowledge and its examples and the type of knowledge to which they apply in various application domains are completely independent of one another.

Application links (A), associating meta-examples with knowledge objects of a domain application, play a pivotal role between the domains. Meta-examples possess "mirror-knowledge," or reification, in the meta-domain, represented in Figure 12 by two-way links. The meaning of these mirror or reification links is simply the following: "To understand the definition of a meta-example (and the meta-concept that it instantiates), consult the model of its mirror-knowledge in the meta-domain." This also applies to meta-procedures and meta-principles.

Meta-procedures, also named "operations on knowledge," are actions applied to knowledge from other domains in order to examine, transform, or communicate such knowledge. Classification, defined as a series of operations to determine the smallest class of a taxonomy to which a particular object belongs, is an example of meta-procedure. To instantiate such a meta-procedure consists in choosing the taxonomy and the object to which we want it applied, for example, a taxonomy of vertebrates and a bat, or a taxonomy of professions and a given individual. The result is a meta-trace of specific operations in the application domain: "The bat satisfies the definition of vertebrates, then of mammals, then of chiropters"; or "The individual satisfies the definition of liberal professionals, then of legal professionals, then of notaries." In Chapter 7, we will present several detailed examples of generic skills represented by meta-procedures.

Meta-principles are generic statements that apply to various domains aiming to regulate the use of other meta-knowledge or to establish relations between them. As action or relational principles, they can be described as "knowledge control principles" or "knowledge association principles."

An example of an operational meta-principle is breaking down a problem: "To solve a complex problem, one can first solve a particular case of it." To instantiate such a meta-principle, we select the knowledge to which it applies, in this case, the problem. Results are meta-statements such as "To build a general procedure for compound interest calculation, first solve the problem using an interest rate of 10%," or "To diagnose a car breakdown, first diagnose the electrical system."

A relational meta-principle such as "If a knowledge object is more general than another, the second is of the same type as the first" involves the meta-concepts "knowledge type" and "knowledge generality." Instanciating such a meta-principle consists in selecting the knowledge to which it is applied. Resulting are meta-statements such as "The concept of vertebrate is more general than that of mammal, therefore the latter is also a concept," or "The law of perfect gases is more general than Gay-Lussac's Law; the first is a principle, therefore the second is also a principle."

2.4 SYNTAX RULES OF THE MOT LANGUAGE

In this section, we will complete our definition of the MOT representation system by summarizing its grammar rules. Such rules help to create well-constructed graphs that, from a semantic point of view, can be interpreted with a minimum of ambiguity. We will use the visual formalism developed in the previous sections to build a *meta-model* of the MOT system.

Modeling the MOT Language

Our purpose here is to describe the representation system of the MOT meta-model as a *conceptual* system, i.e. objects of the system are represented by concepts linked by relations of composition and specialization. In other words, our purpose is not to describe the modeling *process*, with its procedural (how) and strategic (when and why) aspects.

The diagram in Figure 13 summarizes the components of a model using object types. It has the following characteristics:

- A MOT model is composed solely of knowledge and relations.
- Each relation is composed of two knowledge objects (origin) and a link, one knowledge being the origin and the other being the destination of the link.
- There are seven sorts of links: C, S, I, L, P, I / P, and A.
- Each link is identified by a name, a symbol, and a unique expression.
- There are two sorts of knowledge objects: facts and abstract knowledge.
- There are three sorts of facts: examples, traces, and statements.
- There are three sorts of abstract knowledge: concepts, procedures, and principles.
- Meta-knowledge objects are sorts of knowledge objects.

Figure 13. Modeling using object types

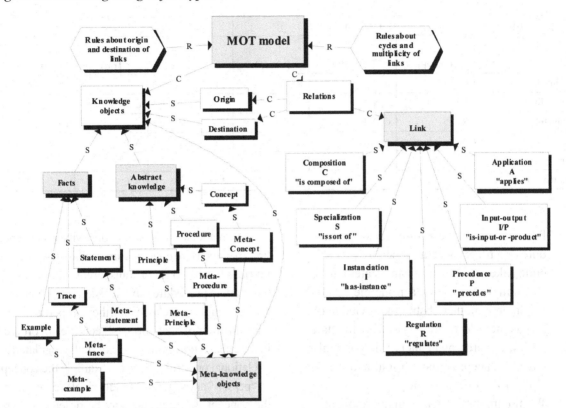

Two groups of principles (grammar rules) are distinguished in the graph: rules about knowledge at the origin and destination of various types of links, and rules that are properties of relations as regards to cycles and multiplicity of links in a graph.

Rules Regarding the Origin and Destination of Links

All links in a model have an origin and a destination (knowledge objects). Table 5 indicates the possible links between knowledge object types with regard to origin and destination.

From this table, we can summarize the following rules:

- A fact (example, trace, or statement) cannot be the origin of a link towards abstract knowledge, except if it is the origin of an application (A) link, thus acting as meta-knowledge.

- Instantiation links can only relate a concept to an example, a procedure to a trace, or a principle to a statement.

- Composition links can only relate knowledge objects of the same type, except for procedures, which can be composed of principles and vice versa (likewise for traces and statements); they can also relate a concept to an example, a procedure to a trace, or a principle to a statement

- Specialization links can only relate abstract knowledge objects of the same type.

- Input-product links can only relate a concept (or example) to a procedure (or trace) and vice versa.

Table 5. Rules regarding the origin and destination of links

Destination > > > > Origin	Abstract Knowledge			Fact		
	Concept	Procedure	Principle	Example	Trace	Statement
Concept	C, S	I/P	R	I, C		
Procedure	I/P	C, S, P	C, P		I, C	
Principle	R	C, R, P	C, S, P, R			I, C
Example	A	A	A	A, C	A, I/P	A, R
Trace	A	A	A	A, I/P	A, C, P	A, C, P
Statement	A	A	A	A, R	A, C, R, P	A, C, R, P

- Precedence links can only relate a procedure or a principle to a procedure or a principle (likewise for traces and statements).
- Regulation links have a principle as their origin and another abstract knowledge object as their destination (likewise for statements, towards other facts); they can also have a concept as their origin and a principle as their destination.
- Within an application domain, application links relate an example, trace, or statement (acting as meta-knowledge) to any another type of abstract knowledge or fact.

The justification for these rules cannot be made individually but in relationship to one another. For example, it would have been possible to accept procedures or principles as components of a concept. We exclude, however, this type of representation for the sake of transparency and convenience. Rather than representing the principle of concept as a component, we prefer to represent it externally to the concept by tracing an R link from the principle to the concept (see Figure 9), or from the concept to the principle; in this way, the semantics is clear, and the principle can be used to regulate other concepts. In the same way, we exclude procedures as potential components of concepts, instead representing them as procedural attachments external to concepts (see Figures 7 and 8).

The reader may also wonder why precedence links between two concepts are excluded. Again, the purpose here is to favor transparent interpretation. Contrary to procedures and decision rules, concepts representing object classes and their properties do not have an order of execution. Objects are not ordered in time per se, unless they are externally regulated by a relational principle. Take for example the concept of "person" and a group of individuals representing the concept.[3] The group may be ordered by age, size, resistance to stress, or other criteria. Such criteria of "precedence" or "ordering" would be more accurately expressed using a relational principle.

Figure 14 illustrates a precedence relation between two people—represented by concept X and concept Y—based on age. We can instantiate these concepts to two individuals, e.g. Judith and Anne, and instantiate the relational principles to the resulting statement. When we want to represent a real-life situation, we only represent true statements, in this case, "Judith is older than Anne." This more accurate visual notation corresponds to the right part of the figure where an entity-relation graph is presented. In this manner, we can represent any binary relation not belonging to the MOT lexicon.

In a more general sense, the reader may wonder why users are not free to choose their own links between knowledge objects. We try to limit this practice to situations having a unique interpretation, such as the one in Figure 14.

Figure 14. An order relation, and it abbreviation, between groups of people

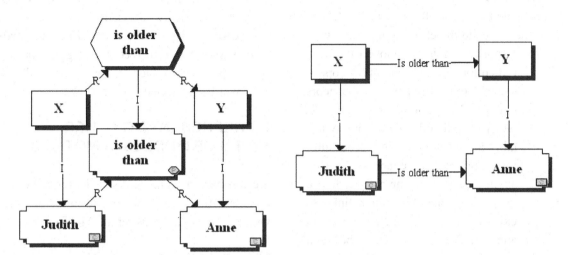

There are many reasons for restricting link types. Firstly, imagine a spoken language without grammar rules, in which nouns, adjectives, and verbs are used in any way and in any order. Sentences would be difficult to interpret, and our ability to communicate would be seriously limited. For the same reasons, we wanted to create a visual language that was as natural and unambiguous as possible.

Secondly, and more fundamentally, we wanted to create a "typology" of knowledge objects and links. Such a choice required that we take into account the "natural" links between three categories of thought—objects per se; actions on, and statements about objects, actions and statements. This is why I/P and R links are defined the way they are.

Finally, if users were completely free to use their own links, we would no longer be able to make a clear distinction and semantic between link types or object types. In Chapter 4, when we present the MOT and MOT+ visual editors in greater detail, we allow for the use of non-typed objects and links in order to simplify the visual representation, as we did in Figure 14—but we so with a cautionary note: Such links can jeopardize the consistency of the model. A model with both typed and non-typed objects and links would be like a hybrid that uses the syntax of different languages; it would also present the same problems. This is why one language or the other should be used, or if both are used, interpretations of the non-typed links should be clearly explained.

Rules Regarding Cycles and Multiplicity of Links

The seven basic relations/links are binary relations, and as such, they have intrinsic properties within any given model, notably as regards the presence of cycles in the graph and the multiplicity of links. As for any grammar rule, there are small number of exceptions:

- **Anti-reflexivity**: The origin and destination of any link must be two distinct knowledge objects. In other words, a link cannot exist from a knowledge object to itself.
  - Exception: A C link can exist from an abstract knowledge object (or a fact) to itself, thus permitting a nesting effect on any number of levels. For example, the concept "group of persons" may be composed recursively of other "group of persons."

- **Asymmetry**: If two knowledge objects are connected by a link, they cannot be linked in the opposite direction by the same type of link (nor with a link of another type).
  - Exception: An I/P link and its opposite may exist between some concepts or examples and some procedures, directly or indirectly. This property notably allows iteration in a procedure: the output of a procedure can be used as an input in the same procedure a number of time. Also, an R link can exist from an concept to a relation and back if the relation holds between objects of the same concept-class (see the example of Figure 17)
- **Transitivity**: If a link connects knowledge objects A and B, and a link of the same type connects a third knowledge object C, then the same link type connects A to C.
  - Exception: Only links C, S, and P are fully transitive, although in general, we will avoid tracing a link from A to C in the model. R and I links are transitive by default, since if A is connected to B by one of these links, B cannot generally be linked to another knowledge object of the same type (except as regards an R link between principles). The I/P link is not transitive, since if A is linked to B and B to C, A and C are necessarily concepts or examples that cannot be connected by an I/P link. It is the same for an A- link, since B and C are not meta-knowledge objects.
- **Uniqueness of the link**: If a link of a certain type exists between two knowledge objects, A and B, no other direct or indirect link of another type may exist between these two knowledge objects in the same model.
- **Cardinality of the set of links originating from a knowledge object**: For a given

link, it is possible to trace one or several links from any knowledge object.
- **Cardinality of the set of links towards a knowledge object**: For a given link, it is possible to trace one or several links towards a knowledge object.

2.5 REPRESENTING OTHER TYPES OF MODELS IN MOT

We complete this chapter by revisiting the visual representations in chapter 1 and modeling each visual representation using the MOT system.

MOT Models of a Semantic Trees and a Conceptual Maps

Compare the MOT model of Figure 14 with the semantic tree presented in Figure 3 in Chapter 1. Unlike the semantic tree that blurs the types of objects, the MOT model specifies two object types—groups of painters and individual painters—and two link types—"sorts-of" groups of painters and instanciation, i.e. examples of a particular group of painters.

Compare the MOT model on Figure 16 with the conceptual map in Figure 4 in Chapter 1. This example is interesting in that it demonstrates how different types of knowledge objects are specified in the MOT system, adding clarity to the model.

Here, agricultural practices, both current and new, are presented as procedures, since they are considered as categories of human activities. In these processes, use of fertilizer or rice production (S links) produce an increase in greenhouse gases such as methane or nitrogen oxide (I/P links). The same is true of new agricultural practices that produce less greenhouse gases. The model also categorizes greenhouse gases and shows that they are inputs to climate change.

Here again, the MOT model is clearer with actions being distinguished from products or inputs to process, which is not clear in the conceptual graph of Figure 4 in Chapter 1.

Figure 15. MOT model of a semantic tree

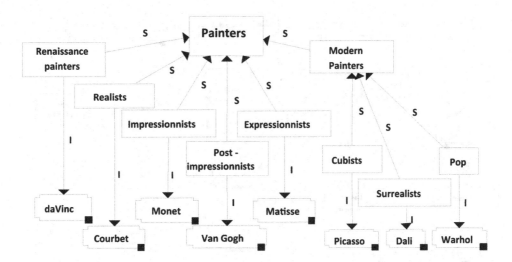

Figure 16. MOT model of a conceptual map

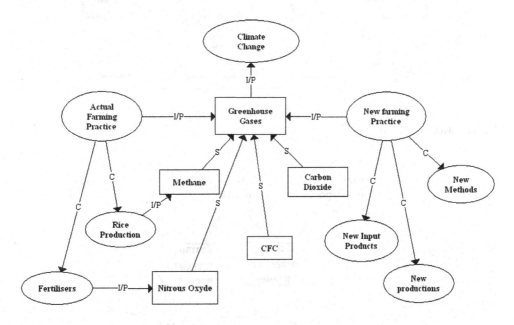

MOT Models of Semantics Networks

Compare the MOT model of Figure 17 with the semantic network in Figure 5 in Chapter 1. The semantic network presents a set of facts. The nodes of the semantic network (in white) are all objects representing different examples of people, numbers, and gender. We have replaced the network links in Figure 5 in Chapter 1 with statements symbols (in gray) that are specific relations to obtain the gender, age, father, mother, or boss of an individual represented on the graph. The MOT

Figure 17. MOT model of a semantic network

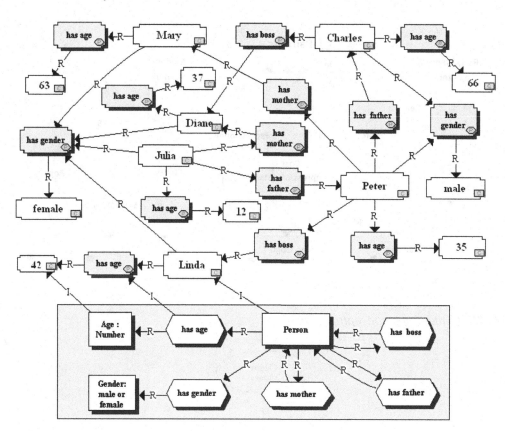

Figure 18. MOT Model of a flow chart

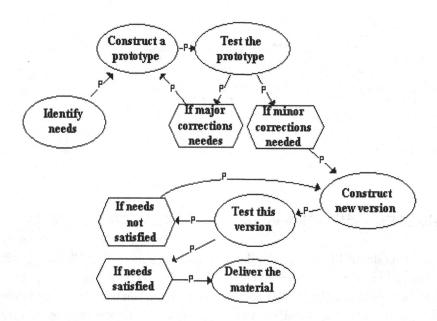

Figure 19. MOT model of a causal diagram

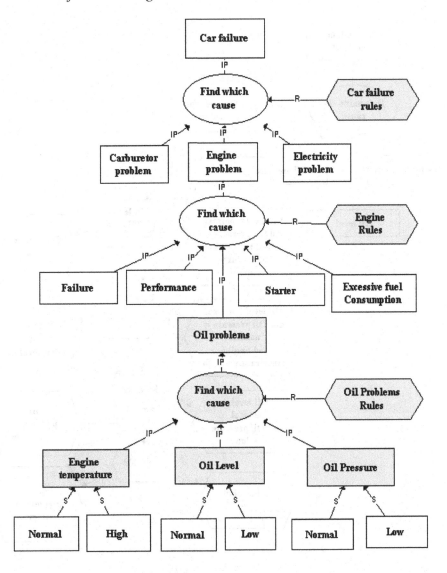

model contains exactly the same information as the semantic network. Compared to Figure 5 in Chapter 1, It clearly shows that we are dealing with facts, with individuals and their properties.

The box at the bottom of Figure 17 also demonstrates that a MOT model is able to reveal the underlying structure of a semantic network. All the facts represented in this network pertain to persons and their attributes, numbers that reveal their age, terms that indicate their gender and other persons that are their mother, father or boss. All

the person-attribute-value triples of the network are obtained by instantiation of the model in the box. On the figure, only the instantiation to the "Linda-age- 42" triple is shown.

MOT Model of a Flow Chart

Compare the MOT model of Figure 18, representing the development of training material, with the second flow chart in Figure 6 in Chapter 1. The main difference is the replacement of one losange

Figure 20. MOT model of a decision tree

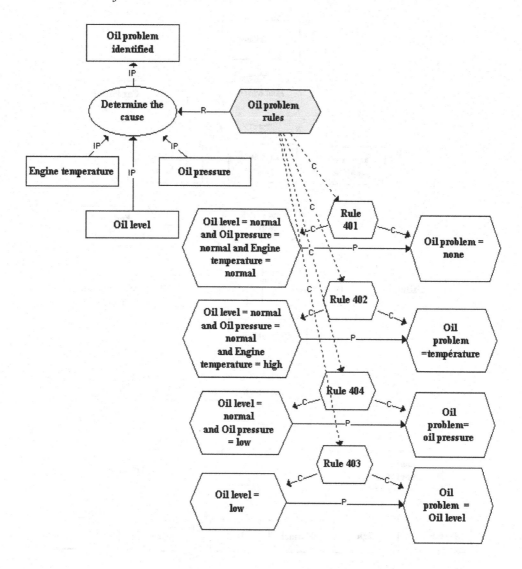

decision box by two principles, one for each branch of the alternative. The graph has more boxes, but the flow is as transparent.

MOT Models of a Causal Diagram and a Decision Tree

Compare the MOT model of Figure 19 with the causal diagram in Figure 7a in Chapter 1, troubleshooting car failure.

Here, the probable causes are presented in the form of concepts linked together by the procedure "find which cause." On the figure, three levels of troubleshooting are shown. This can be termed a *constraint tree* (Paquette & Roy, 1990). For example, to identify the cause of a car not starting, it can be because there is a fuel, engine, or electrical problem. Then, to identify the type of engine problem, we must consider the possibilities of complete failure, poor performance, starter (voltage or spark plug) problems, poor fuel consumption, or oil problems. Finally, to identify the type of oil problem, we must consider oil level, oil pressure, or engine temperature.

Figure 21. MOT model of an inference tree

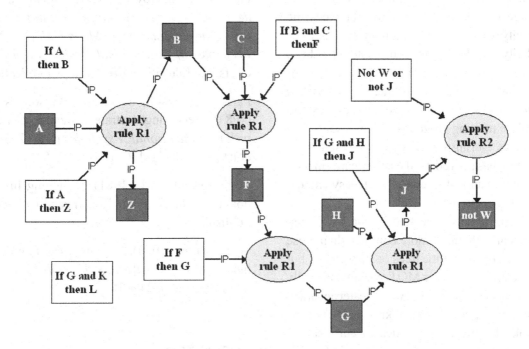

The model also brings to light the principles that regulate the procedures for identifying causes, i.e. sets of rules to be applied in each case. Those pertaining to oil problems are presented as a sub-model in Figure 20 (which corresponds to Figure 7b in Chapter 1), in which the rules are stated as a set four relational principles, each a component of "Oil problem rules."

Each of the four principles has two components:

- a condition that states the properties of the attributes influencing the outcome, in this case, oil level, oil pressure, or engine temperature;
- an outcome that states a value of an attribute, in this case, oil problems.

Decision rules regarding other possible causes for car failure, including engine, fuel, or electrical problems, could be stated in the same way. The model in Figure 19 clearly shows the decision level for each rule set and the role of the rules in the decision process. The sub-model in Figure 20 represents the rules directly, rather than indirectly, through a decision tree.

MOT Model of an Inference Tree

Compare the MOT model of Figure 21 with the inference tree in Figure 8 in Chapter 1. In this case, although we are dealing with statements, we have chosen to represent the situation as a process. The rules are represented by procedures (apply rule R1, apply rule R2), allowing the interpretation to be more transparent. The model takes up more space than the model in Figure 8 in Chapter 1, but it is more explicit. The deduction path can be traced by following the I/P links.

CONCLUSION

In concluding the chapter, we hope to have achieved our initial objective of describing a representation system that is characterized by simplicity, genericity, completeness, ease of interpretation, standardization, and communicability.

There is clearly a compromise between the genericity of a representation system and its simplicity. The MOT modeling system has been used since its inception in 1992 in a variety of settings and applications—modeling of a virtual campus, engineering of university courses and workplace training programs, and as a study tool by students. During these years of implementation, the system has proved itself easy to learn (in only a few hours) and, at a certain level, easy enough for most users to use.

Indeed, models generated by the MOT system appear sometimes more complex than those represented by semantic trees or flow charts, but we have proven that the MOT system can easily reproduce these models, but with greater accuracy and by offering a typology of knowledge objects and links that helps communicate clear ideas.

As demonstrated by the examples in Section 2.6, MOT models reveal elements that are not revealed by other representations. In this sense, they facilitate interpretation, in that the same components being used from model to model and with the same meaning.

Standardization of representation through a precise graphical syntax is an important factor not only for interpretation, but also for communicating ideas contained in the models. The latter must be read and interpreted correctly with a minimum of explanation and comments.

Finally, the generalizability and completeness of the MOT representation system is best demonstrated through a number of examples illustrating its diversity and expressiveness. This is the objective of the next chapter.

REFERENCES

Paquette, G., Crevier, F., & Aubin, C. (1994). ID knowledge in a course design workbench. *Educational Technology, 34*(9), 50–57.

Paquette, G., & Roy, L. (1990). *Systèmes à base de connaissances. Montréal, Canada: Télé-université et Beauchemin. Merrill, M. D. (1994). Principles of Instructional Design.* Englewood Cliffs, NJ: Educational Technology Publications.

Paris, S., Lipson, M. Y., & Wixson, K. K. (1983). Becoming a strategic reader. *Contemporary Educational Psychology, 8*, 293–31. doi:10.1016/0361-476X(83)90018-8

Romiszowski, A. J. (1981). Designing Instructional Systems. London: Kogan Page andNichols Publishing.

Tennyson, R. (1990). Cognitive learning theory linked to instructional theory. *Journal of Structural Learning, 10*(3), 249–25.

ENDNOTES

[1]   The concept of knowledge used here is broader than that used by most books on the topic. It includes not only facts and abstract knowledge—concepts, procedures, and principles—but also mental skills viewed as meta-knowledge. These will be addressed later in the book. In short, knowledge is everything that can be learned by the human mind, including cognitive, motor, and socio-emotional skills.

[2]   It is in relation to an application domain that the attribute values of knowledge objects are described as "meta." In the field that studies knowledge, meta-examples and meta-concepts are simply examples and concepts. The same is true for other types of meta-knowledge.

[3]   Alternately, we could present the concept of historical event by a procedure regulated by actors, thus giving a dynamic meaning to the notion of event. Events would then be procedures connected by P links, and the standard interpretation between procedures or traces would apply.

Chapter 3
Types and Examples of Knowledge Models

Gilbert Paquette
LICEF Research Center, Canada

ABSTRACT

- Basis for a Classification of Models
- Factual Systems
- Conceptual Systems
  - Taxonomies
  - Component-based systems
  - Hybrid conceptual systems
- Procedural Systems
  - Sequential procedures
  - Parallel procedures
  - Iterative procedures
- Prescriptive Systems
  - Definitions, standards, and constraints
  - Laws and theories
  - Decision Trees
  - Control structure of processes
- Processes and Methods
  - Processes
  - Methods and Techniques
  - Collaborative systems

With only a few object and link types, it is possible to construct representations of complex knowledge systems such as the taxonomies, theories, processes, or methodologies used to describe various fields of knowledge. In this chapter, we will present a taxonomy of knowledge models and provide examples of each model type. Our goal is to demonstrate the generality of the MOT representation system by modeling a wide variety of situations usually modeled by other representations, or in some cases, not at all. In so doing, we will develop a library of models from which designers can choose to adapt

DOI: 10.4018/978-1-61520-839-5.ch003

Figure 1. Taxonomy of knowledge: Facts and abstract knowledge

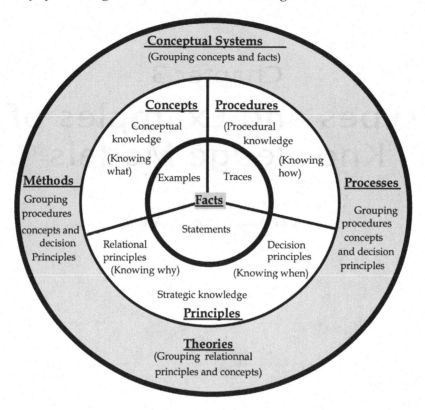

to their own areas of concern.

3.1 BASIS FOR A CLASSIFICATION OF MODELS

A representation system using object types can be used to model a diversity of knowledge systems far greater than the few examples presented so far. The basic knowledge types (concepts, procedures, and principles) and the three fact types can be combined into increasingly complex systems of structured knowledge.

Complex Knowledge Models

Figure 1 identifies four types of composite systems—conceptual systems, theories, processes, and methods—which can be found in all areas

of knowledge and to which we can give precise meanings and representations within a classification of knowledge models.

Conceptual systems consist of a relatively large number of concepts connected through a semantic network. Each concept possesses a number of attributes that are themselves connected through links of generalization, composition, etc.

Conceptual system can be found in all fields of knowledge. In the natural sciences, Linnaeus's taxonomy of plants, though now abandoned, is a well-known example, as are his descriptions of thousands of animal species. In human physiology, the major body systems (respiratory, cardiovascular, skeletal, muscular, and hormonal) their components, and their interrelationships are conceptual systems. In science, the classification and description of three-dimensional solids, the periodic table of chemical elements, and the description of atomic and subatomic particles in physics are other examples of conceptual systems. In the humanities and social sciences, the description of countries, populations and political regimes, the eras and civilizations in which events take place, and the components and functions of economies are all examples of conceptual systems.

Theories are knowledge systems consisting of numerous relational principles (laws or theorems) that connect domain concepts (definitions).

Like conceptual systems, theories are found in all areas of knowledge. The theory of market economics incorporates such laws as the "the law of supply and demand," as well as the conceptual systems that define offer, demand, and economic exchange. The theory of numbers describing types and properties of numbers, the laws and concepts explaining universal gravitation, and the geological principles underlying continental drift are all examples of theories.

Processes consist of procedures performed sequentially, in parallel fashion, or iteratively. Processes also contain input objects and the products of procedures, which are defined by concepts. In processes, the transition from one procedure to another is regulated by strategic knowledge in the form of deterministic decision rules or heuristic rules.

All fields of knowledge contain descriptions of processes that reflect their dynamic aspect, that is, sets of actions that produce results. Such processes include collective writing, reviewing financial statements, the protocols of scientific experimentation, the historical processes leading to the rise and fall of civilizations, and the modeling, sculpting, and painting techniques used in fine arts.

Methods are prescriptive rather than descriptive systems composed of processes, conceptual systems and networks, taxonomies, interpretative systems, and above all, methodological principles or strategies that guide human activity in a given domain.

- All areas of knowledge contain methods. Among the best known, and themselves part of the scientific method, are the experimental methods for observing phenomena, formulating hypotheses, and validating hypotheses. Software engineering, knowledge engineering, and instructional engineering and design are also examples of methods.

A Taxonomy of Knowledge Models

Figure 2 is an overview of this taxonomy; five main classes of models are divided into seventeen sub-classes.

The five main classes of models are defined in Table 1. They are distinguished by the types of knowledge objects and links they contain, with some sub-classes containing only one type of knowledge object.

Although processes and methods are, in a way, extensions of procedural and prescriptive models respectively, they imply a certain balance between conceptual, procedural, and prescriptive elements. For this reason, we have treated them as a separate class. Several examples of the above models were presented in Section 2.6; examples of the various sub-classes will be presented below.

3.2 FACTUAL SYSTEMS

Factual systems, that is, sets of facts, are obtained by instantiating a concept and its components (left-hand example in Figure 3), and more generally, by instantiating one or several connected knowledge objects (right-hand example in Figure 3). Factual systems are often presented in tabular form.

Figure 3 shows two sets of facts. The first is an set of examples derived from the concept "chronology" and its attributes "date," "event," and "period." The second is a set of trace derived from the procedure "multiplication" and its inputs,

Figure 2. Taxonomy of knowledge models

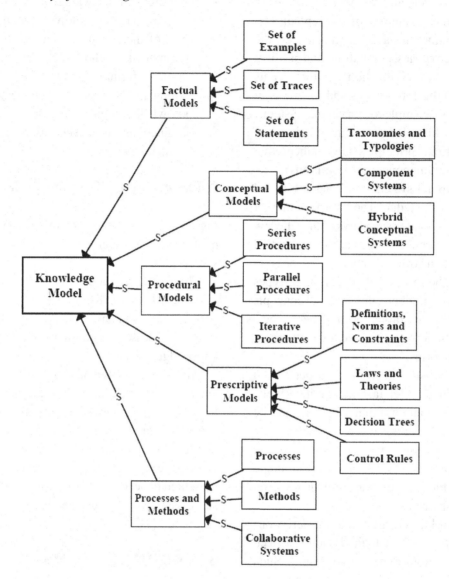

Table 1. Main classes of models

Class	Definition	Examples
Factual models	A majority of knowledge objects are facts.	Procedural traces related to processing a form (the actual actions and the various states of the form thus produced); a network of links between people.
Conceptual models	A majority of knowledge objects are concepts.	Components and sub-components of a car; a taxonomy of the animal kingdom
Procedural models	A majority of knowledge objects are procedures.	A procedure for calculating income tax; a procedure for solving equations for two unknowns.
Prescriptive models	A majority of knowledge objects are principles.	A checklist of conditions for choosing a home according to one's needs; the laws of gravity; the theory of the evolution of species.
Processes and methods	There is an equilibrium between procedures and control principles.	A process or method for project management; experimental methods.

Figure 3. Two factual systems: A group of examples and a group of facts

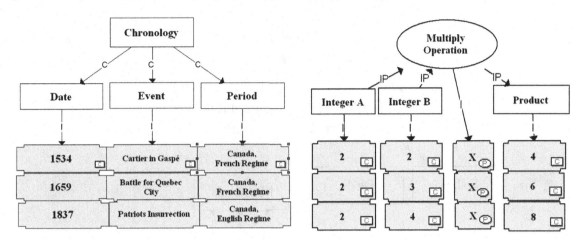

Table 2. Three sub-classes of fact systems

Class name	Definition	Examples
Example set	All the examples are instances of the same "origin concept."	A list of events; a table comparing computers by name, memory size, etc.
Trace set	All the traces are instances of the same "origin procedure."	Addition or multiplication tables; procedures for preparing an income tax return.
Statement set	All the statements are instances of the same "origin statement."	The characteristics of a particular medical doctor.

operations, and products (commonly called a "multiplication table").

The model of the semantic network in Figure 17 in Chapter 2 is an example of a statement set.

3.3 CONCEPTUAL SYSTEMS

Conceptual models are composed almost exclusively of concepts. Consequently, their emphasis is on describing a system's objects and links, the latter being generally those of composition and specialization. Other types of knowledge objects can be included in the model, for example, a procedural attachment (discussed earlier) or a constraint principle (see Figure 7); however, these are used only to clarify the system.

Taxonomies

Taxonomies generally specify concepts related by links of specialization, that is, between classes and sub-classes.

As we descend the hierarchy, concepts generate progressively fewer instances.

Examples of taxonomies can be found in all areas of knowledge: living beings, grammatical categories, administrative units in an organizational chart, types of media, etc.

Component-Based Systems

Component-based systems are composed of concepts related by composition links. Component-based systems are divided into subsystems, which can be further divided and subdivided until components deemed "terminal" are obtained,

Figure 4. Taxonomy of the animal world

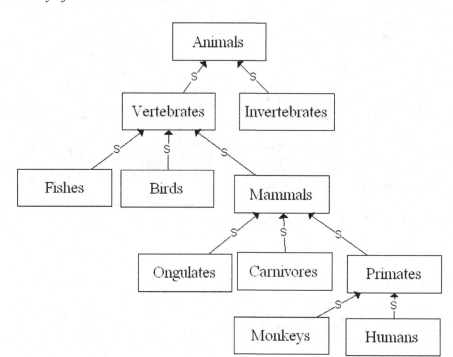

Table 3. Three sub-classes of conceptual systems

Class	Definition	Examples
Typologies and taxonomies	Composed entirely of S links.	A set of classes and sub-classes of mushrooms.
Component-based systems	Composed entirely of C links.	Components and sub-components of a computer.
Hybrid conceptual systems	Composed of both C links and S links.	A system of geometrical figures representing different categories and their attributes.

that is, those requiring no further decomposition. Examples of component-based systems are found in all areas of knowledge—human physiology, mechanics, instructional design, and so on.

Hybrid Conceptual Systems

Hybrid conceptual systems consist mainly of concepts connected by specialization or composition links. Some concepts may be regulated by principles that define the concepts by enumerating their properties. Finally, other concepts may be defined by a *procedural attachment* specifying how the value of one component of the concept can be derived from its other components.

3.4 PROCEDURAL SYSTEMS

Procedural systems form rather complex structures of procedures that describe a set of related actions. There are three sub-types of procedural systems: sequential procedures, parallel procedures, and iterative or recursive procedures.

Figure 5. A component-based system

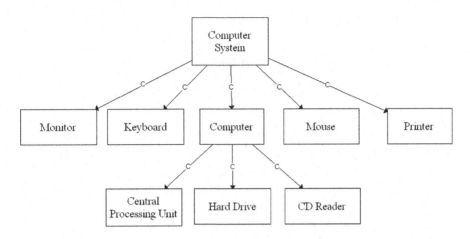

Figure 6. A conceptual hybrid system

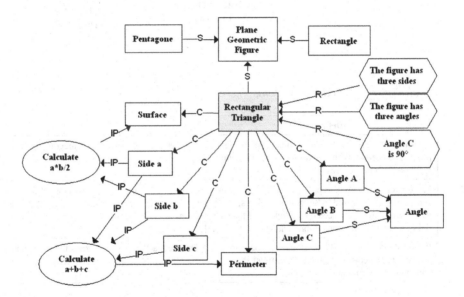

Sequential Procedures

Sequential procedures are connected by single precedence links; a "previous" procedure is followed by a "next" procedure.

Each procedure can be divided and subdivided until a desired level of detail is obtained. Examples include the production steps for an electrical appliance or the topics and sub-topics of an assembly agenda (Figure 7).

Parallel Procedures

Parallel procedures are executed simultaneously. Examples include the production of a newspaper in which the various sections are laid out simultaneously by different people (Figure 8), or a sports league calendar in which several matches take place on the same day and ranking is determined by total points.

Figure 7. A sequential procedure

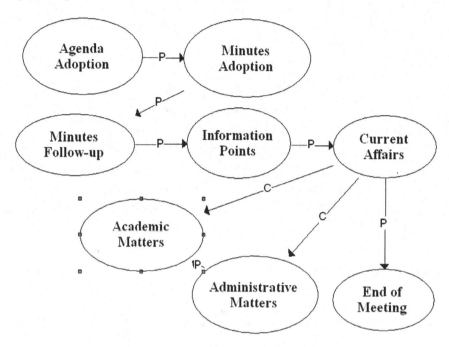

Table 4. Three sub-classes of procedural systems

Class	Definition	Examples
Sequential procedures	All procedures are regulated by P links connecting a previous procedure with a next procedure. The same is true for sub-procedures.	The items and sub-items of a meeting agenda.
Parallel procedures	Procedures are ordered, in part, by P links. One procedure may be followed by several procedures; two procedures may be connected by a link other than a P link. The same is true for sub-procedures.	Collective writing or any project in which some of the work is done in parallel fashion (simultaneously) by different people.
Iterative procedures	P and I/P (input/product) links between procedures are cyclical; a decision principle determines the conditions for terminating the cycle.	The feedback loop of a thermostat; a procedure for dividing a group of people into smaller groups.

Iterative Procedures

Iterative procedures are hybrid in nature and may be of a sequential, parallel, or input/product type. The latter are regulated by principles specifying conditions that, when satisfied, lead to another procedure.

Iteration occurs when one of the conditions of a decision principle continuously returns a procedure until the "stop" condition of another principle terminates the procedure or provides instructions for performing another procedure.

The example in Figure 9 of a thermostat illustrates such a situation. The thermostat is set to a desired threshold temperature as it measures room temperature. If the latter differs only slightly from the threshold level, nothing happens. This is the stop condition.

If the room temperature falls too far below the threshold level, heating starts. Once again, temperature is measured, and if it exceeds the

Figure 8. A parallel procedure

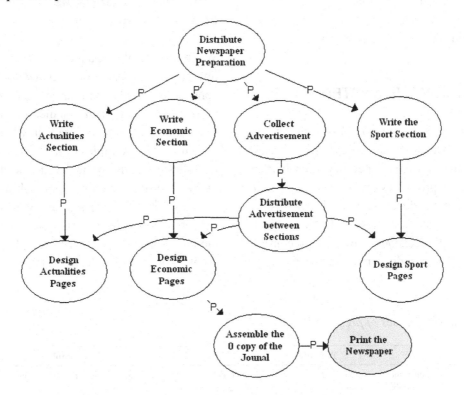

Figure 9. An iterative procedure

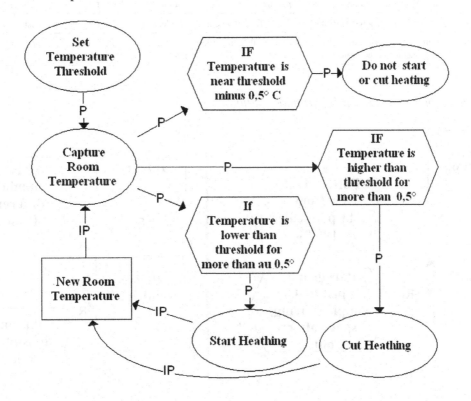

threshold level, heating stops. The procedure continues as long as the temperature is very near the threshold set in the first procedure.

3.5 PRESCRIPTIVE SYSTEMS

Prescriptive systems are composed mainly of principles, or affirmations. There are four classes of prescriptive systems depending on whether they define the properties of an object, establish relations of dependency or causality between concepts (laws and theories), select an object based on multiple decisions, or manage the control flow among the procedures making up a process.

Definitions, Standards, and Constraints

When a principle regulates a concept, it can be interpreted, at least partially, as a *definition* of the concept. It can also be interpreted as a *standard* or *constraint* that each instance of the concept must conform to. In Figure 9 in Chapter 2, we presented two examples of definitions

Rules concerning the origin and destination of MOT models themselves (such as the ones presented in Chapter) are also constraints that contribute to the definition of the concept "MOT model." Other examples are templates or style sheets. For example, the normal font used in this

Table 5. Four sub-classes of prescriptive systems

Class	Definition	Examples
Definitions, standards, and constraints.	Each principle is a statement regulating a single concept to describe a condition that each instance of the concept must satisfy.	Properties that define birds; "accumulated surplus" as defined in accounting.
Laws and theories	Each principle regulates more than one concept through "If…then" relational principles or conditions.	The law of supply and demand; the theorems of plane geometry; the laws of gravity.
Decision trees	Principles are ordered by P links leading to a final procedure.	Guidelines for buying a home or investing money.
Iterative control structures	Principles are not ordered by P links but regulate the order of procedures execution.	Principles of medical diagnostics; principles of project management.

Figure 10. Examples of a standard (left) and a definition (right)

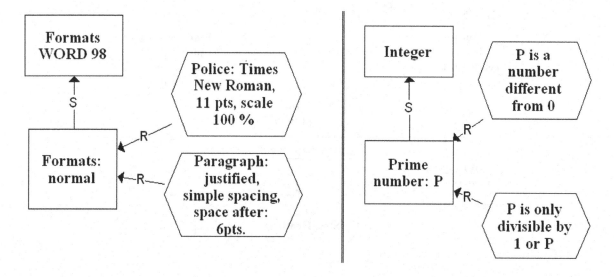

paragraph is defined by the principles illustrated on the left in Figure 10; on the right, the definition of a prime number provides yet another example.

Laws and Theories

Every field of knowledge has its laws and theories. Examples are the laws of gravity in astrophysics, the theory of supply and demand in economics, and the axioms and theorems of geometry establishing relations between points, lines, circles, polygons, etc.

Each of these laws is nothing more than a relational principle stating a cause and effect or a dependency between properties of concepts in the field.

The example in Figure 11 shows a simple theory to determine the duration of an ultrasound treatment in physiotherapy. It involves three concepts: duration, purpose of treatment, and stage of disease. Purpose of treatment can have one of four values: healing, pain relief, adhesion reduction, or edema reduction. Stage of disease can be acute, sub-acute, or chronic. Duration can be set to 3, 5, or 10 minutes.

The theory consists of four laws. Laws 1 and 2 do not involve purpose of treatment. They are relational principles that regulate stage of illness. If the stage is acute, duration is set to three minutes; if the stage is sub-acute, duration is set to 5 minutes.

Note that when a principle precedes another principle (through a P link), the former is always interpreted as a condition and the latter as an outcome (or an action, in the case of a procedure). Laws 3 and 4 are relational principles that regulate all three concepts and involve purpose of treatment when stage of disease is chronic. In such cases, if purpose of treatment is pain relief, duration of treatment is set to 5 minutes; if purpose of treatment is adhesion or edema reduction, duration of treatment is set to 10 minutes.[1]

Decision Trees

The field of expert systems has spread the use of decision trees, which are essentially knowledge bases in the form of rules. As we saw in the automobile example in Chapter 2, such rules are in fact relational principles executed in succession until the system can recommend an action.

Figure 11. A theory of four laws determining the duration of a treatment

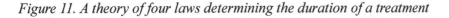
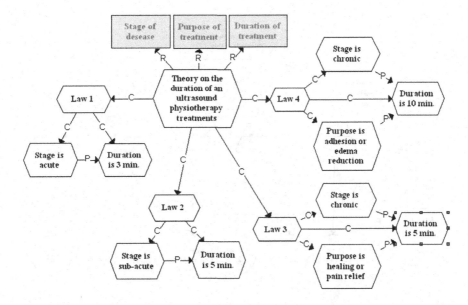

Decision trees are used in many knowledge areas: providing financial advice based on investor profile, identifying weed seedlings, determining immigration status in accordance with citizenship and immigration laws, etc. Figure 12 shows another example of a decision tree (fictitious), determining progressive tax rates for individuals based on their taxable income and whether or not they are married or have children.

The graph can be interpreted as follows:

- It is a prescriptive system divided into three sets of rules according to whether a taxpayer's income is low, medium, or high.
- Each set is subject to a first condition specifying whether the taxpayer is married or single; a second condition specifies whether a married taxpayer has children or not.
- Consequently, each set has three possible paths leading to a final principle; for example, under "Low taxable income,"
    - If the person is married, with children, then the rate is 0%;
    - If the person is married, without children, then the rate is 10%

    - If the person is single, then the rate is 15%.

Control Structure of Processes

In complex processes, the control structure regulating task and sub-task execution is extracted and presented separately. This allows representation of non-linear processes.

For example, designing a dining room involves several phases (represented by procedures): identifying the needs of the client, measuring the space, making a sketch or model of a proposal, adapting the proposal, getting it approved, and then carrying out the project.

Although this process indicates a progression in time, it is not necessarily linear and may require a return to previous phases. The control structure of a process defines the principles that regulate its order of sub-task execution. In our example, the control structure may include the principle, "If the needs of the client are unclear in Phase 1, proceed with the sketch or model, then return to Phase 1 to re-clarify the clients' needs," which would change the normal order of task execution.

Figure 12. A decision tree for calculating tax

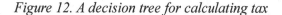

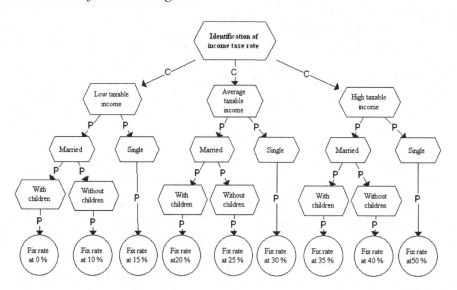

The example in Figure 13 shows a similar control structure for a diagnostic procedure. Notably, the control structure is generic, that is, it can be used to diagnose any system, be it a Hi-Fi sound system or the digestive system of an animal. It can thus apply to a variety of application domains.

The control structure consists of five principles that regulate four sub-diagnostic procedures. The structure can generate and test each component of the target system.

3.6 PROCESSES AND METHODS

Processes and methods are hybrid models incorporating all object types and most link types. They

Figure 13. Principles for controlling a diagnostic procedure

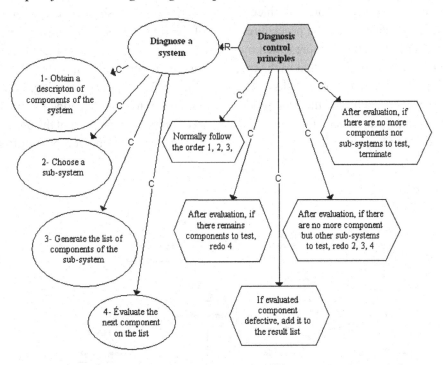

Table 6. Three sub-classes of processes and methods

Class	Definition	Examples
Processes	Models contain simple algorithmic decision principles used primarily for describing operations.	A diagnostic procedure for automobile failure; an industrial process for manufacturing steel.
Methods	Models consist of processes implemented by means of complex decision trees or iterative control structures; concepts are regulated by heuristic action principles or relational principles.	A method for designing and implementing a software program; a method for story writing; a method for figurative painting; a method for instructional engineering.
Multi-agent collaborative systems	Agents and their roles are described by principles that regulate the procedures or processes of the model.	The process of collectively writing a book with each role being clearly defined; a teaching aid system involving various specialists.

are made up of processes, methods and techniques, and multi-agent collaborative systems.

Processes

Processes involve the dynamics of such systems as the operation of a factory, the procedures leading to mechanical or medical diagnosis, the revenue forecasts of a company, or the performance evaluation of a department.

In processes, input/product links are central in connecting the concepts that represent objects to be processed or produced and the procedures that transform them. Procedures, represented by tasks, are connected in such a way that each task becomes the input for another or other tasks in the transformation process leading to the final product, while at the same time respecting a number of constraints defined by principles.

In processes, the transition from one procedure to another is regulated by specific, descriptive decision principles, without which the process could not be understood.

Figure 14 shows a model for the process of diagnosing a sound system. The inputs and products for each sub-process are indicated. The process "Choose and evaluate component" is divided into four main tasks; the final task is divided into five procedures. C links are indicated by dotted arrows.

The main flow of the process is indicated by a series I/P links showing the inputs and products of the procedures. Procedure 4.4 is crucial; it is based on a comparison principle between an observed property value and a standard requirement or norm for proper functioning. If the norm is not met, the component is added to the list of defective components. Note that the observed property may differ from one component to another. For

Figure 14. A diagnostic process

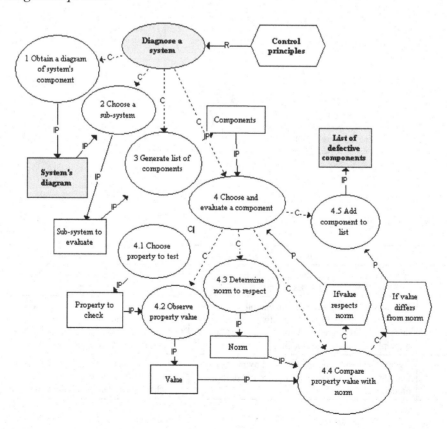

Figure 15. A method for defining a project

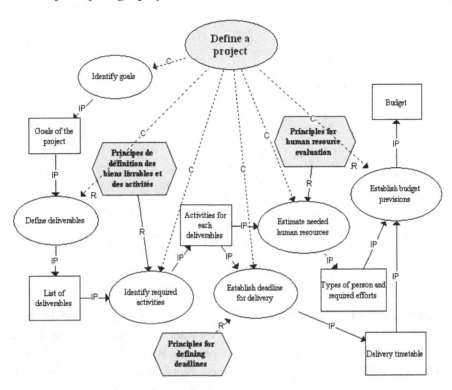

example, it may refer to the image quality of a TV or the sound quality of an amplifier.

The description of the diagnostic process is complemented by a statement of control principles, which can be represented by a sub-model such as the one in Figure 12.

Methods and Techniques

Methods and techniques differ from processes by the magnitude of tasks described (methods and techniques consist of several processes) and by point of view. Techniques generally consist of processes, the products of which be used by more than one method. Techniques and methods aim at creating new objects, rather than systematically producing deliverables. Their point of view shifts from simple descriptions of process control-flows to heuristic principles that regulate various processes. A heuristic principle, unlike a

deterministic principle, does not automatically guarantee the success of a procedure. Rather, it is a suggestion as to how to proceed, which when followed, will generally give good results.

Methods can be found in all areas of knowledge: developing a software program, designing a home or industrial building, planning a city district, instructional engineering, etc.

Figure 15 shows the first-level tasks of another, simpler, method for defining a project. Its three sets of heuristic principles are central and would normally be described in greater detail. In fact, each set would require a prescriptive sub-model possibly involving a large number of decision principles depending on the type of project. For example, the third set might include the following principles: "Resources should be allocated in a balanced way between scheduled phases"; "If deadlines are close to each other, use mostly experienced personnel"; "Allow time for all per-

Figure 16. A collaborative process for drafting a text

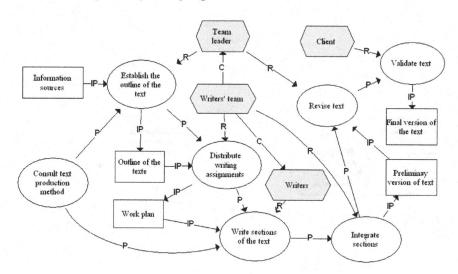

sonnel to participate in project coordination and on-going evaluation."

Collaborative Systems

Most processes and methods require the cooperation and collaboration of several people or agents. For our purposes, cooperation refers to situations in which individuals have separate yet complementary roles, such as in the production of a magazine. Collaboration refers to situations in which people perform a task together by taking similar roles, for example, in the collective writing of a text. In both cases, users must coordinate their actions, though differently, depending on whether they are cooperating or collaborating.

Figure 16 shows a collaborative process for writing a summary draft for a client. Tasks are represented by procedures. Information sources and production items are represented by concepts. Agents are represented by principles: The team leader controls the planning and editing of the text; the client approves the final text; each writer produces a section of the text (cooperation). This is not meant to represent the overall behavior of agents but only their use of principles to control the execution of the task.

Agents are represented by principles since we want to emphasize their role in regulating the process. We could also have represented them by concepts, which would have allowed us to list the attributes of each agent such as name, occupation, or competencies. Nevertheless, the role of agents is described essentially by the principles they use in performing tasks, as this is the aspect we consider most important in this model.

CONCLUSION

It is particularly reassuring to note that the basic principle of the MOT representation system, that is, providing a typology of knowledge objects and links, can lead to a coherent view of our own area of study— knowledge models.

The examples we have shown are relatively simple, but they cover a wide variety of knowledge areas and, above all, a wide variety of model types. More complex examples will be discussed later in this book, notably in Part IV, where we will present models developed in the context of real-life instructional engineering projects. In particular, a description of the MISA instructional engineering method using a complex MOT model will demonstrate the expressiveness of the representation system.

At the end of Chapter 2, we left the question open as to the generality and completeness of the system. It is impossible to demonstrate conclusively that all our objectives have been met. The representation method certainly has its limits. For example, if one wishes to develop highly complex computer systems, on may be better served by more conventional software engineering representations such as entity-relationship graphs or KADS and UML object-oriented models. Nevertheless, MOT modeling can help users to think, to clarify knowledge objects and their interrelationships, and to detect grey areas that require further investigation before undertaking a more technical description of a system.

The taxonomy of models and the examples presented in this chapter do demonstrate, however, the generality of the method in most areas of knowledge. Moreover, the method largely meets our criteria for completeness: It can be used to define basic concepts and associations within a conceptual system and to describe both the dynamic aspect of a domain, through procedural systems and processes, and its prescriptive aspect, including its laws, theories, and methods. Such qualities contribute to making knowledge more than simply a set of static or dynamic descriptions, but also a means of determining how to proceed and why certain phenomena occur.

The visual language presented here is a tool for investigating knowledge. It can be used for summarizing texts, preparing reports, giving presentations, or designing learning systems.

To do this, one needs to acquire basic modeling skills and to be able to graphically represent a variety of knowledge models. This is the objective of the next chapter: to present the modeling tools and techniques (in the sense we have given the word in the present chapter) that are used in the construction of knowledge models.

ENDNOTE

[1] This example is based on the SONODOSE program, developed by the author in collaboration with the Micro-Intel Group, a Québec-based software and multimedia training company.

Chapter 4
Modeling Tools and Techniques

Gilbert Paquette
LICEF Research Center, Canada

ABSTRACT

- The MOT+ Visual Model Editor
- Overview of the Modeling Process
  - Principles defining a model's orientations
  - Principles for selecting a model type.
  - Constructing the initial main model
- Priorizing Knowledge Objects to Be Developed
  - Assessing competency gaps for target populations
  - Creating a multilevel model
- Defining and Co-Referencing Knowledge Objects in Other Domains
- Validating and documenting models

In the previous chapters, we emphasized the "what" and "why" dimensions of knowledge modeling. In this chapter, we will focus on the "how" dimension. We will first present MOT+, a graphic editor that fully respects the syntax and grammar rules of modeling using objet types presented in Chapter 2, Table 5.[1] We will then use this tool as part of a technical description of the modeling process itself.

DOI: 10.4018/978-1-61520-839-5.ch004

4.1 THE MOT+ VISUAL MODEL EDITOR[2]

MOT+ is a model editor enabling users to construct visual models for the various fields of knowledge. With it, it is possible to build four types of visual models: Standard, Flowchart, Educational scenarios and Ontology. In this chapter, we will mainly present and use the *standard* modeling module of MOT+. The Educational scenario (IMS-LD) and Ontology modules will be presented in further chapters.

Upon opening, MOT+ displays the model creation and editing work window. Figure 1 presents the main aspects of this window.

The MOT+ editor has advanced editing capabilities. You can edit most graphic attributes of an object such as color, frame, font, alignment, as well as the relative position of objects through layering, alignment, spacing, etc. The menu bar and the main toolbar contain editing features similar to most advanced software like those in Microsoft or Open Office.

Graphic objects can be associated to any type of document using the OLE standards used in text editors, slide presentations, Web pages, spreadsheets, or database files. These associated documents can be displayed by clicking on the MOT graphic symbol.

Mot+ export tools allows you to convert visual models into formatted Excel spreadsheets, HTML pages, Access databases, XML files, image files, XML OWL, XML IMS-LD files, and Export Project Tree to MSExcel. In particular, exporting to XML provides the possibility for visual models to be processed by software agents respecting for example the IMS LD or OWL schemas.

In the editing toolbar, you can choose the MOT knowledge type such as concept, procedure, principle, example, trace, or statement. You can also choose to draw C, S, I, P, R, I/P or A links between two objects.

The editor also allows you to use a rectangle with rounded corners to represent untyped objects or links defined by the user. Such elements allow the user to create representations that differ from

Figure 1. MOT+ work window

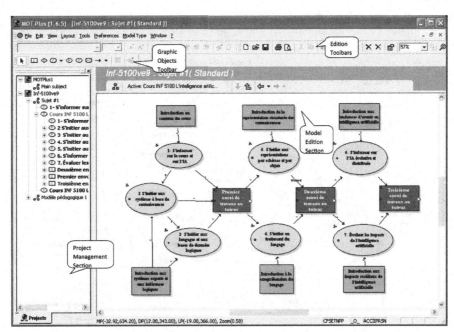

MOT object-type modeling, for example, entity-relation graphs.

An important feature of MOT is the ability to handle *several models* simultaneously through multiple graphical windows. In this way, objects can be transferred from one model to another.

Main Models and Nested Models

Most of the time, a particular model demands the inclusion of many objects and links. In these cases, you may wish to clarify the representation of the project by retaining only one main model while developing nested models. This is one of MOT+ fundamental features. Starting from the main model (level 1), you can build and display a nested model (level 2), if need be, for each of the principal objects in the main model. When the objects of the nested model require detailing, you can build and display a new nested model (level 3), and so on. The models are nested like Russian dolls. This feature enables you to build a multilevel representation of the main subject.

Suppose the ultimate goal is to repair a defective stereo system. To do this, a specialist must perform a succession of tasks. Therefore, we would have the following information:

- Domain: Electronic.
- Purpose of the Model: Represent the tasks required for repairing a defective stereo system.
- Type of Model: To model these tasks a Procedural Model is needed.

The main standard model could look something like Figure 2.

We will now briefly explain this model (which you may have already intuitively grasped) and describe some of the symbols used. The action 'Repair Defective Stereo System' is composed of several procedures numbered 1 through 5 Two of the procedures (1 and 5) are composed of conditions or principles preceding different actions (procedures. A principle followed by procedures is interpreted as an 'if…then…' rule. Other procedures (2, an 3) produce concept objects that are each input to following steps of the procedure.

This level-1 model is the first step in designing a model. It consists establishing an overall view

Figure 2. Example of a procedural model

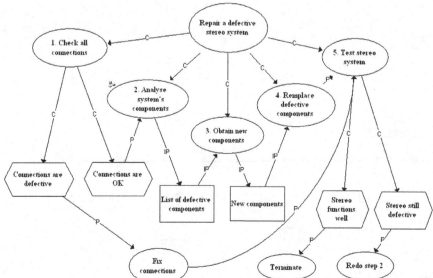

of the subject to be modeled. This view is not encumbered with details that would make the model difficult to understand. However, in many cases, it is important to develop a model further. The way to accomplish this is to build nested models, i.e. level-2 models, associated to each of the main model's objects that require more explanation. Procedure 2, 'Analyse System's Components', was developed into such an explanatory model presented on Figure 3. A symbol in MOT+, appears on the upper left corner of an object to indicate the existence of an associated nested model.

This example demonstrates the benefit of developing into many level-2 nested models associated to the objects since it simplifies significantly the main model.

The nested model is built by breaking down the task 'Analyse System's Components' into four procedures (2.1, 2.2, 2.3, and 2.4). Once

again, we are faced with a procedural Model. The fourth procedure is also broken down into four sub-procedures the last of which 'Add to List of Defective Components' produces the concept 'List of Defective Components', final result of the sub-model's main task (the 'List of Defective Components' is used upward in the main model).

Note that this model contains a new type of object, a fact (rectangle object with inverted corners). For example: 'Kenwood L-05M Amplifier Diagram' is a specific example of the 'Amplifier Diagram' concept.

Furthermore, a new link between two concepts ('S' link) is illustrated in this model, since one concept specializes the more general concept. For example: 'Clarity of Sound' is a sort of 'Attribute'.

Finally, 'if… then' conditions are found in this model. They take the form of principles that make up a procedure's prerequisites ('P' link).

Figure 3. Nested model associated to the 'analyse system's components' process

For example: 'Value Differs from Standard' principle is a prerequisite condition to the 'Add to List of Defective Components' procedure.

One of this model's objects was developed into a level-3 nested model. It is the 'Process Control Structure', a principle ruling ('R' link) the 'Stereo System's Diagnosis Defects' task. Here again, developing the principle into an associated nested model helps to simplify the level-2 upper model. Therefore, the modeling of a subject often entails deploying several nested models associated to specific objects.

Let us see how the nested model associated to 'Control Process Structure' object was developed (see Figure 4)

This model is fairly simple as it mainly represents a set of conditions governing the order of performance of the tasks in the level-2 model. It is a control structure model, similar to the ones presented in chapter 3. The objective here is to illustrate the different conditions governing the order in which the sub-procedures of the 'Analyze

System's Components' objects must be performed. In this model, each condition is expressed as follows: an 'if… then…' statement.

In our example, the control structure (level-3 model) affects the performance of procedures related to the diagnosis (level-2 model), and the results of the diagnosis affect the performance of the main model's (level-1 model) procedures. The main model and objects' Nested models are always nested and dependent on one another. MOT+ actually enables you to create such relationships.

Note that, in this chapter, we often refer to models in a MOT+ document. You must keep in mind that we are not talking about several independent models but one Main Model and a series of nested models stemming from the main model.

Keep in mind that Mot+ is a tool. It is no substitute for your skills as a model designer; however, it will help you to be more efficient when building object models tailored to your needs.

Figure 4. Nested model associated to the 'process control…' knowledge unit

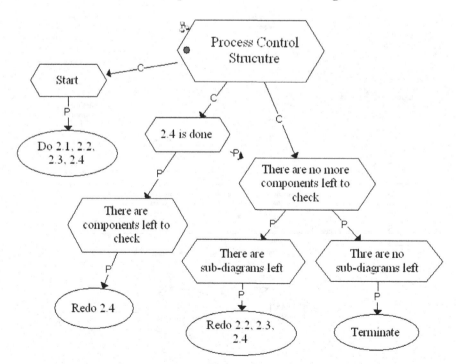

Advanced Features of MOT+

An advanced feature of MOT+ is the ability to *integrate several knowledge domains within the same project*. In Figure 5, an interface (top right window) presents a list of open projects and their domains. One project has four domains. Another project has two domains. Users can add and delete any number of projects and domains within a project.

Unlike the first version of MOT, which was able to handle several domains but within different projects, MOT+ is able to integrate, within a single project, several domains connected by what are called *co-reference* links. Thus, in a single domain, we can describe each object using an associated sub-model (ASM) called a *co-domain*. This is illustrated in Figure 5. The object "Procedure #7" is associated to an instructional model that shows the course units (UA11 and UA12) where this procedure is explained. We can do the inverse as well, i.e. associate each course unit

with a co-domain that is a subset of the knowledge model for the course. This feature gives powerful representational abilities to MOT+

A *marker* function allows objects to be labeled by user-defined symbols. Objects can then be filtered by their associated markers. This feature allows, for example, to create sub-types of concepts, procedures, and principles, or to mark objects by author. Since each model can be presented by a structured drop-down list, objects can be sorted by their marker, i.e. by type, sub-type, author, etc.

Two other advanced features are available:

- Variants can be assigned to models describing the pathways of different actors in task networks. These variants are based on a common model of objects and links. The variants differ from one another by certain objects or links that, if in the same model, would be contradictory. For example, a variant may contain a P link from A to B, while another may contain a P link from B to A.

Figure 5. Co-referencing knowledge objects

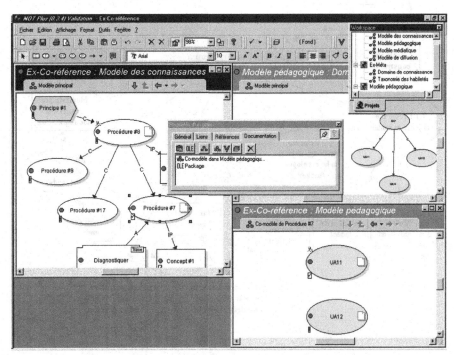

○ A model may also contain many *layers*. This feature is particularly useful in complex models where one needs to describe objects representing many actors, distinguishing for example, the activities of learners from those of instructors. Each layer can be masked or overlapping other layers.

4.2 OVERVIEW OF THE MODELING PROCESS

We will now use the MOT+ editor to represent the technique for modeling using object types. Recall that a technique, as defined in Chapter 3, consists of a set of processes whose products can be used by more than one method. Such processes are regulated by heuristic principles. A heuristic principle, unlike a deterministic or algorithmic principle, does not automatically guarantee the success of a procedure. Rather, it is a suggestion

as to how to proceed, which when followed, will generally give good results

The MOT model on Figure 6 shows an overview of the technique in the form of an upper level process. The purpose of the technique is to construct a model through five main processes. It results in a knowledge model based on the goals and constraints initially set out by the model designer.

The model in Figure 6 is regulated by general principles of progression determining when to implement a particular process. Initially, the model is oriented by an individual or team faced with a representational problem. The goals, raw data, and constraints of the problem then determine the type of knowledge objects and links that will guide the model's development. The final result is a knowledge model that provides a solution to the initial problem according to these goals and constraints.

The modeling process presented here is as broad as possible. Indeed, one may wish to model

Figure 6. Overview of the technique for modeling using object types

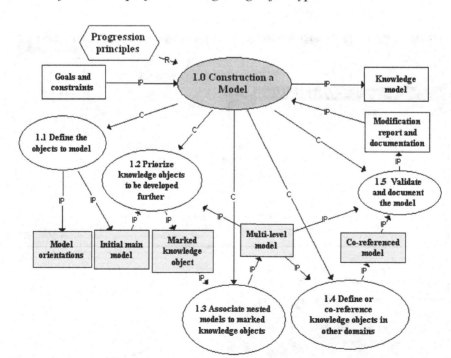

knowledge in a context other than instructional engineering. Although many of our examples are from that field, the technique presented here can be used for other applications, including, for example, re-engineering administrative processes. In such an application, one needs to describe the skills required to carry out process tasks. As well, one needs to associate these tasks to different positions in the organization, considered as a co-domain.

Sub-Processes, Inputs, and Products

As shown in Figure 6, the modeling process is composed of five sub-processes.

- The aim of the first sub-process is to identify the learning objects of the model. To do this, we must define both the orientations of the model and the model type, based on an analysis of the representational problem. From this, we develop a basic model of knowledge objects and skills. At this initial stage, we are concerned only with identifying facts, knowledge objects, and primary links at a single level, i.e. exclusive of lower (nested) sub-models.

- The second sub-process consists in priorizing knowledge objects deemed principal. These are critical knowledge objects that must be learned by target populations. As a consequence, they are good candidates for nested models.

- The aim of the third sub-process is to associate each principal object with a second-level sub-model. The second sub-process is then applied to these sub-models to identify their knowledge objects. If needed, these are in turn associated with third-level nested sub-models. We proceed in this way until a satisfactory coverage of the knowledge domain is attained given the goals and constraints established at the beginning of the modeling project.

- The fourth sub-process consists in referencing knowledge objects of the main model with those of another domain, called a co-domain. A co-domain can be the chapters of a book, the modules of a software program, or the learning units of a course whose contents are defined by the distribution of the knowledge objects. This operation can involve more than one co-domain. This sub-process can be skipped if non co-domain associations are needed.

- The final sub-process consists in testing the model among typical target population users. The validation process focuses on the accuracy, consistency, and completeness of the model with regard to its initial goals and constraints. It allows the model, sub-models, and co-models to be revised, the modifications to be reported, and the model to be documented.

4.3 IDENTIFYING KNOWLEDGE OBJECTS

The first procedure of the technique, "Define the objects of the model," is divided into three main tasks: define the orientations of the knowledge model, choose a model type, and construct the initial model. As shown in Figure 7, each task is regulated by a group of principles.

Initial Data and Model Profile

The modeling process begins by a definition of the representational problem. This definition includes the model's goal, sources of data, a general description of target populations, and the constraints regarding the shape and size of the model. These elements need to be specified in order to begin the modeling process.

The *goal of the model* is a short statement such as "To model Internet search procedures and tools" or "To represent the decision rules for accepting or rejecting products in a quality control test." It must be precise enough to guide the choice for

Figure 7. Sub-process for the identification of knowledge objects

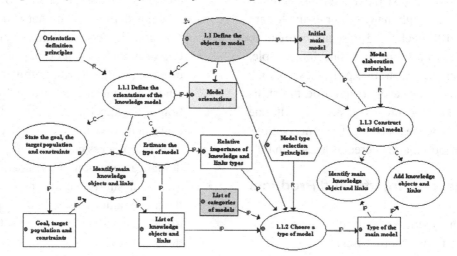

the main knowledge objects and the link types of the eventual model.

Constraints depend on the target populations of the model. Target populations are groups of persons that will use the model. Such groups are distinguished by their information or training needs, their current and target skills related to the knowledge domain under development, their availability, or other constraints that determine the size and levels of the eventual model. From the outset, it may be useful to determine whether the learning goal is merely to apply sensory, memory, comprehension, or practical skills, or whether it is to develop more complex skills such as analyzing, summarizing and evaluating. Skills are also knowledge objects and should appear as such in a model. Normally, using a knowledge model will require both specific and generic skills. These must be applicable in the domain and transferable to other domains.

For example, suppose that a model's target populations requires skills for creating Internet search procedures. In such a case, the model must anticipate more time for knowledge acquisition and thus be more extensive than a model in which users are only required to apply procedures. As well, the model must contain additional principles that allow for the creation of useful and efficient procedures.

Sources of data can be interviews or documents related to the model's goal. Particular attention must be given to current and targeted skills of user populations, task descriptions, and other sources of documentation. An inventory of this data is made to identify the model's principal knowledge objects and link types, and a preliminary list is drawn up. If necessary, this information is validated through interviews with representative members of target populations.

The profile of the knowledge model is a short text based on an analysis of the preliminary inventory of knowledge objects and links. It provides an estimate of the relative number of knowledge objects and links in the model, as well as the model's size; it depends on the model's representational problem and target populations; it dictates whether the model will complex, with multiple levels and relations to other knowledge domains, or simple, with only one or two levels.

For example, if the goal is "To model Internet search procedures and tools," and the skills relevant to the knowledge objects apply to users familiar with office software programs, the model may have the following profile: "The model will consist mostly of procedures (with their input and products); links will be mostly of the input/

product, precedence, and composition type; the model will be limited to two or three levels."

Principles Defining a Model's Orientations

The following principles help carry out the above tasks:

1. *Transition between tasks:* Once the model's goal is identified, the other tasks can be carried out largely in parallel fashion. The estimate of the model's profile can evolve at the same time that the inventory of knowledge objects and links is being made. The library of model types (see Chapter 3) can be continuously accessed, and the model type can be modified as knowledge objects and links are identified and until a level of consistency is achieved for selecting the final model type.

2. *Size of knowledge object and link inventory:* The initial list of knowledge objects should not be too extensive. The purpose of this preliminary analysis is to explore potential model types by specifying the concepts, principles, and procedures they contain and their links. At this point, a great deal of attention is not required for facts or skills, except for principal skills such as those mentioned in the previous examples.

3. *Model profile:* To determine a model's profile, consider the principal skill to be developed in regard to target population constraints. If the time constraints are too strict and target users are new to the domain, expectations regarding skills and the size of the model should be reduced. However, if higher level skills are targeted (analyzing, summarizing, evaluating), processes or methods should be chosen over simple conceptual or procedural models and a larger model should be planned.

4. *Disparity regarding relevant knowledge among target populations.* After examining the representational problem and the sources of data, and if there is more than one target population, one may find that needs of the target populations regarding the model are quite incompatible. If target content or skills are too different, or if current competencies are too disproportional, more than one model can be created and a separate inventory of knowledge objects and links can be compiled for each model.

Principles for Selecting a Model Type

Ultimately, the goal of the model, the preliminary inventory of knowledge objects, and the estimated profile of the model result in a model type chosen from the categories described in Chapter 3. This choice begins the process of modeling from a certain point of view of reality. It also ensures that a standard form of model is used as the starting point.

The following heuristic principles help choose the initial model:

1. *Choosing a conceptual, procedural, or prescriptive point of view.* Choosing a point of view for the knowledge to be acquired depends mainly on the model's goal, the current and targeted competencies of the user population, and the constraints of the latter including those imposed by the client organization. Available sources of information are useful, but a critical eye must be kept, since the prevailing point of view of an organization or domain sometimes needs redefinition.
   - Generally, it is more useful to focus on a conceptual point of view (describing the "what dimension," objects, etc.) when the targeted level of competency is simply an awareness of information. If the objects are more concrete than abstract, a factu-

al-type system is favored, i.e. sets of examples, traces, or statements.

- If knowledge must be used to perform tasks that increase productivity, or if the targeted competency is familiarity with a subject, a procedural point of view is generally favored.
- Finally, if the targeted knowledge is to be used for performing tasks that require creativity or great adaptability or judgment, or if the targeted competency is to acquire mastery or expertise in a particular domain, then a prescriptive point of view is favored.

2. *Choosing a conceptual-type model.* If we opt for a conceptual point of view, the resulting model must consist of either sub-classes (S links) or components (link C).

- The first case is well suited to theoretical models that classify objects, people, or events according to their similarities or differences. Knowledge objects are classified into a hierarchy of classes and sub-classes. Principles that are definition rules specifying the properties of certain concepts can then be added, resulting in a hybrid conceptual system.
- The second case is more suited to systems having many components and sub-components (machines, organizations, etc.). If required, procedures for certain components or definition rules for certain concepts can be added, resulting in a hybrid conceptual system.

3. *Choosing a procedural-type model.* If we opt for a procedural point of view, we must first decide if the model describes a simple or routine procedure or a method involving many concepts and principles. In the first case, we must first determine whether we are dealing with a serial, parallel, or itera-

tive procedure. In the second case, we must choose among the various types of processes or methods. In either case, we will have to choose among several procedural steps requiring control procedures or a prescriptive system akin to a "decision tree."

4. *Choosing a prescriptive-type model.* If we opt for a prescriptive point of view, we must decide on a secondary level for the model to be composed of either relational or decisional principles. In the first case, the principles are used to construct the domain's theory by defining objects and establishing relations between their properties through laws. In the second case, the principles are used to define a decision or control structure for regulating a complex set of possible actions.

5. *Choosing a process- or method-type model.* Each point of view, whether conceptual, procedural, or prescriptive, may evolve into a process or method through the addition of object types initially absent. However, if we know early on that the model will be a process or method, we can develop it along five stages:

- Construct a hierarchy of tasks represented by procedures connected from beginning to end by composition links.
- Specify the input and product concepts for each procedure and, if required, develop certain concepts through specialization, composition, or instantiation (examples).
- Identify the control principles of the process or method and, if required, decompose these principles.
- Develop sets of principles that regulate procedures leading to the final (i.e non-decomposed) procedure, especially in the case of methods and techniques.
- If the model has a collaborative di-

mension, divide task responsibilities among the various agents, resulting in a multi-agent model.

Constructing the Initial Main Model

Establishing a model's orientation and type are the first steps in representing a learning system's knowledge objects and skills. As shown in Figure 7, building an initial main model involves two tasks:

Identify the Principal Knowledge Object

The model type directly determines the principal knowledge object type, be it a concept, procedure, or principle. Choosing the correct principal knowledge object is important because in a way it summarizes the model's goal. For example, "Tele-university" is a concept that can be developed through a hierarchical structure; "Perform an Internet search" is a procedure that can be broken down into more detailed operations. As

shown in Figure 9, it may be useful to specify skills (trace-type objects) that apply (A links) to the main knowledge object and affect the development of the model.

Add Knowledge Objects and Links

Once the principal knowledge object is established, it can be associated with other objects and links chosen according to the model type and selected from the inventory of objects and links. For example, in the case of a conceptual system, the main components and sub-components can be defined and decomposed as required.

Principles for Constructing the Initial Main Model

The following heuristic principles can be used in constructing the initial main model:

1. *Selecting knowledge objects.* The principal knowledge object, additional knowledge

Figure 9. Example of a model showing principal knowledge objects

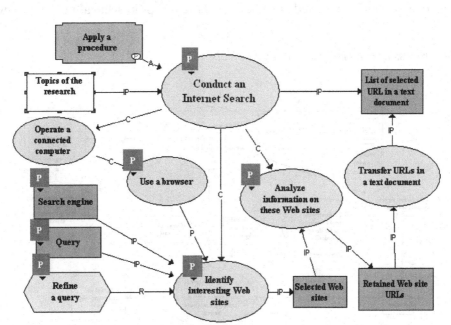

objects, and the links connecting them must correspond to the model type—concepts for a conceptual model, procedures for a procedural model or a process, principles for a prescriptive model.

2. *Selecting links.* Link type also corresponds to model type. For example, taxonomies have S links, component system have C links, procedural systems have P and I/P links, prescriptive systems have R and C links, and processes and methods have mostly C, I/P, and R links.

3. *Scale of the initial main model.* The initial model must contain enough knowledge objects to allow it to be developed according to the estimated size and number of levels. Generally, one should start with an initial model of approximately 10 to 20 knowledge objects.

4.4 PRIORIZING KNOWLEDGE OBJECTS TO BE DEVELOPED FURTHER

The second process of the technique consists in priorizing the principal knowledge objects, first in the initial main model, then in all nested models.

As shown in Figure 8, the process is regulated by a group of principles known as "priorization" principles and divided into four tasks: defining the target population; identifying the critical knowledge objects of the target population; situating the target population competency on a competency scale; and finally, marking the competency gap for each principal knowledge object.

The aim here is to guide the development of the model based on the needs of future users. We want to avoid models that try to be all-inclusive or that contain knowledge objects that are already known, irrelevant, or unnecessary to our modeling goal. We also want to avoid constructing models that are incomplete with regard to that goal.

The use of a progressive competency scale will guide the modeling process to ensure that the target population's ability to read and use the model at a level of detail corresponding to their mastery of the model's principal knowledge objects.

Properties of Target Populations with Respect to Knowledge Objects

During the first process, we were able to identify one or more target population. We can now analyze these groups in detail as the model develops. This

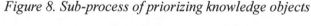

Figure 8. Sub-process of priorizing knowledge objects

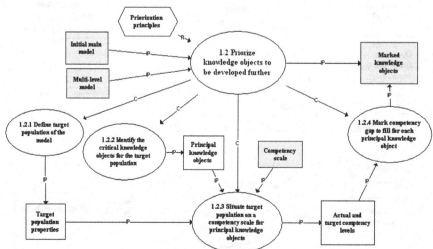

can be in the form of a table showing the main attributes of the target populations, including name, description, previous experience, language, availability (time constraint), and positive, negative or neutral attitudes toward the model's content.

From this table, we can determine which knowledge objects—beyond the principal knowledge object that was the starting point for the model—are the most important for each target population. We then mark this object with a P symbol. In MOT+, as in MOT, this symbol << P >> is created as a comment linked to the principal knowledge object.

The example in Figure 9 illustrates an initial model whose main knowledge object is "Search information on the Internet" for two target populations—managers of a documentation center and documentation technicians. Knowledge objects labeled "P" are defined as principal knowledge objects. This means that at least one target population has a competency gap with regard to these knowledge objects. These knowledge objects will be further developed in nested models, contrary to the other knowledge objects, which are used only to clarify the context of the principal knowledge objects.

Assessing Knowledge Gaps for Target Populations

At this point, we can assess a target population's current and targeted competency level on a competency scale such as the one on Table 1 for each knowledge object. These values are relative and are used to compare target populations for each knowledge object. Nevertheless, they can be interpreted as follows:

- *Awareness.* At this level, a person can explain, in his or her own words, the essential elements of a knowledge object or group of knowledge objects. This level involves mostly skills of recognition and memorization. Further along the awareness scale (S+), a person is able to formulate or have an opinion on the knowledge objet.
  - ○ Examples signaling this competency level:
    - ➤ I know it exists. I've heard about it. I can briefly talk about it.
    - ➤ I know it exists. I've seen it. I've observed it. I can exactly relate what I was told or what I saw.
    - ➤ I know it exists. I've seen its effects. I can form a statement about this knowledge demonstrating that I have grasped the idea.
- *Familiarity.* At this level, a person can apply the acquired knowledge relatively accurately. The person can demonstrate that, for similar problems or situations, he or she can reproduce that particular knowledge, more often than not with advice, assistance, or supervision. A gradual reduction in errors and an increase in autonomy in applying the knowledge are principal factors allowing one to advance along the three familiarity levels of the competency scale. Knowledge objects that require a level of familiarity are often those that involve doing something, i.e. applying a process, procedure, or strategy.
  - ○ Examples signaling this level of competency:

Table 1. A mastery scale

Competency scale										
Level	**Awareness**		**Familiarity**			**Mastery**			**Expertise**	
Value	1	2	3	4	5	6	7	8	9	10
Symbol	S	S+	F -	F	F+	M-	M	M+	E-	E

> ➤ I understand the knowledge and can apply it in a similar context as long as there is considerable support and direction.
> ➤ I understand the knowledge and can apply it as long as there is some support and direction.
> ➤ I understand the knowledge and can apply it thoroughly and without error as long as I have access to occasional help.

- *Mastery.* At this level, a person is able to intelligently apply the acquired knowledge to a variety of situations and adapt it to new situations with a minimum of help. Creativity, the degree of autonomy in adapting the knowledge to a variety of situations, and the ability to accurately communicate this knowledge, are principal factors allowing one to advance along the three mastery levels of the competency scale. Knowledge objects that require a level of mastery are often processes or strategies.
  - ○ Examples signaling this level of competency:
    - ➤ I understand the knowledge and can adapt much of it to a variety of situations with no help.
    - ➤ I understand the knowledge and can adapt much of it to a variety of situations with no help.
    - ➤ I understand the knowledge and not only can I adapt it to other situations with no help, but I can also clearly explain the procedure to others.
- *Expertise.* At this level, a person can participate in the creation of new knowledge objects and is able to explain the rules and heuristics associated with the particular knowledge domain. The capacity to reflect on one's own learning (meta-cognition), the degree of autonomy in creating knowl-

edge objects, and the ability to demonstrate the knowledge domain are principal factors allowing one to advance along the two mastery levels of the competency scale. Knowledge objects at expert levels are usually strategies or methods.

  - ○ Examples signaling this level of competency:
    - ➤ I understand the full extent of the knowledge presented and can apply it in new ways in the domain.
    - ➤ I can explain the rules and heuristics that I use in applying the knowledge.
    - ➤ I can apply the knowledge in new ways in related domains. I can explain the limits of such applications, as well as their rules and heuristics.
    - ➤ I have acquired such knowledge and its applications in two or three related domains: I can explain the limits of these applications in each domain, as well as their rules and heuristics.

Technically, we can estimate the knowledge gap between current and targeted competencies by using a table with the principal knowledge objects (marked P on the model) are listed in the first column. We can draw horizontal bars or lines in which the left end indicates current competency level and the right end indicates target competency level. The distance between the two extremities corresponds to the knowledge gap for that knowledge object for a particular target population. In Instructional Engineering, such knowledge gaps are often called <<learning needs>>.

Table 2 presents estimated competencies gap for two target populations for the model in Figure 9. The first column lists the principal knowledge objects, the second indicates the target populations, and the remaining columns display current and target levels on the competency scale of Table 1.

Here, we make the assumption that managers are less experienced than documentation technicians in matters related to querying a database, and little progress is required on their part; however, more is expected of them regarding their ability to analyze information. The table indicates that the concept "query" and the principles used to refine a query represent a gap of 5 for documentation technicians and only 2 for managers. On the other hand, the procedure of analyzing information on Web sites represents a gap of 3 for managers and 4 for technicians, while both have a targeted competency of 5.

Priorization Principles for Knowledge Objects

The following heuristic principles are used to priorize knowledge objects with regard to competency gaps.

1. *Marking principal knowledge objects.* Marking allows us to decide which principal knowledge objects will be described through a nested model. In constructing nested models, we should continue identifying principal knowledge objects until those with a knowledge gap of zero for all target populations are obtained.

2. *Using skills as a guide.* The skills applying to principal knowledge objects of a model, and to those of nested models, determine the targeted competency level for knowledge objects around the principal knowledge object. In the example presented in this section, for the skill "apply a procedure," familiarity is the targeted level on average, although for some knowledge objects, a level of mastery is targeted (see Table 2). We will then need to decide what the current and target levels of familiarity are for each object.

3. *Relativity among knowledge gaps.* Values for knowledge gaps are not absolute but relative and are based on a comparison of the various knowledge objects and target populations. This is why we recommend creating an overview of the model in tabular form with a comparison of current and targeted compe-

Table 2. Example of a competency table

Knowledge	Target Users	Awareness		Familiarity			Mastery			Expertise	
		1	2	3	4	5	6	7	8	9	10
Analyse information on Web sites (procedure)	Manager			■	■	■					
	Technician		■	■	■	■					
Search Engine (concept)	Manager		■	■							
	Technician			■	■	■					
Use a browser (procedure)	Manager			■	■	■					
	Technician		■	■	■	■					
Refine a query (principle)	Manager		■	■	■						
	Technician		■	■	■	■	■	■			
Quebry (concept)	Manager		■	■	■						
	Technician		■	■	■	■	■	■			
Identify interesting Web sites (procedure)	Manager			■	■	■					
	Technician		■	■	■	■					
Search information on the Internet (procedure)	Manager		■	■	■	■					
	Technician			■	■	■					

tencies for all knowledge objects and target populations. Only by comparing knowledge objects in this way can we assign values, calculate knowledge gaps, and transfer this data to the model through comments, color codes, or labels.

4. *Using skills as a guide.* Note that a small knowledge gap will likely mean that this particular knowledge object is less important in the model and will not require further elaboration, i.e. will have fewer links. A medium gap means that a nested model will be associated with the knowledge object, but probably on a single level. A large gap means that the development of the knowledge object will probably be on several levels. Before completing the priorization process, one should see how the model compares with the initial estimate for shape and size constraints.

4.5 EXPANDING THE MODEL

The third process of the modeling technique consists of elaborating, on several levels, the main model obtained from the first process, according to the prioritized knowledge objects established in the second process.

As can be seen on the graph in Figure 10, this third process is iterative. We first create a second level by associating nested sub-models to knowledge objects of the main models according to their priorization and the intended size of the model. We then apply the process of priorization to the knowledge objects of this second level sub-models. This priorization will guide the development, if necessary, of a third level, and so on.

Two groups of principles regulate this process: the principle of balance among object types and the principle of completeness.

Creating a Multilevel Model

Elaborating a knowledge object by associating it with a sub-model of the same domain is the basis

Figure 10. Sub-process of creating multiple levels

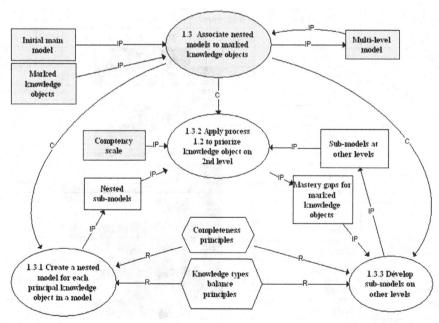

for creating multilevel models. We will now examine the second-level models of the main model in Figure 9, "Conduct an Internet search". Given that we are targeting a medium-scale model, we have chosen not to elaborate the object "search engine." Although the competency gap for "Use a browser" is medium (2 for managers, 3 for technicians), we will not further elaborate this knowledge object.

In fact, knowledge objects with large competency gaps are regulated by the two principles "identify interesting Web sites" and "identify information on these Web sites." We will create a second-level model for each of these procedures. In the first case, the competency gap is average (equal or greater to 4); the objects "Query and "refine a query" are closely related to this procedure. These objects can potentially be developed at a third level.

Figures 11 and 12 show the two second-level models; Figures 13 and 14 are third-level models derived from Figure 11. As such, the multilevel model in our example includes knowledge objects from the following sub-models:

- Level 1: Main model "Search for information on the Internet"
  - Level 2: Nested model "Identify interesting Web sites" (Figure 11)
    - Level 3: Nested model "Request" (Figure 13)
    - Level 3: Nested model "Refine a request" (Figure 14)
  - Level 2: Nested model "Analyze information on selected Web sites (Figure 12)

At this point, we can ask if the procedure has been completed. This of course depends on the orientation, goal, and constraints initially given to the model. We presume that the goal was to improve the skills of two groups of people—documentation managers and technicians—in searching information on the Internet from a list of topics in analyzing this information, and in

creating a summary. We also presume that these users have limited training time, which explains the small size of the model.

In order to answer the question, consider the five sub-models of the overall model, that is the main model of Figure 9 and the models in the four previous figures. The knowledge objects that have the largest competency gaps among the target populations are sufficiently elaborated in second-level models.

- The model in Figure 11 contains a new priorized knowledge, "Formulate a request," which has a large competency gap (Priority 1). This object is elaborated in a nested model along with the object "Request" (Figure 13). The other knowledge objects are not priorized because it is presumed that users of the model are sufficiently familiar with them. The model is therefore elaborated at a sufficient level.
- The model in Figure 12 contains two new priorized knowledge objects, "Analyze a site" and "Site analysis principle," which have medium competency gaps (Priority 2). Together, these objects can form another third-level model. The other knowledge objects of the model, however, do not require further elaboration
- All the knowledge objects of Figures 13 and 14 are familiar to users and do not require further elaboration.

Let us now consider the categories to which these models belong. The main model (Figure 9) is a procedural model since the majority of its knowledge objects are procedures and I/P and P links are favored. Moreover, there is a strict order among the five sub-procedures; it is therefore a sequential procedure. On the other hand, the two second-level models (Figures 11 and 12) represent cycles; they are therefore iterative procedures.

The model for the object "Query" (Fig. 13) is a conceptual system. It shows the components

Figure 11. Second-level nested model for the multilevel model "conduct Internet search"

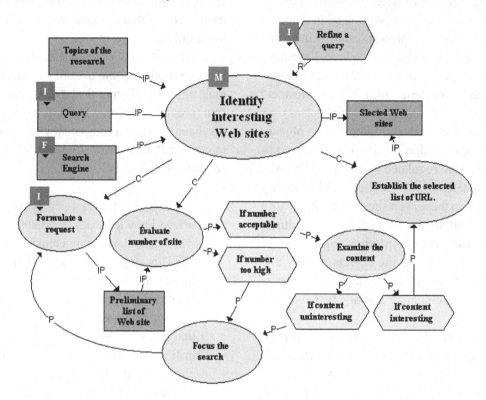

Figure 12. Second-level nested model for the multilevel model "conduct Internet search"

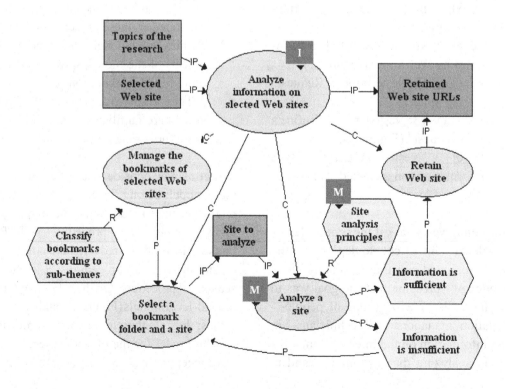

Figure 13. Third-level nested model for the multilevel model "conduct Internet search"

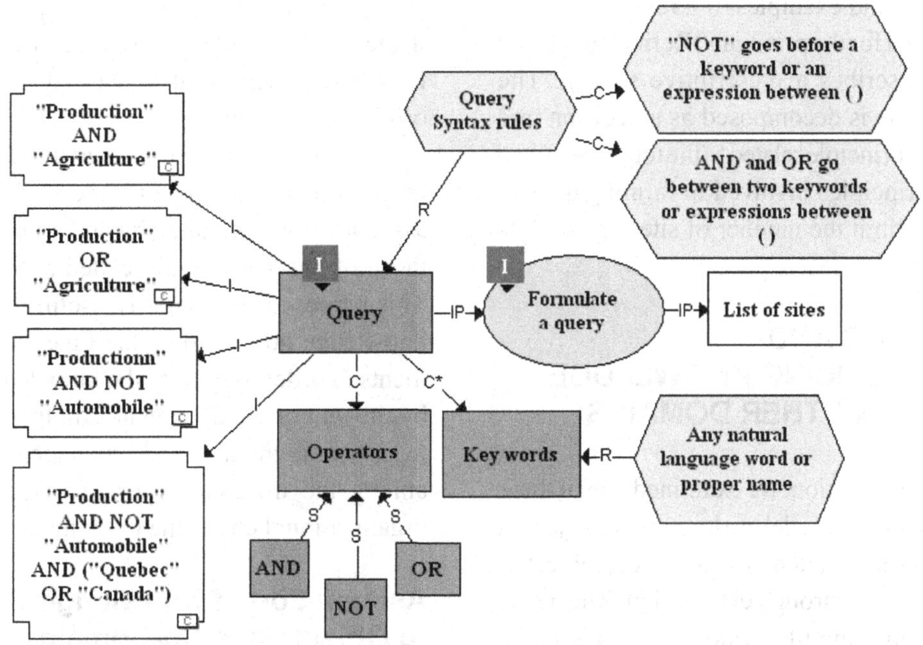

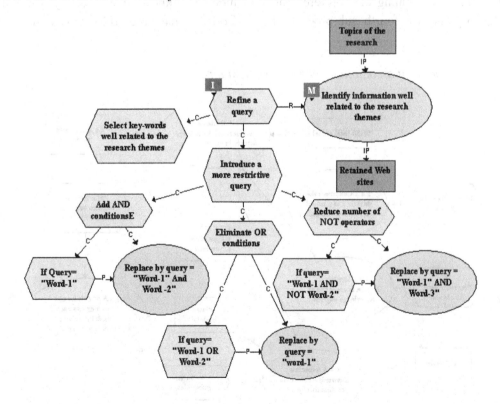

Figure 14. Third-level nested model for the model "conduct Internet search"

of a request, the principles that regulate these components, and examples of a request.

The model for the principle "Refine a request," however, describes a prescriptive system. The main principle is decomposed as a decision tree containing a principle related to the topics searched and three principles involved in forming queries and used to limit the number of sites.

4.6 DEFINING AND CO-REFERENCING KNOWLEDGE OBJECTS IN OTHER DOMAINS

In the previous section, we examined one of three ways to associate a model to a knowledge object. A model can be associated to a knowledge object of the same domain through elaboration. This is the basis for creating multilevel models. In this section, we will present two other methods that involve associating a knowledge object to a sub-model of another domain. Defining or co-referencing knowledge objects is a fourth sub-process of

modeling presented on Figure 15.

Association by *definition* is especially useful if the purpose is to clarify a knowledge object from a different point of view than that of the originating domain.

Association by *co-referencing* needs more elaboration as shown on Figure 15. It consists of associating knowledge objects of one domain to those of another domain called a "co-domain." This process is particularly useful for assigning knowledge objects to units of a course or documents in order to specify the knowledge covered by the unit or the document. Another example is to distribute the tasks of a management process among the different types of personnel of an organizational chart (the co-domain).

Association of Knowledge Objects to Objects in a Co-Domain

We will first consider the method of associating a model to a knowledge object by co-referencing. Co-referencing is used when we want to establish

Figure 15. Sub-process of association between two domains

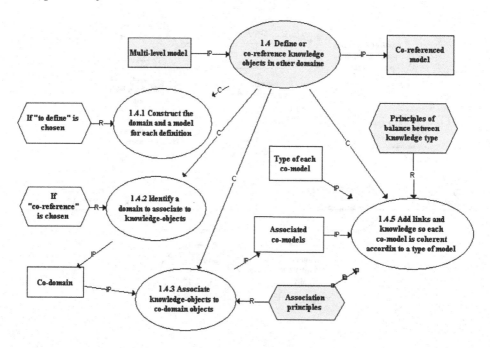

a link of association between two well-defined domains. The two domains can be quite different, such as human physiology and organic chemistry, or project management and software engineering, but our goal is to establish a relationship between them.

Figure 16 shows an instructional model (Learning scenario) for a course on the topic of "Conduct an Internet search." The course is divided into five learning units (LU). Two principles guiding the process path (labeled D) indicate how to select LUs. Each LU can be explained through a nested learning scenario model that is also part of the instructional model, therefore in the same domain. The icons displayed on the ovals representing learning units (little white sheets on the right of the figures) provide links to associated sub-models (ASM) in the knowledge model for the Internet domain presented earlier.

The following Figure 17 shows three of these associated sub-models. The ASM for LU-1 contains the main model that has been presented on Figure 9 with its entire set of nested models, but without models for the concept "Query" or the principle "Refine a request." The second one, presented earlier on Figure 13, is associated to

LU-3, while the third one, presented before on Figure 14, is associated to LU-4. The ASM for LU2 and LU-5 do not appear on Figure 17.

Note that LU-2 will contain the entire "Conduct an Internet search" model because it describes a project involving all the course content. LU-1 contains only the procedural part of the model because it helps learners initiate their project by presenting an overview of the process they have to apply. LU-3 and LU-4 are complementary to the overall model and are thus represented by more specialized models on the concept of "Query" and the principles for "Query refinement". Finally, LU-5 helps learners to improve their general ability to apply a procedure as was shown on Figure 15.

Defining Knowledge Objects of Another Domain

We will provide two examples of this process of a third way to associate a model to a knowledge object different from elaboration or co-referencing. Once again we use our example of information search on the Internet, associating model from definition model to knowledge object on Figure 9.

Figure 16. Teaching model for a course on searching information on the Internet

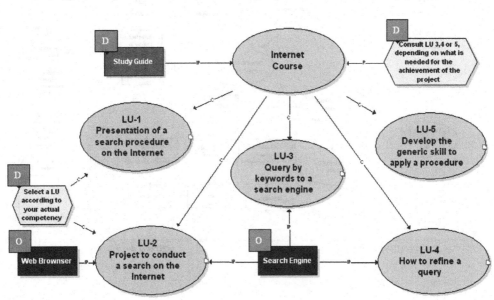

Figure 17. Teaching model and sub-models associated with LUs

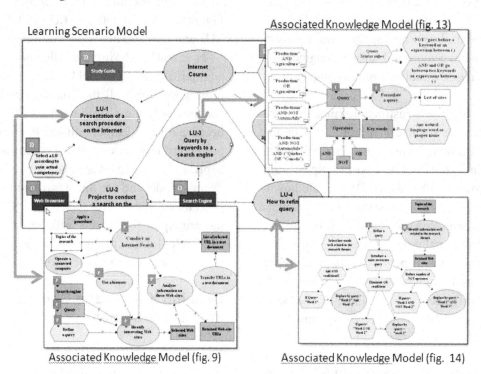

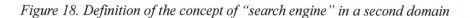

Figure 18. Definition of the concept of "search engine" in a second domain

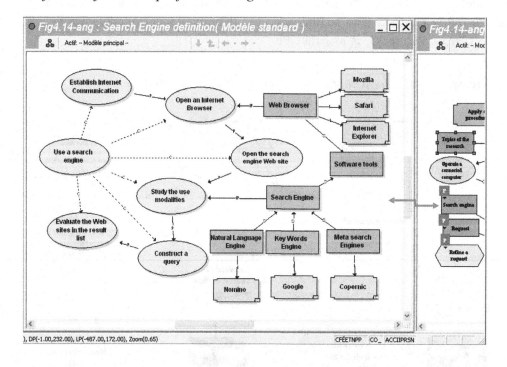

Figure 19.   *Figure 20.*

The first example consists of a definition for "search engine" within the domain of software tools. This knowledge object cannot be elaborated within the main domain since it was not priorized in regard to the model's goal; however, such complementary information may useful to users.

Figure 18 shows two MOT+ windows linked by a definition association. The right window is a portion of the main model in Figure 9. The left window shows a definition of "search engine" in a second domain.

The link between the two domains is represented in MOT+ by an icon (Figure 19) on the knowledge object to be defined by the associated model. Contrary to elaboration models represented by the icon shown in Figure 20 definition models are not required to use the same type of object as the one being defined. Here, the main part of the definition model is partly a procedure "Use a

search engine", while the knowledge object being defined is a concept. The model also contains related sub or super concepts, and also examples of browsers and search engine.

The second example on Figure 21 shows the association of a definition model to the generic skill "apply a procedure" from the main model on Figure 9. As will be explained with more detail in Chapter 6, this skill is a generic process that it can be applied within other domains besides the domain of Internet search. It is therefore necessary and useful to define it within its own domain.

4.7 VALIDATING AND DOCUMENTING MODELS

When a multilevel model is developed and, in some cases, co-referenced by the association of

Figure 21. Definition of an application generic skill

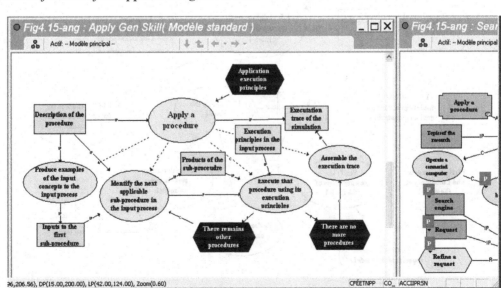

various sub-models to its knowledge objects, we obtain one or several documents that need to be completed and validated. This is the purpose of the fifth and final process of the MOT modeling technique shown on Figure 22.

Validation and Documentation

This sub-process process involves three main tasks: validating the model against its initial goal and constraints (regulated by validation principles), revising the model, and documenting it.

The first sequence of tasks consists of validating the model for potential users and with the person or organization that requested the model. There are here two aspects to consider:

Verifying the completeness of the model. We must ensure that the model contains all knowledge objects required by the modeling goal.

Verifying the accuracy and consistency of the model. We must verify that the knowledge objects and skills are accurately defined and that

the overall structure is consistent in terms of the various principles of the technique, notably,

- *Take in account the competency gaps of the target population.* Each sub-model must take into account the priorization of knowledge objects and contain a sufficient number of objects with respect for the competency gaps to fill.

- *Consistency of models.* Sub-models must relate to one another and correspond to a clearly defined class of models such as those presented in Section 3.

Both types of verification lead to requests for modification of the model. These requests are classified according to whether the sub-model is obtained by elaboration, definition, or co-referencing. In each case, requests are distinguished by whether they aim at improving the accuracy, consistency, or completeness of the overall model.

Figure 22. Sub-process of validation and documentation

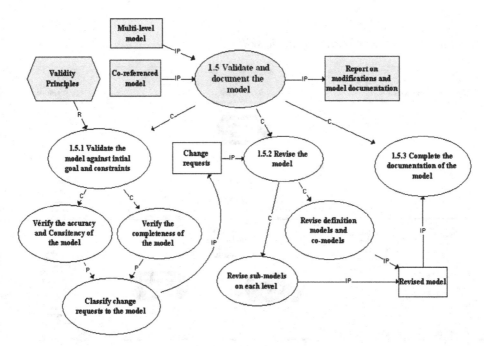

Once classified, requests for modification are included in the validation record, which is then used to complete the second sequence of tasks: *Revise elaboration sub-models* to ensure they include accurate, consistent, and complete knowledge objects; *revise definition and co-reference sub-models* to ensure they too include accurate, consistent, and complete knowledge objects.

The third set of tasks consists of *completing the documentation of the models.* As representative as a graphic model may be, it still may require textual explanations. For this purpose, the model editor offers a variety of features including the ability to add comments, associated texts, and definition or co-reference sub-models. In terms of presentation, the model editor allows users to attach comments or documents directly to a model's objects and links, or incorporate the model into a text such as we have done in the present chapter. It can also be used to build a Web site based on the model's content.

CONCLUSION

Since this chapter concludes the first part of the book, it would be appropriate for us to provide an overview of the material presented so far. In the last four chapters, we examined the concept of knowledge representation and various forms of graphic representation. We then defined a specific method of representation: modeling using object types (MOT). We established the generality of this graphical language—how it can apply to many knowledge domains and represent a wide variety of model types such as taxonomies, component systems, series, parallel or iterative procedures, definitions, laws, theories, decision trees, processes, methods, and multi-agent collaborative systems.

The present chapter has focused on the "how to" aspect of modeling. It presents modeling tools and a modeling technique, itself defined by a MOT model. We hope the reader will now be able to construct models using the MOT editor available on the CICE Web site (www.licef.ca/cice).

The reader's knowledge about modeling will be reused in the rest of the book, beginning with a discussion of the important issues of skills and competencies as well as the problems they help to solve, and followed by a description of a skill-based training/knowledge management strategy. These are the objectives of the next five chapters.

REFERENCES

Paquette, G. (1996 April). La modélisation par objets typés: une méthode de représentation pour les systèmes d'apprentissage et d'aide a la tâche. *Sciences et techniques éducatives*, 9-42.

Paquette, G. (2002). *Modélisation des connaissances et des compétences, un langage graphique pour concevoir et apprendre.* Québec, Canada: Presses de l'Université du Québec.

Paquette, G. (2003). *Instructional Engineering for Network-Based Learning.* San Francisco: Pfeiffer/ Wiley Publishing Co.

Paquette, G., Lundgren-Cayrol, K., & Léonard, M. (2008). The MOT+ Visual Language for Knowledge-Based Instructional Design . In Botturi, L., & Stubs, T. (Eds.), *Handbook of Visual Languages for Instructional Design Languages-Theories and Practices.* Hershey, PA: IGI Global.

ENDNOTES

[1] The MOT editor has been built before the more recent MOT+ version that includes a new << A >>link. To create such a link in the original version of the MOT editor, users must use a non-typed link and mark << A>> on it. The same applies if you need to insert an R link from a concept to a relational principle.

[2] Versions of MOT and MOT+ are available on the companion Web site at www.licef.ca/ cice/

Section 2
Modeling Competencies

Chapter 5
Knowledge, Skills, and Competency

Gilbert Paquette
LICEF Research Center, Canada

ABSTRACT

- Competency Profiles in Practice
  ◦ Competencies in business and the workplace
  ◦ Competencies in the definition of professions
  ◦ Educational competencies
- Analysis of Competency Approaches
- The Concept of Competency

A search on the Internet shows the renewed importance given to competency-based approaches in Education and Administration. Ministries of education, school boards, and teacher training institutes use competency profiles to define school programs or required qualities from the teachers, especially in the use of technologies in education. Consulting companies present their expertise by enumerating competencies, marketing their services in this way. Other companies offer services or computerized tools to help their prospective customers define or manage the competence of their staff, looked upon as the main asset of an organization in a knowledge management perspective. Governmental agencies or professional associations use competency-based approaches to define conditions to the exercise of a profession and to orient their vocational training programs.

Competencies provide learning and training objectives for educational programs and courses. They help define evidence to assess competency acquisition, state requirements for a job in an orga-

DOI: 10.4018/978-1-61520-839-5.ch005

nization to recruit new personnel, or plan instruction to enable persons to fill competency gaps.

Most often, competencies are expressed as simple natural language sentences, stating informally that a group of persons has the "capacity" or the "knowledge" to do certain things. Competency profiles are in general loosely structured collections of such texts that are not always easy to interpret, communicate, or use, especially if the goal is to plan learning events to support the acquisition of new competencies.

According to Kierstead (1998), part of the confusion surrounding the concept of competence can be attributed to the very broad definition given by an influential American author in the field, Boyatzis (1982). He defined competency as an underlying characteristic of a person that is related to a reason, a character, an ability, an aspect of self-image, the social role of the person, or a body of knowledge that he or she uses. We note, however, that this idea already contained the notion of a dynamic relationship between the various components of competency and its related aspects of performance. In organizational sciences, competency is seen as a process carried out by competent persons enabling them, with the resources at hand, to produce effective actions. For example, Le Boterf (1999) provides the following definition: "A competent person is someone who knows how to act appropriately in a particular context by selecting and mobilizing a double resource base: personal resources (knowledge, abilities, personal qualities, culture, emotions, etc.) and network resources (databases, document networks, expert networks, etc.). Knowing how to act appropriately means being able to perform a set of activities according to certain desirable criteria" (p. 38, translated by the author).

In recent years, efforts have been made to facilitate the use of competencies in education and training. For example, the IMS organization, involved in defining eLearning standards, produced in 2002 a Reusable Definition of Competency or Educational Objective (IMS-RDCEO 2002).

It defines an information model for describing, referencing, and exchanging definitions of competencies, primarily in the context of online and distributed learning. Its goal is to enable the interoperability among learning systems that deal with competency information by providing a means for them to refer to common definitions with common meanings. Even though the RDCEO does not provide structural information about a competency, it mentions that "this information may be refined using a user-defined model of the structure of a competency."

We will provide here such a competency model based on knowledge representation techniques.

To do this, we will first present examples of competency profiles and dictionaries used in job training, vocational training, and school curricula. We will then perform a critical analysis, highlighting the diversity of concepts and teaching strategies that underlie the so-called "competency-based approach."

Next, we will discuss and define related concepts such as generic problems, tasks, and skills to provide a structural basis for a definition of a competency.

We will conclude by providing a clear definition of the concept of competency that will allow us to graphically represent competencies and integrate them into a knowledge model.

5.1 COMPETENCIES IN BUSINESS AND THE WORKPLACE

Over the past ten years, the "competency movement" has become widespread in the area of human resources management. Competency profiles, variance analyses, classification and compensation, performance evaluation, staffing, and many other uses of the competency approach are now well integrated into the activities of organizations. In the public sector as in the private sector, the development of competencies is seen as a major factor in productivity and competitiveness.

Figure 1. Objectives of competency management

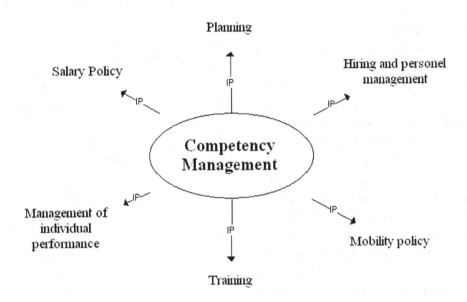

For example, the human resources policy statement of the publicly owned power utility, Hydro-Québec, asserts the following:

"Hydro-Québec, within its overall strategy, considers its employees as an essential resource in fulfilling its vision. Therefore, in order to maintain the competencies required for achieving its business objectives, Hydro-Québec is committed to the following objectives:

- *providing its staff with the best opportunities for professional development to ensure a high level of competency, expertise, and leadership at all times;*
- *attracting, recruiting, and retaining a diversity of skilled employees who share the company's values and are motivated to contribute to its competitive advantage;*
- *preparing for future staffing and ensuring the sustainability of expertise.*

In addition, the company expects employees to "assume responsibility for their development [of their own competencies] and participate in maintaining expertise within the company."

This statement is typical of what is taking place today in large companies. From an internal document of Hydro-Québec's department of human resources, planning, and development, which is responsible for this policy, we found the following definition: "Competency management includes all activities aimed at identifying, acquiring, developing, and maintaining the necessary skills to achieve our business goals." The diagram in Figure 1 illustrates the company's various objectives regarding competency management.

To achieve these objectives, the company has developed a detailed model of target competencies for its employees. This directory includes 50 competency units divided into four categories. One of these units, "Strategic vision," is divided into eleven basic competencies, for example, "Is able to identify important elements and take necessary actions to ensure the present and future success of the company."

By using the directory, the company can create, for each type of position, a competency profile defined as a "principle input for competency management." A competency profile consists of two parts: "personal skills essential for maximum performance" and "technical skills related to the position's area of activity." A competency is defined as a combination of knowledge, skills, and attitudes required to performing a job effectively.

The Hydro-Québec example is quite typical. A similar approach can be found today in most large public and private organizations. For example, the Public Service Commission of Canada, the main recruiting and staffing agency for the Canadian government's civil service has defined competencies as "the characteristics of an individual that underlie performance or behavior at work." These characteristics relate as much to "knowledge abilities, and aptitudes" as to "work styles, personality, interests, principles, values, attitudes, beliefs, and leadership/subordinate styles." The Commission provides a classification of the following competencies traditionally associated with successful on-the-job performance (Table 1).

5.2 COMPETENCIES IN THE DEFINITION OF PROFESSIONS

The professional sector also uses the concept of competency to establish practice criteria, in particular, to develop continuing education programs for members of professions.

For example, in Australia as in other countries, the nursing profession is regulated. Nurses are responsible for ensuring high quality healthcare and practicing in a safe and effective manner. Government agencies at the state and territorial level are responsible for setting competency standards for the expected behaviors of nurses and other professionals. To this effect, the Australian Nursing and Midwifery Council (ANMC) has defined the National Competency Standards for the Registered Nurse, in which 10 competency

Table 1. Competencies model developed by the Public Service Commission of Canada (online 2008)

Communication Competencies	speaking (capturing your audience)
	listening to others
	written communication
	nonverbal (gestural and body language)
Interpersonal Competencies	empathy
	consensus building
	networking
	persuasiveness
	negotiating
	diplomacy
	conflict management (resolving conflict)
	respecting others
	being a team player
Thinking Competencies	strategic thinking
	analytical thinking (analyzing problems)
	committing to action
	applying one's cognitive capability
	identifying the links
	generating creative ideas
Organizational Competencies	planning the work
	organizing resources
	dealing with crises
	getting the job done
	measuring progress
	taking calculated risks
Human Resource Management Competencies	team building which includes: mentoring; motivating staff; staff relations; selection, promotion and development of people
	selection, promotion and development of people
	encouraging participation
	developing talent
	providing performance feedback
	valuing diversity

continues on following page

Table 1. continued

Leadership Competencies	positioning
	organizational development
	managing transitions
	strategic orientation
	developing a vision
	planning the future
	mastering change
	promoting a healthy workplace
Client Service Competencies	identification and analysis of client needs
	service orientation and delivery
	working with clients
	following up with clients
	building partnerships
	committing to quality
Business Competencies	financial management
	business decision-making skills
	working within the system
	using business acumen
	making business decisions
	generating revenue
Self-Management Competencies	being self-motivated
	acting with confidence
	managing own learning
	demonstrating flexibility
Technical/Operational Competencies	performing office tasks
	working with computer technology
	using other equipment and tools
	demonstrating technical/professional expertise
	working with data/numbers

Table 2. Excerpt from standards regulating the nursing profession in Australia. (ANMC online 2009)

ANMC National Competency Standards for the Registered Nurse **Domain: Professional Practice**
1. Practices in accordance with legislation affecting nursing practice and health care
1.1. Complies with relevant legislation and common law
• Identifies legislation governing nursing practice. • Describes nursing practice within the requirements of common law • Describes and adheres to legal requirements for medications • Identifies legal implications of nursing interventions • Actions demonstrate awareness of legal implications of nursing practice • Identifies and explains effects of legislation on the care of individual/groups • Identifies unprofessional practice as it relates to confidentiality and privacy legislation
1.2 Fulfils the duty of care
• Performs nursing interventions in accordance with recognized standards of practice • Clarifies responsibility for aspects of care with other members of the health team • Recognises the responsibility to prevent harm • Performs nursing interventions following comprehensive and accurate assessments
1.3 Recognizes and responds appropriately to unsafe or unprofessional practice
• Identifies interventions which prevent care being compromised and/or law contravened • Identifies appropriate action to be taken in specified circumstances • Identifies and explains alternative strategies for intervention and their likely outcomes • Identifies behavior that is detrimental to achieving optimal care • Follows up incidents of unsafe practice to prevent re-occurrence

units are subdivided into competency elements grouped into four broad areas: "Professional Practice," "Critical Thinking and Analysis," "Provision and Coordination of Care," and "Collaborative and Therapeutic Practice." Nurses must demonstrate these competencies in order to obtain or renew their license. The standards can be used for academic evaluation, performance assessment in the workplace, or on-going measurement of their ability to practice.

These competency standards reflect both the specific features of nursing practice and those it has in common with other professions. The standards identify the knowledge, skills, and attitudes required of nurses and reflect the complex nature of nursing practice. Table 2 shows three competency elements of the first competency section, relating professional practice to legislation. Each competency element is followed by a description of exemplars, i.e. concrete, key examples that are typical of the competency.

The competency-based approach is also used in other areas of professional practice, for example, to identify emerging occupations and trades in the multimedia industry. Table 3 presents a competency profile for the profession of multimedia producer. It is part of a study by *Technocompétences*, a publicly funded private organization dedicated to the promotion of multimedia in Québec. The study involves defining standards for various professions in the multimedia industry through the creation of 14 competency profiles. (Techno-competence, online 2009)

In another area professional practice, Figure 2 presents a competency model for leadership provided by the Los Alamos National Laboratory (LANL), operated by the University of California for the Department of Energy, U.S. Government.

The model includes the knowledge, attitudes, and skills required of managers in most organizations. The development guide for the model describes and provides training activities for 15 competencies. The guide is a tool for professionals who wish to upgrade their skills; it allows them to select courses, publications, and activities that correspond to their learning needs based on tests given by the organization's Leadership Center.

5.3 EDUCATIONAL COMPETENCIES

Ministries of education in several countries have also adopted a competency-based approach to describe curricula or teacher competencies. We will present three examples.

Our first example is the Québec Ministry of Education. In its Inchauspé Report (1997), "Reaffirming the Mission of Our Schools – A New Direction for Success," the task force on curriculum reform recommends "that all compulsory content should be transmitted in two ways: through restructured programs of study and through *cross-curricular competencies.*"

Table 4 is an excerpt of the report showing these competencies to be pursued at all levels of elementary and secondary education. Educators are responsible for helping students to develop the competencies and attitudes contained in this "program of programs."

As well, DISCAS, a private organization carrying out several mandates for school boards and the Québec Ministry of Education, has conducted a detailed analysis of some 9,000 intermediate and final objectives of current elementary and secondary school curricula. The results of this study are presented, in Table 5 as a summary of competencies to be developed through official curricula. (DISCAS online 2009).

While not a theoretical model itself, this reference guide is representative of the current situation regarding school curricula in Québec. It contains 34 competency elements grouped into 7 core competencies. Each element is fully defined and illustrated. The last column contains action verbs describing various skills and attitudes. These are derived from a taxonomy that is also described in detail.

Each skill is defined on a separate information sheet, for example, in the case 'Represent': "Translate information in a symbolic or conventional form or transpose symbolic information from one form to an equivalent form." The information sheet also includes the scope of the definition, key concepts, general assessment criteria, activities, and skills acquisition tools. It includes, as well, action verbs from the competency statement and examples of specific goals from school curricula that target the skill, such as "Correctly *use* the symbols 'cm^3,' 'dm^3,' and 'm^3' or "*Illustrate* the growth of a plant by means of a histogram."

The authors note that the competencies can be associated with the three types of knowledge identified in cognitive psychology: Competency 1 is associated with *declarative* knowledge, Competency 4 with *procedural* knowledge, and

Table 3. Competency profile for the profession of multimedia director

Multimedia Producer: Competency Profile	
Tasks	Professional Competencies
• Assume responsibility for management of the content creation process and the interactivity • Participate in the definition of the specifications of the client's expectations and requirements (once the contract is signed) • Prepare the detailed documentation describing the finished product • Participate in technological choices • Devise the production method • Ensure the cohesiveness of the work • Ensure that the content remains properly adapted to the objectives set and the groups targeted • Document, in writing, the project's progress • Maintain communication between the different team members • Head the project team • Ensure coordination between the client and the project team with regard to the content prepared by the client • Participate in the selection of external suppliers • Review the quality of deliverables obtained from external suppliers • Review the quality of deliverables intended for clients • Ensure that the budget and schedule are respected • Ensure technological and competitive intelligence	**Technical Aspect** • Ability to evaluate, analyze and resolve operational problems • Ability to assess technical and graphic feasibility • Ability to demonstrate autonomy when updating technology-based knowledge • Ability to manage production with audiovisual and computer supports • Ability to oversee quality control • Knowledge of every step involved in production • Knowledge of audiovisual supports • Knowledge of the use of Internet and multimedia technologies, their possibilities and their limitations • General knowledge of multimedia creation tools in technical environments (PC/Mac/Unix) • Knowledge of approaches used for the development, integration and implementation of a Web site **Content Aspect** • Ability to adapt one's product to user needs and habits • Ability to assess the quality of the relationship between the content and the interface design • Ability to integrate interactivity into communication
Behavioral Competencies	
• Leadership • Team spirit • Ability to analyze, summarize, and conceptualize • Interpersonal relationships • Verbal and written communication • Flexibility • Ability to persuade and influence • Methodical approach • Resistance to stress • Openness to criticism and ability to criticize • Creativity	

Figure 2. A leadership competency model for managers

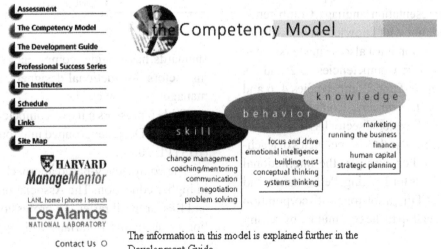

The information in this model is explained further in the Development Guide.

Table 4. Cross-curricular competencies–Québec Ministry of Education

A) Intellectual Skills
• An understanding of phenomena and situations, and the development of a critical mind. • Analyzing and summarizing skills. • Problem solving skills. • The capacity to undertake a project and follow it through to completion. • Development and use of the memory. • Creativity and exercise of the aesthetic sense. • Communication skills. • Assessment and self-assessment skills.
B) Methodological Skills
• The capacity to understand rules and apply them, and to formulate one's own rules. • The capacity to identify and use appropriate sources of information. • The capacity to use appropriate methods to process information (with emphasis on new information and communications technologies). • The capacity to organize work to meet deadlines. • The capacity to work as part of a team.
C) Social Skills
• Everyday application of the rules of life in society. • Intercultural education and respect for differences. • An aesthetic and moral sense. • Application of rules for the preservation of good health. • Environmental education. • An open attitude to international understanding. • Media education.
D) Language-Related Skills
. . . .

Table 5. Competency profile for school curricula in Québec (DISCAS, 2002)

Competency	Competency Elements	Skills and attitudes
1. Basic knowledge understanding	1. Know information 2. Know specific concepts 3. Know general concepts	Identify Describe
2. Language abilities	1. Understand symbols 2. Understand representational systems 3. Understand meaning 4. Translate meaning	Interpret Represent
3. Structural knowledge	1. Categorize items 2. Understand mechanisms 3. Understand laws 4. Understand systems 5. Make inferences	Connect Explain Analyze
4. Procedural knowledge	1. Know operations 2. Know the sequence of operations 3. Know operational standards 4. Perform operations 5. Automate operation	Apply
5. Attitudes	1. Openness 2. Critical mind 3. Solidarity 4. Self-sufficiency 5. Creativity 6. Responsibility	Accept Express Commit
6. Communication skills	1. Understand roles 2. Understand context 3. Understand intentions 4. Understand messages 5. Formulate messages 6. Produce a personal work	Interpret Choose Produce
7. Decision-making skills	1. Use information 2. Set goals 3. Create a plan 4. Solve problems 5. Complete projects	Choose Summarize Commit

Competencies 2 and 3 with *conditional* knowledge. These types of knowledge correspond respectively to concepts, procedures et an principles in the MOT knowledge representation language. Competency 5 is associated, not with knowledge, but with attitudes. A distinction must also be made between knowledge (*savoir*; Competencies 1, 2 and 3), know-how *(savoir-faire*; Competencies 4, 6 and 7), and attitudes (*savoir-être*; Competency 5).

Work in the educational sector has targeted not only curricula, but also the competencies of teachers and trainers. For example, the International Board of Standards for Training, Performance, and Instruction (IBSTPI), a not-for-profit corporation providing leadership to the community by setting standards, has provided competency standards for instructors, instructional designers, and training managers on its Web site.

Table 6 presents a list of competencies for Instructional Designer grouped into four categories (IBSTPI, 2000).

The competency-based approach is also used in higher education. The Association of College and Research Libraries is a professional association of academic librarians with approximately

Table 6. Competencies for instructional designer (IBSTPI, 2000)

Professional Foundations	1. Communicate effectively in visual, oral and written form. (Essential) 2. Apply current research and theory to the practice of instructional design. (Advanced) 3. Update and improve one's knowledge, skills and attitudes pertaining to instructional design and related fields. (Essential) 4. Apply fundamental research skills to instructional design projects. (Advanced) 5. Identify and resolve ethical and legal implications of design in the work place. (Advanced)
Planning and Analysis	6. Conduct a needs assessment. (Essential) 7. Design a curriculum or program. (Essential) 8. Select and use a variety of techniques for determining instructional content. (Essential) 9. Identify and describe target population characteristics. (Essential) 10. Analyze the characteristics of the environment. (Essential) 11. Analyze the characteristics of existing and emerging technologies and their use in an instructional environment. (Essential) 12. Reflect upon the elements of a situation before finalizing design solutions and strategies. (Essential)
Design and Development	13. Select, modify, or create a design and development model appropriate for a given project. (Advanced) 14. Select and use a variety of techniques to define and sequence the instructional content and strategies. (Essential) 15. Select or modify existing instructional materials. (Essential) 16. Develop instructional materials. (Essential) 17. Design instruction that reflects an understanding of the diversity of learners and groups of learners. (Essential) 18. Evaluate and assess instruction and its impact. (Essential)
Implementation and Management	19. Plan and manage instructional design projects. (Advanced) 20. Promote collaboration, partnerships and relationships among the participants in a design project. (Advanced) 21. Apply business skills to managing instructional design. (Advanced) 22. Design instructional management systems. (Advanced) 23. Provide for the effective implementation of instructional products and programs. (Essential)

13,000 members, primarily in the United States. The association has identified a set of targeted competencies for students and faculty in the area of information literacy.

The *Information Literacy Competency Standards for Higher Education* (ACRL online 2009) aims to sensitize university and college students to the need for developing a meta-cognitive approach to learning, making them conscious of the explicit actions required for gathering, analyzing, and using information.

In the competency profile proposed by the association, there are 5 competency standards and 22 performance indicators. For each indicator, the profile also provides examples of behavioral outcomes for assessing to what extent the performance level has been reached. In Table 7, we have omitted these examples.

5.4 ANALYSIS OF COMPETENCY APPROACHES

Behind the ubiquitous notion of competency and the apparent convergence of needs is a wide range of concepts and practices: recruitment and staffing, compensation, skills assessment, individual performance management, career management, etc. In training programs, competency profiles can be used to define learning goals, specify curriculum content and teaching materials, and select teaching strategies, media, and delivery methods.

Competencies are usually presented as statements linking the skills, attitudes, and knowledge required of a group of people. Some of these elements may be excluded, or additional ones may be added. For example, the Public Service Commission of Canada provides a model that extends well

Table 7. Competency profile for information literacy (ACRL)

Information Literacy Competency Standards for Higher Education
Standard One The information literate student determines the nature and extent of the information needed.
Performance Indicators: The information literate student
• defines and articulates the need for information. • identifies a variety of types and formats of potential sources for information. • considers the costs and benefits of acquiring the needed information. • reevaluates the nature and extent of the information need.
Standard Two The information literate student accesses needed information effectively and efficiently.
Performance Indicators: The information literate student:
• selects the most appropriate investigative methods or information retrieval systems for accessing the needed information. • constructs and implements effectively-designed search strategies. • retrieves information online or in person using a variety of methods. • refines the search strategy if necessary. • extracts, records, and manages the information and its sources.
Standard Three The information literate student evaluates information and its sources critically and incorporates selected information into his or her knowledge base and value system.
Performance Indicators: The information literate student:
• summarizes the main ideas to be extracted from the information gathered. • articulates and applies initial criteria for evaluating both the information and its sources. • synthesizes main ideas to construct new concepts. • compares new knowledge with prior knowledge to determine the value added, contradictions, or other unique characteristics of the information. • determines whether the new knowledge has an impact on the individual's value system and takes steps to reconcile differences. • validates understanding and interpretation of the information through discourse with other individuals, subject-area experts, and/or practitioners. • determines whether the initial query should be revised.
Standard Four The information literate student, individually or as a member of a group, uses information effectively to accomplish a specific purpose.
Performance Indicators: The information literate student
• applies new and prior information to the planning and creation of a particular product or performance. • revises the development process for the product or performance. • communicates the product or performance effectively to others.
Standard Five The information literate student understands many of the economic, legal, and social issues surrounding the use of information and accesses and uses information ethically and legally.
Performance Indicators: The information literate student
• understands many of the ethical, legal and socio-economic issues surrounding information and information technology. • follows laws, regulations, institutional policies, and etiquette related to the access and use of information resources. • acknowledges the use of information sources in communicating the product or performance.

beyond the domain of competencies and includes an individual's interest and beliefs (see Table 1). In contrast, statements such as "planning the work" (Table 1), "openness to criticism," and "general knowledge of creation tools" (Table 3) lack sufficient detail in that they describe respectively a skill, an attitude, or knowledge that involve the notion of competency but must be distinguished from it.

Most applications involving competencies have a more clearly defined approach, as underlined by Friedlander (1996). A competency is defined as a combination of knowledge, skills, and attitudes required to perform a role effectively. A "role" is defined as a function performed by a

Figure 3. The meta-concept of competency

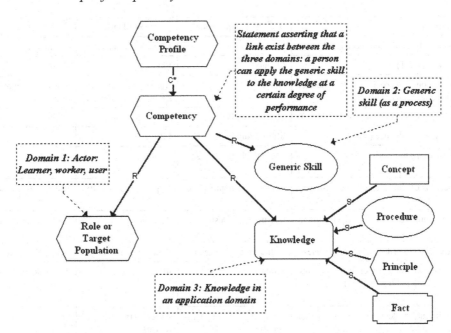

group of individuals in an organization or company, for example, a technician, nurse, or teacher; it depends on general competencies (those that can be shared by other roles) and competencies determined by the tasks the group of individuals must perform or by the problems they must solve. Therefore, the role of a nurse is not the same in a developing country as it is in one characterized by a highly structured health system.

In their analysis of the concept of competency, Bélisle and Linard (1996) present certain positive aspects, of the competency approach in its current form, as well as its theoretical and practical limits.

As for the positive aspects of the approach, the authors note the following:

- It is explicit yet recognizes the implicit nature of work-related knowledge, which until now has been ignored;
- It offers an alternative to recruitment based primarily on scholarly criteria such as type and number of diplomas;
- It provides useful benchmarks and a single, consistent analysis tool previously unavailable to instructors and organizations.

- It is, at first glance, socially forward thinking in that it applies a humanistic, "learner-centered" pedagogy in which learners have greater autonomy and control in their learning process;
- It also provides a useful bridge between action and knowledge by defining qualifications based on observable and measurable behaviors that are clearly defined and categorized.

On the other hand, the authors state that "the method of definition and the notions of knowledge and actions that underlie the approach appear largely at odds with its own objectives and the positive points listed above" (Bélisle & Linard, 1996, p.28).

The desire to standardize competencies and objectively measure specific behaviors can lead to an unnecessary fragmentation of skills and knowledge. "The activity to which the competency refers is thus reduced to an itemized, static, restrictive list of specialized roles, tasks, and ac-

Table 8. Examples of competencies

Statement of competence	Target population	Skill (s)	Knowledge
Identification and analysis of client needs (Table 1)	Manager	Identify and analyze	Client needs
Planning the work (Table 1)	Manager	Plan	Work
Recognizes and responds appropriately to unsafe or unprofessional practice (Table 2)	Nurse	Recognizes and responds appropriately	Unsafe or unprofessional practice
Ability to assess the feasibility of the project (Table 3)	Multimedia Producer	Assess feasibility	Project description
Ability to persuade and influence (Table 3)	Multimedia Producer	Influence	
Analyzing and summarizing skills (Table 4)	Student (elementary/secondary)	Analyze, summarize	
Everyday application of the rules of life in society (Table 4)	Student (elementary/secondary)	Apply in everyday life	Rules of life in society
Analyze the characteristics of the environment (Table 6)	Instructional Designer	Analyze	Characteristics of the environment
Plan and manage instructional design projects (Table 6)	Instructional Designer	Plan and manage	Instructional design project
The information literate student identifies a variety of types and formats of potential sources for information (Table 7)	Student (College/University)	Identify	Types, formats, and sources of information
The information literate student determines whether the initial query should be revised (Table 7)	Student (College/University)	Assess (in order to revise)	Queries

tions, excessive in both detail and length, whose mere juxtaposition is considered reflective of the performance situation" (Bélisle & Linard, 1996, p. 28, translated by the author). As well, competency assessment is often reduced to behavioral indicators chosen from a table of references. Ultimately, a statement of competencies can become a means of control, rather than a basis for development of individuals and groups.

Used in this way, the competency approach becomes abstract and disconnected from the practice of a trade or profession, a learning situation, or shared social and cultural practices. It is closer to Taylor's notion of specialized labor, the methods of behaviorist management, and goal-oriented pedagogy. Moreover, creating competency profiles with such detail requires time and effort that can span several years, while the skills and knowledge themselves can change overnight in some areas. This may explain the relatively limited use of competency profiles in practice, despite the great interest in them and the potential they represent.

5.5 THE CONCEPT OF COMPETENCY

The preceding discussion advocates for a cognitive and constructivist definition and use of the concept of competency. Our goal is to build competency profiles structurally and use them as factors of consistency and quality in learning or management systems that are largely self-managed by their users, adapted to particular contexts and uses, and incorporate important meta-cognitive dimensions of learning and/or working.

Figure 3 presents a MOT model of the generic concept of competency used throughout the remainder of the book. Competency can be described as meta-knowledge because it can be applied in a wide variety of situations or knowledge domains, including all those presented above.

A competency is a statement of principle that regulates the relationship between a target population, a generic skill, and knowledge in a particular domain. These three domains can be each represented by a separate domain model:

- A domain describing the target population that possesses the competency (also called "actors")
- A domain representing the generic skills of the actors, including or not a level of performance of a skill. Later on we will represent the notion of « attitude » as affective/social skills.
- An application domain representing specific knowledge objects to which the actors apply the skills.

The *knowledge domain* is defined by specific concepts, procedures, principles, and facts that are used of an actor playing a role or realizing a task. In the competency profile for a profession such as nursing, knowledge objects would refer to the domain of health or to the domain of nursing practice. In the competency profile of a multimedia producer, knowledge objects would be specific to the techniques, input, and products of multimedia production.

The *skills domain* describes the processes that apply to the knowledge objects and allow them to be perceived, memorized, assimilated, analyzed, summarized, assessed, and so on. With respect to the knowledge in the "application" domain, these processes are "meta-processes," that is they are of a generic nature independent of the application domain and can be applied in other domains. Skills are usually described by action verbs that can be accompanied by adjectives or adverbs depicting an application context or a particular use. For example, in the medical field, a skill could be "make a diagnosis," "make a thorough diagnosis," "or make a diagnosis in an emergency." In each case, the skill can be applied to a variety of knowledge domains such as "skull fracture" or "childbirth."

The *target population domain* contains a description of the actors, their properties, their functions, their tasks, and above all, their expected characteristics (often called wrongly general or behavioral competencies).

We can associate actors with core competencies for performing a role or task, or with current and targeted competencies with respect to a training program. We must distinguish, however, between the terms "actor" and "individual." An actor represents a class of individuals; an individual is an instance of that class.

Table 6 shows the general applicability of this definition by presenting competency statements corresponding to competency profile presented at the beginning of this chapter. In some cases, the competency statement is limited to a skill. Some skills such as "plan" or "assess" are shared by various actors but applied to different knowledge objects. Other skills are distinguished by their context, for example, "apply in everyday life"

CONCLUSION

In this first chapter devoted to competencies and skills, we examined various applications using the competency-based approach and we discussed the advantages and limitations of this methodology. We then proposed a definition of competency involving three main domains: actors, skills, and knowledge.

This definition includes a number of underlying assumptions that situate competencies within the framework of action theories (Bélisle and Linard, 1996):

- Persons for whom we wish to describe competencies are not simple operators or factors to be assessed; they are actors, defined as individuals with their own intentions and their own cognitive and social contexts.
- Competencies describe activities that are 1) specified by a particular function, role, or task, 2) measured by the level of excellence of observed performance, and 3) validated through social sanctions, as in the present models.

- Central to competencies is an association of skills, viewed as generic cognitive processes, and a model that incorporate knowledge objects, thus avoiding a dissociation between knowledge and know-how, and a fragmentation of competencies.
- Skills can therefore be interpreted as knowledge about knowledge and can be used to act upon the latter in different ways. The cognitive and meta-cognitive aspects necessary for thoughtful human action are therefore integrated.
- Competencies can be used to assess individuals, but the criteria are no longer reduced to matching competencies with a list of corresponding behaviors. Competencies are functionally structured and can be used as benchmarks for the development of individuals and not only as a means of controlling behaviour.

The definition of competency that emerges from this chapter entails a structured representation of competencies that requires on a new definition of skills, the subject of the next two chapters.

REFERENCES

ACRL. (2009). *Information Literacy Competency Standards for Higher Education*. Retrieved from http://www.ala.org/ala/mgrps/divs/acrl/standards/informationliteracycompetency.cfm

ANMC. (2009). *National Competency Standards for the Registered Nurse*. Retrieved from http://www.anmc.org.au/docs/Competency_standards_RN.pdf

Bélisle, C., & Linard, M. (1996). Quelles nouvelles compétences des acteurs de la formation dans le contexte des TIC? *Éducation permanente, 127*(2), 19-47.

Boyatzis, R. E. (1982). *The Competent Manager: a Model for Effective Performance*. New York: John Wiley & Sons.

DISCAS. (2009). *Proil de competence de l'élève en apprentissage (tableau-synthèse)*. Retrieved from http://www.csrdn.qc.ca/discas/taxonomie/Profilcompetence.html

Friedlander, P. (1996). Competency-Driven, Component-Based Curriculum Architecture. *Performance and Instruction, 35*(2), 14–21. doi:10.1002/pfi.4170350206

IBSTPI. (2000). *Instructional Design Competencies: A standard*. Retrieved from http://ibstpi.org/Competencies/instruct_design_competencies.htm

IMS-RDCEO. (2002). *Reusable Definition of Competency and Educational Objective*. Retrieved from http://www.imsglobal.org/

Kierstead, J. (1998). *Compétences et CCHA*. Direction générale des politiques, de la recherche et des communications. Commission de la fonction publique du Canada. Retrieved from http://www.psagencyagencefp.gc.ca/arc/research/personnel/comp_ksao_f.asp

Le Boterf, G. (1999). *L'ingénierie des compétences* (2nd ed.). Paris: Éditions d'Organisation.

Public Service Commission of Canada. (2009). Retrieved from http://www.psc-cfp.gc.ca/ppc-cpp/hrm-grh/comptcs-eng.htm

Report, I. (1997). *Reaffirming the Mission of Our Schools – A New Direction for Success*. Retrieved from http://www.mels.gouv.qc.ca/reforme/curricu/anglais/school.htm

TechnoCompétences. (2009). *Multimedia – 14 Profils de competences de professions*. Retrieved from http://www.technocompetences.qc.ca/apropostic/profilsdecompetences/multimedia

Chapter 6
Taxonomies of Problems and Generic Skills

Gilbert Paquette
LICEF Research Center, Canada

ABSTRACT

- Generic Skills as Problem-Solving Processes
- Generic Skills as Active Meta-Knowledge
- Generic Skills within Learning Objectives
- An Integrated Cycle of Skills for Education
- Comparison of Taxonomies of Skills
- Concept of Generic Skill

The aim of this chapter is to define what we call "generic skills," i.e. structured sets of intellectual actions, attitudes, values, and principles that are at the heart of human competencies. We will first examine the various systems that offer different yet convergent views regarding skills.

One multi-viewpoint approach to the concept of skill first analyses the taxonomies of generic problems developed in software engineering. Generic problems correspond to human problem-solving skills as described in cognitive science. Another viewpoint is the concept of active meta-knowledge that situates skills in the realm of meta-cognition, i.e. as knowledge acting on other knowledge. A third viewpoint considers research in education that presents skills in the form of taxonomies of learning objectives in relation to cognitive, affective, social, or psychomotor domains.

We will conclude the chapter with a comparison of the various analysis systems and a definition of generic skills, thus forming the basis for an inte-

DOI: 10.4018/978-1-61520-839-5.ch006

grated taxonomy of skills that will be developed in the next chapter.

6.1 GENERIC SKILLS AS PROBLEM-SOLVING PROCESSES

The notion of "generic" problems, tasks and methods, is at the heart of research in software and knowledge engineering (expert systems). Generic problems, tasks, and methods are three widely interchangeable terms representing different viewpoints of the same reality. They will be given specific meaning using the MOT representation system.

The notion of generic problems or tasks was already present in one of the first reference books about knowledge-based systems (Hayes-Roth, Waterman & Lenat, 1984, Waterman 1986, Paquette &Roy 1990); in this work, we find a first classification of generic problems into ten categories. In pioneer studies about generic tasks at Ohio State University (Chandrasekaran 1983; 1987) these are defined through a problem description and a resolution method, which is a specific information processing algorithm. It introduces the idea of combining a small number of generic methods to solve large classes of more complex problems. Other work on generic problems (McDermott 1988), and the "expertise components" approach (Steels, 1990) must be mentioned.

The KADS method (Schreiber, Wielinga & Breuker, 1993), and its most recent version CommonKADS (Breuker & Van de Velde, 1994), is a synthesis of these studies. It actually constitutes a complete methodology integrating knowledge acquisition for expert systems with concepts of project management, organizational analysis, knowledge and software engineering. In KADS, an engineering software project materializes by building seven models. Four of them are of interest here: the "domain model", the "inference model", the "task model" and the "strategic model".

In the *inference model,* we find a decomposition of the generic task into a task tree and a set of inference schemas associated to the leaves of this tree. The *task model* provides control principles, i.e. rules to manage the order of execution within the tasks. The "strategic model", corresponds to heuristic principles that guide tasks execution. Together, these three models correspond to the notion of a generic process, applicable to various application domains (called "domain models" in KADS).

A **generic problem** is characterized by one or several goals or results to be produced (which are meta-concepts); initial data (also meta-concepts) and a number of operations (meta-procedures) that transform the initial data into results or goals. One recognizes here the notion of a process, one of the categories of problem presented in Chapter 3.

The KADS method defines eight classes of generic problems presented in Table 1.

To each generic problem corresponds a **generic task**, which is a goal to be attained by applying a generic procedure to the input and to produce results, as indicated in Table 1. Breaking down this generic procedure into sub-procedures results in the KADS tasks tree. After a number of levels, terminal-level tasks are reached, to which the KADS method associates an inference schema that details a simple procedure to be executed in a single step.

Figure 1 shows a MOT model for the generic problem of diagnosis similar to the example in Figure 14 in Chapter 3. The Control principles, similar to those on Figure 13 in Chapter 3, correspond to the task model in KADS.

The model is composed of an input: the model of a system of components to be diagnosed. The model main knowledge objects is a generic task, "make a diagnosis", and an expected result or problem solution: a list of defective components. The generic task is broken down into sub-tasks, up to terminal tasks such as "decompose the model", which generates some hypothesis about faulty components. An inference schema, selected in

Table 1: Taxonomy of problems in the KADS method

Generic task	Generic problem	Input (data)	Results (goal)
Classify	Determine an object's category	Classes hierarchy; Object's attributes	Object's classes
Diagnose	Determine the cause of the problem	Symptoms, system's component model	Defective components
Predict	Determine the future state the system	System's components; attributes that will vary	States: classes of the system's possible instances
Supervise	Determine a deviation class between a system's instance and another which is said to be normal	System's components and attributes; normal instances	Instance class according to the difference with the norm
Repair	Modify a system's component so it is in working order	System's model; maintenance standards	Modified model
Plan	Break down the task into steps	Deliverables, sub-tasks, time constraints	Process: sequence of tasks, input and output
Design	Build an object (artifact)	Artifact properties, constraints to be met	Object model
Model	Build a behavioral system model	Goals, constraints, components, viewpoints.	Model of a system's processes and evolution strategies

Figure 1. Example of a generic process: diagnosis

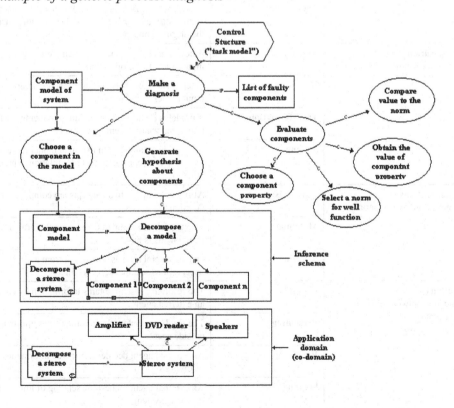

the KADS library, is associated to this terminal task. Using these schemas, the generic task can be applied to an application domain such as "test a stereo system".

The model in Figure 1 uses the concepts of co-referencing presented in Chapter 4. The meta-procedure "Decompose a model" is instantiated to "Decompose a stereo system" which, in the application domain, applies to the stereo system to produce its sub-components: amplifier, DVD reader, speakers.

Each terminal task can thus be associated with an inference schema drawn from the KADS library. The KADS method provides library of inference schemas that can be associated with terminal tasks of generic problems. Table 2 is an adaptation of the library presented in Breuker & Van de Velde (1994) where the operations are described in detail and can be used for programming purposes.

This way of describing generic problems, tasks, and methods is fundamental to software engineering, but is it suitable for describing hu-

Table 2. Inference schemas of the CommonKADS system

Class	Inference schema	Description
Generation operations allow creation of a new knowledge object from another	**Instantiation**	A value is given to all attributes of a concept, thus generating an instance, a facts system.
	Generalization	A concept is identified that, once instantiated, should provide one or several instances.
	Abstraction	A more general concept is obtained from another through elimination of attributes or attributing values to a less attributes than in the original concept.
	Specification	A more specialized concept is obtained from another one by adding attributes or by giving values to more attributes than in the original concept.
Restructuring operations allow transformation of an input model	**Assembling**	A new model is obtained in which the components are the input model to the operation
	Decomposition	A set of sub-models is obtained that are components of an input model
	Transformation	A model is obtained from the input model by adding or removing one or several components.
	Sorting	A model is obtained from the input model by reordering its components according to an order relation, a precedence relation
Differentiation operations generate new knowledge by comparing concepts or models	**Comparison**	Attribute values of two concepts are compared and result in a decision ?
	Matching	Two models are compared and a model formed with common components is built
	Selection	One or several models are chosen from a set, according to a observations sets that serve as filters
Transfer operations allow communication between the process and an external agent (user)	**Obtaining**	The resolving system obtains information by requesting it to an external agent
	Presenting	The resolving system decides to present information to an outside agent.
	Receiving	An external agent decides to provide information to the resolving system
	Sending	An external agent request the sending of information to the resolving system

man activity and especially the concepts of skill and competency as they apply to human actors?

To answer this question, we refer to the founding work of cognitive psychology. We will cite but two authors whose work is strongly consistent with the material presented above.

Like his compatriot Vygotsky (1978), the Russian developmental psychologist Leontiev (1976), advanced the theory that human activity is a voluntary interaction between subjects having intention and who are defined by their social contexts (actors) and material or symbolic objects that these subjects wish to acquire and/ or transform. Leontiev's model consists of three interdependent levels:

- The highest level involves the *elaboration of intentions*. Intentions help to focus attention and set goals based on one's needs, values, and motivations.
- The middle level involves *action as a logical unit of inner transformation*. At this level, strategies and plans are formulated through goals/means analyses based on the above set goals.
- The lower level involves *necessary operations for achieving action plans*. At this level, expertise and basic procedures for often-automated routines come into play.

In KADS language, the three levels correspond respectively to strategic models, inference and task models, and inference schemas. What we call "generic skills" will be represented by a combination of these models in the form of a generic processes.

This theoretical hypothesis converges with the work of American psychologist Bruner (1973), considered one of the founders of cognitive psychology. For Bruner, the full cycle of a deliberate action consists of a transformation from an initial state to a final state (level of action and operations) guided by a certain number of higher mental operations such as:

- *temporal sequencing*, which provides an imprint of the activity's path from initial state to final state.
- *goal-directed sequencing*, or intermediary states
- *autonomous anticipation and voluntary persistence*, which help subjects set and reach states they have chosen for themselves
- the use of strategies that are *sensitive to context* and to changes in the initial intention
- *interactive management* of strategies through internal comparison of expected and actual outcomes and through external evaluation.

This approach is also similar to that of Newell & Simon (1972) in their building computer models of problem solving to better understand human problem solving.

In this framework, skills become components of problem solving methods in the form of processes whose products are intermediate and final goals and whose inputs are initial states or intermediate states resulting from the use of other skills.

6.2 GENERIC SKILLS AS ACTIVE META-KNOWLEDGE

Although many studies involve meta-knowledge, most of the time, the term is not explicitly used. These studies can be found in various domains such as mathematical logic (Thayse, 1988), scientific methodology (Popper, 1967), problem resolution and its teaching (Polya, 1967), education (Romiszowski, 1981), learning environments (Paquette 1991; Merrill, 1994), software and cognitive engineering (Chandrasekaran, 1987, Breuker, Bredeweg, Valente, & van de Velde, 1993), artificial intelligence (Anderson, 1990, Minsky, 1988, Pitrat, 1990, 1993).

Jacques Pitrat has produced an important synthesis in which he distinguishes several meta-knowledge categories and proposes the following definition: "meta-knowledge is knowledge about knowledge, rather than knowledge from a specific domain such as mathematics, medicine or geology." (Pitrat, 1993, p.55, translated by the author)

Romiszowski (1981), talking of meta-knowledge that he calls "skills", expresses very well the simultaneous phenomenon of knowledge acquisition in a particular domain, and meta-knowledge building: "The learner follows two kinds of objectives at the same time - learning specific new knowledge and learning to better analyze what he already knows, to restructure knowledge, to validate new ideas and formulate new knowledge », an idea expressed in another way by Pitrat (1990) "meta-knowledge is being created at the same time as knowledge".

In other words, meta-knowledge develops while it is applied on knowledge in various field. Anybody learning new knowledge uses meta-knowledge (at least minimally) without necessarily being aware of it. However, using meta-knowledge should really be a learner's conscious act. This is what meta-cognition is about (Noël, 1991).

Meta-knowledge is knowledge that eventually leads individuals to improve the way they learn, thus facilitating transfer operations from known application domains to new ones and enabling them to learn more autonomously.

By examining a large corpus of literature, Pitrat (1990) describes the various types of meta-knowledge, which consists in transforming information into knowledge:

- by attributing values to knowledge from other domains: truth, usefulness, importance, knowledge priority, competence of an individual towards a knowledge object, etc.
- by describing "intellectual acts", processes that facilitate knowledge processing in other domains: recall, understanding, application, analysis, synthesis, evaluation, etc.

- by representing strategies to acquire, process and use knowledge from other domains: recall techniques, heuristic principles for problem solving, project management strategies, etc.

Of particular interest for our definition of competency is the distinction between passive and active meta-knowledge: "Some meta-knowledge plays an active role; for example, in a self-regulating system, knowledge about using knowledge allows the system to choose the best testing procedures to improve its immediate effectiveness, while knowledge about discovering knowledge allows it to create new knowledge for improving its future effectiveness (...). Active meta-knowledge requires knowledge about processed knowledge, resulting in a second type of meta-knowledge—properties about knowledge. To store knowledge, it is better to have an idea about the importance and credibility one attributes to it. Active meta-knowledge creates this other meta-knowledge, which is then used by other active meta-knowledge." Pitrat (1990, p.205, translation by the author)

Active meta-knowledge is knowledge that processes other knowledge and, as such, can be integrated into artificial intelligence programs. Pitrat defines six types of active meta-knowledge; their interactions are presented on Figure 2 using a MOT model.

- **Knowledge acquisition** consists in examining and diagnosing available information and knowledge, completing it, if incomplete or inconsistent with other knowledge previously acquired, and reformulating it, as needed, so it may be stored in memory.
- **Knowledge storage** consists in deciding where and how to register knowledge in a structured way in memory so it can become quickly available when needed, following the shortest association chains, without having to systematically scan memory.

Figure 2. Relationships between active meta-knowledge

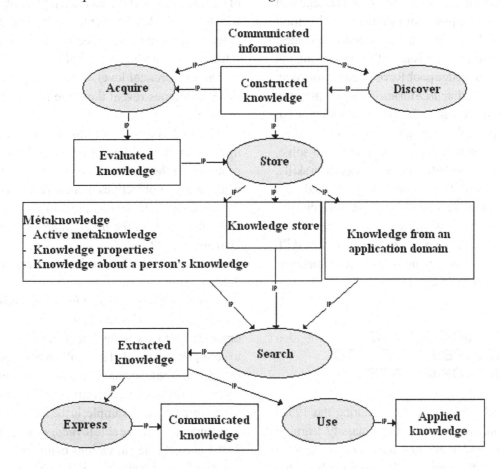

- **Knowledge search** is essentially a set of knowledge reconstruction operations to extract from memory the knowledge needed to solve a problem or accomplish a task.
- **Knowledge discovery** regroups a set of operations like instantiation, specialization or analogy, which allow transformation of acquired knowledge into new knowledge.
- **Knowledge use** regroups a set of operations required to apply knowledge that has been extracted or reconstructed in memory, in order to build a solution for a problem, designing and managing solution plans and results explanation.
- **Knowledge expression,** is the inverse of acquisition, to communicate acquired knowledge to another information process-

ing system, generally a human being; these operations enable us to choose what to say and how to say it, according to the recipient's model.

Figure 2 shows the relationships between different kinds of active meta-knowledge. *Discovery* is the only meta-knowledge that produces new knowledge from raw data or information. *Acquisition* is the meta-knowledge that follows to evaluate knowledge and decide if and how it will be stored in memory. Through the acquisition process, resulting knowledge is structured, reorganized and assessed, notably as regards its validity and interest. *Storage* meta-knowledge help decide how new knowledge from the study domain as well as improved active meta-knowledge will be integrated in memory. The storage actions will facilitate subsequent knowledge identification together with the associated meta-concepts values, evaluated during acquisition, thus increasing the available knowledge pool. Reverse operations may then be followed: *search* for knowledge in memory to communicate it through *express* meta-knowledge and to apply it through and *use* meta-knowledge.

Like the generic problems it serves to solve, active meta-knowledge also corresponds to skills. This approach allows skills to be situated in a "meta-domain," i.e. one that studies knowledge and is parallel to the application domain. This provides us with another perspective on the concept of skill, and a way of representing skills in co-domains of application domains.

6.3 GENERIC SKILLS AS ACTION VERBS RELATED TO LEARNING OBJECTIVES

Theoretical work in education during the 1960s and 70s has led researchers to classify learning objectives and outcomes into three categories or domains: the cognitive domain, involving the knowledge and skills that regulate rational behavior, the affective domain, involving attitudes and emotions, and the psycho-motor domain, involving physical behavior and actions. Authors also talk about multiple intelligences: cognitive and rational intelligence, emotional intelligence, and physical and behavioral intelligence.

As noted by Martin & Briggs (1986, p. 9): "This subdivision was, for the most part, arbitrary since psychologists and educators agree that, in actuality, that is, in teaching and real-life learning situations, no true separation of cognitive, affective, and psychomotor states was possible."

Despite this recognition of the holistic nature learning, practical and theoretical work has concentrated on one domain or the other without taking into account interactions between domains. For example, Joyce & Weil (1980) produced a summary of teaching models for educational practitioners in which each model is presented by its contribution to learning in terms of it effect on the cognitive or affective domain but never both.

On a theoretical level, taxonomies of educational outcomes reveal the same polarization of domains.

The first taxonomy of objectives in the cognitive domain was developed in the 1950's by a group under the direction of Benjamin S. Bloom; a taxonomy of objectives in the affective domain followed, published by Krahtwohl et al. in 1964, and a third one, in the psychomotor domain, by Harrow in 1972.

The first two taxonomies are presented in Tables 3 and 4.

In Bloom's *taxonomy of educational objectives in the cognitive domain* (1956), behaviors are organized into six main categories from simple to complex and divided into sub-categories. Each category can be associated with a set of action verbs that allow the learning objectives or competencies to be expressed, for example, in the following way: The student should be able to *recognize* (Category 1) the correct rules in various contexts" or "The student should be able to *validate* (Category 6) a text without help."

In Krathwohl, Bloom & Masia's taxonomy of *educational objectives in the affective domain* (1964), behaviors are more difficult to classify than in the cognitive domain. The authors use the principle of internalization of values, in which "the ordering of components (of the taxonomy) moves from simple perception to the ability to control one's behavior" (p. 27). The categories are defined in terms of concepts such as emotion, degree of acceptance or rejection, interest, attitude, and appreciation and integration of values.

Various researchers have assessed the hierarchy of categories in both domains. They seem to be more firmly established for taxonomies of the cognitive domain than for those of the affective domain.

Table 3. Taxonomy of the cognitive domain (adapted from Bloom, 1956)

Educational objectives (cognitive domain)	Action verbs
1.00 KNOWLEDGE 1.10 Knowledge of specifics 1.11 Knowledge of terminology 1.12 Knowledge of specific facts 1.20 Knowledge of ways and means of dealing with specifics 1.21 Knowledge of conventions 1.22 Knowledge of trends or sequences 1.23 Knowledge of classifications and categories 1.24 Knowledge of criteria 1.25 Knowledge of methodology 1.30 Knowledge of the universals and abstractions in a field 1.31 Knowledge of principles and generalizations 1.32 Knowledge of theories and structures	Identify, define, recall, recognize, find
2.00 COMPREHENSION 2.10 Translation 2.20 Interpretation 2.30 Extrapolation	Explain, reformulate, interpret, translate, illustrate, distinguish, predict
3.00 APPLICATION	Relate, use, transfer, select, simulate
4.00 ANALYSIS 4.10 Analysis of elements 4.20 Analysis of relationships 4.30 Analysis of organizational principles	Distinguish, classify, categorize, compare, deduce, detect
5.00 SYNTHESIS 5.10 Production of a unique communication 5.20 Production of a plan, or proposed set of operations 5.30 Derivation of a set of abstract relations	Form, write, plan, create, model, produce, construct, repair
6.00 ÉVALUATION 6.10 Judgment in terms of internal evidence 6.20 Judgment in terms of external criteria	Judge, argue, criticize, validate, standardize

Table 4. Taxonomy of the affective domain (adapted from Krathwohl et al., 1964)

Educational objectives (affective domain)	Action verbs
1.0 Receiving (attending) 1.1 Awareness 1.2 Willingness to receive 1.3 Controlled or selected attention	Become aware, pay attention, perceive
2.0 Responding 2.1 Acquiescence in responding 2.2 Willingness to respond 2.3 Satisfaction in response	Show willingness, be involved, take satisfaction
3.0 Valuing 3.1 Acceptance of a value 3.2 Preference for a value 3.3 Commitment (conviction)	Accept, prefer, commit
4.0 Organization 4.1. Conceptualization of a value 4.2 Organization of a value system	Construct, organize
5.0 Characterization by a value or value complex 5.1 Generalized set 5.2 Characterization	Self control

Taxonomies of the cognitive domain are sometimes criticized for over-developing the first category but under-developing the other categories. Other limitations concern the non-inclusion of affective-type constructions. Some categories overlap between the two types of taxonomies, particularly "knowledge" and "reception", and "assessment" and "valuing". The fact remains that these two taxonomies have been and are still widely used in educational practice.

Relatively few studies have dealt with the integration of cognitive, affective, psychomotor domains. There are, however, studies in which the domains are defined somewhat differently than in the work of Bloom.

For example, Gagné (1977) has proposed taxonomy of learning behaviors in five domains, the first three of which correspond to the cognitive domain.

- *Intellectual skills:* ability of learners to use symbols for organizing, interacting with, and understanding the real world.
- *Cognitive strategies:* abilities guiding behavior related to recall, problem solving, and learning.
- *Verbal information:* factual information stored in memory allowing one to name things and facts, memorize sequences, and organize information.

- *Motor skills:* ability to execute movements.
- *Attitudes:* mental state or tendency influencing one's choice of physical or mental actions.

As well, Foshay (1978) describes six learning domains, the last four of which appear to include affective components:

- the *intellectual* domain: similar to Bloom's cognitive domain
- the *physical* domain: psycho-motor skills; development of physical self-concept
- the *emotional* domain: development of feelings and emotions
- the *social* domain: development of social behavior
- the *aesthetic* domain: formal, technical, or expressive sensory response to the examination of an object
- the *spiritual* domain: the search for deeper meaning

These approaches do not seek integration but an exhaustive description of human abilities.

6.4 AN INTEGRATED CYCLE OF SKILLS

The classification of skills proposed by Romiszowski (1981) is different from the one proposed for taxonomies of objectives because it supports an integrated treatment of four categories of skills: cognitive, affective, social, and psychomotor.

His definition of a skill is: "intellectual or physical actions, or even reactions, that a person produces in a competent manner to reach a goal. To do so, knowledge stored in memory is used (...). Any skill may be composed of four activities: perception, planning, prerequisite knowledge recall, and finally, execution of the action (performance)". (p. 253).

He also distinguishes between reproductive and productive skills. Reproductive skills in the cognitive domain correspond to the first three categories of Bloom's taxonomy of the cognitive domain and the first three categories Krathwohl et al's taxonomy of the affective domain. Productive skills correspond to the last three categories of Bloom's taxonomy and the last two of Karthwohl et al's taxonomy. This dual classification results in Table 5, in which the author provides examples for each type of skill.

Table 5. Classification of skills (Romiszowski)

	Reproductive Skills Applying procedures (algorithms)	Productive Skills Applying principles and strategies
Cognitive Skills Decision-making, problem-solving, logical thinking, etc.	Applying a known procedure to a known category of 'problem', e.g. dividing numbers, writing a grammatically correct sentence.	Solving 'new' problems; 'inventing' a new procedure, e.g. proving a theorem, writing creatively.
Psychomotor Skills Physical action, perceptual acuity, etc	Sensori-motor skills, repetitive or automated action, e.g. typewriting, changing gear, running fast.	'Strategy' skills or 'planning' skills ; arts and crafts, e.g. page layout design, 'road sense', playing football,
Reactive Skills Dealing with oneself ; attitudes, feelings, habits, self-control.	Conditioned habits and attitudes, e.g 'attending, responding and valuing' (Bloom taxonomy), approach/avoid behaviors (Mager)	'Personal control' skills, developing a 'mental set' or a value system (Bloom), 'self-actualization' (Rogers)
Interactive Skills Dealing with others	Social habits; conditioned responses, e.g good manners, pleasant tone, verbal habits.	'Interpersonal control' skills, e.g leadership, supervision, persuasion, discussion, salesmanship.

Rather than categorizing skills according to the type of individual response to a stimulus (new knowledge, affective attitudes, social behavior or motor actions), Romiszowski characterizes them according to their functions in the information treatment cycle through which one perceives and transforms knowledge in a given situation.

It is here that Romiszowski departs from the behaviorist approach by examining what happens between stimuli and actions. At first, the non-observable mental actions triggered by stimuli consist in the recall of useful knowledge stored in memory by virtue of the skill's reproductive components. Then, responses are planned through the skill's productive components. This leads to a cycle of skills in 4 phases and 12 basic skills that may or not be present as individual components of complex skills (p. 257). As indicated in Table 6, these four phases describe a cycle of information processing that uses skills belonging to several domains.

This cycle of skills applies to the four domains defined above: cognitive, psycho-motor, affective, and social; it is presented as an analysis tool for identifying causes of poor performance of a complex skill. For example, the inability to diag-nose engine failure or an imperfect dive depends on of the 12 causes, or components of the skills, presented in Table 6.

The author presents the cycle as follows: "It is a language for analyzing skills—a taxonomy if you prefer. But there is no hierarchical relationship of dependency. A complex skill may require, to varying degrees, a combination of the 12 factors or basic skills" (p. 257).

6.5 COMPARISON OF THE TAXONOMIES RELATED TO GENERIC SKILLS

Despite the different goals and approaches, it is possible to establish a comparison between the various taxonomies presented in this chapter. Table 7 presents an integrated comparison based on a list of skills compared with 10 basic categories to be further discussed in the next chapter.

It should be noted that these correspondences are approximate. The purpose of the table is to show an important level of convergence between the taxonomies. The concept of generic processes presented in the first column can be used to recon-

Table 6. Classification of skills proposed by Romiszowski

Phase	Skill	Description
Perception	Attention	Ability to concentrate on a task
	Perceptual acuteness	Ability to recognize the stimulus
	Discrimination	Ability to recognize the stimulus among other similar ones
Recall from memory	Interpretation	Knowledge of the stimulus language
	Procedure recall	Presence of an adequate algorithm in memory
	Schema recall	Presence of relevant concepts and principles in memory
Planning	Analysis	Ability to restructure the problem
	Synthesis	Ability to generate alternative solutions
	Evaluation	Ability to assess alternate implications
Performance	Initiation	Ability to make decisions and act accordingly
	Continuation	Ability to carry through with action
	Control	Ability to self-adapt and self-correct

Table 7. Comparison of skills' taxonomies

Generic processes (competency levels)	Generic problems (KADS)	Inference schemas (KADS)	Active meta-knowledge (Pitrat)	Taxonomy of cognitive objectives (Bloom)	Taxonomy of affective objectives (Krathwohl)	Skills cycle (Romizowski)
1. Pay attention				Knowledge	Receiving	Attention Perceptual acuteness
2. Memorize		Instantiation Obtaining Presenting	Knowledge storage Knowledge Search	Knowledge	Responding	Perceptual discrimination Interpretation
3. Explicitate		Matching Comparison Selection	Knowledge expression	Comprehension	Responding	Procedures recall Schema recall
4. Transpose			Knowledge use	Comprehension		
5. Apply		Specification, Sending, Presenting	Knowledge use	Application		
6. Analyze	Classify Diagnose Predict Supervise	Decomposition Sorting	Knowledge discovery	Analysis		Analysis
7. Repair	Repair	Transformation Sorting	Knowledge discovery	Synthesis	Organization	
8. Synthesize	Plan Design Model	Generalization Abstraction Assembling	Knowledge discovery	Synthesis	Organization	Synthesis
9. Evaluate			Knowledge acquisition	Evaluation	Characterization	Evaluation
10. Self-control			Knowledge acquisition	Evaluation	Characterization	Initiation Continuation Control

cile these classifications. To establish associations between the different systems, we must consider the type of input and product (output) for each term, as well as the process a description of the process to be applied.

Acquisition meta-knowledge is difficult to position because its nature is perceptual as well as evaluative. It involves meta-cognition and the attribution of properties to acquired knowledge. This is the main reason why it is classified at the evaluation and self-control levels.

The libraries of inference schemas and generic problems in KADS are positioned at different levels of granularity. Inference schemas correspond to terminal generic processes operations. On the other hand, KADS generic problems library is of a very high level. Their correspondence is solid as regards to the terms "analysis", "repair" and "synthesis" used in the first column.

6.6 THE CONCEPT OF GENERIC SKILL

We have adopted the concept of (generic) skill as central to the taxonomies presented in this chapter. We will now further develop this concept.

When we acquire specific knowledge in any domain, and while acquiring it, we learn various related skills. For example, we may be able to recognize that a quantity is a fraction but not necessarily be able to apply its definition in everyday life or evaluate whether or not the concept is valid. In a different domain, an individual may be able to recognize a recipe for "canard à l'orange", while another may be able to apply it; however, an expert chef is not only able to apply the procedure, but is also able to evaluate and compare different similar recipes and even invent new ones. In yet another domain, an individual may have an idea of the relative value of a particular type of investment, but a financial expert is able to analyze the client's situation, evaluate different

investment vehicles, and create a portfolio tailored to the client's needs.

The above examples illustrate the following properties of generic skills.

Generic skills vary among individuals and are learned throughout life. Like other knowledge, generic skills are developed at different times in our lives. First, we develop attention and recall skills; then, we learn how to recognize and apply knowledge, perform physical tasks, and work in teams; finally, we learn how to use "higher" skills such as analyzing, integrating, and evaluating knowledge, engaging ourselves, communicating, and adapting. Moreover, we learn to practice a particular skill such as analyzing in increasingly varied and complex domains.

Generic skills are defined in terms of the knowledge to which they apply. Though they exist in themselves, skills are defined in relation to the knowledge to which they apply. Saying that someone is able to make a diagnosis or develop an integrated approach is a simplified way of saying that they are able to exercise these skills in relation to a diversity of knowledge and in domains that may be relatively new to them; nevertheless, they exercise these skills in relation to one or more application domains.

Generic skills are developed through several domains. We develop generic skills, such as the ability to diagnose, through our interactions in several knowledge domains. It is in this sense that they are "generic". We can diagnose simple problems such as paying an overdue bill, or we can diagnose more complex problems such as "debugging" a computer program or assessing a medical condition. Despite their differences, these diagnoses have several characteristics in common, so that mastering a skill in one domain can lead to its transfer, at least partially, in another domain.

Skills are meta-processes. Skills are essentially procedural in nature; they are processes that allow us to perceive, recall, understand, apply, assess, produce, and communicate knowledge. According to the definitions given in Chapter

2 and 3, they are meta-processes in the sense giving by the MOT system to this word. A skill is normally decomposed into sub-tasks that are other skills, their organization being regulated by principles of execution. Each skill also has its own inputs and products that are types of stimuli or knowledge resulting from the application of the skill.

One example is a generic skill "simulate a process". It has a specific process in an application domain as its input and an execution trace of the process as its product, which is the result of the simulation. One of its possible instances is "simulate the procedure to solve a linear equation". This is this instance of the skill that we will use in the Algebra domain in order to solve a particular equation of the form ax+c=b," where a=3, c=8, and b=2. In this case, the simulation trace would be: start with 3x+8=2: a procedure of subtraction of 8 on both sides (first task of the process) yielding 3x = -6; then a division action by 3 on both sides (second task of the process), yielding x = -2.

Psychomotor, affective, and social skills are also learned generic processes applied to knowledge in a variety of domains. All skills are developed through the participation of individuals in the various situations they encounter during their lives. These situations consist of objects, events, people, and interrelations that can be described by facts, concepts, procedures, or principles. For example, a psychomotor skill such as "ride a bicycle" is a process and a cycle of physical actions that lead to a specific goal: keeping one's balance; this result can be described by facts or knowledge. In the same way, an attitude of rejection or disinterest for a certain task, can itself be described by facts and knowledge or by comparing it with knowledge, values, and previous situations stored in memory. Finally, a social skill such as developing solidarity among team members around a common goal can be described as a process that begins with the sharing and comparing of points of view, the agreement on common goals, and the seeking of mutual benefit.

Figure 3. Diagnosis skill applied to an affective situation

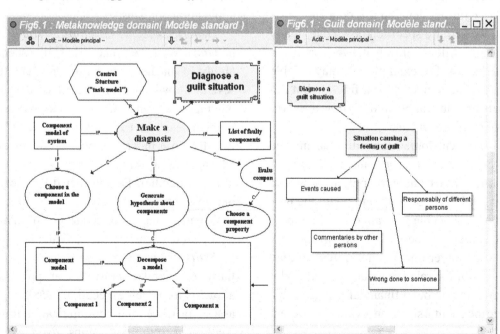

Figure 3 shows a generic process of diagnosis similar to that of Figure 1 but one that applies to a feeling of guilt that may be experienced in a certain situation. The diagnosis consists of decomposing the situation and evaluating each of its components in order to identify the cause of this affective state. This example demonstrates how generic skills are primarily described as a function of information processing, in which a person perceives and translates knowledge into acts and interacts in a given situation, rather than as a response to stimuli such as new information, physical actions, personal and social attitudes, etc. These are rather the product, the result of applying the generic skill to the inputs, whether they are information, physical action or attitudes.

Neurologists tend to situate the higher cognitive faculties in the neo-cortex. Others demonstrate the existence of an emotional memory leaving traces in other regions of the brain called the limbic system (LeDoux 1996; Goleman 1995). Here we make no particular psychological or neural hypothesis about cognition or affect, only seeking a unified way to model generic skills.

What we have here is a unified approach to classifying generic skills, seen as generic processes. Contrary to their traditional use in the definition of learning objectives, skills, as used in this book, are learning objects—knowledge that can be described, analyzed, and assessed per se or in relation to knowledge in other domains. As such, they should be included in knowledge models as targets of learning activities in the same way that knowledge objects are treated in any domain.

CONCLUSION

Many studies in cognitive science, cognitive engineering, and education support the hypothesis proposed here that *human skills can be described as generic processes*. To be sure, the description of skills in this perspective is highly schematic and represents only a portion of reality. Neverthe-

less, representing skills in the form of processes provides a graphical, structural, and operational point of view and one in which skills can be integrated into a competency-driven instructional engineering or knowledge management methodology. Furthermore, to each generic problem or task corresponds a solution method. This method is a generic process that describes the skill that a human or artificial system must apply to solve a problem or perform a task.

Active meta-knowledge also describes generic processes and therefore skills. Viewing skills in this way allows us to situate and study them in a particularly important domain—that which studies knowledge. The relationship between skills and the knowledge to which they apply thus occurs in two domains: the domain of meta-knowledge and an application domain. This view is consistent with the multidimensional nature of human skills and competencies in their regard to different domains of knowledge.

Taxonomies of learning objectives in cognitive, psychomotor, and affective domains also describe skills. These taxonomies can be reused in the development of curricula and learning and assessment tools. Viewing taxonomic categories as generic processes frees them from their behaviourist origins. The stimulus-response aspect is no longer our main area of concern. Beyond the input/product relationship, a generic process model describes its components, its operations, the intermediate products and the principles that regulate the execution of the process. This amounts to describing the *internal functioning* of an actor performing such a skill-process, which is basically a cognitivist viewpoint.

Reinterpreting taxonomies of educational objectives in this way means that we no longer separate the psycho-motor, affective, or social domains, but that we distinguish these views only by the kind of stimulus and respond, not by the internal process that characterizes the generic skill. merely by the way in which a response manifests itself. For example, similar repair processes can be applied to modify a model (cognitive), an attitude (affective), a physical action (psychomotor), or a social behavior.

This is the basis upon which we will develop, in the next chapter, a taxonomy of generic skills substantiated by a library of corresponding generic processes.

REFERENCES

Aloom, B. S. (1956). *Taxonomy of Educational Objectives: the Classification of Educational Goals. Handbook 1: Cognitive domain*. New York: Longman.

Anderson, J. A. (1990). Hybrid computation in cognitive science: Neural networks and symbols. *Applied Cognitive Psychology, 4*, 337–347. doi:10.1002/acp.2350040408

Breuker, J., & Van de Velde, W. (1994). *CommonKads Library for Expertise Modelling*. Amsterdam: IOS Press.

Breuker, J. A., Bredeweg, B., Valente, A., & van de Velde, W. (1993). Reusable Problem Solving Components: the CommonKADS library. In Ch. Löckenhoff, D. Fensel, & R. Studer (Eds.), *Proceedings of the third KADS Meeting* (pp. 251–270). Munich, Germany: Siemens ZFE.

Bruner, J. S. (1973). *La compétence, sa nature et comment on la cultive. Le développement de l'enfant: savoir faire, savoir dire*. Paris: PUF.

Chandrasekaran, B. (1983). Towards a taxonomy of problem solving types. *AI Magazine, 4*(4), 9–17.

Chandrasekaran, B. (1987). Towards a Functional Architecture for Intelligence Based on Generic Information Processing Tasks. In *Proceedings IJCAI-87*, Milan-Italy (pp. 1183-1192).

Foshay, W. R. (1978). An alternative for task analysis in the affective domain. *Journal of Instructional Development, 1*(2), 22–24. doi:10.1007/BF02968231

Gagné, R. M. (1970). *The Conditions of Learning* (2nd ed.). New York: Holt, Rhinehart & Winston.

Goleman, D. P. (1995). *Emotional Intelligence: Why It Can Matter More Than IQ for Character, Health and Lifelong Achievement*. New York: Bantam Books.

Harrow, A. J. (1972). *A Taxonomy of the Psychomotor Domain*. New York: David McKay Co.

Hayes-Roth, F., Waterman, D. A., & Lenat, D. B. (1984). *Building Expert Systems*. Reading, MA: Addison-Wesley.

Joyce, B., & Weil, M. (1980). *Models of Teaching* (3rd ed.). Englewood Cliffs, NJ: Prentice-Hall.

Krathwohl, D. R., Bloom, B. S., & Masia, B. B. (1964). *Taxonomy of Educational Objectives: The Classification of Educational Goals. Handbook II: Affective domain*. New York: Longman.

LeDoux, J. (1996). *The Emotional Brain*. New-York: Simon & Shuster.

Leontiev, A. N. (1976). *Le développement du psychisme* (3rd ed.). Paris: Éditions Sociales.

Martin, B. L., & Briggs, L. (1986). *The Affective and Cognitive Domains: Integration for Instruction and Research*. Englewood Cliffs, NJ: Educational Technology Publications.

McDermott, J. (1988). Preliminary steps towards a taxonomy of problem-solving methods. In Marcus, S. (Ed.), *Automating Knowledge Acquisition for Expert Systems* (pp. 225–255). Boston, MA: Kluwer Academic Publishers.

Merrill, M. D. (1994). *Principles of Instructional Design*. Englewood Cliffs, NJ: Educational Technology Publications.

Minsky, M. (1975). A Framework for Representing Knowledge . In Winston, P. H. (Ed.), *The Psychology of Computer Vision* (pp. 211–277). New York: McGraw-Hill.

Newell, A., & Simon, H. (1972). *Human Problem-Solving*. Englewood Cliffs, NJ: Prentice-Hall.

Noël, B. (1991). *La métacognition*. Bruxelles, Belgium: De Boeck-Wesmael.

Paquette, G., & Roy, L. (1990). *Systèmes à base de connaissances*. Montréal, Canada: Beauchemin.

Pitrat, J. (1990). *Métaconnaissance, avenir de l'intelligence artificielle*. Paris: Hermès.

Pitrat, J. (1993). *Penser l'informatique autrement*. Paris: Hermès.

Polya, G. (1967). La découverte des mathématiques (Vol. 1 & 2). Paris: Dunod.

Popper, K. R. (1967). *The Logic of Scientific Discovery*. New York: Harper Torchbooks.

Romiszowski, A. J. (1981). *Designing Instructional Systems*. New York: Nichols Publishing.

Schreiber, G., Wielinga, B., & Breuker, J. (1993). *KADS – A Principled Approach to Knowledge-based System Development*. San Diego, CA: Academic Press.

Steels, L. (1990). Components of expertise. *AI Magazine, 11*(2), 29–49.

Thayse, A. (1988). *Approche logique de l'intelligence artificielle*. Paris: Dunod.

Vygotsky, L. S. (1978). *Mind in Society: The Development of Higher Psychological Functions*. Cambridge, MA: Harvard University Press.

Waterman, D. A. (1986). *A Guide to Expert Systems*. Reading, MA: Addison-Wesley.

Chapter 7
A Taxonomy of Generic Skills

Gilbert Paquette
LICEF Research Center, Canada

ABSTRACT

- Description of the Taxonomy of Generic Skills
  ○ Receiving Skills
  ○ Reproduction Skills
  ○ Production and creation skills
  ○ Self-management skills
- Generic Skills in Different Meta-domains
- Towards a Library of Generic Skills Processes
  ○ A Generic process for Identification
  ○ A Generic process for Deduction
  ○ A Generic Process for Building a Taxonomy
  ○ A Generic Process for Evaluation
  ○ A Generic Process for Control and Self-adaptation
- Relations between Skills: Specialization and Composition
  ○ Increasing Order of Complexity
  ○ Specialization of the Library
- Analysis of Competency Profiles
  ○ Target Actors for the Profile
  ○ Target Actor's Tasks and Knowledge
  ○ Deciding on Generic Skills

As mentioned in the previous chapter, research in cognitive science, cognitive engineering, and education all support the idea that human skills can be described as generic processes. These processes develop through learning and working situations in various domains where knowledge

DOI: 10.4018/978-1-61520-839-5.ch007

is processed. In their relationship to knowledge, generic skills are the active part of human competencies. Depending on the viewpoint we use, generic skills are problem-solving methods, or active meta-knowledge working on other knowledge, or learning objectives to be acquired. The generic skills framework that will be presented here has been built in order to provide a clear view of the relation between knowledge in any application domain and the "intellectual actions" that enable a person to process and build knowledge. When someone has many such opportunities to exercise generic skills, they the re-construction of their own private universe of generic linkages and connections is made possible.

In this chapter, we will develop an integrated taxonomy of generic skills. It will incorporate previous work in cognitive science, software and cognitive engineering, and pedagogical design, some of which was presented in Chapter 6. It is an integrated taxonomy because it can apply to different manifestations of human activity: cognitive, emotional, social, or motor, representing generic skills in the form of process-type knowledge models constituting an operational library that can be used for projects in instructional engineering.

Figure 1. Taxonomy of generic skills

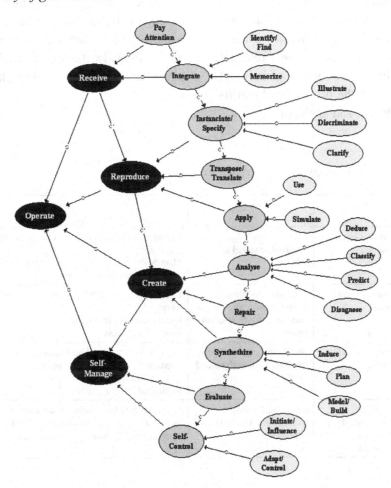

7.1 PRESENTATION OF THE TAXONOMY OF GENERIC SKILLS

Figure 1 is an overview of the taxonomy of generic skills we propose. From left to right, there are three levels, from general to specific.

Each of the general skills (those directly linked to the root) represents a phase in the information processing cycle. Despite differences in terminology, there is a fairly broad consensus regarding the life cycle of generic skills that make up human action and learning.

- The first phase is that of *reception*, in which perception is mobilized in response to external stimuli: attention is placed on objects, information is located in memory to give meaning to each stimulus, and some of the information is memorized.
- This phase is usually followed by a phase of *reproduction*, in which memory is managed in such a way as to select relevant knowledge, in preparation for an eventual response, through the processes of clarification, translation, and application.

- Then, the higher intellectual processes of *creation/production*, analysis, repairing, synthesis, and assessment are mobilized to create/produce a plan for an eventual response and to produce the response or solution itself.
- The expression of this response in the environment leads to the *self-management* of one's mental, physical, emotional, and social actions through mediums of communication such as speech, movement, expressions, etc. The process begins by an assessment of the situation, which helps one to orient one's self, influence others, control the situation, and adapt to the circumstances. This is called the *self-management* phase.

Table 1 synthesizes definition and examples of skills corresponding to these four phases, irrespective of the facts that the inputs and products can be situated at the cognitive, affective, social or psychomotor dimensions of intellectual processes.

Table 1. Main generic skill classes of the taxonomy

Name of the Generic Skill	Inputs	Products	Examples
Receive	Internal or external stimulus	Facts or knowledge retreived or stored in memory	Pay attention to an event, to a movement, to an emotion, to a social context. Identify knowledge, associated impressions. Memorize knowledge, impressions.
Reproduce	Knowledge and models	Facts obtained through instantiation or knowledge obtained through reformulation	Use examples to explain or illustrate a concept, a procedure or a principle. Use a model to explain facts. Simulate a process.
Create	Knowledge and models	New knowledge or models resulting from analysis and synthesis	Classify objects according to a taxonomy. Repair defective system components . Plan a project. Model and build a system.
Self-manage	Knowledge, models, meta-facts or values about knowledge	Knowledge, models, meta-knowledge linked to domain model	Assess knowledge validity or self competence. Initiate a change process after assessing the situation. Apply a generic strategy to improve learning and performance.

Receiving Skills

The first phase is **reception.** Perception is mobilized following an external stimulus, attention is paid to knowledge objects, memorized information is flagged and identified in order to make sense of the stimulus. Then, memorizing takes place. The generic skill to exert such intellectual acts may be considered as an <u>awareness</u> of knowledge objects involved.

At a first level of complexity, persons:

* **Pay attention** to knowledge objects, i.e. simply express a certain response to facts and information that is presented, for instance, participation in activities related to this information and demonstration of interest in the facts presented.

At a second level of complexity, a person starts to integrate the stimuli, data or information by mobilizing two inverse generic skills:

* **Identify/locate** knowledge elements, already stored in memory in relation to the information-related knowledge (type of fact) present in the stimulus.
* **Memorize** knowledge through restructuring mental association, according to already acquired knowledge, and record it in memory in association with existing knowledge or facts that were previously located there.

Reproduction Skills

The second phase is characterized by a set of **reproduction** activities involving knowledge objects, where memory is managed to process knowledge liable to be used to explain, apply and produce more specific knowledge. The generic skill to exert such intellectual acts may be considered as a <u>familiarization</u> with the knowledge objects involved.

At the lowest level, a person **instantiates or specifies** concepts, procedures or principles provided to them in the following ways:

* **Illustrate** concepts, procedures or principles by producing examples, traces or statements obtained through instantiation.
* **Discriminate** between two or several concepts, procedures or principles, by producing instances of each one of them that is not an instance of the others.
* **Clarify** the description of knowledge by adding attributes to concepts, procedures or principles or by showing links that are not explicitly given initially.

At a higher level of complexity, knowledge is redefined to produce a new definition or a new representation in following ways:

* **Transpose** concepts, procedures or principles, by producing knowledge that is similar or presented in another form.

Table 2. Definitions and examples of the reception generic skills

Name of the Generic Skill		Inputs	Products	Examples
Pay attention		Internal or external stimuli	Facts showing attention paid to input stimuli	Pay attention to someone's attitude change or related events
Integrate	Identify/ Locate	Internal or external stimuli	Knowledge located in memory in association with input stimuli	React to the situation description ; Repeat a dance step; recognize a context.
	Memorize	Internal or external stimuli	Knowledge stored in memory in association with stimuli	Record information; avoid repeating socially unacceptable behavior, memorize a melody .

At an even higher level of complexity, the **apply** generic skills go further by the production of elaborated facts systems obtained by instantiating a given model, adding implicit links to the model. This can be done in the following ways.

- **Apply or use** knowledge or models, by producing goal-driven instances.
- **Simulate,** using the model of a process, or a set of principles to systematically produce instances by setting values for certain independent concepts, and obtaining the corresponding values of other dependent concepts.

Production and Creation Generic Skills

The third phase involves higher-level intellectual processes of analysis and synthesis in the **creation** and **production** of new knowledge. The generic skill to exert such intellectual acts may be con-

sidered as a mastery of the knowledge objects involved.

First, let us consider the main analysis intellectual skills such as:

- **Deduce,** i.e. produce a sequence of permitted operations, logically relating initial data to an original goal.
- **Classify** an object by determining taxonomy classes to which it belongs. .
- **Predict** the result of a given process, based on various classes of possible products.
- **Diagnose** a components system, by producing a list of components that do not meet certain performance standards.

At an intermediate level of creation, between analysis and synthesis, we find **repair** skills. Similarly to analysis, repair skills starts with an existing knowledge model, but the result is a modification, an improvement of the model.

Table 3. Definition of reproductive generic skills

Name of the Generic Skill		Inputs	Products	Examples
In-stan-ciate/ Spec-ify	**Illustrate**	Concepts, procedures or principles	Examples, traces or statements obtained by instantiating input	Provide examples of a calculation process. Give examples about gravitational laws.
	Discriminate	Two or several concepts, procedures or principles	Instance of each input that is not an instance of the others	Give examples allowing distinction of one vertebrate family from others.
	Clarify	Concepts, procedures or principles	Knowledge with more links than the one in input	Add attributes to a concept definition to define its meaning. Complete a procedure by adding a step.
Transpose/ Translate		Concepts, procedures or principles	Analogical knowledge or presented in another form	Represent a statement in natural language by a schema or a graph. Describe a situation like an event.
Ap-ply	**Use**	Abstract knowledge or models	Instances of input knowledge obtained to reach a goal	Use a table to calculate interest. Choose a professional category according to the problem to solve.
	Simulate	Models of a process or a system of principles establishing a relation between concepts	Instances produced systematically by instantiating some concepts and getting values for other dependent concepts	Vary ecosystems parameters and examine the impact on populations evolution; Follow up, step by step, the execution of a purchase process in a organization, in different cases.

• **Repair** a system, by replacing some components to achieve better results.

At a higher level of creation, the **synthesis** skills, at the opposite of application and analysis processes, do not take as input an existing model, but aim to construct one from instances, components or partial models. Depending on the type of inputs and products there are many kinds of synthesis skills suche as:

• **Induce** a concept, a procedure or a principle from a set of examples, traces or particular statements.
• **Plan** a process, by producing a set of products that respect time and resource constraints.
• **Model or build** a new model that integrates facts, abstract knowledge or partial models initially provided.

Self-Management Generic Skills

The fourth phase, **self-management** manifests itself through acts that involve generic knowledge, for example assessment of a situation, action or communication, and finally, self-adaptation for behavior control. The skill to exert such intellectual acts may be considered as expertise as regards the knowledge objects involved. Among other things, an individual can:

• **Evaluate** knowledge by attributing values as to its interest, usefulness, relevance, validity, etc. These values are obtained by instancing the corresponding generic concepts.
• **Initiate and influence** one's own or others' evolution, for example by expressing knowledge for a precise goal and one or several recipients, or by accomplishing a series of actions that will lead to knowledge progress, new attitudes, new social behavior, for oneself or others.

• **Control events and adapt to them** by displaying leadership, willpower, perseverance and adaptation capabilities, using knowledge and its assessment to improve one's own or others' knowledge and generic knowledge.

7.2 GENERIC SKILLS AND META-DOMAINS

It may seem ambitious to propose a taxonomy integrating the cognitive, psychomotor, emotional and social domains, while so many practitioners in education use separated taxonomies of generic skills for these meta-domains. We believe on the contrary that it is important to integrate them. As underlined by Martin and Briggs (1986): "This subdivision (in different domains) is relatively arbitrary because the psychologists and the educators agree that, in the reality of educational practice, no real separation between the cognitive, emotional and psychomotor states is possible " (p.10). Martin and Briggs quote in support to this assertion several other authors, notably some having produced important taxonomies such as the ones by Bloom (1975) and Gagné (1970).

Although recent developments in neurophysiology suggest that regions of the brain are specialized in cognition, emotions or psychomotor commands, research in this domain shows evidence of an integration between the various constituents of the brain in each of our activities. As an example, Daniel Goleman (1997) underlines that "our emotional faculties drive us constantly in our choices; they work of concert with the rational spirit and allow - or forbid - the exercise of the very thought processes. Also, the cognitive brain plays an executive role in our feelings." (p. 53)

Table 6 shows that this taxonomy can be interpreted in each of the four meta-domains (cognitive, psycho-motor, affective or social). For example, we can repair theories and movements, as well as attitudes or social relations. What dif-

Table 4. Definition of production and creation generic skills

Name of the Generic Skill		Inputs	Products	Examples
Ana-lyze	Deduce	Goal, data, operations	Series of operation that relate initial data to the goal	Deduce possible options according to budget analysis. Determine the shortest path between two locations.
	Classify	Taxonomy and facts to classify	Taxonomy classes to which each fact belongs	Determine the category of a certain car. Identify the procedure type for a proposed decision mechanism.
	Predict	Processes, classes of process products, process input to be classified	Class of the process products to which the input corresponds	Predict the possible result from a medical intervention according to the patient's characteristics. Predict one's behavior in a certain type of situation.
	Diagnose	Component-based system, norms that regulate each compo-nent,	List of faulty com-ponents compare to norms	Identify one's errors while executing a movement. Find defective components in an electrical system breakdown.
Repair		Models, model com-ponents to improve	New improved model	Reorganize connections in an audio-video system. Prescribe a medical treatment to remedy a health problem.
Syn-the-size	Induce	Set of facts: examples, traces or statements	Concept, procedure or principle where facts are instances	Induce a scientific law linking two or several vari-ables from observations. Build a taxonomy allowing classification of com-puter types.
	Plan	Set of products (con-cepts) and constraints (principles)	Processes generat-ing the products and respecting the constraints	Plan a project execution. Plan a skating session.
	Model/ Construct	Facts, abstract knowl-edge or models	New model that integrates the facts, knowledge and models	Build a complex computer system. Design a course. Draw the architectural plan of a new building.

Table 5. Definition of the self-management skills

Name of the Generic Skill		Inputs	Products	Examples
Evaluate		Knowledge or models	Knowledge attributes (generic concept) associ-ated with each knowledge object or model	Evaluate reliability or validity of statements . Evaluate one's own competence level in a task. Identify self-esteem or confidence needs in a group.
Self-con-trol	Initiate/ Influ-ence	Knowledge or models assessed by their cog-nitive properties	Intervention processes (communication or action); new cognitive properties	Try to convince someone about knowledge validity and usefulness. Initiate an exercise program intended to improve body flexibility. Start to improve attitudes and social climate in an organization.
	Adapt oneself/ Control	Knowledge or models assessed by their cog-nitive properties	Intervention processes (communication or action); modified cognitive pro-cesses (action and strategy)	Decide on developing project management skills. Improve one's learning strategies in a domain. Analyze self or someone else's generic skills and define an improvement program.

Table 6. Generic skills and meta-domains

Generic Skills			Meta-Domains			
			Cognitive	Psycho-motor	Affective	Social
Re-ceive	1	Pay attention	Be interested in a political situation	Perceive a bad position in front of a computer screen	Be favorably impressed by a symphony	Perceive a tense situation in a group
	2	Integrate	Recall or memorize a list of dangerous products	Remember a yoga position or learn a new one	Remember or note a useful strategy for managing anger	Remember or note a method for working in a group
Re-pro-duce	3	Instantiate/specify	Specify a procedure by adding a stage or giving examples	Describe the movements of a well-rehearsed choreography	Distinguish between a joke and an insult	Make a small change to a previously adopted role in a group
	4	Transpose/ translate	Graphically represent a procedure presented orally	Brake a truck based on one's reflexes for braking a car	Flee (or control) a previously experienced unpleasant situation	Take a leadership role in a familiar group situation
Cre-ate	5	Apply	Use a well-known formula for new data	Correctly perform a backhand in tennis using a new position	Control one's anxiety with a known technique	Simulate crisis management through a recognized approach
	6	Analyze	Identify the objectives, data, and constraints of a certain type of problem	Diagnose errors in the execution of a movement	Predict one's emotional response to an action	Analyze and classify group dynamics according to various models
	7	Repair	Add new features to an inefficient method	Correct certain movements of a golf drive	Change one's emotional response to a tense situation	Propose a method for improving the atmosphere in a classroom
	8	Synthesize	Construct a classification or action plan through examples	Learn to juggle three balls for the first time	Adopt a completely new attitude in a difficult situation	Find a constructive way to behave in a group
Self-con-trol	9	Assess	Assess the strength, validity, or relevance of an argument or statement	Compare one's piano playing in a music class	Assess one's emotional state after an argument with friends	Determine the quality of work and productivity of a group one is involved in
	10	Self-manage	Decide to completely change one's way of assessing a situation	Follow a systematic plan for assessing and improving one's physical condition	Manage one's emotional attitudes by assessing them regularly in order to improve one's well-being	Take responsibility for improving the attitudes of participants and the social climate of an organization

ferentiate these four meta-domains is essentially the type of input to a generic skill and its resulting production. If the stimuli or the result concerns rational thought, motor capacities, affectivity or social interactions, we will label the generic skill to be cognitive, psychomotor, affective or social.

More generally, we could say that somebody is "intelligent" on the rational, physical, emotional or social dimension if it he or she is capable of applying in most of cases, all types of generic skills for that dimension. This is basically what the American psychologist Howard Gardner (1993) suggests by taking into account multiple intelligences as the basic conceptual structure of the intellect.

However, in practice, when we analyze the performance of a generic skill in a person, it usually involves a mix of cognitive, emotional, psycho-motor, and social components. When a person perceives a stimulus, all these different functions are usually called upon, and when he or she effectuates a response, it is very often cognitive, emotional, social, *and* psycho-motor.

When we represent a generic skill in the form of a generic process, such as diagnosing, we ignore this aspect. It may be significant, however, when we instantiate the generic skill in an application field (see for example Figure 4 in Chapter 6).

This is for purely practical reasons. Remember that our goal is to provide useful concepts for instructional engineering. When we represent a generic skill without considering the type of intelligence involved, we are not claiming that diagnosing engine failure is the same as diagnosing an emotional state. The diagnostic process is simply a useful model for instructional engineering, allowing one to understand the distinction between generic skills and showing their interactions. It is a tool for instructional engineering, not an exercise in psychology.

7.3 TOWARDS A LIBRARY OF PROCESSES FOR GENERIC SKILLS

We will now present process models for some of the generic skills defined in the preceding sections. These examples are part of a structured and extensible library that concretizes the notions of Generic Skill and Competency. In the following chapters, we will see how this library can be used to build activity scenario, orient knowledge modeling of select resources according to a user's competencies.

A Generic Process for Identification

Perception involves operations that call on the learner actor's senses as well as memory; without memory recall, he would be incapable to recognize facts and knowledge that are presented to him.

The location and identification generic process first mobilizes an attention sub-process in order for the actor to retain some information originating from internal or external stimuli. Figure 2 presents such a process[1].

Then, two other sub-processes are used to process the retained information. The first one searches memory for knowledge that could be associated with new information. We could describe this search as a pathway in a chain of associations from knowledge in memory that contributes to retention of information. The other sub-process preserves the association links that seem relevant and generates the results from the location and identification generic process: association links between existing knowledge and new information.

Memory search and association principles that regulate the generic process can be more or less numerous, complex and efficient, according to the actor's intellectual development, i.e. the extent of actual learning realized. For instance, an actor may search only one domain within three associative links of the information in stored memory, while another will search several domains.

Figure 2. An identification generic process

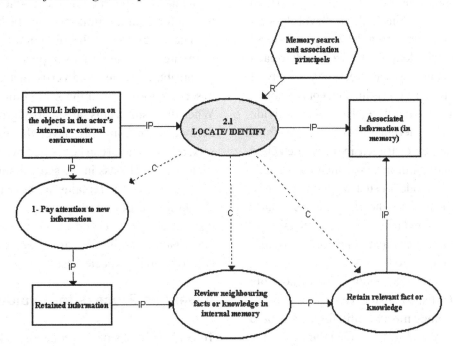

A Generic Process for Deduction

To deduce a solution consists in applying a number of procedures (operators) to instances of concepts called « data », in order to produce an instance of a concept called « goal ». For example, applying algebraic operators to an equation with two unknown variables to infer a solution; applying solutions allowed by the Rubik cube to an initial state of the cube, to get the final state that meets the game conditions ; creating new schedule out of last year's schedule, by applying substitutions that satisfy the new constraints.

Figure 3 is a model of a generic deduction process (6.1), a particular case of the analysis skill process (6).

The first procedure of the generic process consists in examining procedures (operators) that are applicable to data. Then, one of these operators is chosen and applied to data. If the product generated by the procedure is an instance of the concept-goal, there is a one-step solution. Oth-

erwise the process is repeated by looking for an operator to be applied to the product, and so on, until the solution is obtained, i.e. the execution trace of a sequence of procedures transforms data (instances of concept-data) into a goal (instance of concept-goal). Artificial intelligence literature (Laurière 1986, Winston 1984) abounds in such control principles: breath first or depth first search, heuristic evaluation of the distance to the goal, etc.

A Generic Process for Building a Taxonomy

Creating a typology or a taxonomy is a particular modeling process (8.3) that consists in defining a way to classify instances of an abstract knowledge object (concept, procedure or principle), called the taxonomy's object. First, using a set of instances that is as diversified as possible, the object's critical attributes are identified. Then, using conditions involving these attributes, instances are regrouped into two classes or more that are disjoint two by two and cover all possible cases. A taxonomy can then be created by subdividing each first-level class the same way (this is the same as building a one-level taxonomy for knowledge that corresponds to each class). For instance, we can create a taxonomy of buildings by first defining the concepts of home, workplace and public place. Then we subdivide the home class by defining the concepts of family cottage, duplex or triplex in a row, detached duplex or triplex, multiple apartment buildings.

Figure 4 is a model of such a generic process.

The generic process shown on Figure 4 starts with two interrelated sub-processes: selection of independent attributes and selection of a large variety of examples to be classified.

For each retained attribute, a list of possible values is established. If the values are not yet defined, a typology must be built for the attribute by taking it as the object to which the process is applied again, until its values are satisfactorily defined. A table containing the retained attributes values for each example can then be built.

Then, we can sort the table in different ways to create groupings of examples, according to the attributes values, and verify that examples « deserve » to be put in the same grouping class. When the result seems satisfactory, groupings are defined and become first-level classes. If necessary, a second level can be created by subdividing each first-level class in the same manner.

The taxonomy remains to be validated by checking the definition principles: classes are disjoint two to two and cover all cases ; each class gathers similar examples, according to the typology goal (expected use).

A Generic Process for Evaluation

To evaluate one's or someone else's knowledge acquisition consists in diagnosing the under-

Figure 3. A deduction generic process

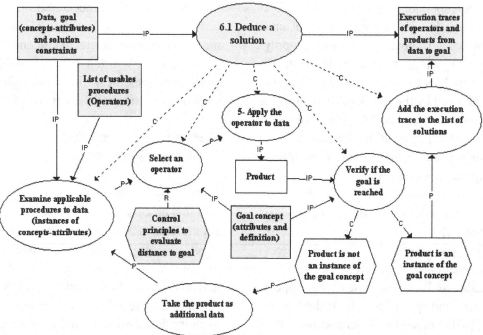

Figure 4. Generic process for building a taxonomy

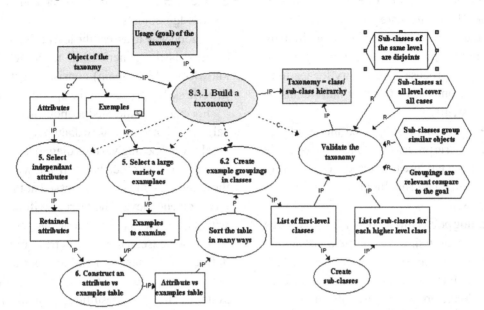

Figure 5. A generic process for evaluating knowledge acquisition

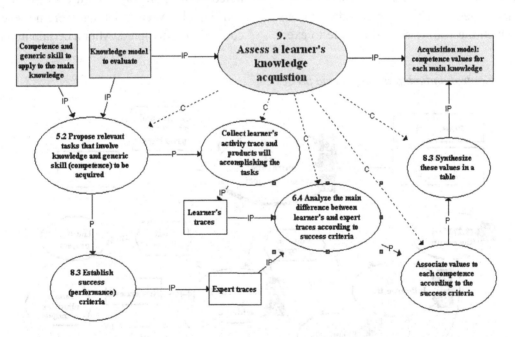

standing level of a person as regards knowledge objects in an application field. For example, one individual knows how to apply a procedure in simple situations, the other, in complex or strange situations. This generic skill is a form of diagnosis, except that the diagnosis result is not a list of objects in the application domain, which would be the defective components of the system being studied, but rather a list of values associated with knowledge. These values are generic concepts that represent the degree of knowledge acquisition by oneself, another person or a group of persons. So this generic process is necessary for learning assistance, to oneself or to other individuals or cognitive systems.

Figure 5 presents a simplified model of this evaluation generic process. It is one of the possible models that can capture the concept of « overlay model » used in several intelligent tutorial systems (Wenger 1987).

The starting point is the model of the knowledge object to be acquired, for example a taxonomy, a components system or a process. Each model possesses a main knowledge object around which other knowledge objects are articulated.

The expression « acquire knowledge » is too vague to be of any use here. We make it more precise by specifying the competence level to reach and a generic skill corresponding to this level, which the learner should be able to exert

on the main knowledge object and its related knowledge objects.

A good way to assess the learner's competence as regards the generic skill to be applied to a knowledge object (main), consists in instancing the generic skill's process in the application domain.

For example, knowledge about the car's electrical system is assessed at a « diagnose » competence level, by proposing various diagnosis tasks to the learner. On the other hand, if knowledge about the same system is to be assessed at the « design » competence level, the learner will be provided with a car's electric system design tasks.

In each case, a « correct » trace of the task is defined, an instance of the appropriate generic process, provided by an expert or built by the system. The trace resulting from the learner's activity is then collected and compared with the « correct » trace. Differences between the two are noted. If there are any, identification of the tasks and links between tasks that were not executed correctly is attempted. After a certain number of

Figure 6. Control and adaptation generic process

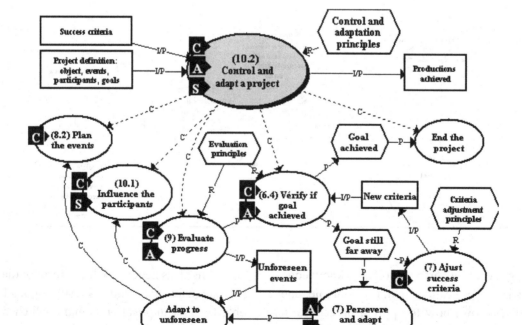

traces, competence values can be attributed to the learner relative to the main knowledge object, and to each component of the skill's generic process being applied to the knowledge object.

A Generic Process for Control and Self-Adaptation

The model on Figure 6 represents a control and self-adaptation generic process (10.2). The corresponding generic problem consists in obtaining the description of a project or change process in a particular domain, as well as success criteria specific to this domain. The generic process produces a model of the new situation created at the end of the generic process.

In the first phase, events are planned and participants are influenced so they coordinate themselves to carry through the project activities and meet the success criteria. Progress is continuously monitored and re-assessed. In the case of unexpected events, adaptation is required, course events are reordered, participant roles are redefined, and even success criteria may be modified.

Regularly, distance to the goal is evaluated according to the success criteria at a given moment. If the distance is too big, the goal is readjusted so that chances of success are increased. An alternative is to change the success criteria.

Planning and evaluation principles are necessary to guide particular tasks. The criteria's adaptation principles are used, for example, to « give some slack » when it becomes clear that success criteria will not be met, and to define, in spite of this, an acceptable success level. Control and adaptation principles monitor the transition between sub-processes, for example, by specifying when progress and success must be assessed or when criteria must be adjusted, or when the generic process should be terminated.

This generic process can be applied in domains as varied as research (cognitive domain), psychosomatic therapy (affective domain), organizational re-engineering (social domain) or sport training such as diving (psychomotor domain).

7.4 RELATIONS BETWEEN GENERIC SKILLS: SPECIALIZATION AND COMPOSITION

The models presented above show an ordering of generic skills form simple to complex. Higher-level generic skills (located in the lower part in Figure 1) usually involve the use of those that precede it. More specifically, the generic process describing a skill contains sub-processes of the generic skills that precede it in the list. Here are some examples:

- The locating/identifying skill of Level 2 involves the attention skill of Level 1 (Figure 2);
- The deduction skill of Level 6 involves the application skill of Level 5 (Figure 3);
- The taxonomy creation skill of Level 8 involves the application skill of Level 5 and the analysis skill of Level 6 (Figure 4);
- The assessment skill of Level 9 involves application, analysis, and synthesis skills (Figure 5);
- The control/adaptation skill of Level 10 involves application, repair, synthesis, and assessment skills of Level 9 (Figure 6).

Increasing Order of Complexity

These examples illustrate that there is an increasing order of complexity of generic skills, at least with regard to the first and second levels of the generic skills tree (Figure 1). In other words, we can refer to levels 1 to 10 as increasing levels of complexity. This assertion is not evident and was sometimes disputed in the case of taxonomies presented in Section 1. For example, the authors of the KADS method have preferred to put emphasis on the organization of sequences of generic tasks than of a hierarchical order among them.

On the other hand, Bloom has insisted on the hierarchical organization between educational outcomes: "Our attempt to order the educational behavior from simple the complex is based on the idea that a given simple behavior can become integrated with another simple behavior to form a more complex behavior. Consequently, our classification can be perceived as that behavior of type A forms a class, behavior of type AB another class and behavior of type ABC still another class" (p.18). One finds a similar preoccupation in the elaboration of the taxonomy of the affective domain. "This organization of constituents seems to describe a process according to which certain phenomenon or value progress from one level of simple awareness to a level where it drives or controls the behavior of a person (Krathwoll et al., op.cit. p.27)."

Experimental studies have tried to verify this hypothesis. Tests have been given to a large number of students containing questions connected to various complexity levels in both taxonomies. With this experimental setting, one should notice a bigger percentage of failure for questions related to the higher taxonomy levels.

As far as the taxonomy of the cognitive domain, according to Martin and Briggs (1986), some studies support to a certain extent the hypothesis of the increasing complexity of levels. The evidence is stronger in the first levels than in the more advanced levels. One finds the same kind of conclusions in the case of the taxonomy of the emotional domain, even though there are fewer studies to support this.

We suspect that the limited evidence coming from certain studies is due to the absence of a meta-knowledge representation scheme for generic skills. For example, certain studies note similar results for analysis on one hand, and for evaluation and the synthesis on the other hand.

Figure 7. Structure of the library of generic skills (specialization and composition relations)

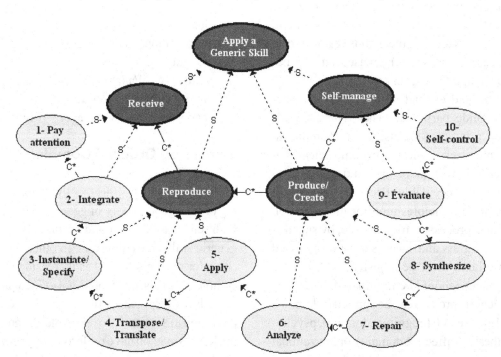

But if one distinguishes synthesis from analysis by the ascent in abstraction, and if one distinguishes evaluation both from synthesis and analysis by the use of meta-values that are properties of knowledge, it is likely that one can maintain the hypothesis of an increasing order of complexity for Bloom's taxonomy as well as for the second layer of our taxonomy.

Here is a clear definition of a generic skill's complexity: *A generic skill A is more complex than a generic skill B if the generic process representing B appears as a sub-process in the model of the generic process A.*

Furthermore, as we descend to higher levels of specialization, the assumptions regarding ordering of generic skills become less likely. For example, it is difficult to say that the generic skills "induce," "plan," and "model/construct" are in order of increasing complexity. Our assumption is thus limited to the four generic skills of the first level and the ten generic skills of the second level.

The graph in Figure 7 demonstrates this notion of an increasing order of complexity through C links, signifying that a higher-level process can contain one or more lower level processes.

Specialization of Generic Skills

We can add further levels of specialization to the library of generic skills beyond the third level in Figure 1 as in the following examples.

Here are four reproduction generic skills. The first two involve forms of instantiating/clarifying; the third involves two specialized simulation skills:

- *Validating a relational principle* begins by first generating a set of instances of the conditions obtained when giving values to its attributes, covering all cases if possible, and then verifying in each case if the condition is true. For example, the following statement can be validated: « If an animal breast feeds its babies and has claws, it is a carnivore mammal » by establishing a set of instances that satisfy the condition (tiger, dog, raccoon) and by verifying that in each case, the conclusion is true.

- *Delimiting a concept* consists in generating a set of *examples*, each resulting from specifying the values of concept's attributes that respect the regulating principles. At the same time, *counter-examples* are generated giving values to the attributes that do not respect the principles. *Near-examples* are particularly useful to delimit a concept, since they result from the specification of the values of a concept's attributes, respecting the regulating principles, except for a small number of cases. For example: robin, sparrow, chaffinch are examples of birds ; « bat » is a near-example of the bird concept, while « dolphin » is a near-example of the mammal concept.

- *Simulating a process* first consists in generating a set of cases, each one gathering an example obtained by instancing each input concept to the process; then, procedures are executed by using values for each case, and action principles are instanced little by little. Execution traces are generated that constitute the simulation product.

- *Simulating a conceptual system* consists in instancing some of the concept's attributes by respecting regulating constraints, in order to examine the values taken by other attributes; for example, the simulation of an electrical system consists in setting up some attributes such as current intensity (I) or resistance (R), and noting the values taken by other attributes such as voltage (V) take based on V=RI (Ohm's law).

Here are two production/creation generic skills involving specialized forms of analysis:

- *Retro-deduce a solution* is a similar approach to deduction, but applied in a reverse way, starting with an instance of the goal-concept (the goal), finding procedures (operators) that can generate it and facts to which a procedure can be applied. This process is repeated backwards, until a set of facts, instances of the initial data-concept is obtained.

- **Monitoring** consists in using a given process, instanciated to get a trace corresponding to a real situation, then classifying this trace according to pre-established categories associated with the corrections to be brought. For example, supervising a nuclear complex consists in collecting values that represent the trace of the process and to determine if the process is safe or on the contrary, if it requires the adjustment of some of the system's parameters.

Here are three production/creation generic skills involving a form of synthesis, in particular, induction:

- **Inducing a concept** consists in examining a set of similar facts and defining an initial concept whose instances contain these facts as examples. Concept definition refines itself when counter-examples or new examples are used, or facts that do not correspond to the current definition of the concept, which can lead to its modification, through specialization, notably by adding conditions to the definition. Near-examples are counter-examples, but they contradict only one aspect of the concept's current definition. One must then wonder if the definition of the concept should be extended to include the near-example as an example, or if it should be restricted to exclude it. Adding new examples of the concept being defined can also lead to generalize the concept in order to « cover » new cases.

- **Inducing a procedure** is a similar generic process that consists in creating an initial procedure that produces expected results from some input data. Then, taking into account new data, to generalize the procedure so it can be applied to many more situations.

- **Inducing a principle or a law** consists in creating a relational principle that sets a relation (explain, summarize) between one or several concepts attributes. The results of the principle being instanced should be true statements, whatever the values of attributes.

Finally, here are four variations of the evaluation generic skill:

- *Prioritizing* consists in taking one or several knowledge objects, or even one or several models, and assigning a value to them as regards their usefulness in some situation: type of users, organization's needs, etc.

- *Validating* consists in assessing the reliability of knowledge, to attribute it a truth probability: does the procedure produce what it should? Does the concept describe what it should? Can the principle be instanciate by true statements, if not, in what cases?

- *Comparing-deciding* consists in comparing two knowledge objects or two models according to criteria of usefulness, reliability, relevance, and keeping the one that seems the most adequate, according to these criteria.

- *Standardizing* consists in modifying a model, according to the results of an evaluation based on criteria such as simplicity, relevance, communicability, and making it conform to these criteria.

We can thus develop the generic skills library through increasingly specialized generic processes to account, for example, for the types of models to which it applies; for example, we can classify, construct, or evaluate conceptual systems, procedures, theories, processes, or methods. We can also obtain variations of basic processes for different domains of knowledge. A diagnosis in auto mechanics is not performed the same way as in medicine. As well, we can obtain variations of processes according to whether they produce or use results in the cognitive, psycho-motor, affective or social domains. Finally, we can obtain variations of processes according to a desired goal, for example, diagnosing some or all faulty components.

Here is an example of increasingly specialized generic skills connected specialization links.

- Produce/Create
  ◦ Synthesize
  ◦ Induce
  ◦ Induce a taxonomy
  ◦ Induce a taxonomy with multiple parents
  ◦ Induce a taxonomy with multiple parents in the animal reign

At the end of a specialization chain, the generic skill may involve only one application domain. In this case, there is no advantage in representing it as a generic skill and one would simply integrate the process as part of the domain knowledge.

Figure 8. Example of a competency profile

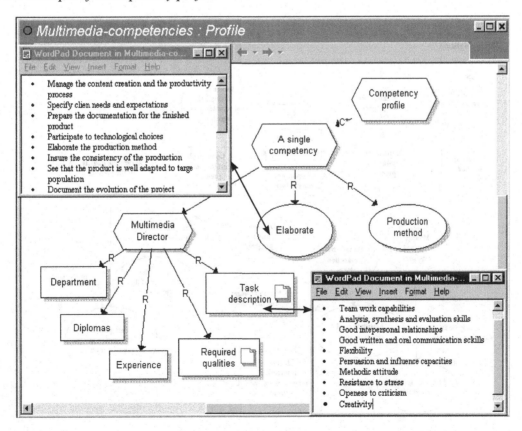

7.5 GIVING AN OPERATIONAL MEANING TO COMPETENCY PROFILES

We will now present a first application of the taxonomy of generic skills presented above. As we have seen in chapter 5, most competency profiles are expressed as more or less precise natural language statements. Their interpretation is often ambiguous because they lack a precise structural definition.

We present here a process to analyze a group of existing of competency statements or to build them in a standard way. This process contains following sub-processes:

- determine one or several target actors for which the competency is defined;

- identify the tasks of these actors, as well as the corresponding knowledge and represent them in a knowledge model;
- identify the skills required by the actors that will be applied to the knowledge.

Identify Target Actors for the Profile

To illustrate this process, we will use as a case study the competency profile of a multimedia director that has been presented in chapter 5. This profile results from a general analysis of the domain of multimedia trades having lead to fourteen actor definitions and their corresponding competency profile. The profile for the multimedia director (see Table 3 in Chapter 5) groups a variety of tasks and competencies that we aim to re-interpret using the same structure presented at the end in

Figure 9. A task and knowledge model for the multimedia director

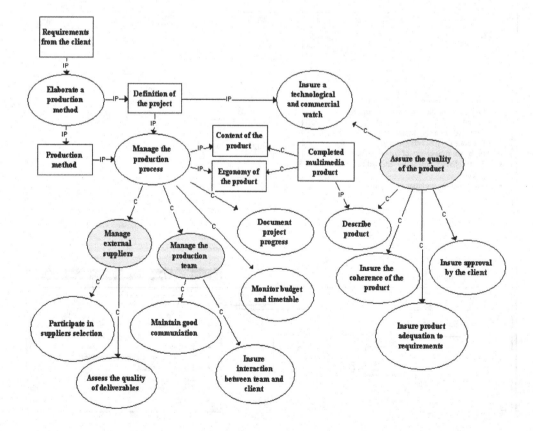

Chapter 5: name of the actor, main generic skill and knowledge to which this skill must be applied.

Figure 8 shows part of a competency model we have built in MOT+ from the profile description in chapter 5. Here the statement would read "A multimedia director must be able to elaborate a production method for a multimedia project". There are of course other competency statements like this in the model. Furthermore, the model is linked to a description of qualities required for the job and a task description that will help identify sub-skills for this job profile.

The task description on Figure 8 is the most important to interpret an existing competency profile or build a new one. The task components are not competency statements but procedural descriptions that help identify the knowledge and the generic skills required from the target actor of the profile. For example: « Document the evolution of the project » contains no generic skills. It rather describes a role, a procedural knowledge the actor will have to apply to some unspecified degree.

Modeling the Target Actor's Tasks and Knowledge

A knowledge model for this domain is essentially procedural based on the tasks definition, but it can be completed by concepts and principles required to achieve the tasks. In this model, three main processes must be governed by the multimedia director: the elaboration of the method of production, the management of the creation / production process and the quality control of the product. Figure 9 presents a partial knowledge model corresponding to the task definition Figure 8. The knowledge elements in this model will provide an anchor to associate the generic skills and competencies required by the actor.

Identify Generic Skills

We can now start to identify the main generic skills that need to be associated to this knowledge model, taking in account the qualities required

Figure 10. An example of a knowledge sub-model and associated generic skills

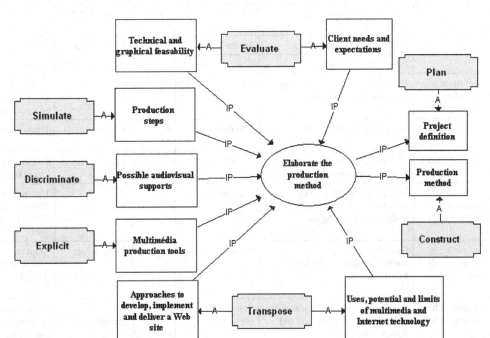

from the multimedia director on Figure 9. This analysis reveals that:

a) *The elaboration of the multimedia production method* requires mainly productive cognitive skills, that is: « analysis, synthesis and evaluation skills » and « creativity».

b) *The management of the production process* requires self-management cognitive skills, as well as affective skills such as « resistance to stress » and « flexibility », and mostly social skills such as « leadership, good teamwork capabilities, interpersonal capabilities, persuasion and influence capacities, openness to criticism».

c) *The quality assurance of the product mainly* requires cognitive skills such as « methodic attitude ».

Now that we know the type of generic skills, cognitive in (a) and (c); cognitive, affective and social in (b), together with their level in the generic skills taxonomy presented in this chapter: creation/production in (a), self-management in (b) and (c), it remains to be more specific on the type of these skills.

To achieve that, we can develop further the knowledge model on Figure 9 to provide more concepts, procedures and principles to which skills can be associates. Figure 10 is one of the sub-models. The central task of this sub-model is to elaborate a method of production and a definition of the project from expectations and requirements of the client. Besides this knowledge, the task requires from the multimedia director the use of knowledge on the technical and graphic feasibility of the project, on the production steps of a multimedia project, on the possible audio-visual supports, on the tools for multimedia creation on PC, MAC AND UNIX, on various approaches to develop, implement and deliver a Web site and

Table 7. Standard interpretation of competency statements from a meta-knowledge point of view

Competency statement		Interpretation			
Initial formulation	**Reformulation**	**Generic skill**	**Type**	**Parent skill**	**Knowledge component**
None	Model a production method	Model	C	8- Synthesize	Production method
None	Plan a project definition	Plan	C	8- Synthesize	Project definition
Capacity to evaluate the technical and graphical feasibility of a project	Evaluate the technical and graphical feasibility of a project	Evaluate	C	9- Evaluate	Technical and graphical feasibility of a project
Knowledge of each production step	Simulate a production process	Simulate	C	5- Apply	Production steps
Knowledge of audio-visual support	Discriminate between properties of audio-visual support	Discriminate	C	3- Instantiate	Properties of audio-visual support
Knowledge of the use, potential and limits of Internet and multimedia technologies	Transpose in the project the use, potential and limits of Internet and multimedia technologies	Transpose	C	4- Transpose	Use, potential and limits of Internet and MM technologies
Superficial knowledge of multimedia creation tools (PC/Mac/Unix)	Explicit the main properties of multimedia creation tools (PC/Mac/Unix)	Explicit	C	3- Instantiate	Main properties of multimedia creation tools (PC/Mac/Unix)
Knowledge on approaches to develop, implement and deliver a web site	Transpose to the project a useful way to develop, implement and deliver a web site	Transpose in a useful way	C	4- Transpose	Approaches to develop, implement and deliver a web site

finally, on the use, potential and limits of the Internet and multimedia technologies.

To each knowledge element, we can associate a skill selected from our taxonomy. For example, for the production method, a suited generic skill is " to construct", for the definition of the project, "to plan ", and so on. For the possible audiovisual supports and the production tools, the multimedia director is not the one who will use them, so he needs a low level of mastery such as "discriminate" or "explicit". In other cases, he must possess a higher level of competency such as "simulate the production steps" or "evaluate the technical and graphical feasibility of the project".

Interpretation Examples

Table 7 presents the overall result of this competency analysis process. It shows the initial competency statement we started from, the reformulation that results from our analysis and the decomposition of each statement in a standard interpretation given by the definition and the meta-models in the generic skills taxonomy. Also, the process has revealed missing or ill-defined competency statements.

CONCLUSION

We have developed, in this chapter, an integrated taxonomy of generic skills. The taxonomy has the following characteristics.

- It allows one to represent generic skills as processes; such processes are generic in relation to the application domains associated with them; they are also generic in relation to generic skill types, whether cognitive, affective, social, or psycho-motor.
- Generic skills can be represented by process MOT models, i.e. models containing a procedure (with its inputs, products, and execution principles) and its sub-proce-

dures (with their own inputs, products, and execution principles).

- Processes representing generic skills can be associated, by co-referencing, with specific application domains in which the cognitive, affective, social, or psycho-motor skill types are indicated by the letters C, A, S, or P depending on whether they refer respectively to rational constructions, affective attitudes, social attitudes, or perceptions of movement.
- Generic skills are structured in relation to each other in a hierarchy from general to specific (through S links) until a final level is reached that is no longer a skill but a process specific to an application domain such as "diagnose a malfunctioning digestive system in a patient."
- The first two levels of the hierarchy in Figure 1 contain generic skills in an increasing order of complexity. For example, the general ability of self-management contains (involves) sub-processes of creation, which in turn contain sub-processes of reproduction, which in turn contain more basic sub-processes of reception. Such ordering is not necessarily valid for the other levels of the hierarchy.

In light of our definition of competency at the end of Chapter 5, we are now able to represent a competency in detail by specifying an application domain (through a MOT model), the generic skill that applies to knowledge in the application domain (through a MOT co-domain), and the actors and target populations that regulate the generic skill (through principles that are defined, as required, by another MOT co-domain). By combining target populations, generic skills, and one or more knowledge objects, we are able to arrive at a clear, constructivist concept of competency.

The next chapter will explore applications of this approach to various instructional engineering tasks such as modeling knowledge, developing task scenarios, selecting resources for actors in a scenario, or modeling actors in order to personalize learning or work environments.

REFERENCES

Bloom, B. S. (1975). *Taxonomy of Educational Objectives: the Classification of Educational Goals*. New York: D. McKay.

Gardner, H. (1993). *Multiple Intelligences: The Theory in Practice*. New York: Basic Books.

Goleman, D. (1997). *L'intelligence émotionnelle*. (Robert Laffont, Trans.).

Krathwohl, D. R., Bloom, B. S., & Masia, B. B. (1964). *Taxonomy of educational objectives: The classification of educational goals. Handbook II: Affective domain*. New York: Longman.

Laurière, J. L. (1986). *Intelligence Artificielle, résolution de problèmes par l'Homme et la machine*. Paris: Eyrolles.

Martin, B. L., & Briggs, L. (1986). *The Affective and Cognitive Domains: Integration for Instruction and Research*. Educational Technology Publications.

Wenger, E. (1987). *Artificial Intelligence and Tutoring Systems - Computational and Cognitive Approaches to the Communication of Knowledge*. San Francisco: Morgan-Kaufmann.

Winston, P. (1984). *Artificial Intelligence* (4th ed.). New York: McGraw-Hill.

ENDNOTE

[1] The numerals before a skill's name are chosen according to Figure 1. For example "pay-attention is numbered 1 and "synthesis is numbered 7.

Chapter 8
Modeling Multi–Actor Activity Scenarios

Gilbert Paquette
LICEF Research Center, Canada

Olga Marino
LICEF Research Center, Canada

ABSTRACT

- Instructional Engineering and Learning Scenarios
  - The MISA Method
  - Process-based delivery scenarios
  - Process-based learning scenarios
- Multi-actor Processes and Workflows
  - Workflow models
  - The Business Process Modeling Notation (BPMN)
  - Basic Elements
  - Control workflow patterns
  - Patterns for personalization
  - Learnflows vs. workflows
- The MOT+LD and the TELOS Scenario Editors
- A Scenario Modeling Process

In this chapter, we concentrate on a very interesting type of model: multi-actor processes. These processes can be found in all domains of human activity, particularly to describe work processes in organizations or learning scenarios. In both cases, we will use the term "activity scenario". These models are characterized by a sequencing of activities, accomplished by one or more actors who use and produce a variety of resources.

We will first present an instructional engineering method, MISA, which enables designers to produce learning or training scenarios. Then we generalize the notion of activity scenario by

DOI: 10.4018/978-1-61520-839-5.ch008

considering work processes, making a distinction between product-oriented and actor-oriented processes. After that, we present activity scenario modeling tools and a first synthesis of the scenario modeling process that can be applied both to learning and work processes. Through this, we discover that competency modeling in a central element of all these processes.

8.1 INSTRUCTIONAL ENGINEERING AND LEARNING SCENARIOS[1]

Instructional Engineering can be defined as "A method that supports the analysis, the design and the delivery planning of a learning system, integrating concepts, processes and principles of instructional design, software engineering and knowledge engineering" (Paquette 2004, p. 56).

Located at the crossroads of these disciplines, from which it inherits most of its properties, Instructional Engineering is a particular systemic method in the field of educational problem solving. It is founded on the System Sciences (Le Moigne 1995; Simon 1973) where a system is defined as a series of units in dynamic interaction, organized in order to achieve specific goals.

The origin of *instructional design* goes back to John Dewey (1900), who, a century ago, advocated the development of an "interlinked science" between learning theories and educational practice. In American literature, this discipline is known as "Instructional Design (ID)", "Instructional System Design (ISD)" or "Instructional Science" (Reigeluth, 1983; Merrill, 1994). In Europe, one of the pioneers of the field used the term "Scientific Pedagogy" (Montessori, 1958).

Since the fifties, the evolution of this new discipline has been carried by influential researchers such as B.F. Skinner (1959), Jerome Bruner (1966) and David Ausubel (1968). In the seventies and eighties, *instructional theories* have blossomed through the work of researchers such as Gagné (1970), Scandura (1973), Merrill (1983), Landa

(1976), Reigeluth and Rogers (1980), Collins and Stevens (1983), to name a few. These instructional design models and theories have been built on solid foundations and present an impressive body of work. However, today it seems necessary to renew the instructional design methods and tools to support the creation of distributed learning systems (DLS) that are heavily dependent on information and communication technologies.

The MISA Method

There is a large set of interrelated decisions involved when we build technology-based learning systems. These are decisions such as the following. What kind of learning delivery model shall we use or what mixture of these models? What kind of learning scenarios do we need for this course? Should it be predefined, offer multiple learning paths or be learner-constructed? Which actors will interact at delivery time, what are their roles, what resources do they need? What kind of interactivity or collaboration should be included? What are the materials that can be reused and are there new ones to build? What kind of standards will be used? How do we take in account the technological diversity between groups of users within the target population?

To cope with all these decisions and others, we have built an instructional engineering method called MISA over a number of years. This method is the result both of research in the field of instructional engineering, but also of the practical experience acquired through the development of many elearning courses or workplace training. This effort started in 1992 and has led to the MISA 4.0 version (Paquette 2001, 2002) and to a Web-based support tool, called ADISA (Paquette et al 2001). The knowledge editor MOT+ is a key element in the method and is embedded in the ADISA system and accessible through a web browser from any workstation linked to the Internet.

A knowledge modeling approach has been used to define the Instructional Engineering method,

Figure 1. The main MISA process and its 6 phases

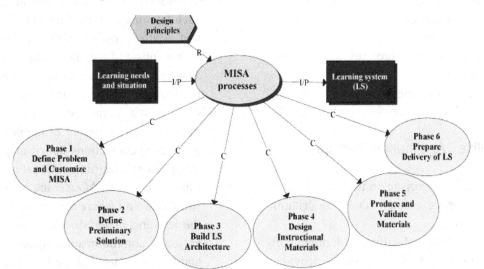

its concepts, its processes and principles. Thus, the method is the result of a knowledge modeling effort in the particular domain of instructional engineering. The way MISA has been built will be discussed further in chapter 21 of this book.

MISA helps develop a learning system (LS) through 6 phases shown on Figure 1: (1) identifying the educational problem, its context and constraints as well as some general orientations; (2) defining preliminary solution; (3) building the LS architecture including the elaboration of the knowledge and competency model as well as the instructional model; (4) designing learning materials, resources or learning objects; (5) modeling, producing and validating these learning materials and (6) specifying the LS delivery model(s) as well as maintenance and quality management processes.

The whole process is guided by a set of design principles that aim at building high quality distance learning systems.

Self-Management and Meta-Cognition Principles

- Explicit association of a target competency (skills+knowledge) to activities guides

the selection of activities for a learning module.
- Provide arious learning paths and personalization options that are self-managed by learners.
- Promote self-management by introducing support tools like progress reports.
- Integrate dxplicit meta-cognitive activities, such as individual and group formative task evaluation.

Information Processing Principles

- Include rich and diversified static and dynamic information resources, clearly related to activities.
- Provide access to search, annotation, and modeling tools to manipulate resources as well as production tools adapted to each task.

Collaboration Principles

- Sustain together collaborative and individual activities.

- Adapt the modalities of collaboration to the generic process in which the collaboration is proposed.
- Allow for both synchronous and asynchronous interactions.
- Provide management tools for coordinating collaborative activities within the LS.

Personalized Assistance Principles

- Encourage heuristic and methodological guidance rather than algorithmic assistance.
- Include multiple facilitators, human, software, check lists, job aids, etc. to provide a flexible learning environment.
- Provide assistance mainly on the learner's initiative.

In each of the phases 2 to 6, MISA also proposes the development along four axes: knowledge, instructional, learning materials and delivery model. Knowledge modeling is the backbone of the method, in each of these four axes.

- The *Knowledge Model* centers on a graphical representation of the content in an application domain. In this model, the domain's facts, concepts, procedures and principles are displayed and interrelated with precise links. Then target and prerequisite competencies are associated to units of knowledge, thus identifying prerequisites and learning objectives for the Instructional Model. Subsequently, knowledge units and competencies are attributed to learning units, instruments or resources used in the learning units.
- The *Instructional Model* is essentially a network of learning events and units, to which knowledge and target competencies are associated. A learning scenario specifying learning and support activities linked

to resources in the environment describes each learning unit. Resources holding content (called instruments) are associated with a subset of the knowledge model.

- The *Learning Material Models* are useful to describe materials (learning objects), their media components, source documents and presentation principles as well as other specifications aimed at graphical designers and learning material producers.
- Finally, *Delivery Models* are produced to show how and where actors use or provide the learning materials and resources such as tools, communication means, services and locations, used in the learning system. Each Delivery Model is a multi-user workflow, where actors use or produce resources, while assuming different roles. These processes correspond to organizational issues, such as group organization, staff assignments, technical help, resource delivery, and so on, which must be prepared to ensure smooth network-based or distance learning deployment.

Process-Based Delivery Scenarios

The multi-actor scenario modeling approach in MISA is applied mainly through the design of the learning scenarios and while building the delivery models.

Figure 2 shows such a delivery model focused on the roles of the trainers, here labeled as tutors. A certain number of graphical conventions help interpret the above graph, both for the human eye and for a computerized support system. The hexagonal figures represent the actors and the oval figures represent the activities or tasks achieved by these actors. An R link from an actor's symbol shows what activities this actor is responsible of. A C link outgoing from an activity indicates sub-activities or components of a more general activity. Finally, the rectangles represent resources, both input resources that help achieve

Figure 2. A delivery model involving a tutor and a learner

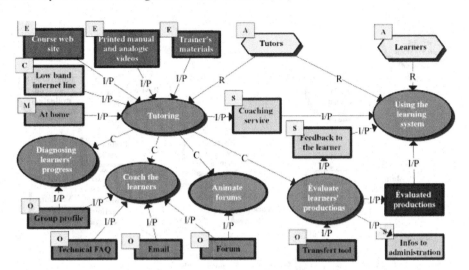

an activity (incoming I/P links to the activity), and productions resulting from the execution of the activities (outgoing I/P links from the activities). Resources can be sets of learning materials (E), tools (O), communications links (C), services (S) or delivery locations (M).

Translating this graph into natural language, we can see that the tutor in involved in tutoring roles and also, together with the learners, is involved in "using the learning system". The tutor has four major roles in this learning system. He diagnoses the learners' progress. He acts as a pedagogical coach to the learners. He animates forums. Finally, he evaluates the learners' productions in the course and giving two services: feedback to the learner and information to the administration.

The tutor has access to the following support materials: the course web site, a printed manual and VHS videos and some trainer's material. He communicates through a low band Internet line and works at home. To support these activities, besides using the materials and the communication links, the trainer will have access to tools: a group profile to assess continuously the progress of the learners; a tool to maintain a frequently asked questions (FAQ) file; email and forum software to animate and support his group of learners; and

finally, a file transfer tool to obtain the learners' productions and send information both to the learners and to the training manager. These tools, materials, communication links and services will form the basis for the trainer's environment in a delivery system.

Process-Based Learning Scenarios

Process-based scenarios are the central products of instructional engineering. They embody the pedagogical strategy and tactics while setting clear relationships between learners and facilitators, together with resources provided in a learning environment.

The competency-based approach we propose for building a learning scenario is based on the fact that specific knowledge in a subject matter and meta-cognitive skills are being constructed at the same time. *A learning scenario for a module should be described, whenever possible, as a generic process, corresponding to a skill.* This skill is to be associated to the knowledge model describing the content to be learned in a module or a learning unit.

In other words, if we want to develop knowledge in a subject matter together with skills like

Figure 3. The basic information processing process

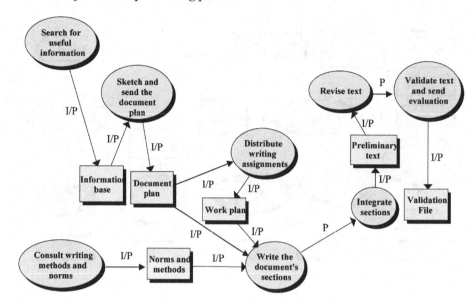

Figure 4. Adding information and production resources to process

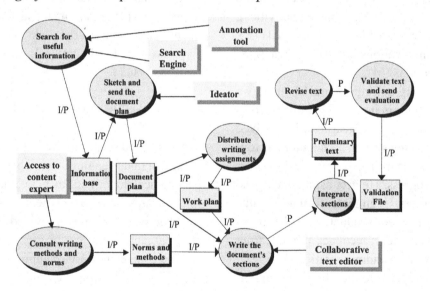

classification, diagnosis, induction or modeling, we should propose classification, diagnosis, induction and modeling problems or projects to the learner, to be applied to information in that subject matter. Then the collaborative activities as well as the information, production and assistance resources will be chosen accordingly. For example, in a classification task, sorting tools in a spreadsheet and collaborative classification activities could be embedded in the scenario, together with assistance taking the form of methodological advice to support the classification process.

Figures 3, 4, 5, and 6 present how we can build a scenario based on a generic synthesis task. This scenario can be used in many subjects, in different application domain.

Figure 5. Adding collaboration rules to the process

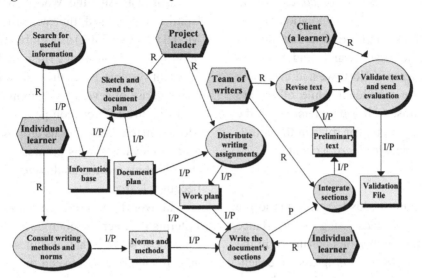

Figure 6. Adding assistance agents to the process

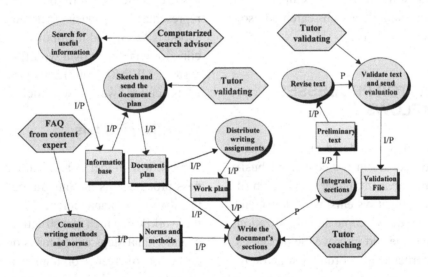

- *Basic flow of activities.* Figure 3 presents the generic process corresponding to one of the synthesis generic skills. It is represented as a MOT model with oval representing learning activities and rectangles representing information sources consulted or produced by learners in an activity, and they are sometimes reused in other activities.

- *Adding tools resources.* Figure 4 shows a certain number of tools for the consultation or the production of information, to be used in some activities. If the Explor@ delivery system is used, the suggestion to use these tools will be made in the web site, but the access to the tools themselves will be achieved through the Explor@ environment.

- *Identifying actor's role for collaboration.* Figure 5 shows how collaboration can be added to the scenario. Before that, the activities could have been intended for an individual learner. Now, we add that some activities are individual while others are done in teams, with some members of the team playing particular roles in the activities, as a project leader or a client.

- Finally, Figure 6 adds to this scenario the intervention of facilitating or assistance actors. Some are persons on-line or in the classroom, validating progress or coaching, others are persons mediated through a "frequently-asked questions" (FAQ) web page, and still others are computerized agents, for example a web-search advisor to help in the first task.

8.2 MULTI-ACTOR PROCESSES AND WORKFLOWS

Workflows have been modeled and tooled for more than two decades in the context of business process management, under the domain of workflow management systems. Workflow management systems allow people and organization to automate, manage and improve the processes that govern interpersonal coordination and collaboration. Processes are the series of day-to-day activities in which people participate and may involve such diverse tasks as planning a project, submitting a travel receipt for reimbursement, getting approval for a proposal, circulating a memo for feedback, tracking customers, or writing software (Bolcer & Taylor, 1998). Workflow management systems help automate the process tasks, get the right information to the right place for a specific job function, integrate information in the enterprise and coordinate the different activities (Hollingsworth, 1995).

In the late 80s, the Workflow Management Coalition proposed the Workflow Reference Model (WfRM, 2002) as a global framework for describing and conceiving Business Process Management systems. Since then, the community has seen the rise of several overlapping standards to deal with the different components of the model. More than ten years after its proposal, the WfRM is still relevant, as was pointed out by Hollingsworth (ibid) and the landscape of standards has become clearer.

The workflow reference model is described in terms of a central component, the workflow enactment service that executes the workflow, and five interfaces between this engine and the other components of the system. Interface 1 gives the enactment engine the definition of a process it has to execute. The definition of a process is "the representation of a business process in a form that supports automated manipulation, such as modeling, or enactment by a workflow management system" (WfMC, 2002) This process definition is also called "workflow model".

Workflow Models

A workflow model is an abstraction of a business process; it is the integrating component of the workflow management system. It includes: the workflow which is a structured organization of individual steps called tasks or activities; the definition of agents or human actors that can execute a particular task; the roles or actor types and the dependencies or transitions which describe the activities execution order and conditions and finally the resources and the external applications that are available to the actor of an activity (Eder & Gruber, 2002; Lei & Singh, 1997).

Very often the terms workflow, workflow instance, workflow model and workflow metamodel are used indistinctively. In the context of an organization, process model and organization model are added to the list of terms used. Lei & Singh (1997) propose an interesting distinction between those terms: the process model is an abstraction of a business process that emphasizes the coordination and interdependence of tasks, the graph of tasks or activities. On the other hand, the organization model is the abstraction of the organization human resources grouping and functions; it establishes actors (human or machine individuals), roles (abstraction of one or more actors, usually in terms of functionality) and their relations. By combining the organization model with the process model, one gets the workflow model; a workflow model is thus a particular process in a particular organization. In terms of the model itself, that means that the activity graph is enriched with information on the roles and actors that should or could perform the activities of the abstracted process. Finally, such a workflow model can be instantiated in a particular time in a particular organizational context. The instantiation fixes all abstract parameters such as exactly who (which actor in the company) will fulfill a particular role of the workflow and with which resources a task will be executed. A workflow model will normally be instantiated several times in different workflow instances. It is the workflow instance that is actually executed with the support of a workflow management system.

The Business Process Modeling Notation (BPMN)

"Much research attention has concentrated on techniques for workflow management, and not enough on techniques for workflow modeling". (Lei & Singh, 1997). Workflow meta-models, workflow description languages and process description languages are terms to designate representational languages in which to express workflow models. As representation languages, workflow meta-models establish assumptions on workflow elements as well as on their relations and relative importance in the workflow design.

Although no workflow representation language is yet widely accepted, various standards are be-

ing proposed. The most widely accepted, BPEL (Business Process Execution Language), XPDL (XML Process Definition Language), WfXML and BPMN (Business Process Modeling Notation) are often compared in terms of their control flow capabilities, that is whether they have native structures to represent 21 well known control pattern such as sequence, parallel split, synchronization, etc. (Aalst et al 2002). It is out of the scope of this book to describe one or more workflow representation languages in detail, but, to give the reader an idea of those high level languages, we will present the basic elements that should be offered by a workflow meta-model and we will exemplify several control patterns in terms of these elements. We will use the BPMN (Business Process Modeling Notation) graphical notation to present the graphical view of each element and each pattern.

Control Workflow Patterns

In this section, we describe basic control patterns, some more advanced branching and synchronization patterns, structural patterns or patterns that affect as a whole the control flow, patterns that deal with multiple instances, patterns based on the workflow being in a particular state or state patterns and finally some patterns that allow for the adaptation of the control flow to particular conditions or events, the personalization patterns. Each pattern is explained by means of the following items: Pattern name, description, diagram and a learning example inspired by the IMS-LD (2003) specification.

Patterns for Personalization

Personalization requirements express changes in the process necessary to adapt an instance to a particular user. In order to adapt the process two elements are used: evaluation gateways and event gateways. Evaluation gateways evaluate conditions to select a branch or a group of branches

Figure 7. Basic BPMN symbols (basic elements)

Elements	Symbol	Description
Participant		An action performer
Group		A group of participants
Role		Defines an expected behavior of an actor (s) during the process definition. This element has two associated attributes: Min participant: Defines the minimum number of participants that can belong to this role Max participant: Defines the maximum number of participants that can belong to this role
Activity		A process activity
Multi-Activity		A process activity instantiated multiple times in execution
Product		A product produced by an activity
Tool		A tool used in an activity
Control link		Simple link between two activities. It establishes precedence in time during execution. The target activity will be launched when the source ends.
Product Dependency Link		A link between two activities. The source activity sends a product to the destination activity. The target activity is started when the product is produced (data flow).
Swim lanes		Swim lanes represent the performer of an activity or groups of activities. It is worth noticing that both a role and a participant/group may be related to a swimlane in the design phase. Also, a participant may be an application
Activity Application Support		An activity supported by one or more tools or applications

in a split point. Event gateways determine the selection of a branch depending on the occurrence of an event.

Learnflows vs. Workflows

For each control pattern in Figures 9 through 15, we have shown that the control flow patterns proposed by the business process engineering community help describe interesting learning patterns. In fact, both domains have much in common. Systems like COW (Vantroy & Peter, 2004) propose the adaptation of a workflow management system to model and execute learning processes. The movement on Educational Modeling Languages (EML) that has led to the IMS-LD specification

has made the learning community reflect on activity structures richer than the simple linear sequences proposed earlier by most commercial e-learning platforms. But how close are learning and workflow processes?

Both e-learning languages and workflow languages tend to solve the same general problem of having actors executing activities and producing something. Therefore, the three main components of such a system in both cases are actor, activity, and product. Moreover, complex processes in both domains require the participation of multiple actors as well ways to coordinate their activities and products, thus both deal with multi-actor activity graphs. Nevertheless, there is one main difference. While business processes are *product centered-*

Figure 8. Basic BPMN symbols (basic elements)

Elements	Symbol	Description
MultiActivity Application Support		A group of activities supported by one or more tools or applications. Does that means one instance of the application is launched per activity instance? Or there is single instance of the application shared by all the activities?
Time Events	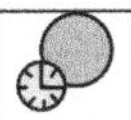	An activity can accept notifications of time limits occurred
Complitition Events	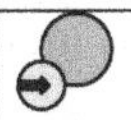	An activity can accept notifications of competition of others activities
Change Value Events	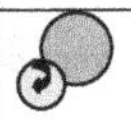	An activity can accept notifications of properties value changes
Condition - XOR	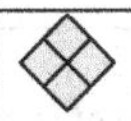	A condition evaluates an expression to determine which action execute. In this case only one action could be executed
Condition – OR		A condition evaluates an expression to determine which action execute. In this case several actions could be executed
Condition – Event		A condition evaluates an expression to determine which action execute. In this case the action executed is the result of the generation of an event
Condition Complex		A condition evaluates an expression to determine which action execute. In this case the action executed is the result of the generation of complex evaluation.
Condition Parallel		A condition evaluates an expression to determine which action execute. In this case all the actions are executed in parallel.
Event		Any kind of event - Start Event
Event - Time		An event triggered as a result of a timeout condition
Event - Notification		A notification event send or received by the platform

processes, learning process are *actor (learner) centered processes*. Let's explore what that means.

In the business process context, what matters most is the product, the final outcome of the process. Main aspects of a workflow system are the product and the efficiency of the process regarding its production. Actors are secondary components; they are seen as resources which importance lies in helping produce the final product. Particular requirements in this context include finding an assignment function from people to roles, decomposing the process in an efficient way, optimizing the quality of actor's production. There are also particular requirements concerning the product: version management, satisfaction of a set of required properties, possibility to be used and consulted outside the workflow system, etc. Workflows do normally represent existing documented enterprise processes. Different instances of a same workflow are identical copies except for actor's assignment to roles and timing information and they should produce quite identical products. Workflow management systems normally include product management as well as different services and tools to manipulate the process (evaluation, measurement, audit, etc.). To support a broad variety of business processes, workflow management systems and workflow models offer a large span of control and synchronization patterns. Finally, they offer

Figure 9. Basic BPMN control patterns

Pattern Name	Sequence
Description	*"An activity in a workflow process is enabled after the completion of another activity in the same process."* [2]
Diagram	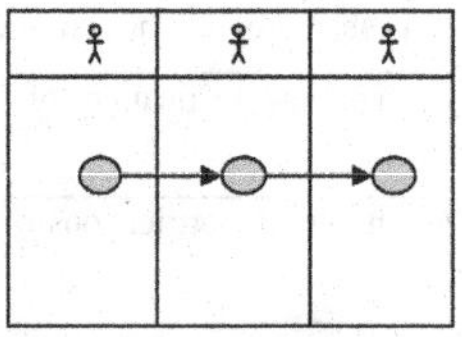
learning Example	Three learning activities defined in an activity structure, executed in sequential order
Pattern	Parallel-split
Description	*"A point in the workflow process where a single thread of control splits into multiple threads of control which can be executed in parallel, thus allowing activities to be executed simultaneously or in any order."* [2]
Diagram	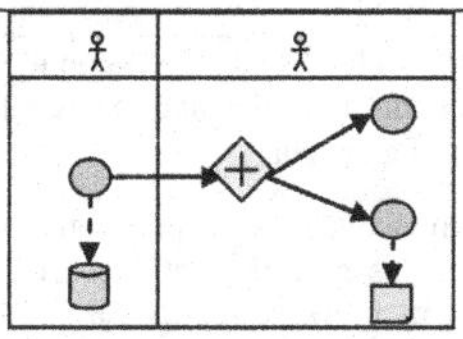
Learning Example	Two students preparing a team project do different activities in parallel: one is reviewing literature on the subject while the second one is doing a survey on it.
Pattern	Synchronization
Description	*"A point in the workflow process where multiple parallel sub processes or activities converge into one single thread of control, thus synchronizing multiple threads. It is an assumption of this pattern that each incoming branch of a synchronizer is executed only once..."* [2]
Diagram	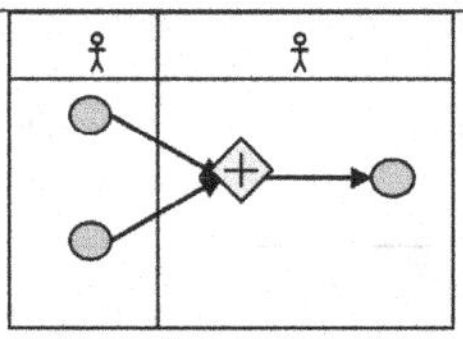
Learning Example	To continue with the next activity, different parallel tasks should be finished: continuing with the preceding example, only when both theoretical and practical data is obtained, students in a team project can start analyzing them.

well-defined interfaces to communicate with other business applications.

On the other hand, the product or goal of an e-learning system is learning by some of the participants. The main actor, the learner, is expected to learn, to acquire new knowledge and competencies, through the execution of structured sets of learning activities. The main component of an E-learning system is the learner actor. The model of this learner is normally part of the system or at least there are ways to pass learner information (learner knowledge and competencies) into the system. The system should allow run time adaptation of the activity based on information on the learner. The whole process and possibly each activity should also have a reference on prerequisites and objectives. Even resources proposed to the actor to execute an activity should take into account the actor's profile and should be described in terms of knowledge and competen-

Figure 10. Basic BPMN control patterns

Pattern	Exclusive Choice
Description	*"A point in the workflow process where, based on a decision or workflow control data, one of several branches is chosen"[2]*
Diagram	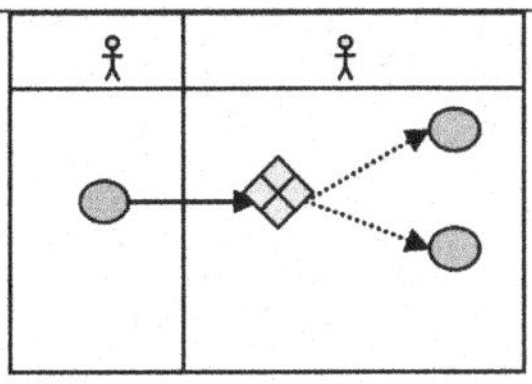
learning Example	Based on the result of an assessment, the learner could pass to the next part of the course or must repeat some learning activities.
Pattern	Simple Merge
Description	*"A point in the workflow process where two or more alternative branches come together without synchronization. It is an assumption of this pattern that none of the alternative branches is ever executed in parallel..."[2]*
Diagram	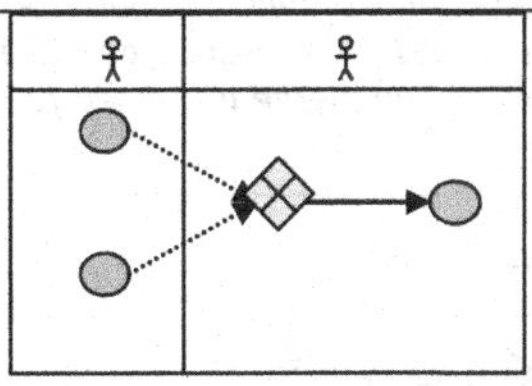
Learning Example	A student has the option to select one and only one activity among two possible ones. After finishing this learning activity a support activity starts its execution.

cies. E-learning processes represent pedagogical models. While existing face-to-face training might inspire an e-learning pedagogical model, new models can exist without a corresponding face-to-face model. In addition, when taking into account personal differences, the model of a same unit of learning is instantiated in different ways for different students.

8.3 THE MOT+LD AND THE TELOS SCENARIO EDITORS

Having established the differences and commonalities between learning scenarios and workflows, we will new discuss the modeling on e-learning processes in terms of Educational Modeling Languages like IMS-LD. We will present two graphical editors well suited for the modeling of high quality reusable learning processes. The second one will provide a synthesis of workflow and educational modeling, in particular by integrating the control patterns presented in the previous section.

In the past few years, a vast movement towards international standards for learning environments has been initiated. Duval & Robson (2001) present a review of the evolution of standards and specifications starting with the Dublin Core metadata initiative in 1995 up to the publication of the Learning Object Metadata (LOM) standard in 2002. A host of other specifications have been published since then. The work on Educational Modeling Languages (Koper 2002), and the subsequent integration of a subset in the IMS Learning Design Specification (IMS 2003) has contributed strongly to integrate Instructional Design preoccupations

Figure 11. BPMN advanced control patterns

Pattern	Multiple Choice
Description	*"A point in the workflow process where, based on a decision or workflow control data, a number of branches are chosen"[2]*
Diagram	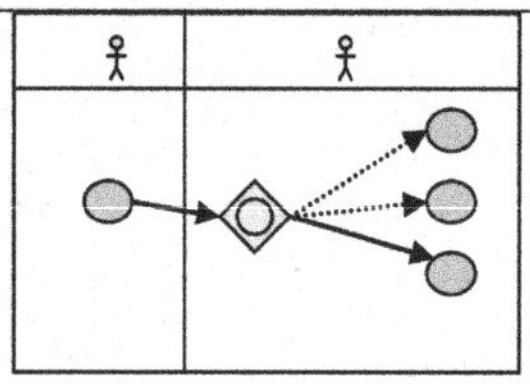
Learning example **Example**	Based on a condition, decide to only execute for instance 3 of the 5 proposed activities. For example, based on student competencies, decide how many exercises he/she should take
Pattern	Multiple Merge
Description	*"A point in a workflow process where two or more branches converge without synchronization. If more than one branch gets activated, possibly concurrently, the activity following the merge is started for every activation of every incoming branch."[2]*
Diagram	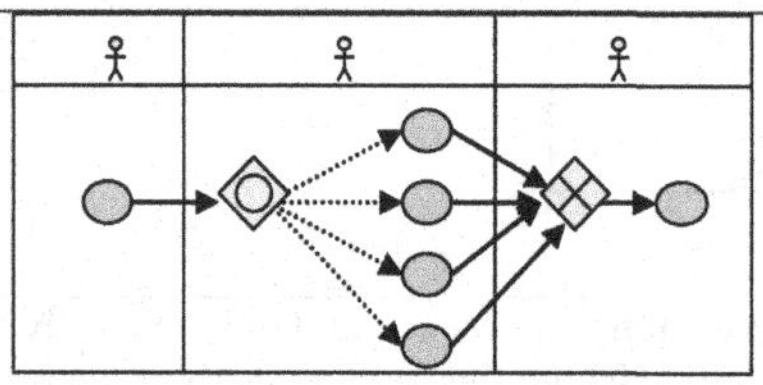
Learning **Example**	An activity assigned to a group could be implemented as a set of multiple instances of the same activity, one per group member. When an instance ends it is necessary to register in a support application the results obtained. This last activity must be done once for each application instances and there are no synchronization requirements because each student may finish his activity at any given time.

into the international standards movement. In particular, it describes a formal way to represent the structure of a unit of learning centered on the concept of a pedagogical method specifying roles and activities that learners and support persons can play using learning objects.

Figure 16 presents a general view of the relationship between instructional engineering methods and tools, and EML/IMS-LD specifications. The IMS-LD specification provides a XML format to describe units of learning, leaving open the choice of instructional methods and modeling tools that can support designers in the process of building learning scenarios. The Instructional

Engineering approach (Paquette 2001) and the Learning Systems Engineering Method (MISA) presented above are especially well suited to help designers build units of learning that can be played on any IMS-LD compliant platform.

In Griffiths and al. (2005) a survey of learning design tools can be found including other graphic editors, showing the interest and adequacy of visual modeling. In the IMS-LD best practice documents (IMS-LD 2003), the UML modeling system is proposed to represent parts of learning designs. Although UML is a widely used standard in software engineering, the different diagrams are not very well adapted to the task of building

Figure 12. BPMN advanced control patterns

Pattern	Discriminator
Description	*"The discriminator is a point in a workflow process that waits for one of the incoming branches to complete before activating the subsequent activity. From that moment on it waits for all remaining branches to complete and "ignores" them. Once all incoming branches have been triggered, it resets itself so that it can be triggered again (which is important otherwise it could not really be used in the context of a loop)"[2]*
Diagram	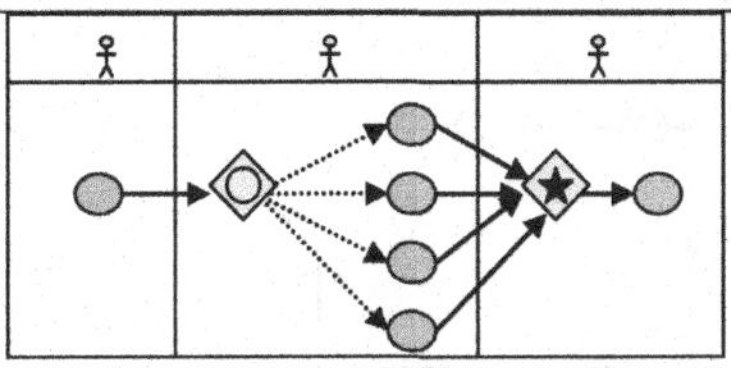
Learning Example	Students are invited to search for the answer to a question. Each do the activity so multiple individual activities are modeled. Once a student gets the answer, the class continues.
Pattern	Arbitrary Cycles
Description	*"A point in a workflow process where one or more activities can be done repeatedly."[2]*
Diagram	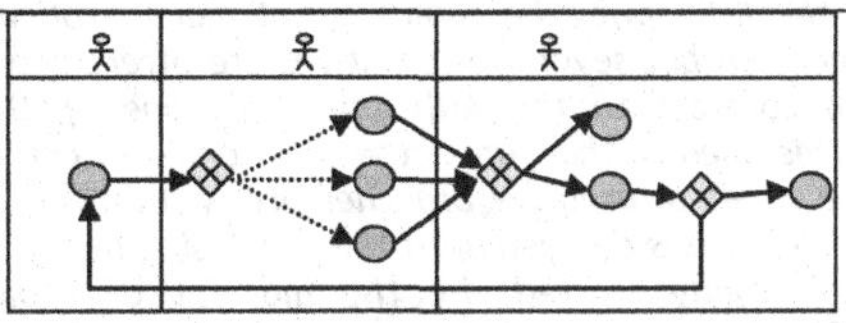
Pattern	Cancellation Activity
Description	*"An enabled activity is disabled, i.e. a thread waiting for the execution of an activity is removed." [2]*
Diagram	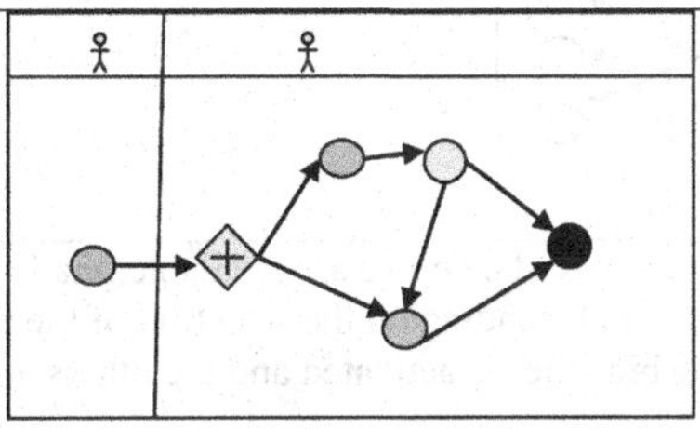
Learning Example	An activity to be held outside could be cancelled due to whether conditions.

learning designs. Another proposal is the LAMS software, which is not LD-compliant but simplifies learning designer's tasks. It is an interesting approach, but not powerful enough to support the complete IMS-LD specification.

In this section, we will present two visual learning design editors that covers all of IMS-LD, while remaining accessible to non computer scientists. MOT+LD is described together with a more recent tool: the TELOS scenario editor. Both

are based on the MOT visual language presented in part I of this book.

The MOT+LD Visual Model Editor

The MOT+LD visual model editor enables designers to describe units of learning and produce a standard IMS-LD XML schema. In Griffiths and al. (2005), this approach is considered *"significant, not only because it provides an example of*

Figure 13. BPMN advanced control patterns

Pattern	Multiples Instances without Synchronization
Description	*"Within the context of a single case (i.e., workflow instance) multiple instances of an activity can be created, i.e., there is a facility to spawn off new threads of control. Each of these threads of control is independent of other threads. Moreover, there is no need to synchronize these threads."[2]*
Diagram	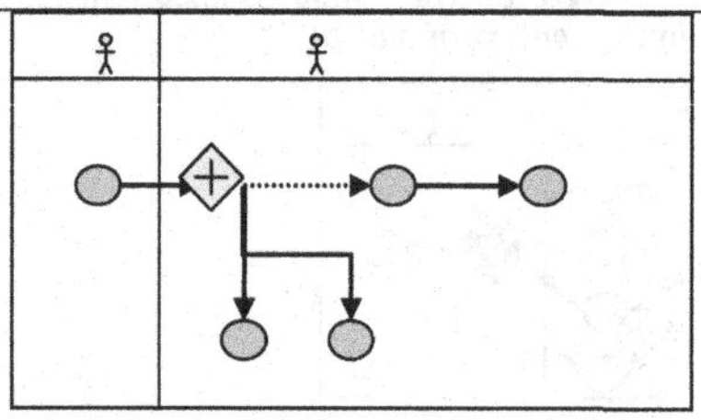
Learning Example	The last activity of a class may be a project. Each student do it on its own and at its pace.
Pattern	Deferred Choice
Description	*"A point in the workflow process where one of several branches is chosen. In contrast to the XOR-split, the choice is not made explicitly (e.g. based on data or a decision) but several alternatives are offered to the environment. However, in contrast to the AND-split, only one of the alternatives is executed. This means that once the environment activates one of the branches the other alternative branches are withdrawn. It is important to note that the choice is delayed until the processing in one of the alternative branches is actually started, i.e. the moment of choice is as late as possible." [2]*
Diagram	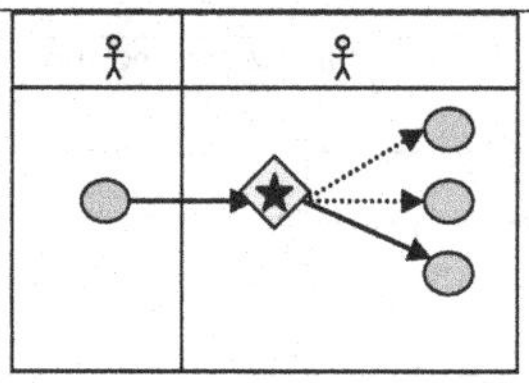
Learning Example	Three different versions of a course are available, made in three different languages. Depending on the selection of the student one of the three possible branches is activated and the others are permanently ignored.

a powerful and expressive high-level LD editor, but also because the structure of LD are mapped onto a graphical language which appears to be very remote from the specification". MOT+LD takes a distance from the specification for usability purposes by educators, preventing the use of XML code or form-based editors, but at the same time producing automatically a completely IMS-LD conformant XML manifest file from the graphs.

Figure 17 shows the MOT+LD graphic symbols used to represent the terms of the specifica-tion. Resources are represented by five kinds of concepts; the LD method components (actions) are represented by seven kinds of procedures; whereas actors and rules are represented by five kinds of principles. Individual objects are repre-sented by individual symbols (also called "facts") representing learning objectives and prerequisites, metadata, items, and four other types of objects needed to describe the conference, send-mail and index-search services.

The same basic links as in the general MOT language can be applied, however we had to

Figure 14. BPMN advanced control patterns

Pattern	Milestone
Description	*"The enabling of an activity depends on the case being in a specified state, i.e. the activity is only enabled if a certain milestone has been reached which did not expire yet. Consider three activities named A, B, and C. Activity A is only enabled if activity B has been executed and C has not been executed yet, i.e. A is not enabled before the execution of B and A is not enabled after the execution of C..." [2]*
Diagram	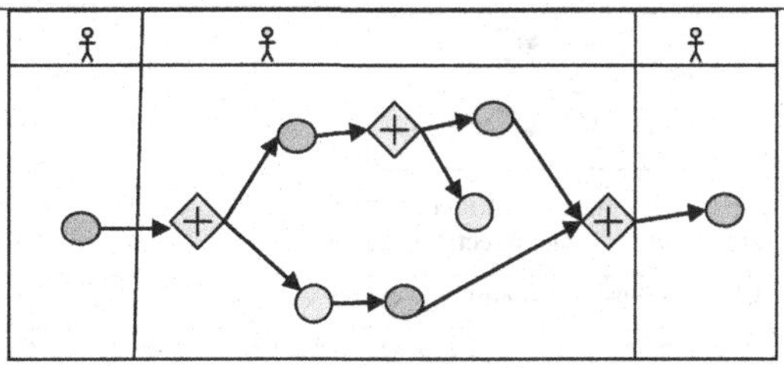
Learning Example	A course is designed to be done in groups of two students. At some point of the process, each of the students must execute in parallel different activities, but one of the activities depends on a partial result obtained by the first student. The two students must synchronize their results before continuing with the following activity.

consider a number of new constraints on the links between subtypes specified in the IMS-LD Information and Binding model (IMS-LD 2003) in order to produce a valid XML manifest file.

Figure 18 underlines the relative complexity of the LD information model (IMS-LD, 2003) but helps to understand it better. It shows a rather straightforward use of the MOT+ C-link. An environment is composed of other environments recursively or of other types of resources, learning objects, outcomes and/or three types of services. Learner and staff roles, and also items can be organized in C-linked hierarchies. Methods are decomposed into plays, which are decomposed into acts, which are decomposed into activity structures. Role-parts are represented in MOT+LD by a role associated to the activity. Finally activity structures can be decomposed into smaller and smaller activity structures until we reach terminal learning activities, support activities or referencer to external unit of learnings (UoL).

The use of input/product I/P-link and precedence P-link is clear and unambiguous. The precedence link is used between procedures only below the Play level. The I/P link is used only below the Act level, from an input resource to a procedure or conversely, from a procedure to its resource outcome. This is more precisely put than the specification itself, since the LD XML file does not distinguish between input resources and outcomes, whereas the outcome is a necessary ingredient of a Learning Design from a designer's point of view.

The instantiation I-link associates learning objectives and prerequisites to a method or to learning activities. Activity structures, learning and support activities, learning and staff roles or resources (except environment and index search) can be associated to items pointing to a location where the physical files are found.

Finally, the regulation R-link associates learner and staff roles to any environment or activity structure, learning or support activity, or it may associate a time limit to any action except a method. It is also used to associate a completion rule to any action except an activity structure and

Figure 15. BPMN personalization control patterns

Pattern	Changes based on Evaluation Gateways
Description	A branching point in the process where the alternative selected is based on the evaluation of expressions. Each transition has associated an evaluation expression. The evaluation gateway evaluates each expression and launches the selected branch if the evaluation result is TRUE.
Diagram	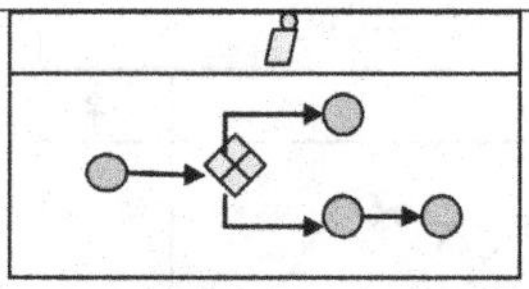
Learning Example	An activity must be omitted if after an evaluation activity the student has at least 90% of his objectives correct.
Pattern	Changes based on completed events with synchronization
Description	A branching point in the process where the alternatives are based on events that occur at that point, rather than the evaluation of expressions using process data (properties) [1].
Diagram	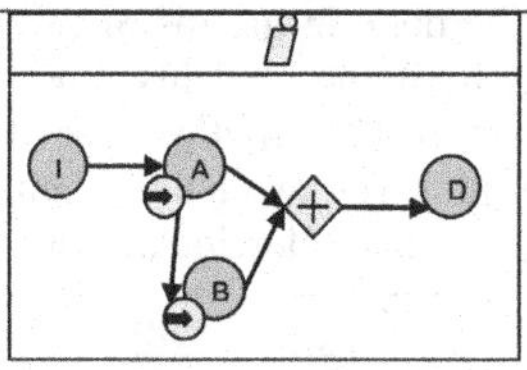
Learning Example	When an activity is completed a notification event is sent to another activity. As a result the receiving activity becomes visible for the learner (In IMS-LD, it changes its visibility mode to show or hide).
Pattern	Changes based on Time- Events
Description	A branching point in the process where the alternatives are based on time events that occur at that point, rather than the evaluation of expressions using process data (properties)
Diagram	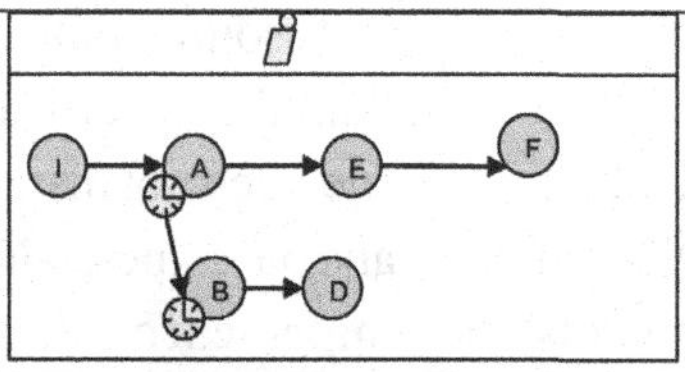
Learning Example	An activity could be done only in a specific period of time. If after that time the activity has not finished, a time event is produced. The new branch of activities is visualized.

a UoL. The number to select rule is R-linked to an activity structure where options are proposed.

Technically, subtypes of the original MOT+ object types were added to the MOT+ editor and standardized labels (as shown on Figures 17 and 18) were added to the lower left corner of the object, in order to distinguish each subtype from the others. The most difficult technical part was to extend the native MOT XML schema and to translate it into the IMS-LD XML standard schema. A post-validation mechanism is built into

the translation program informing the designer whether a rule of the IMS-LD specification is violated and where to find it in the model. The number of possible violations is reduced while designing the model by limiting the choice of possible links between sub-types according to the constraints shown on Figure 18. Also, some of the constraints for metadata association and the description of the services not presented here have been covered.

Figure 16. Interrelations between MISA 4.0, IMS-LD design and Explor@

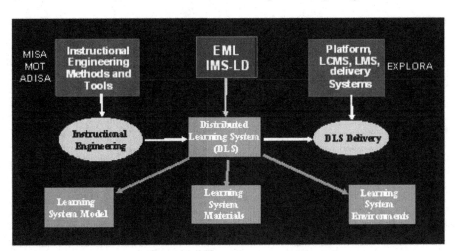

Figure 17. MOT+LD basic vocabulary

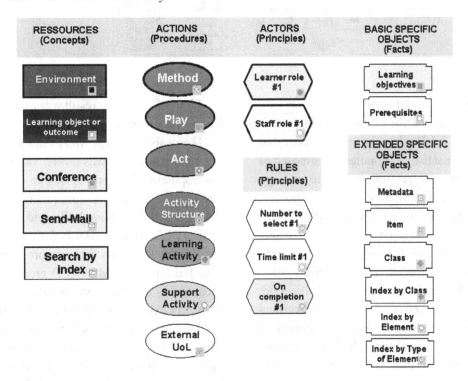

Finally, many examples have been tested, including the well-known complex Versailles example (IMS-LD 2003). The MOT+LD output was exported to RELOAD (RELOAD 2004), a form-based IMS-LD editor. This exercise has shown very small discrepancies between our analysis of the specification and theirs. Minor corrections were made to the MOT+LD editor to arrive at the present version.

Figure 19 presents an example scenario for the second act of a unit-of-learning on solar astronomy (Paquette et al 2006). Act 2 is a discussion on

Figure 18. MOT+LD link constraints

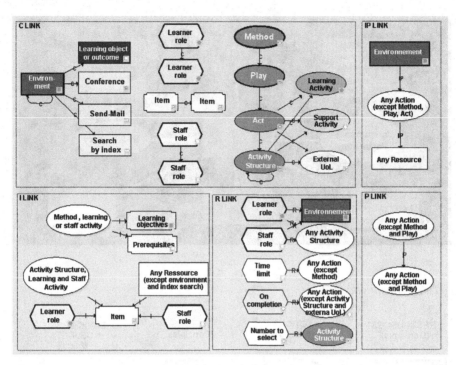

planet properties managed or ruled (*R link*) by a teacher. It is composed of parallel learning activities 2.1.A and 2.1.B where Learners are divided in two teams that use environments composed of a chat tool and different documents to undergo a team discussion to discover planet properties. These activities are supported by staff activities 2.2.A and 2.2.B performed by the teacher where he observes both team discussions and provides to the participants, if needed, additional information (Clues A and Clues B). When these activities end, the flow moves to Activity 2.3 where the learners in both teams reunite to share their discovery of planet properties uncovered in both team discussions. This activity uses a forum managed and moderated by the Teacher.

We were able to execute that scenario by first exporting the visual model to an XML file compliant with IMS-LD. This file was then read into the IMS-LD RELOAD editor to edit the missing level B and C conditions (a feature that was unavailable

in MOT+LD), and the result was executed by the RELOAD Player.

The usability of the MOT+LD Visual Editor at a conceptual level was further validated by the development of a learning design repository by designers of four different universities. Around 50 IMS-LD scenarios were builts and can be found on the IDLD Web site (IDLD-2006). This project has shown, that even with a more user-friendly visual editor such as MOT+LD, creating IMS-LD scenarios is not that easy, even for experienced designers. All of them succeeded with little help, even though they were not initially familiar with IMS-LD, but they reported usability improvements to be made to the editor (Lundgren-Cayrol, Marino, Paquette, Léonard and De la Teja, 2006).

The TELOS Scenario Editor

Before extending the MOT+LD editor to level B and C, we decided to revise completely the architecture of the supporting system to increase its usability and

Figure 19. The MOT+LD version of Act 2 of the Planet Game Unit-of-learning

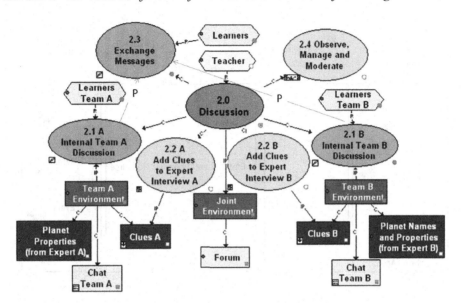

friendliness, and also its generality and efficiency. The new TELOS environment is Ontology-Driven so it embodies a metadata referencing scheme for scenario entities (actors, activities and resources) and scenarios as well. The new Scenario Editor covers all levels of the IMS-LD specification using a smaller number of visual symbols and links. The resulting scenario can be exported to an IMS-LD file or executed within the TELOS environment. TELOS includes a player, the task manager, that provides a visual interface to enable participants to realize their activities and interact with each other and the environment. This environment is produced automatically from the scenario visual graph.

The Visual Scenario Editor is the central piece of the TELOS architecture (Paquette, Rosca, Mihaila and Masmoudi, 2005; Magnan and Paquette 2006) that will be presented in detail in chapter 15. To design it, a comparative analysis has been made between business workflows and IMS-LD learning designs. This work has lead to the identification of 21 control situations for workflows encountered in the software engineering literature (Correal and Marino, 2007) that subsume the properties and conditions in IMS-LD, level B and C.

Based on the MOT+ visual language, the Scenario Editor uses four kinds of objects shown on Figure 20 (Actor, Function, Resource and Condition) with subtypes related to the TELOS technical ontology that drives the system. These symbols are not necessarily in one to one correspondence with IMS-LD terms. For example, the Function symbol can represent Methods, Plays, Acts, as well as Activity Structures. Differentiations between such terms can be made either in the property sheet of the object or be deduced by the export-to-LD parser when it translates automatically a TELOS scenario graph into the IMS-LD XML file.

MOT concept symbols serve to represent all kinds of *Resources*: documents, tools, semantic resource, environment, actor (as a resource), activity (as a resource) and data. MOT procedure symbols represent *Functions* (groups of resources that together achieve a function) that can be decomposed into other functions at any depth level down to activities enacted by humans, or operations performed automatically by the system. Finally, MOT principles serve to represent actors as well as conditions, depicted by two different sets of symbols. The *Actor* symbols represent us-

Figure 20. TELOS scenario editor (TSE) visual symbols

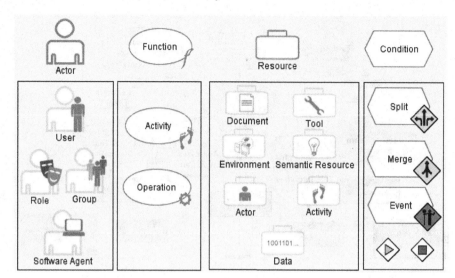

Figure 21. A simple scenario model

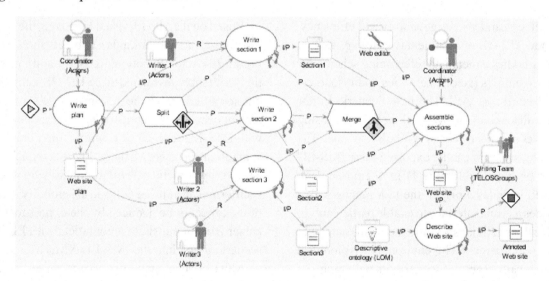

ers, groups, roles or software agents, all seen as control objects that enact the activities using and producing resources as planned by the scenario model. The *Condition* symbols represent control element inserted within the basic flow to decide on the following sequence of activities or operations, including the diamond shapes that define the start and end point for a scenario. A set of subtypes for split, merge and event-based conditions has been programmed into the TELOS editor.

On Figure 21, we see a scenario that combines some of these symbols. A coordinator writes the plan of a Web site document in the first activity. Then, different writers produce three sections performing their activities in parallel. When these are all terminated, the coordinator using a Web editor builds a Web site grouping the different parts, and the group annotates this site using metadata and/or ontologies.

Figure 22. A view of a scenario for act 2 of the Planet Game Unit-of-learning

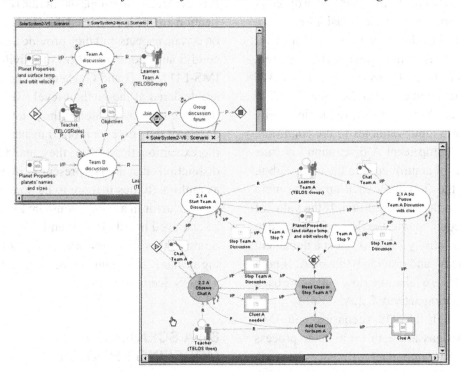

This example shows a split condition after the first activity. Later on, the flow from the activities merges through the merge condition before the next activity takes control. According to the merge condition properties, the "Assemble sections" activity will wait for all the incoming flows to terminate before it is executed. In the Scenario Editor, we see a combination of a control flow and a data flow. The control flow is modeled using the MOT basic P and R links. P links are used for the basic line of execution to indicate the sequencing between Functions, Activities and Operations. R links identify the source of an event (from a user or from the system) that triggers a condition that will alter the basic flow of control. MOT I/P links serve to model the data flow, either from resources to activities where they are consulted, used or processed or from activities to outcome resources.

Figure 22 represents within the TELOS Scenario Editor the second act of the solar astronomy unit-of-learning that was modeled using MOT+LD on

Figure 19. On the left side, we see the upper model of Act 2, where the flow splits into team discussions. The execution waits for both discussions to end and then moves to the group discussion forum where members from both teams and the teachers will all participate.

The right hand part of the figure is a sub-model for the team A chat discussion. It starts with opening the chat tool for team A. Then, the control splits between the learning activity 2.1.A, where team A learners discuss on the planet properties that have been provided to them, and the support activity 2.2.A performed by the teacher where he observes the team A discussion. The teacher's part is highlighted on the figure. After a certain time in activity 2.2.A, the teacher can either produce an event (set a data value) to stop the discussion or provide additional information (Clue A) to help the learners solve the problem. The learners can also decide to stop, either before or after they have received this additional information. A similar pattern rules the discussion for team B, with the same teacher acting as a facilitator for both teams, each with a different set of planet properties as additional information.

The conditions shown on Figure 22 represent level B properties of the IMS-LD specification. The decision "Need Clues or Stop Team A?" depends on its input data and the value "true" or "false" that a teacher action will produce in activity 2.2.A for these input variables to the condition. If the value "Stop team A discussion" is true, then the flow of control goes to the end symbol, after which the flow goes back up to the main act 2 model to the join condition. If the value of "Clues A needed" is true, the flow will proceed to the teacher's activity 2.3.A to select a document named "Clue A" and provide it to team A. If both input variables are false, the flow will come back to the observation activity 2.2.A.

Even though TELOS scenarios and IMS Learning Designs are both multi-actor process models, there are important differences between them for very good reasons. We have decided to keep these differences and add a graph translator to provide import/export facilities between the TELOS scenario editor and standard IMS-LD XML files. This provides a user-friendlier while more powerful scenario editor than MOT+LD.

Another reason is that we wanted to be able to use the Scenario Editor as the main aggregation tool in TELOS. In TELOS, the Scenario Editor can be used at all levels of the system. Engineers have to aggregate existing software components (built possibly with different technologies) to create new ones, in order to extend the capabilities of the system. Technologists have to create or extend a Web platform by building scenarios for designers (instructional design methods) that includes a variety of design tools and documents (Paquette and Magnan, 2008). The constraints introduced in the method structure of IMS-LD do not take these use cases into account.

A second goal was to encompass business workflows as well as instructional scenarios for learners within the same Scenario Editor to enlarge the realm of applications. For workflows, Business

Process Model Notations such as the BPMN specification are more restricted than learning designs on certain aspects, but they provide a larger set of conditions to control the flow of activities. Unlike IMS-LD level B and C where all the conditions are declared at the method level, BPMN conditions are visually located at the point where they are used, thus given a more transparent view of the execution flow. Also, they make important distinctions that are not present in IMS-LD such as multi-activities that are to be done separately by each actor in a group, compare to activities to be achieved by all group member cooperatively. Some of these features are also useful for learning designs, providing a solid foundation to the TELOS Scenario Editor.

8.4 A SCENARIO MODELING PROCESS

In this concluding section, we will present a scenario for designers to help them build learning/work environments and their learning or workflow scenarios. Such a design scenario will present a way to use the skills taxonomy developed in chapters 6 an 7, to guide scenario modeling.

The MISA instructional engineering method presented in this chapter, its operations, products and principles were modeled using an early version of the MOT software. This model of MISA is a general design scenario that we will present further in chapter 21. Presently, a new model of MISA using the MOT+LD and TELOS editors is developed to take in account and generalize the IMS-LD ways of presenting instructional engineering products. A simple design process is provided in the MOT+LD user guide that can be downloaded from the IDLD Web site (www.idld.org). It is a nested model of the design task "Build learning design structure".

Seven steps indicate the main tasks involved in engineering an IMS-LD Unit of Learning:

Figure 23. MISA design scenario: main activities

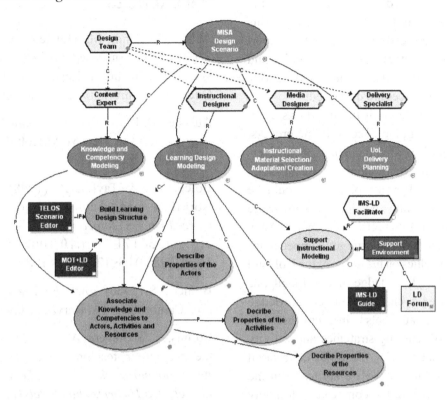

- Decide to adapt an existing LD template or build a new one;
- Add prerequisite and target competencies (educational objectives) linked to the Method object to guide the engineering of the learning design and its method component;
- Specify actor's roles hierarchy, specifying minimum and maximum number of actors for each role;
- Develop the instructional structure (Method, Plays, Acts, Activity structure and Role-parts) as defined by the IMS-LD Information Model;
- Add items (specific files) to resources, activities, roles; add appropriate metadata to learning objects and services;
- Save the model as a LD Manifest and revise, if necessary;

- Export this manifest to a LD Player such as RELOAD or TELOS.

Another design scenario is presented in Figure 23. It is based on four processes (only the second one is developed on the figure) that start in parallel corresponding to four actors that correspond to the design team's role-parts, such as the content expert, the instructional designer, the media designer and the delivery specialist. Each of these actors is responsible for developing one of the four axes of the MISA method.

The instructional designer is the one responsible for the construction of the learning design. He is supported by a staff role where an IMS-LD facilitator coaches designer using an IMS-LD guide and a LD forum included in a community-of-practice environment. Instructional designers proceed to develop the unit of learning using an environment composed of the MOT+LD editor or the TELOS scenario editor, in order to build the LD or workflow model. Then knowledge units and competencies defined by the content expert are associated to actors, learning activities and resources. After that, the properties of actors, activities and resources are described.

Obviously, these are only the main tasks. They are insufficient to guide effectively the process, but they summarize the fundamentals of engineering a LD Model. Many elements are missing. Prerequisites and learning objectives could be obtained by modeling the domain knowledge and associating it to target competencies. Also, the gap between entry and target competencies gives designers clues on the scope of the UoL and its corresponding knowledge model. Finally, as will be discussed in chapter 9, target knowledge and competency statements help orient designers on the types of learning strategies and activity structures to select. For example, conceptual and procedural knowledge are not learnt in the same way; to acquire the competency to apply an administrative procedure is less demanding than acquiring a competency to build and adapt such procedures.

CONCLUSION

In this chapter, we have modeled different kinds of multi-actor activity scenarios. Learning scenarios that promote process-based learning and teaching strategies, business workflows that help organize work and decision activities in organizations, and finally designer's workflow that help coordinate teams that build the learning scenarios or the workflows for other actors to use. In following chapters, we will see other kinds of scenarios that have been modeled graphically using the tools presented in this chapter.

REFERENCES

Aalst, W., Dumas, M., Hofstede, A., & Wohed, P. (2002). Pattern Based analysis of BPML and WSCI. FIT Technical Report, FIT-TR-2002-05 Queensland University of Technology, Australia.

Ausubel, D. P. (1968). *Educational Psychology, A cognitive view*. New York: Holt, Rhinehart & Winston.

Bolcer, G., & Taylor, R. (1998). Advanced workflow management technologies. *Software Process Improvement and Practice, 4*(3), 125–171. doi:10.1002/(SICI)1099-1670(199809)4:3<125::AID-SPIP100>3.0.CO;2-J

Bruner, J. S. (1966). *Towards a Theory of Instruction*. Cambridge, MA: Harvard University Press.

Collins, A., & Stevens, A. L. (1983). A cognitive theory of inquiry teaching. In Reigeluth, C. (Ed.), *Instructional Theories in Action: Lessons Illustrating Selected Theories and Models* (pp. 247–278). Hillsdale, NJ: Lawrence Erlbaum.

Correal, D., & Marino, O. (2007). *Software Requirements Specification Document for General Purpose Function's Editor* (Technical Report V0.4). Montréal, Canada: Télé-université LICEF Research Centre.

Dewey, J. (1900). Psychology and social practice. *Psychological Review,* (7): 105–124. doi:10.1037/h0066152

Duval, E., & Robson, R. (2001). Guest Editorial on Metadata. *Interactive Learning Environments (Special issue: Metadata), 9*(3), 201-206.

Eder, J., & Gruber, W. (2002). A Meta Model for Structured Workflows Supporting Workflow Transformation. In Lecture Notes on Computer Science (Vol. 2435).

Gagné, R. M. (1970). *The conditions of learning* (2nd ed.). New York: Holt, Rhinehart & Winston.

Griffiths, D., Blat, J., Garcia, R., Votgen, H., & Kwong, K. L. (2005). Learning Design Tools . In Koper, R., & Tattersall, C. (Eds.), *Learning Design - A Handbook on Modelling and Delivering Networked Education and Training* (pp. 109–136). Berlin: Springer Verlag.

Hollingsworth, P. (1995). *The Workflow Reference Model.* Technical Report TC00-1003, WfMC.

IDLD. (2006). *Implementation and Deployment of the Learning Design Specification Portal.* Retrieved from http://www.idld.org

IMS-LD. (2003). *IMS Learning Design. Information Model, Best Practice and Implementation Guide, Binding Schemas.* Retrieved October 3, 2003, from http://www.imsglobal.org/learning-design/index.cfm

Koper, R. (2002). *Modeling units of study from a pedagogical perspective – The pedagogical metamodel behind EML.* Retrieved from http://www.eml.ou.nl/introduction/articles.htm

Landa, L. (1976). *Instructional regulation and control: Cybernetics, algorithmization, and heuristics in education.* Englewood Cliffs, NJ: Educational Technology Publications.

Lei, Y., & Singh, M. (1997). A Comparison of Workflow Metamodels. In *Proceedings of the ER-97 Workshop on Behavioral Modeling and Design Transformations: Issues and Opportunities in Conceptual Modeling*, Los Angeles, November 1997.

Lemoigne, J. L. (1995). *Les épistémologies constructivistes.* Paris: PUF.

Magnan, F., & Paquette, G. (2006). TELOS: An ontology driven eLearning OS. Presented at SOA/AIS-06 Workshop, Dublin, Ireland, June 2006.

Mariño, O., Casallas, R., Villalobos, J., Correal, D., & Contamines, J. (2006). Bridging the Gap between e-learning Modeling and Delivery through the Transformation of Learnflows into Workflows . In *E-learning networked. Environments and Architectures: A Knowledge Processing Perspective.* Berlin: Springer Verlag.

Merrill, M. D. (1983). Component Display Theory . In Reigeluth, C. (Ed.), *Instructional Theories in Action: Lessons Illustrating Selected Theories and Models* (pp. 279–333). Hillsdale, NJ: Lawrence Erlbaum.

Paquette, G. (2001). Designing Virtual Learning Centers . In Adelsberger, H., Collis, B., & Pawlowski, J. (Eds.), *Handbook on Information Technologies for Education & Training* (pp. 249–272). Amsterdam: Springer-Verlag.

Paquette, G. (2002). TeleLearning systems engineering: Towards a new ISD model. *Journal of Structural Learning, 14,* 1–35.

Paquette, G. (2004). *Instructional Engineering for Network-Based Learning.* San Francisco: Pfeiffer/Wiley Publishing Co.

Paquette, G., Léonard, M., Lundgren-Cayrol, K., Mihaila, S., & Gareau, D. (2006 January). Learning Design based on Graphical Knowledge-Modeling. *Journal of Educational technology and Society ET&S.*

Paquette, G., Rosca, I., De la Teja, I., Léonard, M., & Lundgren-Cayrol, K. (2001). *Web-based Support for the Instructional Engineering of E-learning Systems.* Presented at WebNet'01 Conference, Orlando 2001.

Paquette, G., Rosca, I., Mihaila, S., & Masmoudi, A. (2006). Telos, a service-oriented framework to support learning and knowledge management . In Pierre, S. (Ed.), *E-Learning Networked Environments and Architectures: a Knowledge Processing Perspective.* Berlin: Springer-Verlag.

Reigeluth, C. M., & Rodgers, C. A. (1980). *The Elaboration Theory of Instruction: Prescription for Task Analysis and Design.* NSPI Journal.

RELOAD. (2004). Retrieved January 23, 2004, from http://www.reload.ac.uk

Scandura, J. M. (1973). *Strutural Learning I: Theory and Research.* New York: Gordon & Breach Science Publishers.

Simon, H. A. (1981). *The sciences of the artificial.* Cambridge, MA: The MIT press.

Skinner, B. F. (1954). The science of learning and the art of teaching. *Harvard Educational Review, 24*(2), 86–97.

Vantroys, T., & Peter, Y. (2004). COW, a Flexible Platform for the Enactment of Learning Scenarios. In *Proceedings of International Workshop on Groupware (CRIWG 2003).* Berlin: Springer-Verlag.

Workflow Management Coalition (WfMC). (2002). *Workflow Process Definition Interface - XML Process Definition Language,* Version 1. Final Draft WFMC-TC-1025. [1] This section summarizes previous articles and books on the subject. For more details, please consult (Paquette 2002, 2004)

Chapter 9
Competency–Driven Scenarios and Actor Modeling

Gilbert Paquette
LICEF Research Center, Canada

Olga Marino
LICEF Research Center, Canada

ABSTRACT

- Competency Gaps and Domain Modeling
  - Performance Indicators for a Competency
  - Competency Gap to Guide Knowledge Modeling
  - Target Competency and Knowledge Model Type
  - Competency Gaps for Actors
- Competency-Driven Scenario Modeling
  - Selection of a Generic Skill's Process
  - Transform the Generic Skill's Model to an Activity Scenario.
  - From Generic Skill's Principles to Assistance in a Scenario
- Competency-based Actor's Roles and Resources
  - Actor's Roles and Generic Skills
  - Coordinating Role Scenarios
- Knowledge and Competency Actors Models
  - A Competency-Based Learner Model
  - A Learner Model That Evolves in Time
  - A Learner Model Having Multiple-Viewpoints
  - A Multi-Viewpoints Evolving Learner Model in Action
  - Initializing the Learner Model for a Learning Process
  - Scenario Adaptation Using the Learner Model

DOI: 10.4018/978-1-61520-839-5.ch009

In this chapter, we will present further applications of the notions of generic skill and competency developed in the previous chapters. The first of these applications is to define the concept of "competency gap" that extends the notion of "knowledge gap" introduced in Chapter 4 to guide the domain modeling process. Then, we show how we can use a model of the generic skill involved in a competency definition, to form the skeleton of an activity scenario. Afterwards, we use competencies to help define the roles and the resources needed by different actors in a virtual learning or knowledge management environment. Finally we use different viewpoints on a user's competencies at the center of a user model that can help personalize or adapt a Web-based environment.

9.1 COMPETENCY GAPS AND DOMAIN MODELING

We present here a more elaborated method to guide the modeling of a knowledge domain than the one presented at the end of Chapter 4 (section 4.4). For this, we will use the concept of performance to define the notion of a *competency gap*, an important concept to guide the knowledge modeling process (Paquette 2003).

Performance Indicators for a Competency

The scale values and the words "awareness", "familiarity", "mastery" and "expertise" that describe levels of knowledge mastery need a more precise definition because the "gap" now applies to competencies (skill + knowledge) instead of just the knowledge part. The general meaning of the levels in the competency scale depends on the level of performance that an actor can demonstrate when he applies the generic skill to the knowledge part of the competency.

A way to evaluate such a performance level is to add to the generic skill part of the competencies, values of performance indicators such as frequency, scope, autonomy, complexity and/or context of use. For example, a competency like "diagnose the source of malfunction of a car engine" could be made more precise by adding performance values at the end of the statement such as:

- *Frequency*: "in all cases (always)" or "in the majority of cases (sometimes)" ;
- *Scope*: "for part of the causes (partially)" or "for all causes (totally)";
- *Autonomy*: "without help" or "with assistance";
- *Complexity*: "for high, middle-range or complexity situations"; or
- *Context of use*: "in familiar or unfamiliar cases".

The usefulness of such indicators is to help built ways to assess the performance level for a competency, using for example questionnaires, interviews or performance observation plans.

Alternative and simpler performance indicators are obtained by linking the broad categories such as "awareness", "familiarity", "productivity" or "expertise" to the performance indicators. One way to combine performance indicators or criteria is shown on Table 1.

Applying this table, we have the following definitions replacing those in section 4.4:

- *Awareness*. At this level, the actor can apply the generic skill to knowledge sometimes, only partially, with assistance, in low complexity and familiar situations.
- *Familiarity*. At this level, the actor can perform the generic skill on the knowledge always, but only partially, with assistance, in low complexity and familiar situations.

Table 1. Performance categories or levels vs. other indicators

Performance Criteria	Awareness (0,0-2,5)	Familiarity [2,5-5.0)	Mastery [5.0-7.5)	Expertise [7,5-10,0]
Frequency	Sometimes	Always	Always	Always
Scope	Partial	Partial	Total	Total
Autonomy	Assistance	Assistance	Without help	Without help
Task complexity	Low	Low	Middle	High
Context of use	Familiar	Familiar	Familiar	Unfamiliar

- *Mastery*. At this level, the actor can perform the generic skill on the knowledge always, without help, totally, in middle range complexity and familiar situations.
- *Expertise*. At this level, the actor can perform the generic skill on the knowledge always, without help, totally, in high complexity and unfamiliar situations.

Competency Gap to Guide Knowledge Modeling

"Competency gap" is a meta-concept applicable in all knowledge domains that we will now define precisely. Such a meta-concept has been implemented in different ways, first in the didactic engineering workbench (Paquette, Crevier and Aubin 1994), into the succeeding versions of the MISA method (Paquette, Aubin and Crevier 1999) and in Explor@-II a learning content management system. It rests on an evaluation of the distance between the initial (or actual) competency of an actor and a target competency using the same performance scale. These tasks can be learning activities as well as tasks in a workflow.

Target competencies are found in competency profiles such as the ones presented in Chapter 5 or in the case study discussed in section 7.5. Then, we need to evaluate the performance level for these target competencies, as well as the initial or actual level for the same competency. For example, if one wants to hire or train multimedia directors, it is necessary to estimate the distance

between the expected initial competencies and the ones defined in a typical profile for a multimedia director. For each competency, a "competency gap" is defined as the difference between the target level and the initial (or actual) level estimated on a performance scale.

Figure 1 shows an example of such level assignments for the competency profile of the multimedia director that has been analyzed in section 7.5. The first competency "Construct a multimedia production method ", presents a rather important gap (around 4.2), because the multimedia director has to master this competence (5.8), while the actual competency is a simple awareness level (1.6).

On the other hand, the second one, "To discriminate between the properties of audio-visual supports ", presents a smaller gap of about 2.3, representing a progress from a high level of awareness to a high level of familiarity. For this competency, we don't expect too much of the multimedia director because he will not have to use the multimedia supports or even select them, since this is the job of some of his team members.

A knowledge (such as "production method") for which the competency gap is large will have to be described by an elaborated model indicating many of its sub-processes, inputs and products, and its regulating principles, possibly on many levels. On the contrary, if the competency gap is very small for a knowledge element, this knowledge part of the competency (such as "audio-visual supports") can be removed from the model with

Figure 1. Competency gaps an actor (multimedia director) on a competency scale

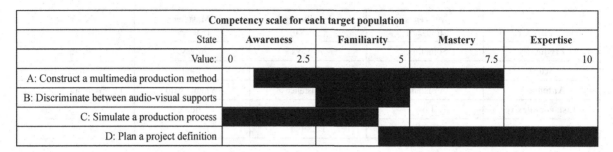

the associated competency unless it serves a clarification purpose towards other knowledge elements around it in the model.

The competency gaps will be used in the same way as in Chapter 4, section 4.4, to guide the construction of the knowledge model in an application domain through the following steps: mark the competency gaps on the main knowledge elements (to which competency is associated); created a nested model for these knowledge elements; repeat these steps until knowledge elements are reached where the competency gap is near zero.

Target Competency and Knowledge Model Type

The competency assigned to the knowledge elements can also guide the modeling process in another way beyond the size of the sub-model or the number of levels of sub-models. The performance part of the target competency can give a clue to the type of knowledge that should appear in the model. Here are some of these heuristic principles.

1. *Target competency performance = Awareness.* In this case, the model should contain mostly facts and concepts, independently of the generic skill involve. For example, a synthesis skill for planning a project might require a few examples (traces) of such a process together with examples of concepts such

as the personnel involved, their efforts in day-persons, and their cost.

2. *Target competency performance* b *= Familiarity.* In this case, the model should contain interrelated facts, concepts and procedures so that the users of the model can consider both the static knowledge and some processes that can be applied.

3. *Target competency performance = Mastery.* In this case, the model should contain not only concepts and procedures, but also some principles that can select what concepts to use or procedures to apply in different situations.

4. *Target competency performance = Expertise.* In this case, the model should contain more principles than in the case of mastery.

Competency Gaps for Actors

When we build a knowledge model, it is not possible in general to assess the actual competency of persons who will use the model, only to estimate an initial competency of a target population who will use the model. This is exactly what textbook authors do when they plan a book.

But when a person starts interacting with a training or a work environment, we can use the concept of a « competency gap » to evaluate its actual competencies.

Figure 2 shows the result of such an evaluation for three persons seeking the job of multimedia producer, for the target competency "construct a multimedia production method". Here the target

Figure 2. Comparing competency gaps of three persons for a target competency

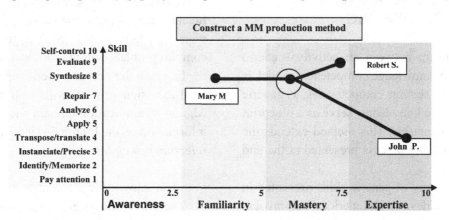

competencies and the actual competencies of these persons are shown on a two-dimensional scale composed of the skill's levels (on the vertical axis) and the performance levels of Figure 1 (on the horizontal axis). The target competency is set at a generic skill's level of 8-Synthesize and at the mastery performance level is set at 7; thus situating the competency for that knowledge at the point (8,7) on the two-dimensional scale.

Using performance criteria such as those on Table 1, it is possible to create questionnaires, exams, interview questions, or test task assignments to verify the actual competency of candidates for the job. With these instruments we can situate each person's actual competency on the two-dimensional scale of Figure 2 with regard to their skill and performance levels.

Figure 2 shows the results of such evaluations.

- Mary M. can perform synthesize (construct) skills for a multimedia production method in a persistent way, but partially, with some help and in simple and familiar examples. She is at a familiarity level for the synthesize skill level for a result 8.5. The competency gap is thus 8.5 – 8.7 = -0.2 which is not bad, requiring little supervision or training.

- John P. cannot perform the skill, but is capable to simulate (apply) a given pro-

duction process at the expertise level. He situates at 5,9 for a competency gap of 5.9 – 8.5 = -2.6 which clearly do not qualify him for the job.

- Robert S. has shown that, not only can he construct a multimedia production method but in addition, he can evaluate its probable results in a persistent, total and autonomous way. His skill's level is 9-Evaluation, at mastery performance level of 7. His competency gap is positive 9.7–8.5 = 2.2, thus exceeding the target competency.

Now suppose we are preparing a work or a training environment for a target group that has the same profile than Mary M. We will need to develop a knowledge model of a moderate size, with many construction process examples to support competency improvement from familiarity to mastery level. On the other hand, if the target population is more like John P.'s profile, the knowledge model will be quite large, developed on several levels, including analysis, repair and construction examples, to help the target population move up their competency level from 5-Application to 8-Construction.

9.2 COMPETENCY-DRIVEN SCENARIO MODELING

The relationship between an activity scenario model and a knowledge/competency model is critical. In this section, competencies, as generic skills applied to knowledge, serve as a blueprint for activity scenarios. This method extends the scenario modeling process presented at the end of Chapter 8.

The taxonomy of generic skills presented in Chapter 7 provides us with generic (meta-) process models that each can be mapped to a process-based activity scenario. Generic skills or processes are thus structured sets of intellectual (cognitive, affective, social or psychomotor) actions that can be instantiated to different knowledge domains. Each generic skill in the taxonomy can be represented as a MOT process by a main (meta-) procedure that is broken down into sub-procedures, to as many levels as needed, until terminal procedures are found that do not need further decomposition. These procedures can become activity or tasks in an activity scenario. For each procedure, there is also a description of input or product generic concepts that feed them or are generated by them; these can correspond to resources and outcomes. Finally, the principles that regulate the transfer of control between the generic procedures can be transformed into assistance given by a human facilitator or through job aids, computerized or not.

Selection of a Generic Skill's Process

In Table 2, "Simulate a process", a sub-skill of the level 5 "Apply skills", is compared to "Construct a process", which is a sub-skill of the level 8 "Synthesize" skills in the taxonomy.

From these descriptions, it is easy to see that an activity scenario in an application domain such as "Information search on the Internet" will be quite different if the goal is to simulate such a process or to construct one. In the first case, a number of walks through the process will probably be sufficient, while in the second case, a project-based scenario where actors are engaged in a more complex problem-solving activity is better suited.

To guide the scenario modeling process, we need to assign generic skills to a main knowledge in an application domain such "Search for information on the Internet". Here are some *skill selection principles*.

- If a knowledge element is fundamental to actors in the target population and these actors have to reach an advanced level of expertise, the level of skill should be high: 7-Repair, 8-Synthesize, 9-Evaluate or 10-Self-manage.
- If a knowledge element is important to actors in the target population, requiring from them a large level of autonomy, the level of skill should be above average: 5-Apply/Use, 6-Analyze, 7-Repair, 8-Synthesize.
- If a knowledge element is useful to actors in the target population, requiring its regular use, the level of skill should be average: 3-Instanciate, 4-Transpose, 5-Apply/Use or 6-Analyze.
- If a knowledge element is sometimes useful to actors in the target population, asking them to retain only the main elements, the level of skill can be weak: 1-Pay attention, 2-Integrate or 3-Instanciate.

Once a generic skill is selected, a process model can be constructed, or selected in a library of skills' model such as the one presented in Chapter 7, to form the basis of an activity scenario.

For example, the MOT graph in Figure 3 provides a precise definition of "Simulate a process". This model starts with a description of the input process that will be simulated. The first subtask is to produce examples of all input objects or concepts. Then, we must find a procedure in the input process that can be applied to some of these inputs and we execute using the principles

Table 2. Comparison of two generic skills

Skill	Input	Product	Process Flow
Simulate a process	A *process*, its procedures, inputs, products and control principles.	A *trace* of the procedure: set of facts obtained through the application of the procedures in a particular case	- Choose input resources objects (data) - Select the first procedure to execute - Execute it and produce a first result - Select the next procedure and execute it - Use the control principles to control the flow of execution
Construct a process	Definition constraints such as relations between inputs and products of the process and/or required steps in the process.	A description of the process: its inputs, products, sub-procedures with their input and output, and the process control principles.	- Assign a name to the procedure to be constructed - Relate this main procedure to a specific input and product resource, respecting the definition constraints - Decompose the procedure, respecting the definition constraints - Continue to a point where well understood small procedures are defined.

that apply to it in the input process. The result is a product that can be used as an input to other procedures that will be executed until we arrive at a terminal procedure of the input process or if all the procedures have been executed. Then, the last task is to assemble the execution trace which the result of the simulation.

Transform the Generic Skill's Model to an Activity Scenario.

We will now use this generic process to build a learning scenario where learners will simulate a process such as "Search information on the Internet". To do this, we lay out a graph corresponding to the generic process, but taking a "learning activity" viewpoint.

Compared to the graph on Figure 3, the one on Figure 4 is specialized using terms specific to the application domain (the Internet). It is also formulated in a "task assignment style" displaying six activities. Based on the generic process inputs and products, the learning scenario starts with a description of the process to simulate and ends by producing a trace report.

Table 3 presents these activities and corresponding elements in the generic process description. Note also the loop between activities 4 and 5 that ends when no more procedure is available for execution.

Of course, the scenario is not yet complete. For example, we could add resources that help actors achieve their tasks, such as a tutorial on query operation or on a final report form. Also, we might specify some collaboration assignments and maybe a description of the evaluation principles that will be used to assess the learner's work.

But the important thing here is that the generic process becomes the founding structure to organize the actor's tasks. In that way, we make sure that he exercises the right generic skill, in this case "simulating a process", while working on the specific knowledge domain, thus building specific domain knowledge and meta-knowledge at the same time.

From Generic Skill's Principles to Assistance in a Scenario

We now use the generic skill's model as a basis to build an assistance scenario describing the activities and products that support actors such as a trainer, a content expert, a designer or a manager will provide to the user of the scenario. To identify the assistance activities ruled by these actors, we go back to the generic process that gave birth to the learning scenario and we identify principles governing the execution of this generic process. Figure 3 supplements the generic simulation pro-

Figure 3. Graph of a generic skill: "simulate a process"

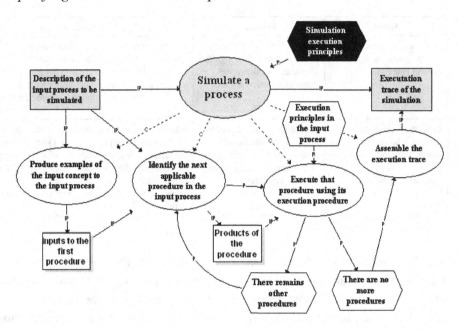

Figure 4. An activity scenario: simulate the "Search the Internet" process

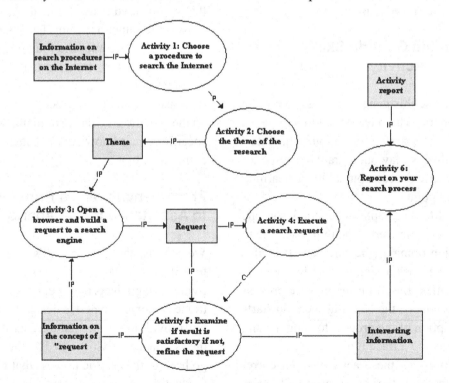

Table 3. Correspondence between learning activities and tasks in a generic process

Activity in the scenario	Correspondence in the generic process
Activity 1: Choose a procedure to search the Internet	Inputs to the generic simulation process, defining the case to be simulated
Activity 2: Choose the theme of the research	First applicable procedure to execute
Activity 3: Open a browser and build a search request	Next applicable procedure to execute
Activity 4: Execute a search request	Execute the chosen procedure
Activity 5: Examine if result is satisfactory; if not, refine the first request; if yes, store interesting information	Decision to continue or not
Activity 6: Report on your search process	Assemble the trace

cess on Figure 1 with generic principles controlling each of the sub-processes.

These principles (hexagons in inverted print) are the basis of the assistance scenario presented on Figure 6. On Table 4, we first state some of the principles on Figure 5 to help decide on a corresponding type of assistance to the scenario users.

Figure 4 presents, the multi-actor complete scenario where the assistance activities and resources are superposed to the user scenario of Figure 4. Every form of assistance corresponds to principles stated in Table 4. It shows three support actors giving different forms of assistance to the users.

This assistance scenario puts in evidence different activities of assistance (in inverted text on the figure) producing help resources for each of six learning activities of Figure 4.

- Three of these assistance resources are materials prepared by a designer, being used as inputs to the first three learning activities.
- Another type of assistance in activity 4, is an interaction by e-mail with an Internet content expert.
- Two other forms of assistance, in activities 5 and 6, involve a trainer animating a forum on the completeness principles of a simulation and also managing a FAQ (frequently asked questions) on the presentation norms for the final report.

Each of these forms of assistance draws its content from the principles describing how the simulation skill can be applied to knowledge processed in the learning unit. A skill's generic process and its execution principles thus define the content of the assistance supplied by a person playing the role of a facilitator, directly or through different types of teaching equipments or tools.

9.3 COMPETENCY-BASED ACTOR'S ROLES AND RESOURCES

We will now discuss the use of generic skills and competencies in defining the roles of the actors in an environment based on an activity scenario, and the selection of resources to help them play their roles.

Actor's Roles and Generic Skills

Figure 6 in the preceding section give us clues to help identify resources for the various actors in the scenario. For example the designer will require a tool to produce and integrate interactive advice, produce texts, videos and Web pages. The trainer will need a forum tool and a frequently-asked question on-line tool. The content expert will need e-mail, textual and video chat to interact with the learners.

We will now extend this approach to show how we can plan the interactions between actors and resource in a virtual work or training environment.

Figure 5. Meta-principles for the management of a simulation processes

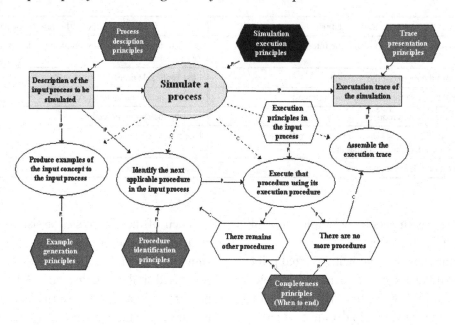

Figure 6. Assistance scenario for the simulation of a multimedia production process

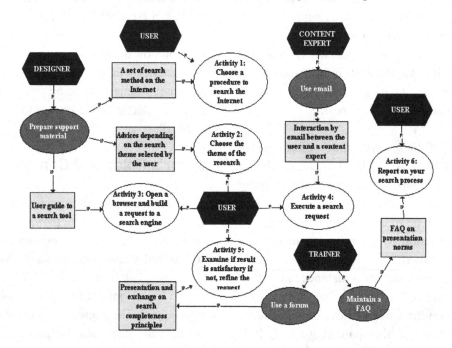

Table 4. Examples of meta-principles and corresponding assistance

Meta-procedure	Examples of meta-principles	Type of assistance
Description of the simulated process	• Inputs and products of the simulated process have to be clearly identified. • Simulated process must be decomposed into its main procedures, if necessary on more than 2 levels. • Principles governing the execution of the process must be identified.	Case studies on a method to describe simulated procedures
Generation of examples (cases to be simulated)	• Every example has to contain a value for each of the inputs of the process to be simulated. • Examples have to cover all the possible cases of execution of the procedure.	Interactive advisor giving help adapted to the examples supplied by the user
Identification of procedures to be applied	• For each of the examples, build a structured list with the products of already executed procedures and add them to inputs. • Eliminate from the preceding list the products that are not inputs of a still unexecuted procedure. • Always choose procedures giving the greatest number of new products for still unexecuted procedures	Texts presenting in detail these principles as well as examples of execution traces
Execution of procedures	• Once a procedure to be executed has been chosen, use its execution principles to obtain new products. • Execution depends especially on the domain of application.	Interaction by e-mail with a content expert
Completeness of the simulation	• If the simulated process is sequential, in parallel or a decision tree, the simulation is completed when every possible branch was executed for at least an example, • If the process is iterative, it contains execution principles telling when to stop cycling; the simulation is completed when each of these stop principles have been tested for at least an example.	Presentation of these completeness principles and dialogue with a trainer to assess completeness of a simulation
Presentation of the execution traces	• Presentation must contain the description of the process to be simulated • Simulated examples must be regrouped in categories according to the structure of the process. • For every example, present the succession of executed procedures and their products.	Contextual help on the presentation of these standards accompanied with examples.

In our previous work, we have built a multi-actor scenario displaying the interaction between the main actors in a virtual campus. Such a model can be easily adapted to a virtual organization. In fact a virtual campus is virtual organization of a special kind, aiming at the delivery of educational activities.

In our virtual campus model (Paquette 2001) we have identified five main actors.

• The *Learner's* main function is to transform information into personal knowledge. The learner achieves knowledge acquisition and construction by managing a learning environment planned by another actor, the designer, through collaboration with other learner agents and assistance from other actors.

• The *Content expert* makes information available to the learner. The corresponding content sources may be persons providing information, but also books, videos, courseware, etc. The learner can also produce information available to others as a result of his/her production activities..

• The *Designer* is the actor planning, adapting and sustaining a telelearning system that integrates information sources (human informers or learning materials), and also self-management, assistance and collaboration tools for the other actors.

• The *Trainer* provides pedagogical assistance or coaching by giving advice to the learner about her individual process and the interactions that may be useful to her based on the learning scenarios defined by the designer.

- Finally, the *Manager* provides organizational assistance to the learner (and other actors) by managing actors and events, creating groups or making tele-services available in order to insure the success of the learning process, based on the scenarios defined by the designer.

In a second step, for each of these actors, we have identified a set of roles that they can play in a virtual campus. These are shown in Table 5. In the last column we have selected a corresponding generic skill from the taxonomy developed in Chapter 6 and 7. This is the basis for defining target competencies needed to perform each actor's role.

Notice that some of the roles are too general to identify a target skill. In this case, these would have to be specified in designing a specific environment. But in all cases it will be possible to use the generic skill to design a role scenario as in section 9.2 and also, by using the skill as a basis for a target competency, to build a knowledge model in an application domain as in section 9.1.

Coordinating Role Scenarios

Consider the role « to solve problem », a role played on various subjects (application domains) by all the actors: learners have to solve problems related to the subject of the course, trainers have to diagnose the progress of their students, designers have to solve instructional engineering problems and so on. A diagnosis process, such as the one described on Figure 15 in Chapter 3 or Figure 1 in Chapter 6 can form the basis of a role scenario for a learner having to solve mechanical failure problems, but also as the basis of another role scenario for a trainer having to diagnose learners' progress problem.

In Table 5, we were not able to assign a generic skill to this role because it depends on the type of problem. Is it a transposition, simulation, classification, diagnosis or design problem? Depending on such a choice, we could assign a precise generic

skill from the taxonomy, and a process model of that generic skill.

Now, let us take a more global viewpoint for actors interacting in Web-based environment for car mechanics composed of four learning units.

- An advanced learner in car mechanics will progress from an information consultation role (memorize, familiarity level), to a problem solver role (diagnose, familiarity level). He will then proceed to a chat discussion to compare result with other learners (synthesize, awareness level) and finally to a self-evaluation role (evaluate, awareness level). In this learning strategy we need four role scenarios corresponding to the generic skills and target competencies, adapted to the subject of car mechanics. With this skeleton of activities, resources can be selected for each of the four roles. The subject of resource selection in scenarios will be discusses in Chapter 12.
- With respect to this pedagogical strategy, the trainer will first act as a coach while the learner searches for information. Then he will use a diagnosis scenario to help learners while they resolve car malfunctioning problems. After that, he will animate the chat discussion where learners compare their solutions and at the end, he will provide feedback to each student on the result of their self-evaluation. The four corresponding skills (respectively: analyze, diagnose, self-control and evaluate) will form the skeleton of the role's activities, specifying the actions to be made and the resources to use or produce.

This example shows the importance of coordinating the actors' role in a multi-actor scenario and the provided based on the identification of the generic skills involved in learners' target competencies.

Table 5. Actor roles in eLearning and corresponding generic skills

ACTOR	ROLES OF THE ACTOR		CORRESPONDING SKILLS
LEARNER (**Transforms information into knowledge**)	Managing his learning scenarios	10	**Self-manage**
	Explore documentation sources	6	**Analyze**
	Solve problems	*	*Depends on problems*
	Achieve a project	10	**Self-manage**
	Produce assessed activities	*	*Depends on activities*
	Self-evaluate activities	9	**Evaluate**
	Interact socially	*	*Depends on interactions*
	Debate in a tele-discussion	8	**Synthesize**
	Communicate information to others	2	**Integrate**
CONTENT EXPERT (**Provides information**)	Present information	3	**Instanciate/Precise Analyze Instanciate/Precise Evaluate Analyze**
	Clarify content	6	
	Manage of mediated knowledge	3	
	Analyze traces of activities	9	
	Analyze documents	6	
DESIGNER (**Builds, adapt, maintain learning systems**)	Analyze Training needs	6	**Analyze**
	Build knowledge models	8	**Synthesize**
	Build instructional scenario	8	**Synthesize**
	Write learning systems plans and cost estimates	8	**Synthesize**
	Simulate and evaluate an environment	5,9	**Apply and Evaluate**
	Produce learning materials	8	**Synthesize**
	Plan the delivery of an environment	8	**Synthesize**
TRAINER (**Facilitates learning**)	Produce diagnosis	6	**Analyze**
	Advise learners on their activities	9	**Evaluate**
	Evaluate learners productions	9	**Evaluate**
	Help learners in using the environment	5	**Apply**
	Animate team and group activities	4	**Self-manage**
MANAGER (**managing actors and events**)	Make decision	10	**Self-manage**
	Control, monitor activities	6	**Analyze**
	Manage delivery operations	10	**Self-manage**
	Setup teams and groups	6	**Analyze**
	Organize experimentation and validation activities	6	**Analyze**
	Coordinate learners assessment	6	**Analyze**
	Manage learning system assessment	10	**Self-manage**
	Insure network infrastructure maintenance	7	**Repair**

There remains the important question of the suitability or adaptation of role scenarios to the actual and target competencies of the individuals involved in each role. For this, we will need a more precise user model. This is the subject of the next section.

9.4 KNOWLEDGE AND COMPETENCY ACTORS MODELS[1]

In the first three sections of the chapter we have studied scenario modeling and knowledge modeling all based on a competency driven approach. In the rest of the chapter we will take a closer look at the model of the person executing the scenario tasks, the actual actor. Indeed, while executing or playing a scenario, the role is instantiated to particular persons whose individual properties should be taken into account to adapt or personalize the process as well as to give the best assistance when required.

The notion of personalization should be understood here as a way to adapt a scenario, or more generally a learning situation (its activities, resources, support agent, etc.) to the cognitive state of a particular user, that is to his/her knowledge and competencies. Our main focus is thus on adapting the activities and resources and not on adapting their form or presentation (as is often the case when talking about personalization in the context of hypermedia).

We present here a model to represent a particular learner, before, during and after a learning scenario; we call this model the learner model. The learner model is based on the competency approach described earlier in this book. Although the focus of the section is on the model of a learner, the user model presented here could be used to describe other actors interacting with processes such as an expert in charge of a knowledge intensive business process or a tutor responsible of assistance activities to learners in an activity scenario.

Before describing the learner model, it is worth stating the three assumptions about learning that guided this model proposal:

• Learning is a lifelong process
• Learning happens in different contexts ranging from formal to informal learning, from academic to professional to personal settings
• Learning takes place through social interaction: several actors and agents interact with the learner in his/her learning process: teachers, tutors, pairs, learning systems, work colleagues, etc.

Based on these assumptions, the learner model is:

• Evolving: its state is changing permanently as the person learns new things. Other than modeling the current learning state, the learner model should keep track of the learning evolution: the previous states as well as the time, action and actors involved in a state transition.
• Open to several learning contexts: the model should be related with all settings in which the learner is learning something he/she wants to keep track of.

• Open to actors and systems involved in the learning process: those actors and systems could state the achievement of a particular competency by the learner thus modifying the learner model state.

Moreover, we believe the learner should be the owner of a model that describes him/her and he/she should be able to decide on restrictions or conditions for consulting or updating his/her model.

A Competency Based Learner Model

The kernel of the learner model, called here the core learner model, is composed of three parts: the learner competencies, the learner productions or portfolio and the learner personal and professional information. Their interrelations are shown on Figure 7.

• *Learner competencies.* The learner competencies are the main elements of the model. Competencies are the set of pertinent competencies he/she has acquired in his/her life. The term "competency profile" has been used in Chapter 5 for this concept. A competency is described in Chapter 5 in terms of a generic skill applied to knowledge in a domain with one or more performance indicators (for instance: give the definition of a polygon in a complete form). In a particular moment, the model will contain the highest competencies, both on the generic skill attained and performance level achieved by the learner. The learner competencies are grouped by domain. The so-called general or core competencies, like those related with leadership, communication and teamwork are also grouped together in knowledge domains that contain, respectively, leadership, communication or teamwork concepts, processes and principles

Figure 7. Competency based learner model

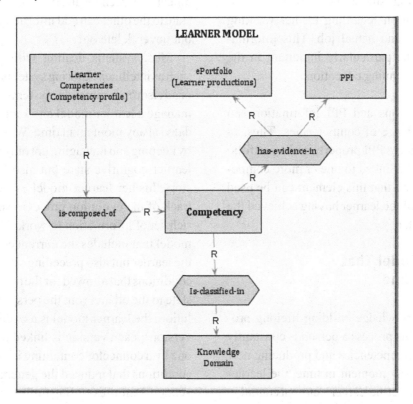

• *Learner productions (E-Portfolio).* The learner model contains also documents produced by the learner that are used or could be used as evidence of his/her competencies. These productions are structured in an e-portfolio. E-Portfolios are "collections of personal information about a learner that represent accomplishments, goals, experiences, and other personalized records that a learner can present to schools, employers, or other entities" (IMS 2004). E-portfolios can be used in four major ways: (1) to describe and demonstrate, (2) to plan, (3) to reflect, and (4) to share its content. The major uses of our learner model are to describe, to demonstrate and to plan, although the other two uses become also very relevant when dealing with open, emerging and collaborative learning environments. E-Portfolios based on these

two major uses are frequently referred to as learning e-Portfolios (IMS Global Consortium 2004, ePortfolio Consortium 2003). Other types of portfolios are personal e-Portfolios, based on self-reflection, and professional e-Portfolios, mainly used for certification and for job search and based on demonstrations and content sharing.

• *Personal and professional Information (PPI).* As stated earlier, learning is a lifelong process that happens in formal and informal learning contexts. The personal and professional information, PPI, is the part of the model that keeps track of information of the learner which, although not directly related to the actual learning process, helps to better know the person behind the learner. PPI includes information about the learner's languages, cultural issues, previous studies, hobbies, etc. as well as information regarding his/her working experience and actual job. This information may be particularly important in the case of continuing education.

Both productions and PPI information can be used as evidence of competencies. Thus, in the learner model, a PPI property and a portfolio production can be linked to one or more competencies, indicating that this element can be used as an evidence of the learner having achieved the referred competency.

A Learner Model That Evolves in Time

Learning is a knowledge building lifelong process. Through this process a person is constantly acquiring new competencies and producing new knowledge. At any moment in time, the learner model should reflect the learner's current cognitive state. A learner model should thus be updated to reflect this evolution. We identify four types of updates to the model: (1) adding a learner production to his/her e-portfolio, (2) adding or modifying information of the PPI, (3) adding or updating a competency, (4) adding a link between an PPI or an e-portfolio element and a competency – that is recognizing an element of the model as an evidence of a competency. It is worth noticing that several updates can take place at the same time: for instance a student project can be used as evidence for several new competencies thus the model should be updated with the new competencies, the new e-portfolio production (the project) and the links between this production and the added competencies. In the next section, we address the question of who is allowed to update the learner model.

Let's underline at this point a choice we have made regarding the learner model evolution. We are working with a monotonic approach of learning, that is, we suppose that a person never

unlearns, which means that a transition from one state to the other can add information to the model but never delete one.

Most systems dealing with personalization such as intelligent tutoring systems (Wenger 1987) or advisor/recommender systems (Winkels 1992) manage a learner model and keep this model updated at any moment in time. We go a step further by keeping and managing not only the last, current learner cognitive state but also his/her learning story, his/her learner model evolution. Keeping track of the evolution process itself gives a very rich set of information to work with. Our learner model that includes the current cognitive state of the learner but also preceding states as well as the conditions that allowed for the transition from one state to the other. From the perspective of its evolution, the learner model is a collection of model versions; each version is linked to the preceding one by a connector containing information on the conditions that induced the generation of the new version. Before exploring further these conditions, let's reflect on the social dimension of learning.

A Learner Model Having Multiple-Viewpoints

We have already stated that learning takes place in the learner's various learning situations, including learning units and their scenarios, and also through social interactions. The core learner model shows an isolated picture of the learner model. But the learner is situated in a rich learning context; learning is a social process where different actors are involved. As shown on Figure 8, the learner interacts with other learners, with tutors and professors and eventually with domain experts, administrative staff and technical support resources. Other than these human actors, the learning context includes all the learning activities, resources and tools that are present in a learning situation. Those elements are grouped in what we named a learning unit. A learning unit may be a standalone activity, a module, a course or a whole

Figure 8. Actors interacting with a learner model

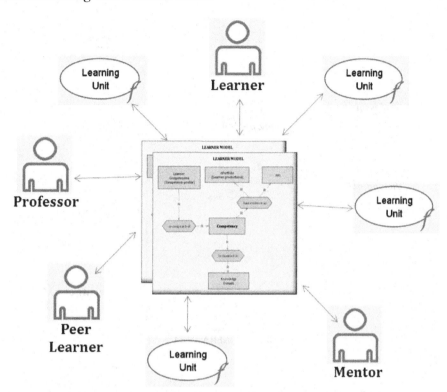

learning program. Moreover, a learner may be taking several courses at the same time, having to deal with different learning units.

These different agents: units of learning and actors interact with the learner and should be allowed to consult the learner model to orient their interactions. On the other hand, through these interactions, agents can state some competencies or evidences for this learner, thus they should also eventually be allowed to register changes in the learner model, such as adding a production, a PPI element or a competency or linking a production to a competency to state that this production evidences this competency. We have here a model that keeps track of all those points of views on the learner, a multiple viewpoints learner model.

A viewpoint is a partial representation of a reality, from an observer's perspective. Two assumptions are possible: either one supposes that the set of viewpoints for an object are consistent, that is if two observers see a same property, they see the same value for this property. The second possibility is accepting inconsistency, which means: viewpoints represent subjective views and a same property may have different values for different observers (Marino, Rechenmann, Uvietta 1990). It would be simplistic to think that all actors and systems interacting with the learner will have the same view of this learner. On the contrary, very often we find two teachers having opposite perceptions of one student's communication or leadership skills. We think that divergent perceptions of a learner's competency represent a very rich source of reflection and should not be avoided. We will use thus the second assumption: although some properties may have the same value for all observers, the model can handle inconsistencies between viewpoints.

Our learner model is a multi-viewpoint model composed of the core learner model and the related

Figure 9. Multiple viewpoints learner model

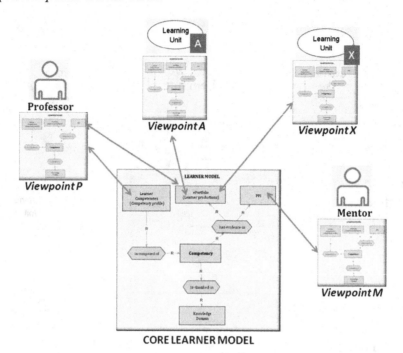

learner model viewpoints. The core learner model includes objective information such as PPI and productions, as well as the learner competencies for which there is a consensus between the various human and machine agents, as well as for the links between those competencies and various evidences. Connected to this core learner model, there are as many viewpoints as there are differentiated observers allowed to modify the learner model (tutors, professors, peers, learning units, etc.). Those viewpoints are not pre-established but settled by the learning context of the learner. A viewpoint contains competencies along with links between those competencies and the learner's PPI and productions.

A Multi-Viewpoints Learner Model in Action

A learner model is thus a collection of ordered and connected versions of a structure composed of a core model and related model viewpoints (Figure 9). We have listed above the type of modifications that can take place in the learner model, which is the answer to the question "what" might be updated. We will know explore further the conditions that activate these modifications, mainly the answer to the questions "when" and "how".

Concerning the "when" question, two types of actors can trigger a modification of the model: the learning systems and the human actors.

The learning system can intervene at four granularity levels. The model evolution can take place:

(1) at the end of a whole learning program (a large learning unit composed of more than one course),
(2) at the end of a course,
(3) at the end of a learning activity (included in a course),
(4) after a resource is used of,
(5) after the learner has created or modified a product.

The choice of using one or the other of these granularity levels can depend on institutional constraints or on the properties of the learning process. For example, one organization might decide to keep track of competencies acquired at the end of a course while another one would like to use the learner model to track the evolution in a course thus allowing for model modification after each activity. Moreover, if the course is based on the elaboration of a project, learner model modifications can be planned after the main milestones of the project.

The human actors can also provoke an evolution of the model by adding information to it. Again, there can be rules stated to allow a human actor to add information to the model at any moment or in particular moments of the learning process.

Let's look now at the question of "how" a learner's modification takes place. When a modification is made by one of the actors in the system (human or system), a new version of the learner model is generated and the connection with the old and the new version includes conditions such as who triggered the modification, at what moment in time and which event activated it (answer to the preceding when question). At that moment a modification mechanism is launched. This mechanism is defined outside of the model, for it should take into account organizational hierarchies and conflict solving strategies. If, as a result of this negotiation mechanism, an agreement is obtained and all concerned actors accept the modification, this modification is reflected in the core model of the new version, otherwise, the modification is only reflected in the view-point of the proposer.

It is worth noticing that the model evolution mechanism can be very complex or quite simple depending on the learning context. For instance, let's think of a situation where a learner is taking only one course and where only the teacher can certify learner's competencies and competency evidences. In this context, no negotiation mechanism is activated and every time the teacher modi-

fies the model, a new version is generated with the update on the core learner model.

Initializing the Learner Model for a Learning Process

When initiating a learning process, several aspects should be defined as to "connect" the model with this learning process:

1. *The competency referential that will be used to assess the learner's competencies.* This information is normally found in the description of the course, mainly in the prerequisites and objectives components of it.
2. *The starting model.* The model should be instantiated with the PPI part as well as with all previous competencies and evidences that concern the chosen competency referential.
3. *The human and software actors that will be allowed to consult or modify the model and the type of action they are allowed to do.* As stated earlier, we believe the learner should have control of his/her model. At the beginning of the training, he/she should decide on access rights for the various actors. This decision could be based on institutional restriction (for instance if a university demands that administrative staff have access to the model, the student can either allow this access or decide to take his/her course elsewhere). The access rights for each actor are formalized in a contract that regulates the interaction between the actors and the model
4. *The negotiation mechanism.* Again, the earner must accept or not the institutional negotiation process; for instance, professor's updates are not negotiated; peers updates must be approved by the professor, etc.
5. *The moments in the training process where the model could be modified* (the answer to the when question).

Scenario Adaptation Using the Learner Model

Using a rich learner model, one can adapt a learning scenario and automatically assist the learner during the learning process. We will look thus here at the link between a learner model and a particular learning unit and how this learning unit, while consulting the learner model can adapt the learning process. The adaptation of this process can be threefold: adapting the learning resources (documents or instruments), adapting an activity or task, and adapting the flow of activities, the scenario itself. It is worth noticing that in all three cases, the scenario should have taken into account those adaptations.

To adapt the learning resources, the system should search for resources that are pertinent to both the task and the learner, either from pre-established learning object repositories or form the Web. To do so, it must align the semantic description of possible resources, with the conditions established in the scenario for that particular activity and with the learner model. As all three will be described in terms of competencies, this alignment means finding the best competency match (see Chapter 12). The contract established for this particular learning unit will decide if the system is to look at the learner model core competencies, at those stated by the particular learning unit or at those from other viewpoints.

To adapt the activity, the scenario should have provided optional versions of the activity, indexed by competencies and again to choose the best activity, a competency equation must be solved.

Adapting the scenario path for a particular learner means either skipping some activities, or adding some activities or choosing from a branch of sequence possibilities, at a particular point in the learn flow. The scenario designer must have foreseen those possibilities together with the conditions (in terms of learner competencies) for the scenario adaptation. When executing such a scenario, the system consults the learner model at each decision point and states if the conditions are satisfied, in which case the path is adapted consequently.

It is important to clarify that the adaptation discussed here focuses on the competency model of a learner. Other useful adaptations, which also take advantage of the learner model can be made regarding cultural issues, learner's preferences and performance while interacting with a learning unit, time spent, resources used, etc.

Finally, let's point out that this chapter doesn't address the key concept of assistance. Automatic assistance as well as system mediated assistance is a key element to help a learner succeed in his learning process. The issue is out of the scope of this chapter but let's just state that all adaptation cases explained in this section can be redefined in terms of assistance. The conditions are evaluated the same way but no action in directly taken by the system. An assistance agent will take control and interact with the learner to allow him/her to decide on the best adaptation to make. Examples of such assistance agents will be given in Chapter 21.

CONCLUSION

This chapter concludes section II of this book devoted to the fundamental concepts of competency modeling. In the first chapter, we have looked at competency profiles in different projects and different areas of human activity. From this, we have defined a competency as a generic skill applied to knowledge in a domain at a certain level of performance. In Chapter 6 and 7, we have focused on generic skills taxonomies seen from multiple viewpoints: as generic processes that apply in various knowledge domains; as a way to model knowledge about knowledge and more precisely cognitive processes that transform knowledge; and finally, as a way to state knowledge mastery objectives, prerequisites or actual state or level of knowledge mastery.

With this strongly structured set of concepts, Chapter 8 and 9 have addressed some of the many ways competencies can be used, for example as a central concept in instructional engineering to built learning scenarios for programs, courses and learning units. The concepts of learning scenario and multi-actor business workflow have been merged into an extension of the previous MOT knowledge editor presented in the first section of this book, together with a scenario modeling process that used prerequisite and target competencies to orient the knowledge and the scenario modeling process.

In this chapter, we have expanded this idea first by extending the concept of competency gap, which is the distance between prerequisite/actual and target competencies on a two dimensional space: the skill's level in the taxonomy presented in Chapter 6, and the performance level obtained by combining a number of performance indicators. This competency gap guides the modeling of the domain knowledge that will be more or less expanded depending on the size of the competency gap. In the second section, we have seen that the skill process part of a target competency provides an initial structure for a learning scenario that will result hopefully in reducing the competency gap. In the third section, we have addressed the association of competency to actors, to help define their role, and to identify the resources they will need to orient and coordinate their action in a meaning full way. In the last section, we have presented a learner's model that can be also used for any actor role. This model is competency-based, grouping progressively individual competencies gained through interactions with learning productions (E-Portfolios) and personal properties that provide evidence for competency acquisition.

This chapter in particular and this section of the book have shown the importance of modeling competencies linked to knowledge in different domains, both for learning, for knowledge man-

agement, and for the development on learning/work environments that can support the evolution of a person's competencies.

The intellectual system developed in this section has been used in many projects that will be presented in detail in section IV of the book. These case studies will provide a good way to deepen the understanding of these concepts while demonstrating their usability in actual practice within various organizations and knowledge domains.

REFERENCES

ePortConsortium. (2003). *Electronic Portfolio White Paper.*

IMS. (2004). *IMS ePortfolio Best Practice and implementation Guide, Version 1.0 Final Specification.* IMS Global Learning Consortium.

Mariño, O., Rechenmann, F., & Uvietta, P. (1990). Multiple Perspectives and Classification mechanism in object-oriented representation. In *9th. European Conference on Artificial Intelligence ECAI.*

Moulet, L., Marino, O., Hotte, R., & Labat, J.-M. (2008). Framework for a Competency-driven, Multi-viewpoint and Evolving Learner Model. In B. Woolf et al. (Ed.), *Proceedings of Intelligent Tutoring Systems, 9th International Conference, ITS 2008,* Montréal, Canada, June 2008 (LNCS 5091, pp. 702-705). Berlin: Springer.

Paquette, G. (2001). Designing Virtual Learning Centers . In Adelsberger, H., Collis, B., & Pawlowski, J. (Eds.), *Handbook on Information Technologies for Education & Training.* Berlin: Springer-Verlag.

Paquette, G. (2003). *Instructional Engineering for Network-Based Learning.* San Francisco: Pfeiffer/Wiley.

Paquette, G., Aubin, C., & Crevier, F. (1999 August). MISA, A Knowledge-based Method for the Engineering of Learning Systems. *Journal of Courseware Engineering, 2.*

Paquette, G., Crevier, F., & Aubin, C. (1994). ID knowledge in a course design workbench. *Educational Technology, 34*(9), 50–57.

Wenger, E. (1987). *Artificial Intelligence and Tutoring Systems- Computational and Cognitive Approaches to the Communication of Knowledge.* San Francisco: Morgan-Kaufmann.

Winkels, R. (1992). *Explorations in intelligent tutoring and help.* Amsterdam: IOS Press.

ENDNOTE

[1] This section is largely based on the Ph.D work of Lucie Moulet (Moulet, Marino, Hotte and Labat 2008).

Section 3
Ontology Modeling and the Semantic Web

Chapter 10
Visual Ontology Modeling and the Semantic Web

Gilbert Paquette
LICEF Research Center, Canada

ABSTRACT

- The Semantic Web - Ontologies and Inferences
  - Semantic Web Technologies
  - Ontologies
  - The Ontology Web Language (OWL)
- The MOT+OWL and MOWL Visual Ontology Editors
  - Class Declaration and Relational Axioms
  - Property Declaration and Attribute Axioms
  - Property Restriction for Class Definition
  - Individuals and Relations
- Ontology Examples
  - An Eco-Agriculture Ontology
  - An Ontology for Learning Design
- A Detailed Ontology For Competencies
  - Main Ontology
  - Generic Skills Sub-Ontology
  - Performance Indicators Sub-Ontology
  - Competency Scale
- Ontology Engineering
  - Ontology Engineering Methods
  - Contribution of the MOT Knowledge Modeling Method

The exponential growth of information available on the Internet makes it increasingly necessary to introduce intelligent agents to facilitate the processing of information and knowledge. A

DOI: 10.4018/978-1-61520-839-5.ch010

few years ago, one of the founders of the Web and current director of the W3 Consortium, Tim Berners-Lee, along with his colleagues (Berners-Lee, Hendler, and Lassila, 2001), proposed to provide the Internet with information whose meaning, beyond its syntax, could be interpreted by a program that would search information in ways that are far more intelligent than now. This new generation of the Internet has been termed "*the Semantic Web*".

We haven't reached that level of sophistication yet, but we're getting closer. Here is an example anyone with an iPhone in 2008 could perform: You know that you will be in Boston next Monday and you will need to go to a computer store to buy some software. You decide to use a voice recognition application such as VLingo and you say to your iPhone, "Boston, Computer Shops, near the airport." It automatically finds several stores with these properties on the Internet and displays them on a map, together with their address. With this information, you can then ask the device, first to phone some of the stores to check the availability of the software. Next, using the iPhone integrated GPS application, you can have an itinerary that will guide you to travel between the airport and one of the stores.

Though there is some intelligence involved in this example, there are two human interventions required. This is because, currently, though computers can analyze Web pages and find information, they have no way, except in rare situations, to process the meaning or infer relationships between links to other pages or applications.

Let us take a more complex example. You learn that your mother has to undergo a series of weekly physiotherapy sessions recommended by her doctor, and you must accompany her. On the Semantic Web, you instruct the agent that looks after your agenda to organize your schedule accordingly. The agent receives information regarding the *treatment* from the doctor's agent, then examines a list of *physiotherapists*, selecting those that correspond to your mother's *insurance*

policy and that are situated within a *radius of 20 kilometers* from her home. Your agent then begins to search *visiting hours* that are compatible with your schedule. Within minutes, it proposes a treatment schedule for your mother.

To accomplish this, the meaning of each page and the terms it contains must be encoded in a web of relationships. In this way, when the agent comes to the page of the physiotherapy clinic, it is able to identify not only keywords such as "treatment," "doctor," "physiotherapist," and "schedule" syntactically, but also that such and such physiotherapist works at the clinic and is available Mondays, Wednesdays, and Fridays during certain times of the year. The page therefore contains a script that can be interpreted by the agent and return a list of possible visiting hours between such and such dates.

10.1 THE SEMANTIC WEB: ONTOLOGIES AND INFERENCES

The Semantic Web is not a new Web but an extension of the actual Internet where an increasing number of pages specify the meaning of the information they contain and are therefore interpretable by a search agent. Given the millions, if not billions, of pages currently available on the Internet, the transition to the Semantic Web will not happen overnight, but it has already begun. It will happen domain by domain by members of a community interested in the same domain and who provide knowledge descriptions (metadata) to the Web pages in their domain.

Figure 1 illustrates the general concept of a semantic Web. Resources available on the Internet, such as data bases, Web sites, texts, images, videos, interactive applications all support elements of knowledge that are described by some metadata listing their properties.

For example, a certain book has an author, has a number of pages, talks about medicine, mainly on heart diseases, has a table of contents that point

Figure 1. The Semantic Web

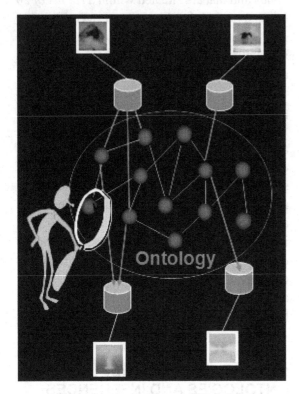

to knowledge in this subject, is related to other books, etc. The values of this book's properties, its metadata, are all taken from an underlying network of concepts and relations between them. A kind of knowledge model like the ones we have encountered throughout this book in its previous chapters. Most of the time, this model will take the form of an *ontology*, a notion that we will discuss in this chapter. Using an ontology, software agents will make deductions starting from search requests using an inference engine on the Internet.

Because of that, ontologies or other kind of knowledge representation languages for the Semantic Web, have to help build formal models. Unlike most of the semi-formal models we have built up until now. Formal models have to be completely unambiguous in order that software agents can process them and make inferences.

Knowledge representation systems developed in artificial intelligence have achieved good results in this area, particularly in the development of expert

systems and the analysis of natural language. Until recently, these systems were centralized, requiring each user to share the same definition of concepts. In addition, items addressed by expert systems have been limited to a small number in order for them to be processed reliably. On the other hand, to develop the Semantic Web, we must accept a decentralization of concepts, a multiplicity of terminology, and large sets of items that can evolve and adapt over time. To achieve this, we need a common representational language for data that can be understood by all kinds of software agents; ontologies (sets of statements) that translate information from disparate databases into common terms; and rules that allow software agents to reason about the information describes in those terms" (Feigenbaum, Herman, Hongsermeier and Neumann 2007) are the building blocks of the Semantic Web.

Semantic Web Technologies

The basic technologies for developing the Semantic Web are available and increasingly applied. The Extensible Markup Language (XML) allows one to create a structured description of the contents of a Web page. The meaning of this content can be specified by a resource description protocol called RDF (Resource Description Framework). RDF represents knowledge in the form of triples written in XML. An RDF triple consists of a subject (resource), a predicate (one of its properties), and an object (a value of the property or a class to which the resource belongs).

For example, in a set of Web pages regarding family ties between a group of people, RDF can be used to represent assertions about these people and their relationships such as "is the brother of" or "is the father or mother of." Thus, from the statements "John is Nathalie's brother" and "Nathalie is Nicole's mother," and the definition rule "If X is Y's brother and Y is Z's mother, then X is Z's uncle," an inference agent can deduce that "John is Nicole's uncle" even if that information is not explicitly written on a Web page. These can be termed "intelligent" agents, since they can infer information that is not explicitly stated.

RDF triples written on the Web represent a network of information in which subjects, predicates, and objects can be specified by URIs (Universal Resource Identifier) much in the same way a URL (Uniform Resource Locator) specifies à link to a Web page. In fact, an URL is a special case of an URI. This mechanism allows users to specify a new relationship simply by specifying its URI somewhere on the Web. Because RDF uses URIs to encode information about a resource, this ensures that the concepts they describe are more than just words in a document; they represent a definition that is available to everyone on the Web.

URIs can also be used to represent concepts by going beyond terminology or even natural language, since all that is required to state is that such and such a term used in a Web page is a synonym for a concept already defined by its URI. This is where the concept of ontology comes

into play. Typically, an ontology is a taxonomy of concepts that describes a set of relationships between the concepts, and a set of inference rules. The taxonomy defines classes and subclasses of objects of the same type. One can then define a number of relationships between these classes and their objects, allowing the sub-classes to inherit properties. The inference rules (or axioms) add a dynamic aspect to the ontology.

Ontologies

Let us illustrate the concept of an ontology with an example. We can describe the occupations of a group of persons through a taxonomy of occupations. Part of this *taxonomy* is represented by the MOT model in Figure 2, in the form of increasingly specialized concepts connected by S links. The class "Persons" is divided into sub-classes such as "Office Worker," "Professional," and "Factory Worker," and the class "Professionals"

Figure 2. An ontology of professions and family relationships

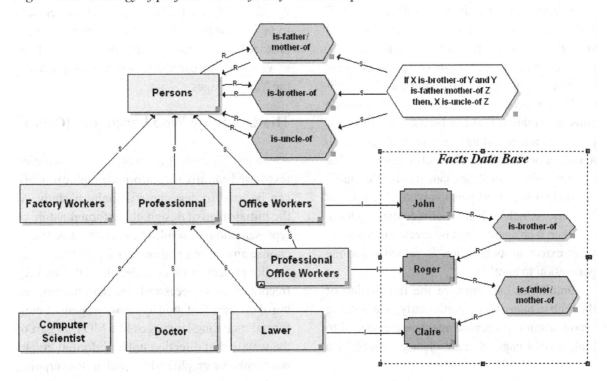

is divided into further specialized sub-classes such as "Lawyer," "Computer Scientist," and "Doctor."

This MOT model also contains the family *relationships* between the persons such as "is-brother-of," "is-father/mother-of," and "is-uncle-of." These properties are represented on the model by principles related to object class, in this case, the same class.

We complete the ontology's definition by adding *inference rules* or *axioms*. In our model, one of the axioms is represented by a principle linking three relationships—the relationship "is-uncle-of" is defined by the relationships "is-brother-of" and "is-father/mother of." Another axiom defines the class "Professional Office Workers" as people who are both professionals and work in an office. On the figure, this class is defined as a subclass that is the intersection of the two other classes (shown by a label in the lower right corner of the graphic object).

Once the ontology is created, we can populate it with instances or individuals and specify the classes to which they belong (by I links) as well as their properties. In our example, the following statements are made: "John is-brother-of Roger" and "Roger is-father/mother of Claire." A set of such statements is called a knowledge base.

A MOT graph such as the one presented here can be converted into XML using the MOT+ editor. If associated with a Web page, the XML code adds information that can be used by scripts or programs integrated into various intelligent Web agents. For example, a search engine capable of processing ontologies can handle the query "provide a list of all persons who are uncles of lawyers," which will return a list containing John. Another Web agent could be created to verify to what extent an occupation is passed from one generation to another.

Ontologies can improve the functioning of the Web in many ways, particularly in increasing search accuracy, because agents are designed to look at only pages that are clearly defined by a URI for which a representation exists, rather than all pages containing vague, undefined keywords.

Ontologies greatly facilitate the creation of programs that can tackle complicated problems whose solutions can be found by visiting more than one page. For example, suppose you want to find the address of a Mr. Cook who you met at a conference last year. You do not remember his name, but you remember that he worked for a client of yours and that his son is a student at your alma mater. A Web agent would examine all the pages of people named "Cook," while avoiding pages related to "cooks," "cooking," "Cook Islands," etc. It will only return pages of people whose URI is on your client list, follow the links to their children's pages, and eliminate those pages for which there is no link to the URI of your alma mater. This type of search is impossible using current search engines and you would have spent much more time browsing on the Internet.

The effectiveness of such Web agents will increase exponentially as more information on the Web is defined semantically (in particular, by ontologies) and more services are automated by other Web agents. In order for these services to be located by Web agents, a communications protocol is required so that a description of the services can be described in a directory much like the Yellow Pages.

The Ontology Web Language (OWL)

Any type of knowledge representation, including text-based narratives or informal graphic models, can be used to describe a domain of study. At the initial stage of design, the informal nature of representation is useful. The mind must be free to choose any representation that seems best suited for the project to be considered. Still, this very freedom does not necessarily facilitate the processing of the representation by software agents. Semi-formal modeling languages like MOT go part of the way in that direction unlike informal graphs built with any graphic editor such as Powerpoint.

The MOT graphic syntax is structured and has a general unambiguous semantic. Using the MOT editor, models can be exported in many formats, including a native XML schema.

Using this schema, software agents can perform different kind of processing, but still some ambiguity remains as we will see in chapter 14. For example, in a control structure, texts within the principles that rule procedures cannot be interpreted in non-ambiguous terms for the process to be performed automatically. In fact, in instructional engineering applications, we had to constrain the MOT graphic language to introduce learning designs in a digitized platform like Explor@-2 (Paquette 2001). Even then, part of the transfer of the design to the delivery platform had to be done manually in order both to prevent enforcing unnatural graphic representations on the users or, at the opposite, leaving ambiguities that prevent the software to execute.

After a phase where informal graphic design has cleared up ideas, we need to move from informal or semi-formal visual representations to formal computable representations. Knowledge in a subject domain can be represented in many ways: taxonomies, thesauri, topic maps, conceptual graphs and ontologies. We are looking for a formal standardized representation that would guarantee computability of the representation of possibly complex domains, not only in simple situations of life or highly constrained domains like mathematics, but in domains as found in the majority of educational situations.

Ontologies are good candidates for that purpose and standard representation languages have been built to support the development of the Semantic Web. OWL, the Ontology Web Language is part of the growing set of World Wide Web consortium (W3C-OWL 2003) recommendations related to the Semantic Web. OWL provides three increasingly expressive representation languages, each providing an XML schema definition to guaranty the compliance of a particular model to the standard form.

- *"OWL Lite* supports those users primarily needing a classification hierarchy and simple constraints. OWL Lite provides a quick migration path for thesauri and other taxonomies. Owl Lite also has a lower formal complexity then the other two representations.

- *OWL DL* supports those users who want the maximum expressiveness while retaining computational completeness (all conclusions are guaranteed to be computable) and decidability (all computations will finish in finite time). OWL DL includes all OWL language constructs, but they can be used only under certain restrictions (for example, while a class may be a subclass of many classes, a class cannot be an instance of another class). OWL DL is so named due to its correspondence with description logics, a field of research that has studied the logics that form the formal foundation of OWL.

- *OWL Full* is meant for users who want maximum expressiveness and the syntactic freedom of RDF with no computational guarantees. For example, in OWL Full a class can be treated simultaneously as a collection of individuals and as an individual in its own right. OWL Full allows an ontology to augment the meaning of the pre-defined (RDF or OWL) vocabulary. It is unlikely that any reasoning software will be able to support complete reasoning for every feature of OWL Full." (W3C-OWL 2003)

Each of these languages is an extension of its simpler predecessor, enlarging what can be legally expressed and what can be validly deduced from the assertions in the ontology. Because of its foundation in description logics, and its computational completeness and decidability, we will concentrate our attention on OWL-DL.

Description Logics (Baader et al 2002) are important knowledge representation formalisms unifying and giving a logical basis to the well known traditions of Frame-based systems (Minski 1975), Semantic Networks (Quillian 1968) and KL-ONE-like languages (Brachman and Schmolze 1985), Object-Oriented representations, Semantic data models, and Type systems. A description logic is a subset of first-order predicate logic that consists of:

- A set of unary predicate symbols used to denote concept (or class) names
- A set of binary predicates used to denote role (or properties) names
- A recursive definition for defining new concept terms from concept names and role names using constructors and axiom restrictions.

Common constructors or restrictions are intersection or conjunction of concepts, union or disjunction of concepts, negation or complement of concepts, value, universal and existential restrictions, enumeration of individuals, inverse relationship between properties, equivalence of classes and properties, transitivity or symmetry of properties, etc. We will examine these concepts in the next section using two graphic languages that are extensions of MOT+ for OWL-DL models.

10.2 THE MOT+OWL AND MOWL VISUAL ONTOLOGY EDITORS

OWL-DL provides a precise XML schema for each component of an ontology but no graphic representation per se. Some ontology editors like HOZO (Sunagawa, Mizoguchi et al. 2003) or PROTÉGÉ (2006) provide partial graphical views of the ontology, but the construction of a model is largely form-based.

This is why MOT+OWL was built: to provide a complete formal graphic representation of all OWL-DL components that can combine the virtue of user-friendly graphical construction with the computational capabilities of a formal specification. In the context of the MOT representation system, ontologies, in particular OWL-DL constructs, correspond to a category of models called theories (see chapter 3). They can thus in principle be modeled graphically using the MOT syntax. In fact, we have specialized our MOT+ language and graphic editor. The specialized MOT+OWL editor uses an adaptation of the objects and links available in the MOT+ editor to cover all the OWL primitives. The MOWL editor is a new version of MOT+OWL accessible on the Web, with export and import capability to the corresponding OWL-DL XML schema.

In the following tables we will present completely the visual MOWL set of graphic symbols with their corresponding XML fragments. The MOT+OWL is very similar. In both cases, three kinds of graphic objects are used to represent classes (rectangles), properties (hexagons) and individuals (rectangles with cut corners). In the general MOT+ language, these correspond respectively to concepts, relational properties and facts. The presentation of the MOWL editor is organized in the following tables

1. Class declaration and relational axioms
2. Property declaration and attribute axioms
3. Property value and cardinality restrictions
4. Individual declaration and relational axioms

10.3 ONTOLOGY EXAMPLES

We will now present three examples of ontologies built with the MOT+OWL editor. The graphic symbols differ slightly from the MOWL symbols presented in Figures 3 to 6, but they cover the same OWL-DL concepts, founded on Description Logic.

Figure 3. Class declaration and relational axioms

Class Declaration and Relational Axioms		
Description	**OWL-DL XML Fragment**	**MOWL Visual Symbol**
Class Declaration Declaration of a class by an identifier	`<owl:Class` `rdf:ID="Class1"/>`	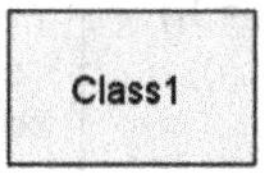
Anonymous Class Declaration of a class without an identifier	`<owl:Class/>`	

Class Intersection **owl:intersectionOf** Declaration of a class as the result of the intersection of two or more classes $(\forall x)$ $(Class3(x) \equiv (Class1(x) \land Class2(y)))$	`<owl:Class`
	`rdf:ID="Class3">`
	`<owl:intersectionOf`
	`rdf:parseType="Collect`
	`ion">`
	`<owl:Class`
	`rdf:about="#Class1"/>`
	`<owl:Class`
	`rdf:about="#Class2"/>`
	`</owl:intersectionOf>`
	`</owl:Class>`
		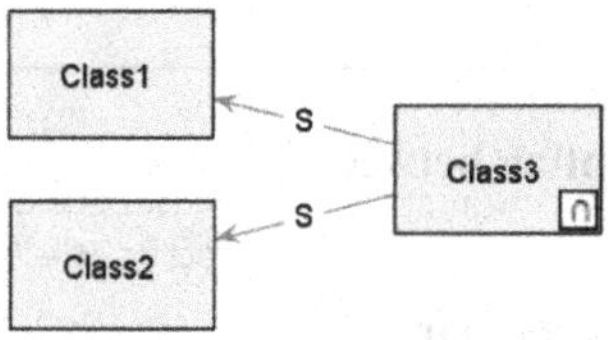 The ∩ symbol on Class3 declares that is is the intersection of super-classes Class1, Class2,…

Class Union **owl:unionOf** Declaration of a class as the result of the intersection of two or more classes $(\forall x)$ $(Class3(x) \equiv (Class1(x) \lor Class2(y)))$	`<owl:Class`
	`rdf:ID="Class3">`
	`<owl:unionOf`
	`rdf:parseType="Collect`
	`ion">`
	`<owl:Class`
	`rdf:about="#Class1"/>`
	`<owl:Class`
	`rdf:about="#Class2"/>`
	`</owl:unionOf>`
	`</owl:Class>`
		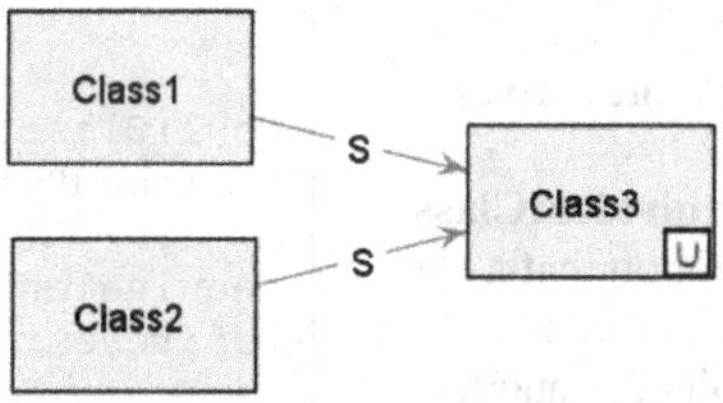 The ∪ symbol signals that Class3 is the union of sub-classes Class1 and Class2..

Complement of a Class **owl:complementOf** Declaration of a class as the complement of another class $(\forall x)$ $(Class2(x) \equiv \neg (Class1(x)))$	`<owl:Class`
	`rdf:ID="Class1">`
	`<owl:complementOf>`
	`<owl:Class`
	`rdf:about="#Class2"/>`
	`</owl:complementOf>`
	`</owl:Class>`

Figure 3. continued

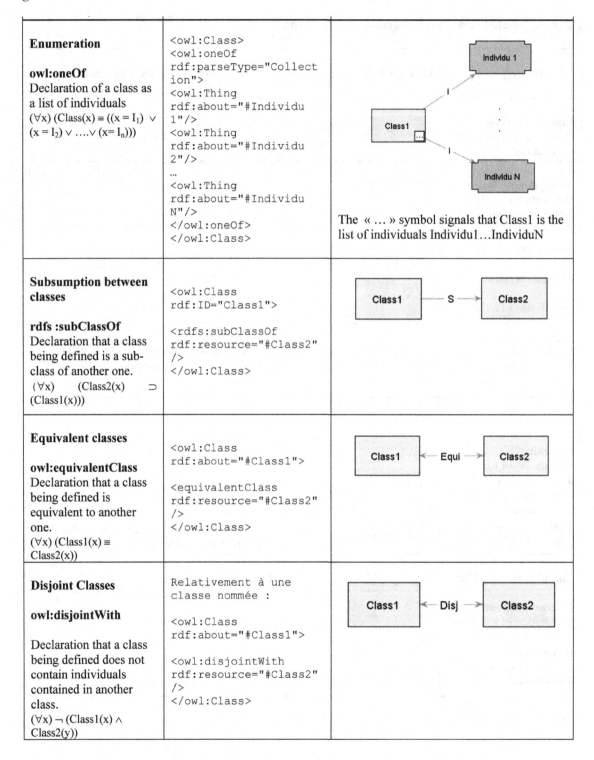

Enumeration **owl:oneOf** Declaration of a class as a list of individuals $(\forall x)\ (Class(x) \equiv ((x = I_1) \lor (x = I_2) \lor ....\lor (x = I_n)))$	```<owl:Class>` `<owl:oneOf` `rdf:parseType="Collection">` `<owl:Thing` `rdf:about="#Individu 1"/>` `<owl:Thing` `rdf:about="#Individu 2"/>` `...` `<owl:Thing` `rdf:about="#Individu N"/>` `</owl:oneOf>` `</owl:Class>```	The « … » symbol signals that Class1 is the list of individuals Individu1…IndividuN
Subsumption between classes **rdfs :subClassOf** Declaration that a class being defined is a subclass of another one. $(\forall x)\qquad (Class2(x)\ \supset\ (Class1(x)))$	```<owl:Class` `rdf:ID="Class1">`  `<rdfs:subClassOf` `rdf:resource="#Class2"/>` `</owl:Class>```	
Equivalent classes **owl:equivalentClass** Declaration that a class being defined is equivalent to another one. $(\forall x)\ (Class1(x) \equiv Class2(x))$	```<owl:Class` `rdf:about="#Class1">`  `<equivalentClass` `rdf:resource="#Class2"/>` `</owl:Class>```	
Disjoint Classes **owl:disjointWith** Declaration that a class being defined does not contain individuals contained in another class. $(\forall x)\ \neg\ (Class1(x) \land Class2(y))$	```Relativement à une classe nommée :`  `<owl:Class` `rdf:about="#Class1">`  `<owl:disjointWith` `rdf:resource="#Class2"/>` `</owl:Class>```	

Figure 4. Property's declaration and relational axioms

Property Declaration and Attribute Axioms		
Description	**OWL-DL XML Fragment**	**MOWL Visual Symbol**
Object Property owl:ObjectPropert y Declaration of a relational property between two classes.	`<owl:ObjectProperty rdf:ID="Property1"/>`	
Data Type Property owl:DataTypePrope rty Declaration of a property of a class that has values of a certain data type.	`<owl:DataTypePropert y rdf:ID="Property1"/>`	

Property Domain and Range
 	
rdfs:domain
rdfs:range
 	
For an Object Property :
$(\forall x)(\forall y)\ (P\ (x,y) \supset (Domain(x) \wedge Range(y)))$
 	
For a <u>datatype property</u>,
$(\forall x)(\forall y)\ (P\ (x,y) \supset (Domain(x) \wedge Datatype(y)))$
	For an Object Property :
	`<owl:ObjectProperty rdf:ID="Property1">`
	`<rdfs:domain rdf:resource="#Domain"/>`
	`<rdfs:range rdf:resource="#Range"/>`
	`</owl:ObjectProperty>`
	
	For a Datatype Property:
	`<owl:DataTypeProperty rdf:ID="Property1">`
	`  <rdfs:domain rdf:resource="#Domain"/>`
	`  <rdfs:range rdf:datatype="&xsd;Datatype"/>`
	`</owl:DataTypeProperty>`
		Example of a property with two domains and three range 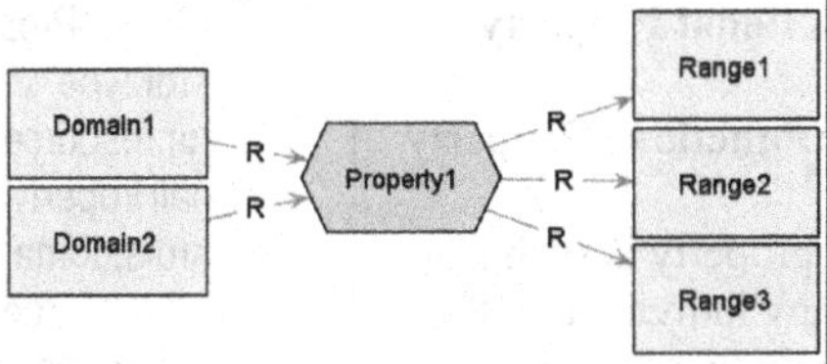
		
		Example of a property with the range being the datatype double. 

Subsumption between properties
 	
rdfs:subPropertyOf
 	
Declaration of a subsumption between a property being defines and another on.
$\forall x)(\forall y)\ (P2(x,y) \supset P1(x,y))$
	`<owl:ObjectProperty rdf:ID="Property1">`
	
	`<rdfs:subPropertyOf rdf:resource="#Property2"/>`
	
	`</owl:ObjectProperty>`
		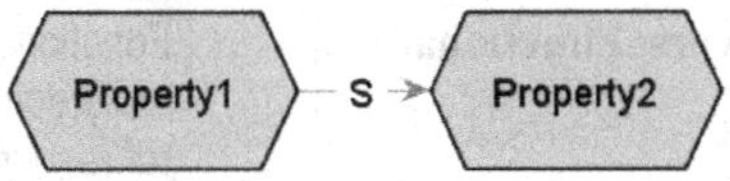

Figure 4. continued

Equivalence between properties
 	
owl:equivalentProperty
 	
Declaration of an equivalence between a property being defines and another on.
$(\forall x)(\forall y)\ (P2(x,y) \equiv P1(x,y))$
	`<owl:ObjectProperty rdf:ID="Property1"/>`
	
	`<owl:equivalentProperty rdf:resource="#Property2"/>`
	
	`</owl:ObjectProperty>`
		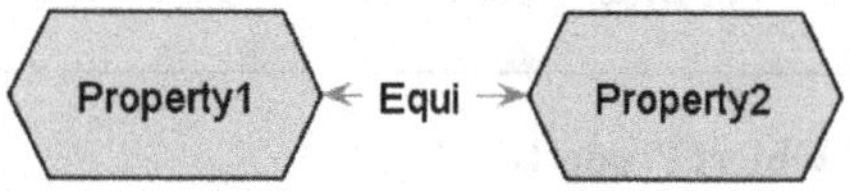 Property1 ← Equi → Property2

Inverse properties
 	
owl:inverseOf
 	
Declaration taht a property being defines is the inverse of another one
$(\forall x)(\forall y)\ (P1(x,y) \equiv P2(y,x))$
	`<owl:ObjectProperty rdf:ID="Property1">`
	`<owl:inverseOf rdf:resource="#Property2"/>`
	`</owl:ObjectProperty>`
		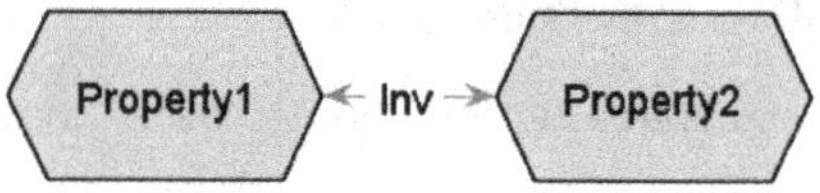 Property1 ← Inv → Property2

Functional Property
 	
owl:FunctionalProperty
 	
The property is such that for any individual in the domain there is only one in the range related by the property.
$(\forall x)(\forall y)(\forall z)\ ((P(x,y) \wedge P(x,z)) \supset y=z)$
	`<owl:ObjectProperty rdf:ID="Property1">`
	`<rdf:type rdf:resource="&owl;FunctionalProperty" />`
	`<rdfs:domain rdf:resource="#...."/>`
	`<rdfs:range rdf:resource="#...."/>`
	`</owl:ObjectProperty>`
		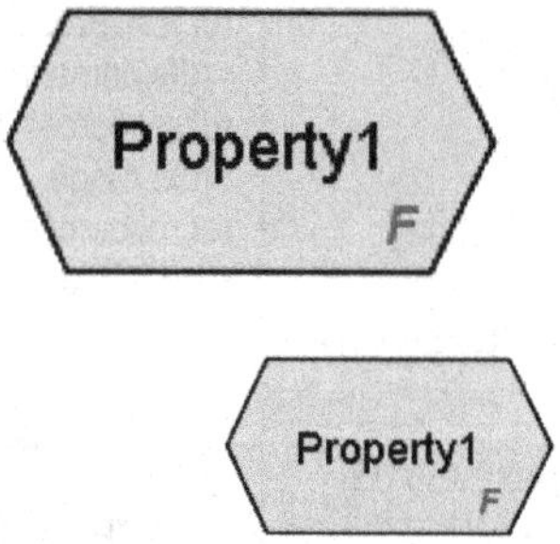 Property1 *F*
		
		Property1 *F*

Inverse Functional Property
 	
owl:InverseFunctionalPr operty
 	
The property is such that for any individual in the range there is only one in the domain related by the property.
$\forall x)(\forall y)(\forall z)\ ((P(x,z) \wedge P(y,z)) \supset x=y)$
	`<owl:ObjectProperty rdf:ID="Property1">`
	`<rdf:type rdf:resource="&owl;InverseFunctionalProperty"/>`
	`<rdfs:domain rdf:resource="#...."/>`
	`<rdfs:range rdf:resource="#...."/>`
	`</owl:ObjectProperty>`
		 Property1 *I*

Figure 4. continued

Transitive Property
 	
owl:TransitiveProperty
 	
The property is transitive
 	
$(\forall x)(\forall y)(\forall z)((P(x,y) \wedge P(y,z)) \supset P(x,z))$
	`<owl:ObjectProperty rdf:ID="Property1">`
	`<rdf:type rdf:resource="&owl;TransitiveProperty"/>`
	`<rdfs:domain rdf:resource="#...."/>`
	`<rdfs:range rdf:resource="#...."/>`
	`</owl:ObjectProperty>`
		 Property1 *T*

Symetrical Property
 	
owl:SymmetricProperty
 	
The property is symetrical
 	
$(\forall x)(\forall y)(P(x,y) \supset P(y,x))$
	`<owl:ObjectProperty rdf:ID="Property1">`
	`<rdf:type rdf:resource="&owl;SymetricProperty"/>`
	`<rdfs:domain rdf:resource="#...."/>`
	`<rdfs:range rdf:resource="#...."/>`
	`</owl:ObjectProperty>`
		 Property1 *S*

Figure 5. Class definition by property restriction

Property Restriction for Class Definition		
Description	**OWL-DL XML Fragment**	**MOWL Visual Symbol**

Universal Restriction
 	
`owl:allValuesFrom`
 	
Declaration that the domain is composed of individual that have all their image by the property, within the range.
 	
$(\forall x)(Class1(x) \equiv (\forall y)(P(x,y) \wedge Class2(y)))$
	`<owl:Class rdf:ID="Class1">`
	`<owl:Restriction>`
	`<owl:onProperty rdf:resource="#Property1" />`
	`<owl:allValuesFrom rdf:resource="#Class2" />`
	`</owl:Restriction>`
	`</owl:Class>`
		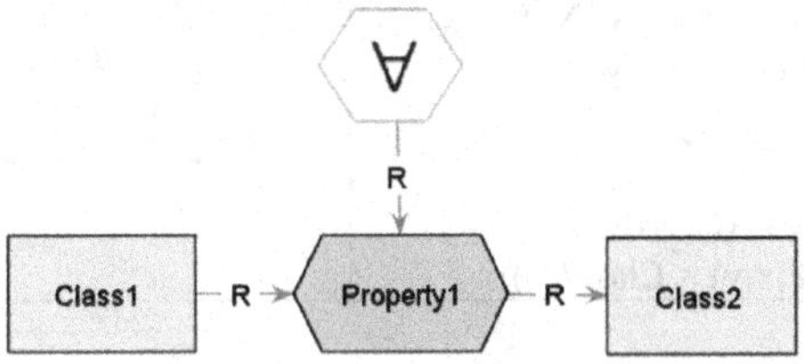 Class1 — R → Property1 — R → Class2

Figure 5. continued

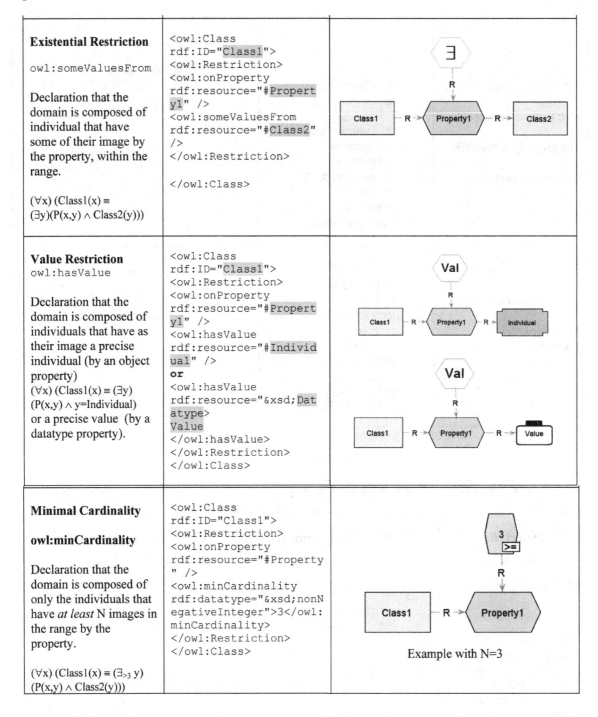

Existential Restriction
 	
owl:someValuesFrom
 	
Declaration that the domain is composed of individual that have some of their image by the property, within the range.
 	
($\forall$x) (Class1(x) $\equiv$ ($\exists$y)(P(x,y) $\wedge$ Class2(y)))
	`<owl:Class`
	`rdf:ID="Class1">`
	`<owl:Restriction>`
	`<owl:onProperty`
	`rdf:resource="#Propert`
	`y1" />`
	`<owl:someValuesFrom`
	`rdf:resource="#Class2"`
	`/>`
	`</owl:Restriction>`
	
	`</owl:Class>`	

Value Restriction
owl:hasValue
 	
Declaration that the domain is composed of individuals that have as their image a precise individual (by an object property)
($\forall$x) (Class1(x) $\equiv$ ($\exists$y) (P(x,y) $\wedge$ y=Individual) or a precise value (by a datatype property).
	`<owl:Class`
	`rdf:ID="Class1">`
	`<owl:Restriction>`
	`<owl:onProperty`
	`rdf:resource="#Propert`
	`y1" />`
	`<owl:hasValue`
	`rdf:resource="#Individ`
	`ual" />`
	or
	`<owl:hasValue`
	`rdf:resource="&xsd;Dat`
	`atype>`
	`Value`
	`</owl:hasValue>`
	`</owl:Restriction>`
	`</owl:Class>`	

Minimal Cardinality
 	
owl:minCardinality
 	
Declaration that the domain is composed of only the individuals that have *at least* N images in the range by the property.
 	
($\forall$x) (Class1(x) $\equiv$ ($\exists_{>3}$ y) (P(x,y) $\wedge$ Class2(y)))
	`<owl:Class`
	`rdf:ID="Class1">`
	`<owl:Restriction>`
	`<owl:onProperty`
	`rdf:resource="#Property`
	`" />`
	`<owl:minCardinality`
	`rdf:datatype="&xsd;nonN`
	`egativeInteger">3</owl:`
	`minCardinality>`
	`</owl:Restriction>`
	`</owl:Class>`
		Example with N=3

Figure 5. continued

Maximal Cardinality
 	
owl:maxCardinality
 	
Declaration that the domain is composed of only the individuals that have *at most* N images in the range by the property.
 	
$(\forall x)\ (Class1(x) \equiv (\exists_{\leq 3}\ y)$
$(P(x,y) \wedge Class2(y)))$
	`<owl:Class`
	`rdf:ID="Class1">`
	`<owl:Restriction>`
	`<owl:onProperty`
	`rdf:resource="#Property`
	`" />`
	`<owl:maxCardinality`
	`rdf:datatype="&xsd;nonN`
	`egativeInteger">3</owl:`
	`maxCardinality>`
	`</owl:Restriction>`
	`</owl:Class>`
		Example with N=3

Exact Cardinality
 	
owl:Cardinality
 	
Declaration that the domain is composed of only the individuals that have exactly N images in the range by the
	`<owl:Class`
	`rdf:ID="Class1">`
	`<owl:Restriction>`
	
	`<owl:onProperty`
	`rdf:resource="#Property`
	`" />`
	`<owl:cardinality`
	`rdf:datatype="&xsd;nonN`
	`egativeInteger">3</owl:`	

Figure 6. Individual's declarations and restrictions

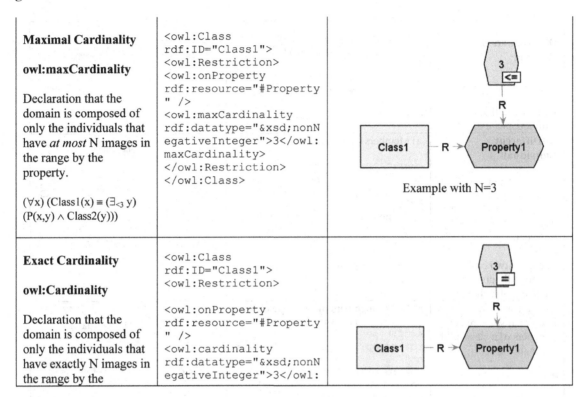

Individuals and Relations		
Description	**OWL-DL XML Fragment**	**MOWL Visual Symbol**

Individual Creation
 	
`owl:Thing`
	First method:
	`<owl:Thing`
	`rdf:ID="Indiviudal2"/>`
	
	Second method:
	`<Class1 rdf:ID="Individual1">`
	`...`
	`<\Class1>`	

Identity Relation
 	
`owl:sameAs`
 	
Declaration that two individuals are identical
	`<rdf:Description`
	`rdf:about="#Individual1">`
	`<owl:sameAs`
	`rdf:resource="#Individual2"/>`
	
	`</rdf:Description>`	

211

Figure 5. continued

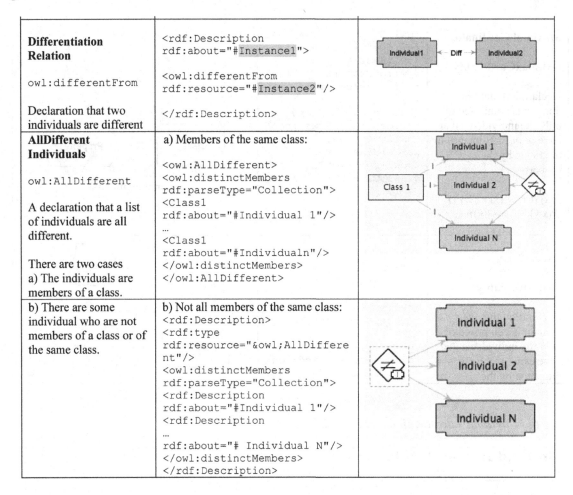

Differentiation Relation
 	
`owl:differentFrom`
 	
Declaration that two individuals are different
	`<rdf:Description`
	`rdf:about="#Instance1">`
	
	`<owl:differentFrom`
	`rdf:resource="#Instance2"/>`
	
	`</rdf:Description>`	

AllDifferent Individuals
 	
`owl:AllDifferent`
 	
A declaration that a list of individuals are all different.
 	
There are two cases
a) The individuals are members of a class.
	a) Members of the same class:
	
	`<owl:AllDifferent>`
	`<owl:distinctMembers`
	`rdf:parseType="Collection">`
	`<Class1`
	`rdf:about="#Individual 1"/>`
	…
	`<Class1`
	`rdf:about="#Individualn"/>`
	`</owl:distinctMembers>`
	`</owl:AllDifferent>`	

b) There are some individual who are not members of a class or of the same class.	b) Not all members of the same class:
	`<rdf:Description>`
	`<rdf:type`
	`rdf:resource="&owl;AllDiffere`
	`nt"/>`
	`<owl:distinctMembers`
	`rdf:parseType="Collection">`
	`<rdf:Description`
	`rdf:about="#Individual 1"/>`
	`<rdf:Description`
	…
	`rdf:about="# Individual N"/>`
	`</owl:distinctMembers>`
	`</rdf:Description>`	

An Eco-Agriculture Ontology

We present on Figure 7 a simple ontology built with MOT+OWL to describe agriculture practices that influence the greenhouse effect. This ontology could serve in a project where student have to find out agriculture alternative practices, in at least five agriculture domains, and then build a transition plan towards the replacement of the old practices by the more ecological ones. The ontology would serve in a browsing mode to access related resources (e.g. annotated by the ontology) and to launch search agents to find persons, information resources and learning activities useful to solve achieve the learning activities.

The upper part of the graph of Figure 7 presents the top levels of three hierarchies of concepts linked by sub-class links "S": *agricultural practices, fertilizers* and *gases*. Some properties of these concepts are shown on the graph. An Agriculture set of practices, such as Rice Production Processes, *has inputs* including fertilizers and *outputs* that can be gases. Fertilizers can also *produce* gases, some of which are *greenhouse gases*. Figure 7 also shows a few of the individuals (or class instances) that will constitute the knowledge base. Here we see an agriculture practice, *Traditional Rice Production*, having among its outputs *methane gas*. It also has *Nitric Oxide* amongst its inputs, a chemical fertilizer that produces *Carbon Dioxide*.

Figure 7. A simple ontology for the eco-agriculture domain

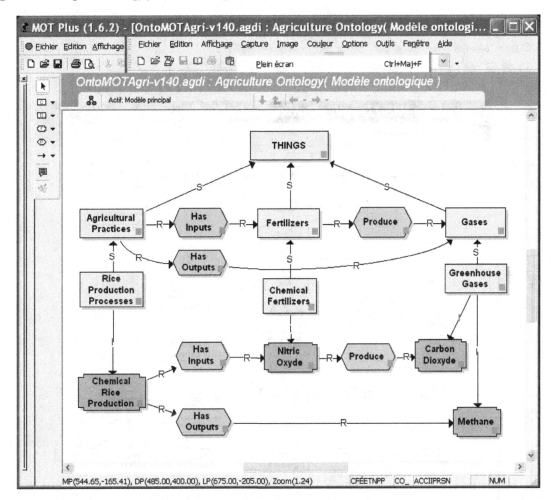

Both of these gases are example of *greenhouses gases* harmful to the environment.

We could now develop this ontology further into sub-graphs to cover the domain more completely and use it to reference the documents and activities in an environment project. For this, sub-graphs of Figure 7 would be associated to actors, activities and resources, in ordre to represent their knowledge.

An Ontology for Learning Designs

With ontologies, we can in principle describe formally any informal model of the MOT taxonomy of models presented on Figure 5, with the restric-

tion that they are amenable to a representation in the description logic at the basis of OWL-DL. It is obvious that ontologies can represent most conceptual models or laws and theory models. It is less evident that they can also describe procedural models sometimes called task ontologies). Procedural and process/methods models are important for our purpose because learning designs for courses or workflows in organizations require the definition of multi-actor processes. We will present here one such model.

The IMS-LD standard specification presented in chapter 8 defines an XML schema for models of multi-actor scenarios or designs. Figure 8 presents a MOT+OWL graph that corresponds exactly to

Figure 8. A simple task ontology for multi-actor learning designs

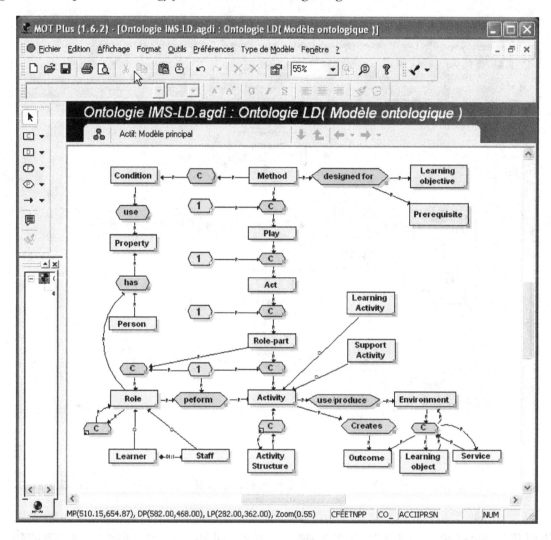

the main conceptual structure of a learning design presented in the IMS-LD information model (IMS-LD 2003, p. 10).

On the figure, C properties correspond to the "is-composed-of" relationship. The ontology model of Figure 8 displays a central class called *"Method"* that is decomposed into at least one *"Play"*, decomposed in at least one *"Act"*, which are composed of at least one *"Role-part"*. A role-part is composed of at least one *"Role"* (that has persons playing it), which perform some *"Activity"*. An *"Activity Structure"* is composed of other Activity structures or Activities, classified

as *"Learning Activity"* or *"Support Activity"*. An Activity use and/or produces an *"Environment"* composed of "Learning Objects" and "Services".

Besides the decomposition of a method in smaller and smaller pieces in a learning design, we notice, on the top of the model, two important properties of a method: a) it is designed for certain "Prerequisite" and "Learning Objectives"; b) it is composed of a number of conditions that "use" "properties" of persons.

This example illustrates how functional relations between components of multi-actor processes such as the method part of a learning

Figure 9. Top level ontology for competency definition

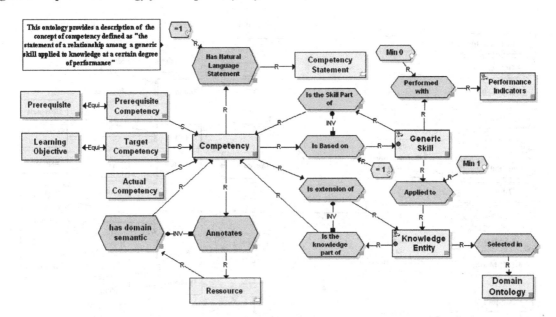

design can be represented by ontologies. Such ontologies can be used to test, for example, the conformance of a specific learning design model to the IMD-LD XML schema (Amorim et al, 2006) and to execute that learning design in the context of ontology-driven system engineering (Magnan and Paquette, 2006). This last question will be addressed in following chapters.

10.4 A DETAILED ONTOLOGY FOR COMPETENCIES

We will now revisit the definition of a competency discussed in chapter 6 and 7 of this book, in order to provide a more precise ontology-based definition.

Main Ontology

The graph on Figure 9 presents the competency ontology expressed in the MOT+OWL Visual language It shows a number of relations that serve to provide a non-ambiguous definition that can be used by humans and software agents (Paquette 2007). [1]

Each *competency* is composed of a single *competency statement,* exactly one *generic skill* that may (or may not) require precisions using performance indicators, and at least one *knowledge* entity selected in domain ontology. The competency statement is a natural language phrase that refers to the other components, stating that the generic skill (with optional performance indicators) can be applied to the knowledge.

The *knowledge* part of the competency can be a concept, an action or a process, a principle or a fact that is selected in a *domain ontology*. In a competency profile for a profession like nursing, this knowledge part will be selected in a health care facts, concepts, procedures or principles. In a competency profile for media producers, the knowledge entity will be one of the techniques, methods, objects or products from the multimedia domain. In general, we will consider that the competency ontology is extended by a domain ontology into which the knowledge part is selected, either as a class or an individual of the domain ontology.

The left part of the graph on Figure 9 shows some of the pragmatic features of the notion of competency. Competencies serve to annotate re-

Figure 10. Extension of the competency ontology to generic skills

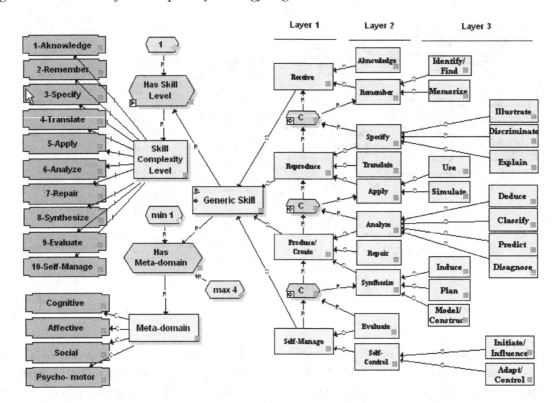

sources, persons as well as media resources, given them a semantic, a meaning, as to the knowledge and skills they own or contain. They can also be declared as actually owned by the resource they annotate (an actual competency) or they can represent a prerequisite to achieve a task, or a target competency, for example a learning objective to be attained. These two relations between "Competency" and "Resource" are inverse properties: competencies annotate resources, and resources have domain semantic (given by a competency).

Generic Skills Sub-Ontology

We will now expand the competency ontology for the generic skill component of a competency requirement. The backbone of this sub-ontology is a generic skill taxonomy that has been presented in chapter 7 of this book. A *generic skill* is a process that can be applied to knowledge in more than one application domain, for example to perceive, memorize, assimilate, analyze, synthesize, or evaluate knowledge objects. A generic skill is described by an action verb, sometimes with performance indicators like "in new situations" or "without help" that serve to make the skill more specific, while remaining independent from any application domain. For example, a generic skill like "establish a diagnosis", or "establish a diagnosis in new situations without help", can be applied in various application domains to knowledge items like "skull fracture", "car motor failure" or "exam failure risk". A generic skill is also selected from a generic skill's ontology that will be considered as an extension of the competency ontology.

Figure 10 presents the sub-ontology for Generic Skills. On the right side of the graph, we see that the taxonomy is ordered by layers (using specialization S links) from left to right, from general to more specialized skills.

Figure 11. Extension of the competency ontology to performance indicators

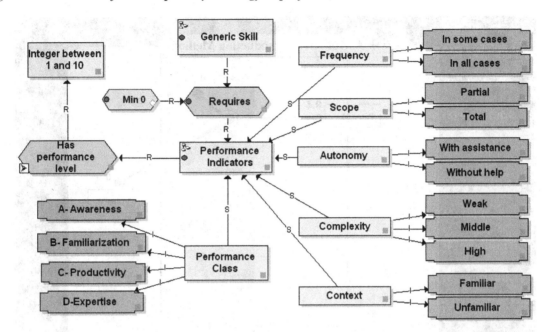

On the first layer a "C" property between the four classes of skills expresses the relation. "is more complex than." We add here a transitivity axiom for the C property by adding an arrow label on its graphic symbol. This property also exists between the 10 classes of skills of the second layer (even though not all C properties are shown), for example between Synthesize and Repair, and between Repair and Analyze. On the other hand, there are no direct C properties between skills of the third layer, only through their second layer parent classes.

These relationships between generic skills are based on the definition of skill's complexity we have given earlier: *"A skill A is more complex than skill B if for any generic process P in class A, there exist a generic process in class B acting as a sub-process of P."* The validity of the "C" relation for the first two layers of the taxonomy has been discussed in Chapter 7 of this book.

Figure 10 shows, on the left side of the graph, a third type of OWL objects representing individuals. The first property, labelled "Has Skill Level" is based on the second layer's total ordering by

complexity. This enables us to assign one and only one number from 1 to 10 representing the complexity level of a generic skill. In OWL terminology, it means that the "has skill level" property is functional. A corresponding axiom is added by a label on the hexagon representing this property.

The second property, labelled "Has Meta-domain" serves to assert that generic skills can have as value "cognitive", "affective", "social" or "psycho-motor", as well as any combination of these values, shown by the "max 4" cardinality axiom affecting the property. In Chapter 7, we have built a complete table showing examples in the cognitive, affective, social and psycho-motor examples for each of the 10 major skills on the second layer of the taxonomy. It shows that this taxonomy can be interpreted in each of the four meta-domains. For example, we can repair theories and movements, as well as attitudes or social relations. What differentiate these four meta-domains is essentially the type of input to a skill and its resulting outputs. If the stimuli or the result concerns rational thought, motor capacities, affective attitude or social interactions,

Figure 12. Situating resources on a skills/performance scale

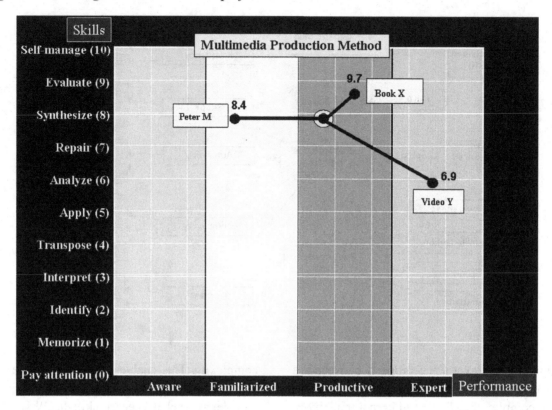

we will label the skill respectively as cognitive, psychomotor, affective or social.

Performance Indicators Sub-Ontology

We now complete the competency ontology by developing a sub-model for the "performance indicator" class of Figure 9. There are many possible performance indicators that are used by practitioners and some that we have explored in our own projects in the last ten years. The indicators on Figure 11 have been found most frequently useful.

For any generic skill, it is possible to add performance indicators such as frequency, scope, autonomy, complexity and/or context of use, by selecting one of the values shown on the figure. For example, a competency like "diagnose the source of malfunction of a car engine" could be

made more precise by adding performance indicators like "in all cases" or "in the some of the cases" (frequency), "partially" (scope), "without help" or "with little assistance" (autonomy), "for high complexity engines" (complexity), or "in unfamiliar cases" (context of use). Some of these values are shown on Figure 7 as instances of the ontology. Other individuals and other values could be added to extend the ontology. The usefulness of such indicators is to help built ways to assess the competency, for example to design exam questions or to register the progress of a novice employee's performing a task.

Alternative and simpler performance indicators classify performance for a generic skill in four broad categories such as "awareness", "familiarization", "productivity" or "expertise", or simply by a number on a 1-10 scale for the performance level. These categories or levels can be direct evaluation results, or they can be calculated from

Table 1. Performance categories or levels vs. other indicators

PERFORMANCE CRITERIA	Awareness (0,0-2,5)	Familiarity [2,5-5.0)	Mastery [5.0-7.5)	Expertise [7,5-10,0]
Frequency	Sometimes	Always	Always	Always
Scope	Partial	Partial	Total	Total
Autonomy	Assistance	Assistance	Without help	Without help
Task complexity	Low	Low	Middle	High
Context of use	Familiar	Familiar	Familiar	Unfamiliar

the other indicators. One way to combine indicators or criteria to define performance classes or levels has been presented in Chapter 9. It is reproduced in Table 1.

An interesting application of such numeric values is the bi-dimensional competency scale presented earlier. By combining the generic skills' levels with the performance levels, such a scale can help situate resources according to their competency for a certain knowledge item. For example, Figure 12 shows such a competency scale for the knowledge of a "multimedia production method". It shows a course having a target competency of 8.6, which means it aims at "Synthesize productively a multimedia production method". For that course, Peter M has an actual competency of 8.4, which means he is "familiar with synthesizing a multimedia production method". Video Y, at a level of 6.9, should not be very useful for that course, except maybe as a refresher, because it focuses on "Analysing at expert level a multimedia production method", which is a lower generic skill level.

10.5 ONTOLOGY ENGINEERING

In this concluding section, we will survey the question of methodologies to help build ontologies. According to Deveddzic (2006), " Ontology engineering denotes a set of design principles, development processes and activities, supporting technologies, as well as systematic methodologies that facilitate ontology development and use

throughout its cycle: design, implementation, evaluation, validation, maintenance, deployment, mapping, integration, sharing and reuse".

Ontology Engineering Methods

Mizoguchi and Ikeda (1996) situate ontology engineering in "Content-oriented research", by opposition to "Form-oriented research" that has dominated the field of Artificial Intelligence, providing formal theory tools for reasoning such as predicate logic. They define Ontology engineering as a "research methodology which gives us [the] design rationale of a knowledge base, kernel conceptualization of the world of interest, strict definition of basic meanings of basic concepts together with sophisticated theories and technologies enabling accumulation of knowledge which is [in]dispensable for modeling the real world". In the last 10 years a large number of Ontology Engineering methodologies have been proposed such as DILIGENT, HCOME, METHONTOLOGY, OTK methodology and ONTOEDIT.

For example METHONTOLOGY is among the most comprehensive ontology engineering methodologies as it is one for building ontologies either from scratch or reusing other ontologies (Gomez-Perez, Fernandez and de Vicente 1996) The framework describes the ontology development process by its main activities, such as, evaluation, configuration, management, conceptualization, integration implementation; a life cycle based on evolving prototypes; and the methodology itself

Figure 13. An ontology engineering process (Staab et al, 2001, p. 29)

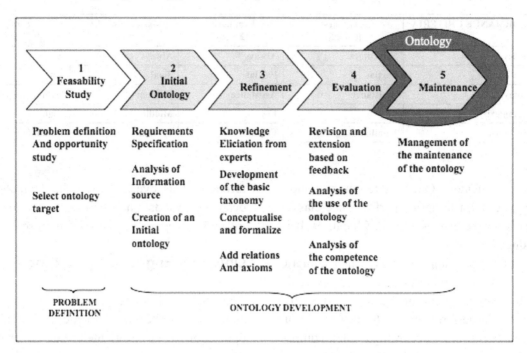

specifying the steps for performing the activities, the techniques used, the outcomes and their evaluation. But this methodology does not provide guidance for decentralized ontology development and do not focus on post development processes.

On the contrary, the authors of the DILIGENT methodology claim that it is "the first methodology to put focus not on the initial development of the ontology, but on the user and his usage of the ontology, and on the changes introduced by the user. "We take the user's own view seriously and enable feedback towards the evolution of the ontology, stressing the ontology's role as a shared conceptualization". Then they describe the main process as composes of five steps: "Consensus Building", "Evolution", "Shared Ontology", "Evolving Local Ontologies" and "Argumentation". (Vendrecic, Pinto, Sure and Tempich 2005).

Similarly, HCONE is an experimental Ontology Engineering Environment supporting the development, maintenance, exploitation, and evaluation of ontologies in the context of emergent knowledge management organizational units:

Communities of practice (CoP) and Communities of interest (CoI). "The aim of HCONE is to fit the practice of these communities, amplify and extend the cognitive and learning abilities of specific humans doing real work. The ultimate goal of HCONE is to support people to develop ontologies and achieve consensus towards commonly agreed and understandable ontologies for effective knowledge management in an organization". (Kotis and Vouros 2006)

Staab, Studer, Schnurr and Sure (2001) were amongst the first to produce an extensive development process for ontology engineering that covers a complete life cycle. The On-to-knowledge methodology is organized around five phases: A "Feasibility Study" is done to define the problem through an opportunity study and the goal of the ontology. Then, an "Initial Ontology" is built by specifying its requirements, analyzing the available information sources and creating a first model. Follows a phase of "Refinement" where concepts are extracted from the experts, a basic taxonomy is built and properties and axioms are formalized. A further step, "Evaluation" is based on feedback from content experts, observation and analysis of the use of the ontology and verification of its competency: verifying if it fulfills its initial goal in helping users achieve their tasks using the ontology. The final phase is the "Maintenance" of the ontology after its delivery, throughout its evolution.

Contribution of the MOT Knowledge Modeling Method

From the point of view developed in this book, building ontologies is constructing a particular kind of knowledge models that correspond to a class in the taxonomy presented in chapter 3 called "*Theories*". Because an ontology is a particular type of knowledge model the MOT modeling process presented in chapter 4 can be specialized as a method for ontology engineering. On this basis, the method is also deployed on five phases.

1. First *identify the components of the ontology* starting with a specification of target population, goals and constraints, in order to build a rough initial ontology. What are the concepts, properties and axioms that should appear in the initial model?
2. Put *priority marks on the objects* in the initial ontology model to determine which ones will have to be developed further into nested models. An interesting way to do this is to evaluate competency gaps of the future users of the ontology towards concepts, properties and axioms on the ontology.
3. *Add nested sub-models* to develop other levels of the initial ontology, particularly to develop further the basic taxonomies and the related properties of their classes.
4. *Co-reference ontology concept or properties* if they need to be related to other existing or to-be-built ontologies. One form of co-referencing corresponds to what is called "ontology alignment".
5. *Validate and document the ontologie.*

Of course, this method for knowledge modeling can be refined further to exploit the particular structure of ontology models, drawing elements from other ontology engineering methods. If so the competency attachments to knowledge objects in the ontology can guide the development of an ontology, as has been explained in section 9.1.

Let us explore that further. Traditionally, intelligent agents (IA) define knowledge objects from a strictly functional point of view. For example, according to Allen Newell, knowledge objects are "anything that can be attributed to an agent in such a way that its behaviour can be computerized according to the principle of rationality." (Newell, 1982). A more recent, alternative approach to knowledge representation with respect to IAs is concerned first and foremost with "modeling real-world systems rather than reproducing what people think and do." (Clancey, 1993). These two approaches reflect two different points of view, i.e. understanding intelligence or providing our systems with more intelligence. It is possible to reconcile these two approaches.

MOT Modeling can be applied for both purposes. In developing an ontology as a non-procedural (declarative) theory independent of a Web agents, ontological engineering assumes that an ontology can be "calibrated" through use cases by agents (persons or software). This is what authors call "competency analysis of the ontology." In other words, the ontology can process data to achieve a competency target. By modeling a domain to target a competency, as defined in the previous chapters, we gain a method for assessing the quality of an ontology based on its goals, and an estimate of the competency gap to fill in order to create a more powerful version of the ontology.

CONCLUSION

This chapter has presented the main concepts at the foundation of the new generation of the Internet called the Semantic Web. We have presented the concept of an ontology and a visual language to build ontologies derived from MOT+ presented in the first three chapters. The MOT+OWL and MOWL tools export any graphical ontology models to OWL-DL XML files and import such standard files into the graphic editor. Using these tools, we have presented a number of ontology models, including a competency ontology based on chapter 6 and 7. Finally, we have discussed methodology issues within the growing field of ontological engineering, underlining the link with the knowledge engineering processes presented in chapter 4.

We have not entered much into the technical details of how the Semantic Web is built, only that it is being constructed though grass-root activities, all using a solid foundation and a common set of technologies to build applications in different areas, providing solutions to real problems. A survey of 23 applications case studies and 12 use cases is available on the W3C web site. They cover many areas: such as Automotive, Broadcasting, eGovernment, Energy, eTourism, Finance, Geographic Information Systems, Health care, IT industry, Life Sciences, Museum, Oil & Gas, Public Institutions, Publishing, Search, Semantic Desktop, Telecommunications, Utilities, and Web Accessibility (W3C – UseCases 2008). Most of these applications use RDF and/or OWL semantic Web technologies.

In the next chapters, we will address a number of important theoretical issues and applications of the Semantic Web framework. And, in the last part of this book some "ontologies in practice" will be presented besides less formal models.

REFERENCES

W3C-OWL. (2004). *Ontology Web Language (OWL), Overview Document.* Retrieved December 10, 2008, at http://www.w3.org/TR/2004/REC-owl-features-20040210/

W3C – UseCases. (2008). Retrieved December 10, 2008, from http://www.w3.org/2001/sw/sweo/public/UseCases/

Amorim, R., Lama, M., & Sanchez, E. (2006) Using Ontologies to model and execute IMS Learning Design Documents. In *Proceedings of the the 6th IEEE International Conference on Advanced Learning Technologies,* Kerkrade, The Netherlands, July 5-7, 2006 (pp. 115-116).

Baader, F., Calvanese, D., McGuinness, D., Nardi, D., & Patel-Schneider, P. (Eds.). (2003). *The Description Logic Handbook.* Cambridge, UK: Cambridge University Press.

Berners-Lee, T., Hendler, J., & Lassila, O. (2001). The Semantic Web. *Scientific American, 284*(5), 34–43. doi:10.1038/scientificamerican0501-34

Brachman, R. J., & Schmolze, J. (1985). An overview of the KL-ONE knowledge representation system. *Cognitive Science, 9*(2). doi:10.1207/s15516709cog0902_1

Clancey, W. (1993). The knowledge level reinterpreted, modelling socio technical systems. *International Journal of Intelligent Systems, 8,* 33–49. doi:10.1002/int.4550080104

Devedzic, V. (2006). *Semantic Web and Education.* Berlin: Springer.

Feigenbaum, L., Herman, I., Hongsermeier, T., & Neumann, E. (2007, December). Semantic Web: How the internet is getting smarter. *Scientific American,* 90–97. Retrieved from http://www.SciAm.com. doi:10.1038/scientificamerican1207-90

Gomez-Perez, A., Fernandez, M., & de Vicente, A. (1996). *Towards a Method to Conceptualize Domain Ontologies.* Workshop on Ontological Engineering, ECAI'96, Budapest, Hungary.

IMS-LD. (2003). *IMS Learning Design - Information Model, Best Practice and Implementation Guide, XML Binding document*. Retrieved October 3, 2003, from http://www.imsglobal.org/learningdesign/index.cfm

Kotis, K., & Vouros, G. (2006). Human-centered ontology engineering: the HCOME methodology. [KAIS]. *International Journal of Knowledge and Information Systems*, *10*(1), 109–131. doi:10.1007/s10115-005-0227-4

Magnan, F., & Paquette, G. (2006). TELOS: An ontology driven eLearning OS. Presented at SOA/AIS-06, Workshop, Dublin, Ireland, June 2006.

Minski, M. (1975). A framework for representing knowledge. In Winston, P. H. (Ed.), *The psychology of computer vision* (pp. 211–227). New York: McGraw-Hill.

Mizoguchi, R., & Ikeda, M. (1996). *Towards Ontology Engineering*. Technical Report AI-TR-96-1, I.S.I.R., Osaka University, Japan.

Newell, A. (1982). The knowledge level. *Artificial Intelligence*, *18*, 87–127. doi:10.1016/0004-3702(82)90012-1

Paquette, G. (2007). An ontology and a software framework for competency modeling and management. *Educational Technology and Society*, *10*(3), 1–21.

PROTÉGÉ. (2006). Stanford Medical Informatics. *Protégé*. Retrieved May 29, 2006, from http://protege.stanford.edu/

Quillian, M. R. (1968). Semantic Memory. In Minsky, M. (Ed.), *Semantic Information Processing* (pp. 227–270). Cambridge, MA: MIT Press.

Staab, S., Studer, R., Schnurr, H. P., & Sure, Y. (2001, January). Knowledge processes and ontologies. *IEEE Intelligent Systems*, 26–34. doi:10.1109/5254.912382

Sunagawa, E., Mizoguchi, R., et al. (2003). *An Environment for Distributed Ontology Development Based on Dependency Management*. Paper presented at the International Semantic Web Conference (ISWC), Florida, USA.

Vrandecic, D., Sofia Pinto, H. S., Sure, Y., & Tempich, C. (2005, October). The DILIGENT knowledge processes. *Journal of Knowledge Management*, *9*(5), 85–96. doi:10.1108/13673270510622474

ENDNOTE

[1] This competency ontology has been adopted by Share.Tec project (www.share.tec.eu) an European project that aims to create a repository of resource across Europe.

Chapter 11
Referencing Resources through Ontology Evolution[1]

Délia Rogozan
LICEF Research Center, Canada

Gilbert Paquette
LICEF Research Center, Canada

ABSTRACT

- A Model of Ontology Evolution
  - Ontology Evolution
  - Process Model for Ontology Evolution
- Compatibility Analysis and Change propagation
  - Preservation of Instances
  - Preservation of the Conceptual Structure
  - Preservation of the Inference Capacity
  - Change Propagation to Semantic References
- An Ontology of Ontology Changes
  - Classification of Change Operations
  - Properties of Change Operations
- Managing Ontology Changes and the Semantic Referencing of Resources
  - A Software Framework for Managing Ontology Changes
  - Managing the History of Ontology Changes
  - Managing the Semantic Referencing of Resources

DOI: 10.4018/978-1-61520-839-5.ch011

Evolution is a fundamental requirement for useful ontologies. Knowledge evolves continuously in all fields of knowledge due to the progress in research and applications. Because they are theories of knowledge in a precise domain, Ontologies need to evolve because the domain has changed, the viewpoint of the domain has changed or because problems in the original domain conceptualization have to be resolved or have been resolved (Noy

& Klein, 2003). Moreover, in open and dynamic environments such as the Semantic Web, the ontologies need to evolve because domain knowledge evolves continually (Heflin & Hendler, 2000) or because ontology-oriented software-agents must respond to changes in users' needs (Stojanovic, Maedche, Stojanovic, & Studer, 2003).

This chapter explores some important issues of ontology evolution. Firstly, it presents a unified model of ontology evolution, that we have modeled using the MOT representation language. Afterward, it illustrates an ontological representation of changes in OWL ontologies. These changes are seen as a local transformation from a previous ontology model to a new one. Both ontologies are expressed using the MOT+OWL visual language presented in Chapter 10. Thirdly, it proposes a framework for managing ontology changes and for managing the semantic referencing of resources, in the Semantic Web context. For this purpose, visual modeling has been used to define the main functionalities of interactive tools to support ontology evolution, with the objective to help maintain a coherent and useful referencing of resources by the ontology.

11.1 A MODEL OF ONTOLOGY EVOLUTION

As any complex processes, ontology evolution requires a model that structures it. Although current researches propose models of ontology construction, these are far from approaching ontology evolution in an elaborated way (Haase & Sure, 2004). Besides, there is no consensus regarding the proposed models of ontology evolution. This is due to the different perspective on what ontology evolution consists. In a centralized context, it signifies the application of changes to an ontology and the exclusive usage of this evolved ontology (Maedche, Motik, & Stojanovic, 2003; Stojanovic, 2004). In a decentralized context, the evolution denotes the identification, the alignment and the

management of multiple versions of a same ontology (Klein, 2004; Klein & Noy, 2003).

The need of a unified model of ontology evolution is thus necessary. This section describes a process model of ontology evolution. It defines the notion of evolution, which is the basis of the model and it provides a description of steps that compose the process of ontology evolution, thus providing a basis for the other sections of this chapter.

Definition of Ontology Evolution

Ontology evolution signifies the timely modification of an ontology according to modifications of its domain, conceptualization or usage. This modification is enacted by the application of changes to an ontology version (V_N) in order to produce a new ontology version (V_{N+1}), while preserving the ontology consistency and role. The *ontology role* refers to the services provided by the ontology and to its usage. For example, in the Semantic Web context, the ontology is used to assure the semantic referencing of resources so that resources can be found by the knowledge they contain. The *ontology consistency* designates the state where all invariants of the ontology model are respected. Invariants are structural and axiomatic constraints that must hold in every stable state of an ontology, any change that invalidates them is inconsistent for example, adding a data property with no value or an intersection axiom on a class that is a subset of only another classe.

Figure 1 illustrates two examples of inconsistent models that could results from a change to an ontology. The first one declare the class "Course Manager" as a subclass of "Designer IMS_LD", while this class was already declared as a subclass of "Course Manager", because of the transitivity of the (S) links. The second example declares "Designer IMS_LD" as a subclass of disjoint classes "PedagogicalDesigner" and "Tutor", which of course means that this class is empty.

Figure 1. Example of an inconsistent change

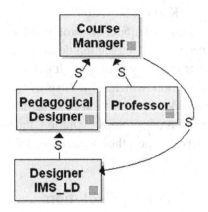 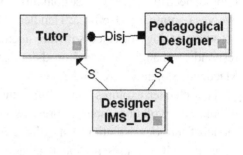

An *ontology change* is a modification brought to an ontology during the evolution from version V_N to a new version V_{N+1}. The changes can be elementary or complex (Klein, 2004; Stojanovic, 2004). At the basis of all evolution processes, an *elementary change* is a simple and non-decomposable change (*i.e.* addition or deletion of ontology elements). A *complex change* is a collection of elementary changes, which form together a logical entity whose signification is unique and clearly defined.

Consequently, every complex change can be decomposed into elementary changes, such as illustrated in Figure 2. In this example, the classes "Pedagogical Designer" and "Professor" in V_N are merged in version V_{N+1} to form the class

"Content Presenter". This complex change can be decomposed in three elementary changes: deleting the first class, deleting the second class, adding the new class "Content Presenter" as a subclass of "Course Manager".

Application of a change can induce inconsistencies in other parts of the ontology (Stojanovic, Maedche, Motik, & Stojanovic, 2002). For example, merging two classes can cause subclasses/properties to be inconsistent. Resolving that problem can be treated as a request for new additional changes, for example deleting subclasses/properties or moving them to another class in V_{N+1}. To illustrate this, let's expands the example of Figure 2. Suppose now that in V_N, "Pedagogical Designer" has two subclasses as shown on Figure

Figure 2. Example of a complex change: merging two classes

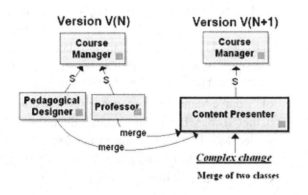 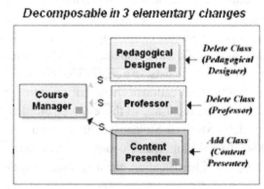

3. Since that class is now merged with "Professor" to form the class "Content Presenter", it is natural to transfer the two sub-classes to the new merged class in V_{N+1}. Also, the class "Professor" had a property, "describes knowledge", in V_N that should probably become a property of the merged class "Content Presenter" in V_{N+1}. We define a *primary change* has a simple or complex change that is not the consequence of any other change, whereas an *additional change* is one that is caused by another change named parent-change.

A MOT Process Model for Ontology Evolution

It is now time to present a process model for ontology evolution. This model, presented on Figure 4 was built using the MOT representation language, to elaborate a unified model of ontology evolution. It consists of eight principal steps, organized in two phases: *evolving the ontology* and *operationalizing the ontology evolution.* Most of these steps must be supervised by ontologists and supported by specialized tools mainly ontology editors, and tools to log, analyze primary changes and recommend changes to the use of the ontology. Such tools will be discussed in the last section.

Evolving the Ontology

This phase is comprised of six steps. During the first step of the evolution model, the ontologists identify and access the ontology version to be modified–the V_N **version**–that is usually archived in a distributed library on the web (Ding & Fensel, 2001).

During the second step, the ontologists identify the changes that should be applied to V_N in order to improve the ontology model so that it correspond better to modifications of ontology domain or ontology usage. They also can identify changes using several heuristics, similar to one that affirms that if a class has only one subclass, then both can be merged (Stojanovic, 2004).

The third and the forth steps are achieved in parallel. On one hand, the ontologists edit the changes previously identified. On the other hand, the effects of changes on the ontology consistency are verified and a method for resolving inconsistencies is provided to the ontologists. The result of these two stages is a verified sequence of elementary and complex changes where certain changes are primary and others are additional.

For an evolution process that is situated in a distributed and multi-actors context, the sequence of changes must be jointly validated by all ontologists. This fifth step provides a method

Figure 3. Primary change of merging two classes and its additional changes

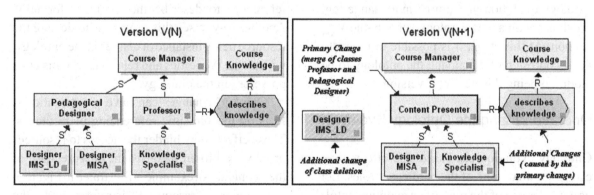

Figure 4. Model of ontology evolution

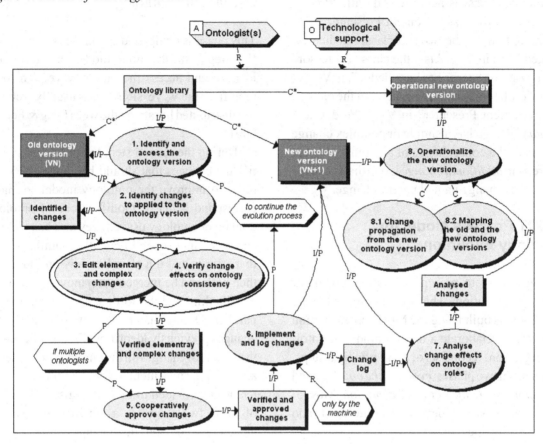

to manage the conflict among changes made by distant ontologists that attempt to modify a shared ontology (Pinto, Staab, & Tempich, 2004; Sunagawa, Mizoguchi, & all., 2003).

The sixth step aims at implementing the changes while preserving the history of the ontology evolution in captured in a change log. We thus obtain a new ontology version–the V_{N+1} version. At this stage, it is possible to return to the second step of the model, the ontology to be modified being this new V_{N+1} version.

Operationalizing the Ontology Evolution

Ontology evolution can cause side effects than can jeopardize some of the ontology's roles. Let us consider one of the roles of an evolving ontology, where it is used to describe the properties

of resources using semantic descriptors. These descriptors, also named *semantic references*, are often knowledge, *i.e.* classes according to the OWL terminology, belonging to one or more ontologies. The *semantic referencing* of a resource consists in associating to a resource one or several semantic references to describe their content formally. Another way to see this process is to declare the resource being instance of classes in the ontology, with all the properties and relations that this class possesses in the ontology.

Ontology changes can have problematic effects on the semantic referencing of resources. These effects may hinder the access to resources or may lead to an inconsistent interpretation of their content. An example is illustrated in Figure 5.

In Figure 5, resource R_1 is referenced by the class "Professor" belonging to V_N version of the

Figure 5. Change effects on semantic referencing of resources

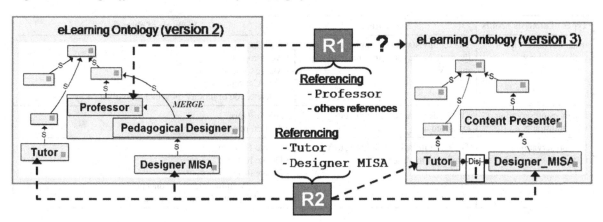

ontology. During the evolution of V_N to V_{N+1}, this class is merged with another class and consequently, it no longer exists in V_{N+1}. This makes the resource R_1 no more accessible for requests like: « Give me a resource which is "Professor"»; the access to R_1 is broken via V_{N+1}. Consider furthermore a resource R_2 that is referenced by the class "Tutor" and "Designer MISA" V_N. If a disjunction axiom is added between these two classes, then the interpretation of R_2 becomes inconsistent via the new ontology version, because R_2 can no more be a member (an instance) of both class at the same time.

To preserve the ontology roles during the ontology evolution, an analysis of the changes must be made. That is the objective of the seventh step of the model. This analysis has to identify the changes that affect the semantic referencing of resources and those that lead to inconsistencies in other dependent ontologies (Maedche, Motik, & Stojanovic, 2003), that is, ontologies that include in their structure a part of the evolving ontology.

The most important result of change analysis is to preserve the ontology roles for the V_{N+1} version. It is the purpose of the eighth and last step of the ontology evolution model.

11.2 COMPATIBILITY ANALYSIS AND CHANGE PROPAGATION

Because of their utmost importance, we will now give more explanations on steps 7 and 8 of the ontology evolution process. In step 7, a compatibility analysis is made between version V_N and V_{N+1} of the ontology, in order to preserve the ontology roles, in particular for the semantic referencing of resources. According to (Noy & Klein, 2003), defining what constitutes compatibility between ontology versions is a major problem since there are several dimensions to take into account. Here, we consider three dimensions: 1) the preservation of instances of the ontology, 2) the preservation of its conceptual structure and 3) the preservation of its inference capability.

Preservation of Instances

The preservation of instances means that there is no instance lost after the ontology evolution. In other words, any resource previously referenced remains accessible using references from the new ontology. Consequently, the instance preservation is ensured when the set of class instances in V_{N+1} is the same or a super-set of the set of instances in V_N. In Table 1, we present three possible results of the instance preservation analysis.

Table 1. Types of analysis results concerning the preservation of instances

Types of analysis results	Explication	Example of changes
Instances preservation without addition	The set of instances belonging to V_n is the same as the set of instances belonging to V_{n+1}	• Add Concept • Add Property • Merge Concepts • Split Concept • - Delete, add or modify the annotation of an entity
Instances preservation with addition	The set of instances belonging to V_n is expanded in V_{n+1}	• Add Instance • Add Property Instance
Non preservation of instances	The set of instances belonging to V_n is reduced or modified in V_{n+1}	• Delete-Concept • Delete Instance • Delete Property Instance • Reclassify an Instance as a concept • - Add Disjoint With for an class axiom

Preservation of the Conceptual Structure

The conceptual structure of the ontology is the set of classes of the ontology and their relationships. It is used as an organized vocabulary to reference the resources or pedagogical elements. This second dimension of the compatibility analysis aims at preserving the referential capacity of the conceptual structure of the ontology. In Table 2, we present the possible results of the preservation analysis of the ontology conceptual structure.

We observe that even if certain changes preserve the ontology instances, they do not necessarily preserve the conceptual structure of the ontology. For example, "Merge_concepts" preserve instances but not the conceptual structure. Conversely "Reclas-

sify an instance as a concept" preserve the conceptual structure with addition but not the instances.

Preservation of the Inference Capacity

The ontology is not only a hierarchy of classes, a conceptual structure. It is a logical system consisting of a set of axioms that constrain the interpretation of the ontology and thus the meaning of the references associated to resources. The set of axioms provides an inference capacity of the ontology. This capacity is preserved when all the facts that may be inferred from V_N may still be inferred from V_{N+1}. In Table 3, we present possible results for the preservation analysis for axioms and the inference capacity of the ontology.

Table 2. Types of analysis results concerning the preservation of conceptual structure

Types of analysis results	Explication	Example of changes
Preservation of the conceptual structure without addition	The set of concepts belonging to V_N is the same as the set of concepts belonging to V_{N+1}	• Add Instance • Add Property Instance • Add class axioms • Delete Property • - Delete, add or modify the annotation of an entity
Preservation of the conceptual structure with addition	The set of concepts belonging to V_N is expanded in V_{N+1}	• Add concept • Reclassify an instance as a concept
Non preservation of the conceptual structure	The set of concepts of V_N is modified in V_{N+1}	• Merge Concepts • - Split Concept

Table 3. Types of analysis results concerning the preservation of inference capacity

Types of analysis results	Explication	Example of changes
Preservation of inference capacity without addition	The set of facts inferred from V_N is the same as the set of facts inferred from V_{N+1}	• Add Concept • Add Instance • Add Property Instance
Preservation of inference capacity with addition	The set of facts inferred from V_{N+1} is a super-set of the set of facts inferred from V_N	• Add Property • Move property from sub-concept to super-concept
Non preservation of inference capacity	The set of facts inferred from V_{N+1} is reduced or modified compared with the set of facts inferred from V_N	• Delete Property • - Move property from super-concept to sub-concept

Taking into account these three dimensions of the compatibility analysis, we can classify the changes applied to V_N in three categories.

- The *compatible changes* completely preserve the roles of V_N. In V_{N+1}, instances are preserved, as well as the conceptual structure and the inference capacity of the ontology.
- The *backward compatible changes* also preserve the roles of V_N, but there is the possibility that not the entire added content in V_{N+1} is used for supporting the ontology roles.
- The *incompatible changes* do not preserve the ontology roles. They either do not preserve instances, or the conceptual structure, or the inference capacity, or two or three of these dimensions.

Change Propagation to Semantic References

We now come back to the last step of the ontology evolution process presented above, when the new ontology version is operationalized. The goal of the operationalization is to ensure that the ontology roles are preserved. As pointed above, any incompatible change may cause some inconsistencies, which in turn may lead to the loss or the malfunctioning of certain ontology roles, for example resource referencing. As for back-

ward compatible changes, the ontology roles are preserved but not all the new knowledge is used. Therefore, in order to ensure the enlargement of ontology roles, it is possible that the ontologists would like to consider the new knowledge added to ontology and use it to add references to resources.

The change propagation to resources is the modification of their *reference links* to ontologies. A reference link is the path that links a resource to a concept or an instance in the ontology. We can have here three situations concerning the modification of a reference link:

- For incompatible changes that do not affect the reference links of objects (links related to the ontological entities untouched by these changes), only the name of the ontology version needs to be modified from V_N to V_{N+1}.
- For incompatible changes that affect the reference links of resources, it is necessary to modify the name of the ontology version as well as the new semantic reference within V_{N+1}.
- For compatible and backward compatible changes, the reference links of objects are not affected. Thus, it is necessary to change only the version name within the reference link. However, when it comes to consider the new knowledge introduced in V_{N+1} by means of backward compatible changes, there is a new possibility to define, if need-

ed, new reference links in order to take into account the new knowledge introduced in V_{N+1}.

11.3 AN ONTOLOGY OF ONTOLOGY CHANGES

In this section, we will summarize the previous discussion by presenting an integrated ontology for ontology changes and role preservation operations. We built such an ontology, not only to summarize these notions in an organized and formal way, but also because we aim to build ontology driven tools to support the process of ontology evolution. Chapter 15 will discuss the question of ontology-driven tools and the last section of this chapter will present some prototypes to achieve that goal.

Regarding the representation of changes, other researchers proposed only taxonomies of elementary changes, although, complex changes have a richer semantic to express high-level modifications of ontologies (Klein & Noy, 2003). The ontology in this section expands the Klein's (2004) and Stojanovic's (2004) taxonomies by adding a typology of complex changes, as well as properties and axioms that formally specify the meaning of each elementary and complex change that we can apply to OWL-DL ontologies.

This ontology has been built using the MOT+OWL visual formalism presented in Chapter 10, that exports to XML files compliant with the OWL-DL standard. The Change Ontology consists of two root-classes: ChangeOperation, which specifies the types of changes and ChangeObject, which represents the ontology objects that can be changed: the ontology, the classes, the properties, etc.

Classification of Change Operations

The ChangeOperation, hierarchy presented in Figure 6 consists of a sub-hierarchy of elementary changes and a sub-hierarchy of complex changes Both sub-hierarchies are declared as disjoint and, by inheritance, each of the elementary operations sub-classes will be disjoint from any complex change sub-classes.

The sub-hierarchy of elementary changes is presented in Figure 7. It contains the generic changes Add_Change and Delete_Change, each of them being decomposed in Figure 8 according to the object being changed (*i.e.* ontology, class and property specified in the ChangeObject hierarchy (presented later).

Figure 8 adds more detail for the sub-hierarchy of elementary change operations. The structure of both generic Add_Change and Delete_Change is

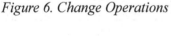

Figure 6. Change Operations

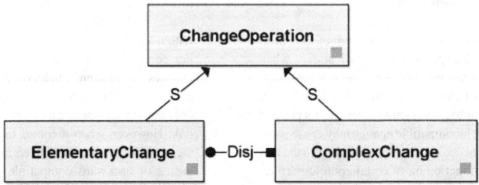

Figure 7. Hierarchy of elementary changes

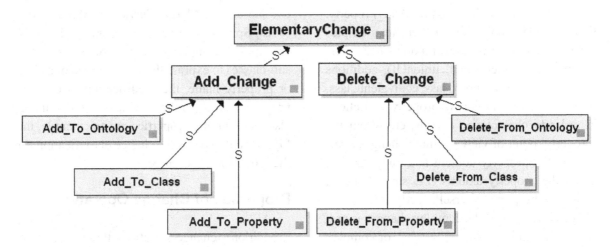

Figure 8. Classification of changes that add elements to an ontology

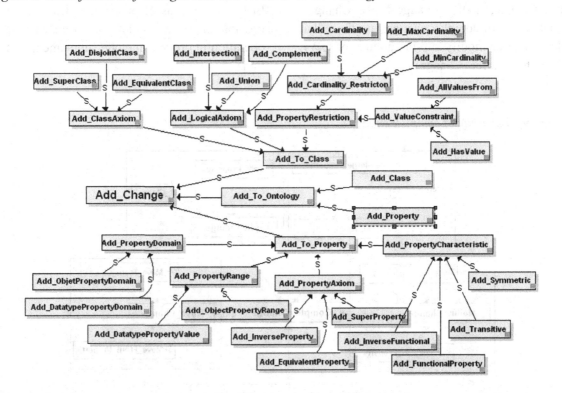

similar. For that reason, the Figure illustrates only the classification of Add_Change changes, the Delete_Change being classified in the same way.

The changes that add elements to the ontology are first classified according to their application object within the OWL-DL language, as in Figure 11. If another ontology language would be used for an evolving ontology, the Change ontology presented here would have to be adapted to the objects in the language.

From the 'ontology' point of view, there are two main changes: Add_Class and Add_Property. From the 'class' point of view there are multiples changes: additions of logical axioms (*i.e.* intersectionOf, complementOf, unionOf), additions of class axioms (*i.e.* superClass, equivalentClass, disjointWith) or additions of property restrictions in order to characterize classes, etc. From the 'property' point of view the main changes operates on the property domain and range as well as on the property axioms (*i.e.* superProperty, equivalentProperty, inverseProperty etc.).

The hierarchy of the complex changes is presented in Figure 9. The main types of complex changes are those that merge, split, modify or move elements of ontologies (Merge_Change, Split_Change, Modify_Change, Move_Change). Others types of complex changes are those that add, delete or modify sub-hierarchies of OWL elements (Subtree_Change).

The changes of merging and splitting have each two sub-classes: Merge_Classes and Merge_Properties, Split_Class and Split_Property. The others types of complex changes have a number of sub-classes to express the modification of a class or property name, the modification of class or property axioms, or the moving of axioms among classes or among properties. As an example, the Figure 10 illustrates the change classification for the type Modify_Change.

Properties of Change Operations

In addition to change operations, the change ontology also consists of a certain number of properties allowing a richer characterization of the changes. In fact, by means of property restrictions, it is possible to extend the definition of each change operation in order to include supplementary notions.

Figure 9. Hierarchy of complex changes

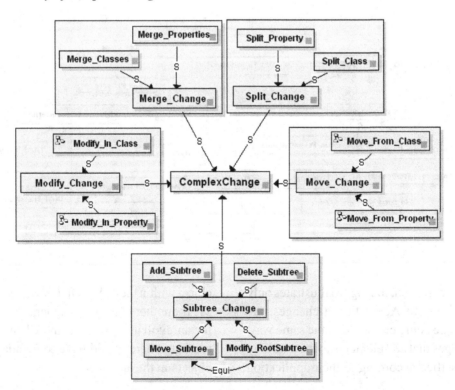

Figure 10. Classification of change operations of the type Modify_Change

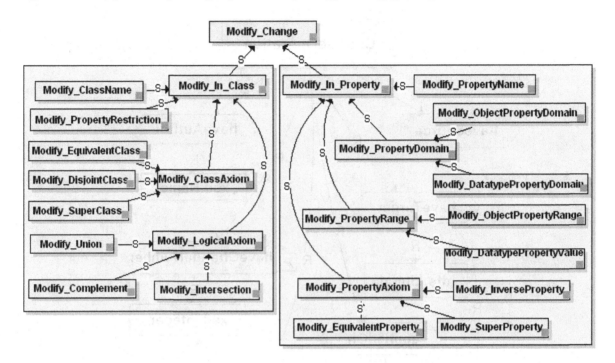

Figure 11 introduces the general properties associated to change operations. The appliedOn property connects the change operations to ontology objects to which they apply. The properties haveSource and haveTarget describe the source and the target of change operations. Both properties have as domain a class of type ChangeOperation and as range a class of type ChangeObject or a value rdfs:Datatype.

Others properties as introduced, as well. The haveChangeNumber property specifies a reference number that indicate the application order of a change. The haveParentChangeNumber property declares the reference number of the parent-change. The haveAuthor property identifies the author of a change.

Restrictions on these general properties may be associated to each change operations in order to characterize it formally. The Figure 12 shows a part of the change characterization for the type Add_Change and for its sub-class Add_Class.

Any operation of type Add_Change is characterized by two general restrictions: an exact cardinality of 0 for the haveSource property, which declares that there is no ontology object as source, and a minimal cardinality of 1 for the haveTarget property, which declares that the target of any addition change comprises at least one ontology object.

Afterward, the type of the target elements for each addition change is declared. The Add_to_Class is declared has the class of Add_Change operations that have as target the change object class. This is done by adding a constraint owl:allValuesFrom on the haveTarget property in order to specify if the target contains only classes. The same method can be followed for all others changes of the type "Add".

The ontology of change operations presented in this section extends previous classification of elementary ontology changes by a taxonomy of complex ontology changes. It also adds to this

Figure 11. Properties of change operations

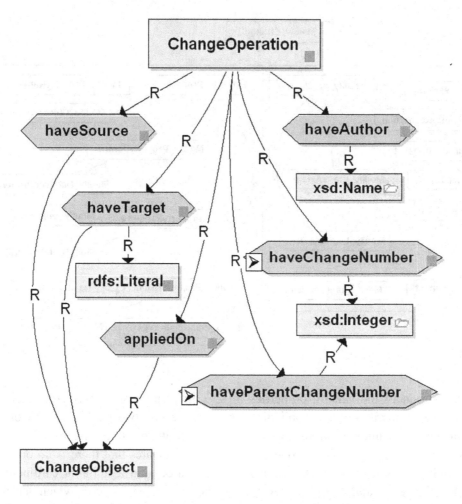

Figure 12. Part of the change characterization for the type Add_Change

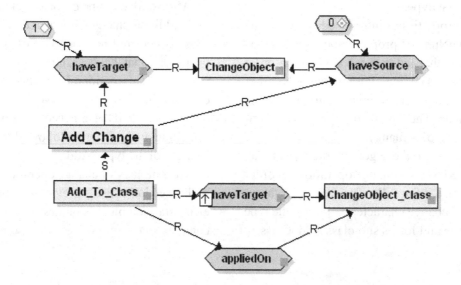

extended taxonomy clear formal definitions of the change operations, with their properties and some axioms on these properties, thus creating an ontology of ontology change.

Such a precise theory of the domain of ontology change can now be used to support the development of tools that will assist the ontologist in preserving the consistency and role of an ontology through its evolution. This is the object of the following section.

11.4 A FRAMEWORK FOR MANAGING THE ONTOLOGY CHANGES AND THE SEMANTIC REFERENCING OF RESOURCES

In section 11.2, we have identified the main steps of a complete ontology evolution process. This process must be supervised by ontologists and supported by specialized tools. However, as we underlined in (Rogozan, 2008), there is a lack of tools to support important steps of the ontology evolution model.

1. At Step 6, there is a need for a tool that provides a uniform and consistent logging of elementary and complex changes as well as the causality relations that exist among them.
2. At Step 7, a tool that can analyse change effects on resources that are semantically referenced by concepts should be made available.
3. At Step 8, we need of tool that preserves the access to and the interpretation of resources via the new ontology version.

To resolve these problems, we propose in this section a framework that groups such tools for managing ontology changes applied to an ontology version V_N. The framework consists of two basic modules–the *ChangeHistoryBuilder* (CHB) and the *SemanticAnnotationModifier* (SAM). with an

ontology editor, such as MOT+OWL presented in Chapter 10.

The Ontology Editor exports ontologies to OWL-DL and is supposed to have functions for change edition, trace and log the history of changes, and for the verification and resolution of inconsistent changes.

CHB provides a support for managing the history of ontology changes. It has two functionalities. The first one aims at logging ontology changes in a manner that make explicit all the evolution semantic. The second one is to retrieve logged changes and to presents them to users to require some action to preserve the consistency or the role of the ontology.

SAM offers to users two services. The first one analyses changes applied to V_N to obtain V_{N+1} in order to inform users about changes that hinder the access to referenced resources or that modify their interpretation. The second service modifies the semantic referencing that is affected by ontology evolution, based on data provided by the CHB system.

Managing the History of Ontology Changes with CHB

Although the management of ontology changes is one of the key issues in successful applications of evolving ontologies, method and tools to support it are almost missing (Haase & Sure, 2004). However, these tools are important to consider for ontology-based referencing of resources since changes affect the way that resource should be handled and interpreted by means of new ontology versions.

There are two major approaches for tracking and managing ontology changes. The first one (Maedche, Motik, & Stojanovic, 2003; Stojanovic, 2004), logs changes during the ontology evolution. Even if this approach may facilitate later retrieval of all performed changes, it presents an important problem: the log-files are stored independently from ontology versions and a tool-oriented lan-

Figure 13. Change management framework

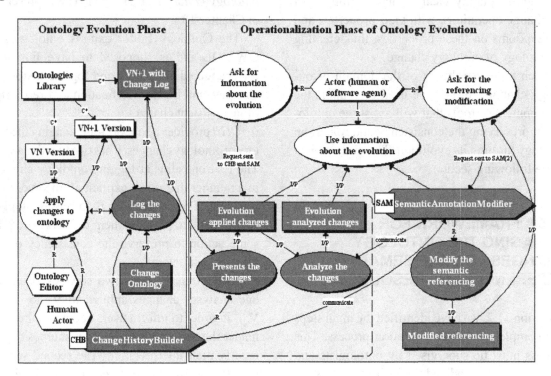

guage formalizes them. Consequently, these log-files are more difficult to identify, to access and to interpret by Semantic Web agents. For that reason, the second approach (Klein, 2004; Noy, Kunnatur, Klein, & Musen, 2004) relies only on a comparison between ontology versions to identify changes. However, it presents a problem as well. It can identify only some elementary changes and therefore, it cannot provide complete information about evolution processes

The *ChangeHistoryBuilder (CHB)* overcomes these two problems: it combines the fact of having access to a log that captures the entire semantic of ontology evolution with the fact of identifying changes starting only from ontology versions. It also can deal with complex changes, in addition to elementary ones. To track and to manage the history of ontology changes, the CHB system supports a four-step process, as illustrated by Figure 14.

Step 1: Capture Changes during Ontology Evolution

The first step aims at capturing in a log-file all changes applied during the evolution from V_N to V_{N+1}. To resolve interpretation problems of log-files generated by different editors, the CHB provides ontology editors with a uniform and common model for logging changes. The CHB model is a set of metadata that aggregates in a common structure all changes (Rogozan & Paquette, 2005). Based on the change ontology, these metadata allow ontology editors to capture specific information about elementary and complex changes, in addition to general information regarding the ontology version. These ontology editors can use the CHB model as a plug-in and thereby generate log-files presenting a normalized and rich description of applied changes.

Figure 14. The fourth-step functioning of the CHB system

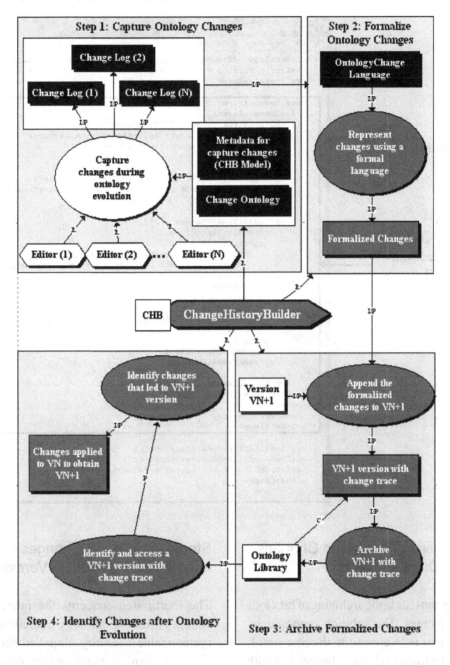

Step 2: Formalize Changes Using the OC+OWL Language

The second step of the logging process supported by the CHB is the formalization of changes that were captured during the previous step. For this purpose, we developed a formalization language, named *OntologyChange* (OC), which is based on a number of XML constructs, labelled oc. When combined to those of OWL, these constructs formally describe all type of changes applicable to OWL-DL ontologies. Figure 15 illustrates how CHB uses these constructs to formalize changes.

Figure 15. An example of a V_{N+1} change ontology version

V_{N+1}Change version

Trace of changes
formalized with
OC+OWL
language

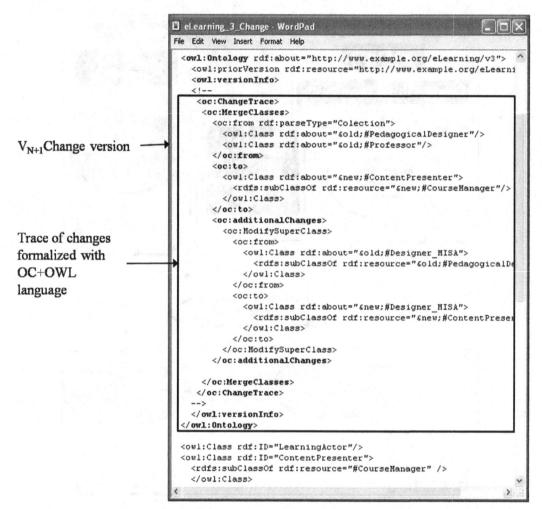

```
 eLearning_3_Change - WordPad
File  Edit  View  Insert  Format  Help
<owl:Ontology rdf:about="http://www.example.org/eLearning/v3">
   <owl:priorVersion rdf:resource="http://www.example.org/eLearni
   <owl:versionInfo>
   <!--
     <oc:ChangeTrace>
      <oc:MergeClasses>
       <oc:from rdf:parseType="Colection">
         <owl:Class rdf:about="&old;#PedagogicalDesigner"/>
         <owl:Class rdf:about="&old;#Professor"/>
       </oc:from>
       <oc:to>
         <owl:Class rdf:about="&new;#ContentPresenter">
           <rdfs:subClassOf rdf:resource="&new;#CourseManager"/>
         </owl:Class>
       </oc:to>
       <oc:additionalChanges>
         <oc:ModifySuperClass>
           <oc:from>
             <owl:Class rdf:about="&old;#Designer_MISA">
               <rdfs:subClassOf rdf:resource="&old;#PedagogicalD
             </owl:Class>
           </oc:from>
           <oc:to>
             <owl:Class rdf:about="&new;#Designer_MISA">
               <rdfs:subClassOf rdf:resource="&new;#ContentPrese
             </owl:Class>
           </oc:to>
         </oc:ModifySuperClass>
       </oc:additionalChanges>

      </oc:MergeClasses>
     </oc:ChangeTrace>
   -->
   </owl:versionInfo>
</owl:Ontology>

<owl:Class rdf:ID="LearningActor"/>
<owl:Class rdf:ID="ContentPresenter">
  <rdfs:subClassOf rdf:resource="#CourseManager" />
  </owl:Class>
```

Step 3: Archiving Formalized Changes in the New Ontology Version

The third step consists in the archiving of previous formalized changes. The solution proposed by the CHB system is to append to the new ontology version the trace of changes formalized with OC+OWL language. $V_{N+1}Change$ denotes this new ontology version with an integrated trace of changes. In this way, V_{N+1}Change contains in addition to the new ontology, all information about its from the preceding version. Figure 15 presents an example of a V_{N+1}Change version.

Step 4: Identifying Changes Starting from the New Ontology Version

The fourth step concerns the interpretation of changes after the ontology evolution. The CHB system is able to identify all applied elementary and complex changes, together with their additional induced changes, by simply reading OC+OWL trace contained in V_{N+1}Change ontology version. Furthermore, all software agents able to interpret OC+OWL language can also identify changes analysing only the content of V_{N+1}Change.

Managing the Semantic Referencing of Resources with SAM

As we have seen previously, ontology evolution can produce side effects that can hamper one of the most important features of the Semantic Web: the ontology referencing of resources that formally describes the resources content. A recent review of the literature on the subject shows, despite the wide range of referencing tools existing nowadays, none of them is able to support an evolving ontology referencing of resources.

In this context, the second system proposed in this chapter is innovative and important. The *SemanticAnnotationModifier (SAM)* provides a support for managing the ontology-based referencing of resources after the ontology evolution. Let us first recall that the semantic referencing process consists of one or several semantic references associated to resources to describe their content formally, each reference being specified by means of a UKI, which is the Web address (a URI) of an ontology component. This is illustrated in Figure 16.

We present the operation model of the SAM in Figure 17 This model underlines the two main services that SAM offers to users. The first one (on the left part of the figure) analyses changes applied to V_N to obtain V_{N+1} in order to inform users about changes that hinder the access to referenced resources or that modify their interpretation. The

second service (on the right part of the figure) helps the user modify the semantic references (*e.g.* UKIs) that are affected by ontology changes.

Here is how SAM operates. Let us consider a user who wants to verify if the semantic referencing of a resource collection is affected by the evolution from an ontology version V_N to a new version V_{N+1}. For that purpose, he sends to SAM a file containing the UKIs (*i.e.* the references to the ontology) associated to these resources. To interpret this UKIs file, SAM decomposes every UKI in order to identify the URI of the ontology versions together with the name of each class used as a reference. Afterward, SAM asks the CHB for the V_{N+1}Change file and extracts all ontology changes that were applied to V_N to obtain V_{N+1}. Because SAM is able to interpret the OC+OWL language, it is also able to 'understand' the trace of changes appended to V_{N+1}Change. Finally, SAM matches each class name specified by UKIs provided by the user to its corresponding name in the change trace.

Based on these operations, SAM presents to user an analysis of changes. First he highlights:(1) changes that breaks the access to resources, (2) changes that give rise to an inconsistent interpretation of resources, and (3) changes that modify the interpretation of resources.

Secondly, SAM provides the user with an analysis of effects for each underlined change. This analysis consists of three elements. The first two

Figure 16. The semantic referencing of a resource

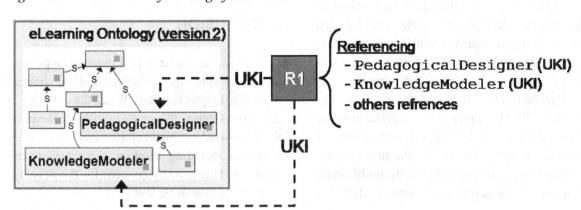

Figure 17. The operation model of the SAM system

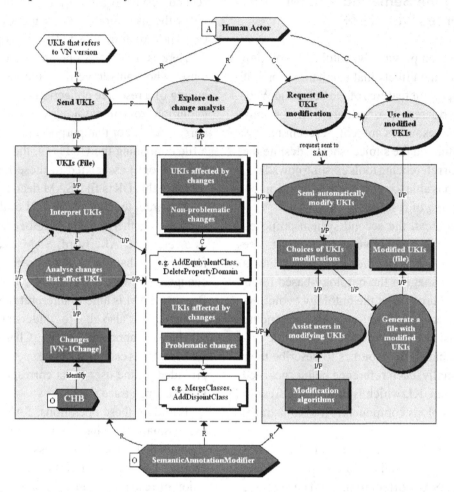

ones deal with the effect of changes on the access to referenced resources or on the consistency of their interpretation. The third one indicates the relation exiting between a class belonging to V_N and the same or other class belonging to V_{N+1}, according to criteria as identity, equivalence, inclusion, generalization, specialization or difference. This last information is particularly useful for understanding how the meaning of a class used as a reference was modified during the ontology evolution.

Starting from the change analysis, the user has the possibility to request the modification to the resource references (*i.e.* UKIs). SAM identifies several possible solutions for the modification of resource references affected by problematic changes. Choosing among the solutions identified

by SAM is the user privilege; it's him that may decide which solution is more appropriated to his context. However, SAM may guide him during the modification process.

CONCLUSION

In this chapter, we have first proposed a process model for ontology evolution. Making changes to an ontology is frequent. When the ontology is used to reference resources in order to describe their knowledge, this evolution can cause many problems including breaking the access to the resource. This is a key concern for the development of the Semantic Web.

We have identified the lack of tools to support ontologists and Semantic Web users that have to cope with ontology evolution. By building an ontology of ontology changes, we provided a clear and formal description of the simple and complex operations that can affect the quality of resource referencing. Based on this representation, we have conceived tools that can supports the persons involved in semantic referencing.

Our next goal will be to evolve the MOWL ontology editor, presented in Chapter 10 to extend its functions for change edition, and for tracing and logging the history of changes. Then these traces will be handed to new versions of the CHB and the SAM modules to integrate assistance support the ontology evolution and the resource referencing processes.

REFERENCES

Ding, Y., & Fensel, D. (2001). *Ontology Library Systems: The key for successful Ontology Reuse.* Paper presented at the First Semantic Web Working Symposium (SWWS'1), Stanford, USA.

Haase, P., & Sure, Y. (2004). *State-of-the-Art on Ontology Evolution*: Technical report, SEKT informal deliverable 3.1.1.b, Institute AIFB, University of Karlsruhe (2004).

Heflin, J., & Hendler, J. (2000). *Dynamic Ontology on the Web.* Paper presented at the AAAI, 17th National Conference on artificial Intelligence.

Klein, M. (2004). *Change Management for Distributed Ontologies.* Amsterdam: Vrije Universiteit Amsterdam.

Klein, M., & Noy, N. (2003). *A component-based framework for the ontology evolution.* Paper presented at the Workshop on Ontologies and Distributed Systems, IJCAI-2003, Acapulco, Mexico.

Maedche, A., Motik, B., & Stojanovic, L. (2003). Managing Multiple and Distributed Ontologies in the Semantic Web. *VLDB Journal - Special Issue on Semantic Web, 12*, 286-302.

Noy, N., & Klein, M. (2003). Ontology evolution: Not the same as schema evolution. *Knowledge and Information Systems, 5.*

Noy, N., Kunnatur, S., Klein, M., & Musen, M. (2004). *Tracking Changes During Ontology Evolution.* Paper presented at the 3rd International Semantic Web Conference (ISWC2004), Hiroshima, Japan.

Pinto, S., Staab, S., & Tempich, C. (2004). *DILIGENT: Towards a fine-grained methodology for Distributed Loosely-controllled and evolvInG Engineering of oNTologies. I.* Paper presented at the 16th European Conference on Artificial Intelligence ECAI-2004, Valencia.

Rogozan, D. (2008). *Management of the ontology evolution: methods and tools for an evolving semantic referencing based on analysis of changes applied to ontology versions (in french).* Université de Québec à Montréal (UQAM)/Télé-université. Montréal: TELUQ.

Rogozan, D., & Paquette, G. (2005). *Managing Ontology Changes on the Semantic Web.* Paper presented at the IEEE/WIC/ACM International Conference on Web Intelligence (WI'05), Compiegne, France.

Stojanovic, L. (2004). *Method and tools for ontology evolution.* Karlsruhe, Germany: University of Karlsruhe.

Stojanovic, L., Maedche, A., Motik, B., & Stojanovic, N. (2002). *User-driven Ontology Evolution Management.* Paper presented at the 13th International Conference on Knowledge Engineering and Knowledge Management (EKAW02), Sigüenza, Spain.

Stojanovic, L., Maedche, A., Stojanovic, N., & Studer, R. (2003). *Ontology Evolution as Reconfiguration- Design Problem Solving.* Paper presented at the 2nd International Conference on Knowledge Capture.

Sunagawa, E., Mizoguchi, R., et al. (2003). *An Environment for Distributed Ontology Development Based on Dependency Management.* Paper presented at the International Semantic Web Conference (ISWC), Florida, USA. [1] This chapter is a synthesis of part of the doctoral thesis of Délia Rogozan (2008) achieved under the supervision of the author.

Chapter 12
Competency Equilibrium and Instructional Scenarios' Quality

Julien Contamines
LICEF Research Center, Canada

Gilbert Paquette
LICEF Research Center, Canada

ABSTRACT

- State of the Art on Instructional Scenarios's Quality
- Competency-Driven Scenario Validation
  - Competency Ontologies
  - Associating Competencies to Resources
  - The Concept of Competency Equilibrium
- Scenario Validation Process
  - From Atomic to Complex Scenarios
  - Tools for Scenario Validation

This chapter focuses on the quality of instructional scenarios. An instructional scenario is a particular kind of aggregated resources composed of learning objects (LO) or resources, actors and activities according to an *Educational Modeling Language* (EML) such as the *IMS Learning Design* or the *TELOS Scenarios Language* (TSL) both presented in Chapter 8.

Among the factors which permit the production of "good" scenarios, one of the most important is the use of Instructional Engineering methods. The case of the MISA method was presented in Chapter 8. Another alternative was presented in Chapter 9 where the elaboration of the scenarios is based on the use of patterns directly in link with the type of cognitive skill aimed by the scenario. Another working example to improve scenario quality was conducted by Psyche, Bourdeau,

DOI: 10.4018/978-1-61520-839-5.ch012

Nkambou & Mizoguchi (2005) where learning and instructional theories guide the use of *IMS Learning Design* educational modeling language. In the present chapter, another alternative for quality scenarios is developed: scenario validation driven by the competencies which are associated with the scenario and its components.

The principles, techniques and methods developed in the field of Instructional Engineering should be further exploited, in order to frame the realization of scenarios, assure their coherence and guide the interconnection of tools, languages and resources that populate the Web and learning objects repositories.

This vision is shared by some researchers in the field. Wiley (2002) advocated that the composition of training with learning objects should fit into an approach of Instructional Engineering. The juxtaposition of learning objects is not sufficient. Baron & Paquette (2007), Devedzic (2006), Knolmayer (2003), Mohan, Greer & McCalla (2003), Karampiperis & Sampson (2004) all advocate that the result of the aggregation of learning objects must "*make sense*" on the educational level.

Baron & Paquette (2007) emphasize the need of a new Instructional Engineering methodology that must take "*account of the standardization of the educational components, the use of the learning objects repositories and the development of ontologies*" (p. 333). They add that this new methodology should be directed by Ontological Engineering in order to define the contents of the activities, the structure of the scenarios, the management of learning material, as well as the course delivery processes.

We begin by summarizing some research projects about the validation of learning objects aggregates and instructional scenarios. Next, the approach of validation by competency equilibrium is introduced and illustrated. We will discuss how a scenario is validated. We shall further discuss the role of *ontological engineering*; how does a *competency ontology* can be used for the validation of scenario equilibrium. Finally, from a technical point of view, we shall discus the implementation of a set of tools and a process to assure the validation of process-based scenarios.

12.1 RESEARCH ON INSTRUCTIONAL SCENARIOS'S QUALITY

Although there is some work on the quality of scenarios in an instructional engineering context (Paquette 2003,; Caeiro-Rodriguez, 2008; Psyché *et al.*, 2005), to our knowledge, there is still limited work on scenario validation.

Melia & Pahl (2007a, 2007b) discuss the following research questions: how can aggregates be validated? How can the invalid aggregates be corrected? These authors propose an architecture named CAVAM (*Courseware Authoring Validation Model*) that integrates four models:

- *Domain Model:* formalization of the domain in the form of a *concept graph*.
- *Goal and Constraints Model*: specification of the objectives of the course and the pedagogical constraints for the domain. The prerequisite relations between concepts are a part of these constraints. The course objectives correspond to a subset of the concepts contained in the domain model. The pedagogical constraints are directly expressed in the domain model by labelled relations between concepts.
- *Learner Model*: the knowledge that the learner possess at the beginning of the course is a subset of the concepts contained in the domain model.
- *Course Model*: it's a formalization of sequences between learning objects. In practical terms, this model is a graph where every learning object is associated to at least one concept of the Domain Model.
- *Validation Model*: specification of what is

valid and what is invalid. It groups the instructional principles, in the form of *production rules*, which the aggregate must respect.

Melia & Pahl distinguish two validation strategies. Firstly, it is the validation of the course prerequisites from the *Goal and Constraints model*. For example, the system verifies if a learner possesses the knowledge required to begin the course. Secondly, the system verifies if the rules in the *Validation Model* are respected by the course. For example, a validation rule can specify that general concepts must be approached before those who are more specific.

Baldoni and his colleagues developed a logical approach to competency-driven curricula validation (Baldoni, Baroglio & Marengo, 2007; Baldoni & Marengo, 2007). It consists of using a constraint-based logical representation to define the competencies associated to courses constituting a curriculum. A curriculum is represented as a sequence of actions to be conducted including the possibility of indicating that certain courses are conducted in a certain order. The courses are represented as *actions* and the competencies as *effects*. The various courses are annotated according to the competencies which they allow to develop and the entry competencies required to follow the course.

The formal and graphical language DCML (*Declarative Curricula Model Language*) supports the modeling of competencies. The model contains a set of competencies and the relations between them represent temporal constraints. The competency is acquired or targeted. A value k which represents the level of mastery associated to every competency, the competency being a knowledge to be acquired. If $k=0$ then there is no learning of the knowledge. Constraints are expressed in *linear temporal logic* (LTL) with regards to the competency. For example, we can express that a competency must be acquired before another competency, that a competency must be acquired just after another competency, that the acquisition of a competency implies the acquisition of another competency. Three types of validation are conducted in a curriculum. On the one hand, the aggregate (the curriculum) presents competency gaps. On the other hand, the aggregate respects the constraints formulated in the curicula model. Finally, in regards to a learner aiming a certain competency, can the curicula meet its needs.

Brusilovsky and Vassileva (2003) present Co-CoA (*Concept-based Courseware Analysis*). This tool is dedicated to the analysis of the aggregates' consistency with the aim of insuring their quality. The aggregates possess three characteristics: they are static, linear and composed of instructional materials. The validation methods exploit two types of annotation on instructional materials. On the one hand, the materials are associated to one prerequisite and objective that can be *strong* or *weak*. For example, a *strong* prerequisite concept needs a detailed presentation of this concept. On the other hand, the materials are annotated according to the instructional role that they will play in the aggregate: presentation, example, guideline, questionnary, etc.

Brusilovsky and Vassileva (2003) envision several validation interventions although their system implements them partially. First, there is a set of consistency rules that serve to check the prerequisites. In particular: 1) The prerequisite presentation: a rule that allows to verify if the prerequisite concepts in the study of a new concept have been previously presented; 2) The prerequisite questionnaire: all the concepts mentioned in the questionnaire were previously studied; 3) The prerequisite exercise: the strong prerequisite concepts approached in the exercises were studied and illustrated by previous examples. For the *weak* prerequisites, consistency rules verify if were either studied or previously illustrated. It is also important to verify that questionnaires are placed in the right place, to estimate the presentation density, to control the difficulty of the exercises and that of the examples.

CoCoA verifies every possible path through the material by simulating the student progress through the materials. The system analyzes every material and the associated annotations, updates the learner model and verifies the equivalence between the contents of the learner model and the materials which appears to the learner during the next stage. The validation tool generates a report which contains both the problems with the content and the situations where the learner has not prerequisites.

OntoGlue is used for the automatic aggregation of learning objects (Santacruz-Valencia, Navarro, Delgado Kloos & Aedo, 2008). Their approach includes the following:

- *Semantic description of learning objects*: needs (prerequisite or required competency) and the competency (targeted) are associated to learning objects using ontological forms, and are named *associated knowledge needs and competencies*.
- *Semantic Search of learning objects*: the search takes place according to the associated knowledge that references the learning objects.
- *Aggregation*: associated semantic to learning objects guide their aggregation. The coherence of the aggregate is analyzed in light of the associated knowledge. Furthermore, they elaborate automatically the metadata of the new aggregate.

The validation takes place during the process of selection of the learning objects that are integrated in the aggregate. For example, during the aggregation of two learning objects, the system verifies if the competency associated to the first one meets the needs of the second. This is conducted in order to guarantee the coherence of the aggregation process in terms of competence and needs.

ELO refers to the type of learning objects which their system can manipulate. The following three types of ELO are distinguished: *Information Unit* (IU), *Content Unit* (CU) and *Didactical Unit* (DU). The IU is an atomic multimedia element which is highly reusable (photo, video, text, animation, etc.). The CU represents an instructional experience (training) associated with needs and prerequisite competencies. The DU adds to the CU learning objectives a summary and a mechanism of evaluation. Some aggregations are not possible, for example, IU and a DU. Two IU results in CU, two CU results in DU, two DU results in a new DU and CU with IU results in CU.

Santacruz-Valencia et al. (2008) propose a mechanism for ELO's comparison on the basis of the knowledge associated to ELO. The needs and the competencies are classes in ontologies. Therefore, the comparison between two ELO is a sort of *ontology mapping*. When the classes belong to the same ontology, the mapping is relatively easy, less when the classes belong to different ontologies. The ontologies are taxonomies and offer a mapping of the ontologies by using algorithms of graph checking.

From this literature review, we draw the following conclusions. Firstly, the competencies or training objectives are represented in a simple manner. According to Baldoni et al. (2007), a competency is a knowledge associated to a numerical value indicating a mastery degree. For Melia & Pahl (2007a, 2007b), the competence is only a concept. Brusilovsky & Vassileva (2003), in their study of the CoCoA system, do not integrate the *competency* term, rather they use *prerequisite* and *objective* terms. In addition, prerequisites and objectives can be either *strong* or *weak*. According to the *OntoGlue* approach (Santacruz-Valencia et al., 2008), the competency is a concept. All of the above formal representations of competency are rather simple and do not provide enough structure to build a more elaborated scenario validation method. Secondly, the various types of aggregate's structure and the impact of this structure on the validation process is only slightly discussed by the different authors.

12.2 COMPETENCY-DRIVEN SCENARIO VALIDATION

In Chapters 5, 8 and 9, we have described the notion of competency and its importance for Instructional Science and Instructional Engineering. In Chapter 5, an operational conceptualization of the notion of competency is proposed. It is the heart of the Instructional Engineering method MISA.

An instructional scenario must be soundly anchored in the targeted competencies. The components of a scenario-learning objects, activities and actors-can be associated to competency. It is important to exploit the corresponding set of competencies in order to verify the coherence of the scenario in light of the objectives which are pursued.

Competency Ontologies

In Chapter 10, based on a cognitive skill taxonomy presented in Chapters 6 and 7, we have presented an ontological formalization of the notion of a competency. The interest in such an ontology is twofold:

1. Providing a formal description of the competence to be able to refer to the learning objects as well as the actors in regards to their competency.
2. Using reasoning techniques for competency management.

Figure 9 in Chapter 10 proposes the first level of the competency ontology that we apply in this chapter. Sub-levels clarify the concepts of generic cognitive skill, knowledge and performance level. A knowledge is a concept, a procedure, a principle

or an instance of these three basic entities. A cognitive skill refers to a metaknowledge which is a generic cognitive process necessary to exploit the knowledge. The cognitive skills are classified in a taxonomy (See Table 1) including ten levels grouped together in four categories.

The learner acquires a certain level of performance regarding the application of cognitive skills to knowledge. The level of performance refers to a degree of progress in the execution of a competency. There are four levels of performance: sensitization, familiarization, mastery and expertise. Every level can be associated to a numerical value. These levels of performance are defined by combining five performance criteria. A competency can be used in: 1) an occasional or continuous manner; 2) an autonomous manner or with assistance; 3) a partial or global manner; 4) in simple or complex situations or 5) in familiar or new situations. For example, the level "expertise" is associated to a competence which is used in a continuous, autonomous, global, complex and new manner.

This competency ontology is the result of nearly fifteen years of research and practice in Instructional Engineering, which led to the elaboration of the MISA method. In particular, the taxonomy of cognitive skills is a synthesis of several other taxonomies previously elaborated in Instructional Engineering (Bloom, 1956) and Knowledge Engineering (Chandrasekaran, 1986). This conceptualization was successfully used in various research projects, among others as a foundation to a self-diagnosis competency system

Table 1. The skills taxonomy (Paquette, 2003)

Receive	Reproduce	Produce/ Create	Self-manage
1. Pay at- tention 2. Integrate	3. Instantiate/ Specify 4. Transpose/ Translate 5. Apply	6. Analyze 7. Repair 8. Synthesize	9. Evaluate 10. Self-control

(Basque & Page-Lamarche, 2007; Brisebois, Ruelland & Paquette, 2005).

Other competency ontologies have been proposed in the domain (Dodero, Sanchez-Alonso & Frosch-Wilke, 2007; Knight, Gasevic & Richards, 2006; Ng, Hatala & Gasevic, 2006; Radevski & Trichet, 2006; Schmidt & Kunzmann, 2006; Sicilia, 2005; Sitthisak, Gilbert & Davis, 2007; Zouaq, Nkambou & Frasson, 2006). Although these researchers proposed clear and simple formalizations of competency, they are not anchored in the field of Instructional Engineering. These ontologies are generally an answer to specific needs of a singular project. We will now introduce three of these ontologies.

Ng et al. (2006) elaborated on a competency ontology in order to develop a learning objects search system (See Figure 1). The learning objects were referenced in regards to this ontology in terms of prerequisite and target competence. The search for learning objects depends on the competency

aimed by the learner, but also on competencies that he has already acquired.

The second phase of their project consisted in developing a dynamic sequencing system of learning objects. In their ontology, the competence was decomposed into three subclasses:

- *Competency Definition*: it specifies information about the competency, for example: its title, its description, metadata respecting the standard RDCEO, and the associated performance criteria.
- *Performance*: a performance level and a performance scale (*proficiency model*).
- *Reference to the Knowledge*: facts and concepts.

The MOWL editor presented in Chapter 10 is used for the model of Figure 1. It shows that this ontology permits a hierarchical organization of the competencies. This hierarchic organization of

Figure 1. Ng et al.'s (2006) ontology

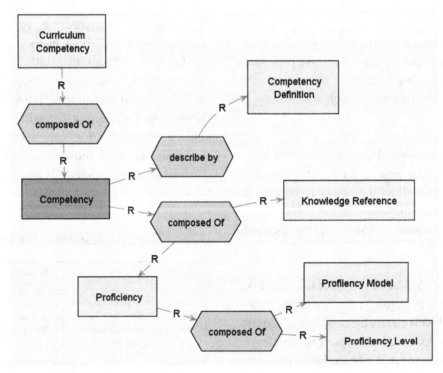

competencies is a characteristic which is absent in the ontology on Figure 9 in Chapter 10. In addition, their ontology offers the possibility of choosing the scale of performance. Finally, there is a mean to connect this formal description of a competence with a standard competency description, by means of the RDCEO standard.

Schmidt & Kunzmann (2006) investigated the link between training practices in companies, knowledge management, performance support and the concept of an *educational semantic Web*. The key element of their approach is a competency ontology which allows one to connect instructional materials with the context of professional tasks. To elaborate their ontology, they consider that a competency is a set of skills, knowledge and capacities. Figure 2 depicts a segment of their ontology.

Like Ng et al.'s (2006) the specificity of this ontology is rgw *competencyType* class connected with the class *competency scale*. It allows one to foresee the specialization of various views of competency according to the nature of the used

competency scale. Also, the properties *consists of* and *subsume* indicate that the competency can be described by sub-competency that can be hierarchically organized.

Sitthisak et al.'s (2007) ontology aims at the development of an evaluation system. One of their ultimate objectives is to offer a personalized support system according to the evaluations' results. The existing systems raise several problems. On the one hand, the existence of different metrics for knowledge, skills and competency used in theses evaluation systems. On the other hand, the fact that the systems cannot exchange the results of the evaluation session. Sitthisak et al.'s research hypothesis was that a competency ontology will facilitate the exchange of evaluations between systems.

Figure 3 shows that the components of the competency are: 1) The individual which possesses the competency (the *owner*); 2) A *proficiency level* of the competency; 3) A *learned capacity* according to the observable behavior of learner; 4) *Evidences* grouping the documents and the

Figure 2. Schmidt and Kunzmann's (2006) ontology

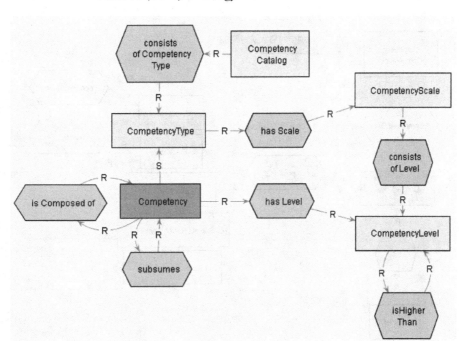

information which demonstrates that the competency has been indeed acquired; 5) The external resources which intervene in the expression of the competency. In addition, the competency can be hierarchically organized to structure all the competencies associated to a training program. This ontology distinguishes itself from the ontology we apply by the following: Firstly, the competency is only associated to an individual possessing it. Secondly, the ontology does not take into account the links between a competency and an activity or an learning object. There is in addition a description of the evidences that the competency is acquired. This theme of *evidence* is not considered by the ontology which we use because the evidences, in TELOS System, constitute a part of the actor model, related to the competencies that constitute also a part of this model (See Chapter 9).

Associating Competencies to Resources

To validate scenarios according to competencies, it is crucial that elements composing scenarios be associated to one or to several competencies. For a learning activity, the associated competencies can be a target competence meant to be achieved at the end of the activity or a prerequisite competency necessary to start the activity. For an actor, a competency can be an acquired competency or a target competency. For a document, or more generally a learning object, a competency can be the competency which we can generally reach by adequately exploiting the learning object or the prerequisite competency necessary to take advantage of this learning object.

There are several ways of studying the link between competency and resource, in particular, by looking at proposed standards. Several standards are defined for competency management in distributed learning environment. RDCEO (*Reusable Definition Competency or Educational*

Figure 3. Sitthisak et al.'s (2007) ontology

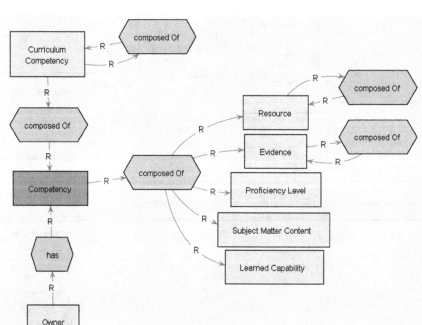

Objective) suggests a standard way to define the competency or learning objective associated with the learning activities. However, this proposition, in version 1.0, remains a summary based on a textual description of the competency, and not a formal or semi-formal representation. Nevertheless, it is possible to connect the description of the competency to an external entity which could be a formal representation of the competency. Furthermore, LIP (*Learner Information Package*) and PAPI (*Public and Private Information for Learners*) are two specifications for storing information about learners. By using them, various training systems can exchange information about learner's competency. Researchers of the domain widely criticize these standards by claiming them to be incomplete, partial and not enough formal (Devedzic, Jovanovic & Gasevic, 2007; Grant, 2006, 2007; Ng et al., 2006; Sicilia, 2005; Sitthisak et al., 2007). In exchange, they propose a combinations or extension of the existing ones.

The approach proposed here is based on a competency ontology and seen as an extension of a standard dedicated competency such as RD-CEO. Figure 4 presents a segment of the TELOS ontology, that will be presented in Chapter 15, that deals with the semantic referencing of resources. Every resource -actor, activity or learning object- includes one or several semantic descriptors. Theses descriptors are the results of semantic

referencing activity of the resource realized with a specific tool. Ontological entities are classes or instances of the ontology. This is an effective mean to formally describe the knowledge and competencies possessed by a given resource or an actor.

For example, the resource Activity 5.3 which is depicted in Figure 5 is an instance of the class TELOS resource. This resource represents *the processes of production of the rice*, instance of a concept describes formally in an ontology. The location of this ontology and the reference is specified by the URI and the data property *hasSemanticRef*.

On Figure 6, we present an example of a competency represented with the ontological editor OWL. The competency named *Competency-Example* is a target competency. It possesses a textual description *Repair rice production process with …* Its knowledge part consists of a single knowledge which is *Rice production processes*. The generic skill is *Repair (7)*, to be applied to the knowledge at the performance level 4 (Familiarization). The resource to which it is associated is a learning activity named *Activity 5.3*. An important constraint during the competency edition is that the elements of knowledge forming the knowledge part of the competency must be descriptors of the ontology (*OWL Descriptors*), describing the resource. This

Figure 4. The link between semantic descriptor and competency

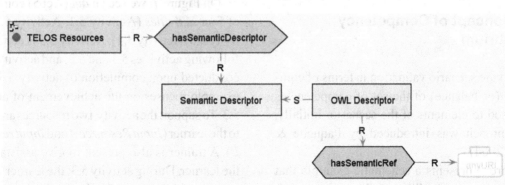

Figure 5. Ontological representation of the resource named Activity 5.3

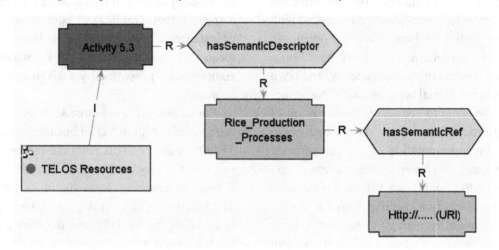

Figure 6. Ontological representation of the competency " competency-example"

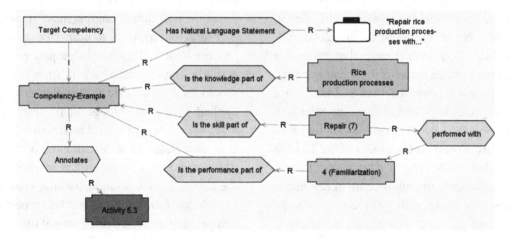

association of ontology references to resources has been presented in Chapter 11.

The Concept of Competency Equilibrium

We plan the scenario validation in terms of equilibrium (or balance) of the set of competencies associated to elements of the scenario. Initially, this approach was introduced by Paquette & Rosca (2004).

Figure 7 presents a schematic example that they have presented to illustrate this new approach

of scenario validation, usign IMS-LD and the MOT+ editor.

On Figure 7, we see an *act* (Act 5) comprised of four *activities* (Activity 5.1, Activity 5.2, Activity 5.3, Activity 5.4). Activity 5.3 is conducted following activities 5.1 and 5.2, and activity 5.4 is conducted upon completion of activity 5.3. This example focuses on the achievement of activity 5.3. To support the activity, two resources are given to the learner (*Input Resource A* and *Input resource B*). A trainer is also present to give assistance to the learner. During activity 5.3, the learner should produce a document (*Product resource*).

Figure 7. Example of equilibrium validation in (Paquette & Rosca, 2004)

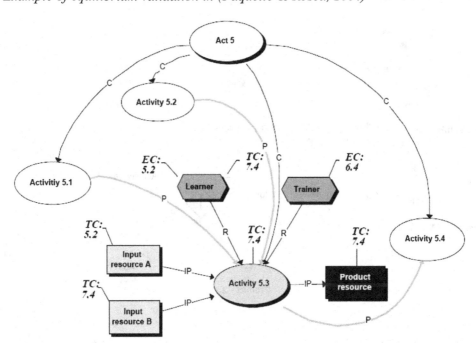

A target competency (TC) and an entry competency (EC) are associated to the input resources, to the learner, to the trainer, to the activity and also to the document which must be produced during the activity. It is important to note that the above competencies are all connected to the same knowledge. The elements that vary are the cognitive skill and the degree of performance. Activity 5.3 aims at competency 7.4, which is Skill = Repair, Performance = Familiarization). A learner that possesses an entry competency of 5.2 (Skill = Apply, Performance = Sensitization) is one that requires assistance. The trainer possesses a competency 6.4 (Skill = Analyze, Performance = familiarization). It is insufficient to help learner to acquire the target competence but the resource B, which has a target competency 7.4, complements the contribution of the trainer. Therefore, we have here a well-balanced instructional scenario.

A case of imbalance is when an activity requires an entry competency, EC1, aims at a target competency TC1, and the knowledge part of both is similar (if the knowledge parts are different,

the situation is less simple. We have to start an inference engine to determine the semantic distance between the different ontology classes or instances entities). Two constraints apply here: the competency that the learner possesses should be superior or equal to EC1 and lower than TC1. If the second constraint is not verified, the learner should not do this activity because he will not increase his competency. The scenario adaptation could then consist of making the activity optional, or even completely abolishing the activity.

The notions of *competency equilibrium* (balance) and *semantic constraints* are needed in order to support scenario validation. They establish a relevant alternative with regards to the existing approaches previously presented. However, this validation approach proposed in 2004 has not been developed to provide a general framework of instructional scenario validation. Indeed, the example supplied by Paquette & Rosca (2004), shown on Figure 8a, are limited and there are many more situations and cases to consider.

Figure 8. A more elaborated case

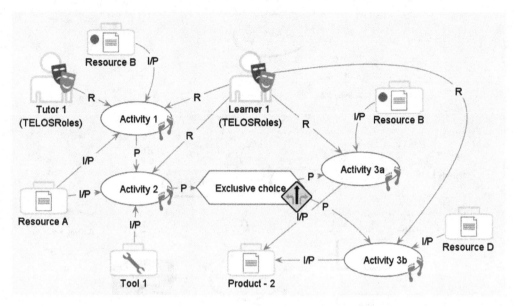

Look for example at the scenario pattern of Figure 8b, where many activities interact with actors and resources.

12.3 PROCESS FOR SCENARIO VALIDATION

The validation of an instructional scenario can take place during its design or during its delivery (or execution). At any time, during its delivery, the scenario can be validated to verify its capability to help reach the targeted competencies or objectives. This dynamic validation notably allows one to envision the adaptation of the scenario to the specific learner's needs and profile. If a learner does not have the adequate prerequisite competencies for participating in an activity, the validation of the scenario with regards to the learner's competencies would lead to an adaptation of the scenario where additional activities would be introduced. Another example consists of the possibility of some actors (e.g. a trainer) modifying certain resources. The validation would then verify that the scenario remains well-balanced with the new resources.

The actors that validate scenarios are primarily instructional designers and learners, however they can also be tutors or trainers. For an instructional designer, scenario validation means verifying if it is balanced to help fulfills the objectives. For a learner, the validation offers the possibility of adapting the scenario according to its own competencies and to its own training objectives which can exceed or be less demanding than those proposed initially. Learners can also play the role of an instruction designer in certain types of training situations such as project-based learning. The learner may elaborate a scenario according to the objectives that he/she has set. The learner may also use the validation tool to ascertain that the produced scenario is balanced. Finally, for the tutor or trainer, scenario validation can facilitate adapting the scenario to a particular learner's or group's need and to adapt the scenario according to his evaluation of the learner progress.

The process of equilibrium validation is an iterative progress from local to global, i.e. from the basic units of the scenario to the whole scenario. In order to proceed, a decomposition of the scenario into simple units is necessary.

Figure 9. Example of atomic aggregates

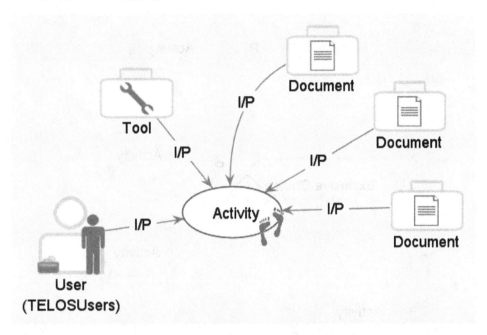

From Atomic to Complex Scenarios

The first level is constituted by *atomic aggregates*. Figures 7 and 9 are examples of these. Any educational modelling language possesses a smaller aggregation unit. In the TELOS educational modelling language, the basic unit is named *activity*. The first validation stage at the atomic level is local, for every activity.

Simple aggregates correspond to particular organizations or patterns of *atomic aggregates*. In the terminology of workflows domain and business processes modelling domain, they are patterns of process control (van der Aalst, Hofstede, Kiepuszewski & Barros, 2003). The three examples of Figure 10 are *simple aggregates* that we find in the TELOS educational modelling language (Marino & Correal, 2006): sequence of several activities, exclusive choice among several activities, and synchronization after two activities.

Complex aggregates correspond to the high-level organizations of simple aggregates. In the TELOS educational modelling language, the situation where a scenario contains one or several *functions* that has its own scenario is an example of complex aggregate. Another example is given in Figure 8.

The validation of a scenario is composed of the following three phases:

1) Validation of the *atomic aggregates*: It consists of verifying if the resources (documents, software tools and actors) linked to a learning activity form a valid set of resources in regards to the competencies (prerequisite and target) associated to the activity;

2) Validation of the *simple aggregates*: it consists of the identification of the simple atomic pattern in the simple aggregate and the verification of competency equilibrium of their combination. This validation uses the results of the first stage;

3) Validation of the *complex aggregates*: it consists of the identification of the simple aggregates composing the complex aggregate and the verification of the competence equilibrium at the level of their interaction. This validation uses the results of the second

Figure 10. Three types of simple aggregates

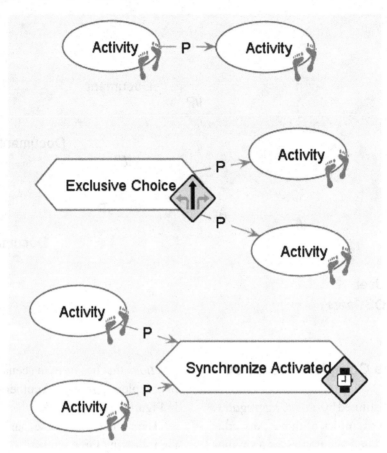

stage.

During the above three stages, a validation report is continuously produced. This report allows the actors to know and analyze the imbalance identified during validation.

Tools for Scenario Validation

Our approach for scenario validation is ontology-based. A validation ontology formalizes, on the one hand, the nature of the atomic, simple and complex aggregates which are specific to an educational modeling language aimed at building instructional scenario. For example, for an atomic aggregate, the ontology contains a formal description of the resources which can be associated to the aggregate,

of the possible products during this aggregate and the links that the aggregate can have with the other aggregates. On the other hand, the validation ontology formalizes the specific *validation rules* for every aggregate. Rules associated to an aggregate assure that the aggregate is balanced in regards to the competency associated to the aggregate and to its components. This ontology is considered to be generic so it can be adapted and used with various educational modeling languages.

Thus, the validation tool is a *knowledge-based system* (KBS). The competencies associated to the instructional scenario and to its components constitute a set of facts formalized according to both the validation ontology and the competency ontology. The validation rules apply to this set of

Figure 11. Tools for supporting the scenario validation process

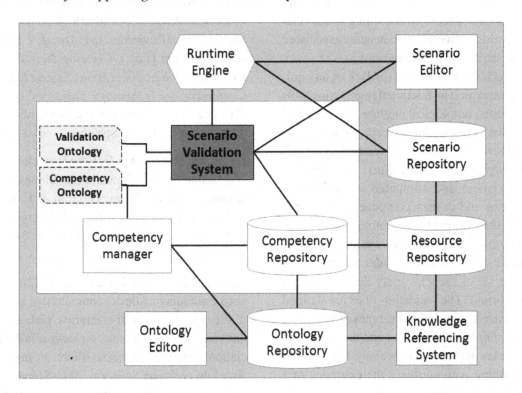

facts in order to diagnose the presence or lack of competency equilibrium in the scenarios.

Figure 11 presents the tools which are used to support the proposed competency-driven scenario validation process. In the white zone, are the tools which are specially developing to support the competency-driven validation process. The *Scenario Validation System* (SVS) is a *knowledge based system* which exploits the *validation ontology* and the *competency ontology*. When validation occurs during the design stage, SVS interacts with the Scenario Editor. When validation occurs during the delivery stage, SVS must also interacts with the runtime engine. Both situations need interaction between SVS and the *Competency Repository* that stores competencies as RDF/OWL files. The *Competency Manager* offers two main functionalities: the edition of competencies and the creation of competency referentials. The edition of a competency requires the selection of

ontological entities in the *Ontology Repository* to be associated to resources in the *Resource Repository*. The various resources (learning objects, actor, etc.) are associated to ontological entities (class, instance) using the *Knowledge Referencing System* (KRS).

CONCLUSION

This chapter presents a new approach to the validation of instructional scenarios, and more generally of learning objects aggregates. It proposes a solution to the integration of instructional engineering principles, techniques and tools in the design of better quality scenarios, participating in the efforts for elearning quality management.

Its originality lies in the concept of *competency equilibrium* (or balance) of an instructional scenario or an aggregate of learning objects. We have presented the general ideas behind a method and tool to validate a scenario according to the relations towards between competencies associated to the scenario and its components.

To check the presence or the lack of an equilibrium, we exploit instructional engineering tools and concepts, ontological engineering tools and also software engineering concepts such as *workflow patterns*. The validation system – SVS – is a *knowledge-based system*. *Facts* are scenarios (or aggregates) and competencies associated to scenarios and to their components. Facts are formalized according to two ontologies: the *validation ontology* and the *competency ontology*. A structured set of *validation rules* allows one to query the set of facts to verify the presence of an equilibrium. The validation rules are defined and organized according to the types of aggregate (*atomic*, *simple* and *complex*) and the validation process takes place in a iterative way, from bottom up, beginning with verifying the existence of a balance for every atomic aggregates.

The development of the required software tools and the evaluation of this scenario validation approach are in progress. However, we believe that this project will provide assistance tools for instructional designers to help them produce better quality scenarios. The question of assistance tools will be treated in Chapter 21 of this book. Furthermore such a validation system can become a first step in a *Scenario Adaptation System* during delivery scenario.

REFERENCES

Baldoni, M., Baroglio, C., & Marengo, E. (2007). Curricula Modeling and Checking . In Basili, R., & Pazienza, M. T. (Eds.), *AI*IA 2007: Artificial Intelligence and Human-Oriented Computing* (pp. 471–482). Berlin: Springer-Verlag. doi:10.1007/978-3-540-74782-6_41

Baldoni, M., & Marengo, E. (2007). Curriculum Model Checking: Declarative Representation and Verification of Properties. In E. Duval, R. Klamma & M. Wolpers (Eds.), *Creating New Learning Experiences on a Global Scale, Second European Conference on Technology Enhanced Learning (EC-TEL 2007),* Crete, Greece, September 17-20 (pp. 432-437). Berlin: Springer.

Baron, M., & Paquette, G. (2007). Technologies, Web sémantique et éducation: quelques défis et tendances. In M. Baron, D. Guin & L. trouche (Eds.), Environnements informatisés et ressources numériques pour l'apprentissage (pp. 315-341). Paris: Hermès/Lavoisier.

Basque, J., & Page-Lamarche, V. (2007). Un outil d'autodiagnostic des compétences au service d'une approche multi-scénarios pédagogiques dans un cours à distance… ou lorsque la différenciation pédagogique cesse d'être un mythe? In Actes du colloque Scénario 2007-Scénariser les activités de l'apprenant: une activité de modélisation, Montréal, Canada.

Bloom, B. S. (1956). *Taxonomy of Educational Objectives: The Classification of Educational Goals, Handbook I: Cognitive Domain*. New York: David McKay.

Brisebois, A., Ruelland, D., & Paquette, G. (2005). Supporting Self-Assessment in a Competency Approach to Learning. In G. Richards (Ed.), *Proceedings of World Conference on E-Learning in Corporate, Government, Healthcare, and Higher Education 2005* (pp. 2828-2835). Chesapeake, VA: AACE.

Brusilovsky, P. L., & Vassileva, J. (2003). Course sequencing techniques for large-scale web-based education. *International Journal of Continuing Engineering Education and Lifelong Learning, 13*(1/2), 75–94.

Caeiro-Rodriguez, M. (2008). poEML: A Separation of Concerns Proposal to Instructional Design. In L. Botturi & G. Stubbs (Eds.), Handbook of Visual Languages for Instructional Design: Theories and Practice (pp. 185-209). Hershey, PA: Informing Science Reference.

Chandrasekaran, B. (1986). Generic tasks in knowledge-based reasoning: High-level building blocks for expert system design. *IEEE Expert, 1*(3), 23–30. doi:10.1109/MEX.1986.4306977

Devedzic, V. (2006). *Semantic Web and Education.* Berlin: Springer.

Devedzic, V., Jovanovic, J., & Gasevic, D. (2007). The pragmatics of current e-learning standards. *IEEE Internet Computing, 11*(3), 19–27. doi:10.1109/MIC.2007.73

Dodero, J. M., Sanchez-Alonso, S., & Frosch-Wilke, D. (2007). Generative instructional engineering of competence development programmes. *Journal of Universal Computer Science, 13*(9), 1213–1233.

Grant, S. (2006). Frameworks of competence: common or specific? In R. Koper & K. Stefanov (eds.), Proceedings of International Workshop in Learning Networks for Lifelong Competence Development, March 30-31, Sofia, Bulgaria (pp. 111-116). Shoumen, Bugaria: INCOMA.

Grant, S. (2007). Towards competence-related interoperability. In TEN Competence workshop, Manchester.

Karampiperis, P., & Sampson, D. (2004). Adaptive instructional planning using ontologies. In D. Sampson (ed.), *Proceedings of IEEE International Conference on Advanced Learning Technologies (ICALT'04),* 30 August-1st September, Joensuu, Finland (pp. 126-130). Washington, DC: IEEE Computer Society Press.

Knight, C., Gasevic, D., & Richards, G. (2006). An ontology-based framework for bridging learning design and learning content. *Educational Technology & Society, 9*(1), 23–37.

Knolmayer, G. F. (2003). Decision Support Models for composing and navigating through e-learning objects. In *Proceedings of 36th IEEE Annual Hawaii International Conference on System Sciences,* Hawaii, USA.

Marino, O., & Correal, D. (2006). General Purpose Function's Editor. Rapport technique, Réseau LORNET, Télé-université du Québec, Montréal, Canada.

Melia, M., & Pahl, C. (2007a). An Information Architecture for Courseware Validation. In *First International Workshop on Learning Object Discovery & Exchange (LODE'07),* Crete, Greece.

Melia, M., & Pahl, C. (2007b). Pedagogical Validation of Courseware. In E. Duval, R. Klamma & M. Wolpers (Eds.), *Creating New Learning Experiences on a Global Scale, Second European Conference on Technology Enhanced Learning (EC-TEL 2007),* Crete, Greece, September 17-20 (pp. 499-504). Berlin: Springer.

Mohan, P., Greer, J., & McCalla, G. (2003). Instructional Planning with Learning Objects. In *Workshop on Knowledge Representation and Automated Reasoning for E-Learning Systems,* Acapulco, Mexico.

Ng, A., Hatala, M., & Gasevic, D. (2006). Ontology-based Approach to Learning Objective Formalization. In Sicilia, M. A. (Ed.), *Competencies in Organizational E-Learning: Concepts and Tools.* Hershey, PA: Informing Science Reference.

Paquette, G. (2003). *Instructional Engineering in Networked Environments.* San Francisco: Pfeiffer.

Paquette, G., & Rosca, I. (2004). An ontology-based referencing of actors, operations and resources in eLearning systems. In [Eindhoven, The Netherlands.]. *Proceedings of Workshop SW-EL, 04*(March), 23.

Psyché, V., Bourdeau, J., Nkambou, R., & Mizoguchi, R. (2005). Making Learning Design Standards Work with an Ontology of Educationnal Theories. In C.-K. Looi, G. McCalla, B. Bredeweg & J. Breuker (Eds.), *Artificial Intelligence in Education: Supporting Learning through Intelligent and Socially Informed Technology (AIED'05)* (pp. 539-546). Amsterdam: IOS Press.

Radevski, V., & Trichet, F. (2006). Ontology-Based Systems Dedicated to Human Resources Management: An Application in e-Recruitment. In R. Meersman, Z. Tari & P. Herrero (Eds.), *Workshops On the Move to Meaningful Internet Systems (OTM'06)*, 29 November-3 December, Montpellier, France (pp. 1068-1077). Berlin: Springer.

Roldan Garcia, M. M., & Aldana-Montes, J. F. (2005). A tool for storing owl using database technology. In *First Int'l Workshop on OWL Experiences and Directions*, Galway, Ireland.

Santacruz-Valencia, L. P., Navarro, A., Delgado Kloos, C., & Aedo, I. (2008). ELO-Tool: Taking action in the challenge of assembling learning objects. *Educational Technology & Society, 11*(1), 102–117.

Schmidt, A., & Kunzmann, C. (2006). Towards a Human Resource Development Ontology for Combining Competence Management and Technology-Enhanced Workplace Learning. In R. Meersman, Z. Tari & P. Herrero (Eds.), *Workshops On the Move to Meaningful Internet Systems (OTM'06)*, 29 November-3 December, Montpellier, France (pp. 1078-1087). Berlin: Springer.

Sicilia, M. A. (2005). Ontology-based competency management: Infrastructures for the knowledge-intensive learning organization . In Lytras, M. D., & Naeve, A. (Eds.), *Intelligent learning infrastructures in knowledge intensive organizations: A semantic web perspective* (pp. 302–324). Hershey, PA: Informing Science Press.

Sitthisak, O., Gilbert, L., & Davis, H. C. (2007). Towards a competency model for adaptive assessment to support lifelong learning. In *Proceedings of TENCompetence Open Workshop on Service Oriented Approaches and Lifelong Competence Development Infrastructures,* 11th – 12th January, Manchester, United Kingdom.

van der Aalst, W. M. P., ter Hofstede, A. H. M., Kiepuszewski, B., & Barros, A. P. (2003). Workflow patterns. *Distributed and Parallel Databases, 14*(1), 5–51. doi:10.1023/A:1022883727209

Wiley, D. A. (2002). Connecting learning objects to instructional design theory: A definition, a metaphor, and a taxonomy . In Wiley, D. A. (Ed.), *The Instructional Use of Learning Objects* (pp. 3–23). Bloomington, IN: Agency for Instructional Technology.

Zouaq, A., Nkambou, R., & Frasson, C. (2006). The Knowledge Puzzle: An Integrated Approach of Intelligent Tutoring Systems and Knowledge Management. In *Proceedings of 18th IEEE International Conference on Tools with Artificial Intelligence (ICTAI'06),* November 13-15. Washington, DC: IEEE Computer Society Press.

Chapter 13
Ontology–Based Software Component Aggregation

Gilbert Paquette
LICEF Research Center, Canada

Anis Masmoudi
LICEF Research Center, Canada

ABSTRACT

- Software Component Aggregation Process
- Metadata for Software Component Referencing
  - Software Component Metadata (SOCOM)
  - The SOCOM Manager
- The Software Components Ontology
  - The SOCOM MOT+OWL Model
  - The SOCOM Ontology in Protégé
- A Framework for Ontology-Driven Aggregation of Components

The topic of Component-Based Software Development (CBSD) has become very important in industry and research in the last 10 years (Allen & Frost 1998; Object Management Group, 2003). In e-learning, an increasing number of organizations have recognized the importance of building learning technologies by aggregating existent pedagogical software components. To support training processes, Web portals and digitized resources need to be provided to actors in each process. This can be done by aggregating, in a process workflow, different kinds of resources accessible on the Web: documents, simulations, videos, software tools, as well as persons interacting through communication tools and services. These resources are all represented by digital components that need to be aggregated in a proper manner.

DOI: 10.4018/978-1-61520-839-5.ch013

Aggregating software components is also a central dimension of the TELOS system that will be presented in chapter 15. In fact, right from the start, the TELOS conceptual architecture documents (Paquette, Rosca, Mihaila & Masmoudi, 2006) proposed a solution to the general resources aggregation problems, whether these resources are actors, documents, learning objects, learning scenarios or workflows, and of course, software components. These documents suggest a generic framework as a conceptual solution for building e-learning. In this chapter, we present an ontology-based approach for the aggregation of a specific resource type, software components.

Aggregating software components poses many challenges: software component characterization, classification, software component identification, software component integration frameworks, software component integration processes and their assessment (Torchiano, Jaccheri, Srensens and Wang, 2002; Szyperski, Gruntz & Murer, 2002; Bechhofer 2003; Izza 2006).

The effort presented here has been mainly conducted within the Canadian LORNET research initiative on distributed knowledge-based computing for the Semantic Web. LORNET researchers have developed software components and integrated them in a support system, TELOS (Paquette & Magnan, 2008), which support actors involved in learning or knowledge management activities, through the use of resource repository networks on the Semantic Web.

In the first section, we present a short review of related work to justify the presentation of a Software Component Aggregation Process (SO-CAP) driven by metadata and ontology models. Metadata management is supported by the SO-COM Web Manager that will be presented in the second section. The metadata presented in this section will help define the SOCOM ontology presented in section 3. Based on this ontology, a software framework will be defined in the concluding section 4, in order to assist software

engineer in the component aggregation process presented in section 1.

13.1 SOFTWARE COMPONENT AGGREGATION PROCESS

Component-Based Software Development (CBSD) is concerned with building complex software systems by integrating previously existing parts called software components. CBSD aims at enhancing the flexibility and maintainability of these systems. It is an approach used to reduce software development costs, and reduce the maintenance burden related to updating large systems (Haines, Carney & James, 1997). The foundation of this approach is the hypothesis that some parts of these systems can be written once rather than many times, and that some software systems can be assembled from existing components, so there is no need to develop them over and over (Allen & Frosts, 1998).

One of the latest trends in systems development is to make greater use of commercial-off-the-shelf (COTS) products. COTS products are commercial components that are ready to use. Component-based systems encompass both COTS products and components acquired through other means, such as non-developmental items. This kind of development becomes feasible due to:

- the increase in the quality and variety of COTS products;
- economic pressures to reduce system development and maintenance costs;
- the evolution and emergence of component integration technologies;
- the increasing amount of existing software that has been designed and implemented to be reused in new development contexts.

Szyperski states that development emphasis moves from programming software to composing software systems (Szyperski, Gruntz, & Murer, 2002). In CBSD. Building systems shifts from writing code from scratch to assembling and integrating existing software components. In contrast to traditional development, component integration is the centrepiece of the CBSD approach. Thus, integration and aggregation are key considerations in the decision to acquire, reuse or build software systems.

Brown suggests four major activities to characterize component-based development approaches:

- component qualification;
- component adaptation;
- assembling components into systems;
- system evolution.

These activities are part of a component-based development process and must be well organized and planned to build complex systems. Many software integration experts consider that technical issues are mature enough, whereas organizational and economic issues are not. Consequently, several issues become important such as integration requirements, standards, component identification, component selection, component metadata repositories, component referencing, component search and retrieval, process development, component architecture (Haines, Carney & James, 1997; Mili, Mili, Yacoub, & Addy, 2002; Seidewitz, 2003).

Most existing literature dealing with characterization of software components focuses on classification, evaluation and selection. Torchiano and Jaccheri propose a classification of software components. A more complex classification is outlined by Morisio and Torchiano. It is based on ten attributes grouped into four areas: source, customization, bundle and role. All these works are detailed in (M. Torchiano, L. Jaccheri, C.-F. Srensens, & A. I. Wang, 2002).

It's important to note that few works deal in a coherent way with component characterization, identification, selection, processes, methods and

frameworks. This is why we have built the software component aggregation process presented in Figure 1. This process model in built using the TELOS scenario editor presented in chapter 8 and discussed more thoroughly in chapter 12. It is model- and metadata-driven and is managed by a software engineer.

Figure 1 illustrates the component aggregation process of two components labelled "component 1"(Cp1) and "component 2"(Cp2). There are six phases in the process.

- *Phase 1.* In the initial meta-tagging phase the engineer gathers metadata on the software component packages he aims to aggregate. He uses the *SOCOM Web Manager* to create two instances in a repository of components that stores metadata on distributed or local components' properties. Technical information about components can be extracted semi-automatically using the SOCOM Metadata Extractor applied to each component's package.
- *Phase 2.* In this categorization phase, the engineer uses the SOCOM OWL ontology that we will present later on, to make request to an inference engine that will use the ontology and some classification rules to categorize the component. The goal here is to decide if the two components can be aggregated and if so, what kind of aggregation can be selected: either collection, coordination of fusion. These terms are defined in the following sections. The result of this phase is an aggregation pattern.
- *Phase 3.* The engineer selects the two components Cp1 and Cp2 for aggregation using the SOCOM Web manager and its search engine. This phase will provide their code and metadata that will be used in the next phase.
- *Phase 4.* Depending on their metadata and the aggregation patterns, the two components will be adapted to fit the specific aggrega-

Figure 1. Software component aggregation process diagram (SOCAP)

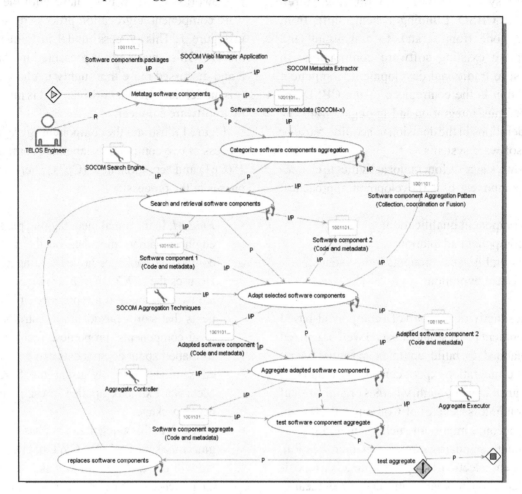

tion context. Different adaptation techniques can be used, such as connectors, wrapping and bridging (Mili, Mili, Yacoub, & Addy, 2002).

- *Phase 5.* This is where the aggregate is produced with its code and metadata. In the case of a Collection or a Coordination aggregate, a component contract will be created using an "Aggregate Controller". The component contract specifies a pattern of interaction, the services provided by each component in the aggregate and the obligations of clients using them, and finally, the environment needed by a component to provide these services (Bachman, 2000).

If the aggregation uses a fusion pattern, the engineer will use reverse and forward model-driven approach (Raistrick, 2004). We reverse engineer Cp1 and Cp2 to obtain their models. Using these models, the engineer tries to design the aggregation solution at the model level, using additional classes and associations to complete the fusion. According to a Model Driven Approach (Kreffe 2003) the engineer will transforms a Platform Independent component Model into Platform Specific component Model(s) and finally, into a code model of the new (aggregated) component.

- *Phase 6.* In the last phase, the engineer tests the aggregate's execution using an "Aggregate Executor". If the test fails, the engineer must alter the aggregate or the components' adaptation, or replace components with others and start over from the beginning.

13.2 METADATA FOR SOFTWARE COMPONENT REFERENCING

The SOCOM Web Manager and its various components is used in all the phases of the SOCAP process presented above. In this section, we will discuss the software component metadata that this manager uses to help search for components and provide their metadata to fuel the aggregation process.

In general, metadata has been defined as data about data, information about data or information about information. For example, a library catalogue contains information (metadata) about publications (data) or a file system maintains permission information (metadata) about files (data), so metadata brings structure to data. Many

machine-readable metadata use generally the XML format. More sophisticated metadata use references to ontologies, in the way presented in chapter 11. A software components ontology will be presented in the next section, based on the present discussion on SOCOM.

SOCOM Attributes

SOCOM is composed of six categories of metadata.

SOCOM static attributes give general information about a software component (SC). They are called static because they often remain the same during the component's life cycle.

- *Component identifier* is the global SOCOM primary key. It varies with the different versions of the product.
- *Product identifier* stays constant across different versions of the same software component.

Figure 2. Two views of the SOCOM Manager

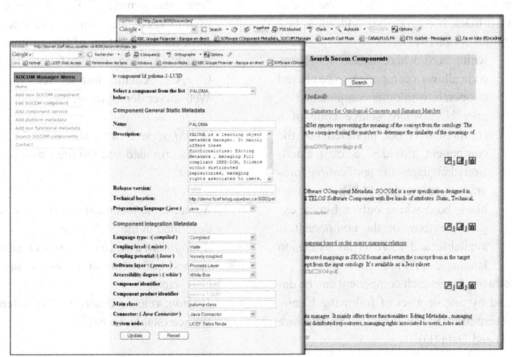

- *Name*: the name or title of the software component.
- *Version*: expresses how the development of a software component has progressed and how much further development it may require. We assume each major version of a product goes through a stage when new features are added (alpha version), then a stage when it is actively debugged (beta version), and finally a stage when all important bugs have been removed (stable version). Possible values of this attribute include pre-alpha, alpha, Beta, Gold release, and Stable-Unstable, among others.
- *System node*: system node (e.g. server, computer) where the component is located.
- Technical location: the URL or URI address that describes the technical location of the SC.
- Description: short description of the SC.

SOCOM aggregation attributes describe metadata that guide the aggregation of components.

- *Component Accessibility*: describes the component in terms of "box". We distinguish black box, grey box and white box (Haines *et al.*, 1997).
  - white box: where access to source code allows a component to be altered to operate with other components;
  - grey box: where source code of a component is not modified but the component provides its own extension language or application programming interface (API);
  - black box: where only a binary executable form of the component is available and there is no extension language or API.
- *Software layer*: each component can be defined by one or a set of following layers: Presentation (P), Business (B), Middleware (M) and Data (D).

- *Coupling level*: describes the potential of a software component to be connected to another one on the same or on different software layers. There are three different coupling levels: horizontal, vertical or mixed coupling. When a component communicates with another component in the same layer, the coupling level is qualified as horizontal, otherwise it's vertical. Coupling level has value "mixed" where a component can communicate with others in the same layer (horizontal) as well as components in other layers (vertical).
- Coupling potential: defines the degree of integration. Loose coupling is where the integration is dependent on a few discrete interfaces. Strong coupling is usually where implementation dependences occur.
- Language Type: language type of the SC's implementation. It can be an interpreted or compiled language.
- Main class: the technical location of the main class that can launch the SC. For example in java: Socom\SocomManager\socomManagerImpl.class.
- Aggregation method: depicts the method used to aggregate a component if it results from the aggregation of two or more SCs. Possible methods include Connector (Java, C++, C#, Scheme, Web service), Launcher, Web server deployment, etc.

SOCOM service attributes describe the set of services provided and required by a software component.

- *Name*: same technical name of the service described in the SC's code.
- *Annotation*: a service description similar to method comments in a class in Java, C#, C++, etc…
- *Version*: release description of referenced service (stable, unstable).

- *Returned type*: type of variable or object returned by the service. SOCOM uses the following subset of XML simple types: « String », « Integer », « Void », « Double », « Collection », and « Boolean ». Other types can be added if needed.

- *Visibility*: similar to method visibility in programming languages, a service can be « Public », « Protected» or « Private ».

- *Type*: for each component, we have two kinds of services: « ProvidedService », « RequiredService ».

- *Invocation mode*: asynchronous when a component service is executed without immediate callback, otherwise synchronous.

- *Required library*: each component may use a set of libraries. For each library, we specify:
  ○ library name;
  ○ library technical location.

- *Services parameters*. Each service needs at least one input parameter. For each parameter, we specify:
  ○ Parameter name: the significant technical name of the parameter.
  ○ Parameter type: similar to service types.
  ○ Visibility: similar to service visibility.
  ○ Parameter rank: position of the parameter within the list needed to call the service. For example, the parameter « id » is the second parameter in the description of the following service: Collection getRessource(String name, Int id)
  ○ Parameter access type: describes the access type to the parameter: « read », « write » or « readwrite ».

SOCOM quality attributes convey information about various qualities of the component that are important for the reuse of the component. Such attributes include performance, reliability, availability, scalability, security, maintainability, versioning, licensing, integrity, etc. The technical name for these attributes is "Non Functional Specification" (NFS).

SOCOM platform attributes are metadata describing the SC's technical environment. They describe the platform on which the SC environments reside: development, deployment, configuration, modeling, data, etc.

SOCOM use cases attributes are domain metadata that describes, the relation between actors and activities where the component is used. Our use case descriptions are similar to UML use case specification models or a TELOS process model.

The SOCOM Manager

Based on these metadata, a version of the SOCOM Manager has been built to store and aggregate software components for the LORNET project. It provides services for metadata edition (left) to integrate new components in the referential and search services to display a list of components, corresponding to a query (right).

13.3 THE SOFTWARE COMPONENTS ONTOLOGY

In this section, we define an ontology in OWL-DL format (W3C, 2003) that helps describe software components semantically, using a set of concepts (classes), properties and axioms. Each software component is considered as an instance of this ontology, which is another way to describe it with metadata based on classes of the ontologies. The advantage of such an implementation is the expressiveness of the Web Ontology Language and its inference capability (Daconta, Obrst & Smith, 2003). This ontology facilitates software component classification and inferences when it is coupled with a DL inference engine and a query language like DIG (Bechhofer, 2003).

The SOCOM MOT+OWL Model

The SOCOM Ontology was build using the MOT+OWL editor presented in chapter 10. Then the ontology was exported to an OWL-DL XML file and read into the Protégé ontology editor where the software components have been declared as instances (individual) to provide them with semantic references, as explained in chapter 11.

Figure 3 shows the top level of SOCOM Ontology. This model incorporates a more detailed description of the metadata in the previous section. Note that the concept "SoftwareComponent" includes properties corresponding to the six classes of attributes presented in the previous section. These properties link the class "SoftwareComponent" to the classes that contain the attributes values of SOCOM.

The class "Aggregate" has a cardinality restriction that indicates that an aggregate is composed of at least two other software components. Since the aggregate is also a component, it is connected to the concept "SoftwareComponent" by a specialization (S) link. Other cardinality restrictions indicate that a component contains only a single

"StaticSpecification", at least one "ServiceSpecification", and at least one "BusinessSpecification".

These classes are further developed and defined in the form of sub-models in the following figures. Figure 4 is a sub-model for the class "ServiceSpecification". The classes in this sub-model represent the attributes of a service provided or required by a component such as name, type (required, provided), return type, version, invocation mode, visibility. Individuals of the model represent the values that some of the attributes may have.

Figure 5 is a sub-model of the class « Service Parameter » present in the « ServiceSpecification » model of Figure 4. For each of the parameters of a service, we give its name, type, order in the list of parameters, its visibility and its type of access.

The model in Fig. 4 also indicates that the concept of service is linked to "BusinessUseCase" by the relation "implements". The concept "BusinessUseCase" is a reference to the sub-model for "BusinessSpecification", shown in Figure 6.

This relationship is important because it allows us to add semantics to the syntactic description of a component, i.e. the business use case it implements. Through this relation, we are provided with

Figure 3. The SOCOM ontology: top level model

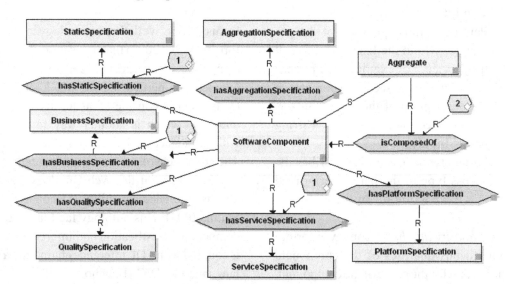

Figure 4. The ServiceSpecification sub-ontology: level-2 model

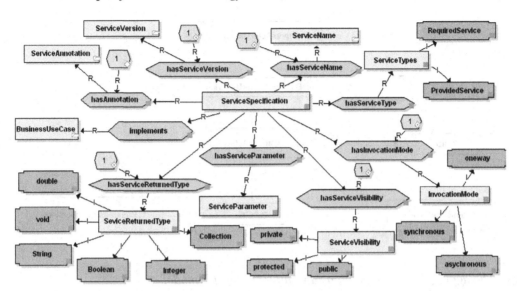

Figure 5. The ServiceParameter sub-ontology: level-3 model

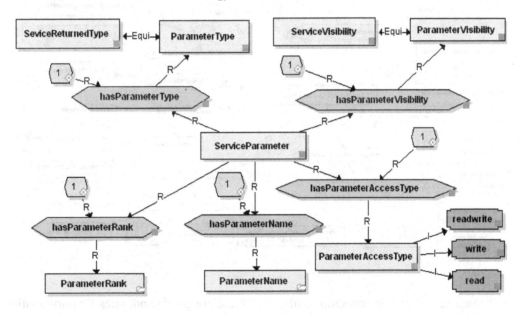

a high level of knowledge regarding the business use case(s) made by the service of the component in question, as outlined by (Renaux, Olivier & Jean-Marc, 2004). Also, the semantics of the service is useful for analysts looking for a particular component in order to aggregate it with others. The business specifications of the component can be used to trace the actor(s) performing a business use case and to describe the latter. Through the model, the definition of the SOCOM component comprises a dual description for each service in the form of technical information provided by the concept "ServiceSpecification" and on business use cases provided by "BusinessSpecification".

The ontology of aggregation specifications shown in Figure 7 is a key element in feasibility

Figure 6. The BusinessSpecification sub-ontology: level-2 model

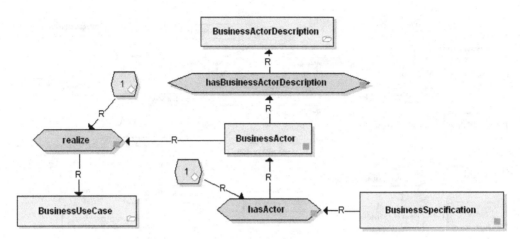

Figure 7. The aggregation specification sub-ontology: level-2 model

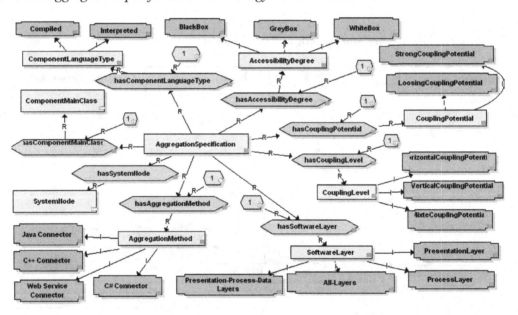

studies on the aggregation of software components. The classes of the model, including degree of accessibility, coupling level, coupling potential, software layer, component language type, and component aggregation method, are used to classify the component and assess its ability to aggregate with other components. In other words, two components having a common set of properties will be in the same class. We can deduce that

these are good candidates for participation in an aggregation process.

The sub-model for "PlatformSpecification", presented in Figure 8, concludes our description of the SOCOM ontology.

From development to usage, each component goes through different types of platforms. Its name, description, document, and operating system, as well as its usage type, characterize each platform during the life of the component. This informa-

Figure 8. The PlatformSpecification sub-ontology: level-2 model

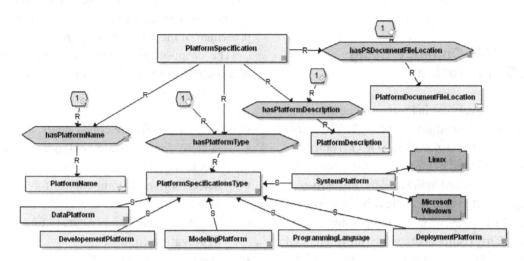

Figure 9. Part of the OWL SOCOM ontology in the Protégé editor

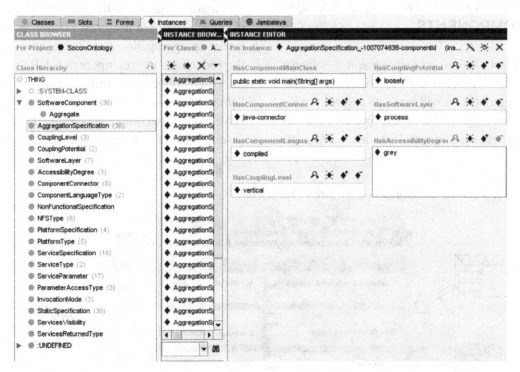

tion can help us in the feasibility studies for the different categories of aggregation.

The SOCOM Ontology Using OWL-DL in Protégé

Figure 9 is an overview in Protégé of the instances and aggregation specifications of a SOCOM ontology component. Classes of the SOCOM ontology are listed on the left of the figure. Instances of the classes are displayed in the middle. Properties of instances selected in the middle column appear on the right. In this way, we have incorporated into the databank thirty components, which are referenced by the metadata provided by the classes of the ontology and their values for a given component.

13.4 A FRAMEWORK FOR ONTOLOGY-DRIVEN AGGREGATION OF COMPONENTS

In this last section, we will present a software framework (D'Souza D.F., & Wills A. C. 1998) grouping tools that will assist an engineer in the component aggregation process presented in section 1. These tools are ontology-driven (Paquette and Magnan 2008) in the sense that their functions are executed by queries to the SOCOM ontology presented in the previous section.

The proposed framework will help users to accomplish, among others, the following functionalities:

*   reference software components,
*   search for software components using metadata,
*   select software components for aggregation purposes,
*   adapt software components to fit a specific aggregation context,
*   create new components,
*   aggregate software components, a
*   replace software components according to the aggregation context.

Figure 10 shows different SOCAF tools or modules. They are designed to support the engineer in aggregating two components, A and B, producing a new component f(A,B) resulting from their collection, coordination or fusion. The *Software Component Storage* is a set of distributed server where the components reside. Their name, description, Web address and other metadata

Figure 10. Software component aggregation framework

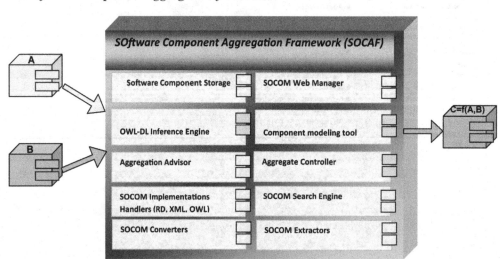

Figure 11. Example of a query to the SOCOM manager

```xml
<asks xmlns="http://dl.kr.org/dig/2003/02/lang">
        <instances id="queryGetSpecificComponent">
                <stringequals val="LGPL">
                        <ratom name=" hasLicenseType"/>
                </stringequals>
                <stringequals val="BlackBox">
                        <ratom name=" hasAccessibilityDegree"/>
                </stringequals>
                <stringequals val="Java">
                        <ratom name=" hasLanguageType"/>
                </stringequals>
                <stringequals val="loosely">
                        <ratom name="hasCouplingLevel "/>
                </stringequals>
                <stringequals val="getLOMResources">
                <ratom name="hasServiceName "/>
                </stringequals>
        </instances>
</asks>
```

are given by declaring them as instances of the SOCOM ontology. They then become a SOCOM component that is described using the SOCOM ontology. Their semantic references are stored as instances in the ontology, in OWL-DL files, accessible by an ontology editor or viewer such as MOT+OWL or PROTÉGÉ.

The SOCOM Web Manager manages SOCOM components. It is a Web application that helps administrators to manage and store software component code (libraries) and their metadata. A preliminary version of the SOCOM Manager has been presented in Figure 2.

This tool uses the *SOCOM Search Engine* to search for software components according to different criteria in component repositories distributed through the Web. We complement the search engine results with an *Inference Engine* to execute specific intelligent queries.

The query shown on Figure 11 is done by an engineer looking for a BlackBox component with LGPL license, implemented in the JAVA language, having a loose coupling potential. This component must have a service called "getLOMResources."

This query is written in the XML DIG format that can communicate with DIG compatible infer-

ence engines like Pellet . Such a OWL inference engine will process the ontology to match the request, directly or by deduction. For example, if a component has another coupling value, it will be discarded because the ontology stipulates that a component has one and only one coupling value. All deductible components will then be displayed to the user.

The aggregation of SOCOM Component is assisted by an entity called the *Aggregation Advisor*, which uses the SOCOM Web Manager and some defined rules to help users decide on aggregation feasibility.

After that, the engineer can design a conceptual aggregate using a *Modeling environment* as a tool used during the aggregation process to model an aggregate from the models of two or more software components. This can be done using UML tools such as IBM-Rational Rose.

The aggregate can be executed by our *Aggregation Executor*, which is an entity that builds and executes aggregates.

Other entities are useful to extract and manipulate SOCOM metadata in different formats such as *SOCOM Converters*, which are a set of useful entities for example to translate between relational database format and OWL-DL XML format.

SOCOM Metadata Extractors are a set of entities that extract technical metadata from the binary code of the software libraries of the component. Because a large proportion of components are Java or C# components, SOCAF provides two Metadata Extractors to extract information from JAR/WAR or DLL files.

CONCLUSION

"Software reuse is the process whereby an organization defines a set of systematic operating procedures to specify, produce, classify, retrieve and adapt software artifacts for the purpose of using them in its development activities." (Mili, Mili, Yacoub, & Addy, 2002, p.6)

This definition has a number of implications. Successful software reuse goes far beyond mere acquisition/implementation of software components. The whole software development lifecycle must be adapted if software reuse is taken seriously. Reuse must also be guided by a well-defined process, as made evident by the "systematic operating procedures" portion of the definition. Moreover, activities which are not typically present in standard software development appear in the definition (e.g. "classify", "retrieve" and "adapt"). Various skills are required in an organization where software reuse is intended. These skills include the librarian, the reuse manager, the domain engineer, the application engineer, and the component engineer.

We believe the ideas presented in this chapter can promote software reuse by reducing the burden associated to reuse for all stakeholders. Domain Engineering can provide the SOCOM specification associated to a component. This specification could actually enhance design documentation provided to Component Engineers for the actual implementation of components. The Librarian can use this metadata to classify and store components in repositories. This metadata will eventually be queried when components are being searched by the Librarian. Application Engineering can also browse and search repositories through metadata.

We proposed in this chapter a process and a supporting framework based on various software component metadata which, once associated with software components, should facilitate their aggregation. Component referencing is an important aspect of a components' repository. With the SOCOM specification and Metadata Extractors components, we obtain different aspects of component information, some of which is automatically extracted from the components' binary code. SOCOM Converters promote the reuse of different formats of our component metadata, namely XML, OWL and relational database. The XML format encourages network exchange of components (e.g. interoperability). The SOCOM ontology facilitates classification and inference when coupled with an inference engine.

In the future, we need to focus on aggregation rules that deal with aggregation feasibility studies. Also, we will exploit alternative ontology representations of SOCOM and their interaction with SOCAM using DL inference engines. In addition, we will analyze component interaction contracts and workflow languages and evaluate their potential contribution into our software component aggregation metadata, SOCAM. We also intend to investigate aggregate execution and different techniques that allow heterogonous component execution. All these activities will enforce our aggregation process and facilitate its implementation and use.

REFERENCES

Allen, P., & Frosts, S. (1998 March). Tackling the Key Issues in CBD. *Select Software Tools.*

Bachman, E. A. (2000). *Volume II: Technical Concepts of Component-Based Software Engineering.* CMU/SEI-2000-TR-008 ESC-TR-2000-007.

Bechhofer, S. (2003). *DIG Specifications, version 1.1.* Manchester, UK: University of Manchester.

D'Souza, D. F., & Wills, A. C. (1998). *Objects, components, and frameworks with UML: the catalysis approach.* Boston, MA: Addison-Wesley.

Daconta, M. C., Obrst, L. J., & Smith, K. T. (2003). *The Semantic Web, A Guide to the Future of XML.* Web Services, and Knowledge Management.

Haines, C. G., Carney, D., & Foreman, J. (1997). *Component-Based Software Development/COTS Integration.* Paper presented at the CBSE 1997.

Kleppe, A., Warmer, J., & Bast, W. (2003). *MDA Explained–The Model Driven Architecture: Practice and Promise.* Boston: Addison-Wesley.

Magnan, F., & Paquette, G. (2006). *Telos: An Ontology Driven eLearning OS.* In S. Weibelzahl & A. Cristea (Eds.), *Proceedings of Workshops held at the Fourth International Conference on Adaptative Hypermedia and Adaptative Web-Based Systems (AH2006),* Dublin, National College of Ireland (pp. 131-139).

Masmoudi, A., & Paquette, G. (2005). *Agrégation de composants dirigée par les métadonnées (ACODIM).* Paper presented at the INFORSID Conference, 2005, Grenoble, France.

Masmoudi, A., Paquette, G., & Champagne, R. (2006, June 1). *Implémentation à l'aide de BPEL de trois processus d'agrégation de composants, dirigée par les modèles.* Paper presented at the INFORSID'06, Hammamet-Tunisie.

Masmoudi, A., Paquette, G., & Champagne, R. (2007). Metadata-Driven software components aggregation process with reuse. *Int. J. Advanced Media and Communication, 1*(1).

Mili, H., Mili, A., Yacoub, S., & Addy, E. (2002). *Reuse based software engineering: techniques, organization, and measurement.* New York: Wiley.

Object Management Group. (2003). *Deployment and Configuration of Component-based Distributed Applications Specification.* Draft Adopted Specification ptc/03-07-02. Retrieved January 24, 2005, from http://www.omg.org/docs/ptc/03-07-02.pdf

Paquette, G., & Magnan, F. (2008). An Executable Model for Virtual Campus Environments. In H. H. Adelsberger, Kinshuk, J. M. Pawlowski, & D. Sampson (Eds.), International Handbook on Information Technologies for Education and Training (2nd Ed.) (pp. 365-405). Berlin: Springer.

Paquette, G., Rosca, I., Mihaila, S., & Masmoudi, A. (2007). TELOS, a service-oriented framework to support learning and knowledge Management. In Pierre, S. (Ed.), *E-Learning Networked Environments and Architectures: a Knowledge Processing Perspective.* Berlin: Springer-Verlag.

Pellet. (2003). *DL compliant inference engine.* Retrieved from http://www.mindswap.org/2003/pellet/

Raistrick, C. (2004). *Model driven architecture with executable UML.* New York: Cambridge University Press.

Szyperski, C., Gruntz, D., & Murer, S. (2002). *Component software: beyond object-oriented programming* (2nd ed.). New York: ACM Press.

Torchiano, M., Jaccheri, L., Srensens, C.-F., & Wang, A. I. (2002). *COTS Products Characterization.* Paper presented at the Conference on Software Engineering and Knowledge Engineering (SEKE'02), Ischia, Italy.

278

Chapter 14
From Semi–Formal Models
to Formal Models

Michel Héon
LICEF Research Center, Canada

Gilbert Paquette
LICEF Research Center, Canada

ABSTRACT

- Levels of Knowledge Formalization
- Meta-Modeling—A Transformation Tool between Models
  - Meta-Models
  - Meta-Models and Modeling Spaces
  - Transformation Process between Models
- Method for Transforming Semi-Formal Models into Ontologies
  - Process of Formalization into a Domain Ontology
  - Import into an OWL Modeling Space
  - Disambiguation of a Semi-Formal Model
- Transformation into a Domain Ontology
- Validation Process
- Illustration of Machine-Assisted Ontology Formalization
  - Producing a Semi-Formal Knowledge Model
  - Formalization of the Model
  - Validation of the Resulting Ontology

Ontological engineering is a methodology that proposes various processes for constructing ontologies (Corcho, Fernández-López, & Gómez-Pérez, 2006; Davies, Fensel, & Harmelen, 2003; Dietz, 2006; Gašević, Djurić, & Devedžić, 2006; Gómez-Pérez, Fernández-López, & Corcho, 2003; T. Gruber, 1993; Guarino, 1997; Horridge, Knub-

DOI: 10.4018/978-1-61520-839-5.ch014

Copyright © 2010, IGI Global. Copying or distributing in print or electronic forms without written permission of IGI Global is prohibited.

lauch, Rector, Stevens, & Wroe, 2004; Uschold & Gruninger, 1996).

Such a process begins with a knowledge elicitation step for the target domain based on the services that the ontology is expected to provide. This step allows for the identification and structuring of the domain's knowledge through documentation and consultation with experts. The next step involves the formalization of knowledge into an ontology. Ontologies can afterwards be processed by software agents using inference engines to deduce facts that were not provided by constructor of the model. The final step, validation, ensures that the ontology is effective in accounting for all useful knowledge needed to satisfy the original objectives.

The nature of the knowledge to be represented and the diversity of its sources (documents, oral and written communications, graphic representations, tacit knowledge, etc.) can make the process of designing an ontology tedious. In particular, in the scientific literature in education and psychology, declarative, procedural, and strategic (or conditional) knowledge is usually discussed (Paquette, 2002; Paris, Lipson & Wixson, 1983), which adds to the complexity of the process.

This chapter contributes to the field of ontological engineering by building a methodology that starts by building semi-formal models and subsequently, transforms this type of model into an ontology. The first section describes the concepts of semi-formal models and formal models, and justifies an ontological engineering methodology based on the transformation of semi-formal models. In Section 2, we will explain the role of meta-models in this methodology. In Section 3, we present the ontological engineering methodology, and in Section 4, we present a concrete example of transformation of a semi-formal model into an ontology.

14.1 LEVELS OF KNOWLEDGE FORMALIZATION

Uschold & Gruninger (1996) classify representational languages into four levels, as shown in Figure 1.

- The *highly informal* level involved the use of natural language, which is the most commonly used in human communications. This type of knowledge representa-

Figure 1. Levels of formalization of knowledge representation languages

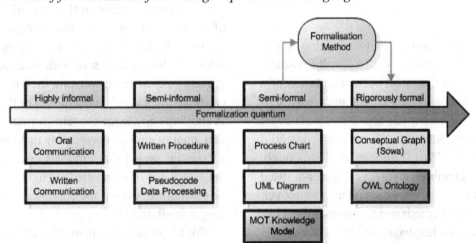

tion, however, presents a high degree of ambiguity, which the human brain is able to decode, in part, but which computer have trouble processing, as evidenced by the difficulties that still exist in the automated interpretation of natural language.

- The *semi-informal* level, involved a restricted and structured form of natural language, for example, the description of algorithms in the stereotyped language known as pseudo-code. These restrictions reduces spontaneity and the degree of expressiveness but enhances the clarity of the representation by reducing ambiguities. The MOT visual modeling language presented in this book, as well as UML, are two examples of semi-formal representational languages. Representations of this type may still contain ambiguities, but the relaxation of language constraints, as compared to formal languages, encourages and stimulates knowledge expressiveness and communication between humans.

- Finally, languages such as conceptual graphs, predicate logic or OWL (presented in Chapter 10), with their rigorously formal levels, provide representations of knowledge that may have reduced expressiveness but, by eliminating representational ambiguity, can be processed by software components.

It is generally agreed that to develop an ontology one must proceed with a feasibility study, specification of the target system, creation of a preliminary ontology, refinement, and finally, revision and modification. (Gómez-Pérez et al., 2003; Staab, Studer, Schnurr, & Sure, 2001; Uschold & Gruninger, 1996). Although well-structured, none of these methods involves computer-assisted formalization and validation steps. Moreover, most of these methods use an informal level of representational language, including documents and interviews with experts, which adds to the

complexity of the ontology formalization step. We propose retaining these sources, but in the context of an initial semi-formal modeling step, one we have applied in a variety of situations, some of which will be presented in chapters 16 and 21. In particular, the co-modeling strategy used by Basque et al. (2008) for knowledge elicitation and the transfer of expertise in organizations brings together experts, novices, and knowledge engineers in the joint development of semi-formal knowledge models. This kind of semi-formal modeling phase is well suited to the consensual aspect inherent to the concept of ontology, according to Gruber (1993).

One might think, in order to save time and energy, it would be preferable to elicit knowledge from a content expert directly in the form of an ontology. On the contrary, we believe that the process of ontology construction must be broken down into two distinct phases: a semi-formal but well-developed knowledge elicitation phase followed by a knowledge formalization phase in which the semi-formal model is transformed into a formal ontology.

Although semi-formal models always contain some elements of ambiguity, their expressive flexibility, especially in their use of visual language, allows for easier access to and identification of tacit knowledge. In this context, spontaneity is not inhibited by the cognitive load associated with the formalization of thought. Also, the use of a representation system that is more convivial than ontologies widens the pool of individuals who are able to represent their knowledge and prevents experts from wasting their time, which can be costly for an organization. The time gained in eliciting knowledge at a semi-formal level is, in fact, quality gain in representing that knowledge. Moreover, semi-formal models created without the assistance of a knowledge engineer can later be formalized, even if the content experts are no longer available.

We begin with the premise that semi-formal models can be formalized into ontologies without losing the distinctions between declarative, procedural, and strategic knowledge types. We further propose a methodology for transforming semi-formal models into formal ontological models through a semi-automated process. This methodology involves procedures, techniques, and a computer-assisted formalization process.

14.2 META-MODELING: A TRANSFORMATION TOOL BETWEEN MODELS

The purpose of this section is to introduce the concepts of "meta-model" and "modeling space" required for describing the transformation between models. These are inspired by the concepts of "Model Driven Architecture (MDA)" (Kadima, 2005; OMG MDA, 2007) and the "Ontological Definition Meta-model (ODM)" " (Gašević, Djurić, & Devedžić, 2006; OMG ODM, 2007).

Remember that a model is an abstraction; an oversimplification of reality, representing the latter's main elements and interactions. A model can be used to replace a theory that is partially or wholly non-existent, simulate and reproduce the interactions of an inaccessible system, or represent a personal or shared conceptualization of a system (Apostel, 1960; T. R. Gruber, 1993). A system is represented by a graphical schematization consisting of entities and relationships. Each entity corresponds to a symbol, a use rule, and more or less formal semantics.

Meta-Models

A meta-relation ("meta" meaning "about") is used in representational systems to connect two entities having the same subject but different levels of abstraction. For example, meta-knowledge (whose subject is knowledge) is knowledge about knowledge (Pitrat, 1990). Similarly, a meta-model is a model about a model. The relation "about" describes a relation of definition

between two objects. The meta-object defines the object. The object is therefore an instance of the meta-object.

Used especially in software development, meta-models can represent 1) a modeling space in the form of domain data models, 2) a domain model using a representational language, or 3) the representation system itself (see Figure 2). Domain data make up Level M0, which consists of the factual representations of domain elements. Domain models, making up level M1, are a first level of abstraction. Level M2 models, also called meta-models, define the representational languages used for modeling the domain. Level M3 models, or meta-meta-models, group together level M2 models, i.e. representation systems. Level M3 models are reflexive, i.e. they are self-defining.

Let us first illustrate the concept of meta-model. In Chapter 2, Figure 2.11, we represented the components of MOT in MOT language. The resulting model was therefore a meta-model of the MOT representation system (Level M2). Note that we could have used any representational language to describe MOT. Figure 3 shows this meta-model expressed in *Unified Modeling Language* (UML). The first part of the figure groups together the higher-level components of objects and relations; the second part describes knowledge types; the third part describes relation types.

According to the UML model, a MOT model consists of one or more "knowledge objects" and one or more "relations." A relation consists of a "source" association and a "target" association, each designating a knowledge object connected by the relation. Much like theories of knowledge representation, MOT offers the possibility of representing knowledge at two levels of abstraction: conceptual ("Abstract Knowledge") and factual ("Fact"). In MOT, knowledge objects are connected together by the link types shown in the figure.

Figure 2. Abstraction level of models

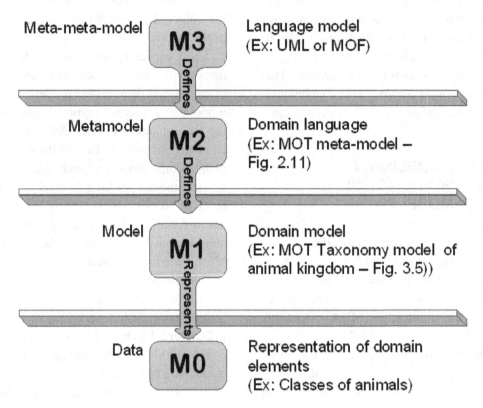

Figure 3. UML representation of higher-level MOT components

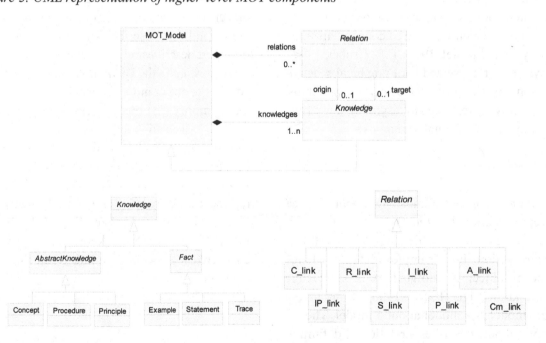

Meta-Models and Modeling Spaces

Let us now define the concept of meta-meta-model. This concept is used for comparing two modeling languages, which is also the purpose of this chapter. For example, suppose we want to compare UML and MOT languages. We must represent them both in the same representational language. This representational language, is at level M3. It could be MOT, UML, or another language, for example the *Ontology Web Language* (OWL). We would represent both the MOT and UML meta-models in this language, thus creating two Level M3 meta-meta-models. The language for representing meta-models (representational language models) is called a *modeling space* (Gašević, Djurić, & Devedžić, 2006).

For a given modeling space, i.e. for a given meta-meta-model, the meta-modeling architecture ensures interoperability between the representation systems (level M2 models). This interoperability supports the translation of a domain model represented by a *source* representation system into a domain model represented by a *target* representation system. The transformation of domain models between representation systems is the main activity supported by this architecture.

A modeling space (MS) is a modeling architecture based on a particular meta-meta-model. Figure 4 shows different types of modeling spaces. The first is the Extended Backus-Naur Form (EBNF), the model that defines the grammar of Java language. It is used for modeling Java programs, which are themselves models for describing representations of reality. The second, RDFS, is the meta-meta-model for OWL language, used to construct OWL ontology models. The third, *MetaObject Facility* (MOF), supports both UML

Figure 4. Modeling spaces (adapted from Gasevic et al., 2006, p. 132)

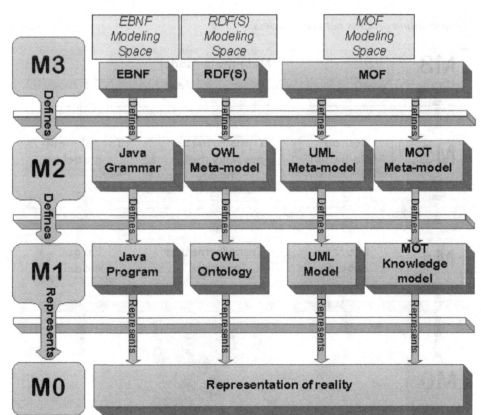

and MOT meta-models, which define the representational language used for constructing their respective models. By applying a single MS, one is able to compare two models that use different representational systems.

Transformation Process between Models

An important application of meta-models and modeling spaces is the transformation between models. This involves the automatic generation of a target model from a source model through the application of transformation rules that regulate the transformation process.

Note that even if the representational rules change from one model to the other, both models are used to represent the same reality. Illustrated in Figure 5, the transformation process generates a target model based on information contained in the source model. Rules for interpreting the

source model's information are determined by the source meta-model (level M2), expressed in the language of the meta-meta-model. Likewise, rules for interpreting the target model's information are defined by the target meta-model, which is also an input to the transformation process.

The *principle of parallel transformation*, shown in Figure 6, has as pre-condition that requires the source and target meta-models to have similar structures, thus facilitating the design of "one to one"-type transformation rules. For example, the meta-class "Concept" of the MOT meta-model can be transposed into the meta-class "Class" of the OWL meta-model; or the meta-class "S_link", which is a relation type, can be transposed into the meta-class "subClassOf." Paquette 82008) used this approach to create the MOT-OWL language so that language is a subclass of MOT models that covers the elements of the OWL-DL ontology language.

Figure 5. Transformation process between models

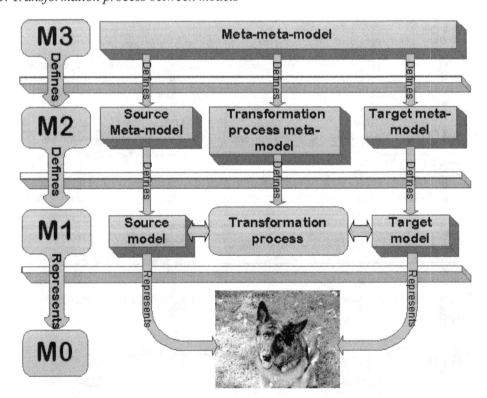

Figure 6. Process of parallel transformation

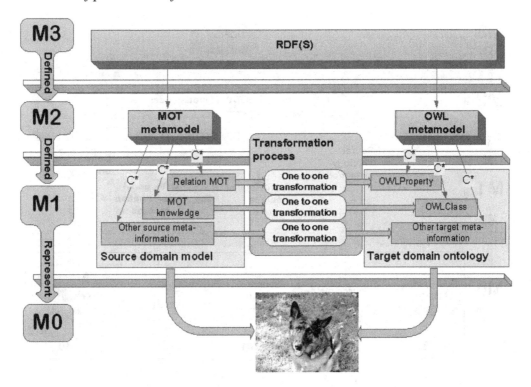

A significant limitation of parallel transformation is that the process is carried out without taking into account the semantics of the languages involved in the transformation. To use the analogy of translation between natural languages, parallel transformation is a process that produces a word-to-word translation without considering the meaning of the words that are translated. Given the diversity of knowledge that can be processed by MOT, and the changes in the level of knowledge formalization required by the transformation process, we feel that the semantic framework offered by MOT language is extremely useful in this respect.

To this end, for the RDF(S) modeling space, we propose the principle of *orthogonal transformation*, which is used to describe OWL ontologies having SWRL extensions for rules. In orthogonal transformation, Levels M1 and M2 of the MOT source model (expressed in the RDF(S) modeling area and thus as an ontology) intercede, as does the source

model itself. As illustrated in Figure 7, the ontology of the MOT meta-model (which describes MOT language), the ontology of the MOT source model (instances of classes in the MOT meta-model), and the MOT source model itself, all act as inputs to the transformation process producing the target model in the form of an ontology. All these models, we repeat, are expressed in the same modeling area.

An interesting feature of this transformation principle is that MOT domain model is represented as a factual element (instances of classes) of the MOT language ontology. The semantics of the semi-formal model is represented by the MOT meta-model ontology. This feature of combining semantic and factual elements allows for the production and application of transformation rules that are based on deductions and inferences contextualized by the source model.

Figure 7. Process of orthogonal transformation

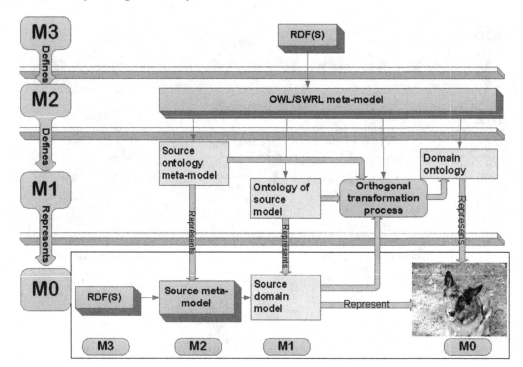

14.3 METHOD FOR TRANSFORMING SEMI-FORMAL MODELS INTO ONTOLOGIES

Based on the above, we will now present the ontological engineering method for transforming a semi-formal model into an ontology model. This method involves three higher-level processes, as shown in Figure 8: 1) design of a semi-formal model, which in fact is a knowledge elicitation step; 2) transformation into a domain ontology, which involves formalizing the semi-formal model into a domain ontology; and 3) semantic and syntactic validation of the domain ontology, which is a pivotal step for determining whether a new iteration is required.

The first process has been the subject of several chapters in this book. It is carried out using a semi-formal model editor such as MOT or UML and helps to produce a semi-formal model that conveys the semantics of a domain. The second and third processes consist in formalizing the semi-formal

model into an ontology and validating its syntax and semantics. The purpose of this validation is to verify that the two models concord. If they do not, the process is repeated until the semi-formal model and the ontology concord satisfactorily. Machine-assisted formalization and validation are designed to support these ontological engineering processes. They are described below.

Process of Formalization into a Domain Ontology

Figure 9 is a sub-model of Figure 8 that shows the central process of formalizing a semi-formal model into an ontology. It is broken down into three tasks: import into a modeling space, disambiguation, and transformation into an ontology

During the import phase, the semi-formal model is translated into the representational language in which the subsequent tasks will be carried out, i.e. OWL. At this stage, no new knowledge is generated. Only the representational language differs.

Figure 8. Incremental method for designing a domain ontology

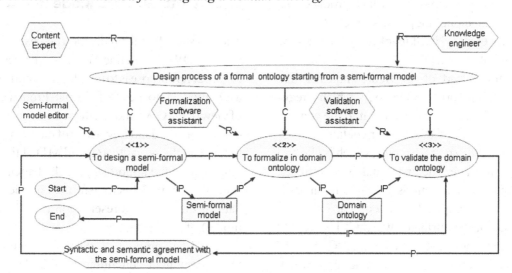

Figure 9. Process of formalization into a domain ontology

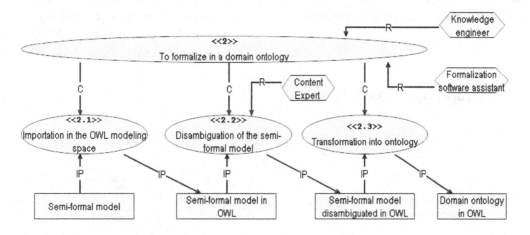

The goal of the disambiguation phase is to reveal ambiguities that may exist in elements of the semi-formal model. This phase is essential for preserving the semantic integrity of the semi-formal model. In the transformation phase, each element of the disambiguated semi-formal model is interpreted and then translated into the appropriate ontological form. Formalization is managed by a knowledge engineer and is computer-assisted. A content expert provides expertise as required, specifically during the disambiguation phase, to help the engineer classify the model's various ambiguous elements

Formalization of a semi-formal model is accomplished in several steps. At each step, the data changes format. To illustrate these changes, we will examine these steps through a typical example. Figure 1 is such an example, which is meant to be general and with no particular significance. Our goal is to simply illustrate the changes in the data independently of an application domain.

Figure 1 is a MOT model combining different types of entities and relations. The dotted entities are facts or instances of abstract knowledge. The bottom line thus indicates that an "Agent" regulates the trace "Processus2," which produces the example "anOutput"; the process is preceded by the trace "Processus1," itself invoked by the example "anInput" of "Concept2."

The upper part of the figure indicates that "Concept2" is a sort-of "Concept3," which is regulated by "aProperty" connecting it to the concept "Concept4." Note that the latter contains two C-links having different meanings, which is allowed in MOT language. The first C-link is an attribute, "Concept6," which comprises the definition of the concept, for example, the concept "cat," which is composed of the attribute "weight." The second link, on the other hand, indicates that "Concept5" is a part of "Concept4," for example "cat," which is composed of a "mouth." The transformation process allows for the disambiguation of these different meanings, as well as the different meanings attributed to the relationship "R-Regulates."

Import into an OWL Modeling Space

The first step of the formalization process—import into the OWL modeling space—is presented in Figure 2. Its purpose is to translate the semi-formal MOT model into the OWL format. From the point of view of the OWL model, the semi-formal model contains all the data (Level M0) of the semi-formal model and the semantics (Level M1) of the MOT language. In the import step, each element of the semi-formal model is transformed into level M0 data in the OWL representation (i.e. the meta-model) of MOT language.

The final product of the import step is an OWL document containing all the elements of the semi-formal model along with their interpretation in the MOT meta-model. Table 1 presents the typical model in Figure 10 both prior to and following transformation. Each entity or relation of the model is represented in OWL by a record of the type subject/predicate/object. The subject

Figure 10. Typical example in MOT language

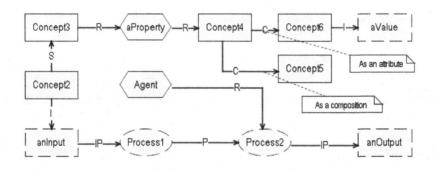

Figure 11. Import of a semi-formal model into an OWL modeling space

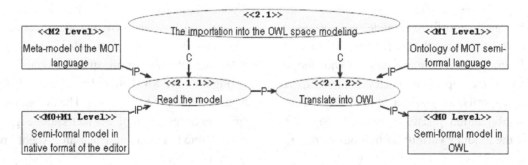

Table 1. Typical level M0 model in an OWL modeling space

Source MOT model	Model imported into OWL
:Agent_114	:Agent_114 **is** metaMot:MOT_Principle.
:Concept2_109	:Concept2_109 **is** metaMot:MOT_Concept.
:Concept3_112	:Concept3_112 **is** metaMot:MOT_Concept.
:Concept4_111	:Concept4_111 **is** metaMot:MOT_Concept.
:Concept5_118	:Concept5_118 **is** metaMot:MOT_Concept.
:Concept6_119	:Concept6_119 **is** metaMot:MOT_Concept.
:Process1_116	:Process1_116 **is** metaMot:MOT_Trace.
:Process2_115	:Process2_115 **is** metaMot:MOT_Trace.
:unIntrant_110	:anInput_110 **is** metaMot:MOT_Example.
:unProduit_117	:anOuput_117 **is** metaMot:MOT_Example.
:unePropriete_113	:aProperty_113 **is** metaMot:MOT_Principle.
:uneValeur_120	:aValue_120 **is** metaMot:MOT_Example.
:LinkC_Concept4_111_Concept5_118	:LinkC_Concept4_111_Concept5_118 **is** metaMot:MOT_LinkC ; metaMot:MOT_connTarget:Concept5_118 ; metaMot:MOT_connDestination:Concept4_111 .
:LinkC_Concept4_111_Concept6_119	:LinkC_Concept4_111_Concept6_119 **is** metaMot:MOT_LinkC ; metaMot:MOT_connDestination:Concept6_119 ; metaMot:MOT_connSource:Concept4_111 .
:LinkR_Agent_114_Process2_115	:LinkR_Agent_114_Process2_115 **is** metaMot:MOT_LinkR ; metaMot:MOT_connDestination:Process2_115 ; metaMot:MOT_connSource:Agent_114 .
:LinkS_Concept2_109_Concept3_112	:LinkS_Concept2_109_Concept3_112 **is** metaMot:MOT_LinkS ; metaMot:MOT_connDestination:Concept3_112 ; metaMot:MOT_connSource:Concept2_109 .

takes the name of the entity or relationship in the MOT model, the predicate is denoted by the word "**is**," and the object is an interpretation with respect to the MOT meta-model.

Disambiguation of a Semi-Formal Model

As seen above, a semi-formal model contains ambiguities that are inherent in the semantics of its representational language. For example, the interpretation of the C-link in MOT has a double semantic as both attribute and part of (component of) a whole. The disambiguation step, presented in Figure 3, is designed to remove such ambiguities by classifying elements of the semi-formal model into a non-ambiguous reference ontology.

Disambiguation of a semi-formal model consists of three steps: typological disambiguation, topological disambiguation, and semantic disambiguation.

Typological disambiguation is the most automated of the three. It associates a semi-formal model component type with an element of a non-ambiguous reference ontology. For example, the component "S_link" (sort-of) is interpreted as a hyponymic relation, and the component "I_link" (instance) is interpreted as a relation of instantiation.

Topological disambiguation is more complex and, in some case, can only be semi-automated. Disambiguation can be defined as a characterization of a model's components by the context in which they participate in a typical structure. For example, the concepts "Concept3" and "Con-

Figure 12. Disambiguation step of a semi-formal model

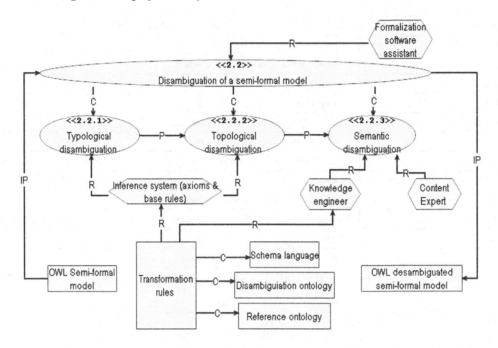

cept4" in Figure 1 are interpreted as "owl:Class," and the principle "aProperty" is interpreted as a (binary) property linking these classes through the following context of disposition: the principle lies between two classes through input R_link and output R_Link.

From the point of view of knowledge engineering, disambiguation based on domain semantics can be tricky since it requires an understanding of the target domain and therefore collaboration with a domain expert. Again, as shown in the example in Figure 1, C-links connect "Concept4" with "Concept5" and "Concept6," and these are

Figure 13. a) Control of ambiguous entities in the reference ontology; b) taxonomy of ontology concepts for the treatment of ambiguous entities in MOT

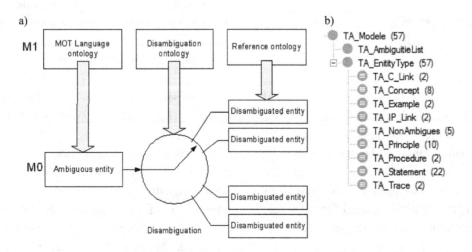

respectively disambiguated by "Concept4 hasAsAttribute Concept6" and "Concept4 hasAsComponent Concept5." This semantic disambiguation requires knowledge of the domain and can only be partially automated.

Disambiguation of a model's entities is analogous to an information control system, as shown in Figure 13a. One by one, each entity of the source model is analyzed according to disambiguation criteria and classified in the reference ontology. The controller is an expert system of axioms and rules that applies knowledge contained in the disambiguation ontology to classify, in the reference ontology, ambiguous entities of the semi-formal model.

The disambiguation ontology consists of a taxonomy used for invoking the system's rules. The concept "TA_AmbiguityList" in Figure 13b is a class containing ambiguous elements of the model. When the engineer believes that disambiguation is completed, he or she applies an inference to the ontology. The non-classified

elements are thus classified under this concept. The concept "TA_EntityType" includes all the disambiguation categories of the MOT semi-formal model elements. Each sub-concept includes the categorization elements of the model's entities for each possible disambiguation. These elements are presented to the engineer in the form of options for semantic disambiguation. For example, the ontology engineer may be asked whether a given concept corresponds to a class by enumeration or by complement, intersection, or union with other classes.

In this approach, the reference ontology acts as an adapter between the source (semi-formal) ontological meta-models and the target domain ontology. This ontology is intended to ensure interoperability between the various semi-formal meta-models since we want to be able to transform into ontologies other semi-formal models besides those expressed in MOT language. Figure 14 illustrates this objective. We note that reference ontologies are OWL formalizations for represent-

Figure 14. Reference ontology for adaptation among meta-models

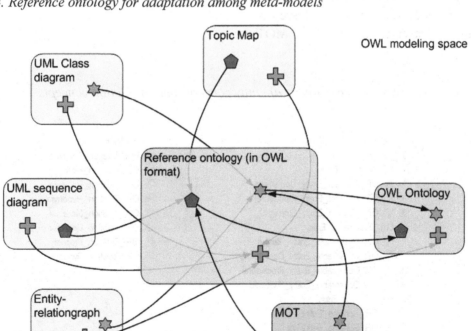

ing MOT models, entity-relation graphs, UML graphs, or Topic Maps, which are various ways of constructing semi-formal models.

The structure of the entity-relation model developed by Chein (1976) is used as a meta-model for reference ontologies. The concepts that make up this ontology are grouped into the classes "OR_Entity" and "OR_Relation." For example, in the transformation, the concepts "MOT" or "Entity-relation graph" are represented in the reference ontology by the OWL class "OR_Abstract_Entity_Procedural_General." When all the elements of the semi-formal model are thus classified, a set of SWRL rules is then applied to the reference ontology to generate the domain ontology.

The taxonomy of reference ontology (RO) classes is shown in Figure 15.

OR_Entity" includes all metaknowledge that can be represented in the domain ontology. It is classified into three general sub-concepts: "OR_Abstract_Entity," "OR_Observable_Entity," and "OR_Schema_Entity."

- The class "OR_Abstract_Entity" includes metaknowledge associated with the representation of abstract knowledge. In MOT language, "MOT_Concept," "MOT_Procedure," and "MOT_Principle" are part of this metaknowledge category.

- The class "OR_Observable_Entity" designates all metaknowledge used for representing observable entities in reality. In MOT language, factual knowledge such as "MOT_Example," "MOT_Trace," and "MOT_Statement" are represented in this class.

- The class "OR_Schema_Entity" is used to classify meta-knowledge associated with data type definitions, for example, integers, real numbers, and character strings.

The class "OR_Relation" designates the meta-relations that are used to connect metaknowledge. Each relation of the semi-formal model is disambiguated and classified according to one of the classes, some of which are structural, such as "Antonym," "Holonym," "Meta," "Operator," "Property," and "Synonym," while others make reference, rather, to relations that designate the path of information, such as "Flux."

Figure 15. Taxonomy of reference ontology a) entity concepts and b) relation concepts

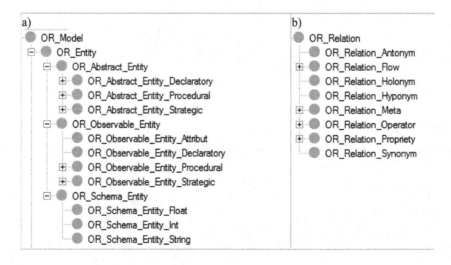

Table 2. Examples of typological and topological disambiguation rules

Type	Rule statement	Interpretation
Identification of a hyponymic relation	metaMot: MOT_LinkS (? ls) → ot:OT_IsEntityType(?ls, oAmbig:Relation_Hyponym)	If the link is an S-link, then there is a hyponymic relation.
Disambiguation of an IP- link between a concept and a procedure	metaMot:MOT_LinkIP(?l_ip) ∧ metaMot:MOT_connSource(?l_ip, ?src) ∧ metaMot:MOT_connDestination(?l_ip, ?dest) ∧ metaMot:MOT_Concept(?src) ∧ metaMot:MOT_Procedure(?dest) → ot:OT_EntityTypeIs(?l_ip, oAmbig:Intrant) ∧ ot:OT_IsEntityType (?src, oAmbig:Declaratory_Entity) ∧ ot:OT_IsEntityType (?dest, oAmbig:Procedure)	If the link is an IP-link whose source is a MOT_Concept and whose destination is a MOT_Procedure, THEN the link is an Input, the source is a Declaratory_Entity, and the destination is a Procedure..
principle between two concepts	metaMot:MOT_Principle(?p) ∧ metaMot:MOT_isSource(?p, ?lrSrc) ∧ metaMot:MOT_isDestination(?p, ?lrDest) ∧ metaMot:MOT_connSource(?lrDest, ?connSrc) ∧ metaMot:MOT_connDestination(?lrSrc, ?connDest) → ot:OT_IsEntityType(?p, oAmbig:Property) ∧ ot:OT_IsEntityType(?connSrc, oAmbig:Declaratory_Entity) ∧ ot:OT_IsEntityType(?connDest, oAmbig: Declaratory_Entity)	IF a principle p is the source of a LinkR (lrSrc) and the destination of another LinkR (lrDest), and if connSrc is the source knowledge of lrDest, and if connDest is the destination knowledge of lrSrc, THEN p is an EntityType Property, connSrc is an EntityType Declaratory_Entity, and connDest is also an EntityType Declaratory_Entity.

Table 3. Classification of the elements of a semi-formal model in a reference ontology following disambiguation

No.	Elements of the semi-formal model following disambiguation
1	:Agent_197 ⇒ oRef:OR_Abstract_Entity_Strategic_Agent, metaMot:MOT_Principle;
2	:Concept2_192 ⇒oRef:OR_Abstract_Entity_Declaratory, metaMot:MOT_Concept ;
3	:Concept3_195 ⇒oRef:OR_ Abstract_Entity_Declaratory, metaMot:MOT_Concept ;
4	:Concept4_194 ⇒oRef:OR_ Abstract_Entity_Declaratory, metaMot:MOT_Concept ;
5	:Concept5_201 ⇒oRef:OR_ Abstract_Entity_Declaratory, metaMot:MOT_Concept ;
6	:Concept6_202 ⇒oRef:OR_ Abstract_Entity_Declaratory, metaMot:MOT_Concept ;
7	:LinkC_Concept4_194_Concept5_201 ⇒ oRef:OR_Relation_Holonym, metaMot:MOT_LinkC ;
8	:LinkC_Concept4_194_Concept6_202 ⇒ oRef:OR_Relation_Property_Attribute, metaMot:MOT_LinkC ;
9	:LinkIP_Process2_198_aProduct_200 ⇒ oRef:OR_Relation_Flux_Product, metaMot:MOT_LinkIP ;
10	:LinkIP_Input_193_Process1_199 ⇒ oRef:OR_Relation_Flux_Input, metaMot:MOT_LinkIP ;
11	:LinkI_Concept2_192_anInput_193 ⇒ oRef:OR_Relation_Instance, metaMot:MOT_LinkI ;
12	:LinkI_Concept6_202_aValue_203 ⇒ oRef:OR_Relation_Instance, metaMot:MOT_LinkI ;
13	:LinkP_Process1_199_Process2_198 ⇒ oRef:OR_Relation_Flux_Precedence, metaMot:MOT_LinkP ;
14	:LinkR_Agent_197_Process2_198 ⇒ oRef:OR_Relation_Property_Regulation, metaMot:MOT_LinkR ;
15	:LinkR_Concept3_195_aProperty_196 ⇒ oRef:OR_Relation_Property_Regulation, metaMot:MOT_LinkR ;
16	:LinkR_Property_196_Concept4_194 ⇒oRef:OR_Relation_Property_Regulation, metaMot:MOT_LinkR ;
17	:LinkS_Concept2_192_Concept3_195 ⇒oRef:OR_Relation_Hyponym, metaMot:MOT_LinkS ;
18	:Process1_199 ⇒ oRef:OR_Observable_Entity_Procedural, metaMot:MOT_Trace ;
19	:Process2_198 ⇒ oRef:OR_ Observable_Entity_Procedural, metaMot:MOT_Trace ;
20	:Inputt_193 ⇒ oRef:OR_ Observable_Entity_Declaratory, metaMot:MOT_Example ;
21	:Prodcut_200 ⇒ oRef:OR_ Observable_Entity_Declaratory, metaMot:MOT_Example ;
22	:Property_196 ⇒ oRef:OR_Relation_Property_Object, metaMot:MOT_Principle ;
23	:Value_203 ⇒ oRef:OR_Observable_Entity_Declaratory, metaMot:MOT_Example

Disambiguation Rules and Axioms

To classify the elements of the semi-formal model, the computer-assisted formalization process uses a set of rules and axioms for both typological and topological disambiguation. Table 2 presents some of these rules as applied to semi-formal MOT language models. The first is a typological rule; the remaining two are topological rules.

Table 3 shows the classification of the semi-formal elements for the typical model in Figure 10 following disambiguation.

Elements 3, 5, and 22 in the table are topological disambiguations. It is interesting to note that an input-product link (items 9, 10), classified by the sole concept "MOT_IP_Link MOT" in the meta-model, can be disambiguated and represented by two separate classes in the reference ontology, either "OR_Relation_Flux_Product" or "OR_Relation_Flux_Input."

Transformation into a Domain Ontology

The final step in the ontology formalization process consists of transforming the disambiguated model into an ontology. Figure 16 presents this step, which consists of applying, in successive order, five groups of rules integrated into the computer-assisted formalization process.

The following are some examples of rules in SWRL format. The first reflects the disambiguation of the C-link between Concept4 and Concept5 in Figure 10. The C-link is interpreted as a "Holonym", i.e. a link between a whole (Concept4) and one of its parts (Concept5). The second rule, based on this holonymic relation and the two declaratory abstract entities, is used to create two elements in the target ontology that have a new property type, "hasAsComponent."

Class creation rule

```
oRef:OR_Relation_Holonym(?lc) ∧
oRef:OR_connSource(?lc, ?src) ∧
oRef:OR_Abstract_Entity_
Declaratory(?src) ∧
oRef:OR_connDestination(?lc,
?dest) ∧
oRef:OR_identifies(?src, ?nameS-
rc) ∧
oRef:OR_identifies(?dest, ?na-
meDest) ∧
swrlb:stringConcat(?no
mPropCompo,?nomSrc,"_
```

Figure 16. Transformation into an ontology

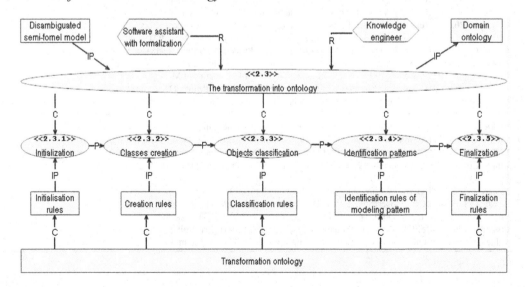

```
hasAsComponent_",?nameDest)
→ swrlbi:invokes("OWLCreatePrope
rtyCmd", ?namePropCompo) ∧
swrlbi:invokes("OWLIsSubpr
opertyCmd",?nomPropCompo,
"metaDom:HAS-AS-COMPONENT")
```

The second example corresponds to the concepts "Concept3" and "Concept4" in Figure 10, related to "Property." The first of the following rules will create this property in the target ontology, while the second rule will add a domain and a co-domain for this property, corresponding to the two concepts of the source ontology.

Class creation
```
oRef:OR_Relation_Property_
Objet(?p) ∧
oRef:OR_indentifies(?p, ?nomP)
→ swrlbi:invokes("OWLCreatePrope
rtyCmd", ?nameP)
Classification of objects
oRef:OR_Relation_Property_
Object(?prop) ∧
oRef:OR_connSource(?prop, ?src)
∧
oRef:OR_connDestination(?prop,
?dest) ∧
oRef:OR_identifies(?prop,
?nameProp) ∧
oRef:OR_Abstract_Entity_
Declaratory(?src) ∧
oRef:OR_ Abstract_Entity_Declar-
atory (?dest) ∧
oRef:OR_identifies(?src, ?nameS-
rc) ∧
oRef:OR_identifies(?dest, ?na-
meDest)
→ swrlbi:invokes("OWLProperty_
AddDomainAndAddImageCmd",
?nameSrc, ?nameProp, ?nameDest)
```

The third example shows how we treat the precedence link between the two trace entities, "Process1" and "Process2," in Figure 10. The first creates an instance of each target trace in the ontology, while the second adds a property "IS-PRECEDENT-OF" between the two traces.

Class creation
```
oRef:OR_Obersvable_Entity_
Procedural(?o) ∧
oRef:OR_identiesy(?o, ?ident)
→swrlbi:invokes("OWLCreateInstan
ceCmd",?ident, "metaDom:MD_Pro-
cedural")
Object classification
oRef:OR_Relation_Flux_
Precedence(?lp) ∧
oRef:OR_connSource(?lp, ?src) ∧
oRef:OR_ Obersvable_Entity_Pro-
cedural (?src) ∧
oRef:OR_connDestination(?lp,
?dest) ∧
oRef:OR_identifies(?src, ?nameS-
rc) ∧
oRef:OR_identifies(?dest, ?na-
meDest)
→swrlbi:invokes("OWLAddProperty
BetweenIndividualCmd",?nameSrc,
"metaDom:IS-PRECEDENT-OF", ?na-
meDest)
```

Validation Process

Validation is a critical step in the process of constructing a domain ontology. In this step, eliciting a domain's knowledge semi-formally has the advantage of producing models in which the pre-formalization of knowledge can be rigorously exploited. The validation of a domain ontology is regulated by two sub-processes—syntactic validation and semantic validation—as shown in Figure 17. These are controlled by the knowledge engineer.

The purpose of syntax validation is to ensure that all elements of the semi-formal model are represented in the ontology according to the rules of the chosen ontology language, in our case, OWL-DL. Syntax validation is carried out in two steps: generating a semi-formal model from the domain ontology; and comparing elements of the generated semi-formal model with those of the source semi-formal model. If they correctly match, then it is true to conclude that the domain ontology syntactically represents all elements of the semi-formal domain model.

Semantic validation focuses on the meaning of the representations that are reflected in the ontology. For example, an error that is sometimes made by designers unfamiliar with MOT language stems from a confusion between S-links ("sort of" [is-a]) and C-links ("comprising" [part-of]). The designers may be tempted to state that "planet" comprises Venus, Earth, Mars, etc., instead of stating that Venus, Earth, and Mars are kinds of (sort-of) planets. Applying an inference to the domain ontology determining that the inverse property of "comprises" is "partOf" would result

in the conclusion that Venus, Earth, and Mars are *parts of* "planet." This type of false conclusion should signal to the engineer and experts that a possible error exists in the semantic representation of the domain.

The first step in semantic validation is the production of formal conclusions through the application of inferences in the domain ontology. Test deduction scenarios can be used to further formalize this step. Comparing the expected conclusions of the engineer and inference expert with the machine-generated ones paves the way for reflection and may, on the one hand, lead the content expert to review the way in which the domain is represented, or on the other hand, terminate the domain ontology construction process.

Gómez-Pérez (2004) presents the following criteria for validating ontologies: *consistency* helps to identify possible contradictions between ontological elements; *completeness* ensures that all ontological elements are either explicitly stated or inferred; *conciseness* is the principle that only elements that need to be defined should be defined; *expandability* is the ability to add new

Figure 17. Syntactic and semantic validation of a domain ontology

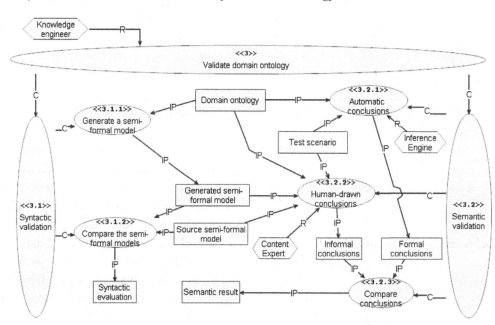

knowledge without changing previous knowledge; and *sensitivity* is the ability to react to changes.

14.4 ILLUSTRATION OF MACHINE-ASSISTED ONTOLOGY FORMALIZATION

In this concluding section, we will illustrate the application of the formalization methodology through an example. The methodology is deployed in three iterative steps: (1) production of a semi-formal model; (2) formalization of the semi-formal model into an ontology; (3) validation of the ontology. This last step involves either terminating the construction of the ontology or formulating a new design iteration. In addition to presenting the application of the methodology, we will examine how not only conceptual, but also procedural and strategic knowledge is treated in ontology formalization.

Step 1: Producing a Semi-Formal Knowledge Model

The purpose of this step is to develop a semi-formal knowledge model. In order to illustrate the assisted process and its ability to detect semantic errors, we have introduced various types of errors and semantic inaccuracies into the model presented in Figure 18. The model was created in MOT language (Paquette 2003, 2008), using the eLi editor[1], which is briefly described in Héon et al. (2009). The errors introduced into the model are based on the "antipattern" concept proposed by Germany & Hendler (2008). Labels guide the treatment of these errors in the ensuing text.

The following outlines the logic that may have produced such a model. Stars, planets, and natural satellites are celestial object. Planets revolve around stars, and natural satellites revolve around planets. Saturn, Mars, and Earth are planets, whereas Deimos and Phobos are natural satellites of Mars; Titan, Tethys, Japet, and Rhea are natural satellites of Saturn. Finally, the Moon is a natural satellite of Earth. There are countless other unspecified satellites. A celestial object is

Figure 18. Example of a semi-formal model to be transformed

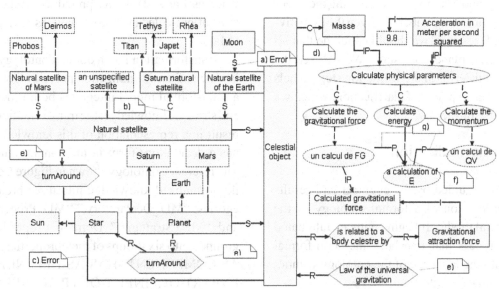

regulated by the principle of the law of universal gravitation. It has as an attribute its mass and is linked to other celestial objects by the force of gravitational attraction. This force is calculated from mass and gravitational acceleration (9.8 m/s^2), Other physical parameters may be calculated, such as energy and momentum.

Before proceeding with the formalization of the experimental model, we must first identify the ambiguities or inaccuracies it contains.

Label a) refers to a commonly observed modeling error—an error in the classification of the represented object's abstraction level. Sometimes, a designer confuses the representation of a concrete object with the abstract class to which it belongs. The concept of "Moon" as a *sort of* "natural satellite of Earth" may be valid, but what should be represented here is that the object is of the *Type* "Moon," i.e. an example of the concept "Natural satellite of Earth" and not a sub-class of it.

Label b) refers to another representational error—the confusion between "S_link" and "C_link." The model states that "Natural satellites" are composed of the "Natural satellites of Saturn." The relation between these two concepts is mistakenly expressed as one of specialization. In the validation step, we will see how this error can be detected and presented to the expert.

Finally, another mistake is reversing the direction of "S_link" (see Label c). Given the transitivity of the S relation, we should conclude that all satellites and planets are stars. We will see the effects of this error in the validation step. Labels d) to g) refer to points of clarification, which we will discuss further on.

Step 2: Formalization

This step is guided by the engineer and results in the production of a formal ontology of the semi-formal model. It begins with an automated import process that translates the semi-formal model into the language of the ontology without transforming the latter.

Afterwards, the semi-automated process of disambiguation provides unique interpretations of the entities of the semi-formal model. Some entities (such as "I_link" and "S_link") are unambiguous, that is, a semi-formal entity corresponds to a single formal entity. In this case, the automated disambiguation is typological.

Some ambiguities require automated processing based on a topological modeling framework. For example, the principles marked by Label e) are subject to this type of disambiguation since a principle between two concepts is interpreted as "owl:ObjectProperty," whereas a principle connected to a concept by "R_link" is interpreted as "owl:class" under the cateogry "AGENT_CONSTRAINT_STANDARD." The same applies to IP_links, which are disambiguated as "owl:ObjectProperty" under the category "Input" or "Output," depending on the direction of the link.

If an object cannot be disambiguated either typologically or topologically, it must be disambiguated manually according to the semantics of the domain. In our example, "C_link" of Label b) and "C_link" of Label d) do not have the same meaning. In the first case, it is expressed as a relation of aggregation ("Natural satellites" are composed of the "Natural satellites of Earth"), whereas Label d) is interpreted as a relation of attribution: celestial bodies have as an attribute "Mass."

Transformation into a domain ontology is the last step of the formalization process. Given that a semi-formal model integrates both procedural and strategic knowledge, the transformation must result in a representation of this knowledge that has a declaratory form in the domain ontology. The reference ontology shown in Figure 6 groups the formalized knowledge into three broad categories: "MD_Declaratory," "MD_Procedural," and "MD_Strategic." Domain properties are grouped into six groups of metaproperties: HAS-AS-COMPONENT, HAS-AS-DEPENDENCY, IS-PART-OF, INPUT-OUTPUT, ALLOWS,

HAS-AS-ATTRIBUTE, REGULATES, and IS-REGULATED-BY. Some metaproperties are inverses of one another; for example, HAS-COMPONENT is the inverse property of IS-PART-OF. In the validation step, we will that the attribution of this inverse property is extremely useful in the interpretation of ontology objects.

Step 3: Validation

We will limit our discussion here to syntatic validation.[2] The main purpose of semantic validation is to compare human conclusions inferred from the semi-formal model with machine conclusions inferred from the domain ontology. The first phase of validation is analysis of the ontology. In the taxonomy of classes for the ontology, the concept "Celestial object" is subsumed under the concept "Star," which would mean that "Earth," a sort of "Planet," is considered a star. This error of classification comes from reversing the direction of the S_link (Label c in Figure 1). The inference engine used in the ontology would automatically detect this inconsistency and lead to correcting the original semi-formal model.

In the scenario represented by Label b), we might interpret that Phobos, a natural satellite, is composed of a natural satellite of Saturn such as Titan. Moreover, a machine inference would state that Titan IS-PART-OF a natural satellite, whereas it would be more accurate to say that Titan and Phobos are both natural satellites.

The formalization of the scenario marked by Label a) indicates that "Moon," a sort of natural satellite of Earth, is a class. This means that we should be able to mechanically instantiate individuals of the type Moon, which in representational terms, is false because the moon is an object and not a class of objects.

Label d) presents a scenario in which a C-link is formalized as an attribute. This would be disambiguated by the distinction that exists between the meta-links HAS-AS-COMPONENT and HAS-AS-ATTRIBUTE.

Label e) presents two use cases of "Principle." The first case, "Law of universal gravitation," is disambiguated in the form "owl:class" under the category "Agent_Constraint_Standard." The second case, "isAbout," is formalized as "owl:OBJECTPROPERTY," whose domain and image correspond to the source and target class "Principle."

Label f) indicates that the entities "calculate FG," "calculate E," and "calculate QV" are traces of the procedural knowledge "calculate gravitational force," "calculate energy," and "calculate momentum." Label g) presents an interesting scenario because it concerns the ontological treatment of procedural knowledge. Through the meta-properties of the reference ontology, the inference engine can deduce that the calculation of momentum HAS-AS-A-DEPENDENCY the calculation of gravitational force and the calculation of energy, in that order.

CONCLUSION

This chapter acts as a link between Parts I and II of this book, focusing on semi-formal modeling, and the chapters of Part III that deal with the Semantic Web and formal ontologies. We have advocated, in this chapter, the advantages of producing semi-formal models during the knowledge elicitation phase and then subsequently transforming them into ontologies in a systematic manner.

This is achieved by applying a specific ontological design methodology, which we described in detail using procedural MOT models. The originality of the methodology lies in the fact that it is supported by a system that assists engineers in the formalization process, and also assists both engineers and experts in the syntactic and semantic validation of the domain ontology. Subsequently, regardless of the types of knowledge or links used in the model, the analysis of possible ambiguities inherent in semi-formal language allows one to construct valid ontologies that are usable on the Semantic Web.

Through the validation of the resulting ontology, the methodology can also be used to assess the quality of semi-formal models that have been transformed into ontologies and from which new domain facts can be deduced. These facts can help to identify problems of interpretation in the original model and thus improve its quality.

The methodology described in this chapter uses the MOT and OWL languages in its application. Nevertheless, it is conceived generically and can be applied to other semi-formal and formal languages.

REFERENCES

Apostel, L. (1960). Towards the formal study of models in the non-formal sciences. *Synthese*, *12*(2), 125–161. doi:10.1007/BF00485092

Basque, J., Paquette, G., Pudelko, B., & Léonard, M. (2008). Collaborative Knowledge Modeling with a Graphical Knowledge Representation Tool: A Strategy to Support the Transfer of Expertise in Organizations . In Okada, A., Shum, S. B., & Sherborne, T. (Eds.), *Knowledge Cartography. Mapping Techniques and Software Tools*. London: Springer-Verlag. doi:10.1007/978-1-84800-149-7_17

Chen, P. P.-S. (1976). The entity-relationship model: Toward a unified view of data. *ACM Transactions on Database Systems*, *1*, 9–36. doi:10.1145/320434.320440

Corcho, O., Fernández-López, M., & Gómez-Pérez, A. (2006). Principles, Methods, Tools and Languages . In *Ontologies for Software Engineering and Software Technology* (pp. 1–48). Ontological Engineering. doi:10.1007/3-540-34518-3_1

Davies, J., Fensel, D., & Harmelen, F. V. (2003). *Towards The Semantic Web: Ontology-Driven Knowledge Management*. Hoboken, NJ: John Wiley & Sons.

Dietz, J. L. G. (2006). *Entreprise Ontology: Theory and Methodology*. Berlin: Springer-Verlag. doi:10.1007/3-540-33149-2

Gašević, D., Djurić, D., & Devedžić, V. (2006). *Model Driven Architecture and Ontology Development*. New York: Springer-Verlag.

Gómez-Pérez, A. (2004). Ontology Evaluation . In Staab, R. S. S. (Ed.), *Handbook on Ontologies* (pp. 251–274). New York: Springer.

Gómez-Pérez, A., Fernández-López, M., & Corcho, O. (2003). *Ontological Engineering: with examples from the areas of Knowledge Management, e-Commerce and the Semantic Web* (1st ed.). New York: Springer.

Gruber, T. (1993). Toward Principles for the Design of Ontologies Used for Knowledge Sharing. *Formal Ontology in Conceptual Analysis and Knowledge Representation*, 23.

Gruber, T. R. (1993). A translation approach to portable ontology specification. *Knowledge Acquisition*, *5*(2), 199–220. doi:10.1006/knac.1993.1008

Guarino, N. (1997). Understanding, building, and using ontologies: A commentary to using explicit ontologies in KBS development. *International Journal of Human-Computer Studies*, (46): 293–310. doi:10.1006/ijhc.1996.0091

Horridge, M., Knublauch, H., Rector, A., Stevens, R., & Wroe, C. (2004). A Practical Guide To Building OWL Ontologies Using The Protege-OWL Plugin and CO-ODE Tools Ed. 1.0.

Kadima, H. (2005). *MDA: Conception orientée objet guidée par les modèles*. Paris: Dumond.

OMG MDA. (2007, April 17). *OMG Model Driven Architecture*. Retrieved September 30, 2008, from http://www.omg.org/mda/

OMG ODM. (2007 November). *Ontology Definition Meta-model: OMG Adopted Specification*. Retrieved May 26, 2008, from http://www.omg.org/spec/ODM/1.0/Beta2/PDF/

Paquette, G. (2002). Modélisation des connaissances et des compétences: un langage graphique pour concevoir et apprendre. Sainte-Foy, Canada: Presses de l'UQ.

Paquette, G. (2008). Graphical Ontology Modeling Language for Learning Environments. In Technology, Instruction., Cognition and Learning (Vol. 5, pp.133-168). Philadelphia, PA: Old City Publishing, Inc.

Paquette, G., & Rogozan, D. (2006). *Correspondance avec le langage graphique MOT-OWL et le langage des prédicats du premier ordre*. Montréal, Canada: LICEF.

Paris, S., Lipson, M. Y., & Wixson, K. K. (1983). Becoming a strategic reader. *Contemporary Educational Psychology, 8*, 293–316. doi:10.1016/0361-476X(83)90018-8

Pitrat, J. (1990). *Métaconnaissance, futur de l'intelligence artificielle*. Paris: Hermès.

Staab, S., Studer, R., Schnurr, H.-P., & Sure, Y. (2001). Knowledge processes and ontologies. *IEEE Intelligent Systems, 16*(1), 26–34. doi:10.1109/5254.912382

Uschold, M., & Gruninger, M. (1996). Ontologies: Principles, methods and applications. *The Knowledge Engineering Review, 11*(2), 93–155. doi:10.1017/S0269888900007797

ENDNOTES

[1] In this editor, facts are represented by dotted figures. I-links originating from concepts, procedures, or principles are sufficient for determining whether these involve examples, traces, or statements, respectively.

[2] Syntax validation is discussed in Héon, Paquette et Basque (2009).

Chapter 15

An Ontology-Driven System for E-Learning and Knowledge Management

Gilbert Paquette
LICEF Research Center, Canada

ABSTRACT

- Principles for an Operation System
- Building the Architecture of TELOS
  - Development Process
  - Use Cases and Requirements
  - Conceptual Architecture
- The TELOS Technical Ontology
  - From Conceptual Framework to Conceptual Ontology
  - From Conceptual Ontology to Technical Ontology
- TELOS Main Tools
  - The Resource Manager
  - The Scenario Editor
- Ontology-Driven Scenario Execution
  - The Task Manager
  - Contextual Views
  - Conditions and Control at Run Time

Between 2003 and 2008, within the LORNET research network (www.lornet.org), our team has been designing and developing TELOS, an innovative operation system for eLearning and knowledge management environments that is driven by a technical ontology. After presenting the underlying principles of this system, we will develop a graphic model of the resulting ontology that captures the conceptual architecture of the system. Next, we will present the main aggregation modeling tool and the way it is related to the TELOS Ontology. Finally, we will illustrate how the ontology is used to drive the system at run-time. The conclusion will discuss the contri-

DOI: 10.4018/978-1-61520-839-5.ch015

bution of this research to the field of ontological engineering of software systems.

15.1 PRINCIPLES FOR AN OPERATIONS' SYSTEM

At the turn of year 2000, new concepts had emerge from various fields such as Web-based programmable learning portals, service oriented frameworks, model-driven and ontology-driven architectures, multi-actor scenarios and workflows. These main technological trends have deeply influenced our work to produce more flexible, powerful, yet user-friendly elearning environments.

We aimed to go one level up, enabling the *aggregation of custom-made platforms* or portals in a way similar to desktop integration that has enabled the interoperation of components from different sources. We have designed the Technology Enhanced Learning Operating System (TELOS) on the same interoperability principles. The TELOS architecture aims to extend portal assembly in ways enabling technologists to built their own platforms. These platforms would foster a variety of distributed learning environments or models such as electronic performance support systems (EPSS), communities of practice, formal on-line training and technology-based classroom, and different forms of blended learning or knowledge management environments.

As the project was starting, *service-oriented frameworks* (Wilson, Blinco and Rehak 2004) such as ELF (2007) or OKI (2007) were proposed to lower the costs of integration, and to encourage more flexibility and simplification of software configurations. Such a framework could also create a broad vocabulary that could be extended to an ontology. The TELOS conceptual framework presented in section 2 would also be designed as a service oriented framework, facilitating the aggregation of services to create custom-made platforms and applications.

This has led us naturally to a *model-driven, ontology-driven architecture* (Kleppe, Warmer and Bast 2003). The main gain of model-driven architectures (MDA) is the generation of the code from the model in successive layers, the model being reusable in other contexts with few adaptations. Ontology-driven architectures (Tetlow et al. 2001; Davies, van Harmelen and Fensel 2002) add to this paradigm an explicit ontology structuring of the objects processed by the system, acting as its executable blueprint. MDA therefore put more emphasis on the platform independent model (PIM), reducing the work on platform specific (PSM) and code models. Ontology-Driven Architectures foster a programming style analogous to the Prolog programming language. Here the declarative part is encoded in the ontology, in our case through OWL-DL statements. The execution part is encoded in queries prepared for an inference engine that processes the queries. The result of a query is to trigger the execution of some of the services.

Another key architectural idea is the concept of *multi-actor learning designs and workflows*, as the main structure of the various environments produced using TELOS. We wanted to avoid some of the weaknesses of our previous virtual campus models and most commercial platforms, where actors only interact within mono-actor environments that do not really take in account collaborative processes. As we have discussed in Chapter 8, this question is now solved partly in workflows modeling languages such as BPMN (Correal and Marino, 2007) and in eLearning design specifications like IMS-LD (2003) Multi-actor learning designs and workflows provide a central aggregation mechanism grouping actors, the operation they perform and the resources they use or produce from or for other actors. Based on this work, a multi-actor scenario editor and execution engine was planned as a central piece of TELOS (Paquette and Rosca 2003; Magnan and Paquette 2006)

15.2 BUILDING THE ARCHITECTURE OF TELOS

Initially, we have tailored the Rational Unified Process (RUP) to the needs of the project. RUP is an adaptable process framework that describes how to develop software effectively using proven techniques. While the RUP encompasses a large number of different activities, it enables the selection of development processes appropriate to a particular software project.

Development Process

As shown on Figure 1 our initial use of RUP was first focused on the business modeling and the requirements processes, each with a few cycles including phases of inception, elaboration, con-struction and transition. This has led to a set of architecture documents, the main one being the Use cases and software requirements documents (UC 1.0). Then the focus has moved to the Analysis and Design process with the construction of the Conceptual Architecture (CA 0.7) and the Conceptual Framework (CF 0.8) documents, which includes the TELOS Conceptual Ontology. The first two years followed the RUP quite closely but with long iteration cycles resulting in a set of architecture documents and throw-away prototypes TELOS-1 and TELOS-2.

In the last three years, the team has reduced the length of the iterations, adopting a process closer to Rapid Prototyping in order to achieve workable prototypes. A number of Software Architecture (SA) documents have been written to support the implementation of the TELOS prototypes. TELOS-3 was the first evolutionary prototype on which we could build the following ones. Each year, a test bed was conducted where users would interact with the available prototype

Figure 1. TELOS development process

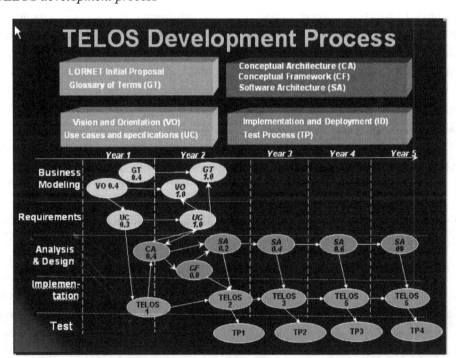

within a carefully planned test process. Prototypes 2, 3 and 4 were demonstrated at the LORNET annual conferences. The last one, TELOS-5, was demonstrated at the ITS-08 conference. This evolution reflects the fact that TELOS does not follow traditional software development processes, being considered as innovative, risky and ambitious by many persons, in other words, a research project.

Use Cases and Requirements

We will now briefly summarize on Figure 2 the Use Cases Specifications and Requirements (UCR 1.0), and the TELOS Conceptual Framework (CF 0.9).

The UCR has undergone 10 iterations, from June 03 to December 04. It groups 30 use case diagrams and descriptions that are packaged as shown on Figure 2. The use cases at the four levels of the system describe how to build, administrate, use and support a Web-based environment, each being used at each cascade level (rows on Figure 2).

Level IV concerns mainly an engineer extending the TELOS Core that will be used by technologists. At Level III, a technologist uses the TELOS Core to produce a platform, technically called a Learning and Knowledge Management System (LKMS). At level II, a designer uses a platform, to build one or more Learning and Knowledge Management Applications (LKMA), usually called "courses", "learning units", "knowledge management workflows", etc. Finally at level I, using one of these applications, a learner or a knowledge worker will acquire knowledge and produce results (homeworks, documents, performance) that can be grouped in a portfolio or a set of Learning and Knowledge Management Products (LKMP).

Generic resource life cycle use cases (columns on Figure 2) correspond to four sub-operations (phases) that occur at each of the four cascade levels. In these, a resource is composed, managed (prepared) for use, used by its intended actors, and analyzed to provide assistance. These operations

Figure 2. Resource life cycle and system cascade actors

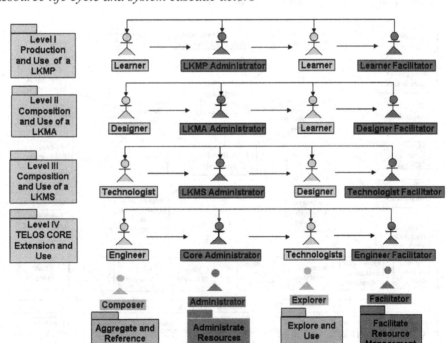

are generally performed in sequence at each of the cascade levels by corresponding actors called respectively composers, administrators, explorers (resource users) and facilitators (acting as analysts to provide assistance and feedback). These operations are generic, being applicable at any cascade level. When they act as composer, learners will have to search for resources in much the same ways as a designer, a technologist or an engineer, even though the content of the resources will differ.

We can use different metaphors to describe these general processes. In a manufacturing metaphor, the resource life cycle corresponds to a process where a product passes through different productions operations. Within the system generation cascade, the TELOS Core is like a factory that produces machine components or complete machines; the products of this first factory are used to build machines that will be used in other factories (LKMSs) to build cars, aircrafts, etc. These transportation machines, will finally be used by their clients to produce some outcome (e.g. to travel).

As a manufacture, the TELOS Core itself starts with a complete set of components to produce LKMS factories, but it will also be open to improvement, adding new processes and operations, to produce more versatile machines.

Conceptual Architecture

Starting with this elaborated set of use cases, the TELOS conceptual architecture (Rosca 2005) and the TELOS conceptual framework (Paquette, Rosca Masmoudi and Mihaila 2005) were built as a service-oriented framework, bringing it closer to a possible implementation. Figure 3 present the main classes of services.

• *Kernel Communication services.* TELOS is built as a distributed architecture on the Internet. To become a node in a Virtual Campus, each user installs a TELOS kernel on his machine that provides

Figure 3. The virtual campus service oriented framework

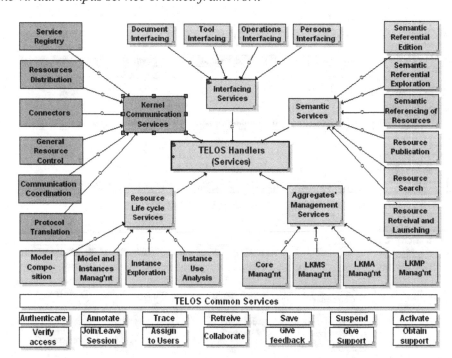

basic communication services with other nodes where resources are distributed. These services include for example a service registry, a repository that locates the resources on the nodes of the network, connectors to provide communication with resources built using different technologies, protocol translation and so on.

- *Resource interfacing services.* Basic resources comprise documents in a variety of media formats, tools to process documents, operations that can perform a process automatically and finally persons managing a set of activities on the network. All these resources usually will require to be interfaced in different ways, for example by a communication agent for format translation, through encapsulation for tracing, etc. They will then be stored in a resource repository in order to be reached and to participate in the learning and/or knowledge management processes

- *Resource life cycle services.* These services provide a number of editors for a composer to build, adapt and aggregate resources, thus producing a model of the resource. The provide tools for an administrator to produce instances of the model, as well as interfaces to help users and facilitators interact with an environment instance.

- *Aggregates' management services.* These services provide management functionalities for the main aggregates (or Web portals) used in the Virtual Campus: Core, LKMSs, LKMAs and LKMPs portals. For example, they will help in the storage, modification, display, evolution and maintenance of versions of TELOS Core, the interoperability between platforms (LKMSs), the management of courses (LKMAs) and the LKMPs such as Portfolios.

- *Semantic services.* These services enable users to query or edit semantic resources,

for example ontologies or metadata, used to reference resources. Resource publication services enable users to package resources with their semantic references, enabling various kind of resource search, retrieval and display. With these services a user can call upon federated or harvested search operations to display documents, tools, operations (including activities and units-of-learning) related to some domain knowledge and competencies.

- ○ *Common services.* We have grouped in this category all the lower level services that are called by the services in the preceding categories. They correspond to operations that all the actors need to perform while participating in the Virtual Campus.

15.3 THE TELOS TECHNICAL ONTOLOGY

In this section we will summarize the general methodology used to develop TELOS. First, we will present the conceptual framework of the TELOS system, and the conceptual ontology derived from it. Next, we will show how this first ontology was adapted to produce the technical ontology that drives the TELOS system.

From Conceptual Framework to Conceptual Ontology

An important goal in the TELOS project was to embed in the system technology-independent models, to help the system survive the rapid pace of technology evolution. Another concern was to favour the reusability of modular components and the flexibility on the system's evolution. For that purpose, the conceptual specifications of TELOS, are not be kept apart from the code of the system as is usually done in software engineering. The TELOS system is able to use ontologies as "conceptual programs". In this vision, the conceptual models are not just prerequisite to the construction of the TELOS system; they are part of the system, as one of its most fundamental layer. These considerations motivated the need for an ontology-driven architecture (ODA).

To achieve that goal, we have translated the use cases and the service-oriented conceptual architecture presented above into an OWL-DL ontology. We have selected to use OWL-DL ontologies (W3C 2004) for a number of reasons. Of the three languages designed by the W3 consortium, OWL-DL has a wide expressivity and its foundation in Description Logic (Baader, Calvanese et al. 2003) guarantees its computational completeness and decidability. On a more practical side, a growing number of software tools have been designed to process OWL-DL XML files and to put inference engines at work to query ontologies in order to execute the processes in a system.

The graph of Figure 4 presents the upper level of the TELOS Conceptual ontology that has been constructed using the MOT+OWL editor (Paquette 2008) presented in Chapter 10. In TELOS, the actors, the operations they perform and the resources they use or produce are all TELOS resources. This is shown on the graph by using S "is-a-sort-of" links. They are represented as classes linked together with properties such as "perform" and "use or produce".

Some classes are further defined in sub-models that present sub-taxonomies of classes and their properties. The graph of Figure 5 shows the taxonomy of TELOS users corresponding to the use cases summarized on Figure 2, related by the "canPerform" property to corresponding operations they perform. The taxonomy of operations is further defined in another Operations' sub-model (not shown here) where the operations are linked with the services (handlers) identified previously in the conceptual architecture (Figure 3).

Another sub-graph describes the taxonomy of resources, including the very important concept of "content" package, which is redefined as resources having semantic descriptions. The upper part of this sub-graph is presented in Figure 6.

From Conceptual Ontogy to Technical Ontology

The conceptual ontology was revised, simplified or expanded to build the TELOS technical ontology shown on Figure 7, that is integrated as code to drive the operation of the system.

First, we had to capture the distributed aspects of TELOS by adding the concept of a "TELOS Node" that was not present in the Conceptual

Figure 4. Upper part of the TELOS conceptual ontology

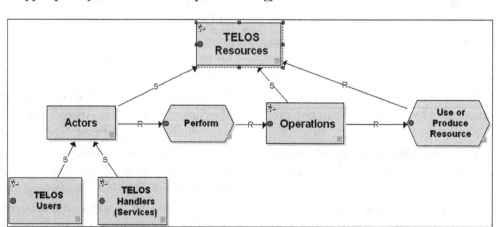

Figure 5. Part of the TELOS conceptual ontology focused on roles and actors

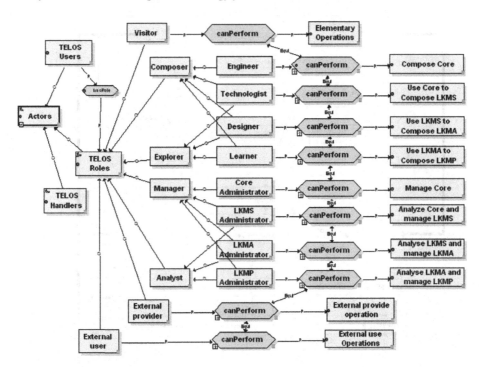

Figure 6. Part of the TELOS conceptual ontology focused on resources

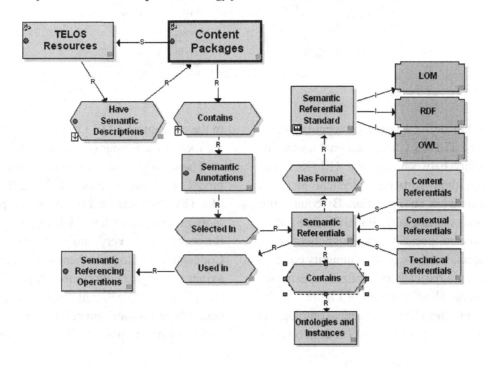

Figure 7. The upper layer of the TELOS technical ontology

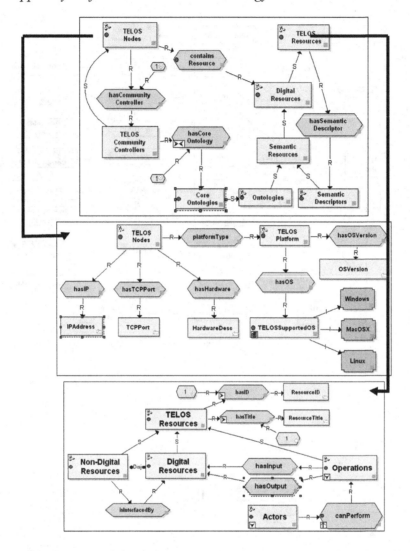

Ontology but defined in the Conceptual architecture. The TELOS Global bus enables the interoperability between different TELOS nodes abstracting their particular physical platform and their network configuration. By connecting TELOS nodes through the Global Bus, we form a dynamic peer-to-peer network. This network may contain special nodes called community controllers, which are basically centralized repositories for resources. The first graph of Figure 7 is the upper level of the TELOS Technical ontology. It presents the concept of a TELOS node in relation to the concept of a TELOS resource, which was the root of the former conceptual ontology.

The second graph on Figure 7 presents a submodel of the previous one defining the concept of a TELOS Node, and the third one presents a more precise, upper level definition of a TELOS Resource that is very similar to the one in the Conceptual ontology. In these graphs, cardinality axioms (hexagons with numbers), disjoint axioms (Disj link) and functional property axioms have been added for more precision. This is essential because this ontology will have to respond to

Figure 8. Part of the sub-ontology for digital resources

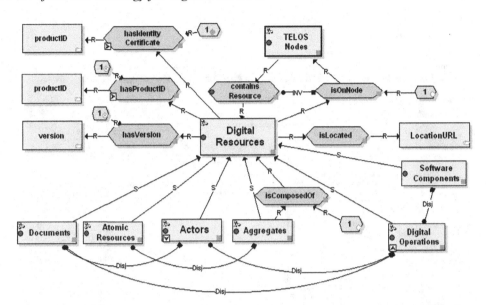

queries using an inference engine that do not tolerate ambiguity.

In these upper layer graphs, we find the inter-relations between the main concepts of *Actors*, *Operations* and *Digital Resources*. The Actors' and the Operations' sub-ontologies are directly imported from the Conceptual ontology presented on Figure 4. The Digital Resources' sub-ontology has undergone more important changes. It is presented on Figure 8. We see that implementation-focused concepts have been added such as *productID* and *locationURL*. Each of the five main sub-classes: *Documents, Atomic Resources, Actors, Aggregates* and *Digital Operations* are detailed in other OWL-DL models no shown here.

The resources are the persistent data of a TELOS node. The "Aggregates" sub-class is particularly important. This type of resource enables users to create new eLearning tools by gluing existing software components and other resources. It also enables users to model collaborative workflows or scenarios aggregating actors, the activities they perform and the documents, the software components they use or produce.

The technical ontology we have just presented forms the heart of the semantic layer if TELOS. It is where all TELOS concepts are declared and related together to define the global behavior of TELOS. The semantic layer also contains the domain ontologies created by users that later enables the referencing of the resources with application domain knowledge and competencies.

15.4 TELOS MAIN TOOLS

Before discussing how the TELOS system uses its semantic layer and its Technical ontology for its operations we will first present de main tools in TELOS. Figure 9 displays the TELOS desktop main interface in a Web browser, with the three main tools open: the Resource Manager, the Scenario Editor and the Task Manager. The MOWL Ontology Editor presented in Chapter 10 is also available from the TELOS desktop.

Figure 9. TELOS desktop main interface

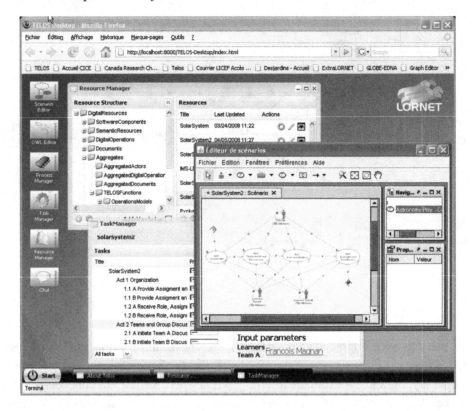

The Resource Manager

The TELOS Resource Manager serves to integrate and manage the resources that actors use or produce in TELOS. These resources are classified according to the technical ontology. On the Figure 9, the "aggregates" class of the technical ontology is expanded and the "My scenarios" class is selected showing the available instances on its right side. Resources can be added, deleted, moved or duplicated within a class or to other classes.

Once a scenario has been selected, the little icons on the right enable any authorized user to *view*, *modify* or *run* the execution of the resource. These functions differ depending on the type to the resources.

- When a resource is open in modify (write) mode, a key icon(Figure 10) is added in the action column to prevent two users to

edit the same resource at the same time. The resource is transferred on the user's local machine and opened with his associated applications (MS Word for a doc file, PowerPoint for a ppt file, etc...) until it is made available again in the resource manager.

- For a scenario the View and Modify functions open the scenario editor presented in Chapter 8, also shown on the second win-

Figure 10. Key icon

dow of Figure 9; the Run option starts the inference engine that will execute the scenario and present it to its users in the Task Manager.

- For an ontology, the View and Modify functions open the ontology in the Ontology Editor presented in Chapter 10.
- Resources of type TELOS Users, viewing or editing opens a User Browser that lets you enter personal information, e-mails, photo, etc....; this information is reachable in scenario execution process, by clickable icons that represent scenario's users. For groups (type Actors/TELOSGroups), a dedicated editor is opened to add or delete individuals from a group.
- Software component can also be integrated into scenarios through operations objects stored in the resource manager. Operations automate some processes during scenario execution. This kind of resource must be a zip archive that contains the binary code of the component plus an XML manifest file that describes its services: name, input parameters, output parameters and arguments order.

The Scenario Editor

The TELOS scenario Editor has been briefly presented in Chapter 8. Let us recall that MOT *Concept* symbols serve to represent all kinds of resources: documents, tools, semantic resources, environments, actors (as a resource), activities (as a resource) and data. MOT procedure symbols represent *Functions* that are aggregates of resources (e.g. scenarios) that together achieve a function. Functions can be decomposed into other functions at any depth down to activities enacted by humans, or operations performed automatically by the system. Finally, MOT principles serve to represent actors as well as conditions, depicted by two different sets of symbols. The *Actor* symbols represent users, groups, roles or software agents, all seen as control objects that rule the activities using and producing resources as planned by the scenario model. The *Condition* symbols represent control elements inserted within the basic flow to decide on the following functions, activities or operations to execute.

Now let us look more closely at the operation of the TELOS Scenario Editor. As a user starts elaborating a scenario model, the top level will be a function (generated by default) that represents the whole scenario that is created. This aggregate will be consequently added as a resource into the

Figure 11. Example of a model and its sub-model

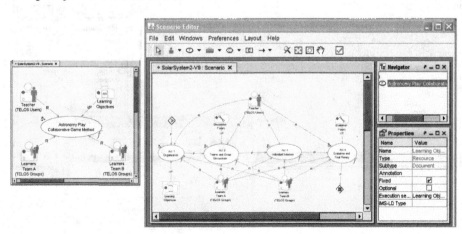

resource manager. At this top level, it is recommended to add and to link to this function all key actors and resources involved in this scenario. Afterwards, the user will add one or more levels of sub-models, to add more details to the scenario, as shown on Figure 11. This sub-model shows that the scenario is composed of a sequence of four acts or modules involving three actors and two forum tools. Learning objectives are presented in the first act.

Each graphic object at any level of the scenario can be described by a property sheet grouping properties like its name, type, annotation, etc., the most important one being its execution semantic.

Figure 12 presents a sub-model of Act 2 that displays a property sheet for the selected object called "Planet Properties land surface temperature and orbital velocity". If we do not tell TELOS what this icon represents in terms of its technical ontology, the system will not be able to process it. This is the role the selected property called "Execution

semantic". By clicking on this field, we open the little window of the Ontology chooser that opens a class of resources, here "Documents" and all the available instances that are member of that class. Here, the resource "Planet Properties A", in fact a Powerpoint presentation on the planets, has been selected to be associated to the selected icon. At runtime, this document will be opened from the Resource Manager. In the same way, the teacher, a TELOS user, and the two teams of learners, will be given an execution semantic. The teacher icon will be associated to an individual user acting as the teacher, and the group icons will be associated to a list of precise learners, previously entered in the resource manager. The same can be said for the two chat tools into which each team will interact. Here, the execution semantic is to simply link the icons to URLs that will open in a browser each chat tool at runtime.

The TELOS scenario language provides a high-level programming visual language for TELOS. This generic language is designed for

Figure 12. A sub-model of a sub-model

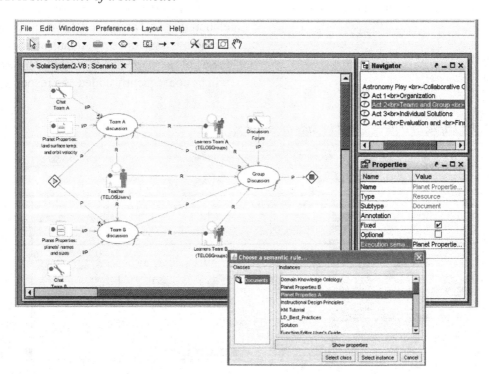

all TELOS users, including students/workers, teachers/designers, technologists and programmers/engineers, when they act, respectively, as composers (see Figure 2) and use composition handlers (see Figure 3) at the different levels of the cascade of TELOS aggregates.

In (Paquette and Magnan 2007) we have presented three examples of scenarios. The first case, presented above, is built by a designer that has constructed the course. The second example is less common, showing how a technologist can combine an existing platform with TELOS tools to extend the functionalities of the design environment. The third one has been built by an engineer aggregating four different components built with different technologies, in order to insert automatically the learning objects found by a Google search into a resource manager.

The example on Figure 13 shows how a technologist can combine an existing platform with TELOS tools to provide a composition environment for a course designer. This design scenario corresponds to the central tasks of the MISA instructional engineering method presented in Chapter 8 (Paquette 2001, Paquette 2004). The figure shows part of this scenario that involves using Concept@, Télé-université's actual course design platform, augmented with the TELOS scenario editor and other components. The little window on the right present the tools used by designers in this design scenario.

The design scenario starts with two parallel functions performed by a designer: design of a course backbone using the Concept@ LCMS and the development of a knowledge and competency model for the course using the TELOS ontology editor. Let us note that actually, Concept@ helps produce an activity tree representing the course plan and its subdivision into modules and activities. This is a common situation in most LCMS (Learning Content Management Systems). This tree structure can be exported to a SCORM package. Then we add to the design scenario an operation that automatically transforms a SCORM

Figure 13. Technologist constructing an augmented LKMS platform for designers

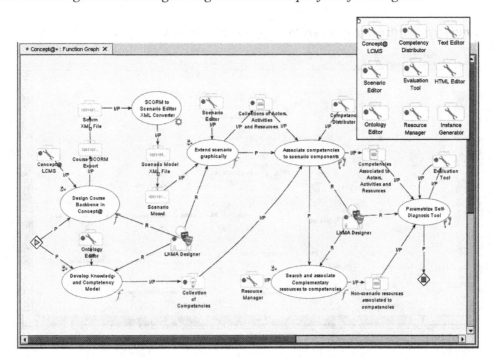

package to the TELOS scenario format. This last XML file can now be imported in the scenario editor and displayed in the form of a scenario graph where it can be expanded.

Many roles can be defined in Concept@ but this exceeds SCORM's mono-actor capabilities. So information about roles/actors is lost when we open the corresponding graph in the TELOS scenario editor. The next design phase proceeds graphically in the TELOS scenario editor to add manually the actors identified in Concept@.

Within the scenario editor more advanced flow of control can also be added to better personalize learning based on the knowledge and competency model. This is shown by the last three steps of the design scenario on Figure 13: associate knowledge and competencies to scenarios components, use a resource manager like PALOMA (see Chapter 18 and 20) to add complementary resources to the scenario targeting the competencies and, finally parameterize the Competency + software (see Chapter 20) for self-diagnosis by the learners of their competencies. We will discuss the question on assistance and personalization in Chapter 21.

A third use of the scenario editor is presented on Figure 14. It has been built by an engineer aggregating a new service encapsulated in an operation called the "Batch LOM Extractor". This operation takes a set of keywords, a number of LOM records to be found and the name of a destination folder in a repository of learning objects managed by the PALOMA software.

The aim of this aggregated operation is first to make a Google query with the given keywords and collect the specified number of Web sites. Then, the next step will apply a text mining algorithm on each websites to extract automatically part of the metadata according to the LOM standard. Then, each of these metadata records will be inserted into the PALOMA folder identified at the beginning. Finally, this folder will open to show to the user the list of LOMs into the PALOMA software interface.

What we see here is the aggregation of software components built by different groups using different technologies. These software components transfer data from one to another. The Google Search Service is launched using a SOAP Web

Figure 14. Engineer constructing an operation aggregating services

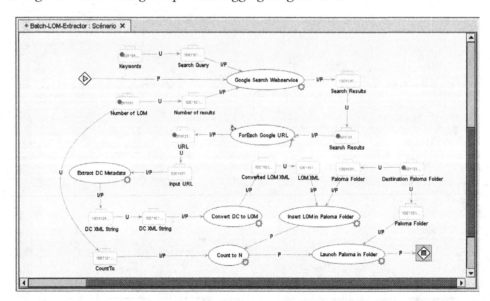

service connector provided by the TELOS kernel. The Metadata Extractor is a C# component linked to the TELOS kernel by a C# connector; it creates a metadata record in the Dublin Core (DC) format. The DC to LOM conversion is a Scheme program linked to TELOS through a Scheme connector. PALOMA is a Java applet linked to TELOS through a Java connector.

This example illustrates the multi-technology aspect of TELOS and the capability of the scenario editor to aggregate software components as if they were one. The resulting aggregate can now be inserted in any scenario as one of its tool.

15.5 ONTOLOGY DRIVEN SCENARIO EXECUTION

Although these scenarios differ greatly by their goals, their component resources and the level of their actors in the view of TELOS on Figure 2, they can all be run by TELOS as long as each resource has an execution semantic based on the TELOS

technical ontology. The Scenario Evaluator is the engine that executes a scenario. It coordinates the interactions between actors, activities/operations/tasks and other resources in the scenario at runtime. It looks at each graphic form in the scenario, obtains their location in the TELOS technical ontology and, with this data, it runs the user interface of the task manager accordingly.

The Task Manager

The *TELOS Task Manager* is the tool allowing a user to interact with running scenarios. To invoke the Task Manager, a user clicks on the Task Manager icon on the desktop or select the Task Manager item in the Start menu. The Task Manager will also be invoked automatically when launching a scenario via the Resource Manager.

Figure 15 shows the Task Manager for the scenario of Figure 11 and 12 at the very beginning. On the left, the tree view shows the four acts of Figure 11. Each can be expanded by the + sign, but none is yet active because the execution

Figure 15. Task manager interface

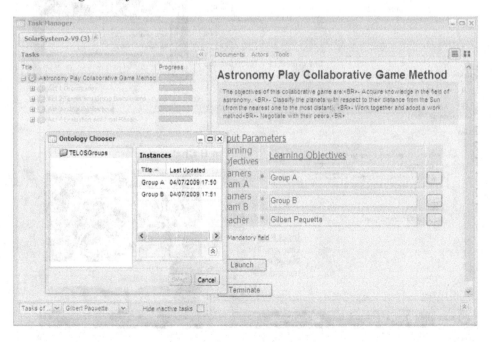

engine is positioned at the function main level. On the right side of the interface, we see an annotation that has been added to state the general description of the scenario, followed by a list of the input parameters of the function specified on Figure 11. The Learning Objective is a concrete document specified at design time so it can already be displayed by clicking on its name.

The other three input parameters, two groups of learners and the teacher, have to be instantiated at run time because their execution semantic is a class of the technical ontology. This is what the administrator has to do in order to launch the scenario: look up in the Ontology Chooser the instances of groups and users available in the resource manager (as shown on the little window

in the front), select a value for each parameter and click on the *Launch* button.

From that moment, the flow of control will move down to the level of the four acts. The first one will be executed, and then the second one and so on, according to the flow of the graph designed on Figure 9.

Interface for Each Actor's Roles

Figure 16 shows the interface in the task manager for team A and team B members at the beginning of Act 2, when they start separate chats to discuss planet properties. It is important for the pedagogy in this scenario that they do not have the same information to analyze. Afterwards, they will

Figure 16. Different views in the task manager for team A and team B

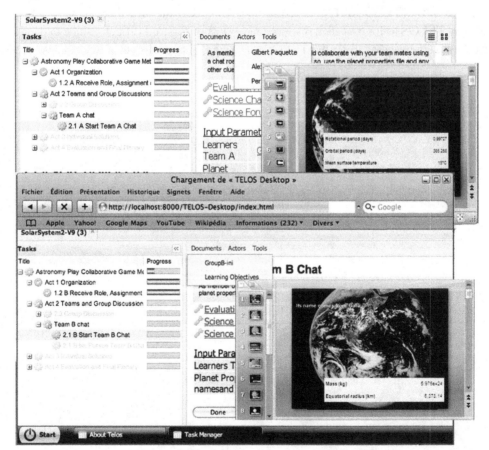

share their information in the forum grouping all students and the teacher.

The essential thing here is that the task manager, guided by the technical ontology, presents adapted task manager interfaces to all the participants in the scenario. The teacher sees everything because he is an actor monitoring all the tasks in this scenario. This enables him to see all the documents, actors and task progress for all the learners involved in the scenario.

On the other hand, as shown on Figure 16, the learners see only the tasks they are involved in and only the document they are suppose to use or produce. For example, learners in team A have terminated activity 1.2A which was their only task in Act 1 and their 2.1A activity is activated. From the Documents menu or from the Input Parameters section to activity 2.1A, they can launch the document shown on the figure that provides information on the rotational periods, the orbital periods and surface temperature of the planets. In the Actors menu, they see for the moment only the v-cards of their co-learners and of the teacher. And from the tools menu, they have access only to the Science chat A tool.

Meanwhile, learners in team B have access to information on other planet properties, their mass and equatorial radius. They can access their own team mate and the teacher in the Actors' menu and they can open their own chat environment in the tools' menu.

Providing Contextual Views

Another interesting feature of the task manager is the graphic view presented on Figure 17 that also uses the structure of the scenario graph and the links between its objects and the TELOS technical ontology. In this mode, the currently selected task is always shown in the center of the graph. Tasks that immediately precede and succeed the current task are displayed, respectively, on the left and right side of the central node. This way, a user can see the task contextually. To see farther tasks, a user can click on another node and the graphical view will adjust itself. The location bar at the top indicates in which sub-graph the current task belong. A user can use the location bar to navigate to upper sub-graphs.

Figure 17. Contextual graphic views in the task manager

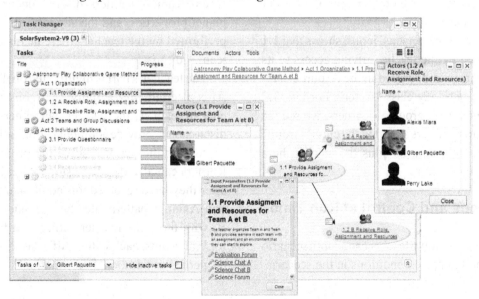

Figure 18. Condition specification and execution at run time

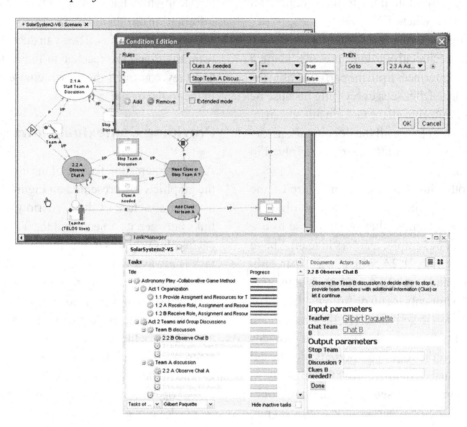

Here, we see a selected activity where the teacher provides the initial objectives, assignments and information to the learners. We see that this task is followed by two parallel learner tasks 1.2A and 1.2B.

Clicking on the persons' icons, shows that 1.1 is performed by the teacher, giving access to its personal information stored in the resource manager in the ontology class "Actor". For task 1.2 A, performed by a group of learners, we see the list of group members stored in the class "Group" of the research manager plus the teacher, here played by the author.

Conditions and Control at Run Time

Figure 18 shows how a teacher can adapt a scenario at run-time thanks to conditions in the scenario.

A sub-model for the team A discussion starts by opening the chat service for team A. Then, the control splits between the learning activity 2.1.A, where team A learners discuss documents on planet properties, and the support activity 2.2.A performed by the teacher where he observes the team A discussion.

The teacher's part is highlighted on the figure. After a certain time activity 2.2.A, observing the chat in team A, the teacher can either stop the discussion or provide additional information (Clue A) to help the learners solve the problem. The learners can also decide to stop, either before or after they have received this additional information. A similar pattern rules the discussion for team B, with the same teacher acting as a facilitator for both teams, each with a different set of planet properties as additional information.

The conditions shown on Figure 18 are rules expressing the equivalent of IMS-LD level B properties. The decision "Need Clues or Stop Team A?" depends on its input data and the value "true" or "false" that a teacher action will produce in activity 2.2.A. If the value "Stop team A discussion" is true, then the flow of control goes to the end symbol, after which the flow goes up to the main act 2 model. If the value of "Clues A needed" is true, the flow will proceed to the teacher's activity where he will select a document named "Clue A". If both input variables are false, the flow will come back to activity 2.2.A. In the task manager, a Web interface, shown on the bottom window, is provided to the Teacher actor to enter a value in the data objects "Stop Team A Discussion" and "Clues A needed". Depending on these values, the condition "Need Clues or Stop Team A" will be executed to orient the flow of activities. The Condition Edition windows on the Figure is where above rules are edited, here showing the rule "If Clues A needed is true and Stop Team A discussion is false, then go to 2.3A Add clues for team A.

CONCLUSION

We now summarize the benefits we expect from this ontology-driven design of TELOS and, more generally, from ontology-driven systems.

1. *Fidelity from Requirements to Code:* Capturing in an ontology the main use cases and conceptual architecture concepts improves the fidelity of the final system with respect to initial requirements. Transforming the Conceptual ontology to a technical ontology embedded in the system ensures that the code will respect the architecture requirements. Also, the ontology-driven aspect of TELOS eases its evolution when

new concepts will need to be integrated in the system.

2. *Global Systemic View.* The technical ontology can be seen as a kind Virtual Campus/Enterprise model. It provides a global view to support the cohesion of the activities, from the upper level where an institution can create a global workflow to coordinate its major processes, to the lower levels of a design scenario-based platform and scenario-based applications. An example of this will be given with the GIT project presented in the first section of Chapter 19.

3. *Extended set of actors.* Compared to the commercial LCMS in operation this new global approach leads to an unlimited set of actors. At any level any number of actors can be defined and really supported.

4. *Better process coordination.* The fact that the system holds a model of the processes and the support resources leads to better process coordination. Especially in distance universities or distributed organizations, this provides a better assurance that the quality of services will be maintained when the personnel changes or it must provide new products to other actors.

5. *Visible scenarios and workflows.* Learning scenarios or workflows can always be consulted in a Web portal interface such as the Task Manager, links between resources, activities and actors can be seen right away. Each user taking an actor's role can visually see the context of the activities he has to perform, what resources to use or produce and with whom he is to interact with.

6. *Flexible and adaptable environments.* Each environment operates according to a technical ontology which is an integral part of the system. This enables very flexible and adaptable environments. If a new kind of actor, activity or resource needs to be introduced, this is done simply by modifying the

instances or classes of the ontology, without changing the main operations of the system.

7. *Resource reusability* is a goal pursued by many advocates of learning object repositories, but it is not that easy to achieve. Using ontologies to annotate each resource within the same framework, and adding connecting operations to take care of possible technology mismatches brings solutions to many reusability problems.

8. *System interoperability*. With TELOS, it is possible to bring different technologies and different platforms to work together. For example, a designer could built a course using a scenario editor in one platform, and transfer it to TELOS to add new functionalities, for example personalized assistance. This process can be designed by defining the aggregation scenario between platforms at the technologist's level.

9. *Modeling for all*. Modeling is not an easy task but it is important enough to make it accessible not only to engineers and technologists, but also to instructional designers, learners and trainers.

10. *Focus on learning and work designs*. Finally, we hope the proposed approach will reduce the technology noise that is often present in eLearning applications when too much time is devoted to solving pure technology problems, instead of focusing on learning problems. We hope the activities will be more focused on pedagogy and on the quality of educational services or knowledge management activities.

These approaches offer new possibilities but also pose additional challenges. The LORNET five year research project having ended, some considerable refinements will happen. We will also need to ensure a user friendliness of the tools that will be novel to most users. But our hope is that the results achieved here will lead the way to future research and developments and fruitful applications to Web-based learning and knowledge management systems.

REFERENCES

W3C. (2004). *OWL Overview Document*. Retrieved from http://www.w3.org/TR/2004/REC-owl-features-20040210/

Baader, F., Calvanese, D., McGuinness, D., Nardi, D., & Patel-Schneider, P. (Eds.). (2003). *The Description Logic Handbook*. Cambridge, UK: Cambridge University Press.

Correal, D., & Marino, O. (2007). *Software Requirements Specification Document for General Purpose Function's Editor* (V0.4). LORNET Technical Documents, LICEF research centrer, Télé-université.

Davies, J., van Harmelen, F., & Fensel, D. (Eds.). (2002). *Towards the Semantic Web: Ontology-driven Knowledge Management*. New York: John Wiley & Sons, Inc.

ELF – e-Learning framework. (2007). Retrieved June 14, 2007, from http://www.elframework.org/

IMS-LD. (2003). *IMS Learning Design. Information Model, Best Practice and Implementation Guide, Binding document*. Schemas.

Kleppe, A. G., Warmer, J. B., & Bast, W. (2003). *MDA explained: the model driven architecture: practice and promise*. Boston: Addison-Wesley.

Magnan, F., & Paquette, G. (2006). TELOS: An ontology driven eLearning OS. Presented at SOA/AIS-06 Workshop, Dublin, Ireland, June 2006.

OKI – Open Knowledge Initiative. (2007). Retrieved June 14, 2007, from http://www.okiproject.org/

Paquette, G. (2001). Designing virtual learning centers . In Adelsberger, H., Collis, B., & Pawlowski, J. M. (Eds.), *Handbook on Information Technologies for Education & Training* (pp. 249–272). Berlin: Springer-Verlag.

Paquette, G. (2003). *Instructional Engineering for Network-Based Learning.* San Francisco: Pfeiffer.

Paquette, G. (2008). Graphical Ontology Modeling Language for Learning Environments. In Technology, Instruction., Cognition and Learning (Vol. 5, pp.133-168). Philadelphia, PA: Old City Publishing, Inc.

Paquette, G., & Magnan, F. (2007). *Learning Resource Referencing, Search and Aggregation At the eLearning System Level.* Presented at LODE Workshop, ECTEL-07 Conference, Crete, September 18-21, 2007

Paquette, G., & Magnan, F. (2008). *From a Conceptual Ontology to the TELOS Operational System.* ITS Workshop on Ontology-based Learning Resource Repositories. Retrieved December 2008, from http://www.lornet.org

Paquette, G., & Magnan, F. (2008). An Executable Model for Virtual Campus Environments. In H. H. Adelsberger, Kinshuk, J. M. Pawlowski & D. Sampson (Eds.), International Handbook on Information Technologies for Education and Training (2nd Ed.) (pp. 365-405). New York: Springer.

Paquette, G., & Rogozan, D. (2006). *Primitives de représentation OWL-DL - Correspondance avec le langage graphique MOT+OWL et le langage des prédicats du premier ordre. TELOS documentation.* Montreal, Canada: LICEF Research Center.

Paquette, G., & Rosca, I. (2003). Modeling the delivery physiology of distributed learning systems. *Technology, Instruction, cognition and Learning,* 1-2, 183–209.

Paquette, G., Rosca, I., Masmoudi, A., & Mihaila, S. (2005). *Telos conceptual framework v0.8. Lornet technical documentation.* Télé-Université.

Paquette, G., Rosca, I., Mihaila, S., & Masmoudi, A. (2006). Telos, a service-oriented framework to support learning and knowledge management . In Pierre, S. (Ed.), *E-Learning Networked Environments and Architectures: a Knowledge Processing Perspective.* Berlin: Springer-Verlag.

Rosca, I. (2005). TELOS Conceptual Architecture, version 0.5. LORNET Technical Documents, LICEF research centrer, Télé-université, Montreal.

Tetlow, P., Pan, J., Oberle, D., Wallace, E., Uschold, M., & Kendall, E. (2001). *Ontology driven architectures and potential uses of the semantic web in systems and softrware engineering.* Retrieved from http://www.w3.org/2001/sw/BestPractices/SE/ODA/051126/

Wilson, S., Blinco, K., & Rehak, D. (2004). *Service-oriented frameworks: Modelling the infrastructure for the next generation of e-learning systems.* White Paper presented at the alt-i-lab '04.

Section 4
Visual Modelling in Practice

Chapter 16
Modeling for Learning

Josianne Basque
LICEF Research Center, Canada

Béatrice Pudelko
LICEF Research Center, Canada

ABSTRACT

- External Representations and Cognitive Tools
- Knowledge Modeling as an Individual Learning strategy
- Collaborative Knowledge Modeling as a Learning Strategy for Distance Education
- Collaborative Knowledge Modeling in Face-to-Face Learning Situations

Some years ago, we have introduced in the pedagogical scenario of a distance university course a learning activity consisting at having students create their own knowledge models with the knowledge modeling software MOT developed by Paquette (2002).

At the same time, was initiated a series of studies[1] aiming at evaluating the learning benefits and exploring the meditating effect of the use of this tool in the learning process, both in individual or collaborative conditions, as well as in face-to-face or distance educational settings. In our research, MOT is mainly used as a mean to support students' text comprehension, but we also proposed this tool to professionals engaged in a vocational university program to help them reflect on how the curriculum knowledge domain is instantiated in their own professional practice. In addition, we provided training sessions to faculties and produced some documentation (available on the web) on the educational uses of knowledge model-

DOI: 10.4018/978-1-61520-839-5.ch016

ing software in higher education (Pudelko & Basque, 2005).

In this chapter, we will first situate the MOT tool among other node-link visual knowledge representation tools used in educational settings. Next, we will describe how we used MOT to support learning in three different learning contexts at the postsecondary level (individual learning by distance learners; collaborative learning in dyads at a distance; collaborative learning in large group in a face-to-face setting) and report some of the results of our studies.

16.1. EXTERNAL REPRESENTATIONS AND COGNITIVE TOOLS

External representations (text, graphic, table, picture, etc.) play a significant role in the teaching/learning process. Learners can be invited either to study external representations elaborated by the teacher or by other authors, or they can be invited to elaborate some themselves. Constructivist and generative learning theories (Duffy & Cunningham, 1996; Grabowski, 1996) tend to favor the second option because students have then to identify the knowledge units to be represented and to provide a substantial effort in searching for how they are related (O'Donnell, Dansereau, & Hall, 2002). This active and deep mental process would help the learner in constructing more elaborate internal structures of knowledge.

To construct any external representation, a representational notation system must be used. Each representational notation system manifests a particular "representational guidance" (Suthers, 2003) in two major ways: (1) it constrains the expressiveness of how the knowledge units can be expressed and (2), it makes some of that knowledge more salient. Hence, representational notation systems structure provide a specific approach how to reason about knowledge domains.

Node-link diagrams constitute a family of external representations which is more and more used for educational purposes. In fact, the construction of node-link diagrams such as concept maps (Novak, 1998; Novak & Gowin, 1984); mind maps (Buzan & Buzan, 1996) or knowledge maps (Holley & Dansereau, 1984) by learners has been proposed as a learning strategy for nearly three decades in the educational field. Since the mid-eighties, much research has been conducted on this issue with students of all educational levels and in several disciplines. In general, research shows that this activity leads to beneficial effects on learning (Horton *et al.*, 1993; Nesbit & Adesope, 2006).

The most popular representational technique explored in these studies is the concept mapping technique proposed by Novak and Gowin in their seminal book *Learning how to learn* published in 1984. A concept map is defined by these authors as "a schematic device for representing a set of concept meanings embedded in a framework of propositions" (p. 15). A proposition is a semantic unit formed by two or more concept linked by words. Then, a concept map is a node-link representation, where nodes denote concepts of a certain knowledge domain, and links denote the relationships among concepts. Concepts are specified by textual labels, which could be a noun, or a noun complemented with one or more adjectives or adverbs for denoting a more specific concept (for example, *living things* instead of *things*). Links are specified by lines, usually arrowed, on which textual labels are also put, more specifically verbs (such as *contain, involve, change, are in, can be,* etc.) or "linking phrases" (such as *then, by, as in, with, that,* etc.). The general spatial layout and the directions of the links aim to express the idea of a hierarchy of concepts, going from the most general to the most specific ones.

The emergence of computer-based concept mapping software in the nineties has provoked a renewed interest in the construction of concept maps by students as a learning activity. Compared to paper-and-pencil, these software tools have much more to offer in facilitating the concept mapping operations, especially in formatting and modifying the maps (Anderson-Inman & Ditson, 1999; Bruillard & Baron, 2000; Lin, Strickland, Ray, & Denner, 2004). Those functionalities encourage users to elaborate and revise their maps and, consequently, help them self-monitor their knowledge construction process.

Moreover, since these tools integrate representational functionalities which guide the user's activity not only at the operational level but also at the cognitive level and even at the metacognitive level, they have been described as "cognitive tools" (Bruillard & Baron, 2000; Kommers, Jonassen, & Mayes, 1992; Lajoie & Derry, 1993), "mindtools" (Jonassen, 2000) and "metacognitive tools" (Coffey, 2007). Such tools facilitate external representations of information and enhance cognitive functioning by making users think harder or differently about knowledge (Kommers, Jonassen, & Mayes, 1992). This notion of cognitive tool is somewhat similar to the notion of "cognitive artefact" proposed in the field of Human-Machine Interaction by Norman (1991) and by other authors involved in Computer-Supported Collaborative Learning (CSCL) (Suthers, 2006) or working within the Activity Theory framework (Engeström, Miettinen, & Punamäki, 1999; Nardi, 2001).

Most concept mapping software tools promote flexibility of expressiveness (Alpert, 2004), that is, they impose minimal constraints on the activity of representing the nodes and the links in the map. For example, Cañas & Carvalho (2004) state that the CMapTools offers a reasonable compromise between flexibility and formalism in knowledge representation" because they believe that "the freedom in the selection of concept and linking phrases gives the tool a lot of its power and makes it user-friendly and easy to learn" (p. 3).

Other authors suggest that a more constrained representational notation system could optimize the beneficial learning guidance offered by concept mapping tools. For example, Kharatmal & Nagarjuna (2006) argue that we should introduce some more "discipline" in the Novakian concept mapping language to assist the learner in specifying valid relationships among concepts. One way to do this is to introduce a typology of links in the representational language, as did Holley & Dansereau, (1984) in their spatial learning strategy called "networking". This limit imposed on the link representation process would help in disambiguating the natural language used to designate links and in making students more aware of the various types of relationships that could be established among knowledge objects (for instance hierarchical, temporal or causal relationships), making these different types of knowledge structures more salient to them.

The MOT knowledge modeling language goes a step further. In addition to a typology of links (which includes six basic generic links), a typology of knowledge objects is proposed, which differentiates "concepts" from "procedures", "principles" and "facts", so that learners must reason not only in terms of interrelated concepts but also in terms of interrelated *types* of knowledge entities. Moreover, some semantic rules determine the type of links that can be drawn among the different types of knowledge entities, as presented in detail in chapter 2.

Thus, the MOT language is much more formalized than most other representational languages used by learners when creating node-link diagrams in educational settings. In fact, the representational notation implemented in the MOT software would be considered a "semi-formal" language in the Artificial Intelligence community. It is not as much rigorously formalized as is the MOT+OWL ontological language (Paquette, 2007) that has been implemented in the recent versions of MOTPlus and MOWL presented in chapter 10, but it is less ambiguous than the typical concept mapping languages used in educational settings,

Figure 1. Degree of formalization of different types of node-link representations

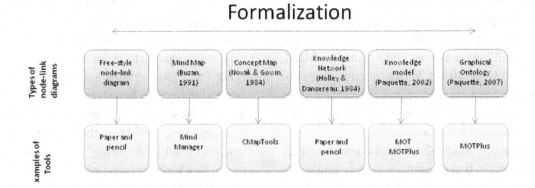

as discussed in part I of this book. In Figure 1, we position different types of node-link diagrams according to their degree of formalization.

Moreover, the MOT tool offers direct guidance to the user by prompting him to conform to the semantic rules of the objet-typed representational language. For example, if the user draws a link between two knowledge entities that is not conform to the MOT grammar, the software will automatically display a default link, that is, the most probable one considering the types of the knowledge entities involved. If the user disagrees with the suggested link, a right-click on the link enables him to select another one from the pool of "permitted" links (the invalid links not being clickable). Thus, the MOT tool not only includes a more formalized knowledge representation language than most computer-based tools for node-link representations, but it also intervenes dynamically in the knowledge representation activity of the user. However, the user may choose to by-pass this limitation by using the "untyped" knowledge object and the "untyped" link which are also implemented in the software.

It should be noted that the MOT software has been developed initially not for educational but for instructional design purposes, that is, to assist the instructional designers in specifying the knowledge content as well as the pedagogical, media

and delivery scenarios of a learning system to be developed (course, module, lesson, program, etc.) (Paquette, 2003). Nevertheless, after using this tool for our own benefit for some years, either as an instructional design tool (Basque, Doré, & Henri, 2000; Doré & Basque, 2002) and as a general modeling tool to assist our thinking on processes, methodologies or concepts in our research activities (Basque, 2004; Basque, Rocheleau, Paquette, & Paquin, 1998; Dufresne et al., 2003), we felt it might be useful as a learning strategy for students. Some evidence to support this hypothesis can be found in studies where there are some kinds of constraints based on typed links or on predefined "micro-structures" made up of combinations of typed links and nodes introduced in the task of building node-link diagrams (Fischer, Bruhn, Gräsel, & Mandl, 2002; Komis, Ergazaki, & Zogza, 2007; Reader & Hammond, 1994; Suthers, Toth, & Weiner, 1997).

The main question that we explored in our research is the following: How does knowledge modeling with a tool using a semi-formal representational language such as MOT may influence learning? As we will see, this question leads us to examine not only the *results* of the activity (i.e. the knowledge models produced by the learners and post-learning measures) but the knowledge modeling *process* and its mediating effect on learning.

16.2. KNOWLEDGE MODELING AS AN INDIVIDUAL LEARNING STRATEGY

Knowledge modeling with MOT in individual learning contexts has been the focus of two of our studies conducted with students in a distance course. Our aim was to enhance text comprehension. Multimedia-based and web-based learning environments flourished in recent years, but this does not mean that text is leaving the educational sphere. In fact, most existing web-based learning environments can still be characterized as essentially text-based. Moreover, they still are quite limited in terms of assistance provided to students (either by human or machine). They are also quite demanding for students in terms of autonomy and meta-cognition. Thus, many researchers in educational technology and distance education stress the need to provide distance learners with powerful cognitive tools aiming to support their knowledge construction process, text comprehension and reflection (Lin, Hmelo, Kinzer, & Secules, 1999; Ruelland & Brisebois, 2002).

In an initial stage, a first exploratory study has been conducted to pinpoint research issues on MOT as a knowledge construction tool in the context of web-based distance education (Basque & Pudelko, 2003). The second goal of this exploration was more pragmatic: feedback was needed from students to help us improve the pedagogical quality of the learning activity in our real-world educational setting at Télé-université. Another objective was to evaluate the adequacy of node-links diagrams as a diagnostis tool in order to identify the main difficulties students had with the course content.

Secondly, Pudelko (2006) conducted a study in which she examined with great scrutiny the tool-mediated thinking of three voluntary students while they were constructing knowledge models with MOT. We will report briefly each of these studies.

In the first study, we analyzed knowledge models produced by students in a graduate distance course delivered on the web, entitled "Cognitive Science and Learning". In one of the course activities, students were invited to construct individually what we call in the context of this course a "knowledge network", which must include at least fifteen key knowledge objects drawn from four texts that are part of course material. MOT was made available to them but it was not imposed, although most students chose this tool to perform this task. Even those that did not use MOT (some used a generic graphical tool or even the graphic functionalities of the Word software) employed the MOT typologies of nodes and links when building their knowledge network. They were also asked to write a short text explaining their network. This work was a graded assignment in this course. The time required to complete the activity, including reading, modeling and writing, was estimated to about 36 hours distributed over four weeks. A textual methodological guide was provided, which included a definition of "knowledge networks", together some examples and a procedure to construct them. Although this assignment was individually produced, peer-tutoring was encouraged: students were invited to ask and answer questions and to share their experience in an online forum all along the activity.

Data examined in this exploratory study (Basque & Pudelko, 2003) come from comments made spontaneously by students in the forum (N=34), a short questionnaire administered to one group (N=17), comments made by students in the last written course assignment requiring them to evaluate the course from a cognitivist perspective (N=18) and the knowledge models themselves (N=34). To obtain a whole picture of the main characteristics of the students' models, we count: (1) the number of typed and un-typed objects and links represented in the models, (2) the number of each category of typed objects and links and (3) the number of sub-models created. Each model was also examined to determine if the MOT syntax was used correctly and whether students simply reproduced the hierarchical structure of the instructional texts as shown by their subtitles or whether they constructed their own representation of key concepts. To refine these exploratory analyses, fourteen models were selected because they were all representing knowledge related to one of the topics covered in the instructional texts (that is, the classical view of the human information process, as described in cognitive science handbooks) and were examined more in depth with a method that we devised (Pudelko, Basque, & Legros, 2003). The method is inspired by the theoretical work of Baudet and Denhière (1991) who proposed a cognitive semantics approach called "analysis in systems" to the study of text comprehension.

Results show that most students expressed positive comments on the knowledge modeling activity and those who used MOT found it easy to learn, user-friendly and useful. There was many more knowledge units represented in their models than the number required (15). Up to 112 knowledge units was counted in a single model (mean: 42 units). From 14 to 102 links (with a mean of 42 links) were counted but the number of links varied greatly in the models. We noticed that they did not simply reproduce the structure of the instructional texts (as denoted by subtitles) and, instead, constructed what seem to be personal interpretations of the meaning of the interrelationships among their selection of key concepts. Many students also made positive comments on the impact of the knowledge modeling activity on their learning and text comprehension. However, it seemed to us that the full potential of MOT as a learning tool was far from being optimized. The MOT syntax appeared not to be so easily understood for all students. For example, a number of students confounded concepts and procedures and labelled some objects with whole sentences denoting their difficulty in isolating the knowledge objects from the links. Our analysis of the

14 models representing the human information processing system showed that students tend to represent this system essentially as a static one, with objects defined by their attributes and related to each other essentially by composition and specialization links, and that they neglected or were not capable of expressing many functional aspects of the human information processing system described in the instructional text.

Surely, the activity was promising but we thought that students probably need more training and practice in elaborating node-link diagrams and in familiarizing themselves with the MOT language and tool. In fact, this has been confirmed since by data collected by questionnaire and interviews with students and tutors (Gérin-Lajoie & Basque, 2006). One example of a training module to knowledge modeling with node-link diagrams for distance learners has been recently designed by one of our graduate students (Gérin-Lajoie, 2008).

We also thought that we needed to explore more in depth what was going on during the knowledge modeling process. In her doctoral thesis, Pudelko (2006), conducted a detailed analysis of the transformations of the external and internal activity structures induced by the use of the MOT tool in students who registered to this same course in a subsequent semester. She based her work on the notion of mediation of cognition by psychological tools as devised by Vygotsky (1978) in his socio-historical theory of cognition and on his Activity Theory, especially as interpreted by Leontiev (1978) and Rabardel (1995). Vygotsky stated that thinking is regulated by external activities, which are instrumented with cultural tools. In that perspective, Pudelko studied the instrumental contribution of the MOT tool in the process of text comprehension by observing the qualitative transformation of this process in one of the three subjects who participated in her study. This subject participated in three knowledge modeling sessions with MOT on a three-week period. In each session, the subject has to read a different short text and to elaborate a knowledge model representing the meaning of the text. Data consist in screen-captures of the student's activity and videotapes of retrospective verbal report interviews.

Results show that the typology of knowledge objects implemented in the software had a beneficial influence on the subject's text comprehension process. For example, the participant represented the term "cognition" initially as a "concept" in his model. It seems that because "cognition" is a noun, it inferred him to think naturally about this knowledge entity in terms of a "static thing". Then, he asked himself "Is cognition a concept or a process?". This self-questioning led him to change this entity into a "procedure" type, referring then not to "cognition" as a "static thing" but as a "process". Hence, the subject added a new property (it is a "dynamic thing") to his initial meaning of the word "cognition", resulting in a more elaborate conceptualization of this knowledge entity. This "dynamization" of substantive words could enhance comprehension of scientific texts, which make frequent use of substantives to refer to processes. Moreover, due to the semantic rules embedded in MOT which determine the type of links that can be drawn between the different types of knowledge entities, changing the type of a knowledge entity in a model leads the subject to make a new series of inferences about the relationships that this knowledge entity has with the other ones represented. For example, representing the knowledge entity "cognition" as a procedure led the subject to represent not only its sub-components (e.g. its sub-processes such as "perception", "encoding", etc.) but also how it is temporarily related (precedes or succeeds) to other procedures (e.g. "actions"), what are its inputs and outputs, etc. The micro-genetic study conducted by Pudelko (2006) brought to light this type of qualitative transformations inferred by the representational properties of the MOT tool into the reasoning chains of the subject.

The results of these studies lead us to think that the use of the MOT tool can be beneficial to text-based learning in scientific domains. Knowledge modeling with this tool would enhance a deep understanding of the meaning of text and consequently would favor significant learning (Ausubel, 1968; Fayol & Gaonac'h, 2003; Graesser, Leon, & Otero, 2002; Kintsch, 2004; Ramsden, 1992).

16.3. COLLABORATIVE KNOWLEDGE MODELING AS A LEARNING STRATEGY FOR DISTANCE EDUCATION

In the last two decades, the socio-constructivist paradigm has become increasingly predominant in the scientific literature in education. This paradigm, which places special emphasis on collaborative learning, is at the core of educational reforms, notably in Quebec, Canada.

The collaborative construction of node-link diagrams by small groups of students or whole classes is a learning activity that fits well with the socio-constructivist paradigm. Thus, a number of researchers began in the nineties to investigate collaborative construction of node-link diagrams (essentially concept maps) in educational contexts (Basque & Lavoie, 2006). With the increasing popularity of distance and online learning at all educational levels and contexts, the remote, computerized collaborative construction of concept maps has also sparked researchers' interest over the last few years.

Studies conducted with primary and high school students showed that such collaborative concept mapping triggers discussions and socio-cognitive conflicts (Doise & Mugny, 1984), which are beneficial to learning (Osmundson, Chung, Herl, & Klein, 1999; van Boxtel, van der Linden, & Kanselaar, 2000). Concept maps have been described as a "linguistic shorthand" of concepts which facilitate sharing of ideas (Kealy, 2001), as "discussion detonators" which help students construct knowledge jointly (Rojas-Drummond & Anzures, 2006), and as a "social glue" that brings learners to share a common conceptual space and to engage in a sustained discourse that replicate interactions in scientific communities, which include co-construction interactions, adversarial interactions and formation of alliances (Roth & Roychoudhury, 1993; Roth & Roychoudhury, 1992, 1994; Sizmur & Osborne, 1997).

Other studies conducted with university students also reveal that social interactions during collaborative concept mapping were quite cognitively engaging and productive (Immonen-Orpana & Åhlberg, 2008; Prezler, 2004; Ryve, 2004; Steketee, 2006). Moreover, some empirical evidence shows that students who constructed concept maps collaboratively outperformed students who constructed concept maps individually or who were engaged in other collaborative activities at post-test learning measures (Chiou, 2006; Czerniak & Haney, 1998; Prezler, 2004; Stoyanova & Kommers, 2002).

Some researchers found that the quality of maps produced at a distance with the use of communication tools (chat tool or audio or videoconferencing) do not differ significantly from maps created collaboratively in a face-to-face (Fischer & Mandl, 2001; Khamesan & Hammond, 2004). The latter authors concluded that "computer-based concept mapping can be used in collaborative learning with remote communication as effectively as with face-to-face communication, although more research is needed to clarify issues how performance is mediated by different CMC [Computer-Mediated Communication] modes" (p. 391).

We contributed to this line of research by investigating the effect of three modes of interaction during a collaborative knowledge modeling activity with MOT on the quality of the models produced and on individual learning. The three modes of interaction included two remote contexts (synchronous and asynchronous) and one face-to-

face context. Learning was measured with a text comprehension pre and post-test.

Forty-eight persons volunteered to participate to this study. They had been randomly distributed into three groups: synchronous distance group (N=16), asynchronous distance group (N=16) and face-to-face group (N=16). To facilitate data collection, we asked participants to come to the university and we simulated the distant conditions by using partitions to isolate each computer workstation and ensure that participants could not see one another. Six to eight subjects participated in each experimental session.

After a short text comprehension pre-test (six open-ended questions) and a 75-minute training period to the MOT software and technique, participants practiced knowledge modeling individually for 20 minutes. Then, they were paired arbitrarily and asked to perform the collaborative knowledge modeling task consisting at representing their understanding of the content of a one-page text on the main components of the Human Information Processing System (Sensory Memory, Short-Term Memory and Long-Term Memory) and the Cognitive Information Process. After having read the text individually for 5 minutes, pairs were allotted 45 minutes to construct their knowledge model using the MOT tool. They had access to a printed version of the text during the activity. At the beginning of the session, one member of each pair was arbitrarily identified as the "editor" of the map, yet participants were told that they could freely change roles during the session. Finally, participants filled out the post-test (identical to the pre-test).

Partners in the *synchronous group* communicated with each other via the NetMeeting software (see Figure 2). Participants in the *asynchronous group* used e-mail to send the co-constructed map to their partner. While waiting for the map from their partner (i.e. the user acting as the editor), participants were instructed to help their partner by sending him/her messages, to think of the next step, or to re-read the text. Pairs in the *face-to-face*

Figure 2. Screen capture of the MOT and NetMeeting windows for the synchronous case

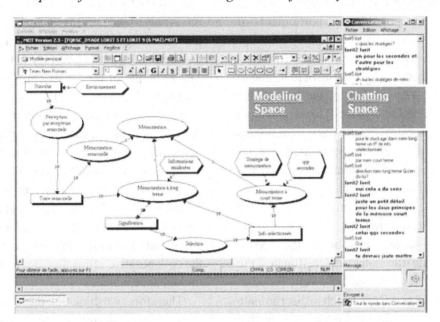

group worked side by side at one computer and used only the MOT software.

Participants' knowledge models were compared to an "expert knowledge model" that was created by a small group of content experts and of MOT experts. Two scores had been calculated. A *Knowledge Objects score* was calculated by summing up the total number of participant's knowledge objects that were also represented in the experts' model, and a *Propositions score* was calculated by adding the total number of experts' knowledge propositions represented in the participant's model; for each proposition, one point was attributed if the same two knowledge objects were paired (regardless of the type of link), one point for each correctly typed knowledge object included in the proposition, one point if the link was correctly typed, and one point for the correct link direction.

In summary, our study shows that the quality of the collaborative knowledge models was superior for pairs working face-to-face at the same computer than for those who communicated asynchronously at a distance, but only in terms of knowledge objects represented (and more

precisely in terms of specification of the type of the knowledge objects), not in terms of the propositions elaborated. No significant difference was found between the scores attributed to the models constructed by the synchronous group and by the face-to-face group, as well as between the scores attributed to the models produced by the asynchronous and the synchronous groups. We also found that groups did not differ on learning as measured by the text comprehension test, although we found a tendency for remote partners who communicated synchronously to have learned more than participants in the two other groups.

If we consider the shared workspace as a "mediating tool" in the activity in the face-to-face and the synchronous distance settings, then the fact that the quality of the knowledge models was not significantly different in these two conditions could mean that the shared visual display in the synchronous context was sufficient enough to establish the basic common ground for communication (Clark & Brennan, 1991) and to compensate for the lack of conversational gesture.

Regarding the significant difference between the scores attributed to the knowledge models constructed by the face-to-face and the asynchronous groups, it is possible that participants of all groups had enough time to identify a similar number of knowledge objects, but only those interacting in face-to-face had sufficient time to negotiate the *categorization* of the knowledge objects represented in the map. This would have been the case because face-to-face participants not only shared a common perceptual and action space but could also interact in a verbal and gestural mode.

Now, how can we explain the fact that we found no significant between-group difference on the Proposition score? It may be that the method used to evaluate the maps underestimates the participants' capacity to elaborate valid propositions and was not sensible enough to discriminate the groups on the quality of the propositions that they co-elaborated. For example, we observed that experts systematically specified (sometimes by inferring them) all the inputs and outputs of each procedure that they represented in their map, while many participants tended to use instead the Precedence link between procedures (and consequently did not represent the inputs and output of the procedures). These propositions were valid, although they were less complete and less informative than the ones represented in the experts' map. However, they were not considered valid in our coding scheme. This could explain, at least in part, the very low performance of subjects on the Proposition score. Besides, the method used to evaluate the concept maps does not tell us much about participants' misconceptions in the target domain, or about the adequacy of the global knowledge structure represented in their models.

Stoyanova & Kommers, 2002) demonstrated that sharing the concept mapping process (which, in our study, was the case in the face-to-face and synchronous contexts) is more beneficial to learning than sharing only the maps constructed individually (which, in our study, was the case of the asynchronous group). In our study, participants

who seemed to have learned the least (although this is only a tendency) are those who either shared the knowledge modeling process the most (face-to-face group), or the least (asynchronous group). The principle of the "least collaborative effort" (Clark & Brennan, 1991) could maybe explain in part these seemingly contradictory results. According to this principle, "in conversation, the participants try to minimize their collaborative effort – the work that both do from the initiation of each communicative contribution to its mutual acceptance" (p.135). We argue that this principle can be observed not only in conversation but also in collaborative *action*: participants try to minimize the collaborative effort they do from initiation to mutual acceptance.

Therefore, we think that the characteristics of the tools used during the activity influence the common grounding process. When constructing a knowledge model collaboratively with MOT, common grounding had to be established not only for the operations of selecting, labeling and linking knowledge objects, but also for the operation of specifying the type of knowledge objects reported in the model. Common grounding could have been equally established for the operations of selecting and labeling of knowledge objects in all three experimental contexts, but, as we already mentioned, partners working at the same computer would have had more time to negotiate about the type of knowledge objects. Consequently, it is possible that their attention has been focused more on the establishment of a common understanding of the MOT representational language than on discussing about the domain-related knowledge, which could explain their somewhat weaker post-test learning performance.

However, we did not conclude that the use of a representational language like MOT is not beneficial to learning and text comprehension. The duration of the task was probably insufficient and the complexity of the task probably too high for novice knowledge modelers to allow participants to take full advantage of the representational language.

16.4. COLLABORATIVE KNOWLEDGE MODELING IN FACE-TO-FACE LEARNING SITUATIONS

The work reported in this section is part of larger research project aimed at (1) developing a blended learning model for higher education inspired by socio-constructivist learning theories, (2) evaluating its incidence on students' persistence at university and academic persistence (Basque *et al.*, 2006). The learning model is developed at the curriculum level and embraces a whole-program approach. The pedagogical scenario of this model is inspired by the experiential learning theory proposed by Kolb (1984), who stated that knowledge is created through the transformation of experience in a four-stage cycle: *Concrete Experience, Reflective Observation, Abstract Conceptualization, Active Experimentation*. Various pedagogical strategies have been developed and associated to these stages: field-practice and mentoring (*Concrete Experience, Active Experimentation*), online learning community of practice (*Reflective Observation*), collaborative knowledge modeling and face-to-face seminars (*Abstract Conceptualization*). We will focus here on the collaborative knowledge modeling strategy.

The learning model has been developed in the context of a graduate program in the field of School Administration offered in a French-Canadian university and in partnership with a School Board (the largest one of the Montreal area). One part of the program was delivered on-site (at the School Board building) and another part at a distance (online community of learning). Although university rules prevent us to change the traditional course sequencing, we managed to integrate as much as possible the pedagogical strategies proposed in this program.

The learning model was tested with two groups of adult students. We will report here the experiment we conducted with the second group only. These students were eleven novice school administrators from the School Board, who had, by law, to complete graduate studies in this field and who had an average of 14 year-long previous teaching experience. At the beginning of the study program, each was assigned a mentor, who was an experienced school administrator in the School Board and whose role was to guide the student for the duration of the program.

Within the framework of this research, our goal, in designing the scenario of the specific strategy of collaborative knowledge modeling, was to support reflection-on-action within the context of professional training, as well as interactions between learners and more experienced working professionals in order to facilitate the externalization of organizational experts' knowledge in line with the learners' needs and knowledge level. The specific objective of this part of the research was to analyze the contribution of collaborative knowledge modeling to the reflective thinking on professional practice in students engaged in a university program.

The collaborative knowledge modeling activity was introduced in one of the course of the program. The specific topic selected by the instructor for the activity was: Budgeting in a School Board. The group of students was invited to collectively elaborate the knowledge model during three meetings of three hours each, at one month intervals. The instructor moderated the sessions and the researcher collaborated in manipulating the software and guiding the knowledge modeling process. The knowledge model was projected on a screen.

The whole process was conducted as follows:

- At the first class meeting, students were introduced to the knowledge modeling technique.
- At the second class meeting, a first high-level generic version of the model was built collectively, based on explanations related to the

topic provided the instructor.

- During the following month, in teams of two or three, students documented one of the knowledge object represented at the first-level of the knowledge model into a sub-model. To perform this task, students collected information from experienced administrators in the School Board.

- At the third class meeting, all the information collected by the different teams were shared, discussed and integrated in the collective knowledge model.

- The fourth meeting was one with the mentor. Each student validated the model with his mentor and questioned him on his "tricks of the trade", that is, his professional strategic knowledge. The student completed the knowledge model, based on the suggestions of the mentor.

- The last class meeting was held to discuss the collected information, to integrate it in the collective model as well as theoretical considerations presented by other instructors during the face-to-face seminars held throughout the program (animated by other instructors).

We interviewed the students and the instructor prior and after the program and collected reflexive texts produced by students, as well as the successive versions of the knowledge model produced collectively. Data also included minutes of an Advising Committee composed of representatives of students, mentors, instructors, researchers and School Board head administrators, that we put in place to help us guide the development and implementation of the study program. Finally, researcher took observation notes.

Data indicates that the students previously perceived the topic of budgeting process tedious and far from their concerns. They found that collaborative knowledge modeling activity was enriching for the following aspects:

- Training in the field: it enabled them to understand the "Why" and the "How" of the budgetary process, as well as its various stages, the interrelationships between actions and the interdependence of the main actors implied in this process;

- Attitude toward the field: students said they were "no longer afraid" of the budgetary process, and that they realized its strategic importance for school management, both for administrative and pedagogical purposes;

- Organizational learning: students said they discovered the richness of the organization's resources. They identified documents and people who could help them in adopting their current and future role in the field. They also recognized the diversity of tasks and responsibilities implied in the budgetary planning and managing processes;

- Socialization: the strategy enabled them to create a network of contacts and even experience friendship with expert colleagues and discover their professional and human qualities;

- Professional valorization: the activity enabled them "to make themselves better known" as members of the community of school administrators in the organization.

Students found collaborative knowledge modeling with MOT cognitively demanding but very productive. According to them, this activity led them to structure their knowledge and to verbalize their thought, and therefore to "think better". They also found that it helped them better identify knowledge areas which required own improvement, to consider different points of view, to work together toward a common understanding of the topic and to stimulate analysis and synthesis. Observations showed that all students contributed to the construction of the knowledge model: they questioned actively the instructor when they found that some knowledge entities or links were unclear and brought new ideas to add to the model.

During meetings with the mentors, the model seems to have helped the mentors to thoroughly describe their ways of doing things as well as the principles and attitudes guiding their practice. The final knowledge model contained 22 sub-maps distributed on three levels. It contained 42 concepts, 51 procedures and 95 principles. Strategic knowledge was thus well represented. The model was declared complete and relevant by students, who said that this type of representation would be an asset to support management practices in the School Board. Several students also expressed their intention to further use MOT for various projects in their schools.

At the end, it appears that the collaborative knowledge modeling strategy was a big success and proved to be one of the most appreciated components of the global pedagogical model for many participants of the study program. The managers of the School Board who participated in the Advising Committee particularly appreciated the community of practice created through exchanges between the trainees and the School Board personnel, which seems to lead to mutual recognition of professional expertise.

This research confirms results obtained in our previous work in the field of knowledge modeling for expertise transfer in organizations (Basque, Imbeault, Pudelko, & Léonard, 2004; Basque, Paquette, Pudelko, & Léonard, 2008). It seems that collaborative knowledge modeling with MOT has a great potential to support construction of professional knowledge also when implemented in a situated learning context, that is, in the context of a professional training program based on a partnership between university and workplace. Our research also shows the advantages of integrating techniques of graphical knowledge representation into teaching strategies, especially when these are designed collaboratively by all the actors of the training program. Future work invites for

further developing resources to support university teachers in implementing this type of innovative teaching strategies strategy.

CONCLUSION

From our work, we conclude that the representational properties of an object-typed knowledge modeling tool may have a substantial epistemic influence when used by learners in their learning process. Most of the time, it seems that they helped learners build knowledge which is valid from a scientific perspective. However, further research is needed to investigate the mediating and the resulting effects of using a constrained knowledge representation language like the one used in MOT (which includes typologies of knowledge objects and of links) on comprehension and learning.

It seems to us that it is necessary to analyze more in depth not only the *result* (knowledge models produced and learning results) but also the *process* of the individual and collaborative knowledge modeling activity. In the individual settings, we need to understand better how internal speech, considered, in a vygotskian perspective, as a "psychological tool of thought" (Carlson, 1997), is guided by representational properties of this tool and how it intermingles with action in this tool-mediated activity.

In the collaborative settings, we similarly need to examine in more depth how actions and communications contribute to interpretations jointly created by partners during a collaborative knowledge modeling activity with the tool. In a recent qualitative analysis of a dyad of adult participants involved in a face-to-face collaborative knowledge modeling activity with MOT, we found that co-learners are actively involved in intense meaning-making and meaning-negotiation processes (Basque & Pudelko, in press). In such a space of shared external representation, questions asked, arguments stated and rules inferred are strongly biased by the representational properties of the modeling software tool and language, as well as by the knowledge modeling technique proposed to learners. In this particular situation, where the knowledge representation tool integrates categorizing constraints for both nodes and links, as well as a grammar that determines valid links between different types of nodes, it is clear that the participants used such constraints to guide their meaning-making and meaning-negotiation actions.

We believe that this type of research contributes to shed some light on the issue of artifact-mediated activity in learning situations and, at the end, can lead us to propose recommendations to designers of cognitive tools and to teachers who propose those tools to their students to enhance learning.

ACKNOWLEDGMENT

We acknowledge Télé-université and the *Fonds Québécois de Recherche sur la Société et la Culture* for financial contribution to some of these studies.

REFERENCES

Alpert, S. (2004). Flexibility of Expressiveness: State of the Practice . In Kommers, P. (Ed.), *Cognitive Support for Learning: Imagining the Unknown* (pp. 253–268). Amsterdam: IOS Press.

Anderson-Inman, L., & Ditson, L. (1999). Computer-based concept mapping: A tool for negotiating meaning. *Learning and Leading with Technology, 26*(8).

Ausubel, D. (1968). *Educational Psychology: A Cognitive View*. New York: Rhinehart & Winston.

Basque, J. (2004). Le transfert d'apprentissage: Qu'en disent les contextualistes? In Frenay, M., & Presseau, A. (Eds.), *Le transfert des apprentissages: Comprendre pour mieux intervenir*. Québec: Presses de l'Université Laval.

Basque, J., Doré, S., & Henri, F. (2000). Facilitating a techno-pedagogical change in higher education: Lessons from the SAVOIR and AMETIST projects. In *Proceedings of the XVIIIth Conference of the International Council for Innovation in Higher Education, November 5-9, 2000, Quebec.*

Basque, J., Imbeault, C., Pudelko, B., & Léonard, M. (2004). Collaborative knowledge modeling between experts and novices: A strategy to support transfer of expertise in an organization. In A. J. Canas, J. D. Novak & F. M. Gonzalez (Eds.), *Proceedings of the First International Conference on Concept Mapping (CMC 2004), Pamplona, September 14-17* (Vol. 1, pp. 75-81). Pamplona, Spain: Universidad Publica de Navarra.

Basque, J., & Lavoie, M.-C. (2006). Collaborative Concept Mapping in Education: Major Research Trends. In A. J. Canas & J. D. Novak (Eds.), *Concept Maps: Theory, Methodology, Technology - Proceedings of the Second International Conference on Concept Mapping* (Vol. 1, pp. 79-86). San Jose, Costa Rica: Universidad de Costa Rica.

Basque, J., Nault, T., Saint-Pierre, M., Toussaint, P., Lajoie, J., Brunet, L., et al. (2006). Un modèle de formation universitaire intégrant le mentorat, la communauté de pratique et la modélisation des connaissances. In *Actes du XXIIIème Congrès de l'Association Internationale de Pédagogie Universitaire: Innovation, Formation et Recherche en Pédagogie Universitaire*, Monastir, Tunisie, 15-18 May 2006.

Basque, J., Paquette, G., Pudelko, B., & Léonard, M. (2008). Collaborative Knowledge Modeling with a Graphical Knowledge Representation Tool: A Strategy to Support the Transfer of Expertise in Organizations. In A. L. P. Okada, S. J. Buckingham Shum & T. Sherborne (Eds.), Knowledge Cartography. Software Tools and Mapping Techniques (pp. 357-382). London: Springer-Verlag.

Basque, J., & Pudelko, B. (2003). Using a concept mapping software as a knowledge construction tool in a graduate online course. In D. Lassner & C. McNaught (Eds.), *Proceedings of ED-MEDIA 2003, World Conference on Educational Multimedia, Hypermedia & Telecommunications,* Honolulu, June 23-28, 2003 (pp. 2268-2264). Norfolk, VA: AACE.

Basque, J., & Pudelko, B. (in press). Intersubjective Meaning-Making in Dyads Using Object-Typed Concept Mapping In P. L. Torres & R. C. V. Marriott (Eds.), Handbook of Research on Collaborative Learning Using Concept Mapping. Hershey, PA: IGI Global.

Basque, J., Rocheleau, J., Paquette, G., & Paquin, C. (1998). An Object-Oriented Model of a Computer-Enriched High School. In T. Ottmann & I. Tomek (Eds.), *Proceedings of ED-MEDIA/ED-TELECOM 98.* Charlottesville, VA: Association for the Advancement of Computing in Education.

Baudet, S., & Denhière, G. (1991). Mental models and acquisition of knowledge from text: Representation and acquisition of functional systems . In Denhière, G., & Rossi, J. P. (Eds.), *Text and text processing* (pp. 155–187). Amsterdam: North-Holland. doi:10.1016/S0166-4115(08)61552-6

Bruillard, E., & Baron, G.-L. (2000). *Computer-based concept mapping: A review of a cognitive tool for students.* Paper presented at the IFIP, Beijing, China.

Buzan, T., & Buzan, B. (1996). *The mind map book.* New York: Penguin Books.

Cañas, A., & Carvalho, M. (2004). Concept Maps and AI: an Unlikely Marriage? In *Proceedings of SBIE 2004 -Simpósio Brasileiro de Informática Educativa.* Manaus, Brasil: SBC.

Carlson, R. A. (1997). Expertise, skill, and everyday action . In *Experienced Cognition* (pp. 242–263). Mahwah, NJ: Lawrence Erlbaum Associates.

Chiou, C.-C. (2006). *Effects of concept mapping strategy on business and economics statistics learning performance.* Retrieved from http://ssrn.com/abstract=918200

Clark, H. H., & Brennan, S. E. (1991). Grounding in Communication excerpt . In Resnick, L. B., Levine, J. M., & Teasley, S. D. (Eds.), *Perspectives on socially shared cognition* (pp. 127–149). Washington, DC: American Psychological Association. doi:10.1037/10096-006

Coffey, J. W. (2007). A meta-cognitive tool for courseware development, maintenance. and reuse. *Computers & Education,* *48*(4), 548–566. doi:10.1016/j.compedu.2005.03.008

Czerniak, C. M., & Haney, J. J. (1998). The effect of collaborative concept mapping on elementary preservice teachers' anxiety, efficacy, and achievement in physical science. *Journal of Science Teacher Education,* *9*(4), 303–320. doi:10.1023/A:1009431400397

Doise, W., & Mugny, G. (1984). *The social development of the intellect.* Oxford, UK: Pergamon Press.

Doré, S., & Basque, J. (2002). *Why not apply an engineering methodology when creating courses?* Paper presented at the American Society for Engineering Education Annual Conference & Exposition (ASEE), Montréal, June 2002.

Duffy, T. M., & Cunningham, D. J. (1996). Constructivism: Implications for the design and delivery of instruction . In Jonassen, D. H. (Ed.), *Handbook of Research for Educational Communications and Technology* (pp. 170–198). New York: Macmillan Library Reference/AECT.

Dufresne, A., Basque, J., Paquette, G., Léonard, M., Lundgren-Cayrol, K., & Prom Tep, S. (2003). Vers un modèle générique d'assistance aux acteurs du téléapprentissage. *STICEF, Numéro spécial: Technologies et formation à distance,* *10*(3).

Engeström, Y., Miettinen, R., & Punamäki, R.-L. (1999). *Perspectives on Activity Theory*. Cambridge, UK: Cambridge University Press.

Fayol, M., & Gaonac'h, D. (2003). La compréhension, une approche de psychologie cognitive . In Gaonac'h, D., & Fayol, M. (Eds.), *Aider les élèves à comprendre: du texte au multimédia* (pp. 5–73). Paris: Hachette.

Fischer, F., Bruhn, J., Gräsel, C., & Mandl, H. (2002). Fostering collaborative knowledge construction with visualization tools. *Learning and Instruction, 12*(2), 213–232. doi:10.1016/S0959-4752(01)00005-6

Fischer, F., & Mandl, H. (2001). *Facilitating the construction of shared knowledge with graphical representation tools in face-to-face and computer-mediated scenarios*. Paper presented at the Euro CSCL, Maastricht.

Gérin-Lajoie, S. (2008). Conception et validation d'un module d'entraînement à la construction de cartes de connaissances, dédié à des étudiants à distance. Télé-université, Quebec.

Gérin-Lajoie, S., & Basque, J. (2006). Training Students at a Distance to Create Concept Maps. In A. J. Canas & J. D. Novak (Eds.), *Concept Maps: Theory, Methodology, Technology - Proceedings of the Second International Conference on Concept Mapping* (Vol. 2, pp. 254-257). San Jose, Costa Rica.

Grabowski, B. L. (1996). Generative learning: Past, present, and future . In Jonassen, D. H. (Ed.), *Handbook of research for educational communications and technology* (pp. 897–918). New York: Macmillan.

Graesser, A. C., Leon, J., & Otero, J. (2002). Introduction to the Psychology of Science Text Comprehension . In Otero, J., León, J. A., & Graesser, A. C. (Eds.), *The Psychology of Science Text Comprehension* (pp. 1–15). Marwah, NJ: Erlbaum.

Holley, C. D., & Dansereau, D. F. (1984). *Spatial Learning Strategies. Techniques, applications, and related issues*. New York: Academic Press.

Horton, P. B., McConney, A. A., Gallo, M., Woods, A. L., Senn, G. J., & Hamelin, D. (1993). An investigation of the effectiveness of concept mapping as an instructional tool. *Science Education, 77*(1), 95–111. doi:10.1002/sce.3730770107

Immonen-Orpana, P., & Åhlberg, M. (2008). Learning, pedagogical thinking and collaborative knowledge building by CMapTools. In A. J. Cañas, P. Reiska, M. Åhlberg & J. D. Novak (Eds.), *Concept Mapping: Connecting Educators - Proceedings of the Third International Conference on Concept Mapping* (Vol. 2, pp. 485-492). Tallinn, Estonia: Tallinn University.

Jonassen, D. H. (2000). *Computers as mindtools for schools: Engaging critical thinking* (2nd ed.). Upper Saddle River, NJ: Prentice Hall.

Kealy, W. A. (2001). Knowledge maps and their use in computer-based collaborative learning environments. *Journal of Educational Computing Research, 25*(4), 325–349. doi:10.2190/VM66-FFUK-KJPD-RYW1

Khamesan, A., & Hammond, N. (2004). Synchronous collaborative concept mapping via ICT: Learning effectiveness and personal and interpersonal awareness. In A. J. Canas, J. D. Novak & F. M. Gonzalez (Eds.), *Proceedings of the First International Conference on Concept Mapping, Pamplona, Spain, 2004*. Pamplona, Spain: Universidad Publica de Navarra.

Kharatmal, M., & Nagarjuna, G. (2006). A proposal to refine concept mapping for effective science learning. In A. J. Canas & J. D. Novak (Eds.), *Concept Maps: Theory, Methodology, Technology – Proceedings of the Second International Conference on Concept Mapping* (Vol. 1, pp. 151-158). San José, Costa Rica: Universidad

Kintsch, W. (2004). The construction-integration model of text comprehension and its implications . In Ruddell, R. B., & Unrau, N. J. (Eds.), *Theoretical models and processes of reading* (5th ed., pp. 1270–1328). Newark, DE: International Reading Association.

Komis, V., Ergazaki, M., & Zogza, V. (2007). Comparing computer-supported dynamic modeling and 'paper & pencil' concept mapping tehnique in students' collaborative activity. *Computers & Education*, *49*, 991–1017. doi:10.1016/j.compedu.2005.12.007

Kommers, P. A. M., Jonassen, D. H., & Mayes, J. T. (Eds.). (1992). *Cognitive tools for learning*. Berlin: Springer-Verlag.

Lajoie, S. P., & Derry, S. J. (1993). *Computers as cognitive tools*.

Leontiev, A. N. (1978). *Activity, Consciousness, and Personality*. Englewood Cliffs, NJ: Prentice-Hall.

Lin, S.-Y., Strickland, J., Ray, B., & Denner, P. (2004). Computer-based concept mapping as a prewriting strategy for Middle School Students. *Meridian: A Middle School Computer Technologies Journal, 7*(2).

Lin, X., Hmelo, C., Kinzer, C. K., & Secules, T. J. (1999). Designing technology to support reflection. *Educational Technology Research and Development*, *47*(3), 43–62. doi:10.1007/BF02299633

Nardi, B. A. (2001). *Context and Consciousness: Activity Theory and Human-Computer Interaction* (3rd ed.). Cambridge, MA: The MIT Press.

Nesbit, J. C., & Adesope, O. O. (2006). Learning with concept and knowledge maps: A meta-analysis. *Review of Educational Research*, *76*(3), 413–448. doi:10.3102/00346543076003413

Norman, D. A. (1991). Cognitive artefacts . In Carroll, J. M. (Ed.), *Designing interaction: Psychology at the human-computer interface* (pp. 17–38). Cambridge: Cambridge University Press.

Novak, J. D. (1998). *Learning, creating and using knowledge: Concept maps as facilitative tools in schools and corporations*. Mahwah, NJ: LEA.

Novak, J. D., & Gowin, D. B. (1984). *Learning how to learn*. Cambridge, UK: Cambridge University Press.

O'Donnell, A. M., Dansereau, D. F., & Hall, R. H. (2002). Knowledge maps as scaffolds for cognitive processing. *Educational Psychology Review*, *14*(1), 71–86. doi:10.1023/A:1013132527007

Osmundson, E., Chung, G. K., Herl, H. E., & Klein, D. C. (1999). *Knowledge mapping in the classroom: A tool for examining the development of students' conceptual understandings* (Technical report No. 507). Los Angeles: CRESST/ University of California.

Paquette, G. (2002). *Modélisation des connaissances et des compétences*. Sainte-Foy, Canada: Presses de l'Université du Québec.

Paquette, G. (2003). *Instructional Engineering in Networked Environments*. San Francisco: Pfeiffer/Wiley.

Paquette, G. (2007). Graphical ontology modeling language for learning environments. *Technology Instruction Cognition and Learning*, *5*, 133–168.

Prezler, R. (2004). Cooperative concept mapping: Improving performance in undergraduate biology. *Journal of College Science Teaching*, *33*(6), 30–35.

Pudelko, B. (2006). *Étude microgénétique des médiations épistémiques d'un outil informatisé de représentation graphique des connaissances au cours d'une activité de compréhension de texte: Propositions pour une approche instrumentale étendue des médiations des outils cognitifs dans l'apprentissage.* Published Doctoral Thesis, UFR Sciences Humaines et Sociales, Université Paris 8.

Pudelko, B., & Basque, J. (2005). Logiciels de construction de cartes de connaissances: des outils pour apprendre. In Dossiers pédagogiques. Montréal, Québec: Profetic, (CREPUQ) Conférence des recteurs et des principaux des universités du Québec.

Pudelko, B., Basque, J., & Legros, D. (2003 April). *Vers une méthode d'évaluation des cartes conceptuelles fondée sur l'analyse en systèmes.* Paper presented at the Environnements informatiques pour l'Apprentissage Humain: Actes de la conférence EIAH 2003, 15 - 17 April, Strasbourg.

Rabardel, P. (1995). *Les hommes et les technologies: Approche cognitive des instruments contemporains.* Paris: Armand Colin.

Ramsden, P. (1992). *Learning to teach in higher education.* London: Kogan Page. doi:10.4324/9780203413937

Reader, W. R., & Hammond, N. (1994). A comparison of structured and unstructured knowledge mapping tools in psychology teaching. In Proceedings of CiP '94, New York.

Rojas-Drummond, S., & Anzures, A. (2006). Oracy, Literacy and Concept Maps as Mediators of the Social Construction of Knowledge Among Peers. In A. J. Canas & J. D. Novak (Eds.), *Concept Maps: Theory, Methodology, Technology. Proceedings of the Second International Conference on Concept Mapping* (Vol. 2, pp. 196-199). San José, Costa Rica: Universidad de Costa Rica.

Roth, W., & Roychoudhury, A. (1993). The concept map as a tool for the collaborative construction of knowledge: A microanalysis of high school physics students. *Journal of Research in Science Teaching, 305,* 503–554. doi:10.1002/tea.3660300508

Roth, W.-M., & Roychoudhury, A. (1992). The social construction of scientific concepts or the concept map as conscription device and tool for social thinking in high school science. *Science Education, 76*(5), 531–557. doi:10.1002/sce.3730760507

Roth, W.-M., & Roychoudhury, A. (1994). Science discourse through collaborative concept mapping: new perspectives for the teacher. *International Journal of Science Education, 16*(4), 437–455. doi:10.1080/0950069940160405

Ruelland, D., & Brisebois, A. (2002). *An electronic performance support system for the eLearner.* Paper presented at the E-Learn, Montreal.

Ryve, A. (2004). Can collaborative concept mapping create mathematically productive discourses? *Educational Studies in Mathematics, 56*(2-3), 157–177. doi:10.1023/B:EDUC.0000040395.17555.c2

Sizmur, S., & Osborne, J. (1997). Learning processes and collaborative concept mapping. *International Journal of Science Education, 19*(10), 1117–1135. doi:10.1080/0950069970191002

Steketee, C. (2006). Modelling ICT integration in teacher education courses using distributed cognition as a framework. *Australasian Journal of Educational Technology, 22*(1), 126–144.

Stoyanova, N., & Kommers, P. (2002). Concept mapping as a medium of shared cognition in computer-supported collaborative problem solving. *Journal of Interactive Learning Research, 13*(1/2), 111–133.

Suthers, D. (2006). Technology affordances for intersubjective meaning making: A research agenda for CSCL. *Computer-Supported Collaborative Learning, 1,* 315–337. doi:10.1007/s11412-006-9660-y

Suthers, D. D. (2003). Representational guidance for collaborative inquiry. In Andriessen, J., Baker, M., & Suthers, D. (Eds.), *Arguing to Learn* (pp. 27–46). London: Kluwer.

Suthers, D. D., Toth, E. E., & Weiner, A. (1997, October 14). *An integrated approach to implementing collaborative inquiry in the classroom.* Paper presented at the Computer support fo collaborative learning, Toronto.

van Boxtel, C., van der Linden, J., & Kanselaar, G. (2000). Collaborative learning tasks and the elaboration of conceptual knowledge. *Learning and Instruction, 10,* 311–330. doi:10.1016/S0959-4752(00)00002-5

Vygotsky, L. S. (1978). *Mind in society: The development of higher psychological process.* Cambridge: Harvard University Press.

Chapter 17
Modeling for Instructional Engineering

Richard Hotte
LICEF Research Center, Canada

Karin Lundgren-Cayrol
LICEF Research Center, Canada

Diane Ruelland
LICEF Research Center, Canada

Gilbert Paquette
LICEF Research Center, Canada

ABSTRACT

- Building a Competency Profile to for a Professional Training Program
  - Building a Competency Profile
  - Instructional Modeling: The Learning Scenarios
  - Media and Delivery Models
- Delivery Models for a Virtual Campus
  - Building Delivery Models
  - Types of Delivery Models
- A Tutoring Scenario for Web-Based Courses
  - Online Tutor's Needs
  - Tutoring Scenario Based on Competency Improvement
  - Tools for Web-based tutoring
- A Design Process Model for Competency-Based Learning
  - Action Research Model
  - Competency-Based Instructional Engineering Model

Instructional Engineering has been presented in chapter 8 and in (Paquette 2004) as a method integrating principles and processes from Instructional Design, Software Engineering and Knowledge Engineering. As such, Visual Knowledge Modelling is at the heart of the instructional engineering where it serves to represent the knowledge, the learning scenarios, the structure of educational material and the delivery processes that support learning. But as we will see in this chapter, Visual

DOI: 10.4018/978-1-61520-839-5.ch017

Modelling can also be used to model the very processes of the learning design activity.

In this chapter, we will present four applications developed with the MOT modelling technique, using or extending the MISA Instructional Engineering method. The first one is an extensive application of the MISA method in order to specify a complete professional training program at the Quebec Bar School, based on a competency profile built through visual knowledge modelling. The second one applies visual modelling to represent a variety of delivery models for virtual campuses, from technology-based classroom and blended learning models, to completely on-line learning models and workplace performance support systems, each model describing the actors, their tasks and the resources they use and produce. The third application focuses on the very important tutoring tasks, proposing a process model to thoroughly support on-line tutors, a central aspect of any delivery model. The last one, focusing on the designers' tasks, is an adaptation of the MISA method itself through an action research process conducted at the Canada School of Public Service. It integrated competency modelling with learning resource management tasks, and their seamless integration into a community of practice environment already used by that organization.

17.1 BUILDING A COMPETENCY PROFILE FOR A PROFESSIONAL TRAINING PROGRAM[1]

This section illustrates the visual modeling approach embedded in the MISA instructional engineering method presented in chapter 8, applied to the elaboration of a professional training program. The LICEF team was contracted by Tecsult-Eduplus, a Montreal-based company, to plan a reconstruction of the complete one-year professional training program for the Quebec Bar School. This one-year program trains law graduates in professional practice in order to be received as lawyers in the Province of Quebec.

The project spanned over a year and a half. Working meetings of our team members with an Expert Committee, composed of 12 experienced lawyers, allowed us to build a relevant knowledge model for the domain of law practice. This model served to identify associated cognitive and socio-affective skills, as well as the performance conditions required of novice lawyers at the start of their professional practice. A set of competencies was elaborated and its content was distributed over a number of courses to set their objectives and select the required knowledge and resources. Later on, a media and delivery model have been built in the form of an on-line training prototype.

This project is certainly the most complete application of the MISA instructional engineering methodology and the MOT knowledge modeling up until now. The process described herein can be applied to other professional training domains where high-level knowledge and competencies are at stake.

Modeling Knowledge

The following paragraphs describe how the knowledge model and the competency profile were created in order to guide the pedagogical development of the program.

Information about the knowledge domain was gathered during group sessions with the Expert Committee and face-to-face sessions with some of its members. All members filed questionnaires in. The consultation of different content documents used in the program served to enrich this information. In working meetings, the teams identified a set of relevant knowledge and, in further steps, the specific cognitive and socio-emotional skills associated with the main knowledge. Moreover, the conditions of performance under which skills should be targeted were also defined.

Systematically, the analysis of obtained data led to a document synthesizing a competency profile that was validated by the Expert Committee. The validation process brought new elements to advance the work and complete the knowledge and competency models. The iterative revision of the different versions of the competency profile led to a list of thirty-five main knowledge elements with their associated target competencies.

Figure 1 illustrates the iterative process that has guided both the design team and the expert committee. This process involves several validation steps under the responsibility of the expert Committee after steps 2, 3 and 4. It is important to note that this is not a linear process, but an iterative one: steps 2, 3 and 4 were repeated for each knowledge area identified by the Committee.

Very soon the discussions focused on the description of the main process and the competencies that a new lawyer has to master early in its professional practice. This is exactly what seemed to be left out by university programs in law faculties, but on the contrary, seemed very pertinent for a one-year professional training program. Making this link explicit between a university degree in law and professional practice was at the heart of the model.

Figure 2 shows the main knowledge model that resulted from these activities. It is a professional process termed "Accomplish professional acts", which is triggered by a service demanded by a client to a lawyer. This process starts by a client-lawyer communication process where interview notes are taken by the lawyer on needs and problems that are identified, resulting in a clarified service demand, which becomes the main input to the second process where a diagnosis is established, guided by the applicable laws and regulations. Afterward, this diagnosis is the input to the third sub-process where the practitioner makes an inventory of possible solutions, selects one with the client, resulting in a written intervention mandate, or abandons the case. In the last sub-process, a client file is opened in order to manage and document the solution that has been selected. The information in this file is governed by the deontological ethic principles that every lawyer must respect.

Throughout the process, basic information on law and jurisprudence is consulted. This is the knowledge that is generally taught in university law curricula and readily available to the learners and teachers at the Quebec Bar School.

Figure 2 illustrates only the main model. It was further developed through nested sub-models on several levels to provide an elaborated view of the conceptual, procedural and strategic knowledge involved in the program. For example the "Sub-

Figure 1. Iterative process of developing knowledge and skills

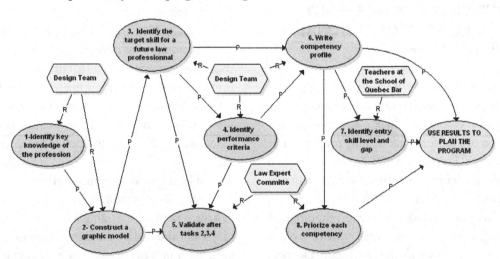

Figure 2. The main professional process knowledge model

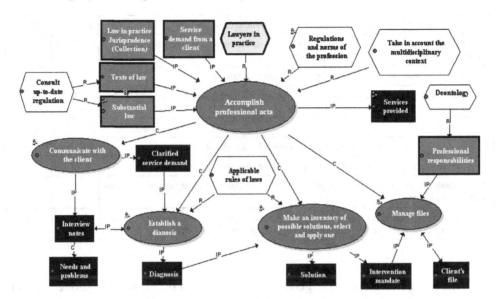

stantial law" input is decomposed into conceptual knowledge models in areas like civil law, public and administrative law, business law, criminal law, ethics, deontology and professional practice, all referring to documents provided by the school.

"Regulations and norms of the profession" groups principles that rule the main process and its sub-processes. Each of these four sub-processes is also developed into nested procedural sub-models like the one in Figure 3.

Figure 3. The "Establish a diagnosis" sub-process

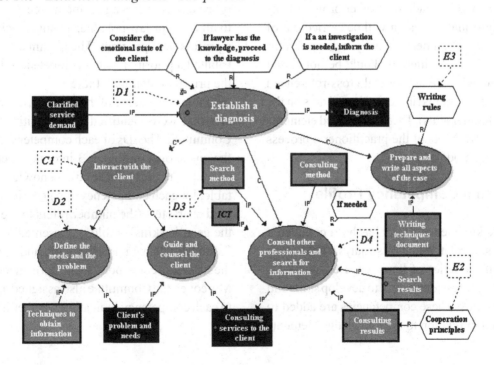

Table 1. Partial table of competencies for the professional training program

Id	Group A: Law concept, regulations and standards of the profession	Priority	Entry	Gap
A1	**(6) Analyze** the *applicable texts of law* to a situation, without help for simple and average complexity situations, with help in complex ones	1	(2)	4
A3	**(3) Specify** the *applicable law regulation*, autonomously in any case	2	(1)	2
A8	**(5) Apply** pertinent *proofs and procedures*, without help for simple and average complexity situations.	1	(2)	3

Id	Group B: Communication with the client	Priority	Entry	Gap
B1	**(6) Analyze** interactions with the client, without help in any communication situation.	2	(2)	4
B2	**(9) Evaluate** the quality of one's capacity to listen to the client, without help in any communication situation	2	(1)	8
B4	**(4) Transpose** in one's social and affectives interactions with the client, principles of communication and human behavior, without help for average complexity situations.	2	(1)	3

Figure 3 shows, amongst others, general principles to be considered for "Establishing a diagnosis." For example, during this process, in addition to the *Service Demand* that has been clarified in the preceding process, the practitioner must always *Consider the emotional state of the client. Establishing a diagnosis* involves three (3) main sub processes. First, one or more interactions with the client are needed in order to define its needs and problems. Second, if necessary, consultations will be made with other professionals and an information search will be carried out of pertinent law documents. Finally, a diagnosis for the case will be written. It should be noted that in this model there are several cross-referenced knowledge elements (indicated by red dots on the knowledge elements). These referenced elements point to other parts of the practitioner's process knowledge model.

Building a Competency Profile

Once the knowledge model has been completed through several iterations, its analysis has helped to identify a series of knowledge elements for which the professionals have to develop skills and competencies. These competencies are added to the model in relation to the knowledge elements

as shown on Figure 3 by dotted rectangles with a label.

Competencies were grouped into five domains based on the knowledge model: A- Law concepts, regulations and standards of the profession; B- Communication with the client; C-Establishment of a diagnosis; D- Elaboration, assessment and application of a solution; and E- Management of case data and quality control. The four last categories show that the knowledge model was mainly procedural, describing the main process common to all areas of law practice, a sound decision for a professional program. The Committee then attributed a priority to each competency shown in the priority column of Table 1.

Table 1 lists some of the thirty-five competencies that were identified and prioritized by the Committee. The IDs of each competency, such as the one shown on Figure 3 in dotted rectangles, are linked to the corresponding knowledge In the table, for each competency, the generic skill is in bold characters (the number refers to the rank in the generic skills' ontology presented in chapter 7, the knowledge part is in italic and the rest of the statement corresponds to performance criteria. Moreover, the Committee also assigned a priority to each competency indicating whether it was 1 =

essential, 2 = important and 3 = very important. This is shown in the third column of Table 1.

To plan the new program, it was important to identify, for every competency, the gap between the entry competency level that the students were required to possess when starting the program, and the target competency level to be acquired at the end of the program. The target level of the generic skill (in parenthesis before the statement) was identified by the expert committee and entry levels were set in a second phase by trainers in the program, shown in the fourth column. The gap between these levels is shown in the last column of Table 1. The gap is an indicator of the effort and time that must be allocated in the future program to attain the competency.

Instructional Modeling: The Learning Scenarios

The estimated competency gap helped define the structure of the new program. From the knowledge model and the information in the competency table, the design team suggested a strategy of gradual and consistent competency learning bundled in thematic blocks or courses.

The gap between the entry and target competency levels proved to be very important for the construction of the program. There were 9 competencies with a gap from 1 to 3, 18 with a gap of 4 or 5; 5 with a gap 6 or 7; and 5 with a gap of 8.

The competencies were distributed into four sequential courses according to their gap. For example, the B2, E4 to E7 competencies (with a gap of 8) were integrated in all four courses to progressively increase the generic skill and performance levels set as objectives to the learners. Competencies A1 and others were distributed into the first two courses because they were supposed to be acquired in previous university courses and thus, were easier (smaller gap) to acquire by the students in the program. Competencies A3 and others were included only in the first learning unit which seems to be sufficient for their acquisition. The target competencies served as learning objectives to be measured by exams and other means of evaluation.

To elaborate further the instructional model, the following main steps were followed. We have first structured the main learning events (LE) in such a way as to identify the links and resources required to perform them as well as the rules governing the progression from one to the other. This was based on the distribution of the competencies to be developed during each block or course. This distribution is presented on Figure 5, in a consistent way with Figure 4. Two integrative exams and a practice stage were added to the four courses.

The originality of this approach is the distribution of competencies in a spiral manner. Competencies such as B1-B4 are the focus of the

Figure 4. Distribution of competencies into courses in the program

Gap	Competencies	Course 1	Course 2	Course 3	Course 4
1-3	A3, A4, A5, A6, A7, A8, B4, C2, C6	x			
4-5	A1, A2, A9, A10, B1, B3, C1, C3, C5, D2, D5, D6, E1, E2, E3, E8	x	x		
6-7	C4, D1, D3, D4, E9	x	x	x	
8	B2, E4, E5, E6, E7	x	x	x	x

Figure 5. Competency distribution into the course structure

Welcome module
Entry exam (to determine if preparatory modules are needed)

	A1 to A3 Regulations and norms	A4 to A9 Substantial law theory	B Communicate	C Establish a diagnosis	D Elaborate a solution	E Management and quality
Course 1 - 5 weeks Description of a client's problem	$A1_4$ $A2_4$ $A3_2$ $A10_1$	$A9_3$ $A4_3$ $A5_3$ $A6_3$	$B1_6$ $B2_9$ $B3_5$ $B4_4$	$C1_3, C2_3$ $C3_3, C4_3$ $C5_5, C6_4$		$E1_1, E2_1$ $E3_1, E4_1$ $E5_1, E6_1$ $E7_1, E8_1$ $E9_1$
Course 2 - 5 weeks Intervention mandate	$A10_2$ $A1_6$ $A2_5$ $A3_3$	$A9_5$ $A4_5$ $A5_5$ $A6_5$	B1 B2 B3 B4	$C1_5, C2_4$ $C3_5, C4_8$ $C5_5 C6_5$	$D1_5$ $D4_4$ $D2_4$ $D6_2$ $D3_8$	$E1_2, E3_2$ $E4_5, E5_8$ $E6_5, E7_5$ $E8_2, E9_3$ $E2_5$
Exam I	*All attained competencies in Block 1 and 2 (middle gray)*					
Course 3, 5 weeks Solution elaboration	$A10_4$ A1 A2 A3	$A7_5$ $A7_5$ $A7_5$ $A8_5$ $A8_5$ A9 A4 A5 A6	B1 B2 B3 B4	C1,C2 C3,C4 C5,C6	$D5_4, D6_4$ $D1_8, D2_6$ $D4_3$ D3,	$E1_4, E3_4$ $E4_3, E5_3$ $E6_3, E7_3$ $E8_4, E9_5$ E2
Course 4, 5 weeks Management and quality control	$A10_5$ A1 A2 A3	A7 A7 A7 A8 A9 A4 A5 A6	B1 B2 B3 B4	C1 C2 C3 C4 C5 C6	$D5_5$ $D6_5$ D1 D2 D3 D4	$E1_5, E3_5$ $E4_9, E5_9$ $E6_9, E7_9$ $E8_5, E9_7$ E2
Exam II, 2 weeks	*All attained competencies in all 4 blocks*					
Stage, 24 weeks	*All attained competencies in all 4 blocks*					

LEGEND: *Light gray: competences being development;*   *Middle gray: competences attained (index = skill level)*
Dark gray: competencies reused after attainment;   *Encircled: Main focus of a block*

first course and they are to be attained (middle gray) at the end of only one course, considering that they have a low competency gap. After that, they are however included in the other courses to maintain competency acquisition (dark gray).

In a similar way, all group C competencies form the basis of the second course, while part of the competencies in the two A groups are also targeted. The rest of group A competencies will be attained in the third course, except A10, skill level 5 who will be attained at the end of the program. In this way, competencies needing more training occasions (higher gap value) are allocated more time. Finally, part of group D competencies form the basis of course 3 while group E is the main basis of course 4.

The following phases of the project were to build, based on the generic skills in the associated competencies, a learning scenario for each course, and within them, for each learning unit. In MISA, the instructional model includes the learner and the teacher activities, the resources needed to carry out each activity as well as the productions resulting.

Figure 6 shows a learning event model (or scenario) for the first course entitled "Problem Description", decomposed into 5 modules or learning units. For each of these modules, the properties: target populations, duration, evaluation weighting, use of collaborative activities, type of learning scenario and mode of delivery are described in a table format, as recommended by the MISA method.

Figure 6. A model for course 1, "problem description"

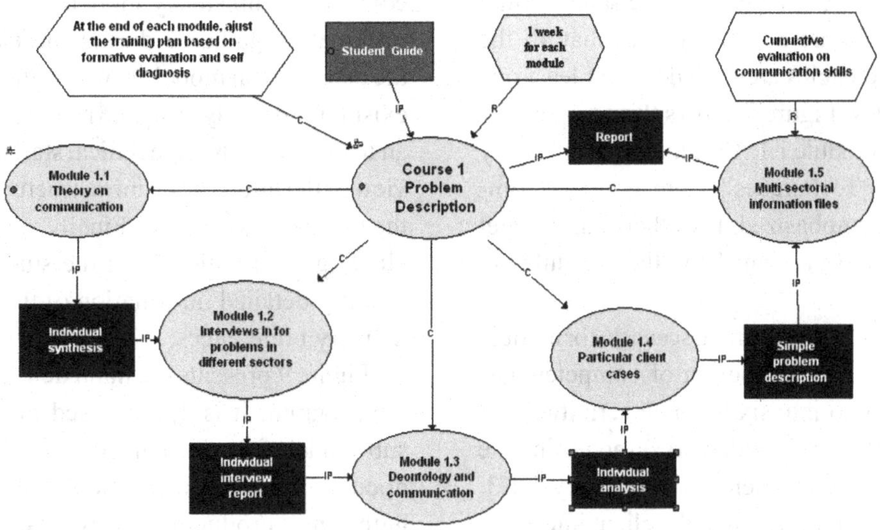

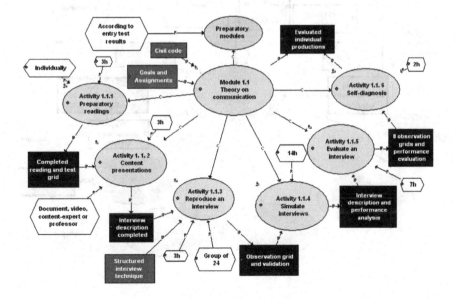

Figure 7. Competency attribution to a course module

	A Regulations and norms	A4 à A9 Substantial law	B Communicate	C Diagnosis	D Elaborate a solution	E Case management and quality
Bloc 1 (5 weeks) Description of a client's problem ==== *Description du problème client*	A1₄ A2₄ A3₂ A10₃	A9₃ A4₃ A5₃ A6₃	B1₆ B2₅ B3₅ B4₄	C1₃, C2₃ C3₃, C4₃ C5₅, C6₄	D1₂ D3₂ D6₂	E1₁, E2₁ E3₁, E4₁ E5₁, E6₁ E7₁, E8₁, E9₁
Module 1.1 (32h) Theory on communication	A1₂ Quebec Law A2₂ Jurisprudence A3₃ Law practice regulations A10₁ Professions' code	A4₂ Civil code	B1₆ Interactions B2₅ Self evaluation B3₅ Client information **B4₄** Interview technique			

Figure 8. The module on the subjects of "communication theory and interview techniques"

351

A finer grain distribution of the competencies is also made for each course in the same format as shown in Figure 5. This ensures that all the course competencies are included in at least one of the modules. Figure 7 shows the competency attribution to module 1.1 "Communication Theory and Interview Techniques". Here, note that competency B4 is emphasized. The other course target competencies are assigned to other modules in this course.

Figure 8 shows the learning scenario for module 1.1 based on this distribution of competencies. It is decomposed into six learning activities that ensure that the learners will work on acquiring the module's target competencies. In activity 1.1.3, 1.1.4 and 1.1.5, it is clear that the client interview technique is the major focus.

Media and Delivery Models

Delivery Models are built in interaction with the development of the media Web-based models.

These two models are both based on the Knowledge and Competency model, but also draw on information gathered during the elaboration of the pedagogical model as well as the inventory of existing and newly designed resources. Moreover, an interview with the technical staff gave an overview of the information infrastructure available at the Quebec Bar School. Finally, a questionnaire eliciting information from the students resulted in fairly detailed information of their media and delivery preferences.

Figure 9 presents the main delivery model for the program. It is decomposed into five nested sub-models for self-management of the program, documentation consultation and information gathering, production activities, presentation and communication activities, and finally, exam organization and evaluation resources.

The model displays all the actors that will participate in some or all of these delivery activities, providing precisely defined services to other

Figure 9. Main delivery model

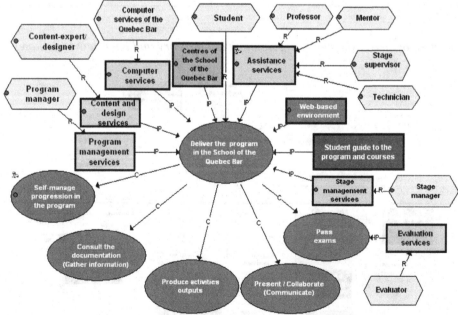

actors in the program. The model identifies the following actors:

- Student
- Professor
- Mentor
- Practical training supervisor
- Practical training manager
- Program manager
- Content-expert/ designer
- Computer professional
- Technician
- Evaluator

The model also shows that the students will carry out the program with the support of a Web-based environment but also carried out in one of the regional centers of the School. In the stage management services, law cabinets, and public services that accept students for an internship will be identified. Typically, the model is a blended learning program where the Web-based environment is used mostly in classrooms and between class meetings.

The four models described in this project correspond to the four axes in the MISA method Presented in chapter 8. They guide a comprehensive and high quality approach to learning system engineering. These visual models served as a mean of communication between the LICEF team and the Expert Committee.

Their main benefit is to help select efficiently a set of pertinent competencies, justify and allocate appropriate time for each competency attainment in the program's pedagogical model, an finally specify adequate resources for each actor involved in the learning environment.

17.2 DELIVERY MODELS FOR VIRTUAL CAMPUSES

In this section, we present a number of typical delivery models such as the one on Figure 9. Along

with the learning and teaching strategy selected, delivery modeling and planning is certainly the most determining factor of the success or failure of a learning system using information and communication technologies. One could argue that delivery is the most important modeling area for educational technologists because it describes the real time use of the learning system, instead of the initial somewhat theoretical view of that system by a subject matter expert or an instructionnal designer. The delivery model is the sole provider of a global and synthetic representation of a learning system needed to manage complex operations involving individuals, resources, information and concepts amalgamated for learning purposes.

Technology-based learning environments involve, not only the materials defined in a media model, but also the information processing tools, the communication means and the services provides by various providers. Some interesting online courses fail regularly due to the mediocre quality of the presentation tools or the orator's poor presentation or communicative skills. Moreover, when learners are in a remote location, the presenter cannot afford this type of deficiencies and methodological help and technical support must be provided.

This situation is even more critical in more advanced models of distributed learning, such as hypermedia self-paced learning, online learning, communities of practice or electronic performance support systems (EPSS). In these cases, disfunctional resources can amplify difficulties and create a « technological noise » that prevents learning and teaching. This technological noise can be measured by the time spent resolving technical problems, the inability to get help when it is needed, the lost of productivity due to a number of tools that are not compatible, etc. Organisational noise also results from poor coordination between the staff that supports as some people lack knowledge and tools regarding their tasks in a given learning event. Finally, a "comprehension noise phenomena" emerges when the environment does not provide observation and feedback facilities on the spot.

We can model delivery situations at different levels:

1. The delivery type of the system: Distributed Classroom, Self-Training on the Web, Online Training, Learning Community of Practice, Performance Support System.
2. The functions within the learning system: competency management, learning assessment, material, resource and collaboration management, etc.
3. The operations performed by certain actors in the context of one or more of these functions, relating the operations to the materials and resources used or produced for other actors.

This section will present a delivery model technique which aims to help solve the aformentioned problems, plus five delivery global delivery models corresponding to the global level of delivery situations. The interested reader can find a discussion of the other elements in (Paquette and Rosca 2003)

Building Delivery Models

According to the MISA method (Paquette 2003), delivery modeling groups three sets of tasks:

1. Stating the orientation principles of the delivery of the learning system;
2. Creating one or more delivery models that emphasize the relatioships between the actors and the resources: material, tools, means of communication, delivery services and locations;
3. Defining a quality control mecanism to be implemented at the creation of the learning system and subsequently upgraded through a learning assessment process and periodical reviews of the content, the materials and the learning environments.

Figure 10 presents an example of a delivery model that has helped plan a Web-based environment for an artificial intelligence course delivered by *Télé-université*. This model highlights the interaction between six types of actors represented as MOT principles and labeled A on the graph: learners, instructors (also called tutors), designers, managers, network administrator, and shipping

Figure 10. An example of delivery model at Télé-Université

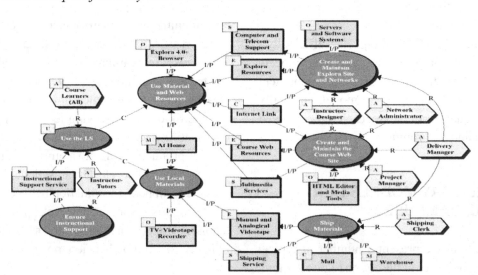

clerks. These actors perform various operations or tasks represented as MOT procedures, using the distributed learning system (DLS) that includes Web content and printed material, ensuring instrucaional support, creating and maintaining the Explor@ LCMS website and the networks, and publishing and updating the course website mailing material.

This model integrates five kinds of ressources, represented as MOT concepts I/P linked to operations in the delivery process:

1. Three sets of material grouped in environments (E): the course website, the Explor@ website (Paquette et al 2000) that manages the actors' environment and the non-computerized ressources such as books and videotapes;
2. Two means of communication (C): the Internet and the regular mail;
3. Many tools (O): IA software, web browser, TV sets and VCR to view videotapes at home, an HTML editor and other media authoring tools to update the website, as well as servers and software to create and maintain the Explor@ environment and the network components.
4. Services (S) offered to the students, such as Instructional support services by Instructor-tutors, Computer and Telecom support,

5. Locations (M) where activity takes place: the participants' home where all learning activities are undertaken and a warehouse from where the non-digitized course material are shipped.

This example concretizes the concept of a Delivery Model. It is a process graph that reveals the interactions between various actors, their functions and the ressources they use or produce. The construction of a Delivery model such as this one can be achieved in the following way.

*   Step 1. First, we must decide if a single or many Delivery Models are required. Then, we specify the purpose of the model(s). There can be various ways to deliver the LS, many types of global physiology, as they have been stated previously in the delivery orientation principles: totally distance learning delivery, self-learning delivery, class-website hybrid delivery, and so on.
*   Step II. Once the purpose of the model is established, each actor and his/her main operations and corresponding R-links are included in the graph. For example, are there many types of learners present in a class or in a remote location? Are they equipped with efficient means of communication? We also create one or many op-

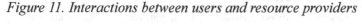

Figure 11. Interactions between users and resource providers

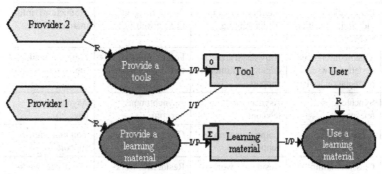

erations done by each type of learners or other actors and we identify the resources needed and produced by each operation.

- <u>Step III.</u> Then, for each of these actors' operations, we identify and link the required material and resources and we relate them using I/P links to each operation already on the graph.

- <u>Step IV.</u> For each resource already on the graph, we identify which actor can provide that resource if not already represented and we represent this new provider on the graph by a hexagon, link the actor to an operation by a R-link, and link that operation to the resource it produces.

- <u>Step V.</u> We then determine the resources these primary providers need and add to the graph the secondary providers who provide these resources to them. In Figure 11, Provider 1 uses a tool provided by Provider 2 to supply the material to the user.

- <u>Step VI.</u> A main delivery model such as the one displayed in Figure 10, can comprise

sub-models. We can create sub-models using a selection filter to display the resources used or produced by a single actor, or to display the multi-actor activities around a subset of the operations involved in the model. This will help plan the various views of the user interface.

Types of Delivery Models

Table 2 introduces the main components of five categories of delivery models. Following that table, a schematic delivery model is displayed for some of the categories. Such a basic collection of delivery models can be used as a starting point, and adapted to the needs, objectives, contexts and constraints of any new learning system. This concept of a library of delivery models can provide adaptable and combinable functionalities to construct an expertise for the engineering, use and analysis of distributed learning systems.

Figure 12 presents a *distributed classroom* model. In this model, five groups of learners occupy five distinct classrooms and the instructor is situated in a sixth room. A technician ensures

Table 2. Categories of delivery models

Main Components	Types of Delivery Models				
	Distributed Classroom	**Self-Training on the Web**	**Online Training**	**Communities of practice**	**Performance Support System**
Learners' Actions	Receive input, ask questions, complete exercises	Autonomous learning, accesses information	Asks questions, cooperation, tele-discussions	Cooperation, tele-discussions, information exchange	Exercises, case studies, simulations
Facilitators	Presenter	Training manager	Trainer, presenter	Group animator	Support manager
Main type of Material	Presentations, videos, information websites	Internet and multi-media training	Productions, informative websites	Productions, informative websites	Activity guide, contextualised help files
Model-Specific Tools	Video-conferencing system, browser, presentation tools	Browser, search engine, multimedia support	Forum, e-mail, multimedia documents	Forum, e-mail, multimedia documents	Computer systems and organizations' data bases
Means of Communication	Synchronous telecom	Asynchronous telecom	Asynchronous telecom	Asynchronous telecom	Asynchronous telecom
Required Services	Technical support	Communication support	Communication support	Communication support	Systems technical support
Delivery Locations	Classroom, multimedia room	Residence, workplace	Residence, workplace	Residence, workplace	Workplace

Figure 12. A delivery model for a distributed classroom

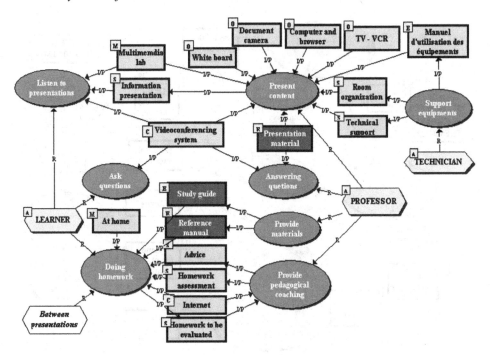

the good function of the equipment and provides a user's guide for this equipment assists the instructor.

The professor here is mainly a content presenter using sophisticated presentation tools. He also answers questions, provides learning materials and gives coaching services. Both the professor and the learners use a videoconference system. Between two presentations, the professor assists learners and assesses their work using the Internet.

The learners' roles consist in attending lectures and asking questions to the instructor using the videoconference system located in the multimedia room closest to their homes. Between two presentations, they use the Internet to consult reference material and documents provided by the instructor. They also use this medium to forward their homework to their instructor.

As a contrast, the model on Figure 13 presents a group of participants involved in an Internet-based learning *community of practice* [Ricciardi-Rigault et al, 1994, Wenger 1998], at their home or their workplace. The members of the group produce

and present information related to a specific task or they solve a specific problem. They use asynchronous forums and/or synchronous tools. This model supports the participants to share knowledge and expertise to build a collection of re-usable documents. Work is completed individually or results from team collaboration. The tele-discussions serves as a forum to exchange on professional praxis. The work is driven by the analysis, assessment and pooling of the members' contributions. An animator in a remote location leads and assists the group helping in the orientation of the work. A web technician provides technical support and helps to build and maintain the collection of documents.

This section has presented delivery models enabling the design of actor-centered environments to support the actor's operations within each function modeled when the system was designed.

In a review of eLearning platforms (Harmbrech 2001), we have noticed that the distance learning support platforms then available were designed for predefined actors. Usually, these platforms

Figure 13. A learning community of practice model

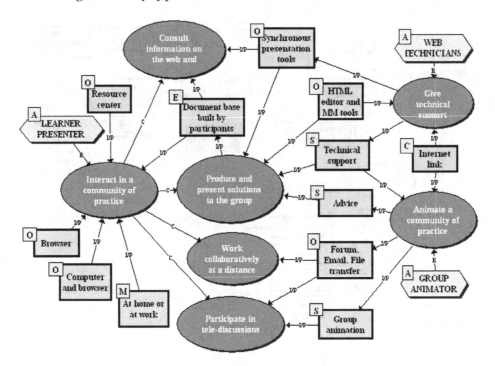

provide a fixed set of tools and resources for an author, a learner, and sometimes, a trainer. Since then, there has been an evolution towards a larger diversity of roles and a greater choice of resources. This is encouraged by specifications like IMS-LD presented in chapter 8 that can be applied to define instructional scenarios as well as delivery models. The TELOS system presented in chapter 15 supports even more a variety of delivery models and a diversification of roles and resources.

TELOS uses graphic delivery models to offer user interfaces at delivery time that are more general and dynamic alternative to hierarchical menus or structures. Such graphic interfaces can be made available for each major function of a learning system. They inform the actors about the context of the operations they perform in different functions, give access to the latest version of the resources produced by other actors, providing ways to update the resources they provide to others.

We believe such workflow-oriented delivery interface solutions will resolve many of the coor-

dination difficulties encountered in all distributed learning systems. Especially in contexts where the actors and resources change regularly, the learners will benefit from constantly knowing where a specific resource or information can be found and with whom they can communicate for information about that resource.

17.3 A TUTORING SCENARIO FOR WEB-BASED COURSES[2]

This section focuses on modeling the tutoring process seen as a support activity to the learning process. The tutor—an intermediate actor within Web-based courses—carries out this activity. He generally acts at delivery time once the educational environment is built, during its real use by the learners. Furthermore, the tutor provides a link between several elements of the educational environment such as the course content, the pedagogical strategy, the social animation activities, the technological aspects of the environment, and the learners' management activities. In fact, a Web tutor should be able to act on different levels: a *cognitive level*, assessing the learning process, analyzing the learner's progress; a *social level*, influencing the improvement of the learners as a group by enabling a group behavior favorable to collective learning, providing support to the organization of the group; and an *emotional level*, motivating and advising learners, while interacting with other actors of the online learning environment.

According to our experience as tutor, tutor trainer, and online course professor-designer, tutoring is based on human collaboration between tutor and learner(s). Such a collaboration process depends mainly on the relational or social competencies of the tutor. In this section, we ask what is the best tutoring process for the tutor to effectively act on these different levels? What are the best ways to build a pedagogical relationship with learners ? And consequently, what kind of tools are needed to support the tutoring process?

Online Tutor's Needs

From 2003 to 2006, we analyzed online pedagogical tutoring processes in a project on tutors, instrumentation and virtual communities, subsided by FQRSC. The tutor's main task is to support adequately the learning process according to a course's objectives and the learners' context, in order to build a pedagogical relationship based on learner-tutor collaboration. As pointed out by Vygotski (1997): "in collaboration with someone the child can always do more than by himself". In this process, the tutor often has to adapt to a social, pedagogical, and technical environment designed and developed by other actors as such professor-designers

We analyzed the needs of tutors using a qualitative survey on Web based courses' involving professor-designers, tutors, and learners from three different educational contexts: a college

(GEGEP@distance), a University (Université de Montréal), and a company (Novisoft). These contexts have been chosen according to two criteria: a good representativeness of various online and distance education contexts, as well as a good integration of a tutoring service in the learning environment. All interviews with Web based courses' designers and tutors were carried out by phone or face-to-face. Moreover, an online forum with learners at whom we had passed an individualized questionnaire also provided data.

Once the data had been analyzed, tutors' needs have been represented as a model, and a tutoring scenario based on several needs has been achieved. For this we used the modeling with typed objects technique (MOT; Paquette 2004), to formalize models and to provide visual graphic representation of them.

Our model is similar to an « ideal-type » representation of the on-line tutoring practice. According to Boudon (1998), the « ideal-type » defines itself as « an integrated set of concepts indispensable to catch the reality. As such, an abstract model is a mean to understand the relationships between concrete phenomena, their causality, and their meaning. It helps to divide the reality in comprehensible components, to select some isolated phenomena, and to describe it according to one and more points of view. ».

We identified three main needs of on-line tutors: training, assistance and recognition or motivation.

Training Needs

The online tutors expressed some training needs at the operational, cognitive and pedagogical levels as Figure 14 points out.

The operational needs are related to organizational and material parameters which determine the online tutoring practice. On one hand, the tutor must know the administrative structure of the educational context where he works to assemble the resources that he needs. On the other

Figure 14. Web-based tutor's training needs

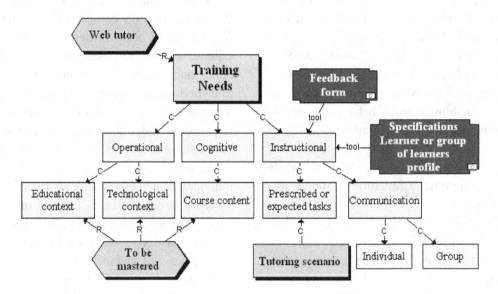

hand, the tutor has to have some technical base (computer, internet connexion, tools etc.) and control other more specific tools that the course uses. The technique control depends mainly on software tools appropriation and a transfer in use. In Web-based courses, the exchange between tutor and learner (s) occurs by phone and software tools as such e-mail, forum, and chat. The tutor must minimally be able to use these communication tools (operational level). Otherwise, he must be able to streamline this use to support learner. In fact, acting in a forum or by email has an important impact on the faith relationship that needs to be built between the tutor and the learner or group of learners, through the communication techniques that the tutor uses.

At the cognitive level, the tutor needs to know perfectly the course content to provide an efficient tutoring. Although the tutor has a general knowledge of the domain in which he tutors, he has to fit in specific contexts by a thorough study of the course using the course material.

Concerning the pedagogical dimension, the instructional design carried out by the courses designer must be understood to communicate efficiently with the learners.

Assistance Needs

As Figure 15 points out, on-line tutors expressed some assistance needs at the information, organizational and human levels. This kind of training, given prior to the tutor's intervention in a course, must be complemented by assistance on all these aspects given to the tutor all along his tutoring activity.

The tutor must be supported by information documents such as guides or other instruments required to understand the designer's pedagogical strategy. It is through this preliminary documentation that the tutor can familiarize himself with the course. This assistance complements the training activities mentioned in the previous section.

At the human level, the tutor can be assisted by his peer tutors with whom he can share some bad or good experiences. This sharing can occur face-to-face or through a virtual discussion space using forums, chats, blogs, etc.

Another form of assistance is the tutoring scenario provided by the professor in charge of the course that has to be adapted to the course context. At the same time, the course content, the tutoring scenario, and the course knowledge goals all support the tutoring activity.

Figure 15. Web-based courses tutor's assistance needs

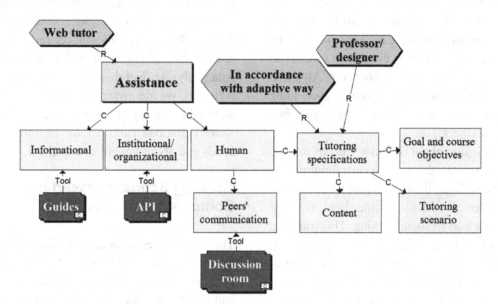

Recognition (Motivation) Needs

The last set of tutor needs concerns his recognition at the institutional, personal (well-being), and interpersonal (appreciation from the designer-professor, learners, and peers) levels. In Web-based education, the tutor appreciation is concerned about his role in course delivery, his contribution concerning learners' contacts and learning progress.

The appreciation of his role is conveyed by the specific status given to the tutor in accordance with the educational context. An on-line educational organization must appreciate the tutor contribution by providing a training service to online tutoring. Moreover, the tutor gains some recognition to the personal and interpersonal level if the course designer associates the tutors in the course improvement process. In this way, he recognizes their knowledge of the course content and the value of their relationship with learners.

Figure 16. Web-based courses tutor's recognition needs

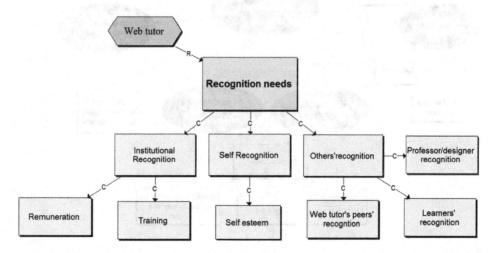

The learners can also to testify in favor of tutor when they are satisfied with his/her tutoring services. Finally, in sharing his experiences with his peers through common discussion spaces the tutor can gain support from his peers. All these recognition elements work towards good tutor self-esteem and an improvement of his contribution with learners.

In conclusion about the tutor's needs model, some assistance needs are similar to training needs. As a matter of fact, these needs are linked, nonetheless different. Coaching a tutor in his tutoring activity can lead to some training. This training, continuous or occasional, do not take away the importance to support the tutor by giving him/her access to a support service to assist him in management problems related to the learners' follow-up and to help him in his relationship with the course professor.

This model reflects to some extent the tutoring practice in Web-based courses context. More specifically, this model classifies most of needs that must be satisfied to offer a top quality tutoring service. This result is limited by the fact that our conceptualization effort is founded on only three different educational contexts that have been included in our survey. The deep interview data analysis offset this lack. Concerning model cohesion, we are aware that each tutor does not demand to satisfy all of these needs. There are some variations from a tutor to another about needs and about how to satisfy them.

Tutoring Scenario Based on Competency Improvement

This section presents a tutoring scenario based on the survey results on tutors' needs just presented. It is based on Duplàa's doctorate work (2003-2006), and on the validation of an online instructors' training that was delivered at the French Université Numérique de Bretagne (2004-2005)

This model is a relational model that leads to a complete appropriation of the tutoring process by the tutor. Figure 17 represents the general model of a tutoring scenario. Each process, in ovals on the

Figure 17. Tutoring scenario-driven knowledge-relational competencies model

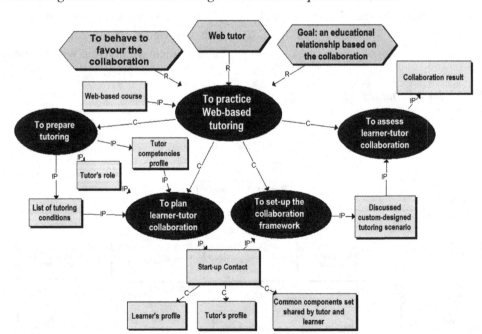

figure, is explained in details by a nested sub-model presented hereafter. This tutoring scenario is based on the tutor ability to self-assess his competencies related to the course which he/she takes in charge, as well as to the learners' profile. We designed and developed this tutoring scenario using a competency engineering approach (Paquette, 2004).

The model is based on collaboration knowledge involved when the tutor establishes a pedagogical relationship with the learner. Its purpose is to satisfy the tutors' needs outlined above.

The model of Figure 17 describes a general tutoring scenario sub-divided in 4 main processes led by the tutor, which are sub-models of the general tutoring process. They are: *To prepare tutoring, To plan learner-tutor collaboration, To set-up the collaboration framework,* and *To assess learner-tutor collaboration.* In brief, this tutoring scenario has as inputs the Web-based course. It is led by competency needs for a facilitating behavior to establish a high-quality pedagogical relationship based on the learner-tutor collaboration.

Preparation Process

To prepare for tutoring constitutes the first process of the tutoring scenario. This first process is formed by three activities as shown on Figure 18. The tutor self-manages his/her activity to improve his/her future results. It is a generic process, adjustable to each specific course content and educational/institutional context.

Planning Bases for Learner-Tutor Collaboration

The second process describes how tutor and learners will interact with each other and state what they need to communicate and collaborate. This first contact between tutor and learners is led by the three following competencies: to be able to pay attention to the others and to take in account information from the environment, to be able to adapt to various educational situations, and, finally, to be able to get in contact with each learner and give requested feedback for a mutual understanding.

Figure 18. The process "to prepare for tutoring"

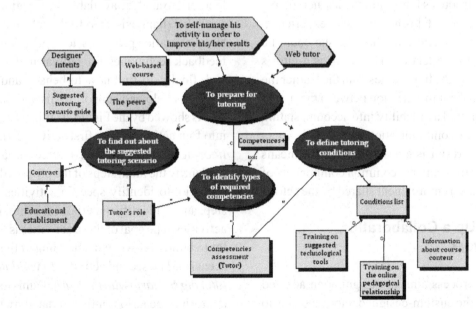

Figure 19. The process "to plan learner-tutor collaboration"

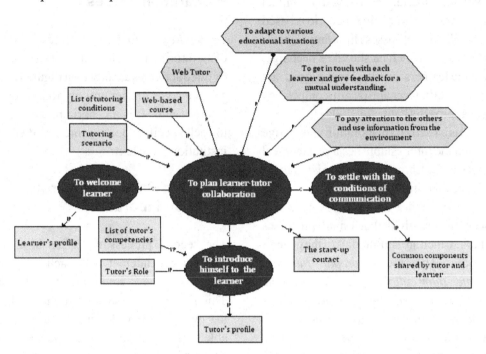

As showed by the Figure 19, this sub process aims at fostering the collaboration between tutor and learners. First, the tutor welcomes the learner to know who he/she is through his/her learning story, his/her motivations, and his/her expectations. The result is a learners' profile. Second,, the tutor introduces himself to the learner to give information about his/her tutoring experience, his/her competencies, and how he/she could be of service to the learner. The result is a tutor's profile. Third, the tutor settles with the learner the conditions of communication between them, taking their mutual availability into account, stating the means of communication to which they can access. The result is a description of the means of collaboration and the common components of the Web-based environment shared by the actors.

Setting Up a Collaboration Framework

The third process aims at designing an adapted version of the custom-designed tutoring scenario

prepared by the professor-designer. This adapted scenario will be used by the tutor and the learner to set-up a mutually agreed collaboration plan. To reach a mutual agreement, the tutor needs four competencies: to synthesize information and communication objectives towards targeted interlocutors, to analyze available information to reach a reliable diagnosis or to find a relevant solution to collaboration problems, to apply relational and feedback techniques for mutual understanding, and, finally, to find how to behave and use this ability as help and support to his action.

As showed by the Figure 20, this process is split into four activities. The first activity *To analyze a tutoring scenario* consists of three sub-activities: to identify the main steps of the proposed tutoring scenario, to identify specific activities for each step, and to identify materials for achieving these activities. The goal of these activities is for the tutor to build his own understanding of the tutoring scenario. The second activity, *To validate his/her tutoring scenario with the learner* aims to produce a tutoring scenario jointly validated by tutor and

Figure 20. The process to set-up the collaboration framework

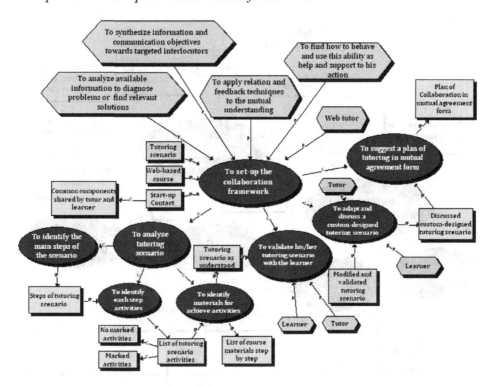

learner. This modified and validated tutoring scenario is used as input to the third activity, which is *To adapt and discuss a custom-designed tutoring scenario*. Finally the fourth activity *To suggest a plan of tutoring in mutual agreement form* leads to a collaboration plan. During all of the learning processes, the support relationship toward the learner will be based on this plan.

Assessing Learner-Tutor Collaboration

The fourth process consists in self-assessing the pedagogical relationship based on the plan of collaboration set-up in a mutual agreement between tutor and learners. This assessment is a reflexive activity, allowing tutor to return on his ability to manage the plan of collaboration through his intervention to the learner.

As showed by the Figure 21 this process aims at improving the quality and the efficiency of the tutor's relationship with the learner throughout

the tutoring process, based on the collaboration plan. First, the tutor assesses the application of the plan by drawing up a list of both positive things and problems throughout the tutoring scenario. Secondly, the tutor self-assesses his/her own competencies and his/her training or assistance needs following his/her collaboration experience in the tutoring process. Finally, the tutor and the learner proceed to a co-assessment of their collaboration to reach a share evaluation result.

The process "to assess collaboration" is a meta-cognitive activity in which the tutor self-assesses his/her approach, his/her knowledge, and abilities during the Web-based tutoring activities. This assessment is achieved at the end of the course. It allows the evaluation of the tutor's personal progress and the up-date of training, assistance and recognition needs.

Figure 21. The process to assess learner-tutor collaboration

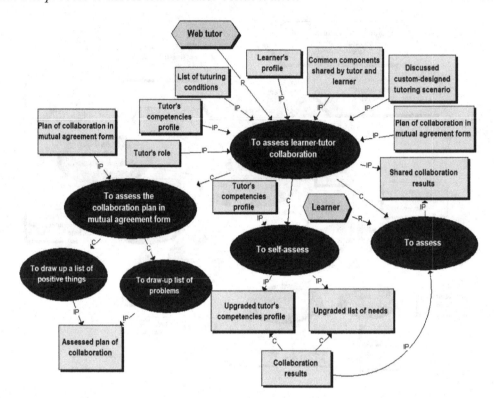

Tools for Web-Based Tutoring

Throughout the Web-based tutoring scenario model the tutor constructs most of the tools he needs to support each of the four processes' activities. These tools are guides, lists, profiles, roles, shared components, and custom-designed tutoring scenarios. From the beginning, the tutor uses the Web-based course and the original tutoring scenario provided by the designer- professor.

Moreover, the technological tools needed to the tutor to achieve his work are composed of the telephone and electronic mail for individual communication and electronic forum for the collective communication. To these tools we can add Social Web software applications such as Blogs Wikis, Facebook, etc. Indeed, most e-learning platform for creating online courses provide, nowadays, a complete set of tools and services that tutor and learners can use how and when they need to for

course development, delivery, and management. A lot of them provide also tools to facilitate communication and collaboration building. The choice of such tools is left to the tutor and learners and are set up when tutor and learners plan their collaboration in the second process.

17.4 DEVELOPING A PROCESS MODEL TO DESIGN COMPETENCY-BASED LEARNING[3]

This section focuses on the adaptation of the MISA method presented in chapter 8, for the design process for competency-based learning environments. It summarizes the work of CICE-LICEF researchers with the Centre for Excellency in Community of Practice (CECP) at the Canada School of Public Service (CSPS). The general mandate of the CSPS is to provide continuous training for all Government departments as stipulated by the "Public Service Modernization Act" (PSMA, 2003).

The Action Research method was used to develop and experiment instructional design (ID) tasks and strategies, in order to adapt them to CSPS needs and context. These tasks and strategies were to be based on a set of competencies. They would reuse learning resources and a Community of Practice approach to learning, these strategies aiming to answer the high demand for training generated by the PSMA.

To elaborate and document the processes conducted by the two teams, the MOT modelling tool and technique was chosen and the MISA method was adapted to the CSPS context. The goal of the modelling process was to identify new tasks required by this context and to facilitate their implementation by instructional designers at the School. A set of documentation elements served

as both idea generation and validation instruments for most of the instructional design activities.

We will now describe two of the MOT models used in this project, a model of the Action Research elements, and then the result of the research, namely, a process model of the Instructional Engineering approach that was carried out. Each model consists of a set of sub-models showing information on who are executing the tasks, what resources are used and produced, as well as principles and rules necessary for accurate execution.

Action Research Model

Action Research involves utilizing a systematic cyclic method of planning, taking action, observing, evaluating (including self-assessing) prior to planning the next cycle (O'Brien, 1998). In this case, it implied that the CICE-LICEF team worked with CEDP course designers, developing a course

Figure 22. The action research process

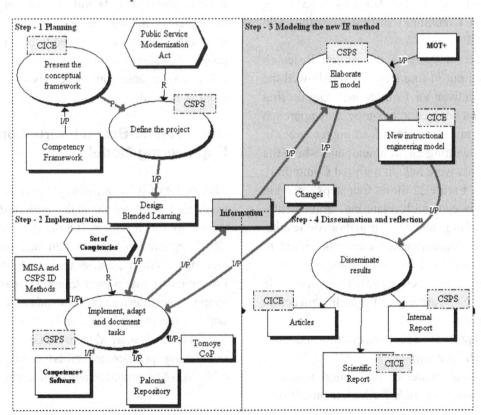

Table 3. Steps in the CSPS project

Step	Description	Products
Planning	The CICE team presented a conceptual framework on how to develop learning modules based on the student's competency level. Selection criteria were developed and applied in order to define the project, which was a set of competencies necessary to design blended learning modules for the instructional designers at the CECP.	• Conceptual framework • Work plan • Project observation description: Design a blended learning course for instructional designers
Implementation	The CECP team described all the entry and target competencies according to the course content. They then matched learning materials to each competency and entered them into the learning resource repository. They used the following tools: Tomoye (the CoP environment), Competency + (for competency management) & Paloma (for resource repository management). They documented the new tasks, which were seen as data for the CICE team Instructional Engineering modeling project.	• Competency profile • Competency distribution table • Course repository • Task descriptions
Modeling the Method	While the CICE team modelled each process including the input and output resources and principles used, the CECP team validated and continued their rapid prototyping approach to build the online course modules using the Tomoye Community of Practice application. This resulted in a six step method and an adaptation process.	• Tomoye Prototype • MOT+ Learning Design Prototype • First draft of new IE model
Dissemination and reflexion	In this phase, the CICE team constructed a docuemented model of the IE method, which was validated by the CECP team. The resulting model is described below.	• Competence based IE Model • Internal report outlining next steps (Ruelland, D., Lundgren, K. 2007) • Scientific Report, articles and book chapter

for training managers on how to develop blended learning modules (Stoyko & Fuchs, 2003) using the Tomoye Community of Practice software in use at CSCP.

The second cycle of the Action Research was carried out in four steps which allowed the teams to deliver an Instructional Engineering (ID) method adapted to a competency approach to learning and the reuse of learning resources in a blended learning environment, and where the online events were held in a virtual Community of Practice. Figure 22 shows four steps recurring in each phase, namely Planning, Implementation, Modelling and Dissemination of results. The various dissemination elements served to provide information for the Planning of the next cycle. In the figure below, the actors responsible (CICE or CSPS) are shown for each main action research tasks.

Table 3 provides a short description and products of each four step.

This visual model of the Action Research phases served as a guide for both teams. It pro-

vided a concise and clear way of sorting out the most important events and resources and document them. It helped both teams to communicate in an efficient way and proved to be an efficient project management tool necessary to assure the AR course of action and to easily make adjustment as needed.

Competency-Based Instructional Engineering Model

The model of the competency-based design (engineering) process is the main result of the above Action Research project. It aims at supplying the CECP organization with a functional, generic and well-documented process that could easily be implemented within their training department to support course design across Canada in accordance with the recent PSMA demand.

This model emerged from the CECP's instructional design practices as well as the main elements of the MISA Learning System Engineering Method

Figure 23. Process model for designing quality competency-based learning

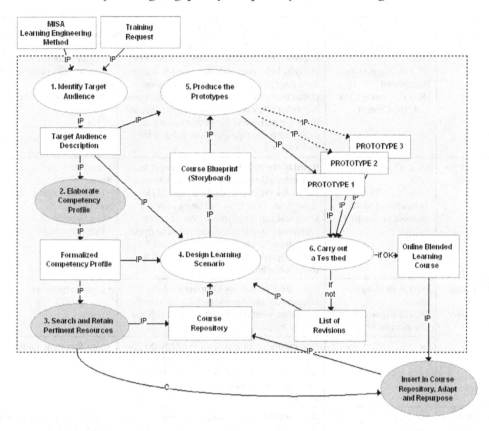

(Paquette, 2002) serving as a guide for quality control of the design (Gauthier, 2006).

As shown in Figure 23, this adapted IE model includes six main processes, which serve to identify the target audience, elaborate a competency profile, search for pertinent resources, design a learning scenario, create a prototype, test and adapt or reuse the course structure and or its resources.

The table below briefly describes each process and the suggested MISA Documentation Elements that are seen as helpful in each process to control the quality.

The following features can describe the originality of this new ID process, as compared to the traditional ADDIE method used in some organizations:

- The target competencies are used to select the learning strategies as well as the learn-

ing resources;

- It integrates the instructional practices particular to the CECP situation, which are blended learning, virtual community of practice and rapid prototyping strategies.

- It uses the MISA engineering method as a framework for quality control.

- It builds on the design, archiving, reuse or repurposing of all kinds of learning resources, i.e., video clips, texts, articles, web sites, or course modules.

- It applies the international specifications IMS Learning Design and IEEE Learning Object Metadata to facilitate reuse and interoperability of the course scenario and its resources.

- Delivers two types of learning environments within which the learners can de-

Table 4. Steps in the CSPS proposed ID process

ID Process	MISA ED	Description	Outcome
1. Identify target audience	DE 104 Target Audience DE 100 Organizational Background DE 102 Training Goal • DE 106 Context	According to the training demand and existing resources, the Instructional designer outlines individual characteristics according to employment descriptions as well as organizational characteristics according to which Government department they belong. Major constraints and needs are also noted. These descriptions are submitted to the repository and indexed for easy retrieval.	• Descriptions of Organisational and Individual characteristics of the target audience. • Metadata description form.
2. Elaborate competency profile	DE 214 Competency Table (using the MISA Taxonomy of Skills ᴾresented in chapter 7	Based on the training demand, the target audience description and the set of competencies chosen for the course, the Instructional Designer formulates entry and target competency levels and gap descriptions. This table also contains a list of potential existing resources for each competency statement. The LICEF tool Competency+ was used to establish the competency profile for the course.	Formalized Competency Profile Table: • Entry and target competency statements • Gap description • Difficulty level
3. Search and retain resources **Adapt or repurpose**	DE 108 Existing Resources DE 212 Knowledge and Competency Model	Using the Competency Distribution Table instructional designers search for resources and define what is to be developed, modified or used as is.	• Course repository
		If an existing course appears to satisfy the demand, adapt or repurpose it according to target audience. The instructional designer analyses what revisions must be made and then may produce a new prototype.	• New Prototype for testing
4. Design learning scenarios	DE 222 Learning Event's Model DE 224 Learning Unit Properties DE 320 Pedagogical Scenarios	According to demand, target audience, content and competencies involved, five consecutive modules were designed. It is to be noted that no compulsory modules or activities exist, nor are any evaluations or grades given. Each learning scenario was also developed using the MOT+ software that lets a designer build a level A of a IMS Learning Design interoperability specification (presented in chapter 8).	• Course Learning Scenarios in IMS-LD format
5. Produce prototype	440 Delivery Model	The CECP used their Community of Practice tool TOMOYE to carry out this part of the design.	• Functional Prototype
6. Carry out a test bed	DE 540 Test Bed Plan DE 542 Revision Log	The CECP has a well-established validation process of their courses, and the only new thing was to test technical compliance.	• Quality-assessed course • List of revisions

velop their competencies and assess their level of accomplishment.

• The learners can undertake suggested learning modules or consult other types of resources, based on the results of their competency self-assessment (just in time, just enough paradigm).

• Carrying out the learning scenario proposed by the instructional designer and receiving learning support by a tutor or mentor.

The tasks described by the model were carried out by the practitioners of the CECP, guided by the

CICE experts, especially as regards competency development, as well as the use of IMS Learning Design and the IEEE Learning Object Metadata. The visual modelling approach proved most satisfactory for both parts.

The CICE team has designed a way of stating a competency that clearly describes its content, skill level as well as indications on how it is to be performed. The challenges were for the CICE team to transfer to the CECP team enough know-how to efficiently and effectively:

- Use the MOT modelling Tool to develop the knowledge and competency model;
- Reference resources and competencies with appropriate metadata using the PALOMA Repository that will be presented in the next chapter.
- State competencies and difficulty levels in order to integrate the competency profile into to the Competency+ tool.
- From this modelling experience the added value of visual modelling was seen to:

- Support the design process by linking the learning competencies to a unit of learning;
- Offer a common base for work that favours collaboration and team work by formalizing the design processes;
- Provide a structure that helps to plan the design decisions;
- Act as a reference for the coordination and management of design projects;
- Facilitate the adaptation of a course by supplying the documentation and the history of the training product.

CONCLUSION

This chapter has underlined the multiple uses of visual modeling for instructional engineering in various organizational contexts. It helped build a competency profile to plan a professional training program for lawyers, prepare plans for the delivery of courses on virtual campuses, design tutoring scenarios in distance universities, or construct an instructional engineering process adapted to a public service school's context.

The strength of visual modeling in all these situations is both in the process and in the product.

As a process, visual modeling fosters and amplifies thinking. It helps classify the type of resources, activities, actors involved in educational environments. It focuses attention on their interrelations, first on a global scale, identifying the most essential elements, and then adding more and more details in nested sub-models, until the situation is clearly defined. This applies to the knowledge and competencies involved in education, as well as to activity scenarios, learning material structure and organization and learning delivery processes. During this process, the various versions of the models serve as a concrete communication artifact between instructional engineering team members.

When stabilized as a product, the models provide the specifications and a solid foundation for the development of learning environments. The knowledge and competency models provide the learning objectives and the content of the future environment. The activity scenario models provide the structure of the learning environments and the actors' interactions. The media model can be given to media specialists as a blueprint that they can use/adapt to build the learning materials. The delivery model will help configure the virtual campus processes to the requirements of a course.

REFERENCES

Boudon, R. (1998). *Études sur les sociologues classiques*. Paris: Presses Universitaires de France.

Duplàa, E. (2006). *On-line instructional relationship*. Doctoral dissertation, Université du Maine, France.

Gauthier, M. (2006). Virtual Communities of Practice (vCoP) at the Canada School of Public Service (CECP). In *Proceedings of I2LOR 2006*, Montréal, November 8-11. Retrieved from http://www.lornet.org/Default.aspx?tabid=644

Gery, G. (1997). Granting three wishes through performance-centered design. *NATO Communications of the ACM, 40*(7), 54–59. doi:10.1145/256175.256185

Harasim, L. (1990). Online Education: An Environment for Collaboration and Intellectual Amplification . In Harasim, L. (Ed.), *Online education: Perspectives on a new environment*. New York: Praeger Publishers.

Harmbrech, W. R. (2001). *Corporate e-Learning: Exploring new frontiers.*

Hiltz, R. (1990). Evaluating the Virtual Classroom . In Harasim, L. (Ed.), *Online education: perspectives on a new environment*. New York: Praeger Publishers.

Hotte, R. (2007). Tutors, Instrumentation and Virtual communities. FQRSC Report File No. 89746. Montreal, Canada: LICEF research Center of TELUQ.

Hotte, R., Duplàa, E., & Lecomte, N. (2005). *La relation pédagogique en ligne. La relation comme entité structurante de la communauté d'apprentissage en ligne.* Communication au colloque Le tutorat: les étudiants à distance en ont-ils vraiment besoin? du GIREFAD, 73ième Congrès de l'Acfas, Université du Québec à Chicoutimi (Chicoutimi), 9 au 13 mai 2005.

IMS-LD. (2003). *IMS Learning Design specification*. Retrieved September 2009, from http://www.imsglobal.org/learningdesign/

LOM. (2003). *Learning Object Metadata*. Retrieved September 2009, from http://ltsc.ieee.org/wg12/

O'Brien, R. (1998). *An Overview of the Methodological Approach of Action Research*. Retrieved from http://www.web.net/~robrien/papers/arfinal.html

Paquette, G. (2002). *L'ingénierie pédagogique. Pour construire l'apprentissage en réseau.* Canada: Presses de l'Université du Québec.

Paquette, G. (2002). Modélisation des connaissances et des compétences. Montreal, Canada: Presses de l'université du Québec

Paquette, G. (2004). Educational Modeling Languages, from an Instructional Engineering Perspective . In McGreal, R. (Ed.), *Online education using learning objects* (pp. 331–346). London: Routledge/Falmer.

Paquette, G. (2004). *Instructional Engineering for Network-Based Learning*. San Francisco, CA: Pfeiffer.

Paquette, G., De la Teja, I., & Dufresne, A. (2000). Explora: An Open Virtual Campus. Actes de la conférence ED-Media 2000, Montréal 2000.

Paquette, G., de la Teja, I., & Léonard, M. (2000). *Presentation of the MISA Learning Engineering Method*. Montréal, Canada: Internal Research Report, Licef Research Centre.

Paquette, G., Lundgren-Cayrol, K., & Léonard, M. (2008). The MOT+ Visual Language for Knowledge-Based Instructional Design . In *Handbook on Virtual Instructional Design Languages*. Hershey, PA: IGI Global.

Paquette, G., & Rosca, I. (2003). *Modeling the physiology of eLearning Delivery Models (Vol. 1*, pp. 1–30). Technology, Instruction, Cognition and Learning.

Ricciardi-Rigault, C., & Henri, F. (1994 June). Developing Tools for Optimizing the Collaborative Learning Process. In *Proceedings of the International Distance Education Conference*, Penn State University, USA.

Rosca, I. (1999). *Vers une vision systémique du processus de l'explication- Récit d'une recherche sur l'intégration de la pédagogie, de l'ingénierie et de la modélisation.* Thèse de Doctorat en technologie éducationnelle, Université de Montréal, 1999. Retrieved from http://www.iro.umontreal.ca/~rosca/index.htm

Ruelland, D., & Lundgren, K. (2007). *Apprentissage mixte en milieu de travail. Collaboration École de la fonction publique du Canada et la Chaire de recherche en ingénierie cognitive et éducative. Rapport de la Phase II, August 2007.* Montréal: Téluq.

Ruelland, D., Lundgren, K., & Bloomfield, D. (2006). *Implementation of IMS-LD and IEEE LOM specifications in the workplace: A Best Practice Study.* Québec: Report for the Canada School of Public Service.

Stoyko, P., & Fuchs, A. (2003). *L'apprentissage @ la portée de tous: Un guide d'apprentissage en ligne pour gestionnaires.* Canadian Center for Management Development. Retrieved from http://www.myschool-monecole.gc.ca/main_f.html

Vygotsky, L. S. (1962). *Thought and Language.* Cambridge, MA: MIT Press. doi:10.1037/11193-000

Vygotsky, L. S. (1978). *Mind in Society.* Cambridge, MA: Harvard University Press.

Wenger, E. (1998). *Communities of Practice. Learning, Meaning and Identity. Learning in Doing: Social, Cognitive, and Computational Perspectives.* Cambridge, UK: Cambridge University Press.

ENDNOTES

[1] Section 1 is a synthesis, written mainly by Karin Lundgren-Cayrol and Michel Léonard, two central LICEF participants in the project.

[2] Section 3 has been prepared by Richard Hotte, based on the following research report: Hotte, R. (2007). *Tutors, Instrumentation and Virtual communities.* FQRSC Report File No. 89746, Produced at the LICEF research Center with a grant by the Quebec Research Fund on Society and Culture.

[3] Section 4 has been prepared by Diane Ruelland and Karin Lundgren-Cayrol, based on the documents produced in an R&D project at the Canada School of Public Services that they have conducted.

Chapter 18
Modeling for Learning Design Repositories

Gilbert Paquette
LICEF Research Center, Canada

ABSTRACT

- A Learning Design Portal
- Learning Design as Learning Objects
- A Case Study: Producing and Reusing Patterns and Learning Designs
  - Description of the Reusability Process
  - Analysis of the process
- An Ontology for Learning Design Objects
  - Main Ontology Model
  - LD Format Relationships
  - Reusability Categories
  - Aggregation Level and Delivery Model
  - Pedagogical Strategies
  - Learner Evaluation Model
  - Using the LD Objects Ontology

The deployment processes of a new technology or a methodology like Instructional Engineering is crucial if we want R&D results and products to reach end users with innovative products and services that produce quality and growth. These preoccupations are at the origin of the IDLD project that provides the main thread of this chapter. This project is based previous projects in the same area: R2R (Paquette, Marino, De la Teja, Lundgren-Cayrol, Léonard & Contamines, 2005) and edusource (McGreal, Anderson, Babin, Downes, Friesen, Harrigan, Hatala, M., MacLeod, Mattson, Paquette, Richards, Roberts & Schafer, 2004).

In the first section we present the IDLD portal (Figure 1) that contains a repository of learning design models and examples. Such a repository groups narratives (lesson plans), MOT+LD mod-

DOI: 10.4018/978-1-61520-839-5.ch018

Figure 1. A view of the IDLD web portal

els and the corresponding XML files compliant with the IMS-LD specification. It contains also an adaptation of the MISA Learning System Engineering Method presented earlier in chapter 8. In section 2, we will present how we have adapted the Learning Object Metadata (LOM) to structure the LD repository, considering LDs as special kinds of learning objects. For this, we had to integrate two classifications schemes into the PALOMA Learning Object manager. PALOMA will be presented with more details in chapter 20. In section 3, we will present a reusability process for decomposing a course into smaller patterns and re-using some of them to compose new courses. In section 4, we will propose an ontology that can help structure learning design repositories and enable more useful queries to such repositories.

18.1. THE IDLD PORTAL

Building LD repositories has been identified as a priority in a Valkenburg Group round table held in January 2004 (Paquette et al, 2004). In order to fulfill this need, the IDLD Web portal has been built. This IMS-LD resource center is now in operation at www.idld.org providing a free access to a repository of learning designs, a suite of tools to support the deployment of IMS-LD, methodological aids to help in its implementation and a number of background documents and related sites.

All object and information in the IDLD Portal can be reuse under a give credit/non commercial/ share alike Creative Commons licence. Knowledgeable persons are invited to use the tools in the Portal and add learning designs to the repository using the PALOMA software.

Besides some basic IMS-LD documentation, the IDLD portal offers a set of *methodological aids* for instructional designers and educators involved in the implementation and deployment of the IMS-LD specification, such as the following:

- A methodological guide to support IMS-LD authoring, validation and execution using the portal's tools or other alternative tools;

- A description of the classes of learning designs in the classifications we have used to provide metadata descriptors for learning designs;

- A set of best practices in the development and use of the learning design repository based on our experience in the project;

- A workflow model to help build units of learning or courses compliant with the IMS-LD specification.

To support the development and use of the LD repository, the IDLD portal presently gives access to four *tools*:

- the MOT+LD graphic editor (Paquette, Léonard, Lundgren-Cayrol, Mihaila and Gareau, 2006) that supports an interactive design process more friendly to designers than form-based editors, but limited to level A of the IMS-LD specification;

- the RELOAD (2006) editor (RELOAD supporting A, B and C levels in a hierarchical form-based format;

- the RELOAD player, embedding the COPPERCORE engine (Martens and Votgen, 2006), that reads IMS-LD manifests and offers a Web-based interface to deliver and execute a LD run;

- PALOMA, a learning object repository management system, extracted from the Explor@ system (Paquette, Miara, Lundgren-Cayrol and Guérette, 2004) that supports the IEEE-LOM and the IMS-DRI

specification for federated search into multiple repositories.

These tools are sufficient to support the implementation process presented below; however, some limitations have appeared in the IDLD test beds, so we aim to extend this tool set with other open source tools that are being developed by us or by other groups. We are in the process to integrate in the portal the new TELOS scenario editor presented in Chapter 15. This editor covers all three levels of IMS-LD and exports the scenario models to XML. TELOS also executes such scenario. When this work is finished, the RELOAD editor can still be used for packaging and the RELOAD player will provide an alternate scenario delivery tool to TELOS.

Figure 2 presents the main process phases (Lundgren-Cayrol & Léonard, 2006) and the tools that we have used to build and reuse the LD repository. In the first phase, our research group's tools, documents and expertise were used by three other teams besides Télé-université, at Concordia University and at Simon Fraser Universities, and also another team at the Canada School of Public Service (see section 17.4) to build standardized learning designs. The two main standards needed for the implementation and deployment of Units of learning are the IMS Learning Design Specification (Koper 2005) and a metadata schema, in our case, the Learning Object Metadata Standard by IEEE, which is integrated into PALOMA.

Using the MOT+LD visual learning design tool presented in chapter 8, the teams involved in the project have build and integrated in the PALOMA Resource Manager, a repository of around 50 learning designs. The IDLD Portal (www.idld.org) gives a direct access to this repository. In a second phase, a test bed was carried out with new instructional designers distributed all over Canada to test the use of the IDLD repository and portal for learning design operations. This test bed yielded ample information not only on implementation and deployment issues, but also on the types of reuse that are potentially viable.

Figure 2. Repository building main process and tool

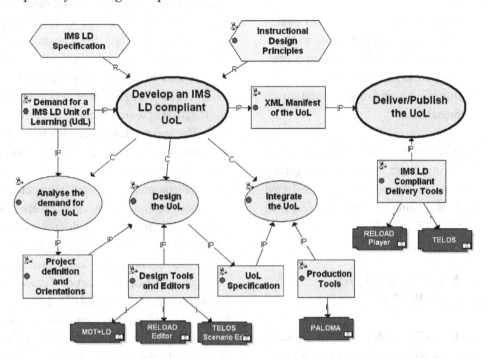

Throughout this process, the instructional designers were involved in the following activities:

1. *Familiarization*: Explanation of main IMS LD concepts and paradigms and the demonstration of MOT+LD editor.
2. *Planning*: Clarification of the context at hand and construction of a plan on how to best implement and deploy IMS Learning Designs.
3. *Preparation*: Analysis of existing courses to be modeled by respecting a number of principles such as:
   a. Constructivist or cognitivist learning paradigms;
   b. Collaborative learning strategies in a blended or online learning setting.
   c. Multi-actor design, making use of content/field experts, teachers moderators etc.
   d. Generic and/or easily adapted learning environment;
   e. Ensure instructional quality by applying a known ID method, i.e., MISA
4. *Implementation*: Model building supported by mentor activities and community exchanges through the following steps:
   a. *Face- to face workshop:* Participant training, where the objective was to explain the constraints required by the IMS LD specification and to demonstrate the MOT+ LD editor tool.
   b. *Exemplification*: Presentation of IMS LD narratives and derived units of learning models and xml files;
   c. *Drafting*: Elaboration of a first draft of the chosen course;
   d. *Face-to face workshop:* Validation of this first model and demonstration of advanced features of the MOT+ LD editor.
   e. *Modeling Support*: Discussion of alternatives to the proposed solutions and continuous coaching in the modeling process.

5. *Validation*:
    a. Exportation of the MOT+LD Level A model as an xml manifest file and testing it in an IMS-LD compliant player, such as RELOAD Player.
    b. Summarizing and documentation of impressions.
6. *Referencing*:
    a. Publishing the Unit of Learning and indexing them using a recognized metadata scheme such as the LOM and integrating the metadata forms in the PALOMA tool.

18.2 LEARNING DESIGN AS LEARNING OBJECTS

The central idea in the PORTAL is to consider learning designs or scenarios, IMS-LD compliant or not, as a special kind of learning objects, which explains the use of the PALOMA Learning Object Metadata (LOM) manager. In this section we will present briefly this tool and the adaptation that

was made to integrate learning designs in learning object repositories. We will also present some examples to show how the learning designs have been described using the LOM standard.

The idea behind this approach is to visualize the construction of a Unit of Learning (UoL) as an aggregation of learning objects of different kinds. A similar approach has been taken in chapter 12. As shown on Figure 3, learning objects can be all sorts of *documents* that carry information using media elements, *tools* that help actors process information, and human or software *actors* that process the information in documents to produce other documents using some of the tools.

Process scenarios or *learning designpatterns* (such as in the central part of Figure 3) are also learning objects composed of a structure of activities, awaiting for actors (red arrows) or documents and tools (yellow arrows) to be specified. When they are at least partly specified (others can be specified only at runtime), then we have a *learning design example*, schematized on the right part of the figure. This schema tells us that an actor will do the first two activities and a group will do

Figure 3. Units of learning through learning object aggregation

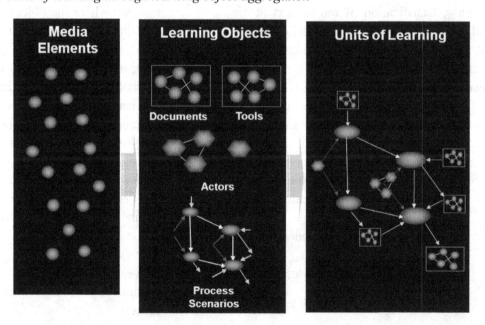

the other two activities. Also, the group will use a document produced by the actor in the second activity in the last activity.

The central component of the IDLD portal is the LD repository. It actually contains around 50 entries, each giving access to products of the learning design implementation process: initial narratives of learning scenarios, visual models of learning designs build with the MOT+LD editor, IMS-LD compliant XML manifests. The visual models and their corresponding XML manifests are either LD examples, where the content resources are specified as items, or LD patterns that are learning design flows without specific content.

We believe that LD patterns are more interesting that other types of learning objects because they are ready-to-adapt multi-actor processes embedding learning and teaching strategies that can be reused in different knowledge domains.

To facilitate search in learning object repositories containing learning design products we

need to classify the LDs according to their main properties. Figure 4 shows a screen from the PALOMA learning object manager. The left part presents a list of available repositories, including the IDLD repository. Other repositories contain description of documents (text, presentations, video, images, etc). They can also contain tools or actors descriptions.

Using PALOMA, a designer car can select the components that will be aggregated to produce a unit-of-learning. The center part of the screen shows a list of designs grouped in the selected folder within the IDLD repository. The larger part of the screen provides a user interface for metadata definition based the 9 sections of the LOM standard specification. This is where people can enter and view metadata on learning objects such as authors, language, intended audience, technological or commercial constraints, etc.

The object actually being referenced is a learning design for a collaborative LD pattern entitled

Figure 4. Learning design classification and metadata association to learning designs

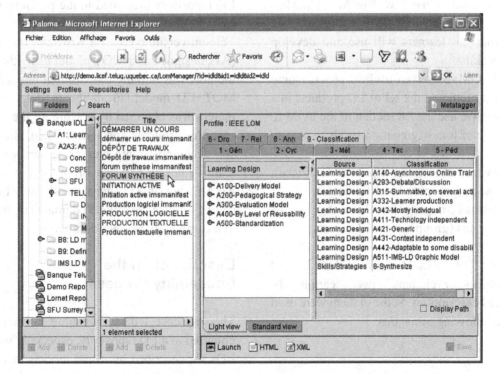

"FORUM SYNTHÈSE". For this LD, the user has already selected metadata from the learning design classification: the delivery model is "Asynchronous Online Training", the pedagogical strategy is "Debate/Discussion", and the evaluation model is "summative", based on "learner productions" that are "mostly individual". These three top level categories of the learning design classification are extracted directly from the MISA method presented in chapter 8. Category A400 of the classification helps specify a level of reusability of a learning design on different aspects. This category is an extension of a proposal by (Currier & Campbell, 2006). Since the LD here is a pattern, it is considered to be "technology independent", "content generic", "context-of-use independent" and "adaptable to certain disabilities". Finally, category A500 describes the type of LD product, in this case an IMS-LD Graphical Model.

Other classifications can also be made available in section 9 of the LOM. In the list of classification descriptors on Figure 4, we see that the last entry shows metadata selected from a classification on cognitive skills and strategies. This classification is also extracted from our work on MISA and has been presented in chapter 7. Here, this metadata asserts that the learners will use and develop synthesis skills.

Other LOM sections are useful to provide some semantic structure to the set of LD products in a repository. We use the 1.8 section of the LOM to specify one of four aggregation levels:

1. Raw media (learning objects and services);
2. Lessons (grouping level 1 objects);
3. Courses (grouping level 2 objects);
4. Programs (grouping level 3 objects).

Section 7 of the LOM also provides a limited set of choices for relations between learning objects LOM descriptions. Some of them were used with the following semantics:

- "is basis for /is based on" indicates the relationship between a narrative or a textual course outline (or lesson plan) and a graphical model or an LD manifest ;
- "has format/is format of" indicates the relationship between a graphic model of a UoL, an IMS-LD manifest or an executable Web site of the same UoL;
- "has part/is part of" will indicate the relationship between a LD product and its components, for example, between a level 3 (course) and a level 2 (lesson) object.
- "has version/is version of" is re-interpreted as the relationship between a pattern and its examples obtained by associating precise items to the abstract objects (environment, activity, role,…) in a LD pattern.

18.3 A CASE STUDY: PRODUCING AND REUSING LEARNING DESIGN PATTERNS

In this section, a reusability process using the LD repository presented in the previous section will be described. In this process an existing Télé-université course on Artificial Intelligence (AI), designed as a MOT model using the MISA method, was initially transformed into a graphic MOT+LD model. From the model, a generic pattern was obtained by erasing all the content-specific resources and terms. Then, the course was decomposed into smaller (lesson or module) learning design patterns. From these patterns, it has been possible to aggregate two new IMS-LD courses, one in the same AI domain and the other in a completely another domain.

Description of the Reusability Process

This use case will demonstrate the reusability potential of a LD repository, especially when the LDs are described by visual models that can be

Figure 5. Inf-5100 initial course module

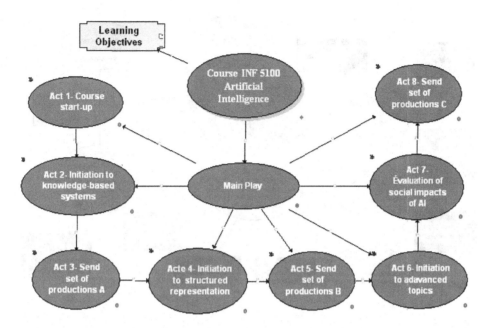

globally viewed and easily modified, decomposed and recomposed.

Transfer to an IMS LD Generic Pattern

An Artificial Intelligence course at Télé-université will serve as an example here. It was developed a few years ago using the MISA method, so a MOT model of its pedagogical structure and scenarios was already available. This model was copied in the MOT+LD specialized editor, as shown on Figure 5. It was then necessary to redefine the object types using those particular to IMS-LD. An alternative, a little more time-consuming would have been to rebuild the graph directly in MOT+LD, which is necessary for courses that have not been modeled graphically.

Figure 6 shows an activity structure, part of Acte2 that shows resources input or output of each activity. In the original model, the instantiated resources were associated to the activities by a direct attachment, which is a standard functionality of the MOT+ editor. In MOT+LD, to respect the format of the IMS-LD specification, it was necessary to introduce IMS-LD "item" elements associated to each resource used in to perform an activity. These item symbols contain the address of a resource. This is where the concrete learning objectives' definitions, the instructions for activities, the texts, the videos and the software can be found and displayed at run time.

To obtain the template by eliminating the contents of the course, we just had to erase the items which carry the contents specific to the AI course. It is afterward sufficient to rename the objects in the graphic template using generic terms instead of AI Terms, so they do not carry any specific meaning. The result a template (or "pattern") reusable in other domains.

Decomposing the Course Pattern

After analysis of the structure of the course, we noted that it could be rebuilt using five basic UoL patterns. Such basic patterns correspond to the concept of "learning nuggets", developed by (Bailey, Mohd, Davis, Fill & Conole, 2006). One example is the activity structure in Figure 6 that

Figure 6. One of the activity structures expressed in MOT-LD format

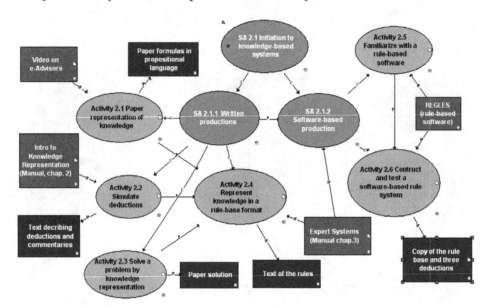

contains two basic patterns: *TEXT PRODUCTION* (for activities 2.1, 2.2 and 2.3) and *SOFTWARE PRODUCTION* (for activities 2.4, 2.5 and 2.6). Another basic pattern is used to *STARTUP* an online course and another one for *HOMEWORK DEPOSIT*. A fifth basic UoL pattern is the FO-RUM SYNTHESIS that was referenced using the PALOMA as shown on Figure 4. Figure 7 represents the main structure of this UoL patterns with a nested model the activity structure in Act 2.

Re-Composing Course Patterns in Various Subject Domains

By re-composing the five basic LD patterns obtained at the preceding step, it is possible to build a new course UoL corresponding exactly to the course pattern produced at step 2, or to change the course structure, re-ordering the activities. This fact confirms the reusability of such patterns. Starting from this new pattern, it is possible to integrate various resources (as IMS-LD items) and thus design a different version of the initial course or a course in a completely different domain. This is done by specifying which resources from

the original course are to be used, thus obtaining another version (or a simplified play) of the initial course "Introduction to Artificial Intelligence".

Figure 8 shows two instantiation of the TEXT PRODUCTION pattern, one in the original subject on artificial intelligence, and the other one in political science. If we compare the two models, we see that the differences are essentially in the items associated to activities or document. These items state each activity's assignment, or point in a LO repository to the videos or texts needed to perform the activities. Another difference is in the names of the activities and documents that are adapted from generic terms to specialized terms in one or the other subject domain.

Analysis of the Process

During the reusability process presented above, the visual representation of LD patterns and examples offered by the MOT+LD editor was of an invaluable support. The MOT+LD editor provides an overview of the learning design that facilitates the construction and the adaptations of scenarios, especially when comparing it to form-based editors,

Figure 7. Forum synthesis, an IMS-LD UoL reusable pattern

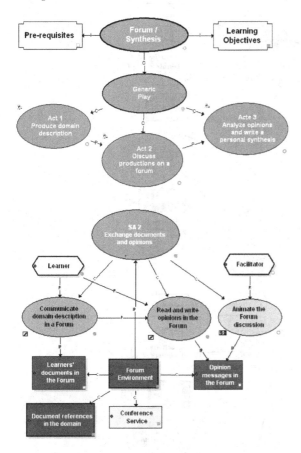

els them side by side, selecting the desired components and copying or dragging/dropping them into the sub-model of an act or an activity structure in the model to be built.

• Once one or several of these transformations are completed, the designer just has to adjust the numbering and text of the objects in the models either to reflect their generic or specific nature, or to identify new components in the resulting model.

At each step, the model can be exported to IMS-LD XML files and both objects can be stored in the LD repository for further reuse. While populating the LD repository in this way, the graphic MOT+LD editor was found very helpful. It is easy to transform graphs, extract sub-graphs or regroup them, then add content items to create new learning designs.

such as RELOAD. Graphical transformations are very simple and little training is needed to make full use of MOT+LD functionalities.

• Transforming an example into an IMS-LD UoL template or vice versa, is done by simply removing item graphic symbols containing pointers to specific resources or adding them on.

• The decomposition of a UoL course template into basic UoLs can be done by simply copying (or dragging/dropping) an activity structure from one model into a new MOT+LD model.

• The reverse operations, re-compositions, are done similarly by placing the two mod-

18.4 AN ONTOLOGY FOR LEARNING DESIGN OBJECTS

In order to add inference capabilities in a LD repository, providing more intelligent processing capabilities, we wanted to *replace the use of classifications in section 9 of the LOM by an ontology* that will be presented in this section. In the context of LOM, relations between the classifications' terms is not possible, only global relations can be made using section 7, as presented above.

Another goal was to reduce the manual referencing of learning objects, which is time consuming with LOM metadata, and even more if the objects are learning design. We need to automate at least partly the referencing process. One way that has been explored by various researchers is to add a natural language parser to extract metadata from text or Web documents automatically or semi-automatically. For LD objects a further possibility exists to *extract metadata from the regular structure of an IMS-LD manifest and by*

Figure 8. Instantiation of a generic text production pattern, in two different domains

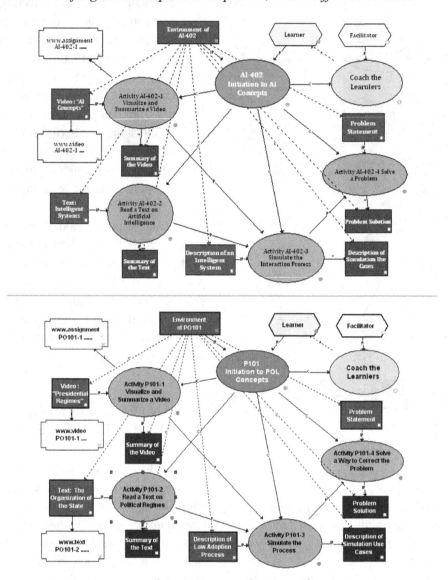

inferences on a LD objects ontology.

In this section, we will present a preliminary ontology for learning designs that provides a more powerful semantic referencing capability than the LOM. We aim to integrate this ontology for *semantic referencing into a IMS-LD editor* such as the TELOS scenario editor presented in chapter 15. This user interface will offer referencing and search services extending the capabilities of the PALOMA LO manager in support of the

various decomposition/re-composition operations presented in section 18.3.

The Main Ontology Model

The main ontology model is presented on Figure 9. It has been built with the MOT+OWL editor presented in chapter 10. It shows the main properties of LD objects: *Format, Aggregation Level, Reusability Level, Delivery model, Pedagogical*

Figure 9. A LD-objects top-level ontology

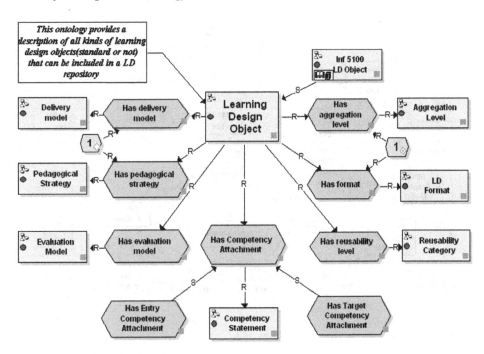

Strategy and *Evaluation Model*. The following figures will present nested sub-models that develop further this main model.

One of the properties of an LD Object is its *Competency Attachment* where an entry (prerequisite) and/or a target (objective) competency attachment can be specified using the *Competency Ontology* presented in chapter 10.

Since there are no cardinality axioms on the Competency Attachment, Reusibility Category and Evaluation Model classes, it is possible that some LD objects lack some of these features. On the other hand, the model tells us that a LD object must have exactly one Aggregation Level and Format and at least one Delivery Model and Pedagogical Strategy.

LD Format Relationships

The subclasses of the "LD format" class and its main relationships are shown on Figure 10. The main sub-classes concern non-standard descrip-

tions and standardised ones using the IMS-LD specification or the SCORM profile.

An IMS-LD format extends a SCORM format. It can provide a basis for non-standard LD objects such as a course plan or a Web delivery version of the LD. Conversely, any non-standard LD can be transformed in IMS-LD format. One example is the MISA model of the AI course in section 18.3. The property "is-a-basis-for" is transitive as shown by the ⇒ symbol on the property symbol.

The lower part of Figure 10 shows the relation between different kinds of IMS-LD objects, distinguishing examples from patterns. From a pattern, one can specify many LD examples by varying the items associated to the different levels of the method defining the LD. Conversely, corresponding to an example, there is only one pattern obtained by removing all the items in the example, at the condition that a controlled vocabulary is used to replace specific names of the objects in the model by generic ones.

Figure 10. The "format" part of the "LD object" ontology

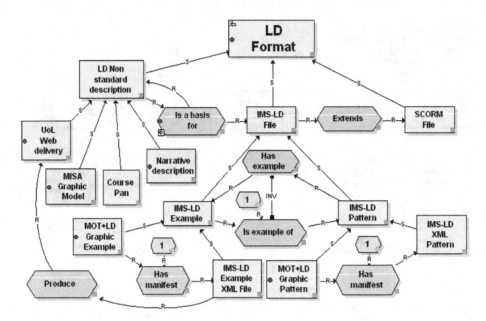

An LD example, or a LD pattern, has a unique IMS-LD manifest, which is the XML file obtained by translating the model in terms of the standard XML schema. A LD example can be used to produce one or more (different by form and presentation) UoL Web delivery interface that can differ by the widgets used, the presentation. Amongst the possible Web delivery interfaces, there is the one we have shown for the TELOS task manager in chapter 15, which provides a user interface for a LD built with the scenario editor.

Reusability Categories

Figure 11 presents a taxonomy for reusability categories that extends a proposal by Currier and Campbell (2006). It specifies four sub-classes covering different aspects: reusability at the technical, content, context levels, and accessibility. These classes are not disjoint, meaning that a particular LD objects can belong to some or all of the classes since there is no restriction in the model of the ontology. But there is a maximum of 4 categories for a particular LD object, because each of the four sub-classes is further subdivided into more specialized classes that are mutually exclusive, which is expressed on the model by "Disj" links.

Aggregation Level and Delivery Model

Figure 12 shows two other parts of the LD objects Ontology. The Aggregation Level reproduces the Learning Object hierarchy in the IMS-LD information model instead of the one provided by section 1.8 of the LOM. The upper object of a Unit-of-Learning (UoL) is called a *Method*, irrespective if the UoL is labelled in the LOM as a program, a course, a module, a learning unit, a lesson or whatever local term is used. Methods are composed of at least one *Play*, Plays of at least one *Act*, and Acts of a least one *Activity Structure*. Activity Structures can be recursively nested on any number of level and finally composed of terminal *Activities* that are either *learning activities* (performed by learners) or *support activities* (performed by tutors or other facilitators). As shown on the model, the property *Has part* is transitive

Figure 11. The reusability categories taxonomy

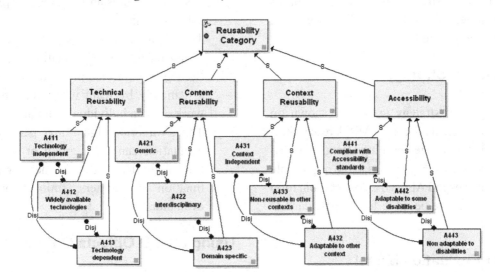

Figure 12. The aggregation level and delivery model taxonomies

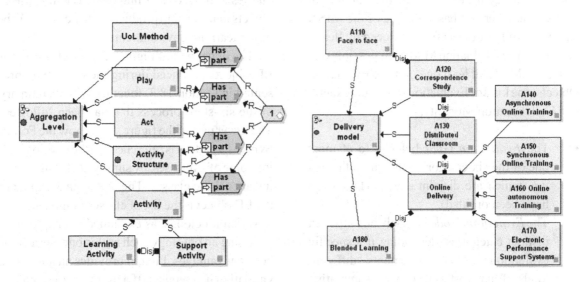

and has a cardinality of at least one. It has the same semantic meaning as the MOT language C link, which is not used in the MOT+OWL language.

The right hand part of Figure 12 present five basic kinds of delivery models: *Face to Face, Correspondence, Distributed Classroom, Online Delivery* and *Blended Learning*. These classes are disjoint two by two. Some of 2-by-2 Disj

links are not shown on the model to improve readability. If a LD uses more than one of these delivery modes, it is classified in the class A180 for Blended Learning. The model also present four sub-classes of Online Delivery. Those are not disjoint classes. This means that a LD object can integrate one, two, three or all four modalities. These categories have been built in the MISA 17 taxonomies of Instructional Engineering products (Paquette, Léonard, De la Teja, Dessaint, Lundgren-Cayrol, 2000)

Pedagogical Strategy

The pedagogical strategy taxonomy shown on Figure 13 also stems out from MISA research. It is a visualisation of the Learning Design classification presented on Figure 4 as a tree of possible metadata entries in PALOMA. Any combination of these classes are possible for a particular LD object.

Learner Evaluation Model

We present on Figure 14 the last part of the LD objects ontology, the learner evaluation model that is also a new version based on one of the MISA taxonomy of LD objects first produced by Ileana de la Teja. The Evaluation Model has possibly one Goal, one Mode, at least one or more Evaluation Objects, one kind of Evaluation Agent and exactly one Collaboration Modality.

- The *Evaluation Goal* belongs to at most one of the six categories shown on the figure, which are disjoint classes (Disj links have been omitted).
- The *Evaluation mode* is exacly one of seven distinct categories, depending if a specific evaluation model implements different kinds of diagnostic, formative, summative or confirmative evaluation contexts. These contexts are also disjoints.
- The *Evaluation Object* is the set of documents or performance data produced by a learner (or a team) that will be evaluated. Theses classes are not disjoint and can be combined. For examples, an evaluation in a computer course can be made through an exam plus some software producer by the learners; an evaluation in a skating course can be based on a skating performance by

the learners, plus an ePortfolio of previous achievements.
- The *Collaboration Modality* adds a precision on how the Evaluation Object has been built, individually, mostly individualy, mostly by team work, only by team work or in an individual/team mixed mode.
- The *Evaluation Agent* that performs the evaluation can be a group or individual trainer, the learner, co-learners or a combination of learners, trainers or other evaluators.

Using the LD Objects Ontology

This ontology can be used, first to reference semantically LD objects, and also to make precise queries to retrieve learning designs and learning objects that can help produce higher quality Web-based learning environments.

The upper part of Figure 15 presents the set of LD objects produced during the case study presented in section 18.3, together with a summary of the six-steps process that has been followed. The lower part of the figure shows how the Forum Synthesis pattern is referenced in the ontology using some of its classes, by simply declaring it as an instance these classes. The metadata assigned to the LD object is the list of classes of the ontology to which it belongs, as explained in chapter 11.

Using an ontology such as this one has a number of advantages. First, it provides an automatic validation mechanism. If a user tries to reference a LD objects with two disjoint classes, it will prompted with this inconsistency. Similarly, if he tries to assign two evaluation goals to the same LD object, he can be prompted to select only one.

Another advantage is the inferencing capability that the ontology provides. Not everything has to be told to the system. For example if a LD object has a class reference, it will be considered has having the class references of all the classes upward in the specialization chain. Using the properties of this class, more related classes can be found and

Figure 13. The pedagogical strategy taxonomy

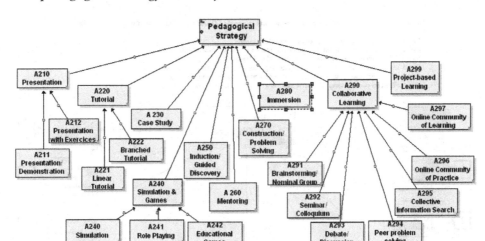

Figure 14. The evaluation model part of the LD objects' ontology

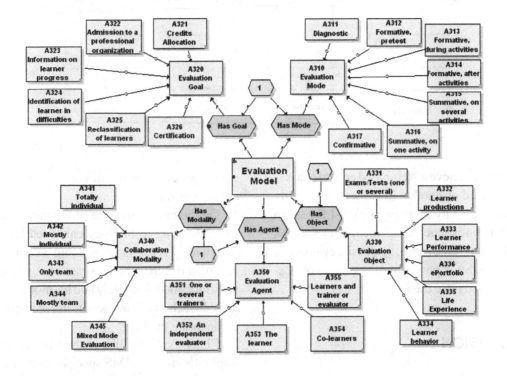

more properties of the objects can be deduced. Similarly, a transitivity axiom on a property can be applied to find out all the related LD objects that are based on a specified LD object.

An inference engine can combine these local built-in inference capabilities. Take for example the following query: *Find all LD objects containing a pattern having a target competency at the analysis skill level or higher.* Such a query will follow all the links in the ontology constrained by restrictions and axioms, listing all the individual corresponding to the query. For example the above

Figure 15. Integration of the case study LD products in the LD objects ontology

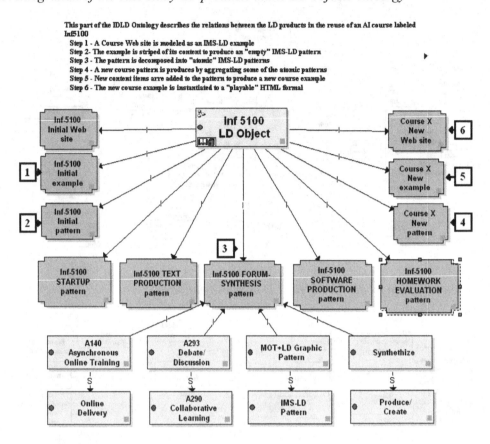

query would retrieve a Web-based course or a lesson plan based on another LD object, containing in one of its activity structure an IMS-LD pattern that has a competency attachment with a skill's part that is analysis, repair, synthesis, evaluate or self-control. Such powerful queries are not possible if we only use the LOM.

CONCLUSION

The work presented in this chapter shows that research in the field of Technology Enhanced Learning has progressed rapidly. On one hand, software engineering concerns such as formal specification, reusability and interoperability have made their way in this community and are here to stay. As a consequence, we are beginning to see

new applications that will improve the quality of online learning.

On the other hand, the problem of designing and delivering technology enhanced learning is now widely recognized as being a complex task in which different dimensions or concepts have to be modelled separately and harmoniously integrated. Such a task implies the use of instructional engineering methods.

Either explicitly like in the MISA method or implicitly, as in the IMS specifications, researchers and practitioners are considering distinct but interrelated concepts such as learning scenarios, knowledge and competency models, learner model, media, resources or learning objects models, evaluation model, assistance model and so on. This separation of concerns has allowed for a better understanding of these dimensions and a more precise specification of technological requirements both at design and at delivery time, allowing new technologies to be effectively tested and integrated into rich learning environments.

The reusability-driven process presented in this chapter, and the ontology for Learning Design Objects is a contribution to address these concerns and facilitate the implementation and dissemination of Instructional Engineering methodology and technology.

The work presented here on learning scenario modeling, decomposition, re-composition and semantic referencing needs to be extended in many directions around the issues of learning scenario patterns and the construction of a larger well-structured LD repository. This might lead us to improve the ontology presented in this chapter. This is another illustration of the need to maintain the semantic referencing of learning objects when the ontology evolves, a question discussed in chapter 11.

Another important research and innovation direction involves partners from the GLOBE community (http://globe-info.org/en), an international effort to federate major learning object repositories around the world. We will develop this subject in Chapter 20, focusing on quality assurance strategies in Learning Object Repository practice.

These preoccupations all converge, from a software engineering point of view, with our development of adaptable ontology-driven learning platforms, such as TELOS, presented in Chapter 15.

REFERENCES

Bailey, C., Mohd, T. Z., Davis, H. C., Fill, K., & Conole, G. (2006). Panning for gold: designing pedagogically inspired learning nuggets. *Educational Technology and Society, 9*(1), 113-122. Retrieved from http://eprints.soton.ac.uk/19642/

Currier, S., & Campbell, L. M. (2006). *Evaluating Learning Resources for Reusability: The "Dner & Learning Objects" Study*. Retrieved February 6, 2006, from http://www.ascilite.org.au/conferences/auckland02/proceedings/papers/059.pdf

De la Teja, I., Lundgren-Cayrol, K., & Paquette, G. (2005). Transposing MISA Learning Scenarios into IMS Units of Learning. *Journal of Educational Technology and Society (Special Issue)*.

IMS-LD. (2006). *Learning Design. Information Model, Best Practice and Implementation Guide, Binding document, Schemas*. Retrieved February 4, 2006, from http://www.imsglobal.org/learning-design/index.html

Koper, R. (2005). An Introduction to Learning Design . In Koper, R., & Tattersall, C. (Eds.), *Learning Design - A Handbook on Modelling and Delivering Networked Education and Training* (pp. 3–20). Berlin: Springer Verlag.

Lundgren-Cayrol, K., & Léonard, M. (2006) *IDLD Modelling Technique*. Retrieved from http://www.idld.org/Methodology/tabid/174/Default.aspx

Martens, H., & Votgen, H. (2006). A Reference Implementation of a Learning Design Engine . In Koper, R., & Tattersall, C. (Eds.), *Learning Design - A Handbook on Modelling and Delivering Networked Education and Training* (pp. 91–108). Berlin: Springer Verlag.

McGreal, R., Anderson, T., Babin, G., Downes, S., Friesen, N, Harrigan, K., Hatala, M., MacLeod, D., Mattson, M., Paquette, G., Richards, G., Roberts, R., & Schafer, S. (2004 March). EduSource: Canada's Learning Object Repository Network. *International Journal of Instructional Technology & Distance Learning*.

Paquette, G. (1999). Meta-knowledge Representation for Learning Scenarios Engineering. In S. Lajoie & M. Vivet (Eds.), *Proceedings of AI-Ed'99 in AI and Education - Open learning environments*. Amsterdam: IOS Press.

Paquette, G. (2004). *Instructional Engineering for Network-Based Learning*. San Francisco: Pfeiffer.

Paquette, G. (2004). IMS-LD: The road ahead. *Canadian Journal of Learning Technologies, 30*(3).

Paquette, G., De la Teja, I., Léonard, M., Lundgren-Cayrol, K., & Marino, O. (2005). An Instructional Engineering Method and Tool for the Design of Units of learning . In Kopper, R., & Tattersall, C. (Eds.), *Learning Design: A Handbook on Modelling and Delivering Networked Education and Training* (pp. 161–184). Berlin: Springer-Verlag.

Paquette, G., Léonard, M., de la Teja, I., Dessaint, M.P., & Lundgren-Cayrol, K. (2000). *Method for Engineering Learning Systems - MISA 4.0 Description of Documentation Elements*. LICEF Research Center, Télé-université.

Paquette, G., Léonard, M., Lundgren-Cayrol, K., Mihaila, S., & Gareau, D. (2006) Learning Design based on Graphical Knowledge-Modeling. Journal of Educational technology and Society ET&S.

Paquette, G., Marino, O., De la Teja, I., Léonard, M., & Lundgren-Cayrol, K. (2005b). Delivery of Learning Design: the Explor@ System's Case . In Koper, R., & Tattersall, C. (Eds.), *Learning Design – A Handbook on Modelling and Delivering Networked Education and Training* (pp. 311–326). Berlin: Springer Verlag.

Paquette, G., Marino, O., De la Teja, I., Lundgren-Cayrol, K., Léonard, M., & Contamines, J. (2005). Implementation and deployment of the IMS learning design specification. *Canadian Journal of Learning and Technology, 31*(2), 85–104.

Paquette, G., Marino, O., Lundgren-Cayrol, K., Léonard, M., & de la Teja, I. (2006) Learning Design Repositories: Structure Ontology and Processes. Presented at TenCompetence workshop, Sofia, Bulgaria, April 2006.

Paquette, G., Miara, A., Lundgren-Cayrol, K., & Guérette, L. (2004). The Explor@2 Learning Object Manager . In McGreal, R. (Ed.), *Online education using learning objects* (pp. 254–268). London: Routledge/Falmer.

RELOAD Project. (2006). Retrieved February 4, 2006, from http://www.reload.ac.uk

Chapter 19
Modeling for Knowledge Management in Organizations

Gilbert Paquette
LICEF Research Center, Canada

Michel Léonard
LICEF Research Center, Canada

Josianne Basque
LICEF Research Center, Canada

Béatrice Pudelko
LICEF Research Center, Canada

ABSTRACT

- Building a Knowledge Management Environment in a Large Company
  - Technical Information Management
  - Tools Involved in the Project
  - Implementing a Methodology
- Transfer of Expertise Through the Co-Modeling of Knowledge
  - Types of Expertise Transfer
  - The Co-Modeling Strategy
  - Participants' Perceptions of Knowledge Transfer and Elicitation
- Modeling a Computerized School
  - Graphic Model of the School
  - Text and Media Versions of the Model
  - Proposed Use of the Model

Knowledge Management has become in recent years a concern of most major organizations. Already, in 2002, a survey by the US Conference Board and the American Management Association had shown that 80% of the thousand largest American companies where implementing some form of knowledge management in their organizations.

Knowledge management embed concepts like "Intellectual Capital", "Learning Organization", "Business Intelligence", "Process re-engineering and decision support" and "Competency Management". It is a cross-disciplinary field using methods and technologies from cognitive science,

DOI: 10.4018/978-1-61520-839-5.ch019

expert systems and knowledge engineering, data and text mining, library and information sciences, document management, computer supported collaborative work (CSCW), communities of practice and organizational science. It is clear that knowledge modeling has a central role to play in such a context.

Knowledge management includes and extends traditional document or data management in many ways. Its goal is to promote the systematic identification, production, formalization, availability and sharing of knowledge in an organization, and also to increase the competencies of its personnel, rather than simply giving them information support. Knowledge management integrates the processing of higher-level knowledge, beyond raw data or factual information. It underlines the importance of principles, models, theories, processes and methods, and helps uncover the tacit knowledge of experts to make it available for learning, working and decision-making.

Because it promotes structured and higher-level knowledge, knowledge management puts much more emphasis than in the past on the knowledge and the competencies of persons working in the organization. It embeds two important processes: knowledge extraction and knowledge acquisition. *Knowledge extraction* transforms the knowledge of experts in a domain into organized information or knowledge resources that can be made available to the whole organization. *Knowledge acquisition* by people in the organization is the inverse process that transforms organizational information and knowledge into new competencies internalized by individual staff members through learning.

Knowledge modeling connects these two processes. Knowledge models, particularly ontologies for the semantic web, are used as knowledge and competencies acquisition tools by persons involved in formal or informal training activities. Knowledge modeling also helps represent use cases of a knowledge management system by describing the actors, the operations that they rule and the resources or learning objects that they use

or produce while processing domain knowledge. This corresponds to activity scenarios as defined in chapter 8. Conversely, actors involved in these use cases will help test, validate or identify improvements and extensions to the knowledge model or the ontology of a domain.

This chapter presents three applications of Knowledge Modeling using the MOT representation language and tools. These applications were performed by the LICEF team in partnership with different organizations. The first one is a project with a large company that aims to create a knowledge management environment to access technical information distributed in 30 different document bases. The second one focuses on the transfer of expertise supported by co-modeling a domain of expertise through collaboration between experts and novices. The third one uses knowledge modeling to describe the processes, the actors and the resources in a typical school, in order to identify the ICT tools that could help best support the organization in its activities.

19.1 BUILDING A KNOWLEDGE MANAGEMENT ENVIRONMENT IN A LARGE COMPANY

The transfer and retention of knowledge is a major challenge within organizations, especially when key resources leave at retirement. A large organization like Hydro-Quebec (HQ) is no exception especially because of the needs created by huge staff mobility and the great number of departures for retirement.

To avoid the lost of knowledge and ensure the continuation of its services, Hydro-Quebec uses Information and Communication Technologies (ICT) tools and methods for the transfer of knowledge. When the intention of an expert to retire is confirmed, one strategy is to transfer of knowledge to a new person, termed "novice" by co-modeling the expert's knowledge. Another strategy is to put in place a knowledge management system facilitating the transfer of information between future retirees and their replacements. The first strategy will be presented in the next section. We now focus on the second one.

Technical Information Management Project

The use of the MOT graphical language at Hydro-Québec and other organizations over years has indicated its user-friendliness demanding a low learning curve. The models produced are available for non-specialists in computers in an interoperable format that can be adapted to the terminology and needs of users. Furthermore, the MOT+ software has the possibility to export ontological models to the standard OWL-DL ontology format. This is considered important asset, for the management of knowledge in this organization.

These facts have helped to refine the initial strategy and its implementation plan for the company. A project called GIT on the management of technical Information (Imbeault 2007) is under development to enhance the knowledge and knowhow of Hydro-Quebec. It is financed by the company, with the following goals:

- To develop methods and tools to formally represent the knowledge of various fields of expertise;
- To develop robust applications and user-friendly interfaces, well adapted to the users and their needs;
- To facilitate the tracing process and access to resources in an industrial context to meet the needs of the enterprise.

The first step of this project is conducted at the Automatic Production Unit covering five disciplines in automation with high technical content, central for the core mission of the company. In particular, it plans to reduce difficulties related to many aspects: the access to technical information; their dispersion in the organization in 30 different

document and data bases; the flow of information between the actors involved in the activities in the field and finally to the integration of the new employees in the organization. The methodologies and tools that are used to are those developed in the Canadian LORNET research network http://www.lornet.org/, managed at LICEF and funded by the Natural Sciences and Engineering Research Council of Canada (NSERC).

They use heavily the Semantic Web technologies presented in chapter 10. Ontology-based systems support a focused and personalized access to information. This approach allows federated search of information that is scattered in different systems, giving the impression to the user of using a single resource bank. Moreover, the use of ontologies facilitates the sharing of information between the actors involved in work processes through shared interfaces and monitoring facilities.

Tools Involved in the Project

Several tools are provided for the implementation of this project. Most of these tools are components issued from the TELOS operating system that has been presented in chapter 15. Some tools will be adapted to the requirements and needs of Hydro-Quebec for this project.

More specifically, two technologies based on the MOT graphical language are used to model the knowledge: domain ontologies and executable scenario processes. The integration of ontological models and scenario models in a single approach provides access to interoperable tools and methods to guide enterprises in the whole process of representation of semantic knowledge.

The following tools are involved in the GIT project:

- The *Knowledge Editor* (MOT+) is used by a designer to model quickly the knowledge and expertise in a semi-formal way (see chapter 14). Thereafter, using this tool, any expert can easily modify or add precisions to this semi-formal level of representation. In addition, this model serves as a basis to define the main classes and properties of the field ontology built with the *Ontology Editor*.

- The *Ontology Editor* presented in chapter 10 is used to produce the ontology model that describes knowledge of the domain, here Automatic Production. An example of such a domain model is shown in Figure 1. It exports the graph to a corresponding OWL-XML format. This formal knowledge model of the domain of expertise enables computer agents to process the knowledge. The domain ontology is the backbone of the *Knowledge Base* that contains semantic references by the ontology to the resources stored in the document and data bases, in way explained in chapter 11.

- The *Semantic Annotator* is the tool that allows the designer and other users, such as

specialists in document management, to enter facts about technical information resources in the knowledge base. It is a web-based tool facilitating the entry of information in a collaborative way.

- The *Scenario Editor* is used for modeling the multi-actor processes' scenarios or workflow, together with the resources required by the activities in each processes. It uses a formalism that can be interpreted by a machine. The model on Figure 2 shows such a scenario modeling interactions between human actors and machine operations that must be coordinated to perform a task.

- Once the scenario is defined in a model, its *Execution* software monitors the process to support and assist people to share the infor-

Figure 1. Part of the automatic production ontology

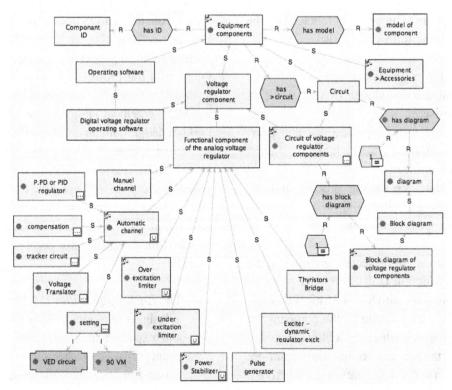

Figure 2. Part of the preventive maintenance process

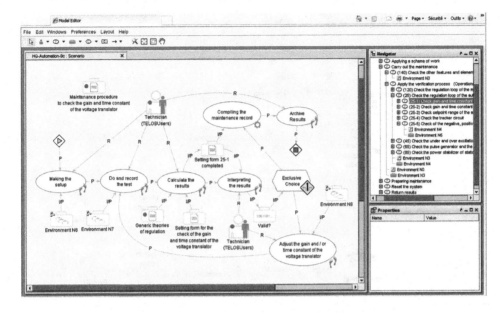

mation and collaborate to achieve the tasks and activities in each process.

- The *Inference Engine* can make inferences from the logical rules outlined in the domain ontology about facts entered in the *Semantic Annotator*. Any search in the *Knowledge Base* for information resources needs to pass through a request to the *Inference Engine*.

- The *Operating System* coordinates all the tools and ensures their interoperability and communication. It provides resource management, to run the tools and support the communication between the various equipments involved in the platform. It is responsible for controlling access to resources from the work processes in execution.

Implementing a Methodology

Humans are at the heart of this project and the implementation of the solution depends entirely on them. The computer systems and tools are there to support the process and make

the task more systematic and effective. Figure 3 illustrates the process of implementing the methodology in a specific area of expertise. This scenario is a formal model showing the orchestration of the Actors and their activities, tools, and resources.

In the first step, using the Knowledge Editor and the Ontology Editor, the designer meets a panel of expert and the manager to build and validate the semi formal knowledge model of the multi-actor process and the formal ontology model of the target field or domain.

In the second step, in collaboration with the specialist in document management, the designer uses the Semantic Annotator to ensure that any appropriate technical support resources are well referenced by the domain ontology. For this, the designer instantiates the ontology concepts and theirs properties with the real resources (facts) distributed in many document management systems actually in place in the enterprise. The gateways with these management systems are made by the Operating system. The result of this step is a Knowledge Base that is validated by a domain specialist.

Figure 3. Process of implementing the methodology in organization

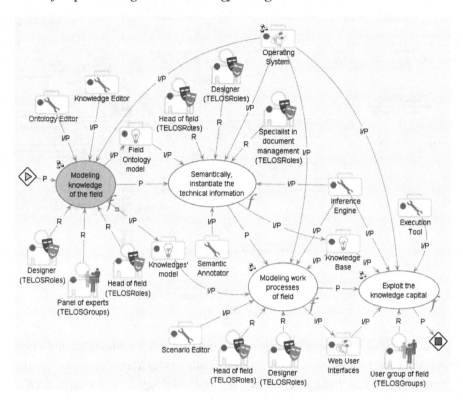

In the next step, the designer uses the Scenario Editor to produce an executable model of the working process (scenario) based on the semi formal knowledge model issued from the first step. He also describes the technical resources necessary to perform the tasks of all actors involved, by linking them to the appropriate element in the Knowledge Base. The designer can control the specific modalities of implementation of the multi-actor process and he can also insert some automatic operations in the process to interact with software already in place in the company.

In the last step, the users interact with the working process through a graphical web interface generated from the scenario by the Execution Tool. Using this interface, they have access to the resources needed for each task and they also have the means to interact with other users involved in the process. Through other web interfaces, the users can make semantic requests to the Knowl-

edge Base to find any referenced information. The Inference Engine tool guides this semantic search.

In summary this process aims to develop methods for the extraction, classification and operationalization of the knowledge contained in a specific domain of expertise, in the form of process-based multi-actor workflows. During the processes, users will assess the applications produced and suggest improvements to the general approach. Eventually, a validated knowledge management process will be embodied in an Web-based environment.

From a technological point of view, recent developments in the Semantic Web, including the work within the LORNET research network, ensure that the semantic approach proposed in the GIT project is feasible. More specifically, two distinctive elements can contribute greatly to the success of a semantic approach in an industrial environment:

- The use of a visual language and user-friendly tools accessible to all users;
- An integrated semantic access to intuitive and engaging interfaces, maximizing the usability of these tools.

By using interoperable standard formats like OWL-DL and multi-actor workflow scenarios, the solution is more easily integrated in an organization's technological architecture and perfectly suited to future technological developments that are always in progress.

This project aims to lay the foundation for knowledge management implementation processes that can be used in later phases of the GIT project at Hydro-Québec, or more generally for Semantic Web applications in other organization.

19.2 TRANSFER OF EXPERTISE IN ORGANIZATIONS THROUGH CO-MODELING OF KNOWLEDGE[1]

Another strategy, experimented by a team at the LICEF Research Center in a few organizations. This strategy is based on small groups of expert and novice employees that co-construct a graphical representation of their tacit professional knowledge using the MOT knowledge editor.

After a first analysis of the theoretical underpinnings of the proposed strategy (Basque & Pudelko, 2004) and some exploratory observations of the potential of knowledge modeling for expertise transfer in a large public organization (Basque, Imbeault, Pudelko, & Léonard, 2004), the team collected data in the context of two action-research studies in workplace settings. The first one was conducted in a large governmental organization and implied three different groups of workers (Basque & Pudelko, 2008), while the second one was conducted in three SMEs in the manufacturing sector (Basque, Desjardins, Pudelko, & Léonard, 2008).

In this section, a distinction between two types of expertise transfer is first made, followed by a presentation of the strategy experimented and of some findings drawn from data collected during the studies.

Knowledge Co-Modeling Using Visual Tools

Since 1999, in the various projects through the Training Institute of Hydro Quebec and the Transenergy division, several training on the MISA Instructional Engineering Method (Paquette 2003) and its MOT modeling tools have been provided to designers and trainers of the company. Moreover, since September 2001, LICEF helped developed a strategy to ensure a transfer of knowledge and skills of experts (technicians, engineers, managers) using the MOT+ modeling software presented in the first part of this book. This software was progressively updated to meet some specific needs of Hydro Quebec. At the beginning, this approach, called knowledge co-modeling, was used with specialized human resources of the Division of Equipment. It was afterwards gradually used in other divisions. More specifically, between 2004 and 2006, the knowledge modeling language and tool has been used successfully to represent knowledge from various experts within the automatic production division, with the specific goal of transferring knowledge from experts to novices

In the first knowledge co-modeling strategy used, pairs consisting of an expert and a novice, model jointly the knowledge in front of a computer equipped with MOT. They represent and link together concepts, principles, procedures and facts related to a specific aspect of the work done by an expert in the organization. This process helps to preserve the expertise of the organization, including the transfer to novices. Also, the product of co-modeling, the models and other related documents are stored by a document management system. Thereafter, the models can be consulted as references for novices who can maintain or adapt them from their own experience of work.

According to a bulletin issued in October 2007 Hydro-Quebec, this process has yielded tangible results that were confirmed by an auditing firm. It offers to the participants a process of empowerment to receive and transmit information. This bulletin cites Robert Lapointe, Director of Human Resources Management at the Hydro-Quebec, Human Resources and Shared Services:

"We have been examining a dozen profiles of jobs, especially in Technical Information, we realize that the process allowed for learning and rapid uptake of specialist expertise. When there was a sharing problem between the expert and the learner, it could assume some responsibilities and take over when the expert would do something else. This resulted in a good success rate of securing certain jobs"

While knowledge co-modeling has proven useful to help novices catch up fast on experts' main knowledge, it is also true that after experts retire, novices need to come back to processes and knowledge's from which their understanding depend.

Types of Expertise Transfer

We need first to distinguish between a "product-oriented" and a "process-oriented" approach to knowledge management, Basque et al. (2008) considered that two types of expertise transfer can be put in place in organizations, which they call Type I and Type II.

Type I Expertise Transfer occurs when workers interact with each other in a more or less formal manner. In this *process-oriented approach*, knowledge is considered *"tied to the person who developed it and is shared mainly through person-to-person contact"* (Apostolou et al., 2000, p. 2), and technology is used to help

people communicate, collaborate and negotiate meaning.

Type II Expertise Transfer occurs when workers consult documents describing some part of the organizational knowledge. In this *product-oriented approach*, technology is used mainly to capture expert knowledge and eventually to store it in an "institutional memory".

The collaborative knowledge co-modeling strategy reported here can be used to support the two types of expertise transfer. As a process-oriented strategy, it promotes expertise transfer during the joint construction of the knowledge model by experts and novices. Through the interaction with experts, novices construct actively their own strategic professional knowledge. As a product-oriented strategy, collaborative knowledge modeling aims at capturing the tacit knowledge of the experts in a graphical semi-formal model (see chapter 16), which will be eventually made available to other employees or will be transformed in a more formal representation, such as an ontology, and will then serve to elaborate an "intelligent" and user-friendly knowledge management system that can eventually be queried in natural language.

In product-oriented type II transfers, co-modeling groups may be composed entirely of experts. However, even in these cases, the LICEF team favors a mix of expertise, since novices are likely to support and broaden the elicitation process regarding expert knowledge through their specialized and informed interventions about the targeted domain. On the one hand, they are motivated to develop their own skills within the domain and, on the other hand, they necessarily possess more skills related to the domain than do knowledge engineers from the outside.

The primary objective of our research and the experimental procedures were designed to respond primarily to the objective of transferring expertise through the co-construction of knowledge models, although we did not exclude the possibility that the resulting models could also serve the objectives of a product-oriented type II transfer.

Furthermore, it was found, during the sessions, that the participants spontaneously adopted a product-oriented approach, expressed through their concerns regarding the quality of the models produced and their usability among other employees. Clearly, there is a need for the organization to clearly distinguish between the objectives of the two different co-modeling strategies.

The Co-Modeling Strategy

The procedure used to implement the co-modeling strategy in organizations includes different steps that can be operationalized differently depending of the goal and the context of the project. The MOT model of Figure 4 illustrates the main generic steps.

- *Specify the domain to model.* In a company, the specification of the target domain usually stems from managers' priorities. A systematic methodology can be used to identify, at a high-level, the most critical knowledge in the organization (Ermine, Boughzala, and Tounkara 2006). At this phase, it is also important that head managers specify the type of expertise transfer

they want to implement in the organization (Type I and/or Type II).

- *Selecting participants.* Groups of less than five participants are recommended. Experts can be workers near retirement possessing strategic knowledge or individuals who possess rare knowledge, which are usually explicitly recognized as experts by their peers. Novices are not necessarily new staff: they can be employees who recently changed position within the organization or individuals who need to extend their knowledge on some work processes to be able to substitute other employees at times. In addition, criteria other than degree of expertise need to be considered to select participants: availability, willingness to share knowledge, familiarity with visual representations, etc. Moreover, participants need to be well informed of the goal and process of the knowledge modeling strategy and be clearly willing to become involved in the activity.
- *Train participants to knowledge modeling.* Training will differ according to the role assigned to the participants involved in the project. If they are to manipulate MOT in order to revise or maintain the

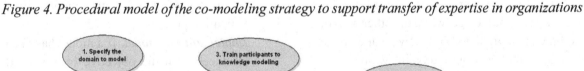

Figure 4. Procedural model of the co-modeling strategy to support transfer of expertise in organizations

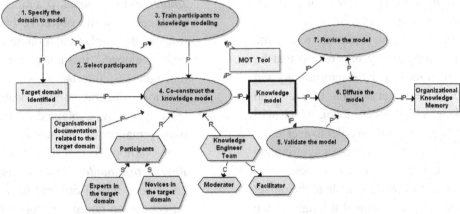

knowledge models after the guided co-knowledge modeling activity, training relative to the MOT software and formalism is necessary. In this case, a two-day session followed by individual and group consultations with the instructor has shown to be effective for basic training. Otherwise, participants' training to the MOT software can be limited to a brief presentation of the typologies used in MOT complemented with a summary sheet. Participants become quite easily and naturally familiar with the MOT language simply by observing how the knowledge-modeling specialist manipulates the software and uses the MOT formalism and semantic grammar.

- *Co-construct the knowledge model.* The duration of the sessions can vary depending on the scope of the target field and the availability of the participants. In the studies reported, an intensive three-day session was put in place, which allows participants to elaborate a global, relatively stable and consensual initial representation of the field. Additional work may be required in order to add details or to extend the scope of the model.

Two knowledge-modeling specialists worked with groups of 2 to 5 persons. The first one (the moderator) interviews participants in order to elicit overtly their knowledge, while the other one (the facilitator) manipulates the software and creates the map, which is projected on the wall.

Prior to the session, the moderator read some documentation supplied by experts, so that he can familiarize himself with the terminology and main aspects of the target domain. He can even develop a sketchy first-level model, which will be suggested to participants in order to accelerate the knowledge modeling process and stimulate discussion at the beginning of the session.

Some decisions should be made at the outset of the session and re-examined throughout the process: type of model that should be developed, level of specificity in the elicitation of the knowledge (developing breadth-first or depth-first?), appropriate level of granularity, etc. Participants are invited to be specific and consistent when labeling knowledge objects, and careful attention is paid to redundancy. At any given moment during the session, the knowledge model can be restructured if participants feel that it should be.

- *Validate the knowledge model.* Once the first version of the model is produced, a validation can be performed by one or more experts who participated in the session and/or peer experts involved in the field. It can be useful to intertwine this validation process with the participants' real work practices: while "instantiating" the knowledge represented in the model based on actual work situations, modifications to the knowledge model can be more easily identified. Electronic documents or URLs can also be attached to knowledge objects in order to provide them with a more detailed and contextual meaning. Moreover, the participants can present their co-constructed knowledge model to their managers and colleagues. This can act as a means of promoting their work, as well as allowing them to deepen their own comprehension of the model and thus supporting the validation process.

- *Implement the model.* If a model has been produced with the objective of a Type II transfer, an implementation strategy must be developed, including access rights management, interfacing with the organization's documents and databases, data security, etc. As explained in chapter 14, a transformation of the semi-formal model to an ontology format should be evaluated.

- *Revise the model.* Once constructed, a knowledge model can and must evolve to reflect the on-going development of individual and organizational knowledge. It is then important to update the model on a regular basis. This task can be performed by individuals with a mandate and (preferably) a group of people endowed with a sufficient level of expertise in the field, while also being familiar with the representational language.

Participants' Perceptions of Knowledge Transfer and Elicitation

Data collected in the two action-research studies (Basque & Pudelko, 2008; Basque et al., 2008) included interviews with participants before and after the 3-day knowledge modeling session, successive versions of the knowledge model elaborated during the session, screen- and audio-captured of the modelling session and researchers' observation notes during meetings with the coordinators of the activity in the settings. Because of limited space, we report only partial results related to participants' perceptions of the effect of the strategy on the knowledge construction process in novices and on the knowledge elicitation process by the experts.

The co-modeling process using MOT was well appreciated by most participants. Both the overall strategy and the modeling language were considered adequate in terms of the objectives. The participants recognized that the process was quite cognitively demanding. The feeling of cognitive effort experienced by participants was related to the necessity of providing precise knowledge explanations, in particular, for "decomposing" knowledge originally considered by experts as impossible or even futile to decompose further.

Since the representational strategy of participating organizations involved constructing models of the type "method and technique" explained in Chapter 3, the focus from the outset was on representing actions (procedures), which were then associated with resources and products (in the form of concepts) and strategic and conditional knowledge in the form of

principles guiding and regulating these actions. Thus, it can be said that the representational property of MOT allowed the participants to focus on actions. When representing an action as a "knowledge object", then it can be decomposed into sub-actions (with the C link) or specialized into different manners to perform this action or into sub-classes of actions (with the S link). The P link (Precedence) can be used to represent sequences between actions.

This representation technique is particularly suitable for expert knowledge, whose structure can thus be reproduced. Indeed, research in cognitive psychology(Chi, Glaser, & Farr, 1988; Chi, Glaser, & Rees, 1982; Ericsson & Charness, 1994; Glaser, 1986; Schmidt & Boshuizen, 1993; Sternberg, 1997) has shown that expert knowledge is structured in the form of mental models in which the various components are closely intertwined, uneasily accessible by consciousness, and therefore difficult to communicate verbally. Experts' mental models imply much procedural knowledge (the know-how), along with knowledge on explicit conditions of its applicability known as conditional or strategic knowledge (the know-when and the know-why), and object schemata which can be instantiated at will (the know-what or declarative knowledge). The novice and the expert then have a useful means for representing their field work as their own procedural model.

This characteristic of the representational language can also bring the novice to interrogate the expert during the co-construction of the knowledge model, the concepts and principles linked to procedures in the model acting as anchors for interaction. Co-modeling generates many discussions, some of which are very lively, involving problems experienced by novices in their recent work. These discussions led some novices to find solutions to these problems on their own and even propose concrete solutions for improving the professional practices of their team. Model definition consists therefore not only in recreating existing knowledge but also, from an individual and organizational point of view, in creating new knowledge.

Novices related how they had become aware of the preferred practices of their organization and how they were able to use this information in their subsequent work. One participant described his meta-cognitive learning experience by explaining how he now approaches work-related problems "through a different lens." In one organization, a few weeks after the experiment, a novice participant was required to complete a job similar to the one modeled and found it much easier because of the learning acquired during the co-modeling process.

A notable result is that even for the experts, the co-modeling process appears to have contributed to the integration and deepening of their expertise. Thus, although no special attention was made by experts regarding the possibility of their acquiring new knowledge during the co-modeling sessions (they mainly saw themselves as "providers of information"), all experts declared during follow-up interviews that they had "seen" something new or better "understood" their way of proceeding or "dealing" with problems. This confirms that the co-modeling process enabled them to use their existing knowledge about actions as objects in the construction of new knowledge models, a process which is also known as "reflective practice" (Schön, 1983, Sternberg, 1999).

Overall, all participants considered that the models produced were satisfactory and adequately represented their area of expertise, given the relatively short time spent in the activity, and despite that the models were considered still incomplete at the end of the three-day co-modeling sessions. They found that the models were not mere repetitions or pooling of knowledge already documented in the organization, but that they were true creations that provided a new perspective on the expertise required for the targeted fields.

The research reported here indicates that co-modeling using the MOT representation language and tools has great potential as a strategy

for transferring expertise between experts and non-experts, since it encourages the explanation of tacit expert knowledge and the construction of knowledge by experts and novices alike during the co-modeling process.

But the results also indicate that to fully benefit from this strategy, participants must feel enabled to use the co-modeling process and the following discussions to explain and, at times, self-explain their knowledge. In this type of strategy, then, modeling is seen as a means rather than an end in itself.

However, it seems that participating organizations did initially grasp the full potential of the strategy as a process-oriented type I transfer of expertise. Some researchers, such as Sveiby (2001), emphasize the different types of knowledge transfer/integration that should be considered in implementing a true knowledge management process within a company. The author indicates that, typically, it is the strategy of establishing an organizational memory that retains most of the attention, to the point where some people equate this strategy with an overall process of knowledge management.

Our data indicate that this was also true for the project's partner companies whose representations and expectations were oriented toward a product-oriented type II transfer. A notable result of the research carried out by Basque and her colleagues is therefore that, despite the participants' product-oriented initial focus many of the comments collected indicate that the main potential of co-modeling, as it was experienced by the participants, was to allow also a process-oriented knowledge transfer occurring during the group modeling sessions themselves.

It is therefore necessary for organizations to recognize the value of this process, not only as a Type II strategy, but also as a Type I strategy, and that they integrate it within their overall strategy of knowledge management.

19.3 MODELLING A COMPUTERIZED SCHOOL

This section present another aspect of modeling for knowledge management in organizations. Here the organization, in fact a high school, is modeled in its main processes, the actors and the documents they consult or produce, in order to help the school management introduce computers and ICT to support its functions. The project was one of the early applications of the MOT modeling methodology, conducted between 1994 and 1998 by a LICEF team (Basque et al. 1998), in two secondary schools as part of the project École informatisée clef en main (The Turnkey Computerized School) developed for Québec's Ministry of Education.

Background of the Approach

The project resulted in the elaboration of a model for the computerized school and a generic model for the integration of information and communication technology (ICT) in schools. Together, the models presented here can serve as a framework for helping schools to make choices appropriate to their specific needs in terms of implementation of ICT, whether as part of teaching and learning activities, educational management activities, or resource document management activities. They process can also be adapted to other kinds of organizations.

By "computerized school" we do not mean an idealized, monolithic vision of ICT in Québec schools, but a systemic and adaptable vision of the various potential uses of ICT in a typical school "rethought" in its entirety and taking into account all of its complexity.

In this perspective, a school can be regarded as an organization in which various stakeholders or actors (students, teachers, non-teaching professionals, managers, school board members, parents, etc.) receive, access, process, manipulate, produce, and communicate information in carrying out various activities such as teaching, learning, and managing. These processes are regulated by a number of principles (pedagogical or managerial) and are implemented using various tools. ICTs, as such, represent a potential for facilitating, enriching, and rethinking how these processes are implemented. They can act as catalysts for redefining the various activities that take place in these kinds of organizations.

The computerized school model was guided by a systemic approach to school management. Under this approach, the school is seen as a system which is part of a larger system and which contains interrelated subsystems. It is therefore important not only to identify the processes of the school but also to specify the links between these processes.

The development of the model was divided into three phases: a graphic representation, a text description of the various components, and a multimedia version incorporating both the graphic and text descriptions.

Graphic Model of the School

A large-scale graphic model consisting of four levels of nested sub-models was developed using MOT. The model contains three types of objects:

* School processes are represented by procedures;
* {Les intervenants qui régissent ces processus ou qui aident à leur exécution sont représentés par des principes.|Stakeholders or Actors regulating or implementing these processes are represented by principles. } Actors can be the various categories of people involved in a school (students, teachers, administrators, professionals, etc.);}
* The inputs and product of the school processes are represented by concepts. These

include printed documents, electronic documents, and computer equipment, as well as the tools that are used to perform the processes (inputs) or that are produced during the execution of the processes (products).

A fourth object type is not part of the proposed model but can be used to adapt the model to a particular school situation. For example, users may want to identify the word processor used in their school (Word, WordPerfect, etc.). They can add this information by instantiating the input "word processor" by a fact-type symbol representing one of the versions of Word or WordPerfect. One could also instantiate procedures to a fact representing a particular process in a school, or instantiate actors to particular people or categories of people in the school.

There are five relation types between these objects.

- Composition links are used to establish a hierarchy of school processes. This hierarchy consists of four levels: 0, 1, 2, and 3 as shown on Figure 5.
- Regulation links connect actors to the processes they "regulate" or for which they are "responsible." For example, "Student" regulates the process "Learning."
- Assistance links, represented by the letter A, connect a actor to a process, indicating that the actor participates in the execution of the processes as an assistant or helper. In Figure 6, the actor "Teacher" assists the actor "Student" in the process "Learning."
- Input/product links connect an input or a product to a process. Figure 7 shows the inputs for the process "Learning."

Figure 5 shows part of the four levels of the task model for School processes.

Figure 5. Hierarchy of school processes

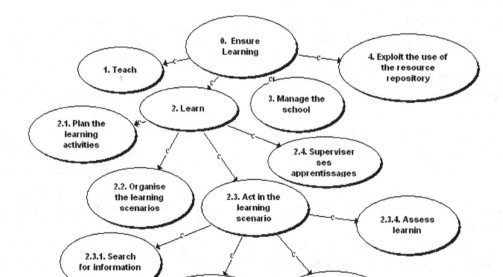

- Level 0 represents the most general level, i.e. the school's mission, simply identified as to "Ensure learning."
- Level 1 consists of four main processes that contribute to achieving this mission, i.e. "Teach," "Learn," "Manage the school," and "Exploit the use of the resource repository (the multimedia center)."
- At Level 2 of the hierarchy, each process is divided into sub-processes. For example, the process "Learning" is divided into four sub-processes, labeled from 2.1 to 2.4.
- At Level 3, each of the Level 2 sub-processes is divided into tasks. A total of 63 tasks are defined in the model.

Figure 6 shows the main stakeholders (actors) and the inputs to one of the process: « Learn ».

Figure 7 illustrates the input and products of task 2.4.1, « Self-learner evaluation of assistance

needs during learning», a sub-process of process 2.4.

Figure 8 shows part of the hierarchy of tools. Specialization links connect two objects of the same type, one being a "sort of" the other. The first is therefore more specific than the second. The arrow proceeds from the more specific object to the more general one.

The graphic model for a computerized school consists of 84 processes, over 300 inputs and products, and up to 10 categories of actors. Given the scale of the model, certain conventions regarding its interpretation needed to be established:

- All inputs/products and actors of a process are "inherited" at a lower level. The concept of inheritance increases the readability of graphs and decreases their redundancy. When reading a graph, therefore, it is important to identify the inputs/products and actors that appear at a higher level. The

Figure 6. Actors and inputs of the process "learning"

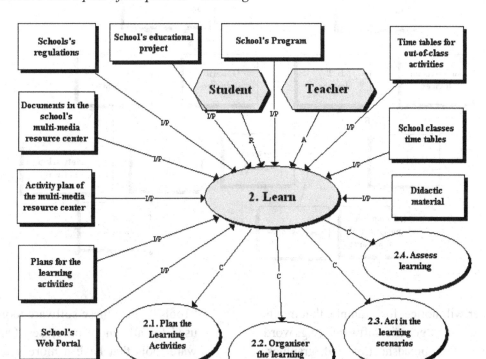

Figure 7. Inputs and products of a terminal task (Level 3)

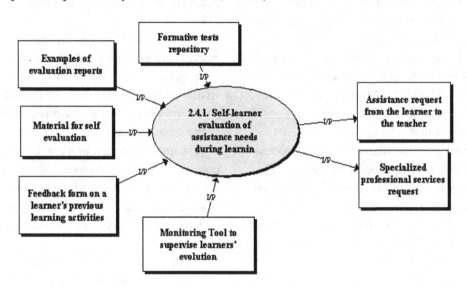

Figure 8. Hiérarchy of tools used in the computerized schools

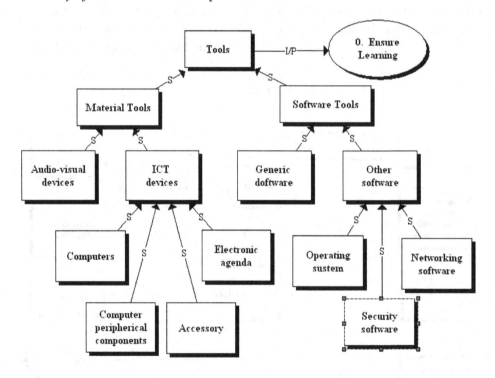

reader will notice, for example, that inputs of the type "'generic software" (e.g. word processing, spreadsheet, e-mail, graphics, browser, and presentation software) appear at Level 0 of the hierarchy (under the input "Tools") since these software tools can be used for all school processes. Other software tools that have a more specific use appear only at the level of tasks (Level 3).

- Inputs/products are defined in generic terms. In ontology terminology, they are classes, not individual objects. Thus, the actual name of a technological tool or generic software is not mentioned in the graph. For example, the term "word processor" is used rather than naming a specific software such as "Word 2007".

- Objects contained in several graphs are identified by a red dot, indicating that they are repeated and cross-referenced. In MOT, by selecting the object and then "Next Reference" in the "View" menu, all graphs containing that object can be displayed one by one. All objects linked to a particular object can also be viewed by carrying out a proximity search on a new page of the model. To do this, you first select the referenced object and then "Insert neighbors" in the Edit menu.

Text and Media Versions of the Model

The graphic model is supplemented by text descriptions in the form of records for each process, sub-process, and task. Each record provides a definition of the process, sub-process, or task. It offers a brief overview of how ICT can help support the process. It lists the most important inputs (including computer tools) and products of the process, and identifies the actor(s) who execute the process or assist in its implementation. The following is an example of a such a record.

In addition to records describing processes and tasks, other records deal more specifically with the various categories of tools identified in the model and provide, for each category, examples of existing tools.

Once the graphic and text versions of the model were completed, a more user-friendly and school-appropriate multimedia version was developed based on the model. This software is

Table 1.

2.4.1 Student self-evaluation of needs
Description This task allows students to recognize difficulties faced at school and to identify available sources of in-school or out-of-school help. Difficulties may be cognitive (understanding, need for tutoring), emotional, or physical. Students can draw upon supplementary learning assessment activities from a bank of formative tests to verify their understanding or acquisition of new knowledge and skills. Using the formative assessment report, corrected evaluation material, and their own learning assessment record, students analyze their needs and submit requests for help from available resources and/or for professional consultation.
ICT Contribution The bank of formative tests can be in electronic form, making it possible to identify the most appropriate tests for each student. Electronic mail offers students a more discreet method for seeking sources of help than by telephone or through personal visits to the office. The school's Web site can also be an important source of information in this regard. As well, a browser will allow students to seek information on the Internet that can help them to better manage their learning experience.

Inputs	Products
• Corrected learning evaluation material • Bank of formative tests • Formative assessment report • Learning assessment record • Learning assessment software	• Student's help request form to teacher • Request for professional consultation

Actors **Responsibility:** Student **Assistants:** Teacher, professional staff

Figure 9. Multimedia version of the model

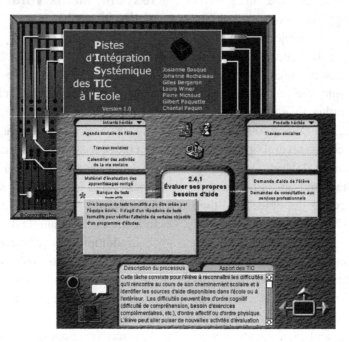

Figure 10. Modelling and tools

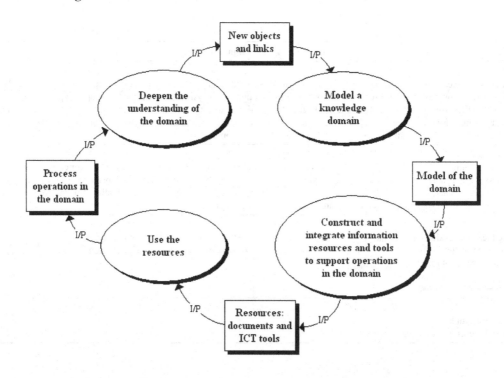

named PISTE: Pistes d'intégration systémique des TIC à l'école (paths for systemic integration of ICT in schools). This version includes inputs and inherited outputs; however, it is intended for consultation purposes only, i.e. it is not "adaptable," unlike the MOT model, which can be instantiated to the particularities of a school.

Proposed Use of the Model

Schools can use the model to develop or regularly revise their ICT implementation plan. Indeed, the model offers a holistic and integrated approach to the typical processes that take place in a school, as well as an overview of the potential uses of various technological tools. Consequently, each school can select the processes, sub-processes, or tasks they consider priorities in their ICT plan. As well, the model can easily provide a snapshot of the many potential uses of a particular tool in the overall processes of a school in such a way as to maximize the effectiveness of the tool.

The model can also provide a snapshot of the computerization of a school's processes at any given moment or a snapshot of its computerization objectives. Indeed, the word "adaptable" in the model's title suggests that schools can make changes to the graphic version of the model as they see fit. Schools can thus omit, add, or change the names of objects or the names of relations between objects of the model to reflect as closely as possible their individual needs. Schools can even add levels to the model if they feel that certain tasks need to be further sub-divided.

CONCLUSION

In this chapter, we have presented three wide-scale projects of knowledge management in organizations using the modeling technique discussed in the previous chapters. The first one uses visual modeling to plan the development of an ontology-driven access to a large company technical information bases. The second one emphasizes the use of co-modeling between experts and novices in various organizations as a way to transfer knowledge between co-modellers and develop the organization's memory. The third one models the generic processes in a school in order to plan the integration of ICT support to its main learning support activities.

Despite their differences, these applications of modeling have much in common. In all three projects, we have built the models first to understand the domain, then to deepen our understanding, better integrate and systematically identify the important knowledge objects and their relationships. We then used the models to provide or build resources to support the knowledge management processes. The MOT model of Figure 10 shows the role of modeling in a cycle of knowledge acquisition and use, which is fundamental in any innovation process within an organization.

A domain's model serves to construct the resources needed to support the operations described in that model. The model facilitates the definition of these resources (tools, documents, services, etc.) by specifying who provides them, who uses them, and in which processes or operations.

Once constructed, these resources are used by the actors for whom they are intended to carry out their various functions in the domain, for the transfer of expertise, the acquisition of competencies, or the management of an organization's work processes.

Monitoring how a domain is processed using these resources allows us not only to validate the model, but also to discover new objects and new links that can lead to a better modeling of the domain. Such a meta-method for research and development has obvious applications for many other domains than the ones presented here.

REFERENCES

Apostolou, D., Mentzas, G., Young, R., & Abecker, A. (2000). *Consolidating the product versus process approaches in knowledge management: The Know-net approach.* Paper presented at the Conference Practical Application of Knowledge Management (PAKeM 2000) - April 12-14, 2000, Manchester, UK.

Basque, J., Desjardins, C., Pudelko, B., & Léonard, M. (2008). *Gérer les connaissances stratégiques dans des entreprises manufacturières de la Monté-régie: Expérimentation de la co-modélisation des connaissances dans 3 PME. Rapport de recherche.* Montreal, Canada: CEFRIO.

Basque, J., Imbeault, C., Pudelko, B., & Léonard, M. (2004). Collaborative knowledge modeling between experts and novices: A strategy to support transfer of expertise in an organization. In A. J. Canas, J. D. Novak & F. M. Gonzalez (Eds.), *Proceedings of the First International Conference on Concept Mapping (CMC 2004), Pamplona, September 14-17* (Vol. 1, pp. 75-81). Pamplona, Spain: Universidad Publica de Navarra.

Basque, J., & Pudelko, B. (2004). La modélisation des connaissances à l'aide d'un outil informatisé à des fins de transfert d'expertise: Recension d'écrits. Montréal, Canada: Centre de recherche LICEF, Télé-université.

Basque, J., & Pudelko, B. (2008). La co-modélisation des connaissances à l'aide d'un outil informatisé. Une stratégie de transfert d'expertise en milieu de travail. Rapport final des expérimentations menées à la Régie des Rentes du Québec. Montréal, Canada: Centre de recherche LICEF, Télé-université.

Basque, J., Rocheleau, J., Winer, L., Michaud, P., Bergeron, G., Paquette, G., & Paquin, C. (1998) *Un modèle adaptable d'une école informatisée.* École informatisée Clés en main du Québec Inc et Centre de recherche LICEF, Télé-université.

Chi, M. T. H., Feltovitch, P. J., & Glaser, R. (1981). Categorisation and representation of physics problems by experts and novices. *Cognitive Science, 5,* 121–152. doi:10.1207/s15516709cog0502_2

Chi, M. T. H., Glaser, R., & Farr, M. J. (1988). *The Nature of Expertise.* Hillsdale, NJ: Lawrence Erlbaum Associates.

Chi, M. T. H., Glaser, R., & Rees, E. (1982). Expertise in problem solving . In Sternberg, R. (Ed.), *Advances in the psychology of human intelligence* (pp. 7–75). Hillsdale, NJ: Lawrence Erlbaum Associates.

Ericsson, K. A., & Charness, N. (1994). Expert performance: Its structure and acquisition. *The American Psychologist, 49*(3), 725–747. doi:10.1037/0003-066X.49.8.725

Ermine, J.-L., Boughzala, I., & Tounkara, T. (2006). Critical knowledge map as a decision tool for knowledge transfer actions. *Electronic Journal of Knowledge Management, 4*(2), 128–140.

Glaser, R. (1986). On the Nature of Expertise . In Hagendorf, H. (Ed.), *Human Memory and Cognitive Capabilitis: Mechanisms and Performances* (pp. 915–928). Amsterdam: Elsevier Science.

Imbeault, C. (2007 November). *Projet GIT, Gestion de l'information technique Automatismes de Production.* Rapport d'étape. Hydro-Quebec internal document.

Paquette, G. (2003). *Instructional Engineering in Networked Environments.* San Francisco: Pfeiffer.

Schmidt, H. G., & Boshuizen, H. P. A. (1993). On acquiring expertise in medicine. *Educational Psychology Review, 5*(3), 205–221. doi:10.1007/BF01323044

Schön, D. A. (1983). *The reflective practitioner: How professionnals think in action.* New York: Basic Books.

Sternberg, R. (1997). Cognitive Conceptions of Expertise . In Hoffman, R. R. (Ed.), *Expertise in Context. Human and Machine* (pp. 149–162). Menlo Park, CA: AAAI Press.

Sternberg, R. (1999). What Do We Know About Tacit Knowledge? Making the Tacit Become Explicit . In Horvath, J. A. (Ed.), *Tacit Knowledge in Professional Practice* (pp. 231–236). Mahwah, NJ: Erlbaum.

Sveiby, K.-E. (2001). A knowledge-based, theory of the firm to guide strategy formulation. *Journal of Intellectual Capital*, *2*(4). doi:10.1108/14691930110409651

ENDNOTE

[1]   The projects reported in section 2 and section 3 were conducted under the direction of Josianne Basque, regular researcher at the LICEF Research Center.

Chapter 20
Modeling for Tools and Environments Specification

Karin Lundgren-Cayrol
LICEF Research Center, Canada

Diane Ruelland
LICEF Research Center, Canada

Geneviève Habel
LICEF Research Center, Canada

François Magnan
LICEF Research Center, Canada

ABSTRACT

- Modeling a Learning Object Management Tool
  - Model Description
  - From the Model to the PALOMA Tool
- Modeling a Resource Repository Management Process
  - The Main Q4R Process
  - Analysis of Organizational Needs
  - Elaboration of the Q4R KIT
  - Use and Maintain LOR Quality
  - The Q4R Feedback Loop to Assure Quality
- Modeling a Competency Self-Management Tool
  - Design Principles
  - Modeling the Process
  - Create a Prototype
  - Evolution of the Model
- Creating an Ontology-Based Learning Environment
  - Developing the Ontology
  - Populating the Ontology
  - Exploitation of the Ontology

This chapter presents a series of projects where the MOT modeling technique was used to specify some software tools, systems or Web-based environments. These activities are similar to those where a software engineer uses visual languages such as UML to specify a tool or a system. The main difference here is that MOT can be used by

DOI: 10.4018/978-1-61520-839-5.ch020

designers who are not necessarily software engineers, as we have pointed out when introducing this representation language in Chapter 2.

As we have also underlined in Chapter 14 on Ontology Engineering, except in simple cases, semi-formal models in MOT+ will have to be transformed in an ontology-based language like OWL-DL, or in software engineering specifications using UML before the tool or system is built. It is also possible, as we will show in the last example of this chapter, that designers can be trained to put their conceptual models already in OWL-DL format using the MOT+OWL or the MOWL ontology modeling tools presented in Chapter 10, leaving the task to computer specialists to integrate later in the ontology the technical elements needed to implement the system.

The following applications are in two groups. In the first three sections, we will see that conceptual designers have used the basic MOT language to built semi-formal process models where the actors are involved in using a tool that they want to see constructed: a learning object repository manager (PALOMA) in the first case, a quality for reuse (Q4R) tool kit in the second case, and a competency self assessment tool (COMPETENCE+) in the third case. In the last section, we will present how the MOT+OWL has been used to build an ontology-driven environment like PONCELET, which serves to teach projective geometry.

20.1 MODELING LEARNING RESOURCE MANAGEMENT TOOLS[1]

The models in this section, designed and produced by the LICEF Team, include models defining various functions of a Learning Resource Manager (LRM). A LRM inspired by these models was first included into the Explor@ Learning Management System (Paquette, Miara, Lundgren-Cayrol & Guérette, 2004) for online teaching and learning. Later on, it evolved to an autonomous tool that is widely used called PALOMA. The LRM

was planned to manage all kinds of resources involved in online learning, including learning events, documents for both learners and teachers, tools and services.

It is important to point out that this modeling experience was carried out before the IMS Learning Object Metadata specification became a standard and that all implications for sharing online resources were not known. The LRM developed here aimed at an institutional resources sharing by professors, tutors and instructional designers.

Model Description

Resource management is a multi-actor process where users finds interesting resources and describes them using an electronic metadata template. Other roles interacts within this process, for example to add or retrieve resources and to reference resources with metadata according to some standard. The set of metadata templates constitutes the repository.

An LRM allows users to search and retrieve resources in different manners (free search, search by specific metadata, thesaurus, etc...). Users are also encouraged to annotate each resource to improve and maintain quality of both resources and the repository itself. It is essential for all actors in online learning to have access to a learning resource repository and an easy to fill-in template to supply metadata, which serves to describe each resource. These constitute information that facilitates search and retrieval.

The model was built with the objective to convey design ideas from the Pedagogical Research Team to the software developers that were to build the LRM. Figure 1 presents the main user process, called "Request Search" for resources and the resulting activities, depending upon whether the result is satisfactory or not. If, satisfactory, three activities are possible and if not, two other activities are suggested.

Figure 1. Model of resource search and retrieve from a repository

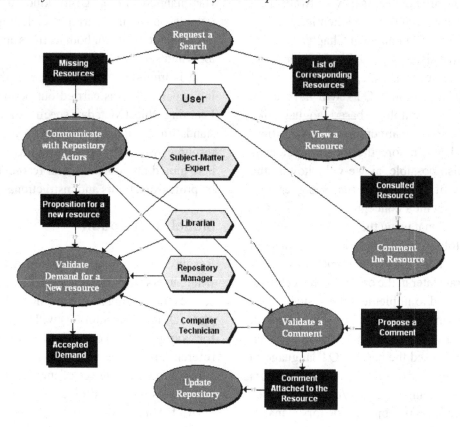

Globally, the model shows the two paths possible after a search has been launched.

If the request is successful (right side of the figure):

- The *"View a Resource"* process implies retrieving the resource once the metadata template has been viewed, either from a distant server or downloading to the local desktop.
- The *"Annotate a Resource"* process involves that the LRM integrates comments made on the resource by the user and validated by a subject-matter expert, librarian or computer technician. Each annotation has a date and user identity and the set of annotations is available for the next user.
- The *"Validate Comments"* process is achieved by various actors, depending if

it concerns the content (subject matter expert), the metadata descriptions (librarian), the structure of the repository (manager), or the technical functionalities of the environment (computer technician).

- The "Update of the repository" is done automatically by the LRM once the actors have signalled that they accept or refuse the annotations.

If the request is unsatisfactory, the following activities are possible (left side of the figure):

- The *"Communicate with Repository Members'* is activated when the result of a search was unsatisfactory. The user may then communicate with a responsible persons available through chat or email. These communication channels allow users to ask or propose new resources, solve technical problems, inform on pedagogical uses of a resource, etc...

* The *"Validate the Demand for new Resource"* process allows the LRM manager to update the LRM to include a new resource or modify a metadata template or again to notify the person proposing that the requested resource that the request cannot be satisfied.

Figure 2 shows the second main process called *"Create and Update a LRM"* which is an activity carried out by a person having an editor's status or role. This process is deployed into four sub-processes, where the editor first enters metadata into an empty electronic template hosted by the temporary Repository.

Once submitted, the template is validated depending on the type of metadata, either by a subject-matter expert for content data, an instructional designer for educational metadata, a librarian for indexing and keyword data, and a computer technician for technical metadata. Once validated, the metadata template is integrated into

the LRM Manager. This software agent updates the LRM and the database and informs whether the new record is accepted or not.

Figure 3 below, details the first process of Figure 2,*"Enter Metadata"*. This sub-model illustrates the process to integrate a resource's description in a metadata template. It is based on the structure of a resource's metadata template, which may be different depending upon the type of the resource. The types of resource shown on the model are based on a resource taxonomy developed at LICEF containing 6 main categories and several elements within. Our metadata template consists of a General section, a Technical section, Accessibility conditions section and a User context section.

A correspondence to the 9 Metadata groups put forth later on by IMS was developed afterward when the LOM specification was made available. The taxonomy of resources available in MISA documentation was integrated as a classification in section 9 of the LOM, helping the user to describe what type of resources is indexed, whether it is a tool/application, material/document, type of communication network, type of learning event, type

Figure 2. Create and update the LRM

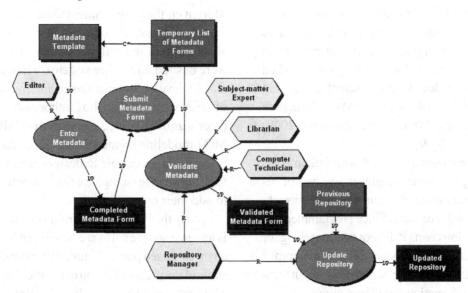

Figure 3. Enter metadata for a resource

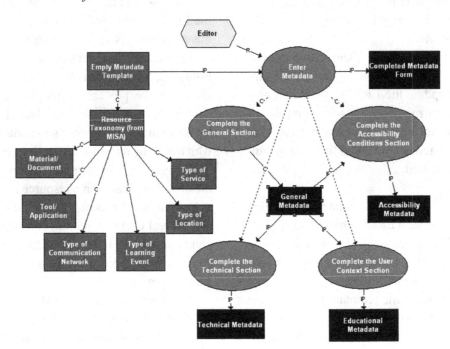

of geographical location and type of services. This taxonomy was later modified to produce a correct xml output for exchange with other systems.

From the Model to the PALOMA Tool

The preceding model as a whole, allowed us to develop most functions and tools necessary in a Learning Resource Manager. They served as a basis for the computer analysis of a LRM in the Explor@ system. The resulting LRM, called PALOMA, includes a federated search engine that uses sub-profiles of the IEEE-LOM standard, such as the CanCore (2009), Scorm Metadata (2009) and Normétic (2009).

We had the programmers exchange on the models by including the system engineer and two of his programmers in some of our modelling sessions to insure the transfer of ideas. Since programmers are used to read flowcharts it did not take very long for them to understand the models and even to improve on them by informing the research team about technological considerations and innovations.

This modelling exercise proved to be a successful communication tool between developers and programmers. The models shows what the different repository actors or end-users should be able to do, the sequence of their actions or use cases, as well as indications on what to include in the interface and what should be automatic. Moreover, the programmers were able to inform the research team about technical constraints such as for example the xml file structure, if exchanges were desired with other systems. They were also able to develop innovations in automatic capture of certain metadata, such as author of the template, dates, size of a file, etc... Compared to UML graphs, MOT modeling seemed to be a good compromise being more accessible to designers as a thinking tool, yet precise enough for the computer analysts to add their own innovations.

Today the PALOMA Learning Object Manager is an open source software which can be added to any web-based portal. Figure 4 shows two screenshots of the present version of the PALOMA-Web. The first one is a process-based template to enter

Figure 4. Paloma repository interface 2009

metadata for a resource and the second one show a federated search result.

PALOMA-Web is presently used by several universities in Quebec, in other parts of Canada, and as a connecting tool for Canadian organizations to GLOBE (http://globe-info.org/en), a consortium of Learning Resources Repositories organizations distributed in all parts of the world.

20.2 MODELING A RESOURCE REPOSITORY MANAGEMENT PROCESS

Learning Object Repositories (LOR) are promising ways to make high quality learning resources and objects (LO) available to individuals as well as to private or public organizations around the

world. The emergence of LOR initiatives, mainly since 2001, has underlined a set of major scientific and technical problems that need to be solved to make LORs a useful reality. The collaboration between researchers and the major LOR initiatives in Canada, USA, Europe, Australia and Japan has made possible a research project, Quality for reuse (Q4R), in order to provide new insights and assistance for innovative educational processes that can be shared and adapted across continents in spite of cultural and/or linguistic barriers. This project terminated in January 2009.

The *Quality for Reuse*, Q4R (www.q4r.org), project aims at fulfilling this vision by providing tools, techniques, procedures, principles and strategies assisting in implementing quality assurance practices for high quality LOR. Furthermore, to fully satisfy this need for quality, a Q4R Workflow model has been built based on our partners' Best Practices as well as our own research and experience. This workflow model has been built in four phases:

- Phase I: Document Best Practices of GLOBE Partners and set up a website and a Wiki
- Phase II: Invite LOR owners to participate by filling out the Best Practice Questionnaire, analyze data and extract valuable strategies.
- Phase III: Elaborate an interactive workflow model and invite partcipants to validate its usefulness
- Phase IV: Test the Quality Assurance model

In addition, a Q4R Repository has been built to provide Q4R Strategies, Instruments and Documents to the actors responsible of setting up a learning objects repository and maintaining its quality.

The Main Q4R Process

Six actor's roles were identified as the most common according to our study involving the examination of about 300 repositories. A role refers to what an end-user can do in the LOR. Each end-user has certain rights depending on his/her role. For example, an Instructional Designer may be both a *Contributor* and a *Reuser* as well as an *Indexer*, whereas a learner might be a *Reuser* but also a *Contributor*. The table below describes major functions and responsibilities for each role.

The main model involving these actors is presented on Figure 5. This model stems from examining the repositories and having 22 of them answering a questionnaire eliciting information about what elements of quality assurance they use at the organizational level: contribution control and at the daily use level, different types of feedback systems, peer-reviews of LO, social tagging, rating systems and annotations.

The model basically consists of 5 main subprocesses, three describing the setting up and maintenance of the repository, and two describing the continuous flow of feedback from all the actors.

These first three processes (upper part of Figure 5) will now be described in further detail.

Table 1. Description of LOR actors roles

Actor Role	Description of tasks
LOR Management Team	This team consists of representatives from all types of stakeholders (administrators, teachers, learners, tutors, moderators, etc.). Its main responsibility is to analyze needs and elaborate quality assurance strategies accordingly. This team is also in charge of getting technical and organizational architecture and the choice and elaboration of policies.
LOR Manager	Clarifies needs, solicits LO contributions, informs end-users about new LO's, maintenance problems, errors, guidelines etc., maintains and monitors quality in the LOR, reports errors and suggestions to the LOR Management Team
LO Contributor	Respects policies, proposes new or existing resources, provides basic metadata of the LO
LO Evaluator	Respects evaluation policies, participates in the design of various evaluation instruments, uses evaluation grids or other instruments to evaluate LOs, informs contributor whether LO is accepted or not, sends accepted LO's to the LO indexer role.
LO Indexer	Respects metadata guidelines and policies, enters and verifies metadata, participates in elaboration of metadata guidelines and reports interoperability errors.
LO User-Reuser	Consults and respects policies, evaluation instruments and guidelines according to need, reports usage of LO as well as quality according to the LOR's annotation criteria or other feedback mechanism.

Figure 5. Q4R quality assurance main model: from analysis to daily use

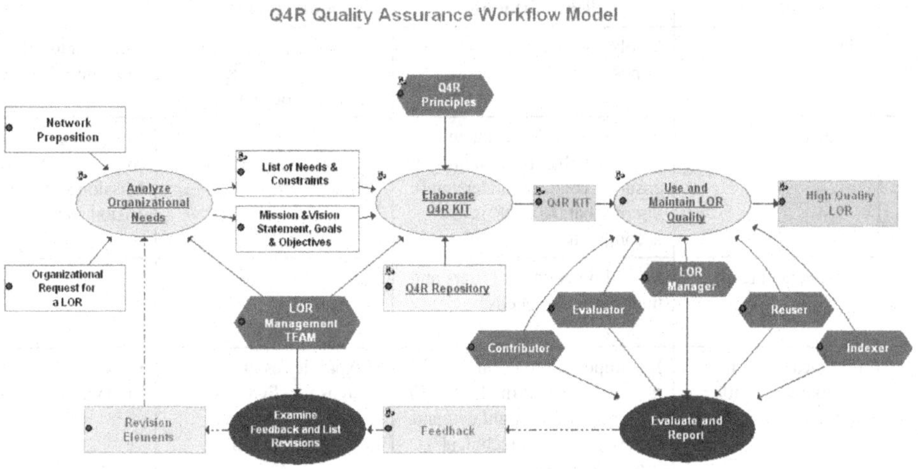

Analysis of Organizational Needs

Analyzing needs is a continuous activity and is triggered either by a proposition from a larger network of repositories or by internal demands. Internal demands often springs from teachers and / or students asking for or suggesting a Repository but also from 'champions' or training managers suggesting using a repository for teachers and learners. As examples of different types of initiatives, we can have an institution asking all its departments to use a repository (Simon Fraser), a nationwide attempt (European SchoolNet; Education Australia) to provide a community of users to join in a share resources repository or a worldwide organization trying to facilitate the sharing of resources regardless of country and cultural diversity (GLOBE).

A very helpful site for this first phase of the LOR management process is the Repositories Support Project (RSP), a major JISC initiative to support the development and growth of the UK repositories network (http://www.rsp.ac.uk/repos/scope). The table below describes the main needs analysis activities, rules of thumb, who should be responsible, resources needed to carry out the activity and what the activity will produce (deliverables).

Elaboration of the Q4R KIT

This second process, presented on Figure 7, is the preparation needed to set-up a repository. It consists in building a Quality for Reuse environment (Q4R kit).

A Q4R Kit is the set of policies, guides, tutorials, tools and job aids that are chosen in order to develop and maintain quality in a Repository that is to ensure that reuse is high. Efforts that aim at developing and maintaining the quality of a LOR cannot ignore the importance of a critical mass of users who are ready to both contribute and reuse the learning objects. To reach this tipping point, or critical mass, that is to ensure reusability, the following points can be considered as important:

- Elaborate change management strategies
- Adopt quality assurance strategies
- Include automatic feedback systems
- Include automatic metadata generation
- Provide easy to understand and applied copyright statements

Table 2. Needs analysis tasks, actors and products

Activity	Responsible	Rule of thumb	Input Resources	Products
Analyze demands for LOR	Manager	Involve as many stakeholders as possible	• Network proposition • Request for LOR within the organization.	Decision to incorporate a LOR into the organization.
Formulate LOR'S goal and objectives	Manager	It is essential to formulate goals and objectives in order to ensure a common understanding of what the LOR is to accomplish.	• Examples of goal, mission and vision statements	LOR's list of goals and objectives Mission statement Vision statement
Identify potential end-users needs	Management team	List all potential end users and their particular needs		
Identify type of LO's to be integrated	Technical staff in collaboration with pertinent end-users	It is important to define the type of LO's that the LOR will host, because it might demand different types of technical infrastructures.	• Example resources, such as i.e., SCORM packages, video, pictures, etc. all kinds	• List of LO's • Compatibility Issues
Identify Repository Communication Channels	Technical staff in collaboration with pertinent end-users	Good communication channels reinforce quality.	For ideas see Q4R Website under the Worldwide Repository page	A choice of Feed back systems • Contact persons • Information • Events Calendar • New resources display system • Newsletter • Award events Etc.
Identify and list constraints	Technical staff in collaboration with pertinent end-users	List joint projects influencing the organizational and / or technical infrastructure needed.	For example, there is a demand for SCORM compliant learning objects and then it is important to provide scorm compliant production and validation software	List of tools pertinent to the decisions in the organization

The management team makes the main decisions here. As summarized in Table 3, they need to decide to join an existing network or not. In this case, there should be a Q4R tool set. If not, or if the decision is to built a new LOR, then the management team will select quality insurance policies, document these policies and built job aids for each role in the process. The Job aids are built by adapting templates provided by the Q4R repository of documents.

Use and Maintenance of LOR Quality

The model on Figure 8 is the third phase of the process. It shows the main activities that each role carries out and how it creates a high quality LOR, may it be a Referatory (stores metadata records and a URL for access to the object itself) or a Repository (stores the object + the metadata record).

The Q4R Feedback Loop to Assure Quality

The feedback loop implies that all users of the LOR participate in evaluating and maintaining the quality

Figure 6. Needs analysis according to demands, propositions or revisions

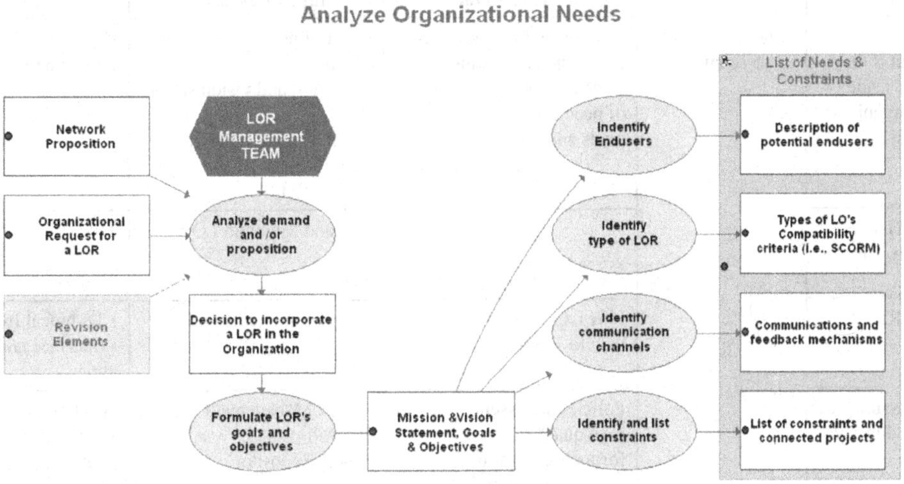

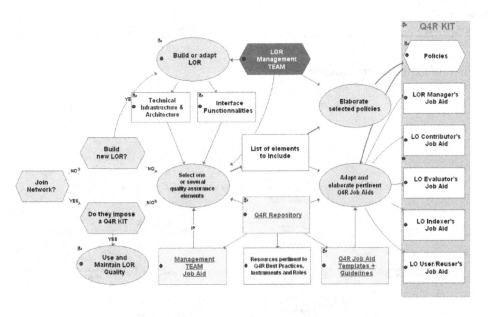

Figure 7. Elaborate the Q4R KIT

of the LOR and its learning objects. To do so the policies should provide guidelines on how the repository should work and what is important. It is therefore key that these are respected. In terms of technical quality it is also essential that all users regardless of their role in the system, report any difficulties or malfunctioning. For this, the LOR Management Team must provide easy to use feedback systems. For example, if a LO is not in working order or a link is broken, this should be automatically reported, but if it breaks after use, it must be reported by the Reuser.

Table 3. LOR preparation tasks, actors and products

Activity	Responsible	Rule of thumb	Input Resources	Products
Join Network? • If yes, find out if they impose Q4R KIT and whether your organization can adopt it.	LOR Management Team	Investigate pros and cons in joining an existing LOR network in the light of needs and constraints, goals and objectives.	• List of needs and constraints • Mission and vision statements • List of goals and objectives • GLOBAL	Decision on whether to build a new LOR or not.
• If the Q4R KIT is acceptable, start using the LOR.			Use and Maintain LOR	
Build New LOR?		If yes, Create a LOR Architecture Team	LOR components	• Technical Infrastructure • Interface and functionalities
Select quality assurance elements desired in your organization.		Policies are essential to high quality, since these put forth criteria for different aspects of quality.	• LOR Management Team Job Aid • Q4R Repository	A list of • Policies • Job Aids • Guides • Tutorials That must be developed
Elaborate desired policies		It essential to create mixed teams including pedagogical, technical and administrative staff.		Documented and ready to use Policies
Adapt and elaborate job aids for each role			Job aid template, or examples of job aids	Adapted job aids for each role

Figure 8. Use and maintain high quality LOR

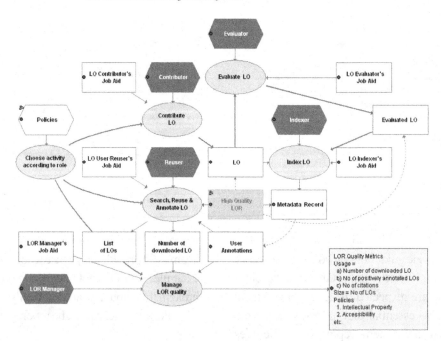

Use and Maintain a High Quality LOR

Table 4. Use and maintain tasks, actors and products

Activity	Responsible	Rule of thumb	Input Resources	Product
Contribute a LO to the LOR - Consult contribution policies - Assure LO pertinence by consulting criteria checklist - Use the LOR interface by consulting guides, community of practice groups, news bulletins etc. - Report any malfunctioning or other type of error in the interface - Make propositions for change	LO Contributor	Always make sure your LO contribution is free of errors and cleared for copyright, that is consult contribution and intellectual property policies.	• Contributor's Job Aids • Q4R Repository	• New LOs conforming to requirements and ready for evaluation • Basic metadata • Suggestions for change • List of errors
Evaluate the LO for inclusion - Evaluate LO according to criteria for each quality dimension - Inform Contributor about the decision and list any changes to be made - Upload LO and inform Indexer - Report any errors or malfunctioning - Make propositions for change	LO Evaluator	- If the decision is to include the LO, then tell the contributor whether there are any changes to be made before being included. - If the decision is not to include the LO, then detail the reasons why according to each quality dimension.	• Evaluator's Job Aids • Q4R Repository: Evaluation grids, rubrics,	• List of accepted and rejected LO's • List of typical malfunctions • Report to the
Index the LO with metadata - Consult metadata guide - Complete and verify metadata record information - Ensure that copyright and usage is indicated by the appropriate metadata - Report any errors or malfunctioning - Make propositions for change	LO Indexer	Be sure you are up-to-date with Metadata guidelines	• Indexer's Job Aids • Q4R Repository: Organizational Metadata Profile	• Metadata record for each LO • List of errors
Search and reuse LO - Search for an LO - Select LO - Reuse LO - Give feedback by annotating LO - Report any errors or malfunctioning - Make propositions for change	LO User/Reuser	It is important to give feedback on resources in order to maintain all types of quality	• Re-User's Job Aids • Q4R Repository	• Annotations • List of errors • Suggestions for change
Monitor and Manage LOR - Solicit Los - Facilitate uploads & downloads - Provide LO editors and players - Communicate important events and news - Report errors to LOR Management Team - Make propositions for change	LOR Manager	- If too many quality rules, the quantity might suffer. - If anything is accepted, quality might suffer. Therefore, it appears that it might be more economic to accept basically anything but to increase possibilities of annotation and other types of feedback. - To do so, find out which is more important quality or quantity, how people use resources, as examples, as is, parts of etc.	• LOR Manager Job Aids • Q4R Repository	• Just in time help • List of available tools and other resources • List of errors • Suggestions for change • News report on events and LO's

All actor roles are involved in the maintenance of the quality of the LOR. They do so by participating in the elaboration of the policies and by respecting these types of quality assurance measures. The policies and metadata guidelines are documents that provide evaluation criteria on the pedagogical, technical, socio-cultural and accessibility/ergonomy dimensions of the LOR.

The LOR Management team is responsible for reviewing at a regular basis the feedback coming in and distributing revision elements to pertinent persons in the organization. This is a continuous activity that helps maintaining quality in the Repository.

20.3 MODELING A COMPETENCY SELF-MANAGEMENT TOOL [2]

This section describes how the use of the visual modeling technique to define a competency self-management process and to build, COMPE-TENCE+, an interactive tool aiming to support competency-based approaches in the workplace as well as in higher education. It is based on the learner self-management model (Ruelland 2000) that is presented in Chapter 21.

Virtual campus, such as the ones developed at LICEF (Paquette, Ricciardi-Rigault, de la Teja and Paquin, 1998; Paquette 2001), is a multi-actor environment shared by designers, tutors, managers, and learners. Among these actors, our attention has focused on the learner for many reasons. On the one hand, many studies have demonstrated that the learner must be actively involved in the self-management process in order to progress and succeed online (Baynton 1992; Burge 1994; Ruelland 2004; Ruelland & Brisebois 2003) and in competency-based approaches (Scallon 2004).

On the other hand, it is generally recognized that for the learner, self-management is a hard and challenging task. Web-based learning environments offer students to acquire knowledge and skills at distance by accessing multimedia docu-ments on Internet and by discussing with peers and trainers via e-mail, forum, chat, etc. These learning conditions provide the learner with a greater amount of flexibility and control over the learning process than traditional classroom settings. They also require the learner to take over some of the teacher tasks, such as defining one's learning needs, setting priorities, controlling one's understanding, accurately diagnosing problem, validating and choosing relevant information to learn.

This situation addresses unfamiliar tasks requiring high-leveled skills related to meta-cognitive strategies such as planning, self-monitoring and self-regulating. Moreover these managerial tasks are not new but become more complex due to the variety of data sources, tools and processes while applying these skills online.

Our strategy was to design a self-management tool to be embedded in a learning environment to support the learner in adopting a proactive attitude and accepting the additional cognitive effort required by learning on-line. Our goal was to formalize the self-management process and design a generic tool adaptable to various learning scenarios and competency repositories.

Competency self-management in an online learning environment is an emerging domain. Various projects were conducted in an iterative process in close collaboration with the workplace as well as the academia. The action research methodology (Gauthier, 1993) carried out in this project includes four major steps: formulating the design principles, modeling the process, creating a prototype and experimenting in the field (Ruelland, Brisebois & Paquette, 2003; Brisebois, Ruelland & Paquette, 2005; Basque, Ruelland & Lavoie, 2006).

Design Principles

As a first step, the following four design principles were drawn from the literature and served as a framework to guide the development of the model and the Competence+ tool

Support the Entire Reflexive Process

From the perspective of research on meta-cognition, self-management is part of a reflexive process which aims at controlling one's activity. It includes the following three procedures: awareness, judgment and decision making. When performed before, during or after an activity, this reflexive process is called planning, monitoring or regulating the activity which allows to close the loop of the reflexive process (Livingston, 1997; Noel, 1997).

Consequently, Competence+ includes all the procedures of a reflexive process. This principle makes a clear distinction between our work and other self-assessment tools that usually don't support the decision procedures nor the self-regulation phase (Basque et al., 2006). To respect the reflexive nature of the process and develop the autonomy of the learner, the assessment of one's competencies is based on a personal meta-cognitive act rather that a quiz or a set of questions (Scallon 2004). The results of the reflexive process are confidential to the learner as the process is for the learner's benefit. Only group data are accessible to the trainer. (St-Pierre, 2004).

Implement a Formative Self-Assessment Strategy

Competence+ presents a formative continuous self-assessment strategy by identifying the learning objectives, the evaluation criteria and the procedures. It is used to help identifying one's learning needs and to adjust the learning strategies (Scallon 2004). Even though the learner might under or over estimate the state of his competency at any time during the learning, he is viewed as the person possessing the most accurate knowledge about his or her competencies. The evaluation results are used to stimulate discussions among peers and tutors. These interactions as well as the awareness emerging from this process are more important for the learning process than the actual results of the self-assessment (Allal 1999; St-Pierre, 2004).

In consequence, a generic qualitative ordinal performance scale adapted from the one presented in Chapter 7 and embedded in a competence ontology (presented in Chapter 10) is integrated to tool. An explanation of the evaluation criteria is available in order to support reflexion, discussion and decision for improvement (St-Pierre, 2004 ; Scallon, 2004). It includes four level of performance (Beginner, Intermediate, Advanced and Expert) defined by combining five learning criteria: autonomy, persistence, completeness, complexity familiarity.

Focus on Competency

The focus on competency self-management (Hotte, Basque, Lavoie-Page, & Ruelland, 2007) is preferred to any of the five other objects of self-management which are: activities, motivation, interaction, time and equipment (Ruelland, 2000).

Create an Online Support Tool

A web-based support tool is required because of the complex data processing it allows as well as the individualized use it offers (Kommers, Jonassen et Mayes, 1992; Mayes, 1993; Brown, Hedberg et Harper, 1994). A general access to the tool is given as the LOM standards are applied to facilitate the reusability of learning resources between platforms. A modular development allows for independent use of each main function.

Modeling the Process

Modeling the competency self-management process was undertaken as a second step to specify the use of the tool. The design principles listed above served to identify the basic knowledge units of the model. The visual modeling MOT technique was used to organize and represent three types of knowledge units as graphical objects. At the basis of the model are the following three reflexive procedures: self-assess the competency on a given performance scale, self-diagnose the strength and weaknesses by comparing the current level a competency with a target level and decide of an action plan to improve the situation using a list of learning resources.

Figure 9 illustrates the basic model of competency self-management. It is a three step model. First a competency profile is provided or built by the learner and he/she evaluates his/her own current competencies. Then, this self-evaluation is compared to some competency target and entry levels to uncover the learner's strength and weaknesses. In the last step, the weaknesses are addresses by selecting learning activities and/or resources in order to compose a work plan to improve the weak competencies.

Create a Prototype

The model of Figure 9 and its sub-models (not shown on the figure) served as a reference document to communicate and discuss the tool's pedagogical requirements with the computer analyst responsible to build the tool. Each and every knowledge unit of the model is transformed into a function or a menu to ensure an efficient use of the tool. Different types of tool elements are created to support the whole cognitive process based on the knowledge type of elements in the model. The concepts in the model determine which information to use or produce while executing a task. The procedures are transformed in executable functions for a task. The principles are guidelines or advices given to guide the execution of a procedure as to why and when to perform a task.

Four prototypes were developed before a generic tool could emerge for self-managing various domains of competencies (Brisebois et al. 2003; Basque et al. 2006; Hotte et al. 2007; Ross & Ruelland 2008). Competence+ consists of three main modules, accessible through navigational tabs, including the Evaluation module, the Summary

Figure 9. Basic model of competency self-management

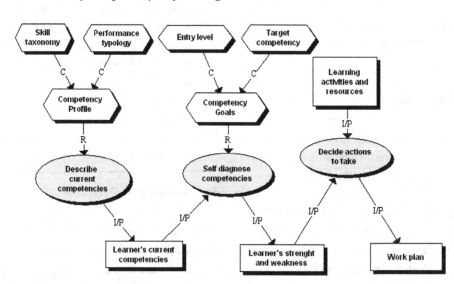

module, and the Action Plan module as illustrated in Figure 10. They correspond to the three main processes of Figure 9.

The *Assessment Module* (first window on the figure) allows students to evaluate their current level for each competency statement listed in the competency profile on the left. By clicking on the performance level that best represents what they believe they are capable of doing, they evaluate their current competencies. The user can access a description of the performance scale at all times, modify the responses one by one, reset all the answers, or save the answers given so far.

The *summary module* (second window) allows the use to visualize her progression towards the expert performance level using a visual progression bar. Each point on the scale represents one point (total four points per statement). Percentages are calculated for each competency and each group of competencies as well as for the overall performance calculated in this manner: Begin-

ner = 0-25%; Intermediate = 26-50%; Advanced = 51-75%; Expert = 76-100%. The student can also consult the detailed summary that presents her strong points and weak points as well as those of the group.

The *Action Plan module* (third window on the figure) offers a big picture view of the competency statements grouped by performance level according to the assessment results. The user can then click on a statement to see resources attached to it. He can set which statement has a higher priority, and access the resource clicking on an hyperlink. After consulting a resource, the user can check the box to indicate that the resource has been consulted.

Test beds have been conducted on four occasions with various target populations to validate the design decisions, the process model and the user interface (Ruelland et al., 2003; Brisebois et al., 2005; Basque et al., 2006; Ross & Ruelland, 2008). The visual model was then used to

Figure 10. Self-assessment modules of COMPETENCE+

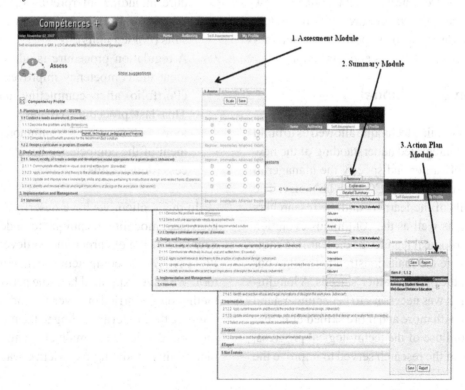

organize the data collected, locate the difficulties in the managerial process and structure the new tasks emerging from the field.

The main findings extracted from the test bed results are the following:

- In general, the main difficulties arose where the procedural support was absent in the prototype; this showed the need for additional functionalities to support the awareness, self-diagnosis and decision activities.
- Some comments showed a difference in perception of the self-assessment process itself. Most participants expected to be tested and receive feedback on their competencies. This finding led us to reconsider the process model and reinforce the "self-assessment" part of the whole process by adding guidelines to this effect.
- Other questions and comments showed a lack of support for the learner to efficiently use the feedback information given by the tool. A better interface with advice as how to execute this procedure must be added, including tools to support human interaction between learners and facilitators.

Evolution of the Model

The visual modeling technique allowed us to build a global and integrated understanding of the new role of the eLearner and specify the managerial tasks to guide the use of COMPETENCE+. The limited skills of the learners and the researchers in that field as well as the continuous evolution of the technological features of the learning environments were the main constraints to align our model with the online learner's needs. A longitudinal research was necessary to better understand the process with more and more skilled eLearner and make full use of the technological progress. Each phase of the research served to improve the

model, which in turn served to improve the use of the tool.

A last version of the model was elaborated to integrate the test bed results. These modifications to the first model are pointed out in Figure 11 as *bolded* graphic objects. Other modifications to the model arose from experiences in the field to associate an ePortfolio grouping resources used by learners to improve their competences (Hotte et al., 2007; Ruelland & Ross, 2008). They are pointed out in Figure 11 as *dotted* graphic objects. An ePortfolio can provide evidence for current competencies.

Here are the main modification to the model:

- A new procedure is included to support the awareness procedure, namely remembering and selecting experiences illustrating a competency (bolded units).
- General guidelines are added to explain and value the "self-assessment" approach embedded in the tool (bolded units).
- Tips are given to help execute each procedure including interpreting the evaluation criteria and analyzing the evaluation results (bolded units).
- A regulation procedure is added to document the competency improvement in the ePortfolio after completing an activity. This last procedure creates the reflexive loop and ensures a continuous management of the competency development process (dotted units).

In this section, we have described the use of the visual modeling technique to understand the new role of the eLearner and to develop COMPETENCE+, a competency self-management tool. We have explained how the action research methodology carried out over a decade allowed to improve the model according to the needs emerging from the field. The main challenge we had to face in this modeling experience was to follow

Figure 11. Competency self-management process revised model

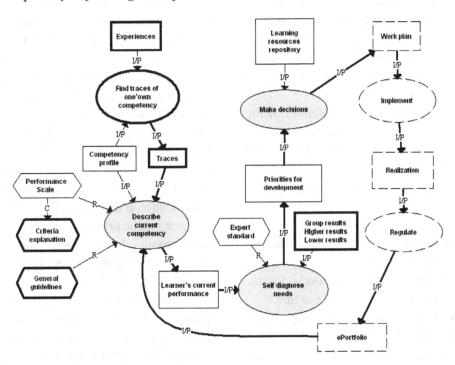

the evolving knowledge of the competency approach and of the technological domain as well as reaching subjects learners with sufficient online experience to collect valuable data at the testbeds.

The self-management model presented here is based on data collected from four research projects conducted at the LICEF Research center. These numerous field testing helped to identified generic needs and to propose a generic tool portable to various activities and target populations. The model is now available for practitioners and researchers as well to develop new online environments, design courses integrating a reflexive approach or elaborate a methodological support.

20.4 CREATING AN ONTOLOGY-BASED LEARNING ENVIRONMENT[3]

The project presented in this section is an experimental platform to help build new interactive media in education. From the formulation of objectives to the mock-up, it was important to have

a grip on content, to categorize, to divide, to tie and structure it. Structuring media resources for Web diffusion, via podcasting or in presence mode has been simplified by adding semantic information from an ontology model to each media unit.

There are three main texts at the origin of the project. First, a course on projective geometry written and taught by Gonzalo E. Reyes explains the basic elements of this mathematical theory. Through videos, schemas, interactive simulators, notes and exercises, learners discover the fundamental theorem of projective geometry: there is only one conic curve. Second, a play, written by Marie La Palme Reyes, "Death and the young man (The last hours of General Poncelet)" brings historical elements in the environment. Dying, General Jean-Victor Poncelet remembers one of the most productive periods of his life, when after crossing the frozen plains of Russia, in winter 1812, he arrives at Saratoff prison, where he lays down the foundations of projective geometry. Finally, an overview of the history of projective geometry is provided, with its early beginnings in the 15th century up to its apogee in the 19th century. These three sources of content are self-contained but are also interconnected through their themes and concepts. With this high volume of rich content, we aimed at offering the users an adaptive navigation experience.

We now outline some key objectives of the project that led us to the consideration of using ontologies to assist the creation and delivery processes of the PONCELET environment. We chose to put emphasis on the following requirements and objectives:

- Offer a multitude of customized learning paths to users.
- Have multiple granularity levels for resources e.g.: play, act, scene, cue line.
- Deal with multiple diffusion support medias e.g.: Web, DVD, podcasting.
- Give us tools to help handle the complexity of managing thousands of multimedia documents.
- Let the users create their own multimedia scenarios.

In the following sections, we will explain how the use of an ontology to classify concepts and resources and their relationships helped our progress on the these issues.

Developing the Poncelet Ontology

The main contributors in the project collaboratively created the essence of the Poncelet ontology. In a small number of work sessions we used an early version of the *MOT+OWL Ontology Editor* presented in Chapter 10, to translate some requirements of the project into OWL class descriptions and OWL properties. The resulting OWL ontology is simple in nature but most importantly it is the most natural structure we could imagine that could accommodate the expression of all necessary knowledge about the concepts of the project.

The MOT+OWL editor lets us define our requirements in OWL with a graphical syntax. We basically build a special kind of graph that represents the structure of the ontology. The graphical nature of the formalism helps habilitate contributors of all backgrounds (with limited knowledge about computers for example) in the creation of the backbone of the project, which is the *Poncelet ontology*.

The first and most natural class introduced in our ontology is the class *PonceletResources* which is to be interpreted as the class of all multimedia resources in the project. This class is then refined into three sub-classes: *PlayResources*, *CourseResources* and *HistoryResources*. Figure 12 shows this with two additional relational properties for *PonceletResources*: the *hasTitle* and *hasLocation* properties. The *hasTitle* associates a title string with each resource and the *hasLocation* associates a URL telling the location of the resource file. The cardinality axioms add that there is exactly one title and one location for each resource.

We can refine the taxonomy of the resources by introducing classes defined by restrictions (an available OWL-DL feature). For example, the *PlayResources* has two subclasses: *Act1Resources* and *Act2Resources* that can be defined as restriction of a property that associates resources to parts of the play.

The three classes are the top level of the Poncelet ontology shown on Figure 13 are *PonceletResources*, *PonceletConcepts* and *PonceletInterfaces*. PonceletConcepts are all the different subjects (mathematical concepts, emotive concepts, philosophical concepts, ...) covered by the *PonceletResources*. Associations of concepts and resources can be expressed by the *isPresentedBy* property. The *PonceletInterface* class represents the graphical user interface elements that let users interact with the resources, or with knowledge inside the ontology. An instance of a *PonceletInterface* would be for example an interface template to display videos in a virtual theater as shown on Figure 15.

Figure 12. A part of the Poncelet ontology graph

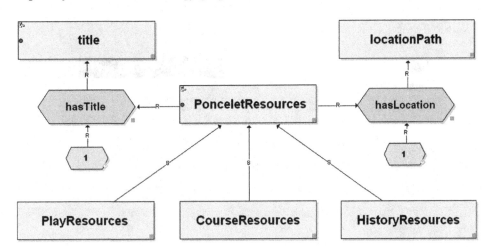

Figure 13. The top level of the Poncelet ontology

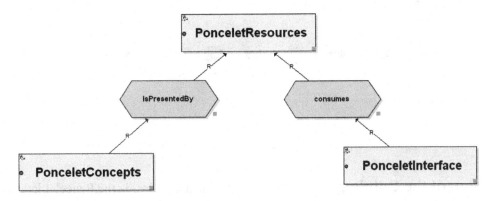

Populating the Ontology

The ontology defined by the previous model and its sub models is the structural backbone of the project. It defines all the necessary concepts we need to realize the project requirements. These concepts must be instantiated by the concrete elements of the project. For example, all multimedia resources of the project must be instantiated as instances of the *PonceletResources* class. This means that about 60 000 instances of PonceletResources must be created and their properties must be filled with the appropriate values.

To accomplish this task, we use a hybrid strategy. First, an automated instances creation process was built to generate instances from a scan of the resources file repository combined with a specific classification methodology in the file repository that enables the inference of the property values of each resource. The second element in the strategy is the use of a specific tool to populate the ontology: the *Semantic Referencer* tool. Figure 14 shows an overview of the *Semantic Referencer* tool.

The Semantic Referencer tool creates generic interface templates to support search, visualization and information input inside the *Poncelet Ontology*. Using the Semantic Referencer, we could input the different property values. For example, associations between resources and mathematical concepts were entered using this tool.

Figure 14. The Semantic Referencer tool

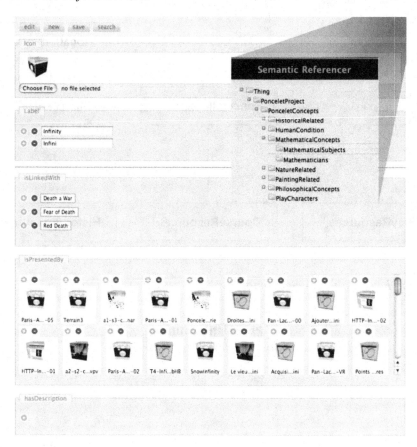

Exploitation of the Ontology

The result of the previous step is a knowledge base for the project. This knowledge base is used to assemble the project material and construct various multimedia scenarios. The scenarios are first built using a standard text editor but we soon thought about providing target users with a graphical tool that lets them design their own multimedia scenarios. This tool named *BrainCuts* lets users create mash-ups of multimedia elements in a Web interface. In the Poncelet project, the mash-ups are restricted inside *PonceletResources* multimedia elements (which can be sounds, actors voices, pictures, movies). *BrainCuts* helps users map and sequence multimedia contents projected on different areas in a 3D virtual environment (e.g., walls of a room). Figure 15 shows the *BrainCuts*

tool in action inside the Poncelet interface.

The whole multimedia project is assembled though interfaces able to play a diversity of multimedia scenarios. The whole knowledge base is delivered to the end users though integrated graphical interfaces that let them navigate inside the project elements.

We reuse the same structure for both authoring and delivery tasks. This gives end users access to a particularly rich and semantically dense knowledge base. All the knowledge needed for the authoring of the project is also made explicitly available to the target users. This is used effectively in the Web environment to enable richer interactivity with the resources.

In conclusion, by giving access to parts of projective geometry theory through the angle of interactive media, the project "A theatrical

Figure 15. PONCELET's user interface

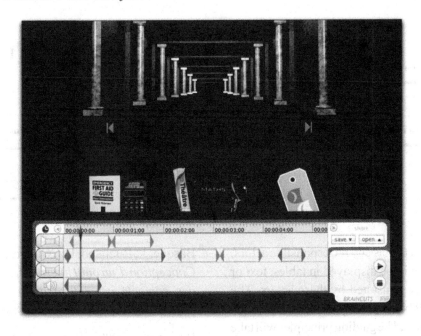

perspective on projective geometry" transports users inside a unique learning experience. We have learned from our experiment that very simple ontologies can be quite useful in the development of a multimedia eLearning project. By providing a unifying framework where all knowledge about the project can be stored inside a unique structure, ontologies provide a solid backbone to which all tasks can be linked and profit from it. The methodology and tools used could be transposed and applied to other projects because the separation between content and technology is well defined. We also learned that an ontology by itself doesn't give very concrete benefits in the project (apart from conceptualization benefits) if it is not combined with the right toolset. The ability to generate tools and interfaces evolving around the ontologies is therefore crucial at this point of time to really profit from this formalism in a concrete way. Readers looking for more details on the project can consult a master thesis on the project (Habel 2009) and a conference proceeding (Habel, Reyes, Magnan and Reyes 2007)

CONCLUSION

In this chapter we have presented four projects where visual modeling has been used to define very different tools, respectively the PALOMA learning object manager, Q4R, a Web-based environment to set-up and maintain high quality learning object repositories, COMPETENCE+, a competency self-management tool and PONCELET, a rich-media open learning environment in mathematics.

A difference must be made between the first three projects, where a process model helped define basic tool components, and the fourth one, where an ontology model drives the system. Figure 16 underlines this difference.

In the first case, the atomic part of a process model (or activity scenario) centers on a task with its responsible actor(s), input and output data, and its guiding principles. The task can be decomposed in sub-tasks for more precision. In the tool or environment, the task and sub-tasks will take the form of menu elements or buttons that trigger the execution of actions that support

Figure 16. Models to define tools

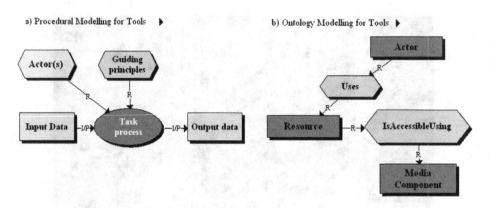

the realization of the task by its responsible actors. The input data will be displayed in tables, text or Web pages to be consulted by these actors. The output data will be entered by the actor(s) using a software interface. The guiding principles will take the form of checks lists, static or dynamic advice given in a static menu or during task execution to help the actors achieve the task (see section 21.2 on advisor systems).

In the second case, the definition elements in the model are not given in procedural form, but in a declarative way, in an ontology model. The ontology declares all the relations between actors, information resources, and media (interface) elements. Unlike procedurals models, the model is not outside the tool but is integrated into the tool. An inference engine will make queries to the ontology to drive the execution of the tool, in a way similar to the TELOS system presented in Chapter 15.

REFERENCES

Allal, L. (1999). Impliquer l'apprenant dans le processus d'évaluation: promesses et pièges de l'autoévaluation . In Depover, C., & Noel, B. (Eds.), *L'Évaluation des compétences et des processus cognitifs, Modèles, pratiques et contextes* (pp. 35–58). Bruxelles, Belgium: De Boeck University.

Basque, J., Ruelland, D., & Lavoie, M. C. (2006). *Conception d'un outil interactif d'autodiagnostic des compétences informationnelles*. Montréal, Canada: Téluq-Université du Québec.

Braincuts. (2009). Retrieved from http://www.categoricaldesign.com/

Brisebois, A., Ruelland, D., & Paquette, G. (2005). Supporting Self-Assessment in a Competency Approach to Learning. In eLearn 2005 proceedings, Vancouver, Canada.

Brown, A. L. (1987). Metacognition, Executive control, Self-regulation, and other more Mysterious Mechanisms . In Weinert, F. E., & Kluwe, R. H. (Eds.), *Metacognition, motivation, and understanding* (pp. 65–116). Hillsdale, NJ: Lawrence Erlbaum Associates.

Brown, N. C., Hedberg, J., & Harper, H. (1994). Metacognition as a basis for learning support software. *Performance Improvement Quarterly*, 7(2), 3–26.

Burge, E. J. (1994). Learning in computer conference contexts: The learners' perspective. *Journal of Distance Education*, 9(1), 19–43.

Cancore. (2009). Retrieved from http://www.cancore.ca/

Gauthier, B. (1993). *Recherche sociale: De la problématique à la collecte de données*. Sainte-Foy, Canada: PUQ.

Habel, G. (2009). *Préparer un cours interactif pour le web, la baladodiffusion et le mode présentiel à l'ère des web 2.0 et 3.0*. Master's thesis, Université du Québec à Montréal.

Habel, G., Reyes, M. L., Magnan, F., & Reyes, G. E. (2007). General poncelet meets the semantic web: a concrete example of the usage of ontologies to support creation and dissemination of elearning contents. In *Proceedings of E-Learn 2007 - World Conference on E-Learning in Corporate, Government, Healthcare, and Higher Education*.

Hotte, R., Basque, J., Lavoie-Page, V., & Ruelland, D. (2007). Ingénierie des compétences et scénarisation pédagogique. *Revue internationale des technologies en pédagogie universitaire, 4*(2). Retrieved October 26, 2008, from http://www.profetic.org/revue

Kommers, P., Jonassen, D. H., & Mayes, T. (1992). *Cognitive Tools for Learning*. Heidelberg, Germany: Springer-Verlag.

Livingston, J. (1997). *Metacognition: An Overview*. Retrieved from http://www.gse.buffalo.edu/fas/shuell/cep564/Metacog.htm

Mayes, T. (1993). Hypermédias et outils cognitifs. In G. I. Baron, J. Baude, & B. de la Passardière (Éds.), Deuxièmes journées francophones hypermédias et apprentissage (pp. 39-47). Paris, France: INRP.

Noël, B. (1997). *Métacognition*. Bruxelles: De Boeck Université.

Normétic. (2009). Retrieved from http://gtn-quebec.org/Normetic

Paquette, G. (2002). *L'ingénierie pédagogique. Pour construire l'apprentissage en réseau*. Quebec, Canada: Presses de l'Université du Québec.

Paquette, G. (2002). Modélisation des connaissances et des compétences. Quebec, Canada: Presses de l'université du Québec

Paquette, G. (2004a). L'ingénierie pédagogique à base d'objets et le référencement par les compétences. Montréal. *Revue internationale des technologies en pédagogie universitaire, 1*(3). Retrieved August 29, 2007, from http://www.profetic.org/revue

Paquette, G. (2004b). *Instructional Engineering in Networked Environments*. San Francisco: Pfeiffer.

Paquette, G. (2008). Graphical ontology modeling language for learning environments. *Technology, Instruction*. [Philadelphia, PA: Old City Publishing, Inc.]. *Cognition and Learning, 5*, 133–168.

Paquette, G., de la Teja, I., & Léonard, M. (2000). *Presentation of the MISA Learning Engineering Method*. Montréal, Canada: Internal Research Report, Licef Research Centre.

Paquette, G., De La Teja, I., Lundgren-Cayrol, K., Léonard, M., & Ruelland, D. (2002). *La modélisation cognitive, un outil de conception des processus et des méthodes d'un campus virtuel. Revue de l'Association Canadienne de l'Éducation à Distance*. ACED.

Paquette, G., Lundgren-Cayrol, K., & Léonard, M. (2008). Visual Language for Knowledge-Based Instructional Design . In *Handbook on Virtual Instructional Design Languages* (pp. 133–154). The MOT.

Paquette, G., Miara, A., Lundgren-Cayrol, K., & Guérette, L. (2004). The Explor@2 Learning Object Manager . In McGreal, R. (Ed.), *Online education using learning objects* (pp. 254–268). London: Routledge/Falmer.

Ross, D., & Ruelland, D. (2008). Rapport du banc d'essai de Compétences+. Montréal, Canada: Centre de recherche LICEF, Réseau Lornet.

Ruelland, D. (2000). *Vers un modèle d'autogestion en situation de télé-apprentissage.* Thèse de doctorat en didactique. Montréal, Faculté des Études Supérieures, Université de Montréal.

Ruelland, D. Ross. D. (2008). Rapport Compétences+: Cas d'utilisation. Katimavik, Chaire de recherche en ingénierie cognitive et educative. Montréal, Canada: Centre de recherche LICEF, Télé-Université.

Ruelland, D., & Brisebois, A. (2003). Rapport d'évaluation du prototype Autodiagnostic. Montréal, Canada: Centre de recherche LICEF, Télé-Université.

Ruelland, D., & Brisebois, A. (2004). Outil d'autodiagnostic des compétences. Rapport du banc d'essai du prototype. Lornet, Montréal, Centre de recherche LICEF, Télé-Université.

Ruelland, D., Brisebois, A., & Paquette, G. (2003). A Performance Support Tool for the eLearner. In *International Conference on Computers in Education* (ICCE2002), Aukland, New Zealand.

Ruelland, D., & Lundgren-Cayrol, K. (2007). *Apprentissage mixte en milieu de travail, Rapport de la recherche-action Phase II.* Montréal, Canada: Réseau Lornet.

Scallon, G. (2004). *L'évaluation des apprentissages dans l'approche par compétences.* Montreal, Canada: ERPI.

Scorm Metadata. (2009). Retrieved from http://www.scormsoft.com/scorm/cam/metadata

ST-Pierre, L. (2004). L'habileté d'Autoévaluation: pourquoi et comment la développer ? *Pédagogie collégiale, 18*(1), 33-38.

ENDNOTES

[1] Section 1 and section 2 has been prepared by Karin Lungren-Cayrol to summarize the work at the LICEF research center on a process to maintain a learning object repository that has led to the development of the PALOMA learning object manager and later and to the Quality for Reuse (Q4R) portal (www.q4r.org) that will be presented in the following section. Other members of the team have made a contribution to this model, especially Ileana de la Teja, Michel Léonard and Ioan Rosca

[2] Section 3 has been prepared by Diane Ruelland, based on her work at the LICEF Research Center on learner's self-management processes and the Competency + tools

[3] Section 4 is based on a summary by Geneviève Habel and François Magnan of their work with other colleagues to specify and develop PONCELET an ontology-based environment on the subject of projective geometry.

Chapter 21
Modeling for Research and Communication

Gilbert Paquette
LICEF Research Center, Canada

ABSTRACT

- Modeling the MISA Instructional Engineering Method
  - Modeling Productions, Tasks and Principles
  - Summary of the MISA R&D Process
- Modeling Assistance for a host system
  - Task-based Advisors
  - Generic Assistance Systems
  - Structure of an Advisor Agent
  - Building Assistance for the ADISA Design Workbench
  - Building Assistance in TELOS
  - Summary of the Advisor System Research Process
- Visual Modeling in Doctoral Research
  - A Thesis on Learners' Self-Management
  - Three Thesis on Cognitive Computing and the Semantic Web
  - Summary of the Research Process

In this concluding chapter, we will give examples where visual modelling techniques have been used in actual research projects. Visual Modelling is particularly useful to the researcher both to organize and guide the research and to communicate its results. Our Research Centre applied this approach in numerous research projects since its creation in 1992.

We will start by showing how visual modelling has helped develop a coherent view of Instructional Engineering that led to the design of the MISA

DOI: 10.4018/978-1-61520-839-5.ch021

method through a number of years. Then we will present another stream of research that has also been supported by knowledge modelling: the development of assistance systems. Finally, we will conclude the chapter by presenting a method that has been used by several doctoral students, in particular by those responsible of the projects presented in section III of this book. These examples will enable us to propose a generic meta-method for research projects and doctoral work that will serve as a conclusion to this chapter.

21.1 MODELING THE MISA INSTRUCTIONAL ENGINEERING METHOD[1]

In many chapters of this book we have presented aspects of the MISA Instructional Engineering Method that make an extensive use of visual knowledge modelling for representing the content, pedagogical strategies, learning materials and delivery processes of learning environments. The reader can refer to chapter 8 for a short introduction to MISA and to the books that have been published on the subject (Paquette 2002, 2004) or to the author's Web site at www.licef.ca/gp.

Here, we are interested in modelling the process and its products that have led to the MISA method and its various tools. Without such a process, refined through the years, it would have been impossible to keep a focused and coherent view on MISA's Evolution and the development of its related tools.

Modelling MISA's Productions, Tasks and Principles

Throughout these research process we asked ourselves, what is it exactly that the designer has to produce, what are the tasks that will enable him to achieve these productions, how are they related, and what are the principles that should guide de-

signers to better quality products. These are quite general question that are present when designing a new methodology, whatever the application domain. These questions led us to build a visual model of MISA with the MOT editor that shows the interrelations between all these elements of the method. In this section, we present the MOT model of MISA 4.0. Another MISA-based model of the method for IMS-LD can be consulted at www.idld.org in the methodological aids section.

The first question was: what is it that an instructional designer supposed to produce? Our answer was: a learning system (or IT-supported environment) in all its dimensions. This led us to a general model of this concept shown on Figure 1. A learning system is composed is produced by an instructional engineering process and is an input to the delivery of the system. It is composed of two elements: a set of specifications or "blueprint", produced using MISA, and the "Physical" system composed of learning materials and support infrastructures.

The role of MISA is to support the production of a blueprint or specifications of a learning system composed of a knowledge and skills model, a pedagogical model grouping learning units and their learner or teacher interrelated activities, a media model to guide the development of the learning material, and a delivery model to define the human and technical infrastructure needed to support the LS when it will be in use.

Analysing these tasks more closely and their interactions, we found out that they had to be developed progressively, as in most method, in a number of phases. We retained the following phases.

- Define the Training Problem and Customize MISA
- Define a Preliminary Solution
- Build the Learning System's Architecture
- Design Instructional Materials
- Produce and Validate the Materials

Figure 1. The learning system concept (Paquette 2001)

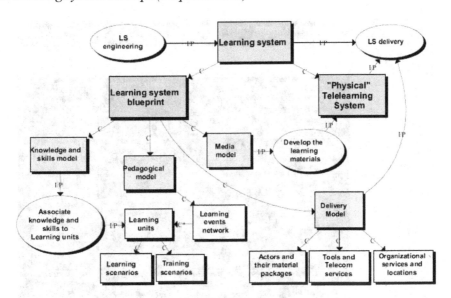

- Prepare the Delivery of the Learning System

Finally 35 main tasks or processes and around 150 subtasks have been identifies. Each main task produces a Documentation Elements (DE) either a graphic MOT model (in bold on the figure) or a form or property table produced using predefined templates. The DEs produced by the instructional designers are distributed into folders for each phase and to each axis.

This bi-dimensional structure of the method and the use of MOT models provide many advantages:

- It makes the engineering process easier to understand and more consistent while facilitating communication between the learning system production team members
- In relation with his specialty and in collaboration with his teammates, each team member may be assigned to a specific DE production. The distribution of tasks and responsibilities is clearly stated so that each team member knows when and what must be done.

- Especially when designing complex LS, the information is represented and organized into a coherent system through graphic modeling and their related DE descriptions.
- All the documentation may be collated into a single report that can include phase folders, axis folders or various combinations of documentation elements (DE) selected by the designer.
- Because of the modularity of the DE system, many LS specification components created by MISA 4.0 may be easily reused from one project to the next one, representing a major saving in terms of effort, cost and resources.
- The LS Engineering Project Management may be structured by phases or by axes or by any combinations of data require to manage the development.

Now let us present the MOT model that gives its unity to the MISA method and provides a way

Figure 2. The structure of the MISA 4.0 instructional engineering method

Phase 1-Definition	100 Organization's Training System 102 Training Objectives 104 Learners' properties 106 Present Situation 108 Reference Documents			
	Knowledge Axis	**Pedagogy Axis**	**Media Axis**	**Delivery Axis**
Phase 2 – Initial solution	210 Knowledge Model Principles 212 Knowledge Model 214 Competencies	220 Instructional Principles 222 Event Network 224 Learning Unit Properties	230 Media Principles	240 Delivery Principles 242 Cost-Benefit Analysis
Phase 3 – Architecture	310 Learning Unit Content	320 Learning Scenarios 322 Activity Properties	330 Development Infrastructure	340 Delivery Planning
Phase 4 – Detailed Design	410 Learning Resource Content	420 Learning Resource Properties	430 Learning Resource List 432 Media Models 434 Media Elements 436 Source Documents	440 Delivery Models 442 Actors and their resources 444 Tools and Telecom 446 Delivery Services and Locations
Phase 5 - Test	540 Test Planning	542 Revision Decision Log		
Phase 6 – Delivery Plan	610 Knowledge/ Competency Management	620 Actors and Group Management	630 Learning System/Resource Management	640 Maintenance/ Quality Management

Figure 3. MISA 4.0 main model

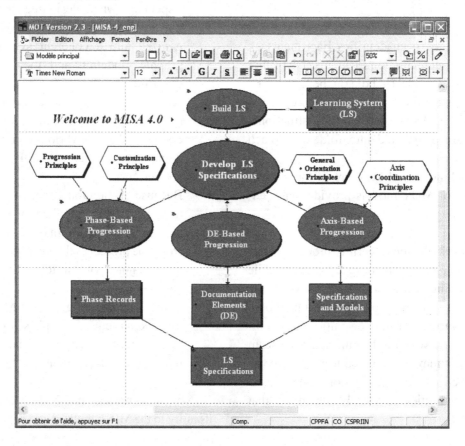

to adapt it and navigate through the different tasks and products. Figure 3 shows the three possible ways to progress in the method and related principles to guide the design tasks.

This model has three sub-models to navigate further depending if the design team wants to navigate through phases, axis or DE elements. The Phase-based Progression sub-model presents a sequence of phases. If phase 2 is selected, the sub-model on Figure 4 is presented, emphasizing that each of MISA's phases may be divided into steps. Each step equates a task that produces a DE or a section of a DE. The DEs produced during a phase can be grouped in the corresponding folder of the phase. It is the method's user who determines which DEs or which DE sections will be included in each folder.

For example, Figure 4 shows the context of phase 2: it is preceded on phase 1 products and will be followed by phase 3. It also shows its content for the four axis: definition of the LS's

Instructional, Material Development and Delivery Orientation Principles, development of the Knowledge Model and the Learning Event Network (LEN). Then, these products will support the analysis of costs, benefits and impacts. The DEs produced during this Phase are grouped in the "Preliminary Solution" folder. Upon client approval of the Preliminary Solution, Phase 3 can be started on this basis.

Going back to Figure 3, the designer can also develop the LS specifications axis by axis or by selecting a DE progression mode. A sub-model for the progression through axis groups all the tasks and DEs into 4 sub-models, one for each axis, showing when products from other axis are needed as input for some of the tasks. Axis coordination principles guide the exchange and reuse of information between products in different axis.

A sub-model for the progression through the products (DEs) presents a bi-dimensional table similar to Figure 1 in order to select one of the

Figure 4. Phase 2 main tasks and DE produced

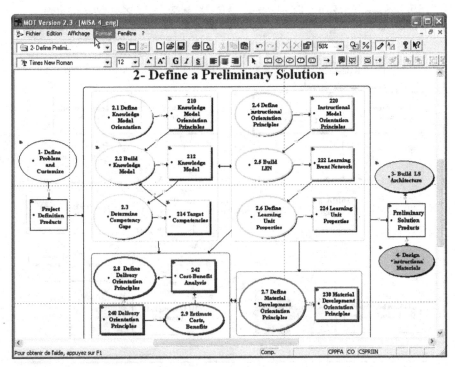

products or DE. Such a selection for DE 212, in this table, or in a phase view such as Figure 4, will open the sub-model shown on Figure 5. This model presents, organized around the DE 212 product, the designer's task to produce it, together with the previous products that influence its design, and the following ones that will be influenced by it.

To complete a documentation element (DE), the designer must use some source data that can originate from different DE's. Once some data has been collected and processed in a DE, they can be useful to different "destination" DE's in which they will be examined in a new perspective.

In the MISA method model, each of the 35 DE's has such a contextual model that helps the designer to make a coherent and efficient LS development.

In this contextual model, the left side indicates the incoming DE's that act as a data "source" useful to build the Knowledge model (DE 212) and the right side of the model shows the destination DE's where the data defined in the Knowledge model can be used or applied. If a designer clicks on one of these products, for example "320 Instructional Scenarios" produced by task 3.3, he will open a new contextual sub-model for this design element. It is then possible to navigate in MOT from DE to DE until the end of the process.

These contextual models are particularly interesting when some validations, tests or LS maintenance management require some data changes in a DE. The designer and the manager can then more easily evaluate the impact on the others DE in the method and the cost of the LS modification.

Organizing a method by building a visual knowledge model ensures the consistency of its various operations. The types of links joining

Figure 5. A contextual model for design element (DE) 212

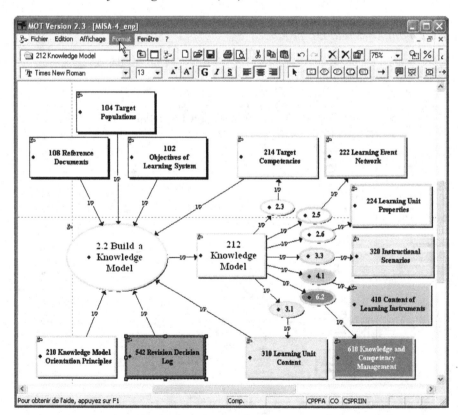

the 35 main instructional design tasks are clearly identified and advice is given to help ensure consistency of the Method's different products. In addition, the Method's general orientation, customization and phase progression principles as well as its axis coordination principles are there to guide LS designers through the process. The model shows clearly for what design tasks these principles are to be applied.

Summary of the MISA R&D Process

As we can see on Figure 6, the development of MISA has been a long process based on three interrelated streams of research: Design methods, Visual Modelling Tools and eLearning delivery systems. Table 1 presents the timeline of these research streams from the point of view of the development of the MISA method.

As shown in Table 1, the whole process started in 1992 on the basis of previous projects on knowledge-based educational environment. A first version of the MISA method (Instructional engineering Method for Learning Systems) was produced in 1994, embedded in a computerized support system for designers called AGD (Paquette, Aubin and Crevier 97; 99). The initial vi-

sion was to *apply knowledge elicitation methods to model the products, processes and principles that instructional designers produce or apply* as they design learning environments or systems.

The method was thereafter validated with instructional designers and content experts in nine organizations and was rebuilt, yielding MISA 2.0, based on results and observations gathered during these validations. In parallel, we extracted and rebuilt a tool for knowledge modelling (MOT) to support central aspects of the method.

After another round of validation, our attention focused on learning object typologies. We defined seventeen typologies on concepts such as knowledge models, skills, learning scenarios, learning materials, delivery models and so on. The MOT models made it easier for the designer to communicate his ideas through a documented model. The *MISA Method was devised and entirely modelled using MOT*, providing a clear visualization of MISA's various processes. In 1998, this effort led to MISA 3.0 in which these typologies and method models were used to present numerous alternatives to the designer on which to build viable design decisions.

Starting with the goal to build a new Instructional Design Web-based tool (ADISA), MISA

Figure 6. Interaction between research projects at LICEF

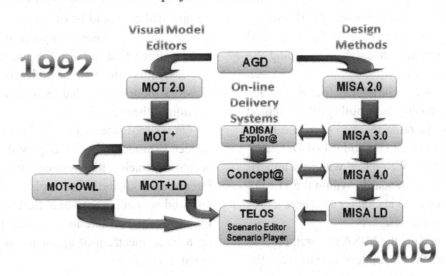

Table 1. Timeline of the research on MISA and related R&D

1987	Beginning of research (at Télé-université) on knowledge-based systems.
1991	Design of a first knowledge-based environment generator (LOUTI).
1992	A Télé-université course on instructional design integrating knowledge modeling.
1992 to 1994	Development of an educational engineering workbench (AGD – Atelier de Génie Didactique) ; Version 1 of MISA and a first Visual Modeling Tool are embedded in AGD
1995	Doctoral thesis on MISA (Françoise Crevier). Trial and validation of MISA version 2.0 and the AGD by some nine organisations and companies.
1995 to 1996	Creation of a first autonomous MOT editor based on the optimization of typed-object modeling techniques developed within the AGD workbench.
1996 à 1997	Production of version 2.0 of the MISA Method using previous trials results. Trial of MISA 2.0 by six instructional design teams at Télé-université.
1998 to 1999	Production of MISA 3.0. This was accomplished in conjunction with the development of the MOT+ editor and of a set of form-based tools to support MISA 3.0. A set of 17 typologies of learning system components or aspects were developed.
1999 to 2001	Development of a Web-based distributed workbench for engineering learning systems (ADISA) in conjunction with Version 4.0 of the MISA Method that integrated the typologies.
2001 to 2003	Multiple applications of MISA and MOT+: Hydro-Québec, Bank of Montreal, Professional Corporations, courses with the Explor@ LCMS, etc.
2003 to 2006	Specialisation of MOT+ to MOT+LD and MOT+OWL. Additional modelling and instructional engineering projects
2006 to 2009	Adaptation of MISA to the IMS-LD specification, development of the IDLD learning design repository, integration of MOT+ and ADISAconcepts into TELOS

evolved to MISA 4.0 during year 2000. This version has been built in coordination with the ADISA support workbench for instructional engineering (Paquette, Rosca, De la Teja, Léonard and Lundgren-Cayrol 2001), which combined the method MISA and the MOT software in a web-based application. The XML files, the results tables in HTML format and the MOT models defined in the workbench could be saved and reused from a computer database grouping the successive versions.

In recent years, we have been focusing on applications, increasing the usability of the method and the tools, adapting them to new eLearning standards such as the LOM and IMS-LD. MOT+ has become totally Web-based with new import/export facilities to standards, within the TELOS framework presented in chapter 15 where it provides scenarios for designers.

Figure 7 presents the MISA research process model. It shows the close interaction between the progressive elaboration of the method and the development of the ICT tools supporting its use and operation. At first, the goal of constructing a support system like AGD favoured a close scrutiny of the design products and the tasks that needed to be supported. We had to be very precise and systematic; otherwise the AGD system could not be operated or would be of no use to designers. In fact, any elaborated computer system needs to be defined first by an information model. In our case, this information model took the form of MOT models. This led us to a first informal version of the method.

On the tool side, within AGD, a module was needed to model the knowledge and the learning scenarios. Such a tool was constructed, closely integrated with the other tools of AGD. Only later did we decide to extract the modelling editor and make it an autonomous tool. This opened up a large spectrum of applications that is still expanding today.

Figure 7. The interaction of R&D activities in the MISA research process

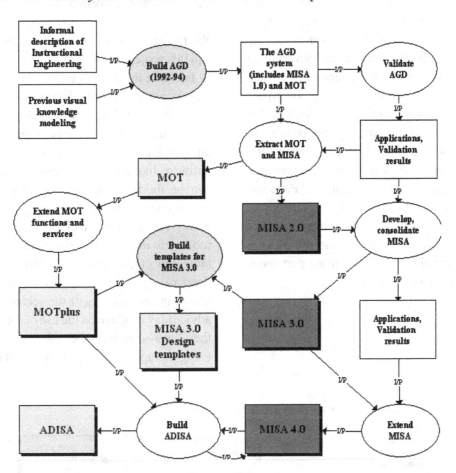

Then, outside AGD, we began to concentrate on the method behind the tool, through a number of applications and tests with partner organizations. This led us to new versions of the method that in turn, had a great influence on the evolution of the tool set.

Another important aspect of MISA research is the testing of the method through the tools. Testing a method is possible without a tool to represent it, but it is difficult to analyse the way the users undergo with the processes. When a method is embodied in a tool, the interaction of users with the tools can be observed directly.

21.2 MODELING ASSISTANCE FOR A HOST SYSTEM

Advising plays a central role in Decision support systems and Intelligent Tutoring Systems. Based on a diagnosis of the activity of a user within an application (called the *host system*), an advisor system compiles some useful advices or explanations, and delivers this assistance to a user.

In this section we summarize a stream of research that has started with the authors doctoral thesis in 1989. In 1992 it was decided to build a companion advisor system for the AGD system intended for designers (Paquette, Pachet, Giroux & Girard 1996). The EpiTalk approach was used to build this first advisor system. It was generic enough to support also learners. In the first case, the host system was a design environment (AGD). In the second case the host system was an eLearning environment such as those produced by a designer using AGD. This led us to integrate advisor capabilities into Explor@ (Girard, Paquette, Miara and Lundgren-Cayrol 1999), an on-line learning delivery system. In a third step, the concept of advisor system was adapted to the ADISA instructional engineering system, in order to integrate some "intelligence" in its operations (Paquette, Rosca, De la Teja, Léonard & Lundgren-Cayrol 2001). More recently, work started to introduce generic assistance capabilities into the TELOS system presented in chapter 15, to support users, whatever their role in the system.

Task-Based Advisors

We present now the research results of the first ÉpiTalk project. ÉpiTalk is a generic tool designed to facilitate the development of advisor systems based on a process model, an activity scenario built with MOT (Paquette and Tchounikine 1999).

Imagine a designer who wants to build an advisor for a given task to be achieved using software like a common spreadsheet. This task can be modeled by an activity scenario such as the ones presented in many chapters of this book. The designer will need to consider the tools provided by the computer environment: table and graph definition, sorting capabilities, database operations. Assistance may focus on one or many subtasks of the scenario. Pieces of advice may be given on the use of the application; they can also address the tasks to be achieved by using the application; or they could address the

Figure 8. A first method to design an advisor system

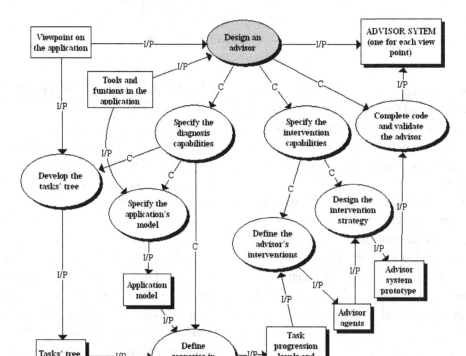

state of knowledge and competencies required or demonstrated by achieving these tasks. Each point of view gives rise to a distinct advisor.

As shown in the MOT model of Figure 8, the designer first chooses a viewpoint on the application. An advisor on a budget analysis task will be quite different from one to support the planning of a project. In both cases, a spreadsheet is used as the host system. Some spreadsheet functions will be useful for the budget task, but not necessarily for the project planning operations. Then, when the viewpoint is chosen, the designer should consider different user scenarios on how to proceed with the task. These are the main inputs to the process, the output being an advisor system for each chosen viewpoint and scenario.

When the designer starts to formalize the advisor, his first steps will be to build a tasks' tree and an activity scenario linking the tasks. The task tree groups the main task and his subtasks on a number of levels down to terminal tasks. It is the backbone of the design of an advisor. Once the designer has completed such a task tree, he should identify in the host system which tools, which documents and what kind of interaction with the host system are relevant to the task. These are the elements that have to be diagnosed upon by the advisor.

This second phase leads first to a model of the interesting part of the application for the task and for the advisor system on the task: the application model. Then, to each sub-task, the designer can add a context that describes progress levels within the task. For a given task, there is an on-going activity necessary to perform the task from the beginning to its completion. Progress levels decompose this activity into ordered stages. Each of these progress levels is an abstraction of a *diagnosis condition*. These conditions refer to the state of the application but mostly to the user's productions. At any time, the user is modeled by the set of its progress level within each task of the task tree.

Then the intervention of the system will rest on an expertise that has to be identified and formalized from the concepts, procedures and problem solving strategies of the task domain or problem type. Some of this expertise can focus on the progress that has been made in a task; that is progress levels associated to each task in the user's model. Another part can evaluate the coherence of the results obtained by the learner by comparing it to some coherence norm. The formalization of this expertise can take the form of a set of individual advices, each with a pattern detection part combining diagnosis conditions and an action part (presenting a message, displaying a tool, etc.) to be performed when a certain pattern is detected.

A Generic Assistance System

Instructional Engineering is not an easy task and it seemed evident right from the start of the AGD/MISA project that the designers using it, or in fact using any instructional design method or tool, would need to be supported by a companion tool that would give them appropriate advice at a right time

Figure 9 present an application of the Epitalk approach to the AGD system. This MOT+ model involves two knowledge domains. On the left, we have the tasks' tree, the tasks being achieved using the tools provided by the hosting AGD system. On the right, we see part of a corresponding advisors' tree.

The links between the two models are co-domain links that can be read as follows: an advisor agent gives advice on a task, and conversely, some task report to an advisor agent on some user actions while accomplishing the task.

The upper part of Figure 9 shows parts of the AGD task graph. The main task, "Design a learning system" is decomposed into a number of levels containing a total of 168 sub-tasks, including the task "model knowledge and activities" which is further decomposed into sub-tasks on the figure(such as "distribute knowledge (into courses, modules and activities of the pedagogical

Figure 9. An example of a tasks' tree and a corresponding advisor's tree

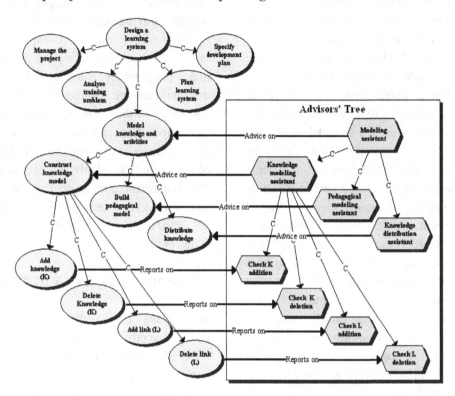

structure)". These tasks are structured together by the model of MISA presented in the first section of this chapter. Tasks like "add or delete knowledge or a links in the model" are terminal tasks, corresponding to direct user actions or set of actions in the host system, here AGD.

To this tasks' tree correspond on the right an advisor's tree that has a similar form. These advisor agents are represented by MOT principles that contribute externally (in an "Epitalk" way) to the control of a corresponding task by giving assistance to the actors responsible for that task (in this case, using a modeling tool).

Conversely the advisor system needs input from actor's action in the host system while enacting a task such as adding a knowledge unit or deleting a link. These inputs are provided by the "spying agents" defined on terminal tasks (insertion points) of the advisor system. This information enables EpiTalk to build a structured memory of the user's actions and progress levels pertaining

to the task. Using as an example the "construct knowledge model" task, Table 2 shows an ordered list of such progress levels in the first column. The second column gives the definition of each level; in the implementation of EpiTalk, this definition is coded and a program inspects the data produced by the user as it manipulates the system.

The third column gives the general meaning of the possible assistance messages when the corresponding conditions are met. Each piece of advice will be given if the user is at or further than the corresponding progress level, but has not reached the next level.

Notice that the second and third progress levels in Table 2 refer to another task "specify learning needs" that is a prerequisite to "construct knowledge model". This is an example of a progression relationship between two different tasks. The present task with its level "initial model sufficient" should be preceded by the task "specify learning needs" at the progress level where it is "Mainly

Table 2. Progress levels and pieces of advice for "construct knowledge model" task in AGD

"Construct knowledge model" and its progress levels		
Progress level	**Condition**	**Associated pieces of advice (if user is further than that level)**
Not started	Default value at start	"Please start using the model editor....."
Model started	**"Knowledge unit list in the user defined model is not empty "**	"Try to complete an initial model containing at least 10 knowledge units" "Specify the learning needs for all client groups before starting to build the model"
Initial model sufficient	**"The model has at least 10 knowledge units for which the learning needs have been specified for all the client groups"**	"The following knowledge units are not linked to the rest of model: ...." "The model is not well balanced for this reason:........." "There are not enough knowledge units because you have too many (courses, modules or learning activities)......."
Model completed and well-balanced	Model contains enough knowledge units (a number sufficient to "cover" each course, module or learning activity already defined) & Model is well balanced, that is relative % of knowledge units that are facts, concepts, procedures and principles is in accordance to the learning needs of the client groups & All the knowledge units in the model are linked to at least another knowledge unit.	"This task is completed for now, you should turn to the development of the pedagogical structure and add some course, module or learning activities"
Mainly achieved	Always false until the user quits the task	

Table 3. State of some components of an advisor

PROGRESS LEVEL IN THE TASK:
"Initial model completed" < = USER < "Model completed and well balanced"
USER PRODUCTIONS:
USER has produced learning needs that are at the SENSIBILIZATION level USER actual knowledge model contains: Facts = 10%; Concepts = 30%; Procedures 35%; Principles = 30%.
EXAMPLE FROM THE ADVISOR'S RULE BASE:
Advice name: "Model-05" • Advice: "Increase the proportion of facts and concepts in your knowledge model by adding new facts or concepts or deleting some procedures or principles". • Additional explanation: "Usually, learning needs at the SENSIBILIZATION level entail mainly factual (more than 30%) or conceptual (more than 40%) knowledge units". • Progress position: between "initial model completed" and "model complete and well balanced" levels • Additional condition: Maximum target for learning needs < = 2.5 and (Facts% < 30 or Concepts% < 40)

Table 4. Progress levels and pieces of advice on the "model and distribute" task in AGD

"Model knowledge and activities" task		
Progress level	**Condition**	**Associated piece of advice (if user is further than that level)**
Not started	Default value at start	**Distr-01** "Start building an initial model and create a first learning event"
Distribute-knowledge ready to start	Knowledge model started & Build pedagogical model started	**Distr -02** "Start developing sub-events of the main learning event and distribute knowledge units in these events...."
Distribute-knowledge started	Knowledge model started & Distribute knowledge started	**Distr -03** "The knowledge model is inadequate for some of first-level sub-events ..."
Distribute-knowledge completed on first level	Knowledge model completed and well-balanced & Pedagogical model completed on first level & Distribute knowledge completed first on level	**Distr -04** "Due to the number of knowledge units in your model, you should consider developing a second-level layer of sub-events"
Distribute-knowledge adequate	Knowledge model completed and well-balanced & Pedagogical model completed & Distribute knowledge completed	**Distr -05** "You should proceed with the "state learning objectives" task.
Mainly achieved	Always false until the user terminates the task	

achieved", that is learning needs are specified for all the knowledge units.

Structure of an Advisor Agent

Each advisor agent on a task is informed by data of the user model used by its assistance rules. This memory component stores the progress level that the user has reached and also the values of his related productions. Table 3 gives an example of the state of an advisor when the initial model is completed but the model is not yet completed and well balanced. This is when a rule such as *"The model is not well balanced for this reason:........."* is ready to fire.

If we go a step higher in the hierarchy, the advices on the "model knowledge and activities" task will become more abstract in nature. As shown in Table 4, the progress levels of this task are defined in terms of progress levels of its sub-tasks, and pieces of advice are focused on the general progress in task achievement.

Building Assistance in the Explor@ LCMS

After completing a companion editor for AGD using the EpiTalk approach, we applied it successfully to another situation. This time the actor being advised was not a designer but a learner interacting with a spreadsheet-based environment where he had to induce simple laws in physics using data tables. This proved the general applicability of the Epitalk approach.

In the meanwhile, in 1999, we had built a platform for distance learning delivery called Explor@. Such systems were to be called later "Learning Content Management System (LCMS)". Explor@ aimed to support a Virtual Learning Centre (VLC) model where five actors were interacting: learner, trainer, designer, content expert and manager. We decided to add a generic advising system to Explor@ based on the EpiTalk approach, in order to support these actors in Web-based environments (Girard, Paquette, Miara and Lundgren-Cayrol 1999).

In this project, we mainly focused on the learner as being the actor to be advised. The host system was any learning environment produced using the Explor@ LCMS. In Explor@, the task tree and an activity scenario are provided by a hierarchical activity structure (AS) build using one of the main tools in Explor@. Another tree, the knowledge structure (KS) could also be built by a similar tool, in order to describe a hierarchy of the concepts to be acquired during the learning activities.

Explor@ also contained an *Advice Editor* that enabled designers to define conditional principles that will update the user model, display an advice or engage a dialogue with the user (Lundgren-Cayrol, Paquette, Miara, Bergeron, Rivard and Rosca 2001).

The advisor system evaluates the user's actions in the host system and assigns, for each activity in the AS or each knowledge unit in the KS, an estimated progress level considered to be done or acquired by the user, called his *belief*, and a targeted progress level called his *goal*. The *user model* at a certain time is simply the set of all beliefs and goals assigned at this time to each activity and knowledge unit.

This user model is updated essentially in three ways: by the designer's predefined rules, by querying the user at run time and by some action the user can take to modify the model. The designer's predefined rules state that if certain conditions are met, the model will be updated to some belief or goal level for a certain activity or knowledge unit. A second way to update the model is when the user is queried. Upon certain answers, other questions can be asked, until the end of a predefined decision tree. Then, depending on the path of the user's answers, the system will be able to update the model or to trigger an action according to the designer's definition in such a case.

The Advice Editor has evolved from being a rather complicated interface to an easy "fill-in-the-form" format intended for the designer. The course designer is asked to enter the instructional

tree structure consisting of nodes (e.g., course modules), sub-nodes (e.g., activity level) and leafs (e.g., terminal task level such as use a resource). Nodes and leafs can be added, deleted or edited at any point. For each node the course designer enters the title of the node, the abbreviation, the URL, the weight of importance (%) and the type of progression within the node (sequential, optional, modular, parallel). The designer then decides whether s/he wants to insert a contextual advice, At the leaf level, the designer enters the above parameters plus information on the level of self-monitoring by the learner.

When the designer has finished entering the static and dynamic advice, the editor can be put in a validation mode, which is the simulation of what the learner will experience once the course is online. The designer can switch from validation to editing mode in order to modify and verify the advisory system, until he is satisfied. This feature has proven very helpful to course designers to determine, before the course is online, whether advice really are inserted at the right place and whether there are enough or too many advice.

When this work is completed by the designer and the learning environment is run, the advisor will manifest itself in the user's interface in three ways:

1. By displaying diagnosis questions and pop-up advice at certains times to the learner while he is navigating in the course site;
2. By making available contextual advice that can be consulted at any time in the Resource Navigator;
3. By displaying progress bars for each activity and knowledge elements.

Building Assistance for the ADISA Design Workbench

In 2002, we have started another project to provide the ADISA design workbench with an assistance system extending the possibilities of the EpiTalk

Figure 10. Generic model of an assistance system

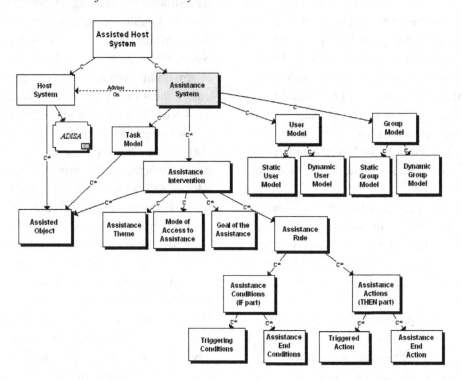

approach. This goal led to a new generic model of an assistance system (Basque, Dufresne, Paquette, Léonard, Lundgren-Cayrol and Prom Tep 2003) that presents refinements of the previous EpiTalk approach

This model takes the form of a MOT conceptual model presented on Figure 10. The figure shows only the upper layer of the model. Sub-models have been developed, but they will only be described textually below and some examples will be given to illustrate an application to the ADISA instructional engineering workbench.

As we can see on the model, we have kept the general EpiTalk approach where the assistance system is defined in relation to a host system and a task model. The host system is an environment like ADISA grouping activities and resources to support users and group achieving a relatively complex task: designing a learning system or environment.

The task model groups a subset of all the ac-

tivities that can be done using the host system. It is the part of the assistance systems that relates to the host system by a task/tool-function association. The task model is basically a hierarchical list of tasks and sub-tasks achieved using the host system. In a similar way to the Explor@ advisor system, the task model can also contain:

- a progress model within each task: sequential, parallel, modular or optional;
- a weights model of the task showing the relative importance of sub-tasks within the task, for example, what percentage of the task a given sub-task represents;
- a time-table model where the duration of each sub-task is specified,.

To be able to adapt to users, the assistance system contains a user and a group model constructed on the basis of the traces of user interactions with the host system. The static user model contains general user properties such as its background, learning styles and preferences or to its role in a task. The dynamic user model contains traces of user activities that will be used by the conditions that trigger the assistance, for example the number time consulting a resource or accessing assistance. The static and dynamic group models contain aggregated results from its individual member's models and also traces of group activities and interactions between group members. It enables a comparison between each user and the other users in a group.

The *assistance interventions* are based on these models. They are composed of an assisted object, an assistance theme, a mode of access to assistance, the goals of the assistance and the assistance rules.

- *The assisted object* is an element of the task model, supported by the host system. It can be a resource, an activity or a knowledge element defined in the host system.
- The *assistance theme* is a way to group the interventions by similarity of goal, in order to facilitate the access to indexed assistance or to build specialized assistance modules on themes like the operation of the host system, task execution, quality of the production (consistence, completeness, pertinence,…), collaboration between users or users' self-management.
- The *mode of access* to assistance determines if the assistance is static or adaptive. Static assistance is not based on the user model. It is always the same, whatever the users actions in the host system. There are two modalities: contextual assistance that provide pieces of advice or information on the task and resources that the user is actually using, or general indexed assistance such as the help files provides by generic software tools. On the contrary, adaptive assistance is founded on the user model. It can also be given in context or in a gen-

eral indexed way. In those two cases, the assistance will be different depending on the user's previous actions.

- Seven types of *assistance goals* have been identified: presentation, explanation, recall, guidance, motivation, verification, feedback.

The *assistance rules* are the central part of an assistance system. Each assistance intervention is define by one or more assistance rules, each composed of one or more assistance conditions (IF part) and a sequence of assistance action (THEN part).

The *assistance actions* either give the assistance or end the assistance. The actions can produce:

- *Adaptation of the user interface*. Such an adaptation can be a modification in the interface of the host system (e.g. the number of choices in a menu is reduced according to the user model); a change in the user model (e.g. the number of times a user access a resource in the host system); information given about the group model (e.g. a bar graph presents the results of a test for each member and an average for the group); the interface of the assistance system (e.g. a progress bar increases to show the progress of a user in a task).
- *Display of an assistance message*. The message is textual or audio-visual and it varies according to the goal of the assistance.
- *Display/launch of an element in the host system*. For example, in ADISA, the action opens a MISA design element in the ADISA interface.
- *Display/launch an external element*: an application, a document, or a notification to other actors of the host system.
- The *ending assistance* actions depend on the type of assistance. If it is a message,

it is simply closed; if it is a host system element, the assistance system has to close that element to return to the preceding state.

The *assistance conditions* of a rule either trigger the assistance or end it. A triggering event (e.g. a user starts a task, produces a document, etc.) is part of the condition. Only if the triggering event happens will the other conditions in a rule be evaluated to decide if the rule will be triggered. Here are the main triggering conditions that can be integrated in assistance rules.

- *Task related conditions*. (e.g an intervention assistance is scheduled at a certain date after the beginning of a task).
- *Conditions on the static user model*. These conditions are based on general properties of the user (e.g. the user prefers a certain access mode to assistance).
- *Conditions on the dynamic user model*. These conditions are based on the previous

actions of the user in the host or the assistance system (e.g. an action can be triggered when the user select, start or complete a task element, passes a long time on a task element or annotates a resource).

- *Conditions on the group model*. These conditions are similar to those on a user model, except they are based on the aggregation of the individuals' models or group properties and previous actions of the group (e.g. all members have declared a low competence for a task (static model); at least two members have participated in a forum (dynamic model).
- *Conditions on the comparison of the user model and the task model*. These conditions evaluate the gap between the user model and the task model (e.g. a user is late on a time table, or tries to complete a task before a prerequisite is completed).
- *Conditions on the comparison of the group model and the task model*: (e.g. conditions where the whole group is late according to

Figure 11. Insertion of an advisor agent in a TELOS scenario

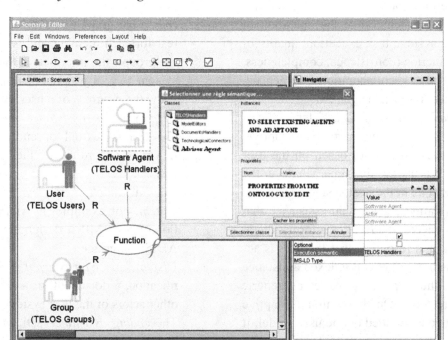

the time table and the progression model for the task).

- *Conditions on the comparison of a user model and the group model.* These conditions evaluate the gap between the user model and the group model (e.g. an intervention is needed when a user is late compared to the progress of the group or if s/he intervenes rarely in group activities compared to other members of the group).

- *Conditions to close assistance.* The user can be offered to close the assistance or the assistance system car retrieve the intervention after a certain period of time.

Building Assistance in TELOS

At the moment of writing this chapter, we have started to apply the EpiTalk approach to build assistance into the TELOS system. In TELOS, host systems are provided by activity scenarios that also provide a task model. In the case of TELOS,

the task model (or the scenario) can be more elaborated than in our previous projects because TELOS is based on the concept of a multi-actor process or workflow. These scenarios can also be intended for any level of the TELOS cascade, for engineers who aim to extend the services given by the system, for technologists who design platforms, for designers who built courses or work scenarios and for the final users who interact in these scenarios.

As explained in chapter 15, it is possible to embed actors called software agents into TELOS scenarios. We will define here a special class of software agents called *advisor agents*. They will be inserted in scenarios to show at what *insertion point* the assistance will be provided. An insertion point is a TELOS function symbol, as shown on Figure 11, or a terminal activity.

But stating that assistance will be given at a certain function or activity is not enough since there can be many actors that intervene in that task. The TELOS ontology (and the IMS-LD model)

Figure 12. Ontological definition of an advisor agent

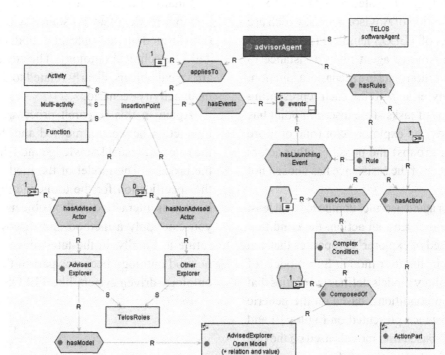

defines actors categories that are "explorers" such as learners or knowledge workers, and facilitators such as coaches, tutors, or technical support staff, in other words, users of the scenario. As a first step, we aim to give the assistance only to actors that are explorers at the exclusion of composers (designers will be assisted in their own scenarios) or administrators that control scenario instances. In the situation of Figure 11, assistance could be given to the user and/or to the Group.

Each advisor is defined essentially by its assistance rules. Rule conditions can check on user preferences (initiator of the assistance, learning style, socio-cultural indicators,...), on previous actions in the TELOS scenario (tasks achieved or progress bars, asked and received assistance,...), on competencies stored in the user model, on a portfolio that provided evidence on a user's competencies, on group collaboration or affective indicators. When conditions are met, the action part of the rules can provide messages to the user, modifications to the user model, advice to facilitators or modification to the scenario.

Figure 12 proposes an extension of the TELOS technical ontology presented in chapter 15 to provide a definition of Advisor agents, which are special classes of TELOS handlers (services). It states that an Advisor agent gives assistance to exactly one insertion point in a scenario: a function, a multi-activity or an activity, each representing tasks or groups of tasks. This insertion point has at least one advised explorer-actor (one or more individuals or groups) and possibly other actors that the designer of the assistance has chosen not to advice.

An Advisor agent has rules composed of at least a condition and at least an action, the condition being composed of explorer's properties that can be consulted in his user model. Sub-models of this main ontology models defines properties that can be used in conditions, based on the generic model of assistance presented on Figure 10 and a competency-based user model based on the one presented at the end of chapter 9.

Summary of the Advisor System Research Process

Let us summarize this research process. The initial phase, involved a process to construct advisor system presented in Figure 8. This process has been embodied in the EpiTalk generic advisor editor. Using this editor, two applications have been made, one for designers using AGD, another one for learners using a physics law induction environment.

After this first phase, a tool to define advising components has been built into the Explor@ LCMS. This new advisor editor refined the initial EpiTalk orientation in order to provide a more accessible tool, but that had a reduced set of functionalities. Advisors for a Job Search environment and advisors for some of Télé-université courses have been built with it.

A third phase began with a three-year research project that resulted in a model of an assistance system partly shown on Figure 10. This model was applied to build an advisor system for the ADISA instructional engineering workbench.

Finally, a fourth phase has started where the previous model of an assistance system has been transformed in an ontology that extends the TELOS technical ontology. The advisors agents are visual objects, clearly related to their context in an activity scenario.

Again in this research process, we see the interaction between a method and its tools and the role that visual knowledge modeling plays in the process. The model of the method provides the specification for the tools and the tools can be seen as interactive method objects. With them, you can apply a method and discover ways to refine it. Finally, in the latest development, the method ontology becomes part of the tool in an ontology-driven system like TELOS.

Figure 13. A learner's self-management process (Adapted from Ruelland, 2000)

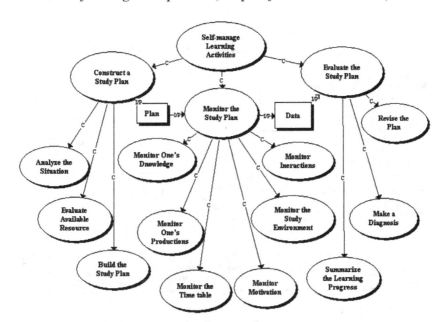

21.3 VISUAL MODELING IN DOCTORAL RESEARCH

The interplay between methods and tools, guided by visual modeling has been applied many times in the doctoral research of students directed by the author. We have mentioned earlier that a prize-winning thesis was produced by Françoise Crevier (1996) on the subject of the MISA method presented in the first section.

Other theses have applied similar approaches, despite the differences between their subjects. We will present here some of these doctoral work, to underline the similarity of the research methodology.

A Thesis on Learners' Self-Management

Another successful Ph. D thesis in Education was accomplished by Diane Ruelland (2000) on the subject of learner self-management. After a number of studies of self-management processes in telelearning environments, she elaborated a

model a learner self-management. The upper part of this model is shown on Figure 13.

The analysis of the learning context in distance learning environments has shown that a learner has to master a number of self-management tasks to succeed. These tasks are complex because of the need to organize interactions and collaboration at using a variety of ICT technologies. On Figure 13 the general process of learning self-management is subdivided in three large sub-processes: construct a study plan, monitor the plan and evaluate the plan.

The first sub-process is normally done at the beginning of course. It encourages a preliminary reflexive activity on how to address the learning activities. In the second process, the learning plan is monitored by the learner on six dimensions: progress in knowledge acquisition, quality of the productions (homework, tests, etc.), time management, state of motivation, mastery of the learning environments and quality of the learner's interaction with peer learners and facilitators. This process is enacted during learning and produces data that will serve to evaluate the plan and the learning progress. Enacted at certain predefined

Figure 14. Identification of self-management tools

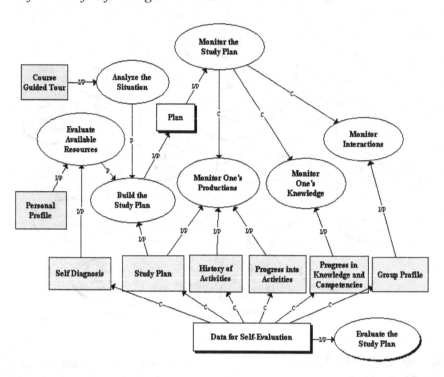

moments (end of a module or a difficult production), this third process favors meta-cognition (Noël 1991), an activity where the learner reflect on his situation and can decide to re-plan a new set of activities, thus starting a new plan-monitor-evaluate cycle.

The model of the self-management process on Figure 13 has been used to identify a number of tools to support the process. Some of them have been implemented in the Explor@ and Concept@ tele-learning delivery systems at Télé-université. Figure 14 presents some of these tools related to components of the self-management process.

The *guided tour* of a course or learning environment is a necessary starting point to analyze the learning situation, in particular to identify the knowledge and competency objectives, and the activities, resources and participants that are available to attain the course's objectives. Then the learner uses the *personal profile tool* to present himself to the other participants. He also uses the *competency self-diagnosis tool* to evaluate its

strengths and weaknesses with regards to the target competencies; such a tool has been presented in the preceding chapter.

The *study plan* plays a central role in the integration of all three sub-processes of learning self-management. It results from the preceding activities and consists in building a timetable integrating individual and collaborative activities and evaluating the amount of work required to achieve them. The study plan provides a basis to help monitor and guide the global learning process.

The four other tools presented on Figure 14 serve mainly to help monitor the learning process by presenting to the learner data to evaluate its progress. The *history* tool provides a trace to the learner, displaying the dates where his activities have been realized. The *progress* tool presents the activity structure of the course together with a progress bar of its achievement. The *knowledge and competency progress* tool presents a synthesis of the evaluation of the learner's production. Finally, the *group profile* tool enables each participant to see the personal profile of each participant in the group and to compare his results with those of the group, It also provide a global view of the group and the individuals progress in the course to the facilitator in order to orient their assistance to the right persons and on the right subjects.

Three Thesis on Cognitive Computing and the Semantic Web

The two above-mentioned thesis are very good examples of the application of Knowledge Modeling to Educational Research. We will now summarize three theses on Cognitive Computing and the Semantic Web. These doctoral research works have been presented in detail in section III of this book, on the subjects of ontology evolution, software components aggregation and ontology modeling.

The doctoral work of Délia Rogozan presented in Chapter 11 has started by building a process model. This visual model, presented on Figure 4 in Chapter 11, has been built using the MOT representation language in order to elaborate a unified model of ontology evolution. It helped identify the delicate operations where support should be given to the ontologists responsible for ontology change. After a further analysis of the ontology evolution process, the conclusion was that there is a lack of tools to support important steps of the ontology evolution model. From the evolution process model, needs have been identified a) for a tool that provides a uniform and consistent logging of elementary and complex changes as well as the causality relations that exist among them; b) for a tool that can analyse change effects on resources that are semantically referenced by concepts should be made available; c) for a tool that preserves the access to and the interpretation of resources via the new ontology version.

To resolve these problems, a framework was proposed that led to the identification of two tools: the *Change History Builder* (CHB) and the *Semantic Annotation Modifier* (SAM). The integration of these tools in the process of ontol-

ogy evolution has been presented in Figure 13 in Chapter 11. Basically, CHB logs the changes in a useful way when the ontology is modified, and SAM uses this information to present referencing adaptations for the ontologist to decide. Essentially, this framework is an advisor system that helps ontologists maintain a sound referencing of resources through ontology evolution.

The doctoral work by Anis Masmoudi presented in chapter 13 has followed a similar path, though with a different subject: the aggregation of software components. On Figure 1 in Chapter 13, a software component aggregation process (SOCAP) has been presented. This aggregation process is based on a software component ontology that provides metadata describing each software component. This metadata helped define a first tool, the SOCOM manager that enables the construction of a software component repository where components can be stored and retrieved according to their metadata. Then other tools have been built into a framework to support the aggregation process. This framework contains an *aggregation advisor* that uses the ontology and the metadata to evaluate if two or more components are compatible for aggregation and if not, make recommendations on how to adapt them.

The doctoral work of Michel Héon, presented in chapter 14, focused on an ontology engineering process based on the transformation of semiformal models into ontologies. This process is presented on Figure 8 in Chapter 14, and the three sub-processes, *design a semi-formal model*, *formalize in a domain ontology*, and *validate the domain ontology*, are presented in Figures 9, 10, and 11 in Chapter 14. Based on this process, a meta-modeling technique is used to help disambiguate the semi-formal model in terms of a reference ontology, with the goal to produce a domain ontology that respects the semantics of the original model. This leads again to an advisor system that uses transformation rules to suggest automatic transformation to the semi-formal model, or propose choices to the ontologist on

Table 5. Comparison of research projects

Research Project	Actors and their products	Method or task process	Assistance rules	Tools and/or framework
MISA Instructional Engineering	Team of instructional engineers – specs of a learning environment	Model of the instructional engineering (IE) method	Rules to ensure coherence relations between IE products	AGD, ADISA, form-based and model support to IE
EpiTalk Advisor systems	Technologist – definition of an advisor system	Adding advisor agents to a host system and a task model	*No assistance to advisor designers has been provided*	Epitalk and Explor@ advice definition tools
Learner self-management	Learners - self-monitored learning process	Model of a self-management of one's learning process	Rules in some Explor@ applications	Personal and group profile, competency self-assessment, progress tools, …
Ontology Evolution	Ontologists – revised resource semantic references	Model of the ontology evolution process	Rules to adapt resource references through ontology change	Change history builder and semantic annotation modifier
Software component aggregation	Software engineers – aggregated components	Model of the software aggregation process	Rules on component compatibility for their aggregation	Software component aggregation framework (SOCAF)
Ontology modelling	Ontology engineers – ontology models	Model of the ontology building process from a semi-formal model	Disambiguation rules for transformation from semi-formal model to ontology	OntoCASE ontology building advisor

alternative possibilities.

CONCLUSION

In this chapter, we have presented a variety of research project that have been conducted using visual modeling. Despite the variety of subjects, there are three constants: the interplay between method modeling and tool definition; the use of visual modeling to represent the method as a process and situate the context of use of the tools; and the use of visual modeling to describe the software framework and the tools themselves. Table 5 synthesizes the main elements of the research projects presented in this chapter.

Figure 15 captures the commonalities of these projects in a generic research process that can be applied to other research areas. We do not pretend it applies in all areas but certainly to the type of oriented research and development that characterizes the LICEF research centre and the CICE research chair.

At the beginning, there is always an actor or a set of actors that we aim to assist by providing a method and a set of tools that will help apply the method. After an inventory of the problem area, the first questions are *who are the actors? what do they have to produce?* Then, with answers to these initial questions, we can start decomposing the products and the main actor's tasks, in order to build a process model or a method structuring these tasks.

The difference between a process model and a method lies in the principles that rule a method. This difference has been underlined in chapter 3. If an advisor system is the final goal, then principles must be added to the process or uncovered from the method in order to formalize some assistance rules, as we have done in some of the projects. This operation requires a more profound analysis and needs not to be done for the entire process but only for the critical tasks in the process or method.

With a set of critical tasks' sub-models, we can start modeling the tools and/or the framework using software engineering techniques. MOT models

Figure 15. A generic research process

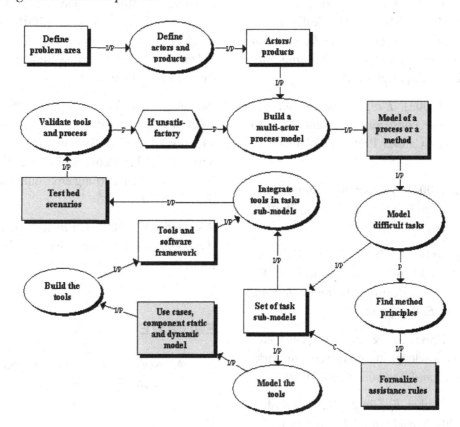

can also be used. By integrating the tools within the tasks sub-model, we can provide precise test bed scenarios for the validation of the process/method and its tools. This validation can start another cycle of process modeling/tool definition, as we have seen in the MISA research process.

REFERENCES

Basque, J., Dufresne, A., Paquette, G., Léonard, M., Lundgren-Cayrol. K., & Prom Tep, S. (2003). Vers un modèle conceptuel générique de système d'assistance pour le téléapprentissage. *Revue STICEF, 10.*

Crevier, F. (1996). *Conception et validation d'une méthode d'ingénierie didactique.* Thèse de doctorat. Sciences de l'Éducation, Université de Montréal.

Girard, J., Paquette, G., Miara, A., & Lundgren-Cayrol, K. (1999). Intelligent Assistance for Web-based TeleLearning. In S. Lajoie & M. Vivet (Eds.), *Proceedings of AI-Ed'99. In AI and Education, open learning environments* (pp. 561-569). Amsterdam: IOS Press.

Lundgren-Cayrol, K., Paquette, G., Miara, A., Bergeron, F., Rivard, J., & Rosca, I. (2001). *Explor@ Advisory Agent: Tracing the Student's Trail.* Presented at WebNet'01 Conference, Orlando.

Noël, B. (1991). *La métacognition.* Bruxelles, Belgium: De Boeck-Wesmael.

Paquette, G. (2001). Designing Virtual Learning Centers . In Adelsberger, H., Collis, B., & Pawlowski, J. (Eds.), *Handbook on Information Technologies for Education & Training* (pp. 249–272). Berlin: Springer-Verlag.

Paquette, G. (2002). *L'ingénierie du télé-apprentissage, pour construire l'apprentissage en réseaux.* Quebec, Canada: Presses de l'Université du Québec.

Paquette, G. (2004). *Instructional Engineering for Network-Based Learning.* New York: Pfeiffer/ Wiley Publishing Co.

Paquette, G., Aubin, C., & Crevier, F. (1999 August). MISA, A Knowledge-based Method for the Engineering of Learning Systems. *Journal of Courseware Engineering, 2.*

Paquette, G., Crevier, F., & Aubin, C. (1994, November). ID knowledge in a course design workbench. *Educational Technology, 34*(9), 50–57.

Paquette, G., Pachet, F., Giroux, S., & Girard, J. (1996) EpiTalk, Generating Advisor Agents for Existing Information Systems. *Artificial Intelligence in Education, 7*(3-4).

Paquette, G., Rosca, I., De la Teja, I., Léonard, M., & Lundgren-Cayrol, K. (2001). *Web-based Support for the Instructional Engineering of E-learning Systems.* Presented at WebNet'01 Conference, Orlando.

Paquette, G., & Tchounikine, P. (1999). Towards a Knowledge Engineering Method for the Construction of Advisor Systems. In S. Lajoie & M. Vivet (Eds.), Proceedings of AI-Ed'99. In AI and Education, open learning environments. Amsterdam: IOS Press.

Ruelland, D. (2000). *Un modèle des processus d'autogestion de l'apprentissage.* Thèse de doctorat, Université de Montréal.

ENDNOTE

[1] A first version of section 1 has been prepared by Michel Léonard.

About the Author

Gilbert Paquette holds a Ph.D from the Université du Maine (FRANCE) in Artificial Intelligence and Education. Researcher at the Center for Interuniversity Research on Telelearning Applications, (CIRTA-LICEF) he has founded in 1992, Gilbert Paquette holds a Canada Research Chair in Cognitive and Educational Engineering, has acted as the Scientific Director of the LORNET Canadian research network and is a professor at Télé-université du Québec in Montreal. In 2007, he has received an Honoris Causa Doctorate from the University Pierre et Marie Curie (Paris VI). He has pioneered strategic projects in the field of knowledge-based systems, instructional engineering and distance education. Recent publications include three books on technology-based learning. He has given invited conferences in many parts of the world and sits on the scientific committee for six Journals, three in France, one in the US and two in Canada. He is "fellow" of the World Technology Network, a group of international experts. He represents Canada on the Globe consortium on learning objects and sits on the scientific committee of the European networks TENCompetence and Share-TEC. He has also founded two companies and has acted as Minister for Science and Technology in the Quebec Government (1982-1984).

Index

A

abstract knowledge 26, 27, 28, 29, 31, 38, 39, 41, 47, 48
activity scenario 145
Actors 303, 304, 306, 312
Actor symbols 306
additional change 220
advisor agents 442, 449, 454
aesthetic domain 115
affective domain 135, 136
Aggregates 300, 304
aggregation advisor 454
Aggregation Level 367, 378, 379
AI domain 373
antecedent 6
Artificial Intelligence (AI) 3, 8, 14, 18, 110, 111, 373, 374, 375, 378, 384
assistance actions 448
assistance conditions 448
assistance goals 448
assistance interventions 447
assistance message 448
assistance rules 443, 447, 448, 450, 456
assistance theme 447
assisted object 447
asynchronous group 325, 327
Asynchronous Online Training 373
attitudes 114
attribute values 25, 29, 31, 48
autonomy 174, 178, 210
awareness 75, 79, 81, 126, 136, 174, 175, 184

B

backward compatible changes 224

C

behavioral intelligence 113
binary predicates 202
blended learning 338, 346, 360, 361, 380
Business Intelligence 386
Business Process Execution Language (BPEL) 153
Business Process Management systems 152
Business Process Modeling Notation (BPMN) 145, 153, 154, 155, 156, 157, 158, 159, 160, 161, 162, 168, 296

capacity 94, 99
Change History Builder (CHB) 454
ChangeObject 225, 228
ChangeOperation 225, 228
change operations 225, 227, 228, 229, 230
close assistance 449
co-domain 71, 72, 73, 86
cognitive domain 113, 114, 115, 135, 136
cognitive engineering 110, 120, 123, 124
cognitive level 351, 352
cognitive psychology 3, 7, 14, 15, 109, 110
cognitive science 106, 120, 121, 123, 124, 386
cognitive skills 242
cognitive strategies 114
cognitive tools 320, 322, 331, 334
collaborative knowledge 325, 326, 328, 329, 330, 333, 393
collaborative learning 319, 324, 325, 333, 336
collaborative systems 61, 62
collective writing 51, 63
commercial-off-the-shelf (COTS) 257, 269, 270
community of practice 338, 349, 351, 361

compatible changes 224

competence 93, 94, 97, 104, 105

competency 174, 175, 176, 177, 178, 184, 186, 187, 188, 189, 190, 191, 192, 193, 207, 208, 209, 210, 211, 213, 214, 215, 216

competency acquisition 93

competency approach 94, 101, 102

Competency Attachment 378

competency-based approach 93, 94, 97, 99, 100, 104

competency equilibrium 239, 248, 250, 251, 252

competency gap 66, 81, 82, 83, 90, 93, 174, 175, 176, 177, 178, 193

Competency Management 95, 242, 245, 255, 386

competency model 147, 345, 383

competency modeling 146

competency movement 94

competency ontology 207, 208, 209, 210, 214, 216, 239, 242, 243, 244, 246, 251, 253, 378

competency profile 93, 94, 95, 97, 101, 102, 103, 208

competency scale 244

competency self-management 418, 420, 421, 423, 429

competency standards 96, 97, 100, 101

competency statement 208

competencyType 244

competency units 95, 96

completeness 25, 47, 48

complex change 219, 220, 225

complexity 174, 175, 201, 209, 210, 211

complex situations 6

Component-Based Software Development (CBSD) 256, 257, 258, 269

component-based systems 49, 53, 54

computability 25

computer engineering 24

Computer-Mediated Communication (CMC) 325, 331

computer programming 26, 30

Computer-Supported Collaborative Learning (CSCL) 320, 333, 336

computer supported collaborative work (CSCW) 386

concept graph 239

conceptual architecture 295, 297, 299, 301, 314, 316

Conceptual Framework 295, 297, 298, 300

conceptual maps 1, 6, 7, 8, 15

conceptual models 52, 53

conceptual ontology 295, 297, 300, 301, 302, 303, 316

conceptual system 49, 50, 51, 54, 55, 76, 77, 83

conceptual trees 9

conclusion 6

conditional knowledge 100

Condition symbols 306

consequence 6

constructivist pedagogy 23

content management 175

Content Unit (CU) 241

context of use 174

contextual assistance 447

contextual knowledge 8

co-reference links 71

co-referencing 86, 87, 90, 109

Course Model 239

creation and production 125, 127, 142

cross-curricular competencies 99

D

data and text mining 386

data management 387

decision tree 58, 59, 60, 61, 76, 83

Declarative Curricula Model Language (DCML) 240

declarative knowledge 100

delivery model 148, 337, 338, 345, 346, 347, 348, 349, 350, 363, 364, 365, 367, 378, 379

delivery processes 433

deterministic decision rules 51

Didactical Unit (DU) 241

digital media 2

Digital Operations 304

Digital Resources 303

distributed classroom model 349

distributed learning system (DLS) 146, 347

diversity 4

documentation element (DE) 434, 436, 437

document management 386, 389, 390, 392, 398

domain knowledge 300, 304, 387

domain model 107, 239, 274, 276, 278, 288

domain ontology 208, 279, 280, 284, 285, 288, 289, 291, 292, 388, 389, 390, 454

dynamic component systems 25

dynamic relationship 94

dynamic user model 447, 448

E

ease of interpretation 25, 47

Educational Modeling Language (EML) 154, 157, 158, 171, 238, 251

educational objectives 113, 120

educational semantic Web 244

e-learning 94, 256, 257, 295, 296, 304, 315, 316, 350, 365

e-learning languages 154

e-learning platforms 154

e-learning processes 156, 157

e-learning system 156

electronic performance support systems (EPSS) 296, 346

elementary change 219, 225

emotional domain 115

emotional intelligence 113

emotional level 351

English 26

entry competency (EC) 247, 248, 253, 254

expertise 79, 80, 81, 128, 174, 177, 178, 242

exponential growth 196

Extended Backus-Naur Form (EBNF) 276

Extensible Markup Language (XML) 198, 200, 201, 202, 206, 207, 214, 215

external element 448

F

face-to-face group 325, 326, 327

factual systems 51

familiarity 75, 79, 81, 174, 175, 176, 178, 184

familiarization 126, 242, 248

feedback loop 416

formal model 390, 393, 395

formal ontology model 390

frequency 174

G

generality 25, 37

generic framework 257

genericity 26, 27, 35, 47

generic problem 106, 107, 109, 113, 118, 120, 135

generic procedure 107, 178

generic process 123, 131, 132, 133, 134, 135, 136, 137, 138, 139, 179, 181

generic skill 106, 110, 118, 119, 120, 123, 124, 125, 126, 127, 128, 129, 131, 133, 134, 136, 137, 138, 139, 140, 141, 142, 143, 144, 174, 175, 176, 178, 179, 180, 181, 183, 184, 185, 187, 192, 193, 208, 209, 210, 211, 341, 342

generic task 107

generic terms 374, 375

Goal and Constraints Model 239, 240

goal-directed sequencing 110

grammar 3, 5, 6

graphic model 295

group model 447, 448, 449

H

haveAuthor 228

haveChangeNumber 228

haveParentChangeNumber 228

heuristic rules 51

hierarchical links 7

human competencies 106

human history 1

hybrid conceptual systems 49, 54, 55

hybrid models 61

I

IDLD project 367

IDLD repository 369, 372

IDLD Web portal 367, 368, 369, 372

incompatible changes 224

inference engine 6, 267, 389, 390, 391

inference model 107

Information and Communication Technologies (ICT) 146, 387, 397, 398, 402, 404

information model 94
Information Unit (IU) 241
instructional designers 434, 438
Instructional Design (ID) 146, 157, 168, 337, 365, 438
instructional engineering 24, 124, 131, 144, 145, 146, 158, 171, 238, 239, 242, 243, 254, 337, 338, 359, 360, 361, 364, 365, 367, 380, 383, 384, 385, 432, 433, 435, 438, 439, 441, 442, 446, 451, 454, 456
Instructional Model 148
Instructional Science 146
Instructional System Design (ISD) 146, 171
instructional theories 146
intellectual actions 124
Intellectual Capital 386, 405
intellectual domain 115
intellectual skills 114
intelligent agents 196, 214
interactive design 369
interactive management 110
interlinked science 146
interpretation 2, 4, 6, 7, 9, 14
invention of writing 1
iterative procedures 49, 56

K

knowledge 1, 2, 3, 4, 6, 7, 8, 9, 10, 11, 14, 15, 16, 17, 18, 19, 20, 21, 93, 94, 96, 97, 98, 99, 100, 101, 102, 103, 104
knowledge acquisition 74, 111, 117, 133, 134, 183, 387, 404, 452
Knowledge Base 389, 390, 391
knowledge co-modeling 392, 393
knowledge discovery 111, 117
knowledge domain 70, 73, 74, 80, 91, 103, 174, 181, 318, 319, 338
knowledge editor 146, 388, 390, 392
knowledge elements 176, 339, 341
knowledge elicitation 272, 273, 278, 292, 438
knowledge engineer 273, 280, 288
knowledge engineering 146, 337, 386
knowledge entity 208
knowledge expression 112, 117
knowledge extraction 387
knowledge gap 174

knowledge management 174, 193, 257, 295, 296, 298, 300, 315, 316, 386, 387, 391, 392, 393, 397, 404, 405
knowledge model 71, 72, 73, 74, 87, 94, 148, 176, 178, 184, 318, 321, 322, 323, 325, 326, 327, 328, 329, 330, 338, 339, 340, 341, 342, 387, 389, 390, 393, 395, 396, 436
knowledge modeling 24, 30, 146, 174, 186, 318, 320, 321, 323, 324, 325, 327, 328, 329, 330, 331, 338, 387, 433, 438, 453
knowledge network 322
knowledge object 24, 25, 26, 27, 28, 29, 31, 36, 37, 38, 39, 40, 41, 42, 47, 48, 51, 71, 72, 73, 74, 75, 76, 77, 78, 79, 80, 81, 82, 83, 86, 87, 89, 90, 107, 120, 125, 126, 127, 128, 129, 132, 133, 134, 139, 144, 320, 322, 323, 325, 326, 327, 330
knowledge representation 23, 24, 94, 100, 198, 200, 202, 214, 215, 272, 274
knowledge search 111
knowledge storage 111, 117
knowledge systems 49, 50, 51
knowledge unit 443, 444, 445
knowledge use 112, 117

L

language ontology 278
LD format 375, 378
Learner Model 239
Learner Verification and Revision (LVR) 9
learning activity 179, 191, 245, 246, 250, 318, 319, 322, 324, 343, 348, 379, 421
Learning and Knowledge Management Applications (LKMA) 298
Learning and Knowledge Management Products (LKMP) 298
Learning and Knowledge Management System (LKMS) 298, 299, 300, 308
learning behaviors 114
Learning Content Management System (LCMS) 347, 439, 444, 445, 451
Learning Design (LD) 238, 254, 367, 368, 369, 370, 371, 372, 373, 374, 375, 376, 377, 378, 379, 380, 381, 382, 383, 384, 385

learning environment 110, 148, 149, 157, 183, 245, 346, 347, 359, 362, 364, 419, 429, 433, 438, 451, 452, 456

Learning Event Network (LEN) 436

learning events (LE) 342, 343, 346

Learning Management 408

Learning Material Models 148

learning materials 433, 438

learning model 327, 328

learning nuggets 374, 384

learning objective 106, 113, 120, 124, 207, 208, 245, 342, 364

learning object (LO) 73, 238, 239, 241, 242, 243, 245, 246, 252, 254, 255, 257, 368, 371, 372, 373, 376, 382, 383, 384, 385, 387, 408, 412, 413, 415, 416, 418, 419, 429, 431

Learning Object Manager 411, 430

Learning Object Metadata (LOM) 157, 368, 369, 371, 372, 373, 376, 377, 379, 382, 408, 410, 411, 420

Learning Object Repositories (LOR) 407, 412, 413, 415, 416, 417, 418, 419

learning object repository management 369

Learning Organization 386

learning process 318, 319, 330, 419, 420

Learning Resource Manager (LRM) 408, 409, 410, 411

Learning Resources Repositories 412

learning scenario 145, 146, 148, 149, 157, 158, 170, 179, 181, 186, 192, 193, 257, 343, 361, 362, 363, 372, 383

learning system 23, 24, 146, 147, 148, 149, 156, 346, 347, 349, 350, 433, 434, 439, 442, 446

Learning System Engineering Method 368

learning theories 319, 328

learning unit 298, 342, 343

lexicon 3, 5, 26, 40

linear temporal logic (LTL) 240

linguistics 3

M

marker function 71

mass communication 2

mastery 75, 78, 79, 80, 81, 127, 142, 174, 176, 177, 178, 193, 240, 241, 242

mental representations 2, 3, 14, 20

meta-cognition 106, 111, 118

meta-concept 175

metadata 197, 198

meta-domains 128, 130

meta-knowledge 106, 110, 111, 112, 113, 116, 117, 120, 124, 136, 143, 181

metal object 29, 30, 31, 33, 34

meta-model 272, 274, 276, 277, 278, 281, 284, 287

meta-object 274

MetaObject Facility (MOF) 276

methodological aids 368, 369

Model Driven Architecture (MDA) 274, 293, 296, 315

model editor 66, 91

modeling 3, 13, 14, 19

modeling architecture 276

modeling process 174, 176, 178, 193

modeling software 318, 330

modeling space (MS) 274, 276, 278, 280, 281, 282

Modeling using Object Types (MOT) 13, 20, 23, 24, 25, 26, 27, 37, 38, 40, 41, 42, 43, 44, 45, 46, 47, 48, 146, 160, 161, 165, 196, 199, 200, 201, 202, 204, 206, 207, 213, 214, 218, 220, 225, 230, 273, 274, 275, 276, 277, 278, 279, 280, 281, 282, 283, 284, 285, 286, 289, 290, 292, 294, 301, 306, 316, 318, 319, 320, 321, 322, 323, 324, 325, 326, 327, 329, 330, 338, 347, 352, 359, 361, 362, 363, 365, 407, 408, 411, 421, 425, 430

model type 66, 73, 75, 77

mode of access 447

Morse code 26

MOT editor 433, 439

MOT graph 179

MOT graphical language 388

MOT model 58, 66, 67, 68, 69, 70, 71, 72, 78, 87, 89, 91, 107, 111, 373, 374, 433, 434, 438, 439, 441, 456

MOT modeling 407, 411

motor skills 114

MOT representation system 24, 25, 26, 37, 48, 49, 63, 387, 397

MOT system 24, 27, 37, 42, 48
multi-actor processes 145, 389
multi-actor scenario 148, 296
multi-agent collaborative systems 62

O

Object-Oriented representations 202
object types 50, 61
online delivery 380
online learning 346, 351, 408, 419, 440
Ontological Definition Meta-model (ODM) 274, 293
ontological engineering 239, 252, 271, 272, 278, 280, 295
ontology 198, 199, 200, 201, 202, 204, 206, 207, 208, 209, 210, 211, 212, 213, 214, 215, 216
ontology change 219, 230
ontology consistency 218, 220
ontology-driven architecture (ODA) 296, 300, 316
Ontology Editor 304, 305, 388, 389, 390
ontology engineering 454
ontology evolution 218, 220, 221, 222, 224, 225, 230, 231, 233, 234, 235, 236
ontology formalization 273, 287, 290
ontology mapping 241
ontology model 389, 390
ontology-oriented software-agents 218
ontology role 218
Ontology Web Language (OWL) 26, 196, 200, 201, 202, 204, 205, 206, 207, 209, 210, 214, 215, 271, 273, 276, 277, 278, 280, 281, 282, 284, 288, 292, 293, 294
operational principles 25, 32, 35
Operations 296, 301, 303, 304, 306
orthogonal transformation 278, 279
OWL 218, 221, 225, 226, 227, 230, 232, 233, 234

P

PALOMA 368, 369, 371, 372, 375, 377, 381
parallel procedures 49, 55, 56
parallel transformation 277, 278
pedagogical constraints 239
pedagogical model 345, 346, 433, 445

pedagogical scenario 318, 328
pedagogical software 256
pedagogical strategy 149, 373, 378, 380, 381, 433
pedagogical structure 374
phenomenon 1, 18
physical domain 115
physiotherapists 197
physiotherapy 197
platform independent model (PIM) 296
platform specific model (PSM) 296
predicate logic 273
premise 6
prescriptive systems 58
primary change 220
procedural attachment 53, 55
procedural knowledge 9, 14, 100
procedural systems 55
Process re-engineering and decision support 386
production rules 239
project management 107, 111
propositional logic 5, 6, 12
psychomotor domain 135

Q

query ontologies 301

R

Rational Unified Process (RUP) 297
reception 125, 126, 144
reference link 224, 225
reference ontology (RO) 282, 283, 284, 285, 286, 287, 291, 292, 454
referencing process 376
relational principle 25, 31, 32, 37, 39, 40, 45, 51, 58, 59, 61
Repositories Support Project (RSP) 415
representation 1, 2, 3, 4, 6, 8, 9, 10, 14, 15, 16, 17, 18, 19, 20, 21
representation system 2, 4, 9, 14, 23, 24, 25, 26, 27, 37, 47, 48, 49, 50, 63, 65
reproduction 125, 126, 137, 144
Resource Description Framework (RDF) 198, 199, 201, 215, 278

S

savoir 100

savoir-être 100

savoir-faire 100

Scenario Editor 389, 390

scientific methodology 110

Scientific Pedagogy 146

scope 174, 192, 210

SCORM profile 378

search agent 197

search engine 82, 87, 88, 89, 200

self-management 125, 128, 129, 141, 142, 144, 418, 419, 420, 421, 423, 424, 429, 431, 447, 451, 452, 453, 454

self-paced learning 346

Semantic Annotation Modifier (SAM) 454

Semantic Annotator 389, 390

semantic approach 391

semantic constraints 248

semantic knowledge 388

semantic network 50, 51

semantic network diagram 8

semantic references 221, 234

semantic referencing 218, 221, 222, 230, 234, 236, 377, 384

semantics 3, 6, 21

semantic tree 1, 6, 7, 16

semantic validation 288, 289, 291, 292

Semantic Web 196, 197, 198, 201, 214, 215, 216, 218, 231, 234, 235, 236, 237, 257, 269, 387, 388, 391, 392

sensitization 242

sequential procedures 49, 55, 56

service oriented framework 296, 299, 316

simplicity 25, 47

skills domain 103

social domain 115, 135

social level 351

socio-affective skills 338

socio-cultural 416

socio-emotional skills 338

SOCOM aggregation attributes 261

SOCOM component 264, 267

SOCOM manager 256, 260, 262, 267, 454

SOCOM Metadata Extractor 258

SOCOM ontology 256, 257, 262, 263, 265, 266, 267, 269

SOCOM OWL 258

SOCOM platform attributes 262

SOCOM quality attributes 262

SOCOM Search Engine 267

SOCOM service attributes 261

SOCOM static attributes 260

SOCOM use cases attributes 262

SOCOM Web Manager 257, 258, 260, 267, 268

software-agents 218

Software Architecture (SA) 297

Software Component Aggregation Process (SO-CAP) 256, 257, 259, 260, 454

software component (SC) 256, 257, 258, 260, 261, 262, 263, 264, 267, 268, 269, 270

Software Component Storage 267

software engineering 146, 158, 165, 337, 383, 384

source representation 276

spiritual domain 115

standard modeling 67

static user model 447, 448

strategic model 107

subject domain 375

support activities 379

support infrastructures 433

support system 23

synchronous group 325, 326

syntax validation 279, 288

synthesis 125, 127, 128, 136, 138, 141, 144

System Sciences 146

T

target competency level 341

target competency (TC) 175, 176, 177, 178, 184, 193, 243, 245, 246, 247, 248

target domain 272, 282, 284

target population domain 103

target representation 276

task model 107

taxonomy 49, 50, 51, 52, 53, 54, 65, 199, 204, 208, 209, 210, 213

technical ontology 295, 300, 301, 303, 304, 306, 307, 310, 311, 312, 314

Technocompétences 97

Technology Enhanced Learning Operating System (TELOS) 295, 296, 297, 298, 299, 300, 301, 302, 303, 304, 305, 306, 307, 308, 309, 310, 312, 314, 315, 316, 350, 369, 377, 379, 384, 388, 432, 439, 441, 449, 450, 451
telelearning environments 451
TELOS Scenarios Language (TSL) 238
temporal sequencing 110
training scenarios 145

U

unary predicate symbols 202
Unified Modeling Language (UML) 273, 274, 275, 276, 279, 284, 407, 408, 411
Uniform Resource Locator (URL) 199
Unit-of-Learning (UoL) 371, 373, 374, 375, 376, 379
Universal Resource Identifier (URI) 199, 200
Use Cases Specifications and Requirements (UCR) 298
user interface 448

V

Validation Model 239, 240
verbal information 114
virtual campus 183, 184, 299, 300, 314, 316, 418
virtual campuse 338, 364
virtual learning 174
Virtual Learning Centre (VLC) 445
virtual organization 183

virtual work 183
visiting hours 197
visual knowledge modelling 337, 338
visual learning 369
visual modeling 218, 273, 337, 338, 364, 432, 438
visual models 66, 67
vocabulary 26

W

Web-based environments 407
Web Ontology Language 262
workflow management 151, 152, 153, 154, 155, 170
Workflow Management Coalition 152, 172
workflow management system 151, 152, 153, 154, 155
workflow model 152, 153, 169
workflow modeling 153
workflow processes 154
Workflow Reference Model (WfRM) 152, 170
workflows modeling languages 296
work processes 145, 146
World Wide Web consortium (W3C) 196, 201, 214, 215

X

XML Process Definition Language (XPDL) 153, 172
XML schema 201, 202, 206, 207